**Textiles for
Residential &
Commercial Interiors**

fb

Third Edition

Amy Willbanks
Vice President of Sales and Marketing
Textile Fabric Consultants, Inc.

Nancy Oxford
President
Textile Fabric Consultants, Inc.
Assistant Professor
Textiles, Merchandising and Design
Middle Tennessee State University

Dana Miller
Associate Professor
Interior Design
Middle Tennessee State University

Sharon Coleman
Associate Professor
Interior Design
Middle Tennessee State University

Second Edition

Jan I. Yeager
Associate Professor
Textiles, Apparel and Merchandising
West Virginia University

Lura K. Teter-Justice
Allied member ASID

Textiles for Residential & Commercial Interiors

Fairchild Books
NEW YORK

Executive Editor: Olga T. Kontzias
Assistant Acquisitions Editor: Amanda Breccia
Editorial Development Director: Jennifer Crane
Associate Development Editor: Lisa Vecchione
Associate Art Director: Erin Fitzsimmons
Production Director: Ginger Hillman
Production Editor: Jessica Rozler
Cover Design: Erin Fitzsimmons
Cover Art: Ken Hayden/Red Cover
Text Design: Tronvig Kuypers
Title Page Art: CELC MASTERS OF LINEN

Library of Congress Catalog Card Number: 2009931287

ISBN: 978-1-56367-651-2

GST R 133004424

Printed in China
TP17

Seventh Printing © 2007
Sixth Printing © 2005
Fifth Printing © 2004
Fourth Printing © 2003
Third Printing © 2002
Second Printing © 2001
Second Edition © 2000
Fairchild Publications, Inc.
Second Printing © 1998 Textile Fabric Consultants, Inc.
First Edition © 1988
Harper & Row, Publishers, Inc.

Contents

Extended Contents

■ The third edition of *Textiles for Residential and Commercial Interiors* reflects the suggestions of several professors who used the second edition. Many of these professors also willingly shared comments offered by their students. Together, their input led to changes in the organization, pedagogy, and scope of the work. The book continues to be, however, written for use by students, educators, extension personnel, practicing interior designers, architects, retailers, and consumers with a professional or personal interest in textile furnishings.

The major objectives for the third edition are:

• to enhance understanding by updating illustrations and adding extensive color photographs

• to examine current and new technologies in the textile industry, including microfibers, nanotechnology, new construction techniques, and new fiber developments

• to expose the students to a wider variety of interior fabrics through use of an optional corresponding swatch kit

• to identify current green/sustainable methods in interior design, including fiber and fabric production, recycling and finishing techniques

• to increase awareness of environmental issues related to the manufacture and use of interior textiles

To achieve a greater understanding of interior textiles requires examining and studying fabrics as well as the information included in the textbook. An optional fabric swatch kit has been developed to correspond directly with the textbook. The residential/commercial interior fabrics include sustainable textiles and are organized in the order they are listed in the textbook. The fabric swatches allow for hands-on experience with interior fabrics. The knowledge gained from this experience will be useful to both the student starting and the professional continuing a career in the interior design industry. (The Interior Design Swatch Kit can be obtained from Textile Fabric Consultants, www.textilefabric.com.)

Because readers will have different levels of knowledge about textiles, the text begins with a focus on textile fundamentals. As requested by users of the earlier edition, all aesthetic, durability, appearance retention, comfort, and health/safety properties are examined in greater

Preface

depth. Fibers, both natural and manufactured, are discussed in greater detail. Newly developed fibers, as well as new fiber processing techniques, are also covered.

The scope of the book has been expanded to include in-depth coverage of institutional textiles, as well as household textile goods. Critically important material has been added on codes, standards, environmental concerns, and green products.

For the benefit of the instructor and the student, there are key terms and review questions for each chapter. Case studies provide a means for the student to analyze a problem. The appendices include a listing of generic manufactured fiber names, formulas for metric conversions, a bibliography, and an extensive glossary. The text is richly illustrated, with line drawings and full-color, detailed photographs of fibers, yarns, fabrics, equipment used in manufacturing, coloring and finishing processes, as well as end products and end-use settings.

The text is presented in five units, with Unit One having a focus on textile fundamentals. Readers having previous formal study of textiles and professionals with knowledge from experience may use this unit for review; others may study the material more thoroughly, to master information built on in later units. Units Two through Five are divided by end-product category. Unit Two includes discussion of upholstered furniture coverings and fillings; Unit Three focuses on window coverings, drapery linings, and textile wallcoverings; Unit Four covers soft floor coverings and cushions; and Unit Five presents material on both functional and decorative textile bath, bedding, and tabletop products used in household and institutional settings.

In larger institutions with extensive offerings, *Textiles for Residential and Commercial Interiors* is appropriate for a course to follow completion of introductory textiles and interior design courses. It can be used in either textiles or interior design departments. In smaller institutions where course offerings may be more limited, the text would be useful in an introductory course with an expansive scope (e.g., apparel textiles and interior textiles, or housing and interior textiles). The book's organization permits the selection of units or chapters dealing with topics in the order preferred by the instructor.

■ We are appreciative of all the companies and individuals who contributed color photographs and illustrations to make this edition more visually appealing. Nancy Oxford, Dana Miller, and Sharon Coleman would also like to give special thanks to coauthor Amy Willbanks, who shot most of the photographs in this edition. Her meticulous attention to detail and amazing organizational skills facilitated the coordination of the entire project.

We are grateful to the many colleagues who provided ideas and helpful comments as we developed this edition. We would also like to thank Textile Fabric Consultants, Inc., for providing facilities, use of photocopying, faxing and scanning equipment, as well as numerous pots of coffee in the production of the new edition of *Textiles for Residential and Commercial Interiors*.

Other readers selected by the publisher were also very helpful. They included: Wendy Beckwith, La Roche College; Jan Cummings, Johnson County Community College; Rita Christoffersen, University of Wisconsin-Stout; Elizabeth P. Easter, University of Kentucky; Karen LaBat, University of Minnesota; Ann Beth Presley, Auburn University; Leanne C. Stone, University of Nevada-Reno; Katherine Wiggins, Madison Area Technical College; Patricia Williams, University of Wisconsin-Stevens Point; and Robyne Williams, North Dakota State University.

As an added benefit to instructors and students, an Interior Design Swatch Kit has been designed to parallel this text. It is available from Textile Fabric Consultants, Inc., 521 Huntly Industrial Blvd., Smyrna, TN 37167; www.textilefabric.com; telephone 800-210-9394.

Amy Willbanks
Nancy Oxford
Dana Miller
Sharon Coleman

Acknowledgments

Textiles for Residential & Commercial Interiors

Photo courtesy of Christian Fischbacher,
www.fischbacher.com.

The Fundamentals of Textiles for Interiors

U NIT ONE focuses on the fundamentals of textiles in the interior design industry. Chapter 1 reviews the nature of the industry, including the sequential flow of product manufacturing and distributing. Economic and environmental factors affecting the industry are also discussed. Chapter 2 identifies criteria influencing interior textile product selection. Scientific and technical associations serving the industry and organizations establishing model building codes are identified. Chapter 3 examines generic fiber names and classifications. Fiber properties related to aesthetics, durability, appearance retention, comfort, and health/safety/protection are identified. Physical external features are also discussed.

Following the normal sequence of production, Chapter 4 examines both natural and manmade fibers. Fiber engineering, fiber modifications and fiber developments are also examined. Chapter 5 focuses on yarns and yarn production. Chapter 6 and 7 examine various methods of fabric production including weaving, knitting, and tufting. Color related variables and methods of color application are discussed in Chapter 8. Conversion or finishing operations, the final process in fabric manufacturing, are discussed in Chapter 9.

The Interior Textile Industry

■ **The interior textile industry**, like the apparel and industrial textile industries, encompasses several segments, each of which is an important link in the chain of production and distribution. Although these segments are composed of many independent firms, there is mutual dependence among firms in different segments: firms in **downstream segments** need suppliers, and firms in **upstream segments** need purchasers. Furniture producers, for example, must have a supply of fillings, linings, and finished fabrics. In turn, they must also have interior designers and architects who are willing to recommend their upholstered products to clients and retailers who are willing to offer them to their customers.

Sharing a common goal—operating profitably—all members of the industry work cooperatively to ensure that the end products offered are widely accepted by contemporary consumers. To secure this acceptance and realize their goal, suppliers, producers, and distributors often support and seek assistance from such auxiliary enterprises as trade associations and advertising firms. While such groups are not directly involved in the manufacturing sequence, they can have a major influence on quality, awareness, and selection of the industry's goods.

Although consumer acceptance or rejection of the products available primarily determines the economic health of the industry and its members, it is also directly affected by such variables as environmental issues and economic factors. Industry executives must be aware of and respond to these variables if their firms are to be financially viable.

Major Segments of the Industry

The major segments of the interior textile industry and their positions in the flow of production and distribution are shown in Figure 1.1. Natural fiber suppliers and manufactured fiber producers initiate the work of the industry; it culminates with the residential and commercial consumer.

Fiber Suppliers and Producers

Natural fiber suppliers recover already-formed or "readymade" fibers, principally from sheep, silk caterpillars, cotton bolls, and flax plants. The responsibility of the supplier is to assist nature and ensure the production of high yields of quality fibers. To be successful, suppli-

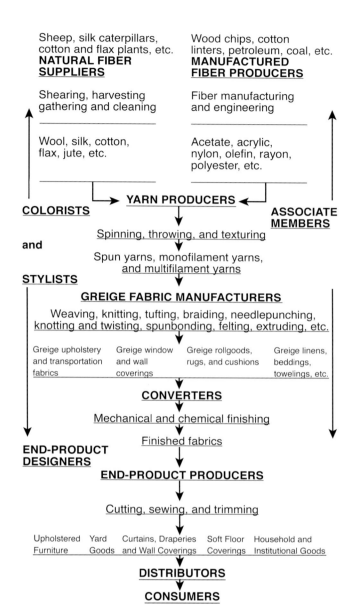

Figure 1.1 The interior textile industry.

ers must cope with the challenges of today's rising costs of labor, feed, pest-control agents, fertilizers, and transportation. They must also contend with growing competition from foreign suppliers and from manufactured fiber producers who are constantly seeking to capture a larger share of the fiber market. Increasingly, natural fiber suppliers must respond to concerns for the environment (e.g., limit runoff of pesticides and fertilizers into water supplies), and they must seek to protect the health and safety of their employees (e.g., reduce pesticide residue on workers' clothing). Also, they must alleviate the apprehension of animal rights activists (e.g., use humane treatment for the fiber-producing animals in their care).

Beginning with such natural materials as wood chips, cotton linters, bamboo, sugar beets, and corn, **manufactured fiber producers** make rayon, PLA, and acetate. Beginning with such natural substances as petroleum and coal, they manufacture acrylic, nylon, polyester, olefin, fiberglass, vinyon, and other fibers used in the interior design industry. Manufactured fiber producers are challenged by the rising costs of petroleum and labor, changing trade balances, and persistent competition from natural fiber suppliers. Like natural fiber suppliers, manufactured fiber producers must be concerned for any negative effects the byproducts of production have on the environment, as well as ensuring the health and safety of their employees.

Fiber suppliers and producers forward staple fibers, filament fibers, and tow to yarn producers. **Staple fibers**, such as wool, cotton, and flax, are relatively short fibers, measured in inches or centimeters. **Filament fibers**—silk and manufactured fibers—are relatively long fibers measured in yards or meters. **Tow** is a bundle of manufactured filaments that has been given a two- or three-dimensional crimp or coil but no twist.

Yarn Producers

Yarn producers are responsible for combining fibers into usable yarn structures. **Spinners** align, spin, and twist staple-length fibers into spun yarns, and **throwsters** combine filament-length fibers into untwisted or twisted multifilament yarns. Tow may be directly combined into yarns or it may be reduced to staple-length fibers (Figure 5.3, p. 87), which are then spun. Yarn producers frequently employ multiple twisting or plying operations to expand the assortment of yarns available to fabric manufacturers.

Fabric Manufacturers

Fabric manufacturers use a variety of **fabrication techniques**, including weaving, knitting, knotting and twisting, braiding, and tufting, to combine yarns into fabric structures. They use such techniques as felting, spunbonding, and needlepunching to produce fabrics directly from fibers, bypassing the yarn stage, and they use extruding to produce polymer film sheeting directly from solutions, bypassing both the fiber and yarn stages. With extrusion operations, the manufactured fiber/film producer is functioning as the fabric manufacturer.

Fabric producers and textile machinery engineers work cooperatively to develop new equipment and devise more efficient fabrication techniques, continually striving to fulfill two major goals. First, they seek to reduce production time and energy consumption and thus to reduce their manufacturing costs. Second, they work to engineer textile structures that will be accepted by and perform satisfactorily for the ultimate consumer.

After fabrication is completed, the results are still unfinished and often bear little resemblance to fabrics selected by professionals and consumers. These unfinished fabrics, known as **greige goods**, are forwarded to converters for finishing, or they may first be sent to dyers and printers.

Textile Colorists, Designers, and Stylists

Textile colorists and fabric stylists may be involved at any stage in the production sequence. Manufactured fiber producers may incorporate dye pigments within filaments as they are extruded; dyers may immerse fibers, yarns, or fabrics in a solution of dyestuff. Printers generally apply colorful patterns to greige goods, although they can produce some unique color styles by printing sheets of yarns and tubes of knitted fabric.

Textile chemists and colorists constantly strive to reduce their utilization of water: the copious amounts of water used in dyeing operations must be purified to minimize pollution. Drying hundreds of pounds of fiber or yarn or thousands of yards of fabric requires sizable amounts of often-costly utilities.

Well in advance of production, **textile designers** and **fabric stylists** must identify the aesthetic features preferred by contemporary consumers. They must be alert for slight shifts in the selection of such fashion-related qualities as fabric weight, textural characteristics, and drapability. They must tally the selections of woven-in patterns and printed patterns, noting preferences for simple and elaborate design motifs, for small-scale and large-scale repeats, and for fiber, yarn, and fabric color styling. Stylists must also accurately interpret and forecast trends and anticipate variations, making certain they are suitable for large-scale production operations. To protect their creative work, textile designers can copyright their work.

Stylists face another challenge: they must ensure that the fabric's service-related properties meet requirements and expectations. This means that stylists must work closely with converters who can change aesthetic and performance qualities during fabric finishing.

Converters

Converters are fabric finishers; they convert greige goods into finished fabrics. Using mechanical treatments and chemical agents, they can alter such appearance features as pile yarn orientation and luster and such performance characteristics as water- and soil-repellency, wrinkle recovery, and shape retention. By applying coatings and fabrics to the backs of carpet rollgoods and textile wall-coverings, converters can improve the functional characteristics and stability of these structures and facilitate their efficient installation.

End-Product Producers

Using fibers, yarns, and finished fabrics, as well as some nonfibrous materials, **end-product producers** construct items that are ready for immediate use or for installation in an interior setting. Some are specifically produced for use in private or **residential interiors**. Other products are specifically designed and constructed to withstand the higher levels of use in public or **commercial interiors**— stores and shopping centers, offices, schools, hospitals, hotels and motels, libraries and public buildings, religious buildings, restaurants and clubs, dormitories, airport terminals, nursing homes, and theaters.

The many interior textile products may be divided into four broad categories, namely upholstered furniture, window and wallcoverings, soft floor coverings and cushions, and household and institutional textiles. The upholstered furniture market includes chairs, sofas, ottomans, and the like, each covered by a textile fabric or such non-textile coverings as vinyl or leather; most items, however, have a textile or cellular foam filling or stuffing. Window coverings range from sheer curtains to blinds and shades containing grasses or metal slats. Wallcoverings may be an elegant moiré taffeta or a rough burlap cloth made of jute. Soft floor coverings range from scatter rugs to wall-to-wall carpet to exquisite Oriental rugs. Carpet and rug cushions or padding may be cattle hair, jute, or olefin. **Household textiles** used in residential interiors include beddings, towelings, and such tabletop accessories as napkins, tablecloths, and runners. When such products are designed and selected for use in hospitality or care-type facilities, they are referred to as **institutional textiles** and the items are required to conform with performance criteria and life safety codes. Among the assortment of products included in each of these categories, there are differences in fiber content, yarn features, fabric structure, color styling, finishes, and product design. In most cases, fabric stylists and **end-product designers** work cooperatively with producers and marketing specialists to plan the combinations needed to meet a variety of consumer needs and desires or to conform with specific requirements set by the design professional or an agency having jurisdiction over an installation.

Domestic producers must compete with one another and with foreign producers; this competition forces them continually to refine their existing products and to develop new and unique items. They must analyze the design, composition, and performance characteristics of their products to confirm that the characteristics offered are those sought by contemporary interior designers, architects, and consumers. At the same time they must contend with the rising costs of materials, labor, and equipment, and seek ways to reduce their consumption, and thus their cost, of energy. Whatever the number and magnitude of the challenges facing them, producers must succeed in meeting them to operate profitably.

It should be noted that some textile firms are organized vertically. These large firms use their own facilities and labor force to complete several sequential production operations. They may, for example, spin yarns, weave fabrics, apply color, convert greige goods, and construct end products. Such corporations normally have the resources needed to support extensive research and development activities and to create and fund effective marketing programs.

Distributors

Several types of retail operations present interior textile products to consumers. Department stores offer home furnishings and household linens, as well as apparel and accessories for all members of the family. Specialty stores offer a limited line of merchandise, such as upholstered furniture or carpet and rugs. Discount stores and factory outlets sell less expensive goods, and mail-order operations offer an ever-expanding assortment of products in a range of prices. Increasingly, consumers have the option of shopping for interior textile products via television or the Internet.

The retailer is sometimes bypassed in the distribution of interior furnishings. An upholstered furniture manufacturer, a wallcoverings designer, or a carpet and area rug producer, for example, may elect to maintain a **product showroom** where merchandise is shown to professional interior designers, architects, and other **members of the trade**. These professionals select products that conform to their clients' aesthetic preferences, serviceability requirements, and interior furnishings budgets.

Design Professionals

Design professionals, primarily licensed, registered, or certified interior designers and architects, select textiles for such hospitality sites as hotels, motels, and restaurants; for such retail establishments as department stores and boutiques; for offices; and for such residences as apartments and homes. Depending upon state legislation, interior designers may become licensed, registered, or certified by passing, for example, the National Council for Interior Design Qualification (NCIDQ) examination. Architects are licensed by individual states. Design professionals may operate their own firms, partnerships, or corporations, or be employed by independent firms of any size. In any case, they normally provide services in accordance with the terms of a contractual agreement made with their residential and commercial clients. The frequent use of such a legal document has given rise to the term **contract design** to describe the work of these professionally trained persons. These legal documents can be an oral agreement between the client and professional or a lengthy written document. Most importantly, contracts establish legal responsibility between a client and design professional.

Interior designers and architects serve as critical links between the industry and the consumer. They have a positive economic effect on the industry when they select new products and when they recommend or specify products that are consistent with their clients' selection criteria. To do their jobs well, they must be familiar with the industry's array of products and be prepared to assess the ability of different products to perform satisfactorily under a particular set of end-use conditions. Designers and architects must be aware of codes governing the selection and installation of products in a facility or in a particular location within a facility. In this work, manufacturers' representatives play an important role in providing information to the designer and architect who are specifying products, especially in commercial projects. Ultimately, the accuracy with which interior designers and architects recommend or specify products helps to determine their professional reputations. It can also have a major influence on the willingness of their clients to be repeat customers of particular interior textile products.

Consumers

The **consumer** is whoever pays for the end product: thus, the consumer may be a person, a group, a corporation, an agency, or an institution. Residential and commercial consumers may prefer to use their own talents and judgment when selecting products, or they may elect to contract for the services of an interior designer or architect. In the latter case, the professionals select, recommend, or specify products, functioning as consultants; their clients, who pay for the merchandise, are consumers.

At this point the work of the industry and the wants and needs of the consumer must coincide. Unless the assortment of products offered by the industry is acceptable to the consumer, the volume of sales will not be high enough for end-product producers to pay their suppliers, cover their operating expenses, and realize an adequate profit. Because a reduction in end-product sales results in a reduction in the amount of fibers, yarns, and finished fabrics needed, it threatens the financial stability of upstream firms as well. Moreover, low profit margins limit the ability of firms to expand. Therefore, all members of the industry strive to ensure that the assortment of products offered conforms to the selection criteria of the contemporary consumer; these criteria are examined in Chapter 2.

Associate Members of the Industry

Various enterprises provide valuable assistance to the textile furnishings industry. While their work is primarily intended to generate profit for themselves and for members of the industry, many of their activities are also useful to students, educators, retailers, and consumers. Among the groups serving the industry are trade associations, publishers, advertising firms, and service organizations. Several of these groups are listed in Appendix C.

Trade Associations

Trade associations are organized to represent, protect, and promote the interests of their members, who provide financial support for the operation and activities of the association. Trade association personnel establish liaisons between their members and various federal and state agencies and legislative bodies. They prepare and distribute educational material and technical literature. They devise marketing programs to increase the recognition and acceptance of their members' products. Some associations also maintain testing laboratories to evaluate and certify the quality of these products.

Some trade associations are composed of firms that compete with one another in the marketplace but also share a common goal. The American Fiber Manufacturers Association, for example, is supported by several independent firms, each of which is competing for sales orders from downstream firms. At the same time, however, these producers recognize the value of cooperating to provide information about manufactured fibers and to extend their use. Other trade associations are made up of firms belonging to different segments of the industry but having a vested interest in the marketing and widespread use of a particular category of products. The Carpet and Rug Institute, for example, works to increase the use of soft floor coverings; Cotton Incorporated works to increase the use of products containing cotton; and the Australian Wool Innovation works to increase the use of products containing wool. The Association for Contract Textiles was established to effectively market contract upholstery fabric manufactured by its members. The organization developed performance standards and promotes the use of symbols to identify fabrics conforming to the standards. (These symbols are shown in Figure 10.4, p. 167.) The Upholstered Furniture Action Council has member firms from throughout the upholstered furniture industry who have a vested interest in fire safety. They joined together to demonstrate that the majority of their member firms would voluntarily participate in improving the ability of upholstered furniture to resist catching fire from a burning cigarette.

Publishers

Writers and publishers provide members of the industry, students, educators, practicing professionals, retailers, and consumers with a wide assortment of articles, books, marketing magazines, technical journals, and trade newspapers focusing on products available for use in interiors. Some of these publications are for the professional preparation of students; some apprise personnel in the industry of new techniques, new products, research findings, marketing plans, and consumer preferences; and some exist to inform the consumer.

Advertising Firms

Industry members use advertising firms and advertisements to introduce and promote new equipment, new components, and new products. Upstream firms direct their advertisements to downstream firms; end-product producers direct their advertisements to members of the trade, to retailers, and to consumers; retailers direct their advertisements to retail consumers. In some cases, the cost of an advertising campaign is shared: for instance, a fiber producer shoulders a portion of the charges assessed for promotions run by an end-product manufacturer.

Service Organizations for Maintenance

In contrast to promoting the sales or improving the safety of a textile product, some organizations have a focus on the efficient, proper, and economical maintenance of the goods. The **Association for Linen Management (ALM)**, formerly the National Association of Institutional Linen Management (NAILM), for example, has members in textile care and environmental services (e.g., hospitals, nursing homes, educational institutions, hotels, motels, etc.). It also has member businesses such as chemical manufacturers and textile manufacturers. The **Dry Cleaning and Laundry Institute International**, formerly the International Fabricare Institute, provides education, research, legislative representation, and industry-specific information to its members on dry cleaning and care procedures related to dry cleaning.

Economic Factors Affecting the Industry

Several of the factors affecting the work and economic health of the textile industry originate elsewhere, in other industries and in government. They nevertheless have a direct impact by favoring or restricting production and expansion in the industry.

Inflation

Inflation (when demand exceeds supply and prices rise) makes it necessary for many consumers to alter their spending and savings patterns. Together with high interest rates on personal loans, inflation forces many consumers to postpone purchases of more expensive durable and semidurable goods, including carpet, upholstered furniture, and automobiles.

Income-related Variables

The demand for textile furnishings is directly affected by the level of income realized by consumers. Their **disposable or real income** is affected by federal and state income taxes and Social Security taxes. A reduction in personal income taxes may result in increased savings, reduced interest rates, and an increased demand for durable goods. On the other hand, a reduction in taxes when interest rates are high may result in increased spending for nondurable goods; consequently, spending for durable and semidurable goods may continue to be delayed.

Fluctuations in the costs of such basic necessities as food, clothing, and shelter, together with the costs of such other things as education and transportation, also influence the demand for interior textile products. These costs alter the **discretionary income** of consumers, increasing or decreasing the amount of income left to spend on the basis of want rather than need.

Energy Costs and Concerns

Concern for energy conservation and the pressure of rising energy costs encourage many residential and commercial consumers to increase their use of soft floor coverings and textile window coverings as insulation materials. In the industry, such energy-related factors have fostered the development of more efficient and economical production techniques and equipment.

Mortgage Interest Rates and Building Costs

Mortgage interest rates and the costs of building materials directly affect the number and size of new constructions. Of course, high rates and costs have a negative effect, slowing construction and reducing the need for such products as carpet, rugs, upholstered furniture, textile wallcoverings, and curtains and draperies. At the same time, the negative impact of such slowdowns may be somewhat tempered by increases in the replacement or refurbishment of these items in existing residential and commercial structures.

Mergers and Acquisitions

Within the industry, mergers and acquisitions can result in companies with greater financial resources, more efficient operations, and a greater number of proficient and skilled personnel. Such large firms are better able to support valuable and necessary research activities, mount effective marketing campaigns, and respond quickly and accurately to changes in consumer needs and wants. They are also more likely to undertake lobbying efforts, the results of which may benefit all members of the industry.

Other Factors

Other factors influencing the economic stability and expansion of the industry include fluctuations in the cost of raw materials, labor, and equipment, and international trade agreements that foster or restrict the import or export of components and end products. In addition, the cost of compliance with mandatory performance and safety specifications generally necessitates an increase in the price of certain products, which can slow their sales, at least temporarily.

An increase in the prices of new automobiles or the cost of gasoline encourages many consumers to select smaller passenger cars. At times, a reduction in car size may have a negative effect on firms producing automotive carpet, as well as on those firms supplying upholstery, tire cord, and interior roof and trunk linings.

Media exposure of styles, materials, and decorating trends, as seen in print, television, and cyberspace, has impacted the demand for goods and services provided by the textile industry. In 1901, Gustav Stickley first began publishing *The Craftsman* to promote architecture and furnishings associated with the up-and-coming Craftsman style. Although magazines related to the decorative arts have been around since the early twentieth century, in recent years a proliferation of weekly, monthly, and bimonthly publications directed toward the consuming public have flooded the market. Magazines targeting specific styles, regions of the country, socioeconomic levels, housing types, materials, and even well-known personalities have appeared, increasing consumer awareness and the desire to have products illustrated or advertised within their covers.

Television has brought home building and furnishing products into even more homes. When the television program *This Old House* first aired on the Boston public television station WGBH in 1979, it became an immediate success. The show began national distribution in 1980, spawning several related television programs, numerous books and book series, and magazines. The popularity of television programming about home construction, remodeling, and decorating has increased rapidly, resulting in the introduction of entire television networks devoted to home decor, gardening, and lifestyle.

Most recently, the increasing interest in environmental issues has resulted in new publications, television programs, Web sites, and a network devoted to sustainable, or "green," design. Such widespread media exposure has a strong impact on consumer awareness of textile and textile-related products.

Environmental Factors Affecting the Industry

Consumers and professionals in many industries are becoming more conscious of environmental concerns, particularly as they relate to textiles. In developing an environmental awareness, consumers and manufacturers are voluntarily reducing the consumption of components and finished goods, reusing materials, and recycling resources. Consumers are separating their garbage and recycling such common materials as glass, plastic, and paper. Members of the industry are seeking to reduce the use of chemicals in processing in order to minimize the subsequent negative effects on **indoor air quality (IAQ)**. Products may carry a reference to a **green standard** to attract environmentally conscious consumers. Since there are no government laws or regulations concerning labeling for environmentally friendly products or what constitutes "green," consumers must evaluate two competing products to decide the validity of manufacturers' claims. Concurrently, organizations such as the Environmental Protection Agency and the Occupational Safety and Health Administration are working to identify or regulate what qualifies as environmentally responsible.

Developments in the Textile Industry

The protection of our environment has become increasingly important. In order to assist in this monumental task, consumers and professional members of the textile industry are seeking new ways to reduce the consumption of raw materials and processing agents, to recycle existing products in a second product, and to reuse existing products in alternative ways. More manufacturers have, for example, increased their use of recycled materials for product packaging. In the industry, every aspect of production and processing is being redefined, from the growing of natural fibers to the recycling of plastic, including drink bottles, for fiber conversion. Some practices are industrywide and some are "quality" practices developed by individual companies.

Reduction of Raw Material Consumption and Processing Agent Usage

In an attempt to reduce chemicals used to grow natural fibers, researchers are experimenting with **organically grown** cotton. In this work, the cotton is cultivated on land that has been chemical-free for a minimum of three years and is nurtured without the use of chemical fertilizers or pest-control agents. Other advances include the development of genetically colored cotton that allows subsequent dyeing processes to be eliminated and reduces the chemicals that exist on the fibers. Design Tex has developed fabrics that are reported to be virtually nontoxic, yet durable, attractive, and in compliance with the Association for Contract Textiles (ACT) standards (see Chapter 14). Developments like these have led to a significant reduction in chemical usage in the industry, making it more environmentally safe.

Reuse of Existing Textile Products

Reusing a product is a second way to eliminate materials that must be sent to a landfill. Many carpet producers, for example, are seeking new ways to use byproducts from carpet manufacturing. They cut surplus carpet into mats for sales to consumers for use as track-off mats to protect floor surfaces or to repair damaged areas. For safety, it is important to use an adhesive tape to properly secure loose mats. Shredded carpet fibers can be used in a concrete mixture for reinforcement. Any reused material preserves available raw materials and eliminates the waste going to a landfill.

Recycling of Existing Textile Products

Recycling is the reconditioning of one product to produce another. Recycling reduces trash that would otherwise go to a landfill and results in a new, environmentally friendly product. A few specific examples of recycling in the textile industry are discussed here.

One of the most successful recycling efforts involves recycling plastics into "green" products. In 1996, Fortrel® Ecospun® fibers were first introduced in the residential furniture industry by Malden Mills. These fibers are produced from recycled plastic bottles that are converted into fibers. In order for the process to be successful, the plastic containers must first be sorted by color and type. In preparation for the conversion process, the bottles are cleaned, crushed, and chopped into fine flakes. The flakes are changed to liquid, then used to produce fibers that are combined into yarns ready for weaving. Standard methods of weaving are used to produce EcoSpun® velvet. It takes some 200 two-liter bottles to produce the 15 to 20 yards of fabric required for upholstering an average sofa. While the fibers are cost prohibitive for the residential market, Malden Mills is successfully producing the fiber for the contract market. Recycled PET (polyethylene terephthalate, better known as polyester) is particularly appealing to the hospitality market because it is extremely durable. Quality fabrics containing the recycled fiber can meet all ACT standards.

Recycling carpet is significant to the industry. Successful recycling programs include the BASF 6ix Again program, DuPont's "Partnership in Carpet Reclamation," and United Recycling. The challenge of recycling carpet begins with collecting the bulky, heavy floor covering and delivering it to a central collection site. In order to be successful, carpet must be sorted by fiber content. Because fibers are nearly impossible to visually identify, the content is determined by melting point, or, more recently, by near-infrared technology. Once the fibers are identified, the carpet is sorted, shredded, crushed, and converted to pellets. The pellets are most often used in industrial, automotive, or building materials. The process is successful in keeping carpet out of landfills, but more research is necessary to develop a cost-effective process for generating new carpet from recycled components (Figure 1.2a and b).

Design Considerations

In order to be more environmentally aware, consumers and interior designers need to know that textiles are often treated with flame retardant agents, stain resistant agents, and other compounds for a wide variety of aesthetic and functional purposes. Even natural products have chemicals applied during cleaning and for such things as mothproofing and stain resistance. Any residue remaining on the textile may emit toxic fumes, reducing indoor air quality. In regard to cleaning agents, there are water-based products that offer less toxicity than petroleum-based products.

The reduction of chemicals used in the growth of fibers or in textile production also assists the interior designer with reducing the problem of indoor air quality. IAQ is a serious issue and is consistently ranked in the top five concerns by the Environmental Protection Agency. IAQ is significant because the average American spends 90 percent of his or her time indoors, thus requiring that sufficient fresh air is circulated throughout the space and potential pollutants are controlled. Pollution may be generated from new furnishings and finishes and the chemicals with which they are treated. For this reason, most manufacturers recommend a **gassing-off** period, which allows the gases to permeate the air and be dissipated while the space is still vacant. These gases are referred to as **volatile organic compounds (VOCs)**.

VOCs are chemicals that contain carbon, which, during evaporation, give off gases, many of which can cause health problems. The term **off-gassing** refers to the release of these chemicals into the air we breathe, both inside and outside. The rate the materials off-gas depends on their molecular makeup and how quickly they vaporize. The amount of volatile material is given a VOC num-

a) Used carpet being recycled.

b) Pellets made from recycled carpet.

Figure 1.2
Photos courtesy of Bruce Quist © 2005 and InterfaceFlor®.

ber, VOC rating, or description of VOC content, either in pounds per gallon or grams per liter or as a percentage by mass. There are thousands of natural and manmade VOCs, some that you can smell and some that are odorless. Many are harmful to humans and the environment. The EPA reports that the amount of volatile material in indoor VOCs can be ten times higher than that found outdoors. As interior designers are concerned with the public's health, safety, and welfare, it is vital that they specify products that support healthy environments. Many new materials and finishing methods are available that contain no or low harmful VOC levels.

Environmental Agencies

In addition to voluntary acts of consumers and manufacturers, several agencies exist in the United States to promote or to regulate issues concerning human well-being in the environment. Some of these agencies are described in this section.

U.S. Environmental Protection Agency (EPA)

The **Environmental Protection Agency (EPA)** was established to protect human health and safeguard the natural environment—air, water, and land—upon which life depends. This protection includes maintaining the quality of air, water, and land.

One of the voluntary programs created by the EPA is EnviroSense: Partners for the Environment. It is the mission of this group to solve environmental problems with common sense. The group facilitates voluntary participation and widespread environmental awareness with corporate partners. It is proving that voluntary guidelines can be successful by committing to programs such as Indoor Air, Indoor Radon, Design for the Environment, and WasteWi$e. Cooperative efforts of consumers and industry members are necessary to continue to achieve improvements in environmental protection and accomplish greater success.

Centers for Disease Control and Prevention (CDC)

The **Centers for Disease Control and Prevention (CDC)** was organized to promote health and quality of life by preventing and controlling disease, injury and disability. In addition to its mission, the CDC is committed to providing a healthy environment in which individuals can achieve personal growth. The organization uses the highest-quality data to make all public health decisions.

Occupational Safety and Health Administration (OSHA)

The goal of the **Occupational Safety and Health Administration (OSHA)** is to save lives, prevent injuries, and protect the health of workers. One of OSHA's primary activities is inspecting the workplace. There are over 2,000 inspectors who investigate complaints. This organization also enforces standards and provides technical support and consultation to employers and employees to ensure safer work environments.

International Organization for Standardization (ISO)

The **International Organization for Standardization (ISO)** is the world's largest nongovernmental developer and publisher of International Standards. ISO is composed of national standards institutes from 157 countries (one member per country). Its main office is located in Geneva, Switzerland. Some member institutions are part of their country's government; others are from the private sector. The ISO 14000 series of standards pertains to comprehensive outcomes of product manufacture and ways in which an organization can minimize its operation's negative impact on the environment.

Greenguard Environmental Institute (GEI)

The **Greenguard Environmental Institute (GEI)** was founded in 2001 to establish an independent third-party product certification program based on established emissions standards and to provide specifying information to design professionals for VOC low-emitting products. The GEI is an American National Standards Institute–authorized standards developer that establishes acceptable indoor air standards for products. Its Greenguard Indoor Air Quality Certification program identifies products and materials that meet the low-emission requirements.

U.S. Green Building Council (USGBC)

The **U.S. Green Building Council (USGBC)** is a nonprofit organization whose mission is to transform the way buildings and communities are designed, built, and operated, enabling an environmentally and socially responsible, healthy, and prosperous environment that improves the quality of life. Composed of more than 15,000 building industry organizations, the membership consists of owners, end users, developers, facility managers, architects, designers, engineers, contractors, building product manufacturers, government agencies, and nonprofit organizations. The USGBC provides green building resources, educational courses, research and statistical information, and the **Leadership in Energy and Environmental Design (LEED)** Green Building Rating System program. Many state and local governments utilize Leadership in Energy and Environmental Design (LEED) for public-owned and public-funded buildings. Federal agencies that participate in the LEED certification program include the Departments of Defense, Agriculture, Energy, and State. LEED-certified projects can also be found in other countries, including Canada, Brazil, Mexico and India.[1]

The Leadership in Energy and Environmental Design Green Building Rating System is a voluntary, national rating system for developing high-performance, sustainable buildings. LEED certification emphasizes state-of-the-art building in five areas: sustainable site development, water savings, energy efficiency, materials and resources selection, and indoor environmental quality. There are nine building rating system categories: new construction, existing buildings: operations and maintenance, commercial interiors, core and shell construction, schools, retail, healthcare, homes, and neighborhood development.

Developed by the USGBC, the **LEED Professional Accreditation Program** is managed by the **Green Building Certification Institute (GBCI)**. Through examination, the GBCI identifies design and building professionals who have the knowledge and skills required to successfully supervise the LEED certification process. **LEED Accredited Professionals (LEED AP)** have a thorough understanding of green building practices and principles and the LEED Rating System (Figure 1.3).

Table 1.1 USGBC Benefits of Green Building	
Environmental benefits:	• enhance and protect ecosystems and biodiversity • improve air and water quality • reduce solid waste • conserve natural resources
Economic benefits:	• reduce operating costs • enhance asset value and profits • improve employee productivity and satisfaction • optimize life-cycle economic performance
Health and community benefits:	• improve air, thermal, and acoustic environments • enhance occupant comfort and health • minimize strain on local infrastructure • contribute to overall quality of life

Source: U.S. Green Building Council (USGBC) Web site "Benefits of Building Green," 2008.

Figure 1.3 Seals: The U.S. Green Building Council (USGBC), Leadership in Energy and Environmental Design (LEED), LEED Accredited Professionals (LEED AP).

Summary

The primary goal of all firms in the interior textile industry is to operate profitably. All members of the industry recognize that this goal depends on consumer acceptance of the end products offered. They strive to secure the initial and repeated selection of their assorted products. In this effort, they often enlist the support of such auxiliary enterprises as trade associations, advertising and publishing agencies, and contract design firms.

To succeed, industry members must cope with competition from other firms and with various external factors. Among the external factors are economic factors that may encourage or retard new construction, pressure from foreign producers, imposed product performance mandates, and growing concern about environmentally safe practices. Whatever challenges are posed by these variables, all industry firms must focus their attention on the wants and needs of contemporary residential and commercial consumers.

Key Terms

Association of Linen Management (ALM)

Centers for Disease Control and Prevention (CDC)

commercial interiors

consumer

contract design

converters

design professionals

discretionary income

disposable or real income

downstream segments

Dry Cleaning and Laundry Institute (DLI)
end-product designers
end-product producers
Environmental Protection Agency (EPA)
fabric stylists
fabrication techniques
filament fibers
gassing-off
green standard
Green Building/Certification Institute (CBCI)
Greenguard Environmental Institute (GEI)
greige goods

household textiles
indoor air quality (IAQ)
inflation
institutional textiles
International Organization for Standardization (ISO)
Leadership in Energy and Environmental Design (LEED)
LEED Accredited Professionals (LEED AP)
LEED Green Building Rating System
manufactured fiber producers
members of the trade
natural fiber suppliers
Occupational Safety and Health Administration (OSHA)

off-gassing
organically grown
product showroom
residential interiors
spinners
staple fibers
textile colorists
textile designers
throwsters
tow
trade associations
U.S. Green Building Council (USGBC)
upstream segments
volatile organic compounds (VOCs)

Review Questions

1. Identify the major segments of the interior textile industry and discuss their interconnectedness.

2. The following is a skeletal profit and loss statement. Discuss what a firm can do with each variable to increase its net profit (e.g., increase sales).

$$\$ \text{ retail sales}$$
$$- \text{ wholesale costs}$$
$$= \text{ operating profit}$$
$$- \text{ expenses}$$
$$= \text{ net profit}$$

3. Discuss the environmental challenges that face natural fiber suppliers and manufactured fiber producers.

4. Why is it critically important that members of the industry monitor slight shifts in both the aesthetic features and the functional expectations of interior textile products?

5. Identify several interior textile products, including those used in residential and commercial interiors. What interior textile products are used in hospitality settings?

6. Differentiate between household textiles and institutional textiles.

7. What challenges face domestic producers, and why must they meet these challenges?

8. Discuss the consequences of offering interior textile products that do not coincide with the wants and needs of the consumer.

9. Discuss the role of interior designers and architects in choosing textiles. What legal ramifications are associated with their decisions?

10. Why would competing firms work cooperatively in a trade association?

11. Explain the critical importance of IAQ. How can the negative effects of interior textiles on the IAQ be reduced?

12. Identify ways the professional designer can strive to protect the environment when selecting textiles.

13. Discuss the benefits of building green.

14. Discuss the recycling of plastic bottles into textile applications.

15. What advantages are offered by Fortrel® Ecospun® fiber?

16. Discuss the external factors that affect the economic health of the industry.

Note

1. U.S. Green Building Council, www.USGBC.org.

CHAPTER TWO

Selecting and Evaluating Textiles for Interiors

Photo courtesy of Christian Fischbacher, www.fischbacher.com.

■ **Each residential and commercial** consumer has a unique set of criteria governing the selection of **textile end products.** Some of these variables relate to appearance and tactile characteristics; some focus on service-related performance; some are concerned with maintenance and installation; some relate to environmental impact; some pertain to human health issues; and some are necessarily determined by cost factors. Consumers and design professionals must work together to determine the relative importance of each criterion and to accommodate those considered most important. Industry firms must be aware of these variables in order to offer products that meet the current selection criteria.

As part of their effort to secure the initial and repeated selection of their products, many firms measure specific properties of the products' components and assess the potential serviceability of the finished items prior to marketing. Initially, this work enables them to make statements about their products' performance on labels and in promotional materials in order to capture the attention of professionals and prospective purchasers. Subsequently, these evaluations help to ensure that their goods will continue to exhibit an acceptable level of **in-use performance,** satisfying consumers and encouraging them to go on selecting the company's products. In many cases, this **quality-control work** involves the use of standard methods of testing and performance specifications published by scientific and technical associations.

Many producers also evaluate their products in accordance with standards established by various regulatory agencies. Products complying with the design or performance specifications set forth in these codes can be used in interiors that come within the scope of legally binding requirements. Design professionals are liable for selecting textiles that meet or exceed the governing codes pertinent to the installation.

Selecting Interior Textiles

Several characteristics considered in the selection of textile furnishings are listed in Tables 2.1 through 2.5. In most cases, the residential or commercial consumer determines the relative importance of these variables, personally deciding whether any compromises can be made. For certain commercial products, however, various regulatory agencies have the authority to require compliance with specific product standards and building codes.

Challenges to Members of the Industry

To remain profitable, firms in the industry must constantly monitor consumer selections, noting and quickly responding to changes in consumer preferences. The aesthetic features currently preferred must be mirrored in the products offered, the service-related characteristics expected must be available, and any mandated design and performance properties must be exhibited. Additionally, required maintenance and installation procedures must coincide with those preferred by consumers, and the price of the product, along with any charges for assembly, delivery, and installation, must not exceed the ability or willingness of the consumer to pay.

Challenges to Design Professionals and Consumers

In order to provide the best solution for the function and aesthetics of the interior, consumers and design professionals such as interior designers and architects, should be informed when making their interior textile product selections. They must, for example, consider the factors affecting the apparent color of textiles to ensure that the color characteristics chosen will look the same when seen in the interior setting. They must understand how the components and structural features of a product influence its functional properties and use-life. Consumers and professionals should therefore be aware of inherent and engineered fiber properties, yarn and fabric features, factors affecting color retention, and the effects of finishing treatments and agents. They should be prepared to identify the activities, conditions, and substances to which the item will be subjected in use, and be able to make reliable judgments regarding the ability of the item to perform satisfactorily when exposed to the anticipated stresses and agents. These several product and end-use variables will be discussed in detail throughout this book.

The task in design is especially challenging because residential and commercial consumers have widely varying and constantly changing aesthetic preferences and performance needs. Designers and architects must be knowledgeable of market trends within the industry. They must be aware of the resources available for reliable information, including trade publications, professional journals, and the Internet.

When contract designers and architects are selecting interior textile products for commercial use, they must ascertain which, if any, agency has jurisdiction over the project, and they must identify all applicable codes affecting their selections. In turn, they must confirm that their planned product selections conform to all mandated selection criteria. Interior designers and architects are, in fact, legally and ethically responsible for choosing textiles that meet all applicable industry and government standards and codes, particularly performance standards and life safety codes. It may be necessary for the design professional to educate the consumer, explaining that codes and safety requirements may preclude the choice of certain aesthetic or structural features with a textile product.

Aesthetic Considerations

Several aesthetic or sensory characteristics are considered in the selection of interior textile products (see Table 2.1). These include such **design elements** as color, line, texture, and form, and such **design principles** as emphasis, rhythm, contrast, and harmony. While the initial visual impact of these features is a primary concern, consideration must also be given to such variables as the effects of end-use lighting on the apparent color, the availability of matching items, and the life expectancy of the fashion features.

Performance and Safety Factors

Among the selection criteria held by consumers are several variables pertaining to performance (see Table 2.2). For some consumers, such functional attributes as indoor air quality, glare reduction, and acoustic control may be critical; for others, texture retention may be of paramount importance; and for still others, durability and wear-life may be high on the list. At the same time, many consumers are increasingly aware of the desirability of having flame-resistant textiles that can widen the margin of safety in the event of fire. For some commercial interiors, flame resistance may not only be desirable, it may be mandatory.

Maintenance Considerations

Products are selected for their appropriateness for an interior, as well as for the enjoyment they will provide during their expected use-life. Part of this enjoyment centers on the type and level of maintenance required and its effectiveness. Proper maintenance of textiles affects their serviceability, in terms of appearance retention, wear, durability, and safety. Dirt that is not removed from carpet, for example, will facilitate an abrasive action between traffic

Table 2.1 Aesthetic Product Selection Criteria	
Variable Characteristics	
Design Elements	form: 3-D form of upholstered furniture, pillows color characteristics: hue, value, and intensity texture: smooth or rough resulting from the fiber, yarn, or fabric structure or from an applied finish pattern: detail, size, and repetition of motifs light: level of reflectance; level of transmittance
Design Principles	scale: size of motifs; fullness of window coverings emphasis: dominant visual characteristic rhythm: repetition of elements contrast: differentiates items in the visual field harmony: pleasing arrangement of parts
Styling Features	color styling: heather, multicolored, solid-colored texture styling: nonpile, cut pile, uncut pile, level, multilevel hand: warm, cool, smooth, rough, soft, harsh drapability: fluid, stiff end-product styling: trimmed, plain, traditional, contemporary availability of matching and/or coordinated items coordination with existing interior and current furnishings life expectancy of fashion features

and the carpet fibers, as well as affect the apparent color. Concomitantly, the aesthetic value of the floor covering would be diminished. Both the consumer and design professional should become aware of proper maintenance, including the cleaning agents and equipment needed.

Health safety and environmental stewardship concerns about cleaning chemicals and processes have become important considerations when selecting and specifying textiles. **Material Safety Data Sheets (MSDS)** identify hazardous chemicals and health and physical hazards, including exposure limits and precautions for workers who may come into contact with these chemicals. Not only are cleaning chemicals identified, but chemicals used in manufacturing processes that pose a hazard to workers

Table 2.2 Performance and Safety Product Selection Criteria

	Variable Characteristics
Functional Properties	insulation, glare reduction, static reduction, fatigue reduction, acoustic control, mobility improvements, safety enhancement
Appearance Retention	color retention, texture retention, resistance to pilling and snagging, soil hiding, soil repellency, soil shedding, soil release
Durability and Wear-life	abrasion resistance, tear resistance, dimensional stability, fuzzing, fiber loss, repairability, warranty availability
Structural Stability	tuft bind strength, delamination strength, stability of yarn twist
Flame Resistance	inherent or applied
Design and Performance Mandates	flame resistance, indoor air quality, structural stability, colorfastness, wear resistance functional properties: acoustical value, static reduction

Table 2.3 Maintenance Product Selection Criteria

	Variable Characteristics
Cleanability	washable, dry cleanable, ease of stain removal, appearance after cleaning
Cleaning Location	on-site versus off-site cleaning
Level of Ironing Required	none, touch-up, extensive
Frequency of Cleaning	daily, weekly, monthly
Cleaning Products Required	toxic, biodegradable, readily available

Table 2.4 Environmental Product Selection Criteria

	Variable Characteristics
Manufacturing Issues	environmental pollution during manufacturing process sustainability
Product Issues	embodied energy life-cycle recyclability impact of cleaning agents

Table 2.5 Cost and Installation Product Selection Criteria

	Variable Characteristics
Initial Cost	product price, accessories prices fees for design professional delivery charges installation charges
Life-Cycle Cost	maintenance costs, including equipment, cleaning agents, and labor warranty costs, insurance costs energy costs interest charges disposal
Installation Factors	site preparation labor, tools, and level of skill needed permanence: movable, removable, permanent

are identified as well. Design professionals review product MSDS when specifying materials to evaluate potential VOC off-gassing problems.

The Occupational Safety and Health Administration (OSHA) requires that MSDS be available to employees for potentially harmful substances handled in the workplace. MSDS are also required to be available to local fire departments and local and state emergency planning officials. These and other maintenance factors are listed in Table 2.3.

Environmental Concerns

Increasingly, many designers, architects, consumers, and manufacturers are showing greater interest in the environment. Their considerations go beyond recycling to encompass concerns regarding environmental impact resulting from the acquisition of raw materials, manufacturing methods, waste production, packaging, distribution, water and energy conservation, maintenance, life-cycle assessment, and final disposal. The term **embodied energy** refers to all the energy used to grow/raise, extract/harvest, and manufacture a product, including the amount of energy needed for transportation, packaging, and recycling or disposal. These and other environmental concerns are listed in Table 2.4.

Cost and Installation Factors

Textile product costs may be categorized by **initial cost** and **life-cycle cost**. Initial cost starts with the cost of the product, as well as the cost incurred for installation, including site preparation, labor, and any accessories that are needed (see Table 2.5). A detailed **project bid** provides prices for each of the products chosen, together with the installation charges, thus enabling the client and designer to ascertain the affordability of the project. If necessary, the project may be completed in phases.

Life-cycle cost is comprehensive and is listed in a formal **project specification.** Consideration is given to several factors, including the initial cost, installation expenses, ongoing maintenance costs, and the anticipated life-span of the product. With life-span in mind, the initial costs may be amortized: for example, an expensive textile product that is expected to be serviceable for ten years could, in fact, be less costly than one whose initial cost was less but whose life expectancy was shorter.

Maintenance procedures should be examined prior to installation to determine that the practices are both feasible and affordable. With commercial installations, interviews with the maintenance personnel would be helpful in determining any deficiencies in equipment. The feasibility of the necessary maintenance procedures must be considered in both residential and commercial installations. Insufficient or incorrect maintenance may lead to premature replacement of a product and greatly add to the long-term cost. Careful consideration should be given to the selection of nontoxic cleaning products that contribute to improved indoor air quality and that do not require dumping contaminants or chemicals into the wastewater system. Together with the cost of utilities, the energy efficiency of a product will result in long-term savings or long-term expense.

Evaluating Interior Textiles

Together with other informed and interested persons, many members of the textile industry participate in the work of several scientific and technical associations. Participants in most of these groups voluntarily share their expertise and opinions to help develop standards pertaining to such things as definitions, recommended practices, methods of testing, classifications, design specifications, or performance specifications. Producers throughout the industry may elect to use these standards when they evaluate their components and end products.

Unless adopted by a **regulatory agency,** standards are not legally binding. A design professional, however, is responsible for using the information to best meet the needs of the client. The Association for Contract Interiors (ACT), for example, suggests that general contract upholstery should withstand 15,000 double rubs with the Wyzenbeek method (see Chapter 14) if it is to give satisfactory abrasion resistance in use; heavy-duty upholstery should withstand 30,000 double rubs. Thus, the ACT standard is a recommendation for satisfactory end-use performance; it is not, however, mandatory.

In the event that an agency having regulatory power adopts a design or performance specification as a requirement, the standard is often then known as a code. Codes are legally binding requirements.

Standard Methods of Testing

A **standard test method** prescribes specific procedures to be followed when making a given measurement, for instance, the measurement of yarn distortion after surface friction. A test method details the selection, size, number, and preparation of the test specimens; describes the test apparatus; specifies test conditions; sets forth test procedures; and lists the observations and calculations to be made in analyzing and reporting the test results. Unless specifically stated otherwise, testing is carried out in a controlled atmosphere of 70 ± 2 °F and 65 ± 2 percent RH (relative humidity). In order to produce accurate and reproducible results, textile researchers and quality-control personnel must strictly adhere to all details included in a standard test method. Performance comparisons can be made only among specimens tested in a like manner. (While the summaries of test methods provided in later chapters are adequate for discussion, they are not sufficient for carrying out testing. Interested persons can read the full text of standard test methods in such publications as the ***AATCC Technical Manual*** and the ***Annual Book of ASTM Standards.*** These publications are listed in the bibliography.) Test methods simulate the conditions to which textile items may be subjected in actual use. Such small-scale laboratory techniques minimize the need for large-scale, long-term, and more expensive evaluation procedures. Standard test methods enable producers efficiently and economically to measure their products' quality and performance.

Many manufacturers use test results as the basis for claims that their products exhibit specific functional and use-life characteristics. They may also analyze test results to determine the advisability of putting their name or other identifying mark on the product label.

Performance Specifications

While analysis of the results of a standard test method may require numerical calculations, it may or may not specify numerical limitations or boundaries pertaining to performance. By contrast, such performance-related requirements are always included in a **standard performance specification.** These requirements represent the minimum or maximum levels—the limits—of performance that the specimens should exhibit when tested in accordance with the designated method.

Design professionals develop performance specifications to establish criteria for project contracts and bidding. This allows the designer to define the product requirements. When textiles are submitted for project approval, evidence of compliance with the specifications is required. Results of the product tests may be requested from the manufacturer or a sample can be tested.

Manufacturers use performance specifications to compare the level of performance recorded for their products with the level recommended in the standard, and, if necessary, to alter the composition or processing of their items accordingly. Compliance with such recommendations ensures that the component or product will exhibit an acceptable level of in-use performance, which in turn will help to secure consumer goodwill and repeat business for the complying company.

Codes

Codes are mandatory practices or mandated performance specifications concerned with the safety and well-being of the general population. Codes are laws enacted by federal, state, and local governments. Individual jurisdictions may write their own laws or rely on the work of government agencies or model building code organizations. Frequently, a regulatory agency will adopt a standard performance specification as a code, in effect turning a recommendation into a requirement. Several state-level fire marshal's offices, for example, have adopted as codes selected standards set forth in the NFPA 101 Life Safety Code®. Some organizations responsible for developing model building codes are discussed later in this chapter.

Because codes are mandatory, the design professional is legally responsible for selecting products that comply with all applicable codes. California Technical Bulletin 133, for example, is a flammability standard that has been adopted as a code by several states. When a designer incorporates a customer's own material (COM) in an occupancy in a state where Cal 133 is the code, the designer must have the fabric tested in accordance with the procedures set forth in Cal 133. The challenge for the designer is to adequately research and accurately specify textile products that meet or exceed all code requirements applicable to the project.

Scientific and Technical Associations

Among the many scientific and technical associations involved in establishing standards, many are of particular interest to producers and consumers of textile furnishing.

American Association of Textile Chemists and Colorists (AATCC)

Founded in 1921, **AATCC** is a technical and scientific society that is internationally recognized for its standard methods of testing dyed and chemically treated fibers and fabrics. AATCC publishes the *AATCC Technical Manual* on an annual basis. The test methods are designed to measure and evaluate such performance characteristics as color-fastness to light and washing, shrinkage, water resistance, flammability, and many other conditions to which textiles may be subjected. While it is beyond the scope of AATCC to set standard performance specifications, the test methods help producers and retailers to ensure the marketability and satisfactory performance of textile fabrics.

AATCC maintains a technical center that serves as a test demonstration center. Its laboratory is equipped with all of the testing apparatus used in AATCC test methods; personnel at the center provide technical support to members engaged in the work of the Association. Members receive the Association's monthly journal, *AATCC Review*, which presents information concerning recent developments in dyes, finishes, and equipment used in the wet processing of textiles, and also includes reports of current research activities in the field of textiles.

ASTM International

Founded in 1898, **ASTM International**, originally known as the American Society for Testing and Materials (ASTM), is one of the largest standards development organizations in the world. Standards developed at ASTM International are the work of more than 30,000 members. The term "materials" in this organization's name indicates that materials other than textiles—such as metals, concrete, and acoustical board—also receive attention from the society's members. The Society publishes the *Annual*

Book of ASTM Standards; this consists of 72 volumes, divided among 16 sections, each focusing on a limited variety of materials, products, or processes. Included in each volume are all proposed, tentative, and formally adopted standards, guidelines, and performance specifications developed for use with the specific materials or processes covered.

The work of ASTM International is carried out by 132 committees. Each major committee is given a letter and number, followed by a general product designation, for instance, D-13 Committee on Textiles. Further numerical designations are used for subcommittees, for example, D-13.21 Subcommittee on Pile Floor Coverings, or D-13.56 Subcommittee on Performance Standards for Textile Fabrics. Standards developed by ASTM International committees are described as "full-consensus" standards. ASTM International members and nonmembers who have an interest in a standard or who would be affected by its application are encouraged to participate in the development of the standard. Each committee and subcommittee has the participation of both producers and users of the products in question, to ensure a balanced representation of all biases and opinions.

National Fire Protection Association (NFPA)

Organized in 1896, the **NFPA** invites the membership of persons concerned with fire safety. NFPA committees establish standards designed to reduce the extent of injury, loss of life, and destruction of property from fire. This work is not limited to the development of test methods and performance specifications for textile products. NFPA standards have also been issued for items ranging from household warning equipment to fire fighters' helmets, as well as for the design of egress facilities permitting the prompt escape of occupants from burning buildings or into safe areas within the buildings.

American National Standards Institute (ANSI)

Unlike the other groups discussed here, **ANSI** is a private corporation, not a voluntary association. ANSI undertakes the development of standards only when so commissioned by an industry group or a government agency. The Institute seeks to reduce the duplication of effort among the many organizations developing voluntary standards and identifies nationally accepted standards. ANSI is the official U.S. representative to the International Organization for Standardization.

Designation and Cross-listing of Standards

Standards developed by the above-mentioned organizations as well as by other associations are issued with fixed designations. For example, ASTM International designates standards by the letter assigned to the committee and an identifying number. Immediately following the designation is a number indicating the year of original adoption or of the last revision; a number in parentheses indicates the year of the last reapproval. However it is designated, the latest edition of a standard should always be used in quality-control and research activities.

Standards developed by one scientific association are often shared with and cross-listed by other associations. ASTM E-84 The Standard Method of Test of Surface Burning Characteristics of Building Materials, for example, is also identified as NFPA 255 and as ANSI A2.5. Cross-listing may indicate widespread acceptance of a standard, but it does not change its voluntary status. Standards developed by these scientific and technical associations are recommendations, not mandates. The associations have no power or authority to enforce the use of standard test methods or compliance with standard performance specifications. Local, state, or federal regulatory agencies, however, often adopt voluntary standards established by these groups; the standard then becomes mandatory.

Agencies Regulating Product Selections

Regulatory agencies are outside of the textile industry but have the power to oversee the selection of many of its products. Some of the federal agencies involved in these activities are identified here. The reader must be cautioned that the jurisdiction, responsibilities, and mandates of all regulatory agencies change frequently. Contract designers and architects must contact the various agencies to confirm their current jurisdictions and requirements.

Federal Housing Administration (FHA)

The **FHA,** a division of the Department of Housing and Urban Development has jurisdiction over the materials used in the interiors of such places as elderly and care-type housing, low-rent public housing projects, and structures insured by FHA. The minimum standards established for materials used in these facilities are set forth in the Use of Materials Bulletin 44d, which is available from the FHA.

Social Security Administration (SSA)

The **SSA,** a division of the Department of Health and Human Services, administers the Medicare and Medicaid programs. In order to participate in these programs, hospitals and extended care facilities must comply with SSA regulations dealing with fire safety and acoustics. Some of these regulations apply to the textile products selected for these facilities.

General Services Administration (GSA)

The **GSA** oversees the selection of materials for federal facilities. Federal Test Method Standard No. 191A, issued July 20, 1978, describes the general physical, chemical, and biological methods used to test textile fibers, yarn, thread, rope, other cordage, cloth, and fabricated textile products for conformity with mandated and performance specifications. Revised and new test methods are issued as needed.

Federal Aviation Administration (FAA) and National Highway Traffic Safety Administration (NHTSA)

The **FAA** and the **NHTSA** are divisions of the Department of Transportation (DOT). The FAA regulates the selection and installation of textile items in the crew and passenger compartments of airliners, and the NHTSA oversees the selection and installation of textile products in automobiles and certain other vehicles. Flammability standards established by these agencies are discussed in Chapter 11.

There are several other agencies regulating the selection of textile products. Some cities have stringent flammability mandates, and virtually all states have established criteria related to the flammability of products used in commercial interiors. The reader must again be cautioned that the jurisdiction, responsibilities, and codes of all regulatory agencies are frequently changed.

The **Consumer Product Safety Commission (CPSC)** is a federal agency concerned with the safety of most consumer products, including the flammability of textile products. The Commission does not, however, set standards pertaining to product selection. Rather, it prohibits the initial introduction of highly flammable products into commerce and thus prevents them from being available for selection. The Commission and its work are discussed in Chapter 11.

Organizations Establishing Model Building Codes

Several organizations establish model codes. The focus of these model codes ranges from plumbing to mechanical features to fire safety. Design professionals should be familiar with the nature of these codes as they plan the interior spaces. Note that once a model code is adopted as law, it becomes a code, that is, a mandate.

International Codes Council (ICC)

In 1994, the Building Officials and Code Administrators (BOCA), the International Conference of Building Officials (ICBO), and the Southern Building Code Council International (SBCCI) established the International Codes Council. The goal of the **ICC** is to develop a single coordinated set of national codes. ICC is also responsible for publishing the International Building Code (IBC) and the International Residential Code (IRC). Each state decides if it will continue with its current codes or adopt the IRC and IBC.

Council of American Building Officials (CABO)

CABO was developed to unify the three nationally recognized model code organizations, BOCA, ICBO, and SBCCI. In the past CABO was dedicated to maintaining the standard for Accessible and Usable Buildings and Facilities. CABO responsibilities will be integrated into the ICC organization.

Building Officials and Code Administrators (BOCA)

BOCA International was established in 1915. It is the oldest professional code association and is used with other codes to protect human safety and well-being in Canada. BOCA also publishes the National Building Code (NBC) and monitors its enforcement.

International Conference of Building Officials (ICBO)

The **ICBO** is a nonprofit service organization. The organization was founded in 1922 and is used in the midwestern and western regions of the United States. Participating cities, counties, and states have control and ownership of the group. ICBO publishes the Uniform Building Code (UBC).

Southern Building Code Council International (SBCCI)

The **SBCCI** supplies government agencies engaged in building codes administration and enforcement with extensive technical, educational, and administrative support. The SBCCI also dispenses information to designers and builders, and publishes the Standard Building Code (SBC), which is used in the southeastern part of the United States.

Summary

Residential and commercial consumers consider many variables when they select textile products. The nature and relative importance of these variables is constantly changing. Members of the industry are challenged to identify the current criteria and to offer products that coincide with them.

To ensure that their products will exhibit an acceptable level of in-use performance and satisfy the consumer, most producers of textile components and end products evaluate their goods prior to shipment. This quality-control work generally involves the use of standard test methods and performance specifications, many of which are developed by members of scientific associations. The use of such standards is voluntary unless they have been adopted by a regulatory agency, in which case products must comply with the criteria set out by the agency before they can be selected for a specific interior.

Key Terms

AATCC Review
American Association of Textile Chemists and Colorists (AATCC)
AATCC Technical Manual
American National Standards Institute (ANSI)
Annual Book of ASTM Standards
ASTM International
Building Officials and Code Administrators (BOCA)
codes
Consumer Product Safety Commission (CPSC)
Council of American Building Officials (CABO)

design elements
design principles
embodied energy
Federal Aviation Administration (FAA)
Federal Housing Administration (FHA)
General Services Administration (GSA)
initial cost
International Codes Council (ICC)
International Conference of Building Officials (ICBO)
in-use performance
life-cycle cost
Material Safety Data Sheets (MSDS)

National Fire Protection Association (NFPA)
National Highway Traffic Safety Administration (NHTSA)
project bid
project specification
quality-control work
regulatory agencies
Social Security Administration (SSA)
Southern Building Code Council International (SBCCI)
standard performance specification
standard test method
textile end products

Review Questions

1. Explain the nature of quality-control work and the reasons members of the interior textile industry engage in this activity.

2. Why is it important that interior textile products exhibit an acceptable level of performance in-use?

3. Explain what is meant by consumer product selection criteria and the importance of these criteria to interior textile product manufacturers.

4. Discuss the challenges faced by the design professional in selecting and specifying interior textile products.

5. Discuss the impact of design elements and principles on textile product selection.

6. What purposes do standard performance specifications have for manufacturers?

7. Distinguish between standard methods of testing and standard performance specifications, and between standards and codes.

8. Characterize the work of such regulatory agencies as the FHA, the FAA, and the CPSC. Then, compare and contrast the focus of the work of these agencies.

9. Explain how organizations that develop test methods for evaluating textiles function.

10. Explain the meaning of "full consensus" standards.

Fiber Classification and Properties

Photo courtesy of Christian Fischbacher, www.fischbacher.com.

■ **Fibers used in contemporary** textile furnishings are chemically the same as those used in apparel and industrial textile products. Wool fibers, for example, are used in fine crepe apparel fabrics, durable upholstery coverings, and thick insulation felt for industrial applications; nylon fibers are used in lingerie, carpet, automobile seat belts, and tires; and polyester fibers are used in ready-to-wear apparel, upholstery, draperies, bedding, and tent fabrics. The characteristics that make a given fiber suitable for a particular end-use application are inherent and/or are engineered by production and processing techniques.

Natural fiber suppliers and manufactured fiber producers allocate millions of dollars annually toward extensive research and development projects. They support these activities in order to remain competitive and to capture a larger share of the fiber market. The results of this work are fibers with improved appearance and performance characteristics, many of which are specifically engineered for use in interior textile applications.

Whether a fiber is natural or manufactured, it is distinguished by its chemical composition and characterized by specific molecular structures and external physical features. Such characteristics are inherent features of natural fibers; they are engineered features of manufactured fibers. In either case, these variables make for the appearance, chemical reactions, and performance properties of fibers.

Because their chemical composition distinguishes textile fibers, they are classified and named on the basis of this composition. A review of the nomenclature will serve to introduce the basic vocabulary used to discuss fibers and to label and promote textile products.

Fiber Classification and Identification

Specific textile fibers are identified by their common or generic name for purposes of discussion or disclosure on a sample or product label. Fibers grouped under the same name are chemically related and tend to exhibit similar properties. Consumers and professionals who are familiar with these names, and with the properties that typically characterize each group, are better equipped to make reliable fiber selections and to identify unnamed fibers.

Classification

A fiber classification system is presented in Table 3.1. Textile fibers are first classified on the basis of how they are produced, whether natural or manufactured. Although some manufactured fibers are produced from natural substances, some of which are inherently fibrous, none can be classified as a natural fiber because the **usable fiber form** is a product of industrial processing.

Within the two broad fiber groupings, further classification may be made on the basis of general chemical composition: for instance, cellulose, dextrose, protein, synthetic, or mineral. Finally, fibers are classified by their **common or generic names**. For purposes of fiber identification and product labeling, the centuries-old common or family names used for natural fibers are considered their generic names (e.g. cotton, wool, silk, etc.).

Generic names or classes for manufactured fibers were established by the Federal Trade Commission in accordance with a congressional directive. Each class is defined in terms of specific chemical composition. A complete listing of the generic class names set forth by the Commission, as well as those promulgated by the International Organization for Standardization, is presented in Appendix A.

The mandatory use of generic names in textile fiber product labeling and promotion is discussed in Chapter 10. Also discussed in that chapter are the powers and responsibilities of the Federal Trade Commission with respect to the commercial activities of the industry.

Identification

In some instances, a professional or a consumer may encounter a fabric of unknown fiber content. The fabric may be, for example, a customer's own material (known as **COM**) and carry no labeling, or it may be commercial yardage that has become separated from its labels. In any case, various testing and examination procedures can help expedite the identification of unknown fibers. Among these techniques are solubility and staining tests, measurement of fiber density, microscopic examination, burning tests, and visual examination. Because some of these procedures require special reagents, microscopes, infrared spectrometers, exhaust hoods, and the like, they can only be conducted in an adequately equipped laboratory. On the other hand, the burning test

Table 3.1 Textile Fiber Classification

NATURAL FIBERS		
PROTEIN (ANIMALS)	**CELLULOSIC (PLANTS)**	**MINERAL (ROCK)**
Alpaca (alpaca)	**Leaf**	Asbestos
Angora (Angora rabbit)	Abaca (manila fiber)	
Camel (Bactrian camel)	Banana	
Cashmere (Cashmere goat)	Henequen	
Cattle hair (cattle)	Pina (pineapple)	
Fur fibers (beaver, fox, mink, sable, etc.)	Sisal	
Llama		
Mohair (Angora goat)	**Seed**	
Qiviut (musk ox)	Coir (coconut)	
	Cotton	
	Kapok	
	Milkweed	
Silk (silkworm)	**Stem (bast)**	
Vicuna (vicuna)	Hemp	
Wool (sheep)	Jute	
Yak	Kenaf	
	Flax	
	Ramie (China grass)	

MANUFACTURED FIBERS			
CELLULOSIC	**DEXTROSE**	**PROTEIN**	**RUBBER**
Acetate	PLA	Azlon	Rubber (natural liquid rubber)
Lyocell			
Rayon			
Triacetate			

NONCELLULOSIC				MINERAL
Acrylic	Melamine	Polyester	Sulfar	Glass
Anidex	Modacrylic	PBI	Vinal	Metallic
Aramid	Novoloid	Rubber (synthetic)	Vinyon	
Elastoester	Nylon	Saran		
Fluoropolymer	Olefin	Spandex		

can readily be conducted by designers, architects, retailers, and consumers, all of whom have access to matches.

To conduct a burning test, the following procedure can be used, with caution:

1. Hold several fibers or a yarn from a fabric with metal tweezers over a fireproof surface to catch ashes and drips.

2. Strike a match away from the body for safety and to avoid inhaling the smoke and fumes.

3. Observe the reaction of the specimen as it approaches the flame, when it is in the flame, and after the ignition source is removed. Note the odor and examine the cooled residue.

Table 3.2 Reaction of Textile Fibers to Heat and Flame

FIBER	APPROACHING FLAME	IN FLAME	AFTER REMOVAL OF FLAME	RESIDUE	ODOR
Natural					
Protein					
Wool	Curls away from flame	Burns slowly	Self-extinguishing[a]	Brittle, small black bead	Similar to burning hair or feathers
Silk	Curls away from flame	Burns slowly and sputters	Usually self-extinguishing[a]	Beadlike, crushable, black bead	Similar to burning hair or feathers
Cellulosic					
Cotton	Does not shrink away, ignites upon contact	Burns quickly without melting	Continues to burn, afterglow	Light, feathery ash, light gray to charcoal in color	Similar to burning paper
Flax	Does not shrink away, ignites upon contact	Burns quickly without melting	Continues to burn, afterglow	Light, feathery ash, light charcoal in color	Similar to burning paper
Hemp	Does not shrink away, ignites upon contact	Burns quickly without melting	Continues to burn, afterglow	Light, feathery ash, light charcoal in color	Similar to burning paper
Manufactured					
Cellulosic					
Acetate	Melts and fuses away from flame	Burns quickly with melting	Continues to burn rapidly with melting	Brittle, irregular-shaped black bead	Acrid (hot vinegar)
Rayon	Does not shrink away, ignites upon contact	Burns quickly without melting	Continues to burn, afterglow	Light, fluffy ash, small amount	Similar to burning paper
Lyocell	Does not shrink away, ignites upon contact	Burns quickly without melting	Continues to burn, afterglow	Light, feathery ash, light gray to charcoal in color	Similar to burning paper
Dextrose					
PLA (Polylactic Acid)	Melts and shrinks away from flame	Melts and burns with slight white smoke	Usually self-extinguishing[a]	Hard tan or gray bead	Slightly acrid odor
Mineral					
Glass	Shrinks away from flame	Melts and glows red to orange	Glowing ceases, does not burn	Hard bead, white	None
Metallic (pure)	May shrink away from flame or have no reaction	Glows red	Glowing ceases, does not burn, hardens	Skeleton outline of fiber	None
Synthetic Manufactured					
Acrylic	Fuses and shrinks away from flame	Burns with melting	Continues to burn with melting	Brittle, irregular-shaped bead, black	Acrid
Modacrylic	Fuses and shrinks away from flame	Burns slowly and irregularly with melting	Self-extinguishing[a]	Hard, irregular-shaped bead, black	Acid chemical
Nylon	Fuses and shrinks away from flame	Burns slowly with melting	Usually self-extinguishing[a]	Hard, tough, round bead, gray	Celery

Table 3.2 Reaction of Textile Fibers to Heat and Flame *(continued)*

FIBER	APPROACHING FLAME	IN FLAME	AFTER REMOVAL OF FLAME	RESIDUE	ODOR
Synthetic					
Olefin (polypropylene)	Fuses, shrinks, and curls away from flame	Burns with melting	Continues to burn with melting, black sooty smoke	Hard, tough tan bead	Chemical or candle wax
Polyester	Fuses and shrinks away from flame	Burns very slowly with melting	Usually self-extinguishing[a]	Hard, tough, round bead, black	Chemical
Saran	Fuses and shrinks away from flame	Burns very slowly with melting, yellow flame	Self-extinguishing[a]	Hard, irregular-shaped bead, black	Chemical
Spandex	Fuses but does not shrink away from flame	Burns with melting	Continues to burn with melting	Soft, crushable, fluffy, black ash	Chemical
Vinyon	Fuses and shrinks away from flame	Burns slowly with melting	Self-extinguishing[a]	Hard, irregular-shaped bead, black	Acrid

[a]Self-extinguishing fibers stop burning when the source of ignition is removed.

Observations from a completed burning test can be compared with the reactions listed in Table 3.2. Other heat-related fiber properties are identified in Table 3.12 and the pyrolytic characteristics of selected fibers are detailed in Table 3.10. If a mixture of reactions is noted when a yarn is burned, a blend may be suspected. Visual characteristics may help the observer to separate different fibers in the yarn and repeat the test.

In some cases, the results obtained in a burning test may not permit identification of the generic class of the unknown fiber; the results will, however, always enable the observer to classify the specimen in a meaningful category, such as protein or cellulosic. Visual examination may help to support further identification.

Fiber Composition, Molecular Structure, and External Physical Features

Fiber Composition

All textile fibers, natural and manufactured, are relatively fine: that is, they are long and thin and have comparatively high ratios of length to width. This structural feature ensures the flexibility required for manufacturing and end-use serviceability.

Differences among textile fibers result not only from their different chemical compositions, but also from variations in the arrangement of their interior molecular units and the nature of their external physical features. Generic fibers vary in their properties according to their chemical compositions. Natural cellulose-based fibers exhibit similar characteristics and properties. Protein-based fibers such as wool and silk also exhibit similar properties.

Molecular Units and Arrangements

With the exception of the inorganic glass and metal fibers, virtually all fibers have carbon (C) and hydrogen (H) atoms. Some fibers, such as cotton, flax, rayon, acetate, and polyester, also have oxygen (O); others, such as wool, silk, acrylic, and nylon, also have nitrogen (N); and wool also has sulfur (S). The various atoms present in each fiber are combined into distinctive molecular fiber-forming units known as **monomers** (from the Greek *mono*, "one," and *mer*, "part"). Through a process known as polymerization, thousands of monomers are linked by strong chemical bonds into extremely long, chain-like units known as **polymers** (from the Greek *poly*, "many," and *mer*, "part"). (A rough analogy would be the linking of thousands of paper-clips into one long chain.) The monomeric units used to form several fibers are identified later in this chapter. Within textile fibers, the polymer chains assume or are made to assume, different types of arrangements. Four of these arrangements are schematically illustrated in Figure 3.1.

When the polymer chains are not aligned parallel to each other, a disordered, **amorphous** arrangement exists. When the chains are aligned parallel to the long axis of the fiber, the arrangement is **oriented**. When the chains are laterally

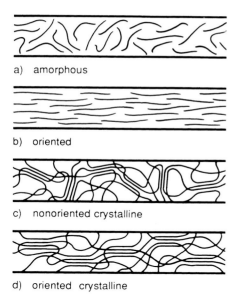

a) amorphous

b) oriented

c) nonoriented crystalline

d) oriented crystalline

Figure 3.1 Molecular arrangements in fibers.

a) overlapping surface scales of wool

Unmercerized Fiber

Mercerized Fiber

b) twisted configuration and wrinkled surface of cotton

c) straight configuration and irregular surface of viscose rayon

d) straight configuration and smooth surface of conventional manufactured fiber

Figure 3.2 Cross-sectional shape, longitudinal configuration, and surface textures of selected fibers.

or longitudinally parallel to each other and closely packed, a high number of chemical bonds or attractions, weaker than the main chain bonds, may form between adjacent chains. Such ordered regions are **crystalline** (Figure 3.1c and d).

The schematic illustration of an amorphous arrangement shown in Figure 3.1a may remind the reader of cooked spaghetti. This analogy can help us appreciate that fibers, such as wool, that have these highly disordered interiors are characterized by relatively high flexibility and low strength: the stronger chemical bonds linking the monomer units are not aligned lengthwise, the direction of stress in textile fibers. By contrast, fibers with an oriented chain arrangement (Figure 3.1b) have their strongest bonds longitudinally aligned, enabling them to bear heavier loads. In any tug-of-war, the winning participants are aligned to offer a collective resistance to the opposing force.

Textile fibers cannot have a totally oriented, crystallized interior arrangement because such fibers would be brittle and inflexible and would snap under stress. Fibers that tend to be highly ordered, such as flax, have relatively low extensibility (ability to extend or be elongated) and flex abrasion resistance (wear resistance). Fabrics composed of such stiff fibers are also less drapable.

External Physical Features

The external features of textile fibers include their cross-sectional shape, their surface texture, their longitudinal configuration, their length, and their diameter. These features, like molecular composition and arrangement, directly influence the properties of fibers.

Cross-sectional Shape

The **cross-sectional shape** of a fiber may be basically round, square, flat, or triangular, or it may be multilobal, having from three to five or more lobes with either slightly concave or deeply indented sides. The effects of cross-sectional shape on the look, stiffness, and tactile characteristics of fibers are explained later in the chapter. The effects of various shapes on the ability of fibers to hide accumulated soil, an important service-related characteristic for fibers used in soft floor coverings, are also discussed in Chapter 3.

Surface Texture

The **surface texture** of textile fibers may be smooth or wrinkled, somewhat rough, or otherwise irregular. Some typical textures are schematized in Figure 3.2. Together with other external features, texture affects the luster and tactile properties of fabric, aesthetic variables that are relatively important selection criteria for many consumers.

Longitudinal Configuration

Lengthwise, fibers may be fairly straight or twisted, or they may have a two- or three-dimensional crimp or coil.

While the form of natural fibers is determined by nature, the form of manufactured fibers is often engineered during fiber or yarn processing. The longitudinal configurations of wool, cotton, rayon, and a conventional manufactured fiber are illustrated in Figure 3.2.

The **longitudinal configuration** of fibers affects such aesthetic features as luster and hand. It also affects such performance properties as elasticity, resiliency, and abrasion resistance. Highly crimped fibers tend to have better resiliency and elasticity.

Length

Textile fibers range in length from a fraction of an inch or millimeter to several miles or meters. Most cotton is $13/16$ inch in length; most wool fibers are between one and eight inches in length; silk filaments approach two miles; and manufactured fibers can be produced to any continuous length desired. Fiber producers classify fiber length as staple or filament. Short fibers that are measured in inches are called **staple fibers**. All the natural fibers, excluding silk, are staple fibers. **Filament fibers** are long, continuous fiber strands of infinite length, typically measured in yards or meters. All manufactured fibers are originally produced as filament fibers but can be cut to staple length.

If other features are equal, longer staples are stronger than shorter staples, and filaments are stronger than staples. In turn, the strength of a fiber helps to determine its abrasion resistance. In addition, yarns made from filaments and longer staple fibers generally appear smoother, and have a cooler hand than do yarns made from shorter staples.

Diameter

The **diameter** or width of a fiber greatly affects a fabric's hand and performance characteristics. Diameter is directly related to end use. Smaller diameter fibers are more pliable, drapable, and softer than larger diameter fibers. Larger diameter fibers are stiffer, crisper, and resist crushing. This is important in carpet fiber production because less crushing means less traffic patterns in carpeting.

Natural fibers are subject to growth irregularities; therefore their diameter is not uniform and cannot be controlled. In natural fibers, the fineness or diameter is a factor in determining the quality of the fiber. Fine fibers are considered to be better quality. The fineness of a fiber is measured in **micrometers** (a micrometer is 1/1,000 millimeters or 1/25, 400 inch). The diameter range for common natural fibers is 10 to 20 for cotton, 12 to 16 for flax, 10 to 50 for wool, and 11 to 12 for silk.[1]

In manufactured fibers, diameter is controlled by the manufacturing process. Manufactured fibers can be produced into any diameter, from uniform to thick and thin throughout their length. The fineness of manufactured fibers is described as **denier**. Denier is the weight of 9,000 meters of fiber or yarn. Filament fiber size (or fineness) is described by **denier per filament** or **dfp**. **Dfp** is calculated by dividing the yarn size by the number of filaments. Fine cotton, cashmere, and wool are 1 to 3 denier. Average cotton, wool, or alpaca is 5 to 8 denier. Carpet wool is 15 denier.[2]

Fiber Properties

To understand a fabric's performance you must first start with the fiber properties. The understanding of textile fibers and their properties is important because fibers are the basic unit of most fabrics. Fiber properties contribute to fabric performance and can predict end-use performance of a particular textile item. Yarn and fabric manufacturers choose the fiber or fibers that most closely match the performance requirements for a particular end use. Each fiber has its own positive and negative attributes/properties. An understanding of fiber properties can lead to better decision making for the consumer.

This chapter section will cover the aesthetic, durability, appearance retention, comfort, and health/safety/protection properties. It should be noted that all fiber properties may by altered in yarn production, fabric manufacturing, color application, and finishing. Some changes are negative and unavoidable; others are positive and intentional. In any event, the properties exhibited by a fiber in finished fabrics and end products may differ from those that characterize the fiber prior to yarn production.

Aesthetic Properties
Luster

The **luster** of textile fibers depends on the quantity of light waves reflected from their surfaces and the direction in which these waves are traveling. Luster is determined by such features as cross-sectional shape, longitudinal configuration, surface texture, and the presence of delustering agents. Figure 3.3 shows that fiber surfaces reflect some portions of incident light waves, transmit other portions, and absorb still other portions. Fibers with round cross sections and smooth surfaces typically reflect large quantities of light rays in one direction (Figure 3.3a), producing a very shiny, lustrous surface. To reduce shine while preserving luster and brightness, fiber engineers create concave shapes, some with marked indentations (Figure 3.3b) and some with slight ones (Figure 3.3c). Light waves striking the indented surfaces are reflected in several directions, producing sheen, not shine.

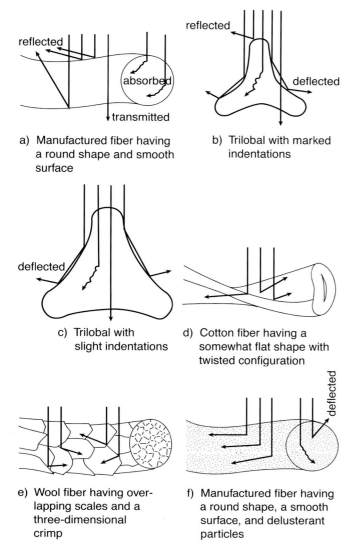

a) Manufactured fiber having a round shape and smooth surface

b) Trilobal with marked indentations

c) Trilobal with slight indentations

d) Cotton fiber having a somewhat flat shape with twisted configuration

e) Wool fiber having over-lapping scales and a three-dimensional crimp

f) Manufactured fiber having a round shape, a smooth surface, and delusterant particles

Figure 3.3 Effects of external features and delusterant particles on fiber luster.

Fibers having crimped or twisted longitudinal configurations will show reduced levels of reflected light. The natural convolutions of cotton fiber give cotton fabrics a low luster (Figure 3.3d). The surface scales and three-dimensional crimp of wool scatter incident light rays (Figure 3.3e) to develop a subdued, matte luster. Manufactured fiber producers often strive to create such soft luster by adding titanium dioxide particles to the polymer solution. Light rays striking the minute, white particles are deflected, dulling the fiber (Figure 3.3f). Incorporating too much delusterant can result in a muddy or chalky luster.

Hand

Hand refers to the tactile characteristics of a fabric. These characteristics include perceived temperature and the level of surface smoothness or roughness. Whether a fabric has a pleasant hand, or feel, is a subjective evaluation that often governs consumer selection. Hand is strongly influenced by the external structural features of the fiber. Fibers with irregular cross-sectional shapes and textured surfaces may feel warm and perhaps harsh or rough. By contrast, fibers with round cross-sectional shapes and smooth surfaces may feel cool and slick when touched (see Figure 3.2).

Drape

Drape is the manner in which a fabric hangs over a three-dimensional form. Fiber size and flexibility contribute to a fabric's drape. Smaller fibers with high flexibility tend to drape easily. The larger and stiffer the fiber, the less likely the fabric is to drape. Yarn twist can also affect drape. Highly twisted fibers tend to be stiffer and drape less. Fabric structure can also affect the amount of drape. Fabrics with a higher yarn count tend to exhibit less drape.

Consumers and designers generally handle sample fabrics and ready-made panels and make subjective evaluations about their drapability. Pleats and folds in panels composed of stiff fibers like flax and glass may not hang freely and evenly, causing the panels to have bows or bulges.

Texture

Texture is the nature of the fiber or fabric surface. Texture is due to the physical structure of the fiber and is identified by both visual and tactile senses. Texture can affect luster, appearance, and comfort. Natural fibers tend to have more texture than manufactured fibers because of their inherent growth irregularities. The cross-sectional shape of manufactured fibers can be changed to allow for differences in texture. Textures can be described as soft, smooth, crisp, or rough. Texture can appear as smooth or rough because of the reflection of light rays (visual) or the surface contour of the fabric (touch).

Durability Properties
Abrasion Resistance

Abrasion resistance is the ability of a textile structure to resist damage and fiber loss by friction. Abrasion may not only diminish the wear life, but it can also cause changes in the textural features and apparent luster of the surface. Abrasion of soft floor coverings can come from the movement of shoe soles, pets, furniture, and equipment across the structure. Abrasive rubbing, especially when accompanied by accumulated grit, can cause carpet and rug fibers to rupture. As split fibers are gradually removed, worn and tattered areas develop and expose the backing. This unsightly problem is more likely to develop first in areas where rubbing actions are concentrated, such as pivotal points in

Table 3.3 Abrasion Resistance of Selected Textile Fibers

Fiber	Level of Resistance
Nylon	Excellent
Olefin	Excellent
Polyester	Excellent
Acrylic	Moderate
Cotton	Moderate
Flax	Moderate
Hemp	Moderate
Lyocell	Moderate
Rayon	Moderate
Wool	Moderate
Silk	Moderate
Acetate	Poor
Vinyon	Poor
Glass	Poor

Table 3.4 Breaking Tenacities of Selected Textile Fibers

Fiber	Grams/Denier Dry	Wet
Natural		
Protein		
Wool	1.5	1.0
Silk	4.5	3.9
Cellulose		
Cotton	4.0	5.0
Flax	5.5	6.5
Manufactured		
Cellulosic		
Acetate	1.2–1.5	0.8–1.2
Rayon (conventional)	0.73–2.6	0.7–1.8
Rayon (improved)	2.5–6.0	1.8–4.6
Lyocell	4.8–5.0	4.2–4.6
Dextrose		
PLA	2.0–6.0	
Mineral		
Glass	7.0	7.0
Synthetic		
Acrylic	2.0–3.5	1.8–3.3
Modacrylic	2.0–3.5	2.0–3.5
Nylon	2.5–9.5	2.0–8.0
Olefin (polypropylene)	4.8–7.0	4.8–7.0
Polyester	2.5–9.5	2.5–9.4
Saran	1.5	1.5
Spandex	0.7	
Vinyon	0.7–1.0	0.7–1.0

traffic paths. Because nylon has excellent abrasion resistance, manufacturers using the fibers are able to offer long-term warranties against significant fiber loss and wear.

Abrasion of bedding products and upholstery comes with use as people slide over the surfaces. Similarly, toweling is abraded as it is moved over glassware or skin. Repeated laundering removes the weakened fibers, and the fabrics get thinner.

The ability of a fiber to resist abrasion depends largely on its strength and elongation. Producers can engineer the necessary strength by controlling the drawing and heat-setting operations used with thermoplastic fibers. Table 3.3 presents the relative abrasion resistance of selected fibers. Abrasion resistance is markedly affected by yarn and fabric structure.

Flexibility

Flexibility is the ability of the fiber to bend repeatedly without breaking. The degree of flexibility or stiffness exhibited by fibers directly affects fabric quality. Flexibility is important in fabrics that will rub against furniture, walls, window frames, or companion panels as they are repeatedly opened or closed. Because fibers displaying low flexibility and elasticity may split and break when subjected to stress, it may be advisable to use them in stationary panels or in infrequently opened casements. Table linens that are repeatedly folded in the same creases may also show wear and tear. This is common with tablecloths and napkins made of flax fiber, as shown in Figure 4.9, p. 55.

Tenacity

Tenacity, or strength, is related to high degrees of polymerization, highly ordered interior arrangements, and/or longer fiber lengths. Shorter fibers with amorphous interiors and/or lower degrees of polymerization exhibit lower tenacity. These variables are given in natural fibers, but in manufactured fibers, these qualities can be engineered during polymerization, spinning, drawing, and heat setting.

The relative terms *weak* and *strong* are often used to describe the strength of textile fibers. These assessments are based on measurements obtained through laboratory testing. Machines equipped to record the length of test specimens at the break point are also equipped to record the grams of force or load that caused the rupture. This information is used to calculate the strength, or breaking tenacity, required to rupture the fiber. The value is reported as grams per denier. Denier indicates weight or mass per unit of length, or linear density. The terms are explained further in Chapter 5.

The breaking tenacities of several fibers are listed in Table 3.4. Although nearly identical to cotton and rayon in chemical composition, flax is stronger than either fiber because of its longer length, higher orientation, and greater crystallinity. Natural cellulosic fibers exhibit greater wet strength, which is a performance variable supporting their wide use in toweling.

Manufactured synthetic fibers exhibit little or no change in tenacity when they are tested wet. This behavior helps make some of the manufactured fibers suitable for end products manufactured for outdoor use, such as awnings, lawn furniture, and outdoor carpeting.

The strength exhibited by a fiber may not be the principal determinant of the strength of the fabric. Weak fibers may be found in strong fabrics, and vice versa. Yarn and fabric structure have a major effect on tenacity. Highly twisted yarns are stronger than low-twist yarns. Higher yarn count also makes stronger fabrics.

Fiber tenacity is an important variable in textile product performance, but elongation must be considered as well in any judgment of potential serviceability.

Elongation

Elongation is the ability of a fiber to be stretched or extended. Elongation depends on the internal arrangement and external structural features of the fiber. Fibers that are highly oriented and crystallized will display minimal elongation (Figure 3.4a). By contrast, fibers having highly amorphous interiors will tend to exhibit high elongation, with the polymer chains straightening and extending under stress (Figure 3.4b). This molecular arrangement and high elongation are characteristic of wool fibers. The molecular arrangement and thus extensibility of most manufactured fibers can be engineered to a great degree by controlling the amount of drawing used in fiber production.

Fibers with a natural or engineered crimp have greater elongation than do fibers with an essentially straight, nontextured configuration (compare Figure 3.4c and 3.4d). For example, the natural crimp of wool augments the extensibility of the amorphous interior. The elongation of cotton derives largely from the unwinding of the natural twist or convolutions. Flax not only has high orientation and crystallinity, but also lacks crimp and so exhibits extremely low elongation.

The extensibility of textile fibers is generally measured at the breaking point. Laboratory equipment used for this is engineered to exert a force while extending the specimen. The machine will then record the breaking load or force in grams and the length of the specimen at the point of rupture. After completion of the test, the elongation of

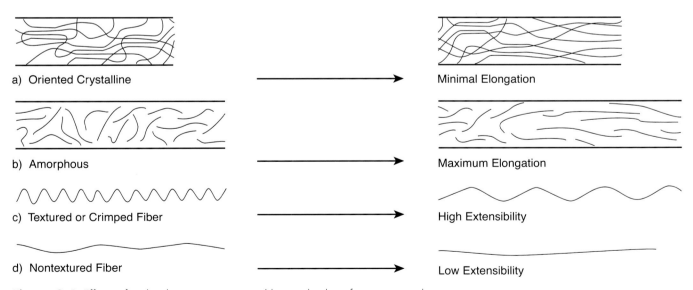

a) Oriented Crystalline → Minimal Elongation

b) Amorphous → Maximum Elongation

c) Textured or Crimped Fiber → High Extensibility

d) Nontextured Fiber → Low Extensibility

Figure 3.4 Effects of molecular arrangement and longitudinal configuration on elongation.

the specimen is calculated and expressed as a percentage of the original length, using the following formula:

$$\% \text{ elongation at break} = \frac{\text{length stretched}}{\text{original length}} \times 100$$

If, for example, a 3-inch length of fiber ruptured when it was 4 inches long, the percent elongation at break is 33.3. (Note that the length stretched is 1 inch, not 4 inches.) Table 3.5 includes elongation measurements for selected textile fibers.

Cohesiveness

Cohesiveness is the ability of fibers to cling together during spinning. Cohesiveness is due to crimp, twist, or the surface contour of fibers. Fabrics made of cohesive fibers are resistant to raveling and yarn slippage. Cotton, one of the shortest textile fibers, is very cohesive because of the convolutions in fiber structure (Figure 3.2). Cotton fibers can make very strong yarns and fabrics because of the cohesiveness of the fiber.

Sunlight Resistance

Sunlight resistance is the ability of a fiber to withstand deterioration by sunlight. Because fabrics and other textile components used in interior and exterior window treatments are exposed to the sun's rays for prolonged periods of time, the sunlight resistance of the fibers used is a crucial service-related property. Consumers and professionals may be more familiar with the negative effects of sunlight on the color component of textile products than with the concurrent loss in fiber tenacity. All fibers are weakened or tendered by sunlight, but some are degraded more rapidly. Over time, the radiant energy of natural light alters the interior structure of fibers, breaking their chemical bonds and reducing the length of their polymer chain. Prolonged exposure to sunlight increases the extent of the damage.

The rate and extent of fiber damage by sunlight is influenced by several factors, including fiber composition, length of exposure, intensity of the light, atmospheric conditions, the presence of colorants, and the use of polymer solution additives. Delusterants can act as catalysts and speed fiber deterioration. On the other hand, ultraviolet absorbers can effectively protect the fiber from harmful rays. This is shown in Figure 3.5, where damage is greatest in the part of the fabric with colorants.

Table 3.5 Elastic Behavior of Selected Textile Fibers

Fiber	% Elongation at Break	% Elastic Recovery from (X%) Strain
Natural		
Protein		
Wool	25–35	99–100 (2), 63 (20)
Silk	13–31	92 (2), 33 (20)
Cellulose		
Cotton	3–7	74 (2), 45 (5)
Flax	3	65 (2)
Manufactured		
Cellulosic		
Acetate	23–45	48–65 (4)
Rayon (conventional)	15–30	82 (2)
Rayon (improved)	9–26	95 (2)
Lyocell	14–18	88 (3)
Dextrose		
PLA	24–32	93 (2)
Mineral		
Glass	3.1–5.3	100 (2)
Synthetic		
Acrylic	34–50	99 (2)
Modacrylic	25–60	100 (1), 55 (10)
Nylon	16–65	100 (5), 99–100 (10)
Olefin (polypropylene)	70–100	97–100 (2), 95 (10)
Polyester	12.0–67.0	67–92 (2), 33 (10)
Saran	15.0–25.0	100 (1), 95 (10)
Spandex	500–700	100 (2), 98 (200)
Vinyon	12.0–125	

Table 3.6 compares the sunlight resistance of selected textile fibers. The loss in tenacity suffered by fibers exposed to light may not be evident until the fabric is cleaned. Consumers may wish to hold the owner of the cleaning establishment responsible for what actually is the result of already weakened fibers rupturing under the cleaning process. For this reason, cleaners may ask customers to sign a statement releasing the firm from responsibility in the event the fabric deteriorates.

Figure 3.5 Sofa faded from sunlight exposure. Courtesy of www.sunmasterstx.com.

Table 3.6 Sunlight Resistance of Selected Textile Fibers

Fiber	Level of Resistance
Glass	Excellent
Acrylic	Excellent
Modacrylic	Excellent
PLA	Excellent
Polyester	Excellent
Lyocell	Moderate
Flax	Moderate
Hemp	Moderate
Cotton	Moderate
Rayon	Moderate
Triacetate	Moderate
Acetate	Moderate
Olefin (Polypropylene)	Moderate
Nylon	Poor
Wool	Poor
Silk	Poor

Insect Resistance

Insect resistance is the resistance to insect damage. Unless wool carpets and rug fibers are treated to be moth resistant, they may be attacked by moth larvae and carpet beetles (see Chapter 9). All domestic wool floor coverings are treated to repel these insects, but residential and commercial consumers must examine the labels of imported products to confirm the use of such treatments. Cellulosic fibers can be attacked by crickets and silverfish. Items of cellulosic nature should be stored clean under dry conditions.

Appearance Retention Properties
Resiliency

Resiliency is the ability of a textile structure to recover from folding, bending, crushing, or twisting. Resiliency is directly related to wrinkle recovery. The resiliency of finished fabrics depends on the behavior of their constituent fibers. If the polymer chains pack closely when the fiber is deformed, new lateral bonds may form and restrict recovery. Such chain packing and bonding are minimized when the polymer chains have large laterally bonded groups, such as those in wool. Fibers with relatively strong lateral bonds, such as those present in spandex and wool, and fibers with a natural or heat-set crimp display better recovery. Stiff fibers, with relatively large diameters and multilobal cross sections, offer greater resistance to wrinkling and exhibit better recovery than do highly flexible fibers.

The resiliency of textile fibers is generally rated in relative terms: excellent, moderate, or poor. Table 3.7 lists the relative performance of fibers frequently used in interior textile products.

To overcome the inherently poor resiliency of cellulose fibers, converters employ chemical cross-linking resins. However, these finishes can decrease fiber strength and abrasion resistance. The use of these finishing compounds is reviewed in Chapter 9.

Compression Resiliency

Compression resiliency, or loft, is the ability of a textile fiber to spring back to its original thickness after being compressed. Compression resiliency contributes to

Table 3.7 Resiliency of Selected Textile Fibers	
Fiber	Level of Resiliency
Wool	Excellent
Polyester	Excellent
PLA	Excellent
Nylon	Good
Acrylic	Good
Olefin	Good
Lyocell	Fair
Acetate	Fair
Rayon	Poor
Cotton	Poor
Hemp	Poor
Flax	Poor

springiness, covering power, and resistance to flattening. It is an important property for end uses such as carpeting, pile upholstery fabrics, and fiberfill applications. The more loft in carpeting, the less it will show wear in high-traffic areas. High compression resiliency in fiberfill batting will allow the air spaces to remain intact, creating a high insulation ability.

Elastic Recovery

Elastic recovery measurements indicate how completely a fiber returns to its original length after being elongated. In standard methods of testing, fibers are generally extended 2 percent of their relaxed length, held in the deformed position for 30 seconds, and allowed 1 minute for recovery. In actual use, fibers are normally subjected to greater deformations for longer periods of time.

Fibers having highly disoriented interior structures typically exhibit an inherent desire to return to their relaxed state. Those having an inherent or heat-stabilized crimp also tend to display better recovery than that shown by noncrimped fibers. Table 3.5 presents the immediate elastic recovery values for several fibers. Measurements taken after longer periods would normally show higher recovery.

Elastic Modulus

The initial resistance to deformation stress exhibited by a fiber is known as its **elastic modulus**. A fiber may have high initial resistance and then yield readily as the stress load increases. Such a response is typical of spandex fi-

bers and partly accounts for their success in foundation garments and swimwear. The superior elastic modulus of spandex provides the necessary holding power, but the fiber can be extended five to seven times its relaxed length by higher stress loads before rupturing.

Unlike spandex fibers, conventional rayon fibers have a low elastic modulus, especially when they are wet or when the level of humidity is high. Under these conditions, the fibers may readily yield to the stress of their own weight and that of the absorbed moisture and lengthen. This lack of fiber stability would cause the panels in curtains and draperies to sag. When the humidity decreases, the fibers and the fabric would shorten again. This phenomenon, variously termed the **elevator effect**, the **yo-yo effect**, and **hiking**, may be quite pronounced with loosely constructed fabrics. Rayon fiber producers have engineered high wet modulus (HWM) fibers that resist deformation under humid or wet conditions. Fabrics composed of HWM rayon fibers will not exhibit the elevator effect and can be laundered as well.

Dimensional Stability/Shrinkage Resistance

Dimensional stability is the ability of a fiber to retain its original size and shape throughout use and care. **Shrinkage resistance** is the ability of a fiber to retain its original shape during care procedures. Some fibers retain shape better than others. A fabric may increase (grow) in size or decrease (shrink) in size. When buying interior textiles, consumers typically do not think of allowance for growth or shrinkage. Shrinkage or growth is related to a fiber's reaction to moisture or heat. Drapery fabrics made of rayon may actually lengthen when the humidity is high and may or may not return to the original length under normal levels of humidity.

Dimensional changes in a fabric often dictate how the fabric is cleaned. Some fabrics can be laundered, whereas others must be dry-cleaned. Natural cellulose fibers exhibit poor dimensional stability, whereas natural protein fibers exhibit high dimensional stability. Manufactured cellulosic and dextrose fibers exhibit dimensional properties similar to those of the natural cellulosics. Manufactured synthetic fibers exhibit very high dimensional stability.

Pilling Propensity

Pilling is the formation of tiny balls of entangled fiber ends on a fabric's surface. The ball of entangled fibers is usually held to the surface of a fabric by one or more fibers. These "pills" are unsightly and a nuisance to remove. Pilling occurs on staple fiber fabrics because the fiber ends entangle due to abrasion. Fabrics composed of short staple yarns are more subject to pilling than fabrics composed of longer staple or filament yarns. High yarn twist and high yarn count can also minimize pilling. Although pills composed of some staple fibers may be removed by subsequent surface abrasion, those composed of stronger fibers tend to cling tenaciously to the fabric.

Oleophilic

Oleophilic fibers exhibit a strong attraction to oily stains. Oleophilic properties are due to a fiber's chemical composition. Fibers that have low moisture absorbency tend to have a high attraction to oils and grease. Textile products made from manufactured synthetic fibers tend to attract oily stains, which can be very difficult to remove.

Soil Repellency

Carpet fibers have been engineered for built-in **soil repellency**, the ability to reduce initial attraction for soil and to retard the rate of soil accumulation. This is accomplished by chemically modifying the fiber. Generally, a fluorocarbon compound is incorporated in the polymer solution. Because this compound lowers the critical surface energy of fibers, dirt, dust, and grime do not readily adhere to their surfaces, and spilled liquids bead up rather than pass through the fibers. Examples of soil-repellent carpet fibers include Anso® IV nylon, produced by Allied Fibers; Trevira® Pentron™ polyester, produced by Hoechst Fibers Industries; and Zefron® 500™ ZX nylon, produced by BASF Corporation.

Soil repellency can also be introduced by coating surfaces of the fibers with fluorocarbon compounds. The agents may be applied to the filaments at the point of extrusion or sprayed over the fibers during conversion of the greige goods. In the latter case, converters must see that the placement of the compound is not limited to the upper portion of the pile yarns. Examples of trade names indicating the application of soil-repellent compounds include Milliguard® Carpet Protector, owned by Milliken & Company; R9000® Soil Shield®, owned by Armstrong World Industries; and Scotchgard® and 3M Brand Pocket Protector, supplied by the 3M Company.

A physical approach for reducing the quantity of soil accumulation involves the extrusion of fibers with an extra large denier per filament. The larger diameter covers more carpet surface area, so fewer of the filaments are required for carpet production.

Continuing the research toward achieving control of soil problems, soil-shedding carpet fibers have been developed. Usually these fibers have a trilobal cross-sectional shape and a rough surface contour that reduces soil adhesion. The microridges effectively "tee up" soil for easy shedding or removal.

Optical Brighteners

Optical brighteners are used to overcome the dulling effects produced by the accumulation of soil. Brighteners are fluorescent compounds. Whether they are incorporated as an integral part of manufactured fibers or absorbed onto exterior surfaces, they increase reflectance by the same mechanism. Incident ultraviolet rays react with brightener molecules, causing them to reflect more light waves. In effect, brighteners convert invisible wavelengths to visible wavelengths, increasing the apparent, not the actual, whiteness or brightness of fibers and fabrics. The effectiveness of most brighteners depends on the quantity of ultraviolet rays reflecting on the textile surface.

Soil Hiding/Soil Magnification

Residential and commercial consumers are extremely critical of textile floor coverings that rapidly accumulate high levels of soil. To overcome such problems and satisfy consumers, fiber chemists and engineers have manipulated fiber cross-sectional shapes and experimented with different polymer additives. **Soil hiding** is the ability of a fiber or coloration to hide or camouflage dirt. The carpet will look cleaner than it is, in contrast to **soil magnification**, in which fibers magnify accumulated soil, and the surface looks dirtier than it is. The peculiar problem of soil magnification occurs when soil particles reflect incident waves through round, nondelustered fibers (Figure 3.6a). Industry researchers first sought to overcome this problem by adding delusterant compounds (Figure 3.6b). As the amount of delusterant is decreased, the soil-hiding power is also increased, but an undesirable muddiness would at some point become apparent in the luster. Researchers then created various nonround cross-sectional shapes that produce an acceptable level of soil hiding as well as the preferred luster and sheen. Light waves are diffused from a multilobal design (see Figure 3.3b).

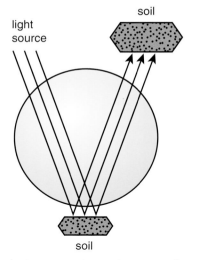

a) Soil magnification by transparent, round cross section.

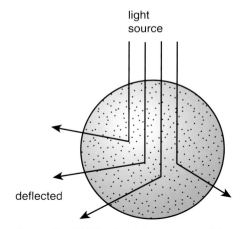

b) Delustering and soil hiding by delusterant particles.

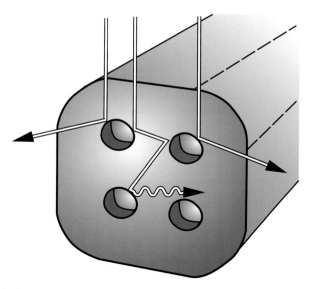

c) Soil hiding by voids and a rounded square cross section.

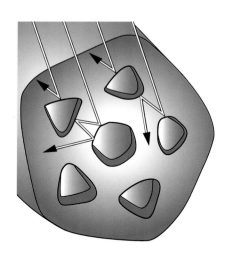

d) Soil hiding by voids and a pentalobal cross section.

Figure 3.6 Effects of cross-sectional shape, delusterants, and microscopic voids on soil magnification and soil hiding. Illustration (d) by Andrea Lau.

Although deeply indented shapes effectively hide soil, their highly concave sides provide crevices or spaces where dirt particles can become entrapped, making their removal more difficult. The modified trilobal design illustrated in Figure 3.3c avoids this problem.

An innovative approach to soil hiding is the introduction of microscopic voids, also referred to as conduits or tunnels, lengthwise within fibers. The interior voids deflect incident waves, obscuring the appearance of soil. Nylon carpet produced with a rounded-square shape and interior voids is illustrated in Figure 3.6c, and that produced with a pentalobal shape and microscopic voids is shown in Figure 3.6d.

Comfort Properties
Absorbency

Absorbency is the percentage of moisture a dry fiber will absorb from the air when at standard humidity and temperature. Comparisons of the abilities of fibers to absorb moisture are based on their moisture regain values, which indicate their abilities to absorb vapor-phase moisture. These values are calculated by the following formula:

$$\% \text{ moisture regain} = \frac{\text{conditioned weight} - \text{dry weight}}{\text{dry weight}} \times 100$$

Dry weight is the weight of the oven-dried specimen. Conditioned weight is determined after the dry specimen has been kept in an atmosphere of 70 ± 2 degrees Fahrenheit and 65 ± 2 percent relatively humidity for a period of 24 hours or until the specimen reaches equilibrium. The increase in conditional weight over dry weight shows the amount of vapor-phase moisture absorbed by the fiber. The difference is expressed as a percentage of the dry weight. Typical moisture regain values are listed in Table 3.8.

Fibers with high regain values, including the natural, manufactured cellulosic and manufactured dextrose fibers, are referred to as **hydrophilic** (water-loving) fibers. These fibers are easily colored with dyestuffs, but they require protective finishes for use in exterior textile products. Fibers with low regain values are **hydrophobic** (water-hating) fibers. These are suitable for use in outdoor applications, but some have virtually no capacity for moisture absorption and are difficult and expensive to dye, limiting their color-styling possibilities. **Hygroscopic** fibers, such as wool, absorb moisture without feeling wet. Wool is more hygroscopic than any other fiber, with a moisture regain of up to 16 percent (see Table 3.8).

The absorbency of fibers has a direct effect on their cleanability. Hydrophilic fibers are more readily cleaned, as they easily absorb the detergent solution. By contrast, hydrophobic fibers and cellulose fibers treated with chemical cross-linking resins may require the application of finishing agents or the use of special laundry aids to improve their cleanability.

Hydrophilic fibers will have a limited buildup of electrical charges on their surface when the level of humidity is high. This lessens their attraction for such airborne soil

Table 3.8 Percentage Moisture Regain of Selected Textile Fibers	
Fiber	Percentage
Wool	16.00
Rayon	13.00
Lyocell	11.50
Flax	10.0–12.0
Cotton	8.50
Acetate	6.00
Nylon	4.00–4.5
Acrylic	1.3–2.5
Polyester	0.4–0.8
PLA	0.4–0.6
Vinyon	0.50
Olefin (Polypropylene)	0.00
Saran	0.00
Glass	0.00

particles as pet hair, dust, and lint. On the other hand, these fibers may be more easily stained by waterborne substances, such as staining agents in grape juice or red wine. In wool, an invisible film known as the cuticle covers the scales and provides temporary protection; staining can be avoided by quickly sponging up spilled fluids.

Some hydrophobic fibers, including nylon, polyester, and olefin, are quite resistant to waterborne stains but are subject to oilborne staining. Converters often apply fluorocarbon compounds to greige goods composed of these fibers to minimize this problem.

Several carpet fibers, including acrylic, polyester, and olefin, have comparatively low moisture regain values (see Table 3.8). If other characteristics are appropriate, these fibers may be used in carpet to be installed outdoors. Drawing and heat setting are used to increase the crystallinity and reduce the absorbency of nylon, making the fiber suitable for use in such products as outdoor carpeting and artificial turf for sports stadiums. Fibers with comparatively high regain values, such as wool, may have reduced static electricity problems when the level of relative humidity is high, but they absorb more moisture and require longer drying times when exposed to wet cleaning agents.

Fibers used in the backing layers of structures to be installed below ground level should have low absorbency

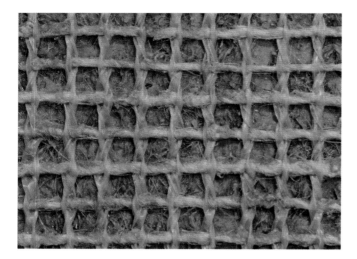

Figure 3.7 Olefin carpet backing.
Courtesy of Amy Willbanks, www.textilefabric.com.

to resist microbe damage and odor. The lack of absorbency of olefin fibers supports their selection for such installations. In contrast, the moisture-induced degradation exhibited by jute makes it inappropriate for such use.

Polyester, with a low moisture regain, is often blended with cotton for use in towels and bath mats. Whereas polyester fiber increases the durability of polyester/cotton blends, the high moisture regain of cotton gives the products increased absorbency. Cotton towels are usually softer than polyester/cotton blended towels.

Wicking

Wicking is the ability of a fiber to transport moisture along its surface by capillary action, as a lamp wick transports flammable fluid upward to the site of the flame. Olefin has inherent wicking, which supports its extensive use in carpet backings, needle punched carpeting, and upholstery slipcovers (Figure 3.7). Currently, fiber chemists are working to improve the wicking ability and absorbency of several noncellulosic fibers.

Heat Conductivity

Heat conductivity and heat transmittance are synonymous terms used to refer to the rate at which a material conducts heat. Most textile fibers have low rates of conduction and contribute to the insulative power of textile structures. Although the transfer of heat is influenced by the conductivity rate of the fiber used, it primarily depends on the thickness of the textile structure. This interrelationship is discussed in detail in Chapter 26. Natural cellulose

fibers tend to exhibit high heat conductivity, whereas natural protein fibers exhibit poor heat conductivity. Blankets made of wool fiber are known for their exceptional heat retention and insulating power.

Covering Power

Covering power is the ability of a textile structure to cover or conceal an area without undue weight. The effectiveness with which fibers cover a surface depends on structural features, such as cross-sectional shape and longitudinal configuration, along with specific gravity.

Fibers having round cross-sectional shapes cover less surface area than do fibers of equal volume with flat configurations. This difference is schematically illustrated in Figure 3.8. Fibers with a natural or engineered crimped configuration cover more surface area than do straight fibers. The effect is more evident when the multidimensional fibers are grouped into yarn structures (Figure 5.1, p. 85).

Density/Specific Gravity

To obtain maximum cover with minimum weight, a fiber with a low specific gravity should be selected. **Specific gravity** is the **density** (mass, or amount of matter per unit of volume) of a fiber relative to that of water at 4 degrees centigrade, which is one. Fibers having a specific gravity

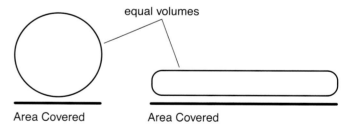

Figure 3.8 Effects of cross-sectional shape on covering power.

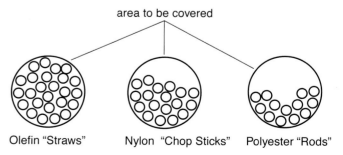

Figure 3.9 Schematic representation of the effect of specific gravity on covering power.

Table 3.9 Specific Gravities of Selected Textile Fibers	
Fiber	Specific Gravity
Glass	2.5–2.7
Saran	1.68–1.75
Lyocell	1.56
Cotton	1.52
Flax	1.52
Rayon	1.50–1.52
Polyester	1.22–1.38
Modacrylic	1.30–1.37
Vinyon	1.37
Wool	1.34
Acetate	1.32
Silk	1.25
PLA	1.24–1.25
Acrylic	1.14–1.19
Nylon	1.14
Olefin (Polypropylene)	0.91

greater than one are heavier than an equal volume of water; those with a specific gravity less than one are lighter and will float on water. Table 3.9 presents the specific gravities of fibers used extensively in interior textile products.

If the diameters of two fibers are equal, the fiber with the lower specific gravity will cover more area with less weight than will the fiber with higher specific gravity. Covering power is an especially critical value when sizable amounts of fiber are used in structures designed to cover large areas, like window, wall, and floor coverings.

As shown in Table 3.9, the specific gravity of glass, 2.50–2.70, is higher that that of all other fibers commonly used for interior applications. Thus, window coverings of glass would weigh more than identical fabrics composed of other fibers. For this reason, glass fiber generally has been used in open casements (Figure 17.18, p. 292). Fiberglass is now being replaced with FR (flame retardant) polyester because of its durability, indoor air quality, cleanability, and cost effectiveness.

The weight and cost of textile floor coverings relate to the specific gravity of the fiber used. An analogy can demonstrate how this is so. Drinking straws represent olefin fibers, wooden chopsticks represent nylon fibers, and glass stirring rods represent polyester fibers; these items, with their obvious differences in density, were chosen to reflect the specific

gravities of the fibers (see Table 3.9). If equal weights of the three are given, as Figure 3.9 shows, the lowest amount of cover will be provided by the polyester rods and the highest amount of cover by the olefin straws. To develop coverage equal to that of olefin, more or larger nylon and still more or larger polyester fibers would have to be used. The weight of the floor covering will increase in either case, as probably would also its cost. As fiber engineers have improved the absorption and reduced the heat sensitivity of olefin fibers, their use in interior floor coverings has increased.

The relationship between fiber density and denier is partly responsible for the success of nylon over polyester in the face yarn market. Figure 3.10 shows a nylon fiber and a polyester fiber of equal deniers. Manufacturers could produce more carpet covering more surface area with fewer filaments and less weight with nylon than with polyester. Increasing the diameter of the polyester to equal that of the nylon would also increase the weight and cost. Because stiffness increases and resiliency improves as fiber diameter grows larger, it follows that a polyester carpet must be heavier and thus more costly than a nylon carpet.

Health/Safety/Protection Properties
Chemical Resistance

The **chemical properties** of textile fibers help determine the end-use serviceability of interior textiles. An inherent chemical property may limit the suitability of a fiber for some end-use applications, and it may dictate the use of finishing agents. The chemical properties of fibers, like their physical properties, can be measured in the laboratory, following the procedures set forth in standard test methods.

Various pollutant gases destroy colorants (see Chapter 14), and, after combining with moisture, they can destroy textile fibers. When vapor-phase moisture within fibers, yarns, or folds in panels reacts with such gases as sulfur oxide and nitrogen oxide, weak sulfuric acid and weak ni-

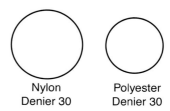

Figure 3.10 Effect of fiber density on denier and fiber diameter.

Table 3.10 Pyrolytic Characteristics of Selected Textile Fibers

	TEMPERATURES				HEATS OF COMBUSTION (BTUs/LB)	LIMITING OXYGEN INDEX
	DECOMPOSITION°		IGNITION			
FIBER	°F	°C	°F	°C		
Natural						
Protein						
Wool	446	230	1,094 (Self-extinguishing)	590	9,450	25.2
Cellulose						
Cotton	581	305	752	400	7,400	17–20
Mineral						
Asbestos			Fireproof			
Manufactured						
Cellulosic						
Acetate	572	300	842	450	7,700	18.4
Rayon	350–464	177–240	788	420	7,400	18.6
Mineral						
Glass	1,500	815	Noncombustible			
Synthetic						
Acrylic	549	287	986	530	1,300	18.2
Aramid	Decomposes above 800 °F (427 °C)					
Modacrylic	455	235	Will not support combustion; self-extinguishing			
Novoloid	Decomposes (converts to carbon)	and resists over 5000 °F (2760 °C); does not burn				
Nylon	653	345	989	532	12,950	20.1
Olefin (Polypropylene)						18.6
Polyester	734	390	1,040	560	9,300	20.6
Saran	168	76	Will not support combustion; self-extinguishing			
Vinyon			Will not support combustion; self-extinguishing			

tric acid will be formed. Indoors, droplets of these compounds may be described as **interior acid rain**. Gradually, the acids attack the chemical bonds within the fibers, interrupting the polymer chains and weakening the fibers. The effects of this degradation may not become evident until laundering or dry cleaning, and they may be more pronounced with cellulosic fibers.

Pyrolytic Characteristics

The production of textile fibers must be long and thin for pliability and flexibility. This physical form results in high ratios of surface area to volume. Thus, for their volume, all textile fibers expose a disproportionately large amount of surface area to the atmospheric oxygen needed for combustion reactions. As the same time, their various chemical compositions result in differences in their pyrolytic characteristics and relative flammability.

In the cyclic combustion process (see Chapter 11), the supply of available oxygen continually decreases. Without sufficient oxygen in the burning area, and with the source of ignition removed, some fibers **self-extinguish**. The amount of oxygen required to support the combustion of a fiber is measured and reported as the **limiting oxygen index (LOI)**. Fibers with a LOI above 21 percent self-extinguish after combustion reduces the level of oxygen below the normal 21 percent concentration and the source of ignition is removed. Under the same conditions, fibers having a LOI below 21 percent continue to burn until they are consumed (Table 3.10).

Textile fibers burn at different temperatures and have different **heat of combustion values**. These values specify the amount of heat energy generated that could cause burn injuries as well as maintain the temperature required for further decomposition and combustion. The heats of combustion, ignition temperature, and other pyrolytic characteristics of selected fiber groups are listed in Table 3.10.

Flammability

Fibers are described as flammable, flame resistant, noncombustible, or fireproof. A **flammable fiber** is relatively easy to ignite and sustains combustion until it is consumed. A **flame-resistant fiber** may have, for example, relatively high decomposition and ignition temperature, a slow rate

of burning, or a high LOI value. **Noncombustible fibers** do not burn or contribute significant amounts of smoke. Noncombustible fibers are not fireproof, however, because they can melt and decompose at high temperatures. A **fireproof fiber** is unaffected by fire. Table 3.11 includes a listing of the relative flammability of several fibers.

Thermoplasticity

Thermoplastic fibers soften when heated, permitting manufactured fiber producers to use heat setting as an engineering tool. In this application, thermoplasticity is a positive fiber characteristic; but **thermoplasticity** is a negative characteristic when a fiber is heated to its melting point by such items as lit cigarettes, glowing embers, candle flames, and overly hot irons. When such an unfortunate event occurs, the fiber shrinks and melts. Subsequently, the molten polymer cools into an unsightly, hardened mass, producing a permanently damaged area in the fabric. The softening and melting points for thermoplastic fibers are listed in Table 3.12. The table also lists temperatures recommended for ironing fabrics composed of several fibers. Not all fibers are heat sensitive in that they soften and melt when heated; however, all fibers are susceptible to heat. They will decompose, scorch, melt, or otherwise react to elevated temperatures.

Table 3.11 Relative Flammability of Selected Textile Fibers			
Fireproof	Noncombustible	Flame-Resistant	Flammable
Asbestos	Glass	Aramid	Cotton
		Novoloid	Flax
		Wool	Hemp
		Modacrylic	PLA
		Vinyon	Lyocell
		Saran	Rayon
		Silk	Acetate
			Triacetate
			Acrylic
			Nylon
			Polyester
			Olefin (Polypropylene)

Table 3.12 Effects of Heat on Textile Fibers

Fiber	Softening Point °F	Softening Point °C	Melting Point °F	Melting Point °C	Safe Ironing Temperature °F	Safe Ironing Temperature °C
Natural						
Protein						
Wool	Does not soften		Does not melt		300	149
Silk	Does not soften		Does not melt		300	149
Cellulose						
Cotton	Does not soften		Does not melt		425	218
Flax	Does not soften		Does not melt		450	232
Manufactured						
Cellulosic						
Acetate	400–455	205–230	500	260	350	177
Rayon	Does not soften		Does not melt		375	191
Mineral						
Glass	1,350+	732+				
Synthetic						
Acrylic	450–497	232–258	Degrades before true melt		320	160
Aramid	Does not melt		Carbonizes above 800 °F			
Modacrylic	300	149	Degrades before true melt			
	shrinks at 250	121				
Novoloid	Does not melt		Carbonizes above 5000 °F			
Nylon	445	229	500	260	350	177
Olefin	230–239	110–115	260	127	Do not iron	
Polyester	460–490	238–254	480–550	249–288	325	163
Saran	240–280	116–138	260	127	Do not iron	
Vinyon	170	77	260	127	Do not iron	
	shrinks at 150	66				

Heat Susceptibility

Although the natural fibers, along with rayon, lyocell and PLA, are not **heat sensitive**, and thus cannot be permanently set with heat, they are nonetheless susceptible to heat. Exposing natural fibers to elevated temperatures, especially for prolonged periods, may cause degradation and discoloration. For example, excessively high ironing temperatures weaken and scorch cotton and linen fabrics.

Microbe Resistance

Antimicrobial agents are chemicals that provide microbe resistance either by killing bacteria or fungi or by retard-ing its normal activities. Bacteria and fungi are extremely simple vegetative plant forms that lack chlorophyll. Bacteria can react with perspiration to cause odor and can cause infection and slow the healing process. Fungi, such as molds and mildew, produce stains and odors. Some microbes use fabrics as a staging point, a place to multiply and build their numbers while they prepare an invasion of the next host who touches the fabric.[3]

Antimicrobial treatments can resist a microbe either by killing the pest or keeping the microbe below a certain level. You do not get odor control by applying a higher dose than necessary. **Spectrum** refers to the array of microorganisms vulnerable to a particular antimicrobial. The end use of a textile product determines which spectrum is appropriate. For example, healthcare facilities would require the broadest spectrum of antimicrobials.

There are also environmental concerns about their effect of antimicrobial treatments on the environment because the purpose of an antimicrobial treatment is to destroy the microbes. Antimicrobials can affect the environment when a chemical is produced, when it is applied to the fabric, and when that fabric is laundered. On the other hand, microbe resistant finishes can have a positive effect on the environment, extending the usable life of the fabric, keeping it out of the landfill. Odor-reducing antimicrobials lead to less frequent laundering at lower temperatures which is also a benefit to the environment.

In the U.S. antimicrobial treatments must be registered by the Environmental Protection Agency (EPA). Registration requires the specific end-use for the antimicrobial. Not only are the chemical themselves controlled, but regulatory bodies also control what claims can be made for the treatments. The EPA makes a fundamental distinction between protecting the textile and protecting the person. For example, the manufacturer can claim an antimicrobial will protect a fabric from developing odors due to bacteria, but cannot claim the antimicrobial will protect the user from bacteria.[4]

One of the fastest growing areas for antimicrobial textiles is the medical/healthcare/nursing home sector. With the rise of hospital-borne and antibiotic-resistant infections, healthcare facilities have become interested in using antimicrobial fabrics in bedding, sheeting, window treatments, upholstery, cubicle curtain, and uniforms to control textile contamination. Converters are now able to apply these agents with others in a single operation, reducing production time and expense while affording fibers greater protection.

Electrical Conductivity/Static Propensity

The electrical properties (static propensity) and moisture absorbency of fibers determine the level of static generated by a soft floor covering. Static development is initiated by the frictional heat energy created by the rubbing of soles on carpet and rug fibers. The heat energy causes negatively charged electrons to transfer from the fiber surfaces to the body, where they accumulate. When the person touches the electrical conductor, such as a metal doorknob, the accumulated electrons rapidly flow from the body to the conductor. It is this sudden discharge of high energy potential that results in electrical shock. The level of voltage on the body when contact is made with a conductor determines

the severity of the shock. Almost no one is sensitive to the discharge of 2,500 or fewer static volts. When the charge level is between 2,500 and 3,500 static volts, almost everyone will feel a shock. The lower end of this range is known as **the threshold of sensitivity**.

Electrical conductivity describes the relative ease with which a fiber conducts or resists the flow of electrons. Fibers that keep electrons flowing, minimizing their accumulation, are classified as **conductors**. Olefin, acrylic, and modacrylic are conductors; metal fibers are especially good conductors. Fibers that offer higher resistance to the flow of electrons are **insulators**. These fibers, which include nylon, wool, and polyester, allow pools of electrons to form on their surfaces, readily available for transfer.

The amount of heat energy available to cause electron release is also determined by the manner of walking. Slow, light-footed walking generates less heat energy than a rapid, heavy gait. Great amounts of heat energy and high levels of electron release accompany scuffing and shuffling because these movements involve vigorous rubbing of the fiber surfaces. Like fibers, shoe sole materials vary in the ease with which they release electrons.

Fibers displaying high moisture regain values will show fewer static problems when the level of humidity is relatively high. Moisture encourages the flow of electrons and limits their pooling on fiber surfaces. Controlling levels of relative humidity is a year-round practice in such interiors as computer rooms and medical facilities. This control helps ensure that sensitive equipment does not malfunction as a result of extra electrical charges picked up from the floor covering. The ability to increase relative

Figure 3.11 Antron® carpet fiber with a conductive carbon black core combined with soil-hiding filaments.
Photo courtesy of INVISTA Sarl.

humidity is particularly helpful in winter months, when interiors may have levels as low as 5 to 10 percent.

One of the first techniques devised to improve fiber conductivity was to add a compound, such as polyethylene glycol, to the polymer solution prior to extrusion. Such additives can contribute to soil hiding as well as static reduction properties.

Another technique to improve fiber conductivity is the use of coated filaments. By enclosing a nylon filament in a sheath of conductive material, such as silver, and plying these coated filaments with other fibers, some companies have developed an effective way to keep electrons from pooling. X-Static®, marketed by Sauquoit Industries, is produced in this manner. A similar technique is used to make Zefstat® products, produced by BASF Corporation. In these structures, however, the position of the components is reversed. The conductive material, aluminum, forms the core, and a colored polymer compound is used as the coating.

Electrical conductivity can also be increased by periodically incorporating fine metal filaments in floor coverings. Metal fibers placed at regular intervals in textile floor coverings effectively drain away electrons. These extremely fine fibers, in staple or filament form, can be added by themselves, spun with staple carpet fibers, or thrown with multifilament yarns. Examples of fine stainless steel fibers are Brunsmet®, produced by Brunswick Corporation, and Bekinox® produced by the Bekaert Steelwire Corporation. When spun yarns of Bekinox® are plied with wool, nylon, or polyester yarns, the blended yarns are distinguished by the name Bekitex®.

Some fiber producers have capitalized on the conductivity of carbon black by incorporating the compound into nonuniform filament structures. These filaments are categorized as bicomponent or conjugate fibers, fibers composed of dissimilar compounds. DuPont has developed a conductive filament whose core of carbon black is surrounded by a round sheath of nylon. This fiber is combined with several soil-hiding fibers (Figure 3.11).

Commercial carpet manufacturers incorporate fibers containing carbon black (used as a lightning rod down the side). This conjugate fiber is 5 percent carbon black and 95 percent nylon. The round cross-section fiber is plied with soil-hiding trilobal Ultra® nylon to form the yarn bundle used in carpet production. A diagram of a microscopic view is shown in Figure 3.12.

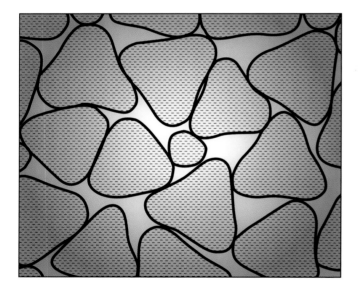

Figure 3.12 Conductive fiber used with Ultron® nylon. Illustration by Andrea Lau.

Summary

The aesthetic, durability, comfort, appearance retention, and health/safety properties of textile fibers depend greatly on their chemical compositions, the arrangement of their internal molecular units, and the nature of their physical external features. Residential consumers, contract designers, and architects should consider fiber properties when selecting or specifying interior textile products, to ensure that the constituent fibers exhibit properties suitable for the end-use application.

Key Terms

abrasion resistance
amorphous polymer chains
antimicrobial agents
apparent whiteness or brightness
breaking tenacity
chemical properties
cohesiveness
COM
common name
colorants
compression resiliency
conductors
covering power
cross-sectional shape
crystalline polymer chains
delusterants
denier
denier per filament (dpf)
density
diameter
dimensional stability
drape
dye pigments
elastic modulus
elastic recovery
electrical conductivity
electrical resistivity
elevator effect
elongation
Federal Trade Commission (FTC)
fiber toughness
fibrillation
filament fibers

fireproof fiber
flame-resistant fiber
flammable fiber
flexibility
fluorescent compound
fluorocarbon compound
frictional heat energy
generic name
hand
heat conductivity
heat of combustion values
heat sensitive fiber
heat transmittance
hiking
hydrophilic fiber
hydrophobic fiber
hygroscopic fiber
inherent color
insect resistance
insulators
interior acid rain
limiting oxygen index (LOI)
linear density
longitudinal configuration
luster
micrometer
microscopic voids
moisture absorbency
moisture regain values
monomers
moth resistance
noncombustible fiber
oleophilic fiber

optical brighteners
optical properties
oriented polymer chains
pilling
pollutant gases
polymer
polymer additive
relative humidity
resiliency
self-extinguishing fiber
shrinkage resistance
soil hiding
soil magnification
soil repellency
soil shedding
specific gravity
staple fibers
static propensity
stiffness
sunlight resistance
surface texture
susceptibility to heat
tenacity
tendered
texture
thermoplastic fibers
thermoplasticity
threshold of human sensitivity
usable fiber form
vapor-phase moisture
wicking
yo-yo effect

Review Questions

1. Explain how generic classes are defined. Are there similarities among fibers within the same class? Are there differences, as well?

2. When will the burning test for fiber identification be useful? What is one distinctive reaction that will support the identification of protein fibers?

3. What is one distinctive reaction that will support the identification of a cellulosic fiber? To visually distinguish between cotton and rayon or lyocell, what features should be considered?

4. What is one distinctive reaction that will support the identification of a thermoplastic fiber? Name

a thermoplastic fiber that smells like celery when undergoing the burning test. Name a thermoplastic fiber that smells like hot vinegar.

5. Explain the meaning of *self-extinguishing fiber*. How could a self-extinguishing fiber provide a margin of safety in the event it was ignited?

6. Explain the influence of polymer chain orientation on fiber strength. How can the level of orientation be increased?

7. Identify some textural features of textile fibers that affect their hand, their luster, and their ability to adhere to one another.

8. Which fibers occur naturally in staple length? in filament length? Are manufactured fibers produced in staple or filament length?

9. Arrange the following in the sequence of production: polymer chains, atoms, usable fibers, and monomer. What is the responsibility of the natural fiber supplier in this production? the role of the manufactured fiber producer?

10. What is meant by the term "apparent" when used with whiteness and brightness? Distinguish between "apparent" and "actual" whiteness and brightness.

11. Distinguish between "soil hiding" and "soil magnification."

12. Explain the effectiveness of delusterants in hiding soil.

13. How do interior fiber voids obscure the appearance of soil?

14. How important is the "hand" of a textile product to consumers? Is hand largely subjective? What fiber features influence the hand of a textile?

15. How do the effects of abrasive forces on textile products show up to the consumer? How are abrasion and pilling related? How do fiber producers engineer fiber toughness? Why is it critical to select a fiber having relatively high abrasion resistance for use in soft floor coverings?

16. Distinguish between specific gravity and density.

17. What influence does specific gravity have on the covering power of a textile? Why is covering power an important consideration for textile structures used to cover large surface areas?

18. How do the weight and cost of textile floor coverings relate to the specific gravity of the fiber used?

19. Explain the relationship between fiber density and fiber denier.

20. Why can fabrics of high wet modulus rayon fibers be laundered instead of dry cleaned?

21. Explain the influence of the molecular arrangement and physical structural features of fibers on their extensibility and their recovery.

22. Identify interior textile products whose serviceability is improved by having fibers exhibiting a high level of resiliency.

23. Discuss the influence of fiber stiffness on the resiliency and abrasion resistance of textile fabrics.

24. How can one predict fabric performance?

25. The breaking tenacities of cotton and flax are higher when the fibers are wet. Does this have an influence on their end-use performance?

26. What constitutes "interior acid rain" and how does it affect interior textile products?

27. Differentiate among these terms: flammable, flame resistant, noncombustible, and fireproof.

28. When is thermoplasticity of a fiber an advantage? When is it a disadvantage?

29. Can products composed of cotton be heat set?

30. Cite end-use applications where textile products should be resistant to microbes.

31. Distinguish between hydrophilic, hydrophobic, and hygroscopic fibers, and cite benefits and limitations of each fiber type.

32. How is soil repellency introduced to manufactured fibers?

33. What is the role of fluorocarbon compounds in soil reduction?

34. Summarize the sequence leading to electrical shock.

35. Discuss static control techniques that use fibers.

Notes

1. Sara J. Kadolph. (2007). *Textiles*, 10th Edition. Hoboken, NJ: Pearson Education. Pg. 21–22.

2. Ibid., p. 22.

3. Maria C. Thiry, "Unsung Heroes: Antimicrobials Save the Day," *AATCC Journal*, Vol. 9, No. 5, May 2009, 20.

4. Ibid., p. 22.

Natural Fibers
Production
Natural Cellulosic Fibers
Minor Natural Cellulosic
    Fibers
Natural Protein Fibers
Natural Fiber Engineering

Manufactured Fibers
Production
Manufactured Cellulose Fibers
Manufactured Dextrose Fibers
Manufactured Protein Fibers
Manufactured Synthetic Fibers

**Manufactured Fiber
Engineering**
Fiber Variants
Fiber Modifications
Fiber Developments

Textile Fibers

CHAPTER **FOUR**

Natural Fibers

Natural fibers are found in nature and used in the same form from which they are found. Natural fibers are classified according to their origin and include those made from plant, animal, or mineral sources (see Table 3.1, p. 26). Plant fibers are **cellulosic** in nature and include such fibers as cotton, flax, hemp, jute, and sisal. Animal sources are **protein** in nature and include wool, silk, and specialty wools, such as mohair and cashmere. Mineral fibers are found in the ground and include asbestos. Formerly, **asbestos** was used in such interior applications as insulation around pipes and in walls and ceilings because of its fire resistance. Its use has been discontinued because the fiber is a known carcinogen.

The production of all fibers, natural and manufactured, follows this highly simplified sequence:

atoms → monomers → polymer chains → usable fibers

For most natural fibers, this entire sequence is carried out by animals or plants; an exception is asbestos, which is a mineral.

Production

The production of natural fibers is accomplished by nature with human assistance but without direct human involvement. Sheep, silk caterpillars, cotton and flax plants, and other organisms synthesize the monomers, form the polymer chains, and produce the usable fibers. The contribution of suppliers is important but limited. They must nurture and protect their animals and plants, keeping their sheep and caterpillars healthy and fed and their cotton and flax plants fertilized, weed-free, and protected from harmful insects. Wool fleeces must be shorn from the sheep, silk filaments must be unwound from the cocoons, flax fibers must be removed from the flax stalks, and cotton fibers must be separated from the seeds in the bolls. Once the fibers are recovered, they must be cleaned, sorted, and graded prior to yarn production.

Natural Cellulosic Fibers

All plants contain fiber that gives them strength. The main ingredient in plant fibers is cellulose, a carbohydrate found in all plant life. Plant fibers include those made from the seed, stem (bast), or leaf of a plant. Natural plant fibers will have many common fiber properties because they all contain cellulose. Properties common to all natural cellulose fibers include high absorbency, low flame resistance, high moth resistance, low resiliency, and low mildew resistance. Natural cellulose fibers exhibit no static buildup and are stronger when wet. However, each fiber differs in the amount of cellulose, the physical structure, and the molecular arrangement. This gives each fiber slight variations in its properties and chemical reactions.

Cotton

Cotton is a seed fiber obtained from the boll of the cotton plant. Cotton fiber is the most important natural fiber throughout the world and is used in both the interior and apparel industry. It is generally believed that the first cultivation of cotton was in India. Cotton cultivation spread to Egypt, China, Mexico, and Peru. Cotton was grown by the American Indians in the early 1500s and in the southern colonies as soon as they were established. For the next several hundred years, cotton fibers were separated from the seed by hand. This was very time consuming and tedious, and only about 1 pound of fiber could be separated from the seeds in a day. Samuel Slater, an English mill worker, migrated to America in 1790 and built the first cotton mill from memory. With the invention of the cotton gin in 1793 by Eli Whitney, cotton could now be separated from the seed much faster, and volume was increased for each worker from 1 pound to 50 pounds per day. The cotton gin made it possible to supply large quantities of cotton fiber to the fast-growing textile industry.

Cotton is grown in climates in which the growing season is long and hot. Adequate rainfall or irrigation is also required. Currently, there are four prominent types of cotton being grown commercially around the world. They are Egyptian, Sea Island, American Pima, and Upland. In the United States there are 14 major cotton growing states that produce Upland cotton. These states comprise a region known as the Cotton Belt and include Alabama, Arizona, Arkansas, California, Georgia, Louisiana, Mississippi, Missouri, North Carolina, Oklahoma, South Carolina, Tennessee, Texas, and Virginia. American Pima Cotton is grown in Arizona, California, New Mexico, and Texas. The major producers of cotton are the United States, China, India, Pakistan, Turkey, and Brazil.

Cotton fibers grow on bushes 2 to 5 feet high. In approximately 5 to 7 weeks, flower buds appear on the

Figure 4.1 Cotton boll.
Courtesy of Amy Willbanks, www.textilefabric.com.

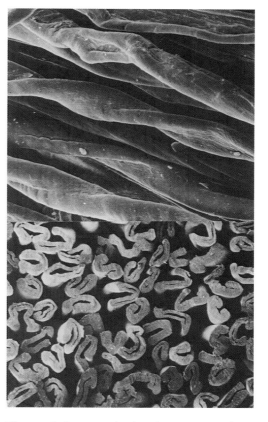

Figure 4.2 Longitudinal and cross-sectional views of cotton fiber.
Courtesy of Shirley Technologies Ltd, www.shirleytech.co.uk.

plants. In another 3 weeks the buds open. After about 3 days, they wither and fall off, leaving small green pods called cotton bolls. Cotton fibers begin growing inside the boll. The boll splits open when the cotton fibers mature and the fluffy fibers are exposed (Figure 4.1). Cotton fibers range in color from white to cream. After cotton is picked, it is taken to the gin, which separates the fiber from the seed. The **ginning process** also removes foreign matter, such as burs, leaves, stem, dirt, and parts of the boll. The ginned fiber, called **lint**, is pressed together and made into dense bales weighing approximately 500 pounds. These bales are sold to spinning mills for yarn production. The remaining seeds are covered with very short fibers called **linters**. The linters are separated from the seed and used in manufactured fiber production (such as rayon and acetate), paper, and plastic production. Linters are also processed into batting for padding mattresses, furniture, and automobile cushions. The seeds are used for livestock feed or processed into cottonseed oil, meal, and hulls.

Cotton fibers are staple-length fibers that range from ½–2 ½ inches, depending on the variety. Longer-length fibers are considered to be better quality because they can be made into stronger, smoother, and softer fabrics. Convolutions (or ribbonlike twists) characterize the cotton fabric (Figure 4.2). A microscopic view shows these twists that are unique to cotton. The cross-sectional shape of cotton is kidney shaped. There are four distinctive parts of the cotton fiber (Figure 4.3). The **lumen** is the central canal and provides the nutrients to the fiber. The twists and convolutions of cotton fiber are due to

the drying out of its liquid and the collapsing of the central canal. This twist forms a natural crimp that makes cotton very cohesive. Despite its short length, cotton is one of the most spinnable fibers. The **secondary wall** is made up of layers of cellulose. These layers are deposited daily while the cotton plant matures. The cellulose grows in reverse spirals, further contributing to the convolutions. The **primary wall** is the outer covering of the cotton fiber. The **cuticle** is a waxlike covering on the primary wall.

Cotton is relatively strong and has a soft hand and a pleasing appearance. Unlike wool, cotton lacks strong cross-linking bonds to stabilize the fiber and contribute to resilient behavior. To compensate for this, chemical cross-linking resins are used to impart resiliency and wrinkle recovery. Cotton has excellent moisture absorption, is stronger wet than dry, and dries quickly, good features for household and institutional textiles. Because convolutions in the fiber deflect light rays (Figure 3.2, p. 29), the fiber

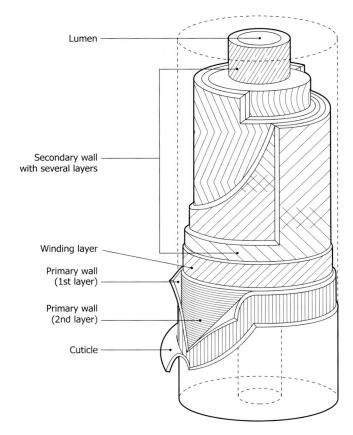

Lumen

Secondary wall
with several layers

Winding layer

Primary wall
(1st layer)

Primary wall
(2nd layer)

Cuticle

Figure 4.3 Diagram of layers in cotton fiber.
Courtesy of Kerri Charlton, International Textile Center, Texas
Tech University, 2001.

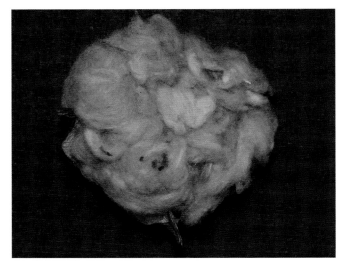

a) Naturally colored FoxFibre® cotton fiber.

b) Naturally colored FoxFibre® upholstery fabric.

Figure 4.4 FoxFibre®.
Courtesy of Amy Willbanks, www.textilefabric.com.

has a matte luster. The luster, strength, and moisture absorption of the fiber can be increased with mercerization (see Chapter 9). Because cotton is flammable, it may be desirable or necessary to use a flame-retardant finish. Cotton will also decompose with prolonged exposure to sunlight and is negatively affected by mildew, especially in humid climates. Cotton is resistant to moths but harmed by silverfish.

The uses of cotton include curtains, draperies, bedspreads, comforters, throws, sheets, towels, tablecloths, table mats, napkins, bath mats, shower curtains, carpets, rugs, and upholstery fabrics.

Although conventional cotton is a natural fiber, it has a negative impact on the environment. Farmers in the U.S. apply nearly $1/3$ pound of chemical fertilizers and pesticides for every pound of cotton harvested. When all the cotton producing states are tallied, cotton crops account for more than 25 percent of all pesticides in the United States. Some of these chemicals are among the

most toxic classified by the Environmental Protection Agency. In developing countries, where regulations are less stringent, the amount of pesticides and insecticides and their toxicity are often greater than in the United States. Cotton is also a very water intensive crop, requiring a minimum of 15 to 20 inches per year. In areas where there is not enough rainfall, irrigation is used. Soil erosion is a problem as well because of the tilling of the land. Cotton also depletes the soil of nutrients, so crop rotation must be practiced.

Figure 4.5 Organic cotton upholstered sofa. Custom Green furniture by Viesso, www.viesso.com.

Organic cotton is grown without synthetic chemicals and meets the standards established by certifying organizations to ensure fairness in the market. Organic cotton is grown using natural methods of farm management, including the introduction of beneficial bugs to eat harmful insects. Compost, natural fertilizers, and crop rotation practices are used to nourish the plants and keep them healthy. Organic cotton significantly reduces pesticides and soil erosion. **Green cotton** describes a cotton fabric that has not been bleached or treated with any other chemicals common in finishing and dyeing. **Natural-colored cotton** grows in different colors, which eliminates the need for dyeing. Grown in South American and Central America for centuries, naturally colored cotton has gained importance in the home furnishings industry. Found increasingly in bath towels, bedding products, and upholstery fabrics, naturally colored cotton is found in shades of brown and green. Sally Fox has developed and patented FoxFibre®, an organically grown, natural-colored cotton in hues of brown, green, and a new redwood color (Figure 4.4a and b).

Organic cotton is used to make sheets, towels, shower curtains, throw pillows, table linens, pillowcases, duvet covers, upholstered furniture (Figure 4.5), crib and baby linens, mattress pads, and bath mats. Organic cotton can be USDA certified (organically grown), but the processing of the textile fiber is not covered. The green and organic cotton industries are experiencing rapid growth and expect a phenomenal increase in sales.

There is also debate over the **genetically modified (GM) cotton seeds** that have been developed. Several agricultural companies have introduced GM seeds that are resistant to natural pests, which reduces the use of pesticides and herbicides. Some argue that this practice will contribute to the sustainability of cotton, but others argue that it is harmful to the food chain. Other types of genetically modified cotton include flame retardant, water repellent, and durable-press treated.

A highly innovative insulation company recycled jeans and other denim apparel and converted the cotton to create its UltraTouch™ Natural Cotton Fiber insulation. The apparel was collected by colleges around the country as part of the Cotton Incorporated "Dirty Laundry Tour." The insulation was then donated to Habitat for Humanity homes. Cotton is also being recycled and made into mulch to prevent land erosion and encourage grass growth.

Flax

Flax fiber is obtained from the stem of the flax plant. **Linen** refers to cloth made from the flax fiber. **Linens** typically describe sheets, towels, tablecloths, napkins, and related products but are commonly made of other fiber contents. Today, flax is considered a luxury fiber as a result of its limited production and relatively high cost.

Flax fiber is the oldest of all domestically produced fibers. Flax is thought to have originated in the Mediterranean region of Europe. Remnants of linen have been found among the remains of the Swiss Lake Dwellers, who lived in the Stone Age. Linen cloth was used to wrap the mummies in the early Egyptian tombs. Medicinal uses for flax can be traced to the Ancient Greeks. In the United States early colonists grew flax for home use, and commercial production of the flax fiber began in 1753. However, with the invention of the cotton gin in 1793, flax production began to decline. After the 1940s, flax production in the United States almost dropped to zero.

The flax plant grows to approximately 4 feet high and is usually planted very densely to minimize branching (Figure 4.6). When approaching maturity, after about 70 to 100 days, small blue or white flowers are produced, depending on the variety. The strands of flax fiber are embedded longitudinally in the stem of the plant. The flax stalks are harvested by pulling up their roots to preserve the full length of the fiber, which extend below the ground. The stalks are then bundled and dried. A series of steps separate the fiber from the stem. **Rippling**, the first step,

pulls the stalks through a coarse metal comb to separate the seeds. The next step in flax fiber production is **retting**, which is a rotting process that separates the fiber from the woody portion of the stalk. In the **breaking** stage, the retted stalks are broken open by passing them through corrugated rollers. The next step is **scutching** and involves the removal of the woody portion of the stalk. **Hackling** pulls the fiber bundles through rows of metal tines that align the fibers for spinning (Figure 4.7). The flax seeds are used in the food and feed industries and in the production of linseed oil.

Today, a few individual mills grow flax fiber in North Dakota, South Dakota, and Minnesota. The major producers of flax are Belgium, France, the Netherlands, Ireland, Italy, and Germany.

Flax is a staple fiber that ranges from 12 to 24 inches in length. Short flax fibers are called **tow**. The longer, better quality flax fibers are called **line**. A microscopic view shows the fibers to be multicellular, with polygo-

Figure 4.7 Flax that has been hackled. Courtesy of CELC MASTERS OF LINEN.

Figure 4.6 Flowering field of flax plants. Courtesy of CELC MASTERS OF LINEN.

nal rounded edges (Figure 4.8). Like cotton, flax fibers also contain a lumen, which carries nutrients to the plant during growth. Individual flax fibers are characterized by **nodes**, markings similar to the cross markings on bamboo and corn plants. The nodes help keep the dried fiber from collapsing and help create a more lustrous fiber than cotton. The longer fibers also contribute to flax's strength. Flax fibers are light ivory to dark brown in color. The polymer chains within flax fibers are highly oriented. Flax has longer polymer chains and a higher level of crystallinity than cotton, making the fiber stronger but more brittle and less flexible than cotton fiber. (Linen products have a crisp appearance). Flax is stronger when wet and exhibits excellent absorbency, hence its use in table linens. Flax has extremely low elongation, poor elastic recovery, low flexibility, and low abrasion resistance. Its low flexibility is a problem, especially when fabrics of flax fiber are repeatedly folded on the same crease line for storage, as is the case with tablecloths and napkins (Figure 4.9).

Flax burns easily, is highly resistant to UV damage and insects, and more resistant to mildew than cotton. Flax is used in upholstery and drapery fabric, wallcoverings, toweling, bedding, tablecloths, table mats, and napkins (Figure 4.10).

Flax has a much less negative environmental impact than cotton. Flax production requires fewer chemicals and less water. Soil erosion can be a problem because of harvesting, as the flax plant is pulled from the roots. Significant amounts of water are used in the retting process, but the water can be recycled. Dew retting is also popular, which allows the plants to rot naturally by laying them on the ground and leaving them for several weeks, exposed to dew and rain.

Hemp

The **hemp** plant is a stem fiber similar to flax, jute, and ramie. Hemp is harvested for its fibers, seed, and seed oil. Because of its high processing costs and limited quantities, hemp is about 100 percent higher in cost than cotton. About 75 percent of hemp grown worldwide is being turned into textiles.

Although hemp clothing and other consumer goods have only recently gained popularity in the past several years, the use of hemp dates back the Stone Age, with hemp fiber imprints found in pottery shards in China more than 10,000 years old. Hemp has played a very important part in American history. In the early 1600s, hemp was considered such a vital resource that laws were passed ordering farmers to grow it. George Washington and Thomas Jefferson

Figure 4.8 Longitudinal and cross-sectional views of flax fiber. Courtesy of Shirley Technologies Ltd, www.shirleytech.co.uk.

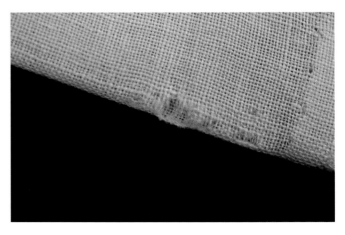

Figure 4.9 Folded linen fabric showing breakage. Courtesy of Amy Willbanks, www.textilefabric.com.

Figure 4.10 Sofa upholstered with linen fabric.
Courtesy of Drexel Heritage.

both grew hemp on their plantations. The Betsy Ross flag, the Gutenberg Bible, the Declaration of Independence, and Lewis Carroll's *Alice's Adventures in Wonderland* were written on 100 percent hemp paper.

Hemp clothing, home furnishing products, and food products are completely legal in the United States. However, the cultivation of hemp had been illegal in the United States since World War II, until legislation in the late 1990s allowed for minor production. Hemp production has been the subject of a worldwide controversy that involves farmers, government enforcement agencies, supporters of legalized drugs, and manufacturers of textile, food, and paper products. The controversy stems from the existence of several varieties of the hemp plant, *Can-*

nabis sativa, one of which is the marijuana plant. The ban made no distinction between the different kinds of hemp. Industrial hemp used for textiles cannot be used as a drug because it contains only about 0.3 percent THC (delta-9-tetrahydrocannabinol, the active hallucinatory ingredient in marijuana) whereas marijuana contains at least 5 to 30 percent THC. Hemp proponents are trying hard to overcome the obvious image problem.

For the first time since World War II, hemp seeds have been planted legally on American soil. A total of 19 states have introduced hemp legislation. The legislation in Hawaii, Minnesota, and North Dakota permits the production of industrial hemp, provided farmers obtain licenses from the U.S. Drug Enforcement Administration (DEA). Currently, the majority of hemp products are imported into the United States. Hemp sold in the United States comes primarily from China, Hungary, Romania, El Salvador, and Chile. Hemp is also legally cultivated in Australia, England, Canada, and New Zealand.

Hemp fibers come from a tall shrub of the mulberry family that can grow to 20 feet in height. The bark layer contains the long fibers that extend nearly the entire length of the stem. The interior of the stalk is hollow, surrounded by a layer of woody fibers called hurds (Figure 4.11). Hemp hurds are used in various applications, such as animal bedding, composites, building materials, and paper. Hemp can be grown on a wide range of soils but tends to grow best on land that produces high yields of corn. The soil must be well drained, rich in nitrogen, and nonacidic. Unlike cotton, hemp grows in many climate zones. Hemp averages between 6 and 15

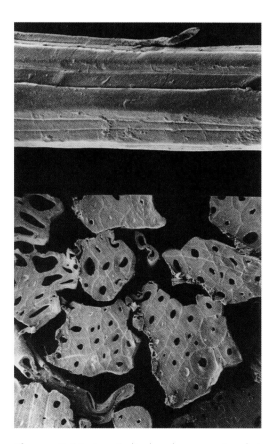

Figure 4.11 Longitudinal and cross-sectional views of hemp fiber.
Courtesy of Shirley Technologies Ltd, www.shirleytech.co.uk.

feet in height in about 4 months of growth. Harvesting stalks for high-quality fiber occurs as soon as the crop is in flower. Once a hemp crop has matured and been harvested, hemp fibers are separated from the stalk through the retting process, much like flax. Hemp fibers are dark tan to brown.

Hemp exhibits high luster because of its long fiber length, ranging from ¾ inch to several inches. Hemp fibers are similar to flax fibers in feel and texture. Like cotton and flax, hemp can withstand high temperatures. Hemp fiber is one of the most durable and strongest natural textile fibers. Hemp fibers are longer and stronger than cotton, with eight times the tensile strength and four times the durability of cotton. Hemp fibers are more absorbent and more mildew resistant, and they hold more insulation power than cotton. Hemp can absorb moisture up to 30 percent its weight at 100 percent humidity and dries very quickly. Hemp fibers are more absorbent to dyes, which, coupled with the fiber's ability to withstand ultraviolet rays, means that hemp fabrics are less prone to fading than cotton fabrics. Hemp fibers are easily damaged by strong acids, exhibit a high resistance to alkalis, are difficult to bleach, and are highly resistant to moths and other insects.

Hemp fiber is used in toweling, bedding, window coverings, curtain panels, wallcoverings, tablecloths, napkins, rugs, and carpeting (Figure 4.12b and c). Antimildew and antimicrobial properties make hemp fibers very suitable for sails, awnings, and floor coverings. Hemp seeds and flour are being imported into North America and used in food products, such as tortilla chips, pretzels, beer, salad dressings, cheese, and ice cream.

Hemp oil is used in body-care products, such as lotions, moisturizers, and shampoos. Hemp oil is very high in unsaturated fatty acids and cannot be used for frying.

The pollution of soil and water by fertilizers and pesticides used in growing cotton has been a constant battleground for environmentalists. Because of its unique nature, hemp can easily be grown organically. Hemp is naturally resistant to mold, bacteria, and insects. Hemp is grown without pesticides, herbicides, or agricultural chemicals.

Hemp is a high-yield crop, maturing in about a hundred days and producing significantly more fiber than flax or cotton in equivalent space. The life cycle for timber to make paper pulp and rayon can be a hun-

a) Hemp plant.

b) Hemp herringbone upholstery fabric.

c) Hemp hot pad.

Figure 4.12 Hemp plant and products.
a) Courtesy of CELC MASTERS OF LINEN. b) Courtesy of Amy Willbanks, www.textilefabric.com. c) Courtesy of Amy Willbanks, www.textilefabric.com.

dred years. The hemp plant has a deep root system (thus preventing soil erosion), removes toxins, and aerates the soil to the benefit of future crops. On a per acre basis, hemp yields 250 percent more fiber than cotton and 600 percent more fiber than flax without the need for toxic chemicals. The entire plant can be used, from seed to foliage, for use in such diverse products as building materials, insulation, paper, and food. Another green aspect to hemp fiber is that its dense growth makes it a prime contributor to weed control and elimination. Hemp can displace wood fiber and save forests for watershed, wildlife habitat, recreation, and oxygen production. The

rediscovery of this renewable resource has made it the fiber of choice for future textiles, personal care products, building materials, and fuel.

Jute

Jute, a bast fiber, is one of the most popular fibers in the world. It is also one of the least expensive. Jute fiber grows to a height of 15 to 20 feet. Extraction of the fiber is by the same basic method as for flax and hemp. Jute can be harvested within 4 to 6 months and is considered a high-yield fiber. Bangladesh is the world's largest producer and exporter of jute. Jute is grown throughout

India, China, Pakistan, Nepal, Myanmar, and Thailand. The jute fiber is yellow, brown, or gray in color.

Jute is less uniform than flax and has a much rougher surface. A microscopic view shows the rough surface and irregular cross-sectional shape (Figure 4.13). **Jute** exhibits excellent absorbency, high covering power, poor flexibility, low elongation, and low elastic recovery. The majority of jute fiber goes into making rope, cordage, twine, and bagging. **Burlap** is a common fabric often used for coffee and sugar bagging. Jute fiber is also used for carpet backing (Figure 4.14a), curtains, chair coverings, wallcoverings, area rugs (Figure 4.14b), and backing for linoleum. Jute has many advantages in residential and commercial textiles because of its strength, colorfastness, sound and heat insulation, and low thermal conduction. Its antistatic and UV protection are also advantageous. The use of jute has decreased in the past because of competition from manufactured fibers, such as olefin. As consumers demand more green fibers, the use of jute has been on the rise in interior products.

a) Jute carpet backing.

b) Jute rug.

Figure 4.14 Jute products.
Courtesy of Amy Willbanks, www.textilefabric.com.

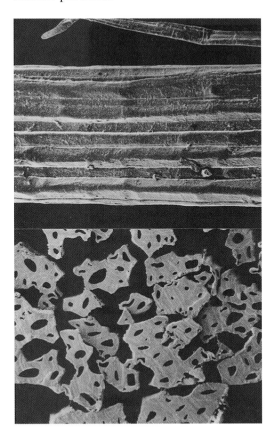

Figure 4.13 Longitudinal and cross-sectional views of jute fiber.
Courtesy of Shirley Technologies Ltd, www.shirleytech.co.uk.

Relatively modest amounts of fertilizer, herbicide, and pesticide are required for jute cultivation, especially in comparison to cotton. When jute is rotated with other crops, it can improve the health of the other crops and reduce their risk of attracting pests and disease. Jute products are 100 percent biodegradable and recyclable. Olefin, nylon, and polyester are typically used in place of jute because of their outstanding durability properties and versatility.

Ramie

Ramie, a bast fiber from the ramie plant, is also known as grass cloth, rhea, or China grass. Ramie has been grown in China for thousands of years. In the past, the separation of ramie from the plant stalk was very labor intensive.

However, newer, less expensive means of separating the fiber have been developed, and ramie is becoming more commercially important each year.

Ramie is a tall perennial shrub that can be harvested several times a year. Ramie grows in hot, humid climates. The major producers of ramie are China, the Philippines, and Brazil. Ramie is a pure white fiber similar to flax. Its cross-sectional shape (Figure 4.15) resembles that of flax, showing a multicellular fiber with a thick and thin longitudinal shape.

Ramie is higher in luster than flax because of its longer fiber length. Ramie is highly resistant to mold and mildew as well as to rotting. Because of its high molecular structure, ramie fibers are stiff and, like flax, will break if folded repeatedly. Ramie exhibits poor resiliency, poor elongation, and poor elastic recovery. Ramie has moderate abrasion resistance and elongation. Ramie exhibits natural resistance to mildew, insects, and ultraviolet light, and it dries very quickly. It is also one of the stron-

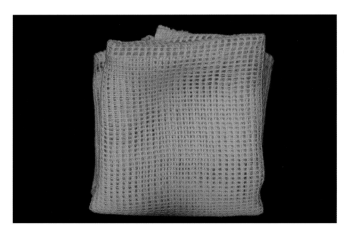

Figure 4.16 Ramie washcloth.
Courtesy of Amy Willbanks, www.textilefabric.com.

gest natural fibers. With these characteristics, ramie is a choice for outdoor mats for the green fiber market. Ramie is used in tablecloths, napkins, window treatments, bath products, and pillows as well (Figure 4.16).

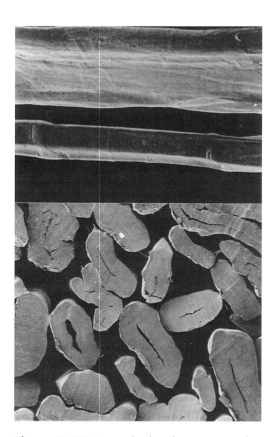

Figure 4.15 Longitudinal and cross-sectional views of ramie fiber.
Courtesy of Shirley Technologies Ltd, www.shirleytech.co.uk.

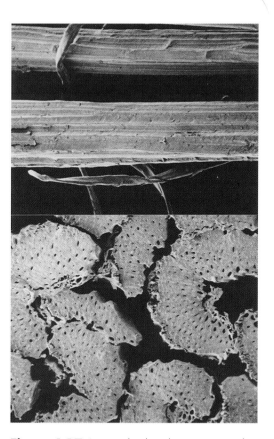

Figure 4.17 Longitudinal and cross-sectional views of sisal fiber.
Courtesy of Shirley Technologies Ltd, www.shirleytech.co.uk.

Sisal

Sisal fiber is the most popular natural leaf fiber, obtained from the leaves of the agave or yucca plant. The sisal plant consists of a rosette of sword-shaped leaves about 3 to 6 feet tall. The sisal plant has a lifespan of 10 years. The leaves are harvested and transported to a decortication plant to extract the fiber. Mexico, Africa, South America, and Brazil are the leading producers of sisal (Figure 4.17).

Long a favorite carpeting material for porches and sunrooms, sisal is moving into the more formal rooms of the home. Sisal works well in any room in which you would use fine wool carpets. Sisal does not build up static, nor does it trap dirt. It is a strong, durable fiber and resistant to sea water. Its outstanding weathering properties make it suitable for use in outdoor settings. Dyes are re-

Figure 4.18 Sisal rugs.
Courtesy of RUCKSTUHL AG, www.ruckstuhl.com.

markably colorfast, but strong sunlight will fade the color over a period of time. Sisal area rugs (Figure 4.18) should not be used in kitchens, as grease stains can be difficult to remove.

Products made from sisal are rapidly increasing: carpets, area rugs, outdoor mats, bags, table linens, home furnishing upholstery fabric, and window treatments (Figure 4.19). Sisal is used in the automobile industry as an environmentally friendly substitute for fiberglass. Sisal is also used in home furnishings as a substitute for horsehair.

Minor Natural Cellulosic Fibers

Abaca fiber comes from the leaf stem of the abaca plant, a member of the banana family. It has a natural luster because of its long fiber length. It is off-white to brown in color. Strong and durable, abaca fiber is used for placemats for indoor/outdoor use and production of wicker furniture.

Piña fiber is obtained from the leaves of a pineapple plant grown mainly in the Phillipines. It is used to produce very lightweight, sheer fabrics. Piña fiber is used for placemats, embroidered tablecloths, and clothing.

Henequin fiber is grown in Africa and Central America. It is a smooth, straight yellow fiber that is used for better grades of rope, twine, and brush bristles.

Coir fibers are seed fibers obtained from the fibrous mass between the outer shell and the actual nut of the coconut. The fibers are removed by soaking the husk in saline water for several months. Coir fibers are extremely stiff.

Figure 4.19 Sisal ottoman/cat cube.
Courtesy of Viesso, www.viesso.com.

They are resistant to abrasion, water, and most weather conditions. These properties make coir suitable for indoor and outdoor mats, rugs, outdoor carpeting, and brushes (Figure 4.21). These products are extremely durable. Sri Lanka is the major producer of coir fiber.

Kapok is obtained from the seed of the Java kapok tree. Kapok is a hollow fiber, very lightweight and soft. Historically, kapok had been used for upholstery padding and pillow fiberfill. Kapok exhibits very low durability and therefore has limited use in the interior textile industry. Many of the manufactured fibers are now used for these applications as a substitute for kapok.

Other minor cellulose materials are used in the home furnishings industry on a very limited basis. *Rush* or *marsh grass*, *sea grass (China grass)*, *palm grass* and *cornhusks* are used to make area rugs, upholstery covering, window treatments, wallcoverings, and wicker furniture. These fibers give products an interesting and natural texture (Figure 4.20).

Figure 4.21 Coir outdoor rug.
Courtesy of RUCKSTUHL AG, www.ruckstuhl.com.

Natural Protein Fibers

Natural protein fibers are of animal origin. Wool and silk are the two major natural protein fibers. Protein fibers have common properties because of their similar chemical composition. Properties common to all protein fibers include high resiliency, low density, high absorbency (hygroscopic), flammability resistance, and weaker wet strength.

Silk

Silk is a natural protein fiber and is known for its softness, comfort, and luster. **Sericulture** is the growth of silkworms and the production of cultivated silk. Sericulture is a tedious, labor-intensive industry.

The discovery of silk began between 2700 B.C. and 2600 B.C., by the Chinese empress Xi-Ling-Shi. Concerned about the imperial mulberry grove, Emperor Huang Ti appointed Xi-Ling-Shi to investigate the tiny white worms that were devouring the tree's leaves. Gathering a bundle of cocoons, the empress accidentally dropped a silkworm cocoon in her hot tea. She noticed that the cocoon separated into long, slender filaments. The empress learned to reel the silk filaments into yarns and weave the yarns into beautiful garments. Sericulture spread throughout China, and silk became a precious commodity highly sought by other countries. China maintained its virtual monopoly over silk for 3,000 years. Silk reached Korea around 200 B.C., smuggled out of China by Chinese immigrants. Sericulture reached Japan through Korea in the early part of the third century A.D. Soon the silk industry began in the Middle East. The Persians mastered the art of silk weaving. Gradually, the silk industry became wide-

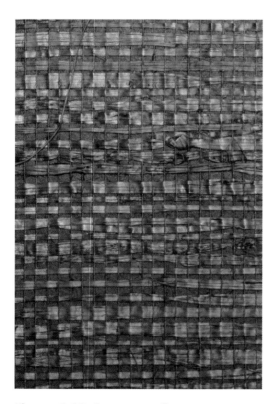

Figure 4.20 Sea grass wallcovering.
Courtesy of Amy Willbanks, www.textilefabric.com.

spread in Europe. Today, the leading producers of silk are China, Japan, and India.

Silk is a natural animal fiber produced by the larvae of a silk caterpillar, often referred to as a silkworm. Cultivated silk is the only natural fiber found in filament form. It is a natural protein fiber composed of fibroin. Silk fiber is long and thin and has a smooth surface. Silk has a triangular cross-sectional shape (Figure 4.23).

After several thousand years of captive breeding, the silk caterpillar, *Bombyx mori*, evolved into a blind moth that cannot fly and lives for only a few days, during which it lays about 500 eggs and then dies. The egg hatches in approximately 10 days and becomes a larva. The silkworm larva will eat mulberry leaves almost nonstop for 35 days, increasing its weight 10,000 times, from a tiny speck to a large grub. Once full grown, the larva begins spinning a cocoon (Figure 4.22). This stage of silkworm life is called pupating. The silkworm produces liquid silk, a fibroin protein compound, from two glands inside the worm. The fibroin, forced from openings in the silkworm's head, hardens on contact with the air. A water soluble gum, called **sericin**, keeps the two stands of silk joined and provides a gluelike substance to hold the cocoon together. By revolving its head in a figure eight fashion, the silkworm surrounds itself with silk filament up to 1 mile in length in less than 3 days. The silkworm matures into a moth and breaks through the cocoon to start the life cycle again.

When the cocoons are to be harvested for the silk filaments, they are exposed to heat that will end the life of the silkworm and preserve the filament intact. In **reeling**, the sericin is softened in warm water, and skilled technicians collect the filament ends and unwind the cocoons. **Throwing** is used to skillfully combine several filaments into multifilament silk yarns. Any staple-length silk, known as **noil**, is recovered and combined into silk spun yarns.

Silk may be sufficiently whitened by boiling the filaments in a detergent solution. This operation is known as **boiling off** and removes the sericin. If the sericin is left in place, the silk is marketed as **raw silk**. **Tussah silk** is a type of raw silk (Figure 4.24). **Duppioni silk** is a type of silk that is a result of two silkworms spinning their cocoons together. Duppioni silk fabrics have irregular yarns that have a thick and thin appearance.

Weighting is a textile manufacturing process particular to silk and involves the application of metallic salts to add body, luster, and physical weight to silk fabrics. If not done properly, weighting can damage the silk fabric. **Pure silk** describes a 100 percent silk fabric that does not contain any metallic weighting compounds.

Figure 4.23 Longitudinal and cross-sectional views of silk fiber.
Courtesy of Shirley Technologies Ltd, www.shirleytech.co.uk.

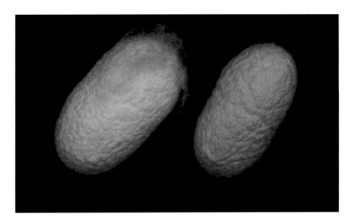

Figure 4.22 Silk cocoons.
Courtesy of Amy Willbanks, www.textilefabric.com.

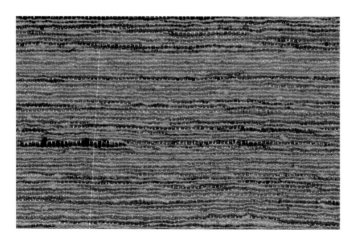

Figure 4.24 Tussah silk drapery fabric.
Courtesy of Amy Willbanks, www.textilefabric.com.

Figure 4.25 Silk upholstered bench.
Courtesy of Drexel Heritage.

Silk is one of the strongest natural fibers and has medium elongation and moderate abrasion resistance. The increased orientation and crystallinity contribute strength to the fiber. Although the lower abrasion resistance does not support the selection of upholstery fabrics of silk, they nonetheless are used when luxury and luster is sought. Although silk is weakened or **tendered** by sunlight, it is used when historical restoration calls for authenticity in document fabrics. Dry cleaning or hand washing is generally recommended for cleaning fabrics of silk, not only to avoid damaging the fiber with strong alkaline solutions, but also to prevent fastness problems with unstable dyestuffs.

Silk is used in window treatments, upholstered furniture (Figure 4.25), bedding, wallcoverings, and decorative table accessories.

There are alternatives to cultivated silk for consumers who are concerned about the ethics of destroying the silkworm to harvest the fiber. For those who love the feel, luster, and excellent aesthetic properties of silk, there are more ethical options. Some silk producers allow the moths to emerge from the cocoon and then salvage the damaged cocoons. There are also many species of wild caterpillars that produce silk cocoons used in the production of upholstery fabrics. The larvae feed on oak leaves instead of mulberry leaves. The filament fiber is broken into staple fibers by the emerging moth. This silk is often called **peace silk** or vegetarian silk.

Wild silk production is uncontrolled. Whereas cultivated silkworms feed exclusively on mulberry leaves, wild silkworms feed on oak leaves. The cocoons are harvested after the moth has emerged. Because the cocoon is dam-

aged by the emerging moth, wild silk is only found in staple form. The silk is much less uniform than pure silk and is usually brown and tan in color. A common variety of wild silk is Tussah silk (Figure 4.24).

Silk is biodegradable and will decompose in landfills. Sustainable and eco-friendly silks that use low-impact and fiber-reactive dyes are available. Several organizations are helping develop programs to assist poor rural communities in conservation efforts and economic development. Programs include developing the wild silk industries and marketing silk fabric that is produced according to Fair Trade principles, which protect workers involved in all phases of producing the cloth.

Scientists in Japan have been experimenting with naturally colored silks by genetically engineering the pigment transport system of the silkworm. Red and flesh tone colors in silk fiber have been produced. The color of the silk can be decided at the production stage. No chemical dyes are used, thus lessening pollution and saving water and energy.

Wool

Wool fiber comes from the follicles of a sheep's skin. Wool fiber's combined properties cannot be duplicated by any other natural or manufactured fiber: flame resistance, thermal retention, felting ability, initial water repellency, and ability to absorb moisture without feeling wet. Wool fiber production began during the Stone Age, about 10,000 years ago. Primitive man living in Mesopotamia had been using sheep for food and clothing for centuries. Between 3000 and 1000 B.C. the Persians, Greeks, and Romans distributed sheep and wool throughout Europe as they continued to improve breeds. The Romans took sheep with them as they built their empire in what is now Spain, North Africa, and the British Isles. They established a wool plant in what is now Winchester, England as early as 50 A.D. Sheep were first introduced into what is now the southwest United States in 1519 by Spanish troops under Hernán Cortez. Wool was the most widely used textile fiber before the Industrial Revolution. Today, sheep thrive in all 50 states and in most countries of the world. Sheep can live on rough, barren land or in high altitudes that other animals cannot withstand because of lack of vegetation; sheep can survive and flourish on weeds and vegetation other animals will not eat, converting to protein a group of natural resources that would otherwise be wasted. The major producers of wool are Australia, New Zealand, China, and Argentina.

The first step in the processing of wool is **shearing**, or removing the fleece from the sheep (Figures 4.26 and 4.27). In most parts of the world, sheep are sheared once a year, in early spring or early summer. A shearer can shear a sheep in about 30 seconds, using electric hand clippers. Long, smooth strokes very close to the skin are used in order to preserve the length of the fiber. The shearer will peel away the fleece in one piece. The best wool comes from the shoulders and sides of the sheep.

After shearing, the fibers are **scoured** to remove sand, dirt, plant material from the environment, and dried body excrement. A set of rakes moves the fleeces through a series of scouring tubs of soap and water. Raw wool can contain as much as 30 to 70 percent of these impurities. A byproduct of this scouring process is the grease from the fleece. This grease, or **lanolin**, is separated from the wash water, purified, and used in creams, soaps, lotions, cosmetics, and other pharmaceutical products.

Wool fibers range in length from ½ inch to 6 inches. The wool fiber is composed of three distinctive parts. The **medulla** is the center of the fiber and contains hollow, honeycomb-shaped cells (Figure 4.28) that give wool its excellent insulating power. The **cortex** is the central fiber, containing long, cigar-shaped cells called cortical cells. The cortical cells on each side of the fiber react differently to heat and moisture. This causes the fiber to bend and turn, giving wool a natural three-dimensional crimp. The outer structure, or **cuticle**, is

Figure 4.26 Sheep shearing. Courtesy of the British Wool Marketing Board, www.britishwool.org.uk.

Figure 4.27 Side view of half-shorn fleece. Courtesy of www.icebreaker.com.

composed of overlapping scales. The scales are covered by a thin, porous, waxlike membrane that repels water yet absorbs perspiration (Figure 4.28). Wool fibers range in color from various shades of black, brown, tan and ivory. The quality of wool is determined by fiber length, diameter, luster, color, and age of the sheep. The grade of the fiber determines the type of product for which the wool will be used. Merino sheep are the most valued for their wool. Merino wool is 3 to 6 inches in length and has a soft hand.

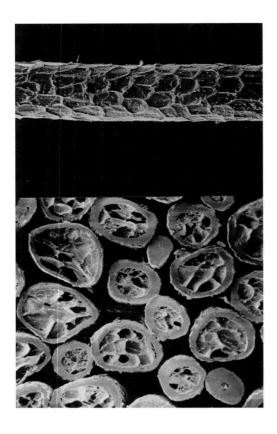

Figure 4.28 Longitudinal and cross-sectional views of wool fiber. Courtesy of Shirley Technologies Ltd, www.shirleytech.co.uk.

The natural crimp of the wool fiber produces excellent loft and resiliency. The crimp acts as a spring and increases the resiliency and elasticity. After extension, the crimp will return to its original shape, which make wool an excellent choice for carpets. Traffic patterns will not show because the fibers exhibit high recovery to crushing. The loftiness of the wool fiber entraps dead air and acts as a natural insulator, making wool one of the warmest natural fibers. The three-dimensional crimp also acts as an excellent sound insulator, or sound-absorbing fabric. Wool carpeting and draperies will absorb sound and insulate as well. Wool carpeting and rugs may be used to reduce noise in enclosed areas (Figure 4.29).

Wool fiber is hygroscopic, taking up moisture in vapor form. Tiny pores in the cuticle allow vapor to pass through to the center of the fiber. Wool can easily absorb up to 30 percent of its original weight in moisture without feeling damp or clammy. The wool fabric remains absorptive and comfortable inside because its outer surface releases moisture through evaporation to the outer atmosphere. The

scales on the cuticle also give wool both a natural water and stain repellency.

The physical structure of the outer scaly layer of the wool fiber contributes to the wool's unique property of **felting** (Figure 4.28). Under the mechanical action of agitation, friction, and pressure in the presence of heat and moisture, the scales on the edges of the wool fiber interlock. This prevents the fiber from returning to its original position. The felting property of wool is both an advantage and disadvantage. Controlled shrinkage of a wool fabric is called **fulling** and creates a softer finish and more covering power for woven wool fabric. Felting is also an advantage because it provides a wide variety of felt fabrics for hats and industrial uses. Felting is a disadvantage because it makes washing of untreated wool fabric difficult. Untreated wool fabric must be laundered by hand or dry-cleaned.

Wool is naturally self-extinguishing because it contains moisture in each fiber. Instead of burning freely when touched by a flame, wool chars. When the flame is removed, the fire goes out almost immediately. Wool is known for its durability as well. The fiber's high elongation and excellent elastic recovery contribute to wool's high durability. The crimp and scale structure also makes wool fibers cohesive in the spinning process, producing very strong yarns.

Wool stays cleaner longer than other fabrics. Because the high moisture content allows for less static, wool does not attract lint and dust. Wool's coiled fibers and their shinglelike structure also help keep dirt from penetrating its surface.

Several chemical finishes can be applied to wool, depending on its end use. Products labeled "Superwash," a trademark owned by the Australian Wool Innovation, are 100 percent wool that can be washed using ordinary laundry detergent and machine dried. A mild chemical treatment is applied to the outer surface of the fiber, forming a microscopic film that essentially coats the scales. This reduces fiber entanglement and eliminates the felting shrinkage that occurs in nontreated wool products. Wool can also be treated to make it highly resistant to moths, stains, moisture, and fire.

Woolen fabrics are made from fibers that are 1 to 3 inches in length that have only been carded. Woolen fabrics exhibit more loft, or bulkiness; higher thermal retention, resulting in more warmth; and more covering power, for better insulation. **Worsted** fabrics contain yarns 3 to 6 inches in length that have been carded and combed, resulting in a finer, smoother, thinner fabric with a crisp hand.

Although wool fibers and products are relatively expensive, these characteristics make wool fiber highly desirable for upholstered furnishings, draperies, wallcoverings, blankets, and carpeting.

Wool fiber is often recycled for use by taking wool yarn or fabrics and converting them back to a fiber in a process called **garneting**. These wool fabrics must be so

Figure 4.29 Wool rug.
Courtesy of RUCKSTUHL AG, www.ruckstuhl.com.

Figure 4.30 Alpacas.
Courtesy of *Wild Fibers Magazine*.

Figure 4.31 Angora goats.
Courtesy of *Wild Fibers Magazine*.

labeled according to the Wool Products Labeling Act. Recycled wools have been used in carpeting for decades and are increasing in use because there is simply not enough wool for use on a worldwide scale.

Although it requires special production procedures and certification, **organic wool** represents a growing market in the wool industry. For wool to be certified as organic, it must be produced in accordance with federal standards for organic livestock production. These include: (1) livestock feed and forage used from the last, third gestation must be certified organic; (2) the use of synthetic hormones and genetic engineering is prohibited; (3) the use of synthetic pesticides (internal, external, and on pastures) is prohibited; and (4) producers must encourage livestock health through good environmental and management practices. Organic wool is very limited in supply; much of it comes from Australia and New Zealand.

Organic wool is also getting attention from companies that produce bedding material. There are several manufacturers that produce organic wool blankets. Other manufacturers are offering mattresses made from organic wool.

In the United States, organic wool is produced in New Mexico, Montana, Maine, Vermont, and New Jersey.

Specialty Wools

Specialty wools are obtained from the goat, camel, and rabbit families (Table 3.1, p. 26). These fibers have very limited use in the interior industry because of their high cost and limited supply. With the exception of mohair, the specialty wool fibers are less durable than sheep's wool. Many of these specialty wool fibers are blended with wool to add softness, texture, color interest, or prestige value.

Alpaca fibers are obtained from the hair of a domesticated animal of the camel family (Figure 4.30). Alpacas are native to the Andes Mountains. The fibers are soft, fine, and lustrous. Alpaca fiber is softer than llama fiber and is used in upholstery fabrics and rugs. Alpaca fibers are typically used in their natural colors, which include a range of whites, browns, grays, and blacks.

Mohair is the fiber of the Angora goat. The goats (Figure 4.31) are sheared twice a year. Mohair is a very resilient fiber, having fewer scales and less crimp than wool. Mohair fibers are smoother, with fibers up to 12 inches in length, giving them a lustrous appearance. Mohair is also a fine fiber and has better abrasion resistance and resiliency than wool. Because it resists crushing, mohair is used in upholstery fabrics and floor coverings. Its high insulation properties, sound absorbency, and flame resistance make mohair an excellent choice for draperies. Its thermal retention properties help blankets retain their heat. South Africa is the largest producer of mohair fiber, supplying more than half of the world's total production. Other major producers are the United States and Turkey.

Angora is the fur of the Angora rabbit. This domesticated rabbit is raised in the United States, France, Italy, and Japan. The fiber is obtained by plucking or shearing. Angora fiber is very soft and smooth. The smoothness of the fiber contributes to its low cohesiveness. For this reason, angora is often blended with sheep's wool. Angora fiber has a high thermal retention and is used in blankets and bedding products.

Camel's hair is the fiber of the two-humped Bactrian camel and provides the best insulation of all the specialty wools. The Bactrian camel originally came from North Afghanistan. Today, they are found living in Turkey, and as far east as China, and as far north as Siberia. In the spring of every year, the fiber is gathered by hand, when the camels shed their outer hair and undercoat. A camel produces about five pounds of fiber per year.

Llama fibers, like alpaca fibers, are also obtained from the hair of a domesticated animal (Figure 4.32) of the camel family. Llama fibers are coarser and less strong than alpaca fiber. Also, other characteristics that differentiate the llama from the alpaca is the llama's larger size and longer head. Llama fibers are used on a limited basis, for rugs. As of 2007, there were more than seven million llamas and alpacas in South America.[1] Due to their importation from South America in the late twentieth century, there are now more than 100,000 llamas and 7,000 alpacas in the United States and Canada.

Cashmere fiber is the fleece of a cashmere goat[2] (Figure 4.33) and is one of the softest, most expensive fibers produced. The fiber is obtained by combing the domesticated animals during the molting season. Cashmere fibers are used for bedding and blankets. More than half of all cashmere fiber is produced by China, followed by Mongolia, Afghanistan, and Iran.

Quivit is the fiber from the underbelly of the domesticated musk ox (Figure 4.34). These animals are raised in Alaska and Canada for their rare and luxurious fiber. The fiber sheds naturally and is separated from the coarser hairs by hand. Quivit fibers are soft as cashmere and warmer than wool.

Vicuna fiber is obtained from the hair of the vicuna, a rare wild animal of the camel family. Vicuna fiber is the softest, finest, and rarest of all specialty fibers. Vicunas are found in Peru, Chile, Argentina, and Bolivia. Vicunas were hunted to the brink of extinction for their prized fiber and eventually declared an endangered species in 1974. Sanctions forbidding trade in vicuna were established, along with antipoaching efforts. Now, vicuna is making a dramatic comeback and is sought by premium-fiber processors in South America, Europe, and Asia. Vicunas are

Figure 4.32 llama.
Courtesy of Minnesota Minis, www.minnesotaminis.com.

Figure 4.33 Cashmere goats.
Courtesy of *Wild Fibers Magazine*.

Figure 4.34 Musk ox.
Courtesy of *Wild Fibers Magazine*.

sheared similarly to sheep, and commercial harvesting of vicuna fiber is allowed, but international export of the animals, and hunting of them, is illegal.

Yak fiber is produced from a large ox (Figure 4.35) that is found in Tibet. The soft inner coat is used for garments and blankets. This soft and short fiber is hand plucked from the chest and belly.

Natural Fiber Engineering

With natural fibers, appearance and performance engineering must be accomplished by working with already-formed fibers having a given set of inherent properties. Thus, converters, not fiber suppliers, are generally responsible for altering the inherent characteristics of these fibers. While some treatments, such as the application of moth-repellent agents and cross-linking resins, produce chemical changes within the fibers, they are nonetheless introduced during conversion of the greige goods. This work is discussed in Chapter 9.

Manufactured Fibers

Currently, four major groups of manufactured fibers are produced. These include the cellulose fibers, dextrose fibers, synthetic fibers, and mineral fibers. Not all fibers that have been invented continue to be available. Among those no longer produced in the United States are triacetate, azlon, anidex, lastrile, nytril, and vinal. Some of these fibers may be manufactured overseas and imported into the domestic market.

Figure 4.35 Yak.
Courtesy of Spring Brook Ranch, Jim Watson, springbrookranch.com.

Production

Virtually all manufactured fibers are produced in this sequence:

obtain fiber-forming substances → form polymer solutions → incorporate polymer additives → extrude and solidify filaments → draw → heat set

For manufactured fibers, the chemist becomes responsible for production at the monomer stage, even when nature provides the monomers and polymers.

Obtaining Fiber-forming Substances

Most fiber-forming substances are obtained by one of three techniques: extract them from fibrous materials, synthesize them from nonfibrous natural materials, and combine inorganic compounds.

Extracting Cellulose and Dextrose Polymers To produce rayon, acetate, lyocell, and PLA, the chemist extracts cellulose and dextrose material from natural products such as wood chips, cotton linters, bamboo plants, corn, and sugar beets. Although these materials are fibrous, wood fibers lack the flexibility needed for textile processing and end-use applications. Cotton linters are too short to be spun into quality yarns. The dextrose is extracted from both corn and sugar beets and then converted to lactic acid, which is then converted to fiber form.

Synthesizing Monomers To produce polyester, nylon, acrylic, olefin, and other manufactured synthetic fibers, the chemist must first synthesize the monomers from such nonfibrous natural materials as natural gas, oil, and coal. Subsequently, the monomers are polymerized in vessels resembling pressure cookers. During this step of the process, the chemist can often control the **degree of polymerization**, that is, the extent to which the monomers link to form polymer chains. When high strength and abrasion resistance are needed, for example, the chemist will form longer chains.

Combining Inorganic Compounds Manufactured mineral fibers, including glass and metal fibers, are inorganic fibers. Glass fibers are formed by heating silica sand, limestone, and other compounds until they fuse and liquefy; distinctive fiber-forming units are not produced. The resulting solution is normally converted into marbles that can be inspected for clarity. Today, glass fibers have diminished use because of the weight and relatively low flexibility.

True metal fibers are made from such substances as gold, silver, copper, and stainless steel. The expense of gold and silver, of course, precludes their widespread use; other structures have been developed to simulate their appearance.

Forming Polymer Solutions

The second step in the production of manufactured fibers is the formation of a solution of the fiber-forming substance. In some cases, a solvent is used to dissolve the polymer compound; in other cases, heat is used to melt the substance.

Incorporating Additives

After the polymer solution is formed, the producer may incorporate **additives** to engineer specific properties. Such additives include dye pigments for superior colorfastness, optical brighteners to improve apparent whiteness and brightness, ultraviolet absorbers to minimize light degradation, flame-retardant agents to reduce flammability, delusterants to reduce light reflectance and hide accumulated soil, and antistatic agents to increase electrical conductivity.

Extruding and Solidifying Filaments

Filaments are formed in a mechanical spinning operation. This type of spinning should not be confused with yarn spinning, the combining of staple-length fibers into textile yarn structures.

The spinning operation involves the extrusion of the polymer solution through a device called a **spinneret**. As schematized in Figure 4.36, a spinneret is similar to a shower head. In the same manner as pressure forces water through a shower head, pressure forces the polymer solution through the minute openings in the spinneret.

The openings in spinnerets are often no more than a few ten-thousandths of an inch in diameter, but their size can be varied to produce finer or coarser filaments. This enables the producer to regulate the flexibility of the filaments, to increase or decrease the area that the filaments will cover, and to control the amount of surface area per unit of volume the filaments present for soil adhesion. In some spinning operations, the shape of the apertures is designed to produce filaments with specific cross-sectional shapes.

Four basic spinning techniques are used to extrude and solidify filaments: wet spinning, solvent spinning, dry spinning, and melt spinning.

Wet Spinning In **wet spinning**, a solvent is used to dissolve the polymer. The solution is extruded through the spinneret into an acidic, aqueous bath where the solvent is extracted and the extruded strands coagulate or harden. Wet spinning is used in the production of rayon and some acrylic and spandex fibers.

Solvent Spinning **Solvent spinning** is similar to wet spinning in that a solvent is used to dissolve the polymer and the solution is extruded through a spinneret into a fluid bath. The bath, however, is not water based; it is a solvent that is recovered for continued use. Solvent spinning is used in the production of lyocell, a relatively new cellulosic fiber.

Dry Spinning In **dry spinning**, a highly volatile solvent is used to dissolve the polymer compound, producing the spinning solution. The solution is extruded through

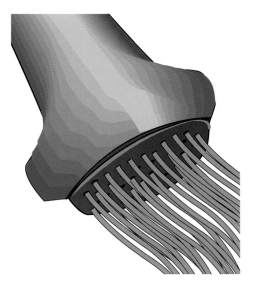

Figure 4.36 Spinneret device for spinning manufactured fibers.

a spinneret into a warm air chamber where the solvent evaporates, solidifying the fine filaments. Dry spinning is used in the production of acetate, triacetate, and some acrylic, modacrylic, spandex, and vinyon fibers.

Melt Spinning   In **melt spinning**, heat is used to melt the polymer, producing the liquid spinning **dope**. The liquid is extruded through the spinneret into a cool air chamber where the filaments harden as they cool. Variations in aperture shapes are often used in melt spinning as the filaments retain the shape of the openings. Melt spinning is used for the production of polyester, nylon, olefin, and glass fibers.

Drawing

Because most extruded filaments are disordered, they must be drawn or stretched to increase the orientation of their polymer chains and their degree of interior order. The drawing operation may be carried out by the fiber producer or by the throwster.

Drawing lengthens the filaments and reduces their diameters, aligning the chains and causing them to pack more closely. These changes increase the likelihood that crystalline regions will result from extensive lateral bonding. As the degree of interior order increases, there are parallel increases in strength and stiffness and decreases in extensibility and the rate at which such substances as water, dye, and finishing agents will be absorbed. Producers develop an appropriate balance among these properties by controlling the extent of drawing, always limiting the operation to avoid producing a totally oriented and crystallized arrangement.

Drawing or stretching an extruded filament introduces strain within the fiber, like that created within an elastic band when it is stretched. If an unstabilized drawn filament were exposed to conditions such as water and heat that encourage the release of this imposed strain, the polymer chains would relax, reverting back to the undrawn, amorphous arrangement. This would be accompanied by a shortening of the fiber, a reaction like that of an elastic band returning to its original length after the stretching force releases it. In order to prevent this interior relaxation and loss of length, manufacturers generally stabilize drawn filaments by exposing them to controlled amounts of heat.

Heat Setting

Heat can be used to stabilize or set **thermoplastic or heat-sensitive fibers**—fibers that soften and shrink when exposed to a controlled amount of heat, and melt when exposed to an excessive amount of heat. With the exception of rayon, lyocell, and the high-temperature resistant aramid and novoloid fibers, most manufactured fibers are thermoplastic.

In the **heat setting** operation, the fiber is heated to its **glass transition temperature**. At this temperature, lateral bonds within the fiber are disturbed and the polymer chains can shift their positions. In order to prevent excessive shrinkage, the heated fiber is held under some tension. As the fiber cools, new bonds form to "lock" the polymer chains into their new position, stabilizing the length of the filament.

Heat setting will be postponed until the yarn stage when the filaments are to be given a two- or three-dimensional crimped or curled configuration. It will be postponed until the greige good stage when a three-dimensional, embossed design is planned, or when the converter intends to improve the alignment of the yarns and stabilize the dimensions of the fabric. Whenever heat setting is performed, it must be carried out at approximately 50 °F higher than the temperatures that may be encountered later in processing, laundering, or ironing. Exposure to temperatures higher than those used for heat setting will overcome the initial set and stability of the textile item.

Manufactured Cellulosic Fibers

In the 1800s and early 1900s, chemists eagerly sought to invent a fiber to substitute for the luxurious but costly silk. Early tries included a fibrous but explosive combination of cellulose and nitrogen. Subsequently, chemists created an **artificial silk** in the late 1800s, and the fibers were commercially produced in the United States in 1910. Because of negative connotations associated with the term artificial, fiber producers wanted to discontinue its use, and the name **rayon** was coined and used in the mid-1920s. Further work resulted in two additional cellulose-based fibers, **acetate** and **triacetate**, being introduced to consumers in 1924. The production of triacetate fibers in the United States, however, was discontinued in the mid-1980s. In the early 1990s a fourth cellulose fiber, **lyocell**, was created. **PLA**, a fifth manufactured cellulose fiber, was introduced in 2003.

Acetate

The Federal Trade Commission defines acetate as "a manufactured fiber in which the fiber-forming substance is cellulose acetate. Where not less than 92 percent of the hydroxyl groups are acetylated, the term *triacetate* may be used." Triacetate is no longer produced in the United States.

Production of acetate begins with cellulose, generally from trees, cotton linters, or bamboo. Therefore, these fibers are often referred to as cellulose-based fibers. The fibers are dry spun.

Fabrics of acetate have high drapability and the look and feel of silk, but are more reasonably priced (see Figure 4.37). A major problem is **gasfastness**. With exposure to such gaseous pollutants or air contaminants as oxides of nitrogen or sulfur, acetate dyed with disperse dyestuffs permanently changes color: blue turns pink, brown becomes yellowish, and green converts to a reddish hue. This unsightly problem, known as **fume or gas fading**, can be prevented with solution dyeing as described in Chapter 8. Fume fading is an especially important consideration for such interior textile products as drapery and upholstery fabrics. Should the original color of such items be lost, the harmony of the interior would be destroyed, necessitating an unplanned, costly, and disruptive replacement.

Acetate was the first manufactured fiber that was thermoplastic or heat sensitive. Although heat setting can be used, its use is restricted to preserve high flexibility and drapability. Consumers must be cautious with ironing temperatures to avoid melting the fibers.

Lyocell

Lyocell was introduced to consumers in 1991 and originally marketed as a type of rayon. In 1996 the FTC officially approved lyocell as the new generic name for "a solvent spun fiber that is obtained by an organic solvent spinning process." Lyocell is a cellulose fiber made from the wood pulp of trees grown on managed tree farms, where the trees are constantly replanted. Unlike rayon, virtually all the chemicals used in the production process are reclaimed and recycled. Environmentalists have heralded lyocell as a new fiber that represents a milestone in the development of environmentally sustainable textiles.

Lyocell shares many properties with other natural cellulose fibers, such as cotton, flax, and silk. Short, staple-length fibers give a cottonlike look to fabrics. Long filament fibers are successful in silklike uses. Lyocell blends well with other fibers, including wool, silk, rayon, cotton, flax, nylon, and polyester. Fabrics made of lyocell have exceptional strength, a luxurious hand, and excellent drape. Lyocell is breathable and comfortable, and it resists wrinkling and shrinking (Figure 4.38). Unlike other natural fibers, lyocell is stronger when wet and exhibits better dimensional stability when laundered. Lyocell is much stronger than rayon when wet. This property of high wet strength allows fabrics made of lyocell to be machine washed successfully.

Tencel® is the trade name owned by Lenzing Fibers Inc., of Germany. Lenzing is currently the only producer of lyocell. Production costs are greater than for cotton, making products made of lyocell more expensive.

Figure 4.37 Satin fabric made from acetate fiber. Courtesy of Amy Willbanks, www.textilefabric.com.

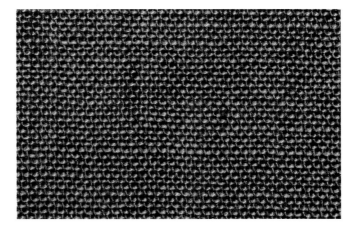

Figure 4.38 Chambray fabric made of Tencel® lyocell. Courtesy of Amy Willbanks, www.textilefabric.com.

A new variety of textiles has come on the market with the development of fabrics containing active, health-promoting substances that survive the manufacturing process and remain in the fiber even after repeated washing. These textile innovations also include odor- and bacteria-reducing effects. **Seacell®** is a modified lyocell fiber with a natural anti-inflammatory and skin protection additive: seaweed. The minerals contained in seawater accumulate in seaweed. This explains the high concentration of trace elements, vitamins, and minerals. The porous, open structure of the Seacell® fiber promotes humidity intake and release as well as a healthy reaction between the fiber and the skin. The garment absorbs what your skin expels, while your skin absorbs the healthful elements carried in the fibers. The fiber also neutralizes odors. This makes Seacell® an excellent choice for sheeting and toweling products. Seacell® is produced in two versions: Seacell® Pure, for the pure effect of the seaweed, and Seacell® Active, which holds an additional antimicrobial effect that occurs by adding silver.

Rayon

According to the Federal Trade Commission, rayon is "a manufactured fiber composed of regenerated cellulose, as well as manufactured fibers composed of regenerated cellulose in which substituents have replaced not more than 15 percent of the hydroxyl groups." Rayon fibers may be a conventional type (e.g., viscose or cuprammonium), or an improved type (e.g., medium or high strength or high wet modulus [HWM]). The conventional cuprammonium rayons are no longer produced in the United States.

The basic wet spinning process has been continuously used for the production of conventional viscose rayon fibers since the 1940s. The term *viscose* comes from the viscous, syrup-like polymer solution formed. In order to compete more effectively in the fiber market, rayon fiber producers have altered the viscose process, including the spinning operation, to produce improved fibers with higher strength and/or a higher wet elastic modulus. Fabrics made of the HWM fibers resist deformation under humid or wet conditions, exhibiting better dimensional stability than the conventional types, and can be laundered.

Conventional viscose rayon fibers have relatively low strength and poor dimensional stability, properties requiring that dry cleaning be used. The fibers are soft, absorbent, and drapable, and, because they have the luster and sheen so prized with silk, they are often used in lieu of the more expensive fiber. Rayon is used in curtain and drapery fabrics, upholstery fabrics, table linens, and blankets. It also is used in such window treatment trimmings as cords and galloons. One of the advantages of rayon over cotton is its resistance to shrinkage, a notorious problem for cotton. Rayon is less likely to fade or to form pills as a result of friction.

Modal® is a registered tradename of Lenzing AG, a German company that specializes in regenerated manufactured fibers. Whereas rayon may be made of the wood pulp of a number of different trees, Modal® is a variety of HWM rayon derived exclusively from beech trees. Modal® is very soft and is popular for household textiles, such as bedding, upholstery, and towels. Many companies market Modal® as "completely natural." This type of advertising can be misleading to the consumer because it implies that Modal® is a natural fiber. This is incorrect, as Modal® is a type of rayon, and the fiber undergoes harsh chemical processing in its production.

Bamboo, although commonly marketed as a natural fiber, is actually nothing more than rayon, as defined by the Federal Trade Commission. Historically, viscose rayon has been manufactured using a process in which fairly toxic chemicals convert the cellulose into a soluble compound, which is in turn regenerated into almost pure cellulose. In contrast to viscose rayon, bamboo rayon uses a new method for converting plant cellulose into a usable fiber. Instead of wood pulp as the principle product, this rayon is produced using bamboo plants. A woody grass native to almost every continent, bamboo is among the fastest growing plants on earth. Bamboo can grow up to 3 feet in 1 day. Bamboo grows naturally without the use of pesticides, herbicides, or fertilizers. It reaches maturity quickly and can be harvested in about 4 years, compared with many species of trees, which can take 20 to 30 years to mature. Bamboo does not require replanting after harvesting because its vast root system continually sprouts new shoots. The major producer of bamboo is China.

The fiber is smooth, strong, durable, and long lasting. It also has antibacterial and antimicrobial properties, making it an excellent choice for towels and bedding (Figures 4.39 and 28.3, p. 427). Bamboo rayon is highly absorbent and wicks water away from the body faster than cotton. Bamboo rayon is very soft and comfortable.

Bamboo rayon is used to make sheets, towels, rugs, bath mats, carpeting, flooring, window shades, placemats, window coverings, wallcoverings, and other decorative accessories. More and more designers are introducing

Figure 4.39 Rayon (made from bamboo) blended with cotton sheets.
Courtesy of Amy Willbanks, www.textilefabric.com.

bamboo-fiber home collections offering bamboo bedding and bath towels.

Manufactured Dextrose Fibers
PLA

In 2003 Cargill Dow Polymers introduced "NatureWorks PLA," a manufactured dextrose fiber produced from corn. The Federal Trade Commission issued a new generic name, PLA (polylactic acid), to the new fiber. The Federal Trade Commission defines PLA as "a manufactured fiber in which the fiber-forming substance is composed of at least 85% by weight of lactic acid ester units derived from naturally occurring sugars."

PLA is made from the dextrose extracted from corn, an annually renewable resource. The dextrose is fermented to produce lactic acid. The water is then removed and converted to fiber form. PLA is not a new polymer, but the recent advances in the fermentation of glucose have led to a dramatic reduction in the cost of the lactic acid used to make the polymers. For the first time these fibers can be made from a renewable resource while at the same time compete in the marketplace in relation to cost and performance. PLA products have a combination of features similar to those of cotton, such as wrinkle resistance, superior hand, and excellent absorbency and resiliency. PLA's soil-resistant properties make it ideal for use in carpeting in both commercial and residential settings. PLA exhibits high UV resistance, which promotes its use in outdoor furniture and furnishings applications. **Ingeo™**, meaning "ingredients of the earth," is also a registered trademark of Cargill (Figures 4.40, 4.41, and 4.42). The natural flame resistance of Ingeo™ makes it

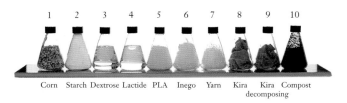

Figure 4.40 The production cycle stages of Ingeo® Kira™.
Courtesy of Herman Miller.

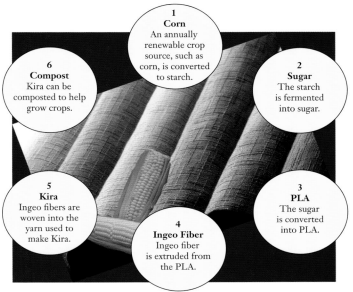

Figure 4.41 The production cycle stages of Ingeo® Kira™.
Courtesy of Herman Miller.

Figure 4.42 Ingeo® Kira™ panel fabric.
Courtesy of Herman Miller.

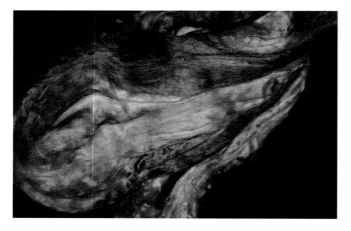

Figure 4.43 SoySilk®.
Courtesy of Amy Willbanks, www.textilefabric.com.

Figure 4.44 Azlon/hemp blend upholstery fabric.
Courtesy of Amy Willbanks, www.textilefabric.com.

well suited for home furnishing fabrics. It is ideal for applications for rugs, carpeting, and office furniture. Ingeo™ offers the performance of synthetics with the comfort of natural fibers. Cargill Dow has plans to introduce PLA with an array of corn-based products, including carpeting, wall panels, upholstery, interior furnishings, and outdoor fabrics.

Environmental groups have questioned the eco-friendliness of PLA, as it is produced from genetically engineered corn. Cargill Dow researchers are working on techniques to use many other sources of plant material as the base for the fiber.

Composting can be considered the ultimate recycling, turning waste fibers back to the earth. Some manufactured fibers are designed to be composted at the end of their useful life spans. PLA is one of the most well known of these fibers. Recycling fibers like polyester and nylon cost time and money, and crated its own environmental footprint. Composting is environmentally responsible and leaves no harmful byproducts.[4]

Manufactured Protein Fibers

Azlon is defined by the Federal Trade Commission as a "manufactured fiber in which the fiber-forming substance is composed of any regenerated naturally occurring proteins." **SoySilk®**, a registered tradename of the azlon fiber, is made from the residue of soybeans from tofu manufacturing (Figure 4.43). **Soy** was cultivated in China before 3000 B.C., and its use was popular in the 1940s. Henry Ford often touted the virtues of soy and wore a suit made of soy in 1937. Because soy is an environmentally friendly fiber made from tofu manufacturing waste (soybean protein is extracted from the residual oils of soybean cake),

the production process uses resources that would otherwise go unused. Soybeans are a sustainable crop that can be grown successfully with little to no pesticides. China, the largest producer and exporter of textiles, has begun mass producing soy-based yarn. SoySilk® has a soft hand and is very durable. Soysilk® exhibits good colorfastness and excellent absorbency and comfort. Soy products are found mainly as sheets in the interior furnishings industry. **Silk Latte®**, another registered tradename for azlon, is made from milk protein. Silk Latte® also has a very soft hand. It is not as durable as Soysilk® and therefore not used as much in home furnishings. Because of its low cost compared with natural silk, Silk Latte® is used in blends to resemble the more expensive silk fiber. These fibers are gaining popularity among hand knitters for sweaters, blankets, hats, and scarves. An azlon/hemp upholstery fabric is shown in Figure 4.44.

Manufactured Synthetic Fibers

Manufactured synthetic fibers are derived from such materials as natural gas, oil, and coal. Because of the initial synthesis of the monomers, the term **synthetic** was applied to these fibers. Manufactured synthetic fibers offer easy appearance properties, such as wrinkle resistance and easy care. Known for their durability, synthetics also offer resistance to moths and mildew. Synthetics have a low moisture absorbency, which makes them excellent for end uses that call for water repellency, such as outdoor furniture coverings. Synthetics are also widely used in upholstery and drapery treatments, carpeting, and bath/bedding products (Figure 4.45). Modifications in fiber production have greatly improved the properties of these fibers.

a)

b)

c)

Figure 4.45 Sunbrella® acrylic fabric used on indoor and outdoor furniture. Sunbrella® photos provided by Glen Raven, Inc.

Acrylic

Acrylic fibers are defined by the Federal Trade Commission as "a manufactured fiber in which the fiber-forming substance is any long-chain synthetic polymer composed of at least 85% by weight of acrylonitrile units."

The fibers are derived from elements taken from natural gas, air, water, and petroleum. After synthesis of the monomers, the polymer solution is formed, additives are included, and the filaments are dry or wet spun.

Acrylic fibers are prized for their ability to be engineered to resemble wool, imitating them more successfully than any other fiber. Here, the more economical manufactured fiber offers the convenience and cost-savings of laundering rather than dry cleaning; an inher-

ent resistance to moths, carpet beetles, and the outdoor elements; and superior resistance to the damaging rays in sunlight. These various properties support the use of acrylic in carpet and rugs, curtains and draperies, and as awnings and coverings for outdoor furniture. Sunbrella® is a popular acrylic fabric used in indoor and outdoor furniture (Figure 4.45a, b, and c). Acrylic's low specific gravity and high bulkiness makes it successful in end uses that require warmth without the weight, such as blankets. Acrylic blankets are soft, warm, lightweight, and machine washable. Foamed acrylic is also applied as a coating to drapery fabrics and linings for sound and heat insulation, temperature control, and room darkening features (Figure 17.32, p. 298).

Aramid

The Federal Trade Commission defines aramid as "a manufactured fiber in which the fiber-forming substance is a long-chain synthetic aromatic polyamide in which at least 85% of the amide linkages are attached directly to two aromatic rings." Because these fibers have high temperature and flame resistance, they are increasingly used in aircraft upholstery and carpet. The relatively high stiffness, however, precludes their widespread use in interior furnishings. High cost is also a contributing factor to their limited use in residential fabrics.

Glass

Glass is referred to as a manufactured fiber in which the "fiber forming substance is glass." Because of their fire resistance, glass fibers are used in sheer drapery casements, and window and drapery treatments. Because the broken ends can cause skin irritation, bedding and upholstery are rarely used. Fabrics of fiberglass do not require frequent cleaning because the fibers resist soil. Spots and stains in window treatments can be wiped off. Glass is considered a heavy fiber and this weight may require a commercial type curtain rod.

Modacrylic

The Federal Trade Commission definition of modacrylic is "a manufactured fiber in which the fiber-forming substance is any long-chain synthetic polymer composed of less than 85% but at least 35% by weight of acrylonitrile units." Thus, a significant portion of the fiber, from 15 percent to 65 percent, is a second monomer or **copolymer**. Such compounds as vinyl chloride, vinylidene chloride, or vinyl bromide are used.

Modacrylic fibers are resilient, abrasion resistant, quick drying, flame resistant, and heat sensitive (Figure 4.46). Their relatively high flame resistance supports their use in scatter rugs and in window covering fabrics for such commercial interiors as theaters, hospitals, schools, and restaurants. Their thermoplasticity allows them to be shaped and heat set, as in the case of wigs. It also allows them to be used effectively in simulated fur for apparel and upholstery applications.

Nylon

Nylon fibers were the first truly synthesized manufactured fibers. They were unceremoniously introduced into the consumer market in 1938 as a replacement for boar's bristles in toothbrushes. Thereafter, they were introduced in sheer hosiery, as a replacement for silk and rayon. With the outbreak of World War II, however, nylon was quickly withdrawn for use in war material.

Nylon may be produced with a single monomer or with two monomers. Nylon 6, for example, is manufactured from a single monomer, caprolactam: the "6" indicates that the compound has six carbon atoms. Nylon 6,6, the more common copolymer type manufactured in the United States, is made from adipic acid and hexamethylene diamine, each having six carbon atoms. After the monomers are synthesized from petroleum or natural gas, air, and water, they are polymerized and melt spun, drawn, and heat set.

Because nylon is melt spun, the fibers retain the shape of the spinneret holes, making it possible to engineer selected features into the fibers. These features range from a change in hand to a change in luster and soil-hiding ability.

Drawing and heat setting are controlled to engineer the desired amount of strength, elongation, abrasion resistance, and resiliency. The strength and abrasion resistance of nylon fibers support their use in carpet and rugs and upholstery fabrics (Figure 4.47). Curtains, bedspreads, and scatter rugs made of nylon are easily laundered and retain their dimensional stability and resiliency. The low moisture absorbency of the fibers gives quick drying items but encourages static buildup. Because of the demand for recycled fibers and the

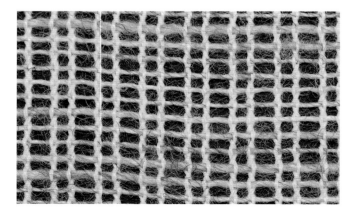

Figure 4.46 Modacrylic casement fabric.
Courtesy of Amy Willbanks, www.textilefabric.com.

Figure 4.47 Nylon carpet samples.
Courtesy of INVISTA Sarl.

popularity of recycled polyester, several manufacturers are offering recycled nylon products. Recycled nylon fibers are used in apparel, carpeting, and window treatments. One of the biggest problems in the recycling of polyester is that even a 100 percent nylon fabric cannot be recycled if it has a polyurethane coating on the back. Most of the time, recycling nylon is cost-prohibitive since they often have coatings, finishes, and blends. The fiber industry has come a long way in their recycling efforts. The infrastructure is now in place to easily collect and sort the raw material.[3]

Olefin

The name **olefin** is assigned to "a manufactured fiber in which the fiber-forming substance is at least 85 percent by weight of ethylene, propylene, or other olefin units." Their resistance to rot and weather adds to their success as a fiber in outdoor carpeting. Their heat sensitivity requires careful temperature control in drying and ironing, while their extremely low moisture absorption makes olefin products quick drying. Olefin is also referred to as **polypropylene** or **polyethylene**. Although these are not generic names, many producers identify olefin by these terms. Olefin fibers are generally melt spun and solution dyed. They are chosen for both indoor and outdoor carpet and upholstery fabric because of their abrasion resistance (Figure 4.48). Their resistance to rot and weather adds to their success as a fiber in outdoor carpet. Olefin fibers generate low static electricity, a plus for use in carpeting.

Some interior designers prefer olefin to other fibers because of its positive performance characteristics and low cost. Olefin is moisture resistant and chemical resistant, stain resistant, abrasion resistant, colorfast, and extremely lightweight. Olefin is the lightest textile fiber.

Olefin has almost completely replaced jute in carpet backing because of its low cost, easy processing, and excellent durability (Figures 22.3 a,b,c and 22.4, p. 351). Olefin is also used for draperies, wallcoverings, slipcovers, and automotive interiors.

Introduced in 1981, after 7 years of research and testing by Carnegie, Xorel® olefin fabrics have revolutionized the upholstered furniture and wallcoverings industry. Xorel® fabrics are inherently flame resistant and stain resistant. No topical chemical treatments are necessary to provide these properties. This eliminates the need to use and dispose of the chemicals needed for this process. Because Xorel® fabrics exhibit remarkable stain resistance and ease of maintenance, they are an excellent choice for upholstered furniture, wall panels, and wallcoverings. Xorel® fabrics have an exceptionally long life cycle (backed by a 7-year performance warranty), and do not require period replacement as do most textiles exposed to high-traffic commercial areas. Xorel® fabrics exhibit excellent colorfastness and show no signs of fading after years of use. For indoor air quality, Xorel® fabric releases insignificant levels of VOCs. These fabrics are also resistant to microbes, which has increased its use for commercial applications. In hospitals and health care facilities, the fabric's antibacterial properties create a safe environment for both worker and patients.

Lastrol, a generic subclass of **olefin**, has much higher elongation and elastic recovery properties than regular olefin. Lastrol can stretch up to 500 percent of its original length. It is used as fitted upholstery fabric coverings.

Polyester

Although polyester has been available in the domestic market only since 1953, its importance has grown dramatically for both the apparel and interior textile industries, excluding the soft floor coverings market where nylon is dominant. The Federal Trade Commission defines polyester as "a manufactured fiber in which the fiber-forming substance is any long-

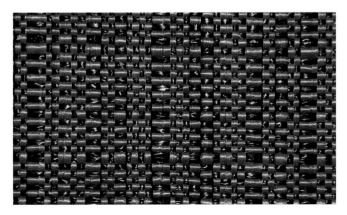

Figure 4.48 Olefin upholstery fabric.
Courtesy of Amy Willbanks, www.textilefabric.com.

Figure 4.49 Polyester sheer.
Courtesy of Amy Willbanks, www.textilefabric.com.

Figure 4.50 Sofa upholstered in recycled polyester. Courtesy of Viesso, www.viesso.com.

chain synthetic polymer composed of at least 85 percent by weight of an ester of a substituted aromatic carboxylic acid, including but not restricted to substituted terephthalic units, and parasubstituted hydroxy-benzoate units."

Thus, polyester fibers are copolymers, and like nylon and olefin, are melt spun, giving the producer the ability to engineer fiber properties by controlling the shape and form of the fibers. With drawing and heat setting, the strength, elongation, abrasion resistance, resiliency, and dimensional stability of the fiber can also be controlled.

Polyester is used in soft floor coverings, curtain and drapery fabrics and linings, bedding, wallcoverings, and table linens (Figures 4.49). The fibers are frequently blended with cotton or rayon for use in household and institutional textiles, including toweling.

Recycled plastic bottles are now being transformed into fiber produced for the home furnishings market. In 1993, Wellman, Inc., introduced EcoSpun, a revolutionary fiber made from 100 percent recycled plastic soda, water, and food containers. Until EcoSpun, no company had developed desirable or appealing post-consumer recycled fibers. The fibers are made from post-consumer PET containers. Because these are primarily food containers, the raw materials used to produce the plastic are rigorously controlled by the Food and Drug Administration and thus considered extremely high quality polyester. To be made into fiber, the plastic is cleaned, chopped, melted and then extruded into fibers. From coast to coast, predominant retailers, such as Saks, Macy's, Wal-Mart, and Blue Ridge Mountain Sports are carrying recycled home textiles. The message today is that recycling now extends far beyond simply stacking newspapers, metal cans, and plastic bottles in local recycling bins. With the growing prevalence of these fabrics hitting the market, consumers are proving that recycling can be fashionable, literally, and that it is environmentally proactive to purchase products made of recycled materials (Figure 4.50). Figure 13.6 (p. 219) shows an upholstery fabric made of 58 percent recycled post-consumer polyester/42 percent virgin wool.

Saran

Saran was first introduced into the commercial market in 1941. The Federal Trade Commission defines saran as "a manufactured fiber in which the fiber-forming substance is any long-chain synthetic polymer composed of at least 80 percent by weight of vinylidene chloride units."

As shown in Table 3.9 (p. 41), saran is a relatively heavy fiber. The fiber also has a relatively low softening point (Table 3.12, p. 44). With its resistance to chemicals, water, mildew, and sunlight, the fiber is frequently and successfully used for the webbing and coverings on patio chairs. It also is used for fabrics installed in public transportation vehicles.

Spandex

Spandex is defined by the Federal Trade Commission as "a manufactured fiber in which the fiber-forming substance is a long-chain synthetic polymer comprised of at least 85 percent of a segmented polyurethane." These elastomeric fibers are widely appreciated for their high elongation, high elastic recovery, and high holding power in such apparel items as swimwear, hosiery, and sock tops. In recent years, their superior elasticity supports their use in upholstery fabric that is applied to curved furniture forms.

Vinyon

Vinyon is the generic name for which the fiber-forming substance composed of "at least 85 percent by weight of vinyl chloride units." Vinyon in film form is often called **vinyl** by both manufacturers and consumers. Vinyon fibers have excellent resistance to chemicals, bacteria, and insects. They are used as flame-resistant fibers in blankets, draperies, and carpeting. Because of its excellent weather resistance, vinyon is used in tarps, awnings, and outdoor furniture.

Manufactured Fiber Engineering

For more than three decades, the primary focus of manufactured fiber research has been on fiber engineering, not on fiber invention. This work has resulted in the refinement of production procedures and the development or identification of polymer additives that can produce fiber variants. Technological advances are often described as belonging to a particular "generation" of manufactured fibers. Other developments in fiber engineering continue today.

Fiber Variants

A **fiber variant** is chemically related to other fibers in its generic class, but it is distinguished by one or more features. Among several polyester fibers, for example, one variant may have a round cross-sectional shape, a relatively large diameter, and a comparatively high degree of orientation; another may have a pentalobal cross-sectional shape, be inherently flame resistant, and dull; and yet another may be inherently antistatic, have a relatively small diameter, and be bright.

The availability of hundreds of fiber variants enables end-product manufacturers to be highly selective when they choose fibers. In turn, this helps them to offer products that conform closely to the selection criteria of contemporary consumers.

Fiber Modifications

Members of the industry recognize **generations** or levels of manufactured fiber development. Each new designation has been used to distinguish major scientific breakthroughs from earlier achievements. Such distinctions were used extensively in the promotion of noncellulosic fiber variants, especially those intended for use in soft floor coverings.

First Generation   The first level of manufactured fiber development is considered to be the level of invention. Following the invention and commercial production of the cellulosic fibers, research chemist Wallace Carothers developed the foundations of high polymer chemistry. His pioneering work led directly to the development of nylon. As knowledge of polymer science grew, fiber chemists manufactured such other fibers as acrylics, modacrylics, olefins, polyesters, spandexes, and vinyons.

Second Generation   The second phase of manufactured fiber development saw the refinement of the several general groups of fibers. Their aesthetic features were enhanced and their performance properties improved. Some of the technologies used included modification of fiber cross sections for soil hiding, alteration of fiber diameters for controlled stiffness, and inclusion of such polymer additives as delusterants, dye pigments, antistatic agents, and flame-retardant compounds. Experimentation and evaluation provided greater understanding of the effects of varied amounts of drawing on fiber performance. Heat-setting procedures were perfected and used to improve resiliency and dimensional stability. Texturing methods were developed to introduce multidimensional configurations to smooth, straight filaments, enabling producers to control such things as covering power, resiliency, pill formation, and fiber cohesiveness.

Third Generation   The third generation included such developments as the production of bicomponent fibers, biconstituent fibers, and blended filaments. **Bicomponent fibers** are made by combining two generically similar compounds into one filament; **biconstituent fibers** are made by combining two generically dissimilar compounds into one filament; and **blended filaments** are made by combining two generically dissimilar filaments into a single yarn structure immediately after extrusion. Other developments of this generation included the processing techniques that enable producers to offer manufactured fibers having the aesthetic features of natural fibers.

Fourth and Advanced Generations   In the fourth and advanced generations, fiber technology became increasingly sophisticated. Fibers were engineered to exhibit specific service-related characteristics, many of which were appropriate for a limited assortment of products. Fiber cross-sectional shapes, for example, underwent further modification to provide soil shedding as well as better soil hiding and controlled levels of luster in soft floor coverings. Innovative filament compositions and designs very nearly overcame static problems. Newer polymer additives provided inherent stain and soil repellency. Fibers having hollow or tubular shapes provided higher insulation without added weight. The inventions of the high-temperature and flame-resistant aramid and novoloid fibers were other developments of the fourth or advanced generation.

Fiber Developments

Microfibers, used in the apparel industry for years, are fast becoming a part of the home furnishing industry. Microfibers are manufactured fibers with a denier of less than 1, which is the size of silk. Although the filaments are superfine, strength is exceptional. Both heavyweight and lightweight fabrics can be sueded or sanded without affecting the strength. Yarns made from microfibers contain more filaments than regular yarns, producing fabrics with more breathability. With more filaments comes more surface area as well. This allows printed fabrics to be vivid, with more clarity and a sharper contrast. Microdenier yarns produce soft, fluid, silky fabrics with exceptional drapability. A microfiber lets a comforter retain its loft, fullness, ample shape, and airiness. Window coverings drape exceptionally well. Manufacturers claim that microfibers have the comfort and feel of natural fibers with the strength and easy care of manufactured fibers. Microfibers have been met with great enthusiasm from both designers and consumers.

Two methods are commonly used to make microfibers. One method is to make the microfiber from two polymers and then split them into their components. Another is to dissolve away one polymer of a bicomponent fiber, leaving fine fibrils of the second one. In both instances, a thicker fiber is first spun but ends up as an ultrafine microfiber.

Using **nanotechnology**, tiny molecules are permanently attached to the fiber without clogging the fabric weave. This leads to superior performance characteristics for fabrics, such as spill resistance, stain resistance, microbe resistance, and static resistance. Moisture-wicking characteristics can also be improved using nanotechnology. Whereas many traditional treatments use a coating, through nanotechnology the chemical can be directly bound to the fiber. A permanent bond is established that does not affect the hand, look, or color of the product.

Developments in fiber engineering continue today. Numbered generations, however, are not widely used in marketing. On the other hand, such other marketing tools as trade names and logos are extensively used for purposes of promotion and marketing (see Chapter 10).

Summary

All textile fibers have a similar physical form; they are relatively long and thin. But there are numerous differences among fibers—their molecular arrangements, cross-sectional shapes, longitudinal configurations, length, and chemical compositions. Differences in chemical composition serve as the basis for classifying fibers into useful generic groups or classes.

The synthesis and production of all fibers includes the combining of atoms into monomers, the linking of monomers into polymers, and the forming of a fine, usable strand.

With natural fibers this sequence is carried out without direct human involvement, but subsequently inherent characteristics may be altered during fabric conversion. With manufactured fibers the sequence of synthesis and production is controlled by the fiber chemist and producer, who can introduce specific characteristics during production. Such fiber engineering has become increasingly sophisticated, enabling the producer to offer fibers that exhibit the aesthetic and performance features preferred or required by residential and commercial consumers.

Key Terms

abaca fiber	breaking	dry spinning	glass transition
acetate	burlap	Duppioni silk	temperature
additives	camel's hair	fiber variant	green cotton
alpaca	cashmere fiber	flax	hackling
angora	cellulosic	FoxFibre®	heat setting
artificial silk	coir fiber	fulling	hemp
asbestos	copolymer	fume or gas fading	henequin fiber
azlon	cornhusks	garneting	Ingeo™
bamboo	cortex	gasfastness	jute
bicomponent fiber	cotton	generation	kapok
biconstituent fiber	cuticle	genetically modified cotton	lanolin
blended filaments	degree of polymerization	seed (GM)	Lastrol
boiling off	drawing	ginning process	

line	noil	scutching	thermoplastic or heat-
linen	olefin	sea grass	sensitive fiber
linens	organic cotton	Seacell®	throwing
lint	organic wool	secondary wall	tinting
linters	palm grass	sericin	tow
llama fiber	peace silk	sericulture	triacetate
lumen	piña	shearing	Tussah silk
lyocell	protein	silk fiber	upland cotton
manufactured fiber	primary wall	Silk Latte®	vicuna
medulla	pure silk	sisal fiber	weighting
melt spinning	quivit	solvent spinning	wet spinning
microfiber	ramie	soy	wild silk
Modal®	raw silk	SoySilk®	wool
mohair	reeling	specialty wools	woolen
nanotechnology	retting	spinneret	worsted
natural-colored	rippling	synthetic	yak
cotton	rush grass	Tencel®	
nodes	scoured	tendered	

Review Questions

1. Cite both positive and negative properties of wool.

2. Why is silk not vulnerable to moth attack (as long as the fiber is clean)?

3. Discuss the positive and negative features of genetically modified cotton.

4. Identify properties of cotton that support its use in household and institutional textiles.

5. Distinguish among the following terms: *flax plant*, *flax fiber*, *linen*, and *linens*.

6. Why has the use of asbestos been discontinued?

7. Trace the production sequence of manufactured fibers. Explain how fiber engineering is accomplished during the production.

8. Are there similarities between wet spinning and solvent spinning?

9. Explain the drawing operation and why the fiber producer carefully controls the process.

10. How does heat setting benefit the consumer? Are there concomitant challenges?

11. Cotton, rayon, and lyocell are cellulosic fibers, each having the same anhydrous glucose monomer. Why aren't these fabrics called natural cellulosic fibers?

12. What advantages do acrylic fibers offer over wool fibers?

13. What fiber features can be engineered by using a particular shape for the spinneret openings? Which fibers retain the shape of the openings?

14. What properties support the use of olefin and saran fibers in outdoor textile applications?

15. Summarize the achievements in each "generation" of manufactured fiber development.

16. Why is hemp considered to be more environmentally friendly than cotton?

17. Define microfiber, and state the advantages of using microfibers in home furnishings.

18. Discuss the manufacture of PLA, and list negative and positive properties.

Notes

1. South Central Llama Association, "Llama Facts," 6/5/2007.

2. Animal Welfare Information Center, "Information Resources for the South American Camelids: Llama, Alpaca, Guanaco, & Vicuna," 2004–2008. Beltsville, MD.

3. Maria Thiry. (2009). "Everything Old Is New Again: Recycling, Recycled, and Recycled Fibers." *AATCC Review*, vol. 9, no. 3. pp. 21–22.

4. Ibid., p. 27.

CHAPTER **FIVE**

Textile Yarns and Yarn-like Structures

■ **All textile yarns, like textile fibers,** must be relatively long and thin to provide the flexibility required in manufacturing and use. However, yarns can have marked differences in their degrees of twist, textural characteristics, complexity, and relative fineness. The fineness of yarns can be measured and reported in numerical terms. These numbers, along with other notations, are used in designations of yarn construction.

Simple yarns, structures having minimal design value, are typically used in carpet, rugs, towels, sheets, and tabletop accessories. By contrast, decorative, complex yarns are often used in textile wallcoverings and in upholstery, curtain, and drapery fabrics. Complex yarns have slubs, loops, and other irregular textural effects that add tactile and visual interest. This chapter describes the production and qualities of the widely used simple and complex yarns.

Although most interior textile products are composed entirely of textile yarns or fibers, some are composed in whole or in part of yarn-like structures. Although these components are handled like textile yarns, they are not formed by conventional yarn production processes, and several contain no fibers.

Yarn Production

One type of yarn, known as a **monofilament yarn**, is actually manufactured by the fiber producer. In this process, a single filament is treated as a yarn structure. For strength and stability, the filament has a relatively large diameter and is drawn and heat set. Monofilament yarns are often used in the production of lightweight, transparent window coverings. They are also used as strong sewing thread in the construction of many interior textile products. In this application, the filaments may be clear or smoke-colored so that they will assume the color of the textile structure being sewn and produce an inconspicuous seam.

While fiber producers manufacture monofilament yarns, **throwsters** produce multifilament yarns and **spinners** produce spun yarns. Throwsters may use a texturing process to introduce such characteristics as bulk and cohesiveness to groups of filaments, some of which are then reduced to staple lengths and spun.

Throwing

The great length of silk and manufactured filaments allows them to be directly combined or "thrown" together into multifilament yarn structures; no textile yarn spinning process is required. If drawn manufactured filaments are supplied, the throwster needs only to gather and twist several of the fine strands. If undrawn filaments are supplied, the throwster must combine drawing and twisting. For a limited number of applications, throwsters will produce untwisted multifilament yarns.

Texturing

Texturing processes introduce multidimensional configurations to otherwise parallel and smooth filaments. Such physical changes may decrease strength, but they can impart elasticity, create a softer, warmer hand, help to simulate a natural appearance, and increase fiber cohesiveness. They also increase the **bulk or apparent volume** of the grouped filaments to provide greater covering power, as showing in Figure 5.1. In use, fabrics composed of textured yarns have reduced levels of pilling and better dimensional stability and resiliency, and retain their original appearance for a longer period of time than do fabrics made of staple fibers.

Among the texturing processes used with interior textile product components are false-twist coiling, stuffer-box crimping, knit-de-knit crinkling, air-jet texturing, and gear crimping. These processes are schematized in Figure 5.2. Yarns textured by these and other techniques are known as **bulked continuous filament (BCF) yarns**.

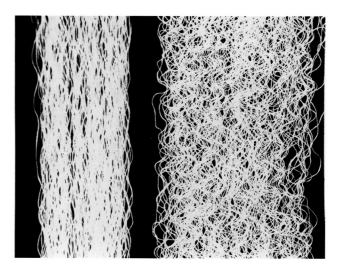

Figure 5.1 Identical skeins of nylon filaments showing increase in apparent bulk or volume produced by texturing. Courtesy of Ascend Performance Materials.

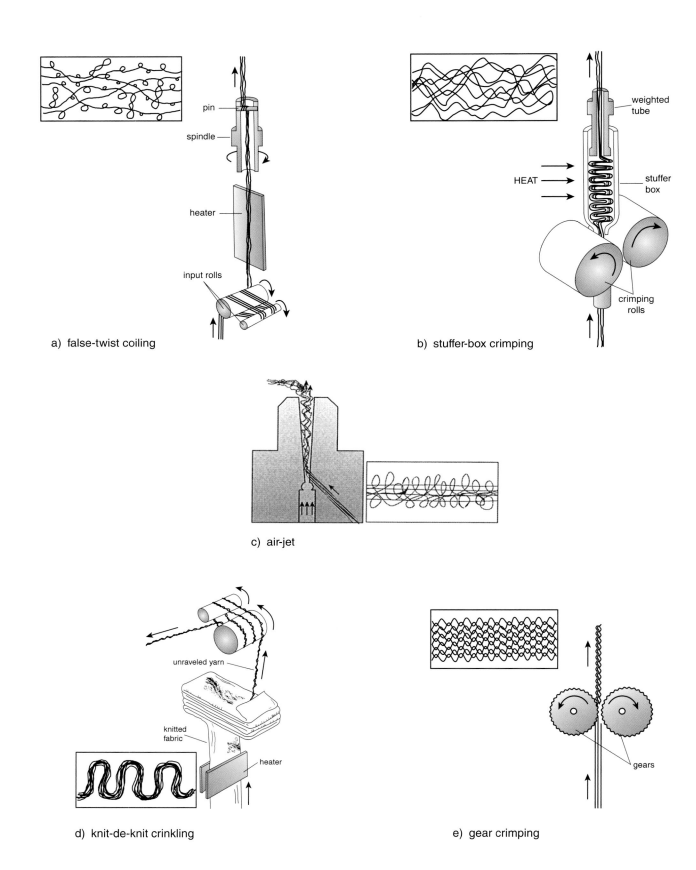

a) false-twist coiling

b) stuffer-box crimping

c) air-jet

d) knit-de-knit crinkling

e) gear crimping

Figure 5.2 Yarn texturing processes.

False-Twist Coiling

In **false-twist coiling**, the yarn bundle is twisted, heated, and untwisted in one continuous operation. A heat-set coil within each filament results; the yarn itself has no twist (hence the name "false-twist"). This is one of the least expensive methods for adding bulk.

Stuffer-Box Crimping

The **stuffer-box crimping** technique is so called because the yarns are rapidly stuffed into a heated, box-like chamber. Because the yarns are withdrawn slowly, they buckle and back up on themselves. The three-dimensional crimp is permanently set by the heat. The stuffer-box method is a fast and inexpensive method for carpeting yarn.

Knit-De-Knit Crinkling

Knit-de-knit crinkling produces a crinkled or wavy configuration. Multifilament yarns are first knitted into a fabric. The fabric is then heat set and subsequently unraveled ("de-knit"). The knitting gauge (the number of loops per inch) determines the size of the yarn waves. This technique is frequently combined with the application of dyestuffs to produce uniquely colored and textured yarns for soft floor coverings (Figure 8.7, p. 128).

Air-Jet Texturing

In **air-jet texturing**, filament yarns are fed over a tiny blast of air that forces the filament into loops. This type of yarn is also called air-textured or air-entangled.

Gear Crimping

In **gear crimping**, intermeshing gears introduce a two-dimensional crimp to filaments. Heat can be used to permanently set the crimped configuration.

When filaments are to be reduced to staple lengths and spun into yarns, they are first grouped into a rope-like bundle known as **tow**. This untwisted bundle is then textured, generally by gear or stuffer-box crimping, to impart the **fiber cohesiveness** required for the production of spun yarns. The textured tow is stretched or cut into staple fibers of the desired length, generally from 1 to 6 inches. The staple fibers in Figure 5.3 were cut from gear-crimped tow.

Spinning

Staple-length fibers are converted into usable yarn strands by processing them through various spinning systems, including the cotton, woolen, worsted, and linen systems.

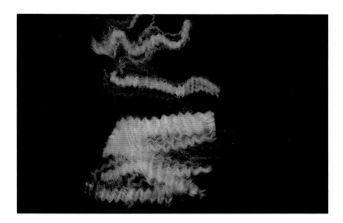

Figure 5.3 Staple-length fibers cut from gear-crimped tow. Courtesy of Amy Willbanks, www.textilefabric.com.

Formerly, the system used depended upon the type of fiber being spun; today, as manufactured fibers are increasingly used to simulate natural fibers, the choice of spinning systems is largely based on the length of the staples being processed. In any case, the basic procedures used in the several systems are similar, with each successive operation producing a structure that is more yarn-like.

Cotton System

The following highly simplified summary identifies the basic procedures used in the **cotton spinning system** and describes the changes produced in each step:

1. **Opening and cleaning:** loosening, cleaning, and blending the cotton fibers.

2. **Picking:** fluffing the compacted fibers into a loose, disoriented mass.

3. **Carding:** initially aligning the fibers in a somewhat parallel fashion and forming a card sliver, a long, loose strand that is approximately 1 inch in diameter.

4. **Combing:** further aligning the fibers and separating the shorter staples before forming a comb sliver.

5. **Drawing out:** reducing the diameter of the sliver to produce a roving, a long, fine strand that is approximately ¼ inch in diameter.

6. **Spinning and twisting:** reducing the diameter of the roving and twisting the resulting fine strand into a usable spun yarn.

The cotton system is used for spinning fibers that are approximately ½ inch to 1½ inches in length. Yarns with relatively long and highly aligned fibers are known as **combed yarns**; those having both long and short staples and relatively little fiber alignment are called **carded yarns**. Today, polyester and rayon staples, alone or blended with cotton, are frequently spun on the cotton system.

Woolen and Worsted Systems

The basic equipment in the woolen spinning system is designed to handle fibers from 2 to 3 inches in length; that in the worsted system is designed to handle fibers from 3 to 5 inches in length. Spinners can adjust the equipment, however, to spin the longer staples frequently used in interior textile yarns. **Woolen yarns**, like carded yarns, have varied lengths of staples and less fiber alignment; **worsted yarns**, like combed yarns, contain only long staples that are highly aligned.

Because spun yarns have many fiber ends protruding from their surfaces, their level of light reflectance is less than that of multifilament yarns. Spinners use this characteristic to advantage when they process staple-length acrylic, nylon, and olefin fibers on the woolen system to produce yarns with a subdued, mellow luster, imitating natural wool.

Linen System

The linen spinning system is designed to align and twist flax tow fibers, which are approximately 12 inches in length, and flax line fibers, which are approximately 24 inches in length. Tow fibers are spun into relatively heavy yarns for use in such interior textile products as wallcoverings, upholstery, and drapery fabrics, while line fibers are spun into fine yarns for use in such items as woven table linens, bed sheets, and lace doilies. Groups of aligned flax fibers in Figure 5.4 resemble strands of human hair prior to yarn twisting.

Yarn Twisting

Twisting must be used for all spun yarns, and while it is optional for multifilament yarns, it is generally used to stabilize the fine, parallel filaments. Whatever the type of yarn, twist can be specified by its direction and level.

Direction of Twist

The letters S and Z are used to describe the direction of twist in all textile yarns (Figure 5.5). A left-handed or counterclockwise twist is called an **S twist**; the fibers ascend from right to left and align with the central portion

Figure 5.4 Aligned flax fibers prior to drawing out and twisting.
Courtesy of CELC MASTERS OF LINEN.

of the letter. A right-handed or clockwise twist is termed a **Z twist**; the fibers ascend from left to right and again align with the central portion of the letter. Neither direction offers an advantage over the other.

Level of Twist

The level or amount of twist used in yarn formation is denoted by the number of **turns per inch** (turns/inch or tpi). Multifilament yarns may have as few as 2 or 3 tpi, while spun yarns often have as many as 30 or 40 tpi. Optimum levels have evolved from years of experience and yarn testing by spinners and throwsters.

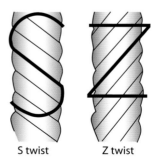

S twist   Z twist

Figure 5.5 Direction of twist in textile yarns.
Illustration by Andrea Lau.

Spun yarns with a relatively low level of twist are comparatively soft, large, weak, and dull. Up to a point, increasing the twist will produce a concomitant increase in yarn firmness, fineness, strength, and luster. When more than about 40 tpi are used, kinks and ridges may form, reducing the elasticity and strength of the yarns. Such surface irregularities may deflect incident light waves, dulling the yarns in much the same way as coils dull fibers.

Throwsters and spinners use a variety of techniques to control the aesthetic features and service-related qualities of yarns and expand the assortment of yarns available to producers and consumers. They may vary the level of twist used, introduce decorative effects, or combine various numbers and types of yarn strands. The resulting yarns are then classified and named on the basis of their structural characteristics.

Yarn Classification and Nomenclature

Yarns produced by throwing or spinning textile fibers are classified and described by the number of their parts and their design features. A brief outline will serve to introduce the classification system used with textile yarns and the extensive number of names used for decorative yarns.

I. Simple Yarns
   A. Single
   B. Ply
   C. Cord
   D. Cable
   E. Rope
   F. Hawser
II. Complex Yarns
   A. Singles
      1. Slub
      2. Thick-and-thin
      3. Speck/Tweed/Flock
   B. Plies and cords
      1. Plied slub
      2. Flame
      3. Spiral
      4. Corkscrew
      5. Nub/Knot/Spot
         a. Seed
         b. Splash
      6. Ratiné
      7. Bouclé
      8. Loop or curl
      9. Gimp

Simple Yarns

Yarns having a smooth appearance and a uniform diameter along their length are classified as **simple yarns**. Simple yarns may be composed of a single yarn or a number of single yarns twisted or plied together in various ways.

Single, Ply, and Cord Yarns

Simple single yarns are produced in a single spinning or throwing operation, or, in the case of monofilament yarns, in a single extruding operation. Although simple multifilament yarns are composed of multiple filaments, they are classified as single yarns. Twisting or plying two or more single yarns together forms **simple ply yarns**. Twisting two or more ply yarns together forms **simple cord yarns**. These yarns are illustrated in Figure 5.6.

As long as the fineness or size of the components is not reduced, plying increases yarn strength. So that ply and cord yarns will be balanced and smooth, each successive twisting or plying procedure uses about half the amount of twist as the previous one and S and Z twists are alternated. The

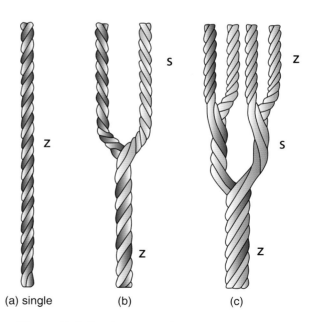

Figure 5.6 Simple yarns and yarn twist.
Illustration by Andrea Lau.

standard practice followed in designating the construction of these yarns is discussed later in this chapter.

Cable, Rope, and Hawser Yarns

When simple cord yarns are plied, the resulting structure is called a **cable yarn**; when cable yarns are plied, the new structure is called **rope**; and when rope strands are combined, the structure becomes a **hawser**, a structure that is strong enough to anchor a ship. Rope structures composed of sisal or hemp fibers frequently appear in hand-woven chair seats.

In comparison with complex yarns, simple yarns have minimal design value. Spinners and throwsters can, however, combine various hues and shades of fibers and yarns to enhance the visual interest of simple yarns. Such distinctive yarn color styles as heather, marled, and ombré, and the methods used to produce them, are described in Chapter 8.

Complex Yarns

Yarns with variations in the level of twist used along their length, three-dimensional decorative features, or components with different fiber contents are called **complex yarns**. The unique combination of features characterizing each of these decorative yarns determines its yarn name.

Complex Single Yarns

Complex single yarns may be spun, filament, or a combination of both. A **slub** or **thick-and-thin** yarn has both fine and coarse segments along its length. In spun yarns, these differences in diameter are produced by varying the level of twist used in the final spinning operation (Figure 5.7a). Because fewer twists per inch are used for the coarse areas, they are softer and weaker than the finer, more twisted areas. In filament yarns, the differences in diameter are produced by varying the extrusion pressure during the formation of the manufactured fiber, producing variations (Figure 5.7b). **Speck** yarns, often called **tweed** or **flock** yarns, are produced by periodically incorporating small tufts of contrasting colored yarns during spinning. The colored tufts interrupt the smoothness of the yarn, creating visual interest (Figure 5.7c). Speck (tweed or flock) yarns are found in upholstery and drapery fabrics. (Figure 13.1b, p. 217).

Complex Plies and Cords

Complex plies and cords are formed by twisting together two or more single yarns that may themselves be simple or complex structures. Frequently, distinctive

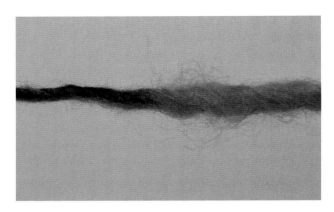

a) Slub yarn with staple fibers.

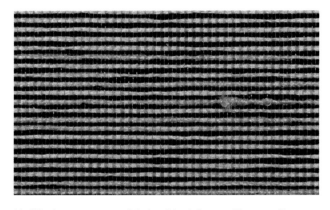

b) Window casement fabric with slub yarn filament fibers.

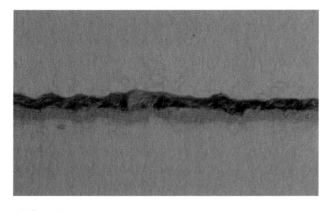

c) Speck/tweed yarn.

Figure 5.7 Complex single yarns.
Courtesy of Amy Willbanks, www.textilefabric.com/Yarns provided by Yarn Mavens, Inc. and Jack Donovan and Company.

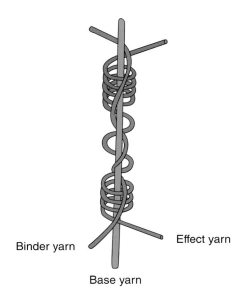

Binder yarn   Effect yarn

Base yarn

Figure 5.8 Basic components of complex ply and cord yarns. Illustration by Andrea Lau.

forms of twisting are used to produce complex structures from simple components. Because the basic textural and design features of a complex yarn can be produced by using single or plied components, many textile authorities make no distinction between complex ply yarns and complex cord yarns.

Basic Components As shown in Figure 5.8, complex plies and cords may have three distinct components. The **base yarn**, which is also known as the core, foundation, or ground yarn, provides stability and determines the yarn length. The **effect yarn**, which is also known as the fancy yarn, contributes the novelty or decorative appearance. The **binder or tie yarn** secures the effect yarn to the base yarn. Some complex yarns have only two of these components.

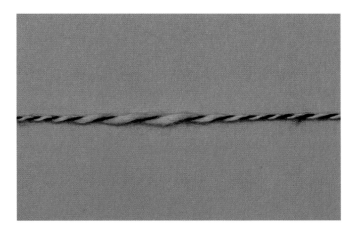

a) Plied slub.

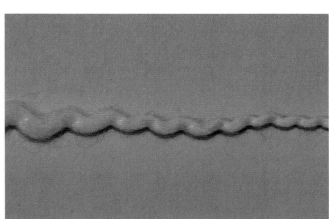

b) Flame.

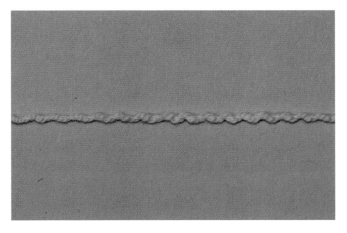

c) Spiral.

d) Corkscrew.

Figure 5.9 Complex two-ply yarns.
Courtesy of Amy Willbanks, www.textilefabric.com/Yarns provided by Yarn Mavens, Inc. and Jack Donovan and Company.

Complex Yarn Names and Descriptions Complex plies and cords are distinguished by their appearance and structural features. These features determine the name assigned to the yarn.

Plied slub yarns, pictured in Figure 5.9a, are formed by twisting two slub yarns together. As shown in Figure 5.9b, twisting a simple yarn around a single slub yarn that has large and elongated areas of low twist produces a **flame yarn**.

The components of **spiral and corkscrew yarns** differ in their construction, fiber content, level of twist, degree of luster, or size. Together they create a visual spiral. (While plying simple yarns that differ only in color would produce a spiral appearance, such yarns do not come within the definition of spiral and corkscrew yarns. They would be classified as simple, two-ply yarns.) For greater emphasis on the visual spiral, a spun yarn may be combined with a filament yarn, or a yarn-like metallic strand may be combined with a spun yarn. Although many textile authorities use "spiral" and "corkscrew" as synonyms, a distinction may be made when yarns of different sizes are plied. As shown in Figure 5.9c and d, "spiral" applies when the heavier yarn twists around the finer yarn, and "corkscrew" when the finer yarn twists around the heavier yarn.

Imaginative forms of plying can produce complex yarns from simple components. **Nub yarns**, which are also called **knot** or **spot** yarns, have tightly compacted projections at irregular intervals along their lengths. These three-dimensional nubs are created by wrapping a simple yarn several times around a base yarn. **Seed yarns** have small, compacted nubs and **splash yarns** have larger, elongated nubs. Examples of yarns with nub effects are shown in Figure 5.10.

Several complex yarns have loop-type textural effects. These include spike, ratiné, bouclé, and loop yarns. **Spike or snarl yarns** are composed of yarns having different levels of twist. During the plying operation, the more highly twisted yarn is introduced at a faster rate, causing the extra length to form well-defined kinks or loops. **Ratiné yarns** (Figure 5.11a) have uniformly spaced loops of equal size. In their production, a fuzzy effect yarn is fed faster than the base during the plying sequence, producing small, tightly spaced loops that are almost perpendicular to the base. Some ratiné yarns are produced with a smooth effect yarn, causing the projections to assume a diamond shape similar to that in rick-rack trim. **Bouclé yarns** (Figure 5.11b) have pro-

a) Nub yarn.

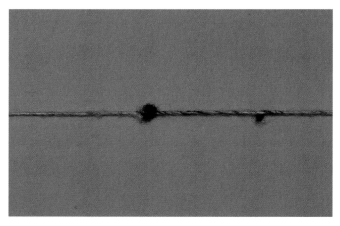

b) Seed yarn.

c) Splash yarn.

Figure 5.10 Complex yarns with nub effects. Courtesy of Amy Willbanks, www.textilefabric.com/ Yarns provided by Yarn Mavens, Inc. and Jack Donovan and Company.

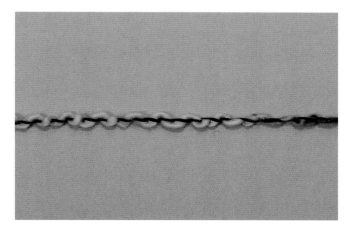

a) Ratiné yarn.

b) Bouclé yarn.

c) Loop yarn.

d) Gimp yarn.

Figure 5.11 Complex yarns with loop effects.
Courtesy of Amy Willbanks, www.textilefabric.com/Yarns provided by Yarn Mavens, Inc. and Jack Donovan and Company.

nounced, closed loops that vary in size and spacing. **Loop or curl yarns** (Figures 5.11c and 15.4, p. 258) have open, airy loops. Frequently, the effect yarns are loosely spun of mohair fibers.

Gimp yarns (Figure 5.11d) are formed by spirally wrapping one yarn around another, or by braiding three or more strands around one central yarn; in either case, the core yarn is completely covered. Gimp yarns frequently have yarn-like metallic strands on the exterior; such decorative yarns are occasionally used to embellish towels and such other interior textile items as tablecloths and wall hangings.

Core-spun and covered-core yarns are special types of gimp yarns having a rubber or spandex filament as the core component. When staple-length fibers are spun around the elastomeric filament, the structure is called a

core-spun yarn; when filaments are wrapped or braided around the filament, the structure is called a **covered-core yarn**.

Designation of Yarn Construction

ASTM D 1244 Standard Practice for Designation of Yarn Construction includes recommendations for describing the structural features of simple yarns (the standard does not cover the description of complex yarns). Three basic notations are used to designate the construction: yarn number, direction of twist, and number of components.

Yarn Number

Yarn numbers designate the fineness or size of yarns. They are determined according to various yarn numbering systems, but the number or count of one system can be converted to its equivalent number in other systems.

Indirect Yarn Numbering Systems

In **indirect yarn numbering systems**, the yarn number or size is based on length per unit of mass (weight), and the yarn diameter decreases as the yarn number increases. These systems are traditionally used for spun yarns.

Cotton Count (cc) System   The **cc system** is used to determine the yarn number of yarns spun on the cotton spinning system. The cc yarn number is equal to the number of 840-yard lengths or hanks of yarn produced from one pound of fiber. For example, a cc of 1 means that one 840-yard hank of yarn was produced from one pound of fiber, while a cc of 50 means that 50 hanks or 42,000 yards of yarn were produced from one pound of fiber.

Linen Lea (ll) System   The **ll system** is used to determine the yarn number of yarns produced on the linen spinning system. In this system, the ll number is equal to the number of 300-yard hanks of yarn produced from one pound of fiber.

Woolen Run (wr) System   The **wr system** is used to determine the yarn number of yarns produced on the woolen spinning system. The wr number is equal to the number of 1,600-yard hanks of yarn produced from one pound of fiber. Some spinners may choose to use the woolen cut (w/c) system instead of the wr system. In the w/c system, the yarn number is equal to the number of 300-yard hanks of yarn produced from one pound of fiber.

Worsted Count (wc) System   The **wc system** is used to determine the yarn number of yarns on the worsted spinning system. The wc number is equal to the number of 560-yard hanks of yarn produced from one pound of fiber.

Direct Yarn Numbering Systems

In **direct yarn numbering systems**, the yarn number or size is based on mass (weight) per unit of length, and the yarn diameter increases as the yarn number increases. These systems are generally used with silk and manufactured filaments.

Denier (den) System   In this system, the **den number** is equal to the weight in grams of 9,000 meters of a mono-filament or multifilament yarn. A den number of 200, for example, means that 9,000 meters of yarn weighed 200 grams.

Tex System   In this system, the **tex number** is equal to the weight in grams of 1,000 meters of a monofilament or multifilament yarn. This system is recommended by the International Organization for Standardization. While the system is finding some acceptance for international trade purposes, many experienced technicians are resisting its universal adoption because they are more familiar with the denier and indirect yarn numbering systems.

Because converting yarn numbers or counts determined in one system to equivalent numbers in other systems is laborious and time consuming, selected conversions are presented in Table 5.1. For conversion of yarn counts or numbers not included in the table, readers may consult ASTM D 2260 Standard Tables of Conversion Factors and of Equivalent Yarn Numbers Measured in Various Numbering Systems.

Describing Single Yarns

Information pertaining to the construction of single spun yarns is stated in this order: the yarn number and the numbering system used, the direction of twist, and the amount of twist (e.g., 50cc S 15 tpi). For single multifilament yarns, the letter f followed by the number of component filaments is inserted after the yarn number (e.g., 10 den f40 S 3 tpi). Monofilaments are designated as f/1.

Describing Ply Yarns

Two groups of data are used to describe ply yarns. The first group describes the single yarn components, listing the information as directed in the previous paragraph. The second group describes the ply yarn, stating the number of single yarn components in the plied yarn and the direction and the amount of plying twist. The two groups are separated by a small "x": An example is 50cc S 15 tpi x 2 Z 7 tpi.

Describing Cord Yarns

A third group of notations is used to describe cord yarns. This group follows the groups used to describe the single and ply components and states the number of ply yarns and the direction and amount of twist used to form the cord.

Table 5.1 Yarn Number Conversions

Cotton Count (840 yd per lb)	Linen Lea (300 yd per lb)	Woolen Run (1,600 yd per lb)	Worsted Count (560 yd per lb)	Denier (g per 9,000 m)	Tex (g per 1,000 m)
Coarsest					
0.357	1.000	0.188	0.536	14,890.0	1,654.0
0.667	1.867	0.350	1.000	7,972.0	885.2
1.000	2.800	0.525	1.500	5,315.0	590.5
1.905	5.333	1.000	2.857	2,790.0	310.0
3.333	9.333	1.750	5.000	1,595.0	177.2
3.810	10.67	2.000	5.714	1,395.0	155.0
40.00	112.00	21.00	60.00	132.9	14.80
50.00	140.0	26.25	75.00	106.3	11.80
60.00	168.0	31.50	90.00	88.58	9.84
531.5	1,488.0	279.1	797.3	10.00	1.11
Finest					

Courtesy of Celanese Corporation.

Some downstream producers prefer designations of yarn construction to be stated in an order opposite that described (i.e., cord-ply-single or ply-single). Interested readers may refer to ASTM D 1244, **Practice for Designation of Yarn Construction**, for a review of these and other notations.

Formation of Yarn-like Structures

Several components incorporated in interior textile products are yarn-like structures. While some of these strands are composed of textile fibers, and are generally referred to as yarns, they are produced with techniques other than throwing and spinning.

Chenille Yarns

Chenille yarns are actually narrow strips cut from a leno-woven fabric. In leno-weave interlacing, illustrated in Figure 6.12 (p. 107), pairs of warp (lengthwise) yarns are crossed in a figure-eight fashion around the filling or weft (crosswise) yarns. The warp yarns are simple and highly twisted, and the filling yarns are simple, low-twist strands. After weaving, the fabric is carefully cut lengthwise between the leno-entwined warp yarns, producing fuzzy, caterpillar-like structures (Figure 5.12). Locking precut lengths of fibers between plied base yarns can also produce chenille yarns; this avoids the initial weaving operation and cutting procedure.

Felted Wool Yarns

Research projects sponsored by the Australian Wool Innovation have led to the development of unique wool yarns for use in soft floor coverings. One technique exposes loosely knitted strands of wool rovings to heat, agitation, and moisture, causing felting shrinkage and converting the strands into yarn-like structures. In this way—by capitalizing on the inherent tendency of wool fibers to shrink and matt together—manufacturers produce wool carpet yarns while avoiding the expense and time involved in conventional spinning, twisting, and plying. This helps to offset the relatively high cost of the fibers in the finished product.

Figure 5.12 Chenille yarn cut from leno-woven fabric. Courtesy of Amy Willbanks, www.textilefabric.com.

Metallic Yarns

Metallic yarns, in contrast to metal filaments, are formed in various ways. Frequently, silver-colored foil is encased between clear polyester film sheeting. The layered structure is then slit into thin, yarn-like strands. The highly reflective strands may be used alone or in combination with conventional textile yarns.

Polymer Tapes

Polymer ribbons or tapes are produced by extruding a polymer solution as a wide sheet of film, much like sandwich wrap but thicker. The film sheeting is then slit into long strands of the desired width (Figure 5.13). These structures, often referred to as fibrillated ribbons or fibrillated tapes, are usually composed of polypropylene (olefin) or saran. Fibrillated polypropylene (olefin) tapes predominate in backing fabrics produced for use with pile floor coverings (Figure 22.3b, p. 351), and they are colored and used extensively as the face yarns in carpet designed to be installed outdoors and in laundry rooms, locker rooms, basements, and barns.

Other Structures

Various natural substances are converted into yarn-like structures and used for such products as hand-woven

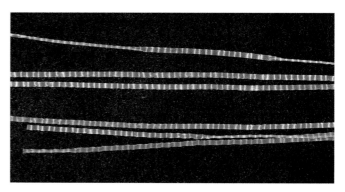

Figure 5.13 Fibrillated polymer tapes.
Courtesy of Amy Willbanks, www.textilefabric.com.

chair seats and backs. **Natural rush** strands are produced by twisting two or three flat cattail leaves into a long unit. Sea grass, also known as *Hong Kong grass*, is used for wallcovering because of its interesting textures (Figure 4.20, p. 62). **Cane** is retrieved from the rattan, a climbing palm. The outer bark is shaved and cut into various widths, ranging from ⅛ inch or less to ⁵⁄₁₆ inch. **Kraftcord** is traditionally made of paper produced from cellulose recovered from titiaceous plants, which are related to lime plants. The heavy cord-like strands have been used in the back of layers of woven floor coverings.

Summary

Spinners use various systems to align and twist staple-length fibers into spun yarns, and throwsters use simple twisting operations to combine filament-length fibers into multifilament yarns. Throwsters may also use a texturing procedure to impose a multidimensional configuration on filaments, increasing their elasticity, cohesiveness, or apparent volume. Spinners and throwsters can vary the level of twist and employ several plying operations to produce an extensive assortment of yarn styles, many with decorative and distinctive effects.

The construction of simple textile yarns is described in accordance with practices outlined in standards established by such voluntary scientific associations as ASTM International and the International Organization for Standardization. These designations typically include the yarn number, direction of twist, and number of components. Informed persons can interpret a yarn's designation and learn several important facts about its features without actually examining the yarn itself.

Various yarn-like structures supplement the supply of spun and thrown yarns available to fabric producers. Some of these structures, including felted wool rovings and chenille yarns, are composed of fibers; others are composed of such materials as paper, grass, and film-coated foil.

Key Terms

air-jet texturing
base yarn
binder or tie yarn
bouclé yarns
bulked continuous filament (BCF)
    yarns
bulk or apparent volume
cable yarns
cane
carded yarns
carding
cc system
chenille yarns
combed yarns
combing
complex plies and cords
complex single yarns
complex yarns
core-spun yarn
cotton spinning system
covered-core yarn
den number
direct yarn numbering systems
drawing out
effect yarn
false-twist coiling

fiber cohesiveness
flame yarn
flock or flake yarns
gear crimping
gimp yarns
hawser
indirect yarn numbering systems
knit-de-knit crinkling
knot yarn
kraftcord
ll system
loop or curl yarns
metallic yarns
monofilament yarn
natural rush
nub yarns
opening and cleaning
picking
plied slub yarns
polymer ribbons or tapes
ratiné yarns
rope
seed yarns
simple cord yarns
simple ply yarns
simple single yarns

simple yarns
slub yarns
speck yarn
spike or snarl yarns
spinners
spinning and twisting
spiral and corkscrew yarns
splash yarns
spot yarns
stuffer-box crimping
S twist
tex number
texturing
thick-and-thin yarns
throwsters
tow
turns per inch
twisting
wc system
woolen yarns
worsted yarns
wr system
yarn numbers
Z twist

Review Questions

1. Identify the advantages textured yarns bring to textile end-products.

2. Describe the techniques used to texture filaments.

3. Does one direction of yarn twist, S or Z, offer an advantage over the other?

4. Why is the level of twist decreased and the direction of twist alternated in successive twisting or plying procedures?

5. Explain the importance of twisting spun yarns.

6. Differentiate between the types of complex yarns.

7. What yarn features are changed as the level of twist is increased?

8. Differentiate between indirect and direct yarn numbering systems.

9. Here is an example of notation used to describe a yarn: 50cc Z 30 tpi x 3 S 15 tpi x 2 Z 7 tpi. Is the yarn a ply, cord, or cable? How many single yarns are used? What yarn numbering system is used? How many ply yarns are used?

10. Describe the production of chenille yarns. Would this process make these yarns more or less expensive than conventional yarns, and why?

11. Distinguish between metallic yarns and metal fibers.

12. Describe the difference in single, ply, and cord yarns.

Fabricating Textiles for Interiors: Weaving

Photo courtesy of Amy Willbanks, www.textilefabric.com.

■ **Fabrications are ways to** produce fabrics, and each of the several fabrication techniques used to produce textile fabrics creates a structure with distinctive aesthetic and structural features. Because these features affect the serviceability of the fabric, as well as its installation and maintenance requirements, they influence the suitability of the fabric for various end-use applications. The method of fabrication also has a direct effect on the cost of the end product, an important criterion in the selection of most residential and commercial interior textile products.

With the exception of soft floor coverings, most textile fabrics are produced by interlacing yarns in one of several fabrication operations. Among these operations are basic or biaxial weaving, pile weaving, and triaxial weaving. In basic weaving, a set of warp yarns and a set of filling yarns are interlaced at 90-degree angles to each other, to produce an essentially flat, two-dimensional fabric. In pile weaving, one or more sets of additional yarns are interlaced with the base warp and filling to create a pile or depth layer. Three sets of yarns are used in triaxial weaving; the yarns are interlaced at 60-degree angles to produce a flat fabric.

Weaving

Basic or **biaxial weaving** operations involve the crosswise interlacing of one set of yarns with a second set of yarns that is held parallel and tensioned on a loom. Each successive crosswise yarn is passed over and under selected lengthwise yarns in a predetermined interlacing pattern. To a large extent, the complexity of an interlacing pattern reflects the loom used to produce it. Simple interlacing patterns are executed on simple looms, and complex interlacing patterns are executed on complex looms. In any case, all looms have some common features, and all woven fabrics have some common components.

Yarn Components and Positions

Most woven fabrics have one set of lengthwise yarns, known as the **warp yarns**, and one set of crosswise yarns, known as the **filling yarns**, the **weft yarns**, or the **woof yarns**. (Multiple sets of yarns are used in some decorative interlacing patterns.) One warp yarn is often referred to as an **end**, and one filling yarn as a **pick**. The **true bias**, which is at a 45-degree angle to the warp and filling yarns, exhibits higher elasticity than other directions in fabric. A

quality woven fabric is **grain-straight**: all the warp yarns are perpendicular to all the filling yarns (Figure 6.1). Conversion operations used to correct the yarn alignment in off-grain fabrics are discussed in Chapter 9.

Selvages are the narrow (¼ to ¾ inch) lengthwise edges of woven fabric. They are designed to prevent or minimize raveling. Fabrics produced on conventional looms have **conventional selvages**, whereas those produced on newer types of looms may have **tucked-in, compacted**, or **leno-reinforced selvages** (Figure 6.2). When composed of thermoplastic fibers, fabrics woven on newer looms often have a **fused selvage** produced by heat-sealing the edges.

The closeness or compactness of the yarns in woven fabrics is numerically reported as the **fabric count**. Specifically, fabric count is equal to the number of warp and filling yarns in one square inch of greige goods. The number of warp yarns is listed first (e.g., 90 × 84). When one number is given—a frequent practice with bed sheets—a **balanced construction**, that is, an equal number of warp and filling yarns, can be assumed. (Fabric count should not be confused with yarn count.)

The **compactness of construction** used in weaving helps to determine the appearance and serviceability of

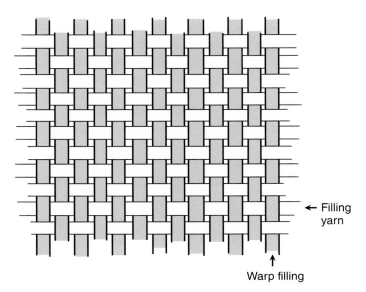

← Filling yarn

↑ Warp filling

Figure 6.1 Components and features of a grain-straight biaxially woven fabric.
Illustration by Andrea Lau.

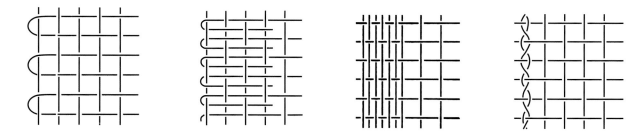

Figure 6.2 Selvages found on biaxially woven fabrics.
Illustrations by Andrea Lau.

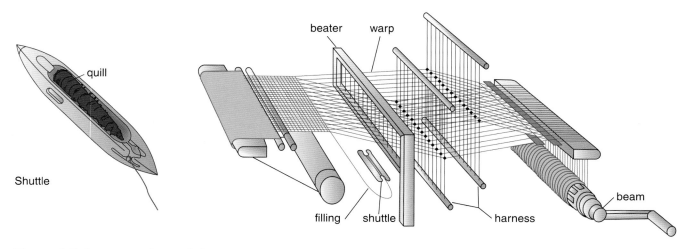

Figure 6.3 Basic parts of a simple loom.
Shuttle is reproduced by permission of Kosa. Loom is reproduced by permission of Brickel Associates Inc.

fabrics, as well as their cost. The compactness of curtain and drapery fabrics, for example, influences their decorative characteristics, their ability to reduce glare, their ability to minimize heat gain and loss, and their cost.

Loom and Weaving Fundamentals

Looms used in weaving operations vary in width and efficiency, as well as in complexity. Some looms are constructed to weave fabrics in widths of 36, 45, or 60 inches; others to weave narrow trimmings efficiently; still others to weave such wide structures as sheeting, blanketing, and carpet. Today, some looms are capable of weaving multiple widths of fabric simultaneously (Figure 28.2, p. 426).

To execute even a simple interlacing pattern, a loom must have components and control mechanisms to systematically raise and lower specific warp yarns, insert the filling yarns, align each successive filling yarn, and advance the warp yarns and woven fabric as the opera-

tion progresses. A complex interlacing pattern requires a loom with additional components and sophisticated control mechanisms.

Parts of a Simple Loom

The component parts of a simple loom are shown in Figure 6.3. **Loom beams** hold the supply of warp yarns. The warp yarns are threaded through **heddles**, thin metal, nylon, or string strips with eye-like openings. The number of heddles required depends on the complexity of the interlacing pattern, the compactness of construction, and the fabric width. **Harnesses** hold the heddles and move up and down, shifting the position of selected warp yarns. The **reed**, a comb-like device with openings called **dents**, helps to keep the warp yarns aligned and ensure grain straightness. The number of **dents per inch** in the reed determines the compactness of the warp yarns. The reed is locked into the **beater bar** or **lay**, which moves forward and backward to beat or lay each new pick into position. A **cloth beam** holds the woven fabric.

On industrial looms, before each warp end is threaded through a heddle, it is threaded through a **drop wire**, a small, curved metal device. If a strained warp yarn breaks during weaving, its drop wire drops, immediately stopping the operation and preventing an unsightly flaw in the fabric.

On conventional looms, the filling yarn is wound on a **bobbin** or **quill** that is carried by a canoe-shaped **shuttle**, shown in detail in Figure 6.3. The devices used on newer looms to carry the filling picks are described later in this chapter.

Threading the Loom

In preparation for drawing-in or threading the warp yarns on the loom, large packages of yarn, known as **cheeses**, are mounted on a **creel frame** (Figure 6.4). Hundreds of yarns are taken from the cheeses and wound evenly on a beam. The yarns are then treated with a hot starch or sizing compound in an operation known as **slashing**. This treatment makes the yarns smoother and stronger, enabling them better to withstand the weaving stresses. It should be noted that warp yarns are usually simple yarns. Complex yarns generally lack the strength needed to withstand the weaving tension, and their decorative effects could be abraded by the drop wires, heddles, and the reed.

The loom beam full of slashed and dried warp yarns is placed on the loom. Each end is then unwound, threaded through a drop wire, an eye in a heddle, and a dent in the reed, and tied onto the cloth beam. A pattern draft or point design serves as a guide for drawing the warp yarns through the heddles.

Pattern Drafts **Pattern drafts** or **point designs** are graphic representations of an interlacing pattern only; they do not indicate yarn size or fabric count. Blocked paper is used to record the planned interlacings. Each lengthwise division of the draft paper represents one warp end and each crosswise division represents one filling pick; each block thus represents the perpendicular crossing of the yarns. When an end passes over a pick, the intersection is darkened; when an end passes behind a pick, the intersection is left blank.

A plain-weave interlacing pattern is shown in Figure 6.1. Because each end passes over and under successive picks in this weave, the draft resembles a checkerboard. It is apparent that more involved interlacing patterns have more elaborate drafts (Figures 23.3a, p. 362, and 27.16a, p. 410).

Following the draft of the plain weave, for example, the technician would draw-in or thread all even-numbered warp yarns through the heddles on one harness and all odd-numbered warp yarns through the heddles on a

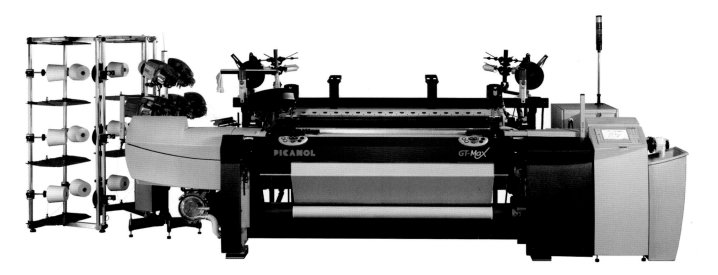

Figure 6.4 Warping: Winding yarns from "cheeses" mounted on a creel frame onto warp beams. Photo courtesy of Picanol.

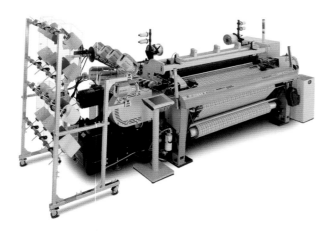

Figure 6.5 Rapier loom.
Courtesy of ITEMA Weaving.

Figure 6.6 Metal rapier used to carry the pick.
Courtesy of ITEMA Weaving.

second harness. The need for more heddles and harnesses with more complicated interlacing patterns will be understood after the basic weaving operation is reviewed.

Basic Weaving Operation

Whether a simple or a complex interlacing pattern is being woven, the weaving sequence includes four steps: **shedding**, **picking**, **battening**, and **taking up and letting off**.

Shedding   In shedding, some harnesses are raised, lifting the warp yarns threaded through heddles held by these harnesses, and some harnesses are lowered, lowering the remaining warp yarns. This creates a V-shaped opening called the **shed**. Mechanized attachments automatically position the harnesses on industrial looms, whereas artisans selectively depress foot-controlled treadles and hand-controlled levers to regulate shedding on hand looms.

Picking   In this step, one or more picks are propelled or carried through the shed. Conventional looms, often called **flying shuttle looms**, have stick-like attachments that hammer the shuttle and send it "flying" through the shed. Because these looms are comparatively slow and create a great deal of noise, they are being replaced with quieter, more efficient looms.

Newer, so-called **shuttleless looms** have ingenious devices for inserting the picks. A rapier loom (Figure 6.5) uses a **rapier** (from the French for "sword"), a flexible or rigid metal tape, to "thrust" the picks (Figure 6.6). One

rapier carries the pick to the center of the shed. Here, it is grasped by a second rapier and carried through the remaining width of the shed.

Other shuttleless looms use a jet of air or a jet of water to "shoot" the picks, and still others use small projectiles to "grip and pull" the picks. A projectile grips a cut end of a pick and is propelled through the shed, pulling the trailing pick into position. When the projectile reaches the far side of the shed, the grip is released, the pick is cut, and the two ends are turned and tucked into the next shed. Because a jet stream of air disperses rapidly, early air jet looms were relatively narrow. Today, however, air jet looms are capable of weaving wide bed sheeting as they have auxiliary jets to support the picks through the sheds.

Battening   In this step, the beater bar or lay moves forward, pushing the inserted pick and aligning it parallel to the other filling yarns. This procedure helps to ensure uniform spacing of the filling yarns and good crosswise grain in the fabric.

Taking Up and Letting Off   The last step in the weaving sequence includes two concurrent procedures. Woven fabric is taken up on the cloth beam, and more warp yarn length is let off from the loom beam.

This four-step sequence is repeated until the supply of warp yarns is exhausted. In each successive shedding operation, however, the positions of the harnesses are changed prior to picking.

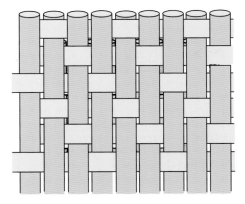

a) Warp-faced twill weave.

b) Filling-faced twill weave.

Figure 6.7 2/1 twill weave interlacings. Illustrations by Andrea Lau.

Because the number of harnesses limits the complexity of the draft that can be followed in drawing-in the warp yarns, it also limits the variety of sheds that can be formed. More than two harnesses are required for interlacing yarns in patterns other than the plain weave and its variations.

Basic Interlacing Patterns

The basic interlacing patterns include the plain, twill, and satin weaves. Each of these weaves has one or more variations. The variations can be produced by slightly altering the shed patterns used, by varying the number of picks inserted in each shed, and by using warp and filling yarns of different sizes.

Plain and Plain Weave Variations

The **plain weave** is also known as the **tabby** or **homespun weave**. The notation used to describe the interlacing pattern is 1 × 1. This indicates that one warp yarn and one filling yarn alternately pass over one another (Figure 6.1). The plain weave is the simplest of the weaves, requiring only two harnesses to be produced. Other examples of plain weave fabrics are shown in Figure 13.1, p. 217.

Variations of the basic plain weave include the basket, warp-rib, and filling-rib weaves. The basket variation involves slightly altering the pattern of drawing the warp yarns through the heddles and changing the number of picks inserted in each shed. The rib weaves use an unbalanced fabric count or a combination of yarns with different yarn counts.

Basket Weave

In the **basket weave**, two or more warp yarns, side by side, interlace with one or more filling yarns. When two warp yarns alternately pass over and under one filling yarn, the pattern is described as a 2 × 1 basket weave (Figure 6.8a). Interlacing two warp yarns with two filling yarns is a 2 × 2 basket weave (Figure 6.8b). When the loom is threaded for this pattern, the first two warp yarns are drawn through heddles on one harness, the next two warp yarns are drawn through heddles on the second harness, and so on. Each shed has alternating groups of two warp yarns raised and two warp yarns lowered. The 2 × 2 interlacing is then executed by inserting two picks in each shed.

Warp-Rib Weave

The **warp-rib weave** creates a rib effect lengthwise in the fabric. The ribs may be produced by combining warp yarns having different counts or by using a combination of interlacing patterns. **Dimity**, a warp-rib woven fabric often used in drapery sheers, is pictured in Figure 17.10, p. 289. Ribcord, a warp-rib weave commonly used in window shades and bedding products, is shown in Figure 17.11, p. 289.

Filling-Rib Weave

Filling-rib weave fabrics generally have a 1 × 1 interlacing, but they are distinguished by crosswise three-dimensional ribs or ridges (Figure 13.3, p. 218). The ribs are produced by using a higher number of ends than picks per inch or by incorporating larger yarns in the crosswise direction. These larger yarns may result from extruding filaments or spinning yarns with oversized diameters, plying several single yarns, or grouping several single yarns together without twist.

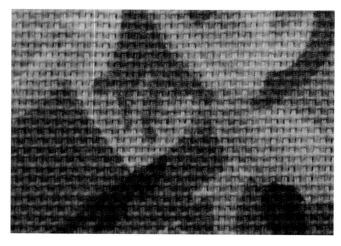

a) 2 × 1 interlacing.

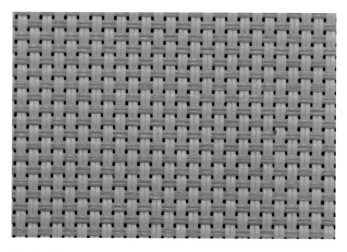

b) 2 × 2 interlacing.

Figure 6.8 Basket weave interlacings.
Courtesy of Amy Willbanks, www.textilefabric.com.

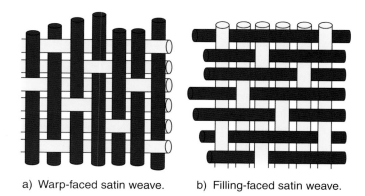

a) Warp-faced satin weave.   b) Filling-faced satin weave.

Figure 6.9 Satin interlacing patterns.
Illustrations by Andrea Lau.

Twill and Twill Weave Variations

The interlacing patterns used in **twill weaves** are more involved than the patterns used in the plain weave and its variations. Looms must have three or more harnesses to execute twill interlacing patterns.

Notations used with twill weaves describe the interlacing pattern of each warp yarn. The 2/1 notation describing Figure 6.7a, for example, indicates that each warp yarn passes or floats over two filling yarns, under one filling yarn, over two filling yarns, and so on. (Students should note the difference between the notation used for the basket and the twill weave, e.g., a 2 × 1 basket and a 2/1 twill.)

In a 2/1 interlacing depicted in the draft shown in Figure 6.7b, each filling yarn passes over two warp yarns and under one filling yarn, over two warp yarns, and so on.

Angle and Direction of the Visual Diagonal

To create the **visual diagonal** characteristic of twill-woven fabrics, each warp yarn must be interlaced one filling yarn above or below the filling yarn interlaced by the adjacent warp yarn. The angle of the visual diagonal depends on the pattern of interlacing and the compactness of construction. Increasing the length of the warp float and increasing the number of warp yarns per inch, for example, increases the angle. The diagonal can be **regular** (at a 45-degree angle), **reclined** (at a less than 45-degree angle), or **steep** (at a greater than 45-degree angle). This diagonal is an appearance feature only; the warp and filling yarns always interlace at a 90-degree angle in basic weaving.

As noted in Figure 6.10a and b, the direction of the visual diagonal is described as either right-hand or left-hand. **Left-hand twills** have a diagonal pattern that descends from left to right; **right-hand twills** have a diagonal that descends from right to left.

Even and Uneven Twill Interlacings

In twill interlacings, each warp or filling yarn must float or pass over a minimum of two yarns before interlacing. When the warp yarns float over a greater number of filling yarns than they pass behind, they cover a greater por-

a) Right-hand twill weave.

b) Left-hand twill weave.

c) Even-sided twill weave.

Figure 6.10 Twill weaves and twill weave variations. Courtesy of Amy Willbanks, www.textilefabric.com.

tion of the fabric surface, and the fabric is described as an **uneven warp-faced twill**. When the filling yarns float over a greater number of warp yarns than they pass behind, the fabric is described as an **uneven filling-faced twill**. The difference between a warp-faced twill and a filling-faced twill can be seen by comparing Figure 6.7a and b. When an interlacing pattern has equal amounts of warp and filling yarns covering the fabric surface, as illustrated in Figure 6.10c, the fabric is described as an **even twill**.

Twill Weave Variations

Herringbone is a twill weave variation created by changing the direction of the twill weave. The direction is continually reversed across the width of the fabric, as shown in Figure 13.6, p. 219. This process creates a striped chevron pattern in the fabric, repeating in the lengthwise direction. Herringbone is sometimes called an alternating twill weave. **Houndstooth** is a twill weave in which the interlacing pattern varies to create a unique star pattern in the weave (Figure 13.5, p. 219). Houndstooth fabrics are sometimes called broken twill weaves.

Satin and Sateen Weaves

Like warp-faced twill fabrics, **satin** fabrics have floating warp yarns. In satin interlacings, however, a visual diagonal does not appear because adjacent warp yarns do not interlace with adjacent filling yarns.

Satin interlacing patterns require more shed variations than do basic twill patterns. To produce the satin weave depicted in Figure 6.9, five harnesses would need to be threaded. This pattern is described as five-shaft construction, indicating that each warp yarn is floating over four picks and under the fifth.

Satin-woven fabrics are characterized by high luster and sheen, primarily produced by the reflection of large amounts of light from the smooth, uninterrupted surface areas of the floats, but also frequently augmented by the use of bright fibers (Figure 6.11a). The level of luster will be reduced if abrasion ruptures the floating yarns during use.

Sateen Weave

In **sateen** interlacing, the filling yarns float over the warp yarns (Figure 6.11b). This weave, which is also known as the **filling-faced satin weave**, is frequently used to produce drapery lining fabrics (see Chapter 17).

a) Satin: warp-faced satin weave.

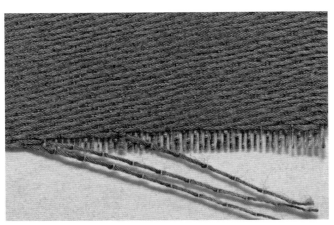

b) Sateen: filling-faced satin weave.

Figure 6.11 Satin and sateen weaves.
Courtesy of Amy Willbanks, www.textilefabric.com.

Decorative Interlacing Patterns

The relative simplicity of the basic weaves and their variations can readily be appreciated when they are compared to the decorative weaves, in which several simple weaves and multiple sets of yarns are often used. The decorative weaves include the dobby, the surface-figure, the leno, and the Jacquard weaves. Because decorative appearance features are often important selection criteria, these complex interlacing patterns are used extensively in the production of interior textile fabrics.

Dobby Weave

Dobby weaving is used to interlace yarns into fabrics having small, geometric motifs. Although the motifs are comparatively simple, dobby looms must have as many as twenty or thirty harnesses to produce the variety of sheds required.

In order to ensure accurate weaving of the motifs, the technician must carefully follow the pattern draft when drawing the warp yarns through the many heddles held by the several harnesses. During weaving, the positions of the harnesses for each shed are mechanically controlled by a unit attached to the side of the loom. This unit has a pattern roll similar to the paper music roll used with player pianos. The holes punched in the pattern roll determine which harnesses will be raised and which harnesses will be lowered, as the holes punched in the music roll determine which keys will be played.

Surface-Figure Weaves

Surface-figure weaves are executed on a dobby loom, using extra yarns to produce raised figures while the base fabric is being woven. These interlacing patterns, including dot or spot weaving and swivel weaving, are used to produce several curtain fabrics (see Chapter 17), and the dot or spot technique is used to produce assorted upholstery fabrics (Figure 13.10, p. 221).

Dot or Spot Weave

In **dot or spot weaving**, extra yarns are periodically interlaced with the base yarns to create a small dot or figured spot. Between the decorative figures or dots, the extra yarns are floated on the back of the fabric. When the floating yarns are left in place, the fabric is known as an **unclipped dot or spot fabric**; when the floating yarns are cut away, the fabric is known as a **clipped dot or spot fabric**. When the base fabric is sheer, the floats should be clipped to avoid linear shadows, especially when the fabric is intended for use as a window covering. Either side of a clipped dot or spot fabric can be used as the face side (Figure 17.16, p. 292). The floating yarns should be left unclipped in opaque fabrics to minimize the possibility that the dots or spots will be removed by in-use abrasion and cleaning.

Swivel Weave

In **swivel weaving**, extra yarns periodically swivel around or encircle the base yarns to create small, secure dots.

Some imported **dotted swiss** is produced with this interlacing technique, but the relatively slow rate of production precludes its widespread use.

Leno Weave

Looms with special attachments are used for the **leno weave**, in which paired warp yarns cross as they encircle and secure the filling yarns. As sketched in Figure 6.12, the warp yarns do not twist around one another; one yarn in each pair always passes in front of the second yarn. Although the individual warp yarns are not parallel, the paired groups are, and the structure is essentially biaxial.

Marquisette, a transparent, leno-weave window covering is pictured in Figures 15.4 and 17.17, pp. 258 and 292. **Casements** with leno interlacings are pictured in Figure 17.18, p. 292.

Jacquard Weave

Jacquard-woven fabrics often have extremely complex interlacing patterns combining two or more simple weaves, multiple sets of yarns, and strategically placed colors. Typically, the pattern repeats are large and composed of various motifs, each having finely detailed curved and

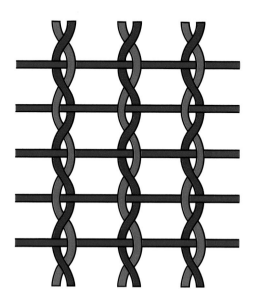

Figure 6.12 Leno-weave interlacing.
Illustration by Andrea Lau.

swirled shapes. It is apparent that the Jacquard loom (Figure 6.13) must have the capacity to form an almost unlimited variety of intricate sheds and to facilitate the selection of specific colors of picks.

As explained earlier, the variety of possible shed patterns can be explained by increasing the number of harnesses. For intricate Jacquard patterns, however, the number of sheds required to complete one repeat may be so large that hundreds of harnesses would be needed. Not only would a loom so equipped be massive in size, but drawing-in the warp yarns would be difficult. To avoid these problems, Jacquard looms have a system of cords and hooks in lieu of harness frames.

Each warp yarn is threaded through a cord heddle that is linked to a needle by a rod and hook apparatus. In effect, each cord heddle functions as a miniature harness that can be raised and lowered independently of all the other heddles. The position of each cord, and thus of each warp yarn, in a shed is controlled by a programmed card resembling that formerly used with computers or, increasingly, by computer tape. One programmed card is key-punched for each shed in the pattern repeat. Figure 6.13 shows the several cards suspended above the loom.

In the Jacquard weaving operation, a programmed card is brought into position and the needles shift forward. When a needle encounters a hole in the card, the hook is permitted to rise, carrying the warp yarn upward; when a needle encounters a solid portion of the card, the hook is not permitted to rise and the warp yarn remains down. The picking, battening, and taking up and letting off weaving procedures follow. The second card is then brought into position, and the four-step weaving operation is repeated. This sequence is continued until the pattern repeat is completed. A second repeat is then woven, again using the programmed cards to control the interlacings.

Today, computer software is increasingly used to design the intricate motifs and to control the complex shedding used in Jacquard weaving. Jacquard woven upholstery fabrics are pictured in Chapter 13, and Jacquard woven drapery fabrics are pictured in Chapter 17. The use of Jacquard mechanisms in the weaving of Wilton carpet is explained in Chapter 23.

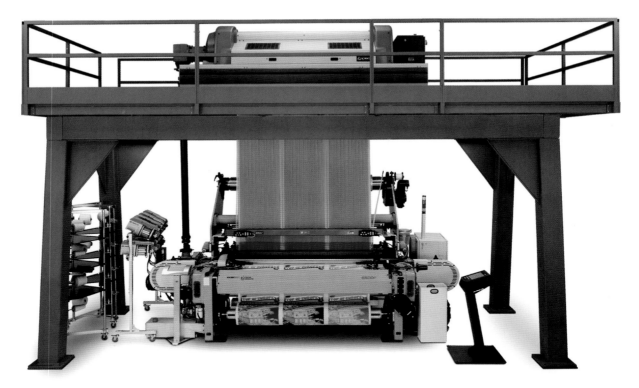

Figure 6.13 Jacquard loom.
Courtesy of ITEMA Weaving, sultex.com.

Pile Interlacing Patterns

Woven pile fabrics are constructed by interlacing three sets of yarns: one set of warp yarns and one set of filling yarns for the base fabric and one set of warp or filling yarns for the pile layer. In the finished fabrics, the pile yarns are more or less perpendicular to the base yarns, introducing a dimension of height to otherwise two-dimensional fabrics (Figure 13.21, p. 255).

Filling Pile Weaves

Filling pile fabrics, including corduroy and velveteen, are produced by incorporating an extra set of filling yarns. Corduroy has lengthwise ridges of pile yarns, called wales, whereas velveteen has uniformly spaced pile yarns; the manner of interlacing the pile yarns differs for each fabric.

Producing Corduroy

To produce **corduroy**, the filling pile yarns are floated over a number of base warp yarns and then interlaced with others. For wider **wales**, which are often preferred for interior applications, the pile yarns may be floated over five or six base yarns before they are interlaced. Each successive pile yarn must cross over and under the same base warp yarns to ensure that the floats are aligned in lengthwise rows. For high pile density, two, three, four, or more pile yarns may be interlaced before a base filling is interlaced.

After the weaving operation has been completed, thin metal guides are used to lift the floats as circular knives cut them. When wide and narrow wales are planned, the floats are cut off-center. The surface is then brushed to raise the cut ends, forming the lengthwise wales and exposing the fabric areas that had been covered by the floats.

During fabric conversion, the pile yarns are laid in one direction, introducing a surface feature known as pile lay, pile sweep, or fabric nap. This reorientation of the pile yarns (illustrated in Figure 9.3, p. 145) alters the reflective characteristics of the surface, as well as the tactile features. Finishing techniques such as embossing can also be used to reorient the pile (Figure 6.14).

Producing Velveteen

Velveteen construction differs from that of corduroy in three major ways. First, the filling pile yarns used are usually much

Figure 6.14 Embossed corduroy.
Courtesy of Amy Willbanks, www.textilefabric.com.

finer than those used in corduroy. Second, each successive pile yarn crosses over and under different base warp yarns to avoid having the floats aligned in lengthwise rows. Third, the pile yarns are floated over no more than two base warp yarns, and more floats are used per inch. Collectively, these construction features produce a short, dense pile layer without wales. As with corduroy, the floats are cut, raised, and laid in one direction after the weaving operation has been completed.

Warp Pile Yarns

Warp pile fabrics are made by incorporating an extra set of warp yarns during weaving. Three kinds of weaving operations are used to produce these fabrics.

Doublecloth Construction Technique

The **doublecloth construction technique** produces two lengths of **velvet** in one weaving operation. As shown in Figure 6.15, the pile layers are formed by alternately interlacing the extra set of warp yarns with the base yarns forming the upper fabric and with those forming the lower fabric. The interlacing pattern is controlled to avoid the formation of crosswise wales. As the weaving progresses, the pile yarns joining the two fabrics are cut, and the two fabrics are taken up on separate cloth beams.

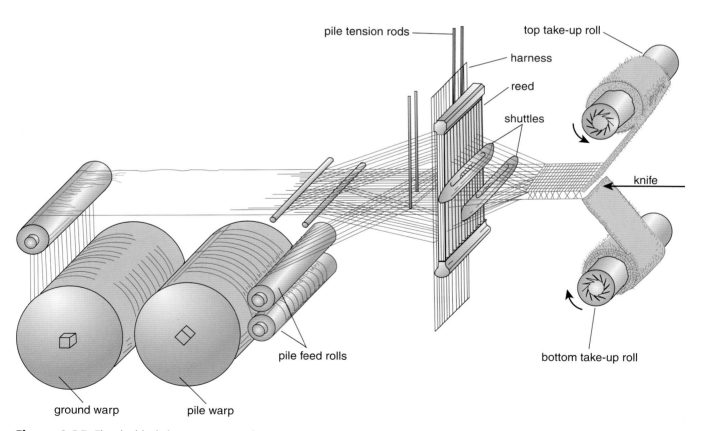

Figure 6.15 The doublecloth construction technique.

The pile yarns may be interlaced in such a manner that the pile tufts have a V-shaped configuration or a W-shaped configuration. In the **V pattern** (Figure 6.16a), each pile yarn is anchored by one base filling, while in the **W pattern** (Figure 6.16b), each pile yarn is anchored by three base yarns. The W form is inherently more stable, but the V form can be stabilized by weaving the base compactly and applying an adhesive coating to the fabric back. Using a high pile density with either pattern will improve texture retention and abrasion resistance during the product's use.

Producing Friezé and Grospoint Velvet

The **over-the-wire construction technique** is used for weaving some pile upholstery fabrics and some carpet. In this procedure, illustrated in Figure 6.17, wires are used to support the pile yarns during weaving. The height of the pile layer can be controlled by the height of the wires used. The wires are withdrawn after several successive

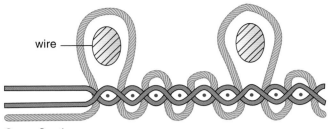

Cross Section

Figure 6.17 The over-the-wire construction technique.

rows of pile loops have been woven. When a cut pile surface texture is planned, the wires have a knife blade on one end; the wires have rounded ends when an uncut pile surface is planned.

The over-the-wire construction technique is used for **friezé** and **grospoint** upholstery fabrics (see Figures 13.24, p. 226, and 13.25, p. 226, respectively). It also is used for weaving **velvet carpet** (see Chapter 23).

Producing Terry Toweling

The warp pile weaving operation used to produce terry toweling (Figure 28.1, p. 426) is known as the **slack tension technique**. During weaving, the base warp yarns are held under regular (high) tension, and the pile warp yarns are held under slackened tension. As the reed moves forward in the battening operation, it compacts the filling picks and pushes the slackened yarns into pile loops on the fabric surface. For greater durability, the number of picks per crosswise row of loops may be increased from three to four or five, but the number of picks must be limited to preserve the number of pile loops available for absorption. A Jacquard mechanism may be used to produce elaborate, multicolored patterns in the pile layer (Figure 28.2. p. 426).

Triaxial Weaving

Triaxial weaving is a fabrication technique in which two sets of warp yarns and one set of filling yarns are interlaced at 60-degree angles rather than 90-degree angles. Whereas selected warp yarns are raised and lowered in basic shedding operations, in triaxial shedding operations all yarns in each set of warp yarns are alternately raised and

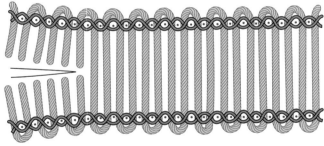

Cross Section

a) V interlacing.

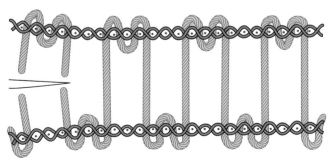

Cross Section

b) W interlacing.

Figure 6.16 V and W forms of pile interlacing patterns.

Figure 6.18 Triaxial interlacing pattern.

lowered. This results in one set of warp yarns always passing over the filling yarns and the other set always passing behind the filling yarns, as illustrated in Figure 6.18.

Triaxially woven fabrics are strong, yet lightweight. This feature, along with stretchability and high resistance to tearing, supports the increased use of these fabrics for upholstered furniture and automobile seat coverings.

Summary

Among the fabrication techniques used to interlace textile yarns or yarn-like structures are basic weaving, pile weaving, and triaxial weaving. Relatively simple interlacing patterns, like the plain, twill, and satin weaves and their respective variations, can be executed on comparatively simple looms. By contrast, complicated interlacing patterns, like those followed in the dobby, surface-figure, leno, and Jacquard weaves, must be produced on complex looms with sophisticated control mechanisms.

Pile weaving operations use a minimum of three sets of yarns. Two sets are interlaced to form the base fabric, while the third set is simultaneously incorporated to form a pile or depth layer. Such woven pile fabrics as corduroy, velvet, terry, and carpet are used for a wide variety of interior applications.

Three sets of yarns are also used in triaxial weaving operations. In this technique, the yarns are interlaced at 60-degree rather than 90-degree angles. Triaxial weaving is increasingly used by fabric producers to expand the assortment of greige goods available to down-stream firms.

Key Terms

balanced construction	conventional selvage	even twill
basket weave	corduroy	fabric count
battening	creel frame	filling pile fabric
beater bar	dents	filling-faced satin weave
biaxial weaving	dents per inch	filling-rib weave
bobbin	dimity	filling yarns
casements	dobby weave	flying shuttle loom
cheeses	dot or spot weave	friezé
clipped dot or spot fabric	dotted swiss	fused selvage
cloth beam	doublecloth construction technique	grain-straight
compacted selvage	drop wire	grospoint
compactness of construction	end	harnesses

heddles
herringbone
homespun weave
houndstooth
Jacquard weave
lappet weaving
lay
left-hand twill
leno weave
leno-reinforced selvage
loom beam
marquisette
over-the-wire construction technique
pattern drafts
pick
picking
plain weave
point designs
quill

rapier
reclined diagonal
reed
regular diagonal
right-hand twill
sateen
satin
selvages
shed
shedding
shuttle
shuttleless looms
slack tension technique
slashing
steep diagonal
swivel weave
tabby weave
taking up and letting off
triaxial weave

true bias
tucked-in selvage
twill weave
unclipped dot or spot fabric
uneven filling-faced twill
uneven warp-faced twill
V pattern interlacing
velvet carpet
velveteen
visual diagonal
W pattern interlacing
wales
warp pile fabric
warp-rib weave
warp yarns
weft yarns
woof yarns

Review Questions

1. Differentiate between biaxial and triaxial weaving.

2. Identify the features of a grain-straight fabric.

3. Explain the function of each part of the loom in the basic weaving process.

4. Why are complex yarns rarely, if ever, used as warp yarns?

5. Why are shuttleless looms replacing flying shuttle looms?

6. Would hydrophilic fibers be used in fabric being woven on water jet looms?

7. Name some specific advantages offered by air jet looms.

8. Explain the following notations: 2×1, 2×2, 4×4, 2/1, and 2/2.

9. Differentiate between the three basic weaves.

10. How is the visual diagonal created in twill weaving?

11. Why is the sateen weave sometimes referred to as the filling-faced satin weave?

12. When should the floats be clipped in dot or spot weaving? When should they be left unclipped?

13. Why are harnesses not used on Jacquard looms?

14. How is corduroy produced?

15. Name three differences between velvet and corduroy.

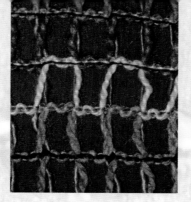

Fabricating Textiles for Interiors: Other Techniques

CHAPTER **SEVEN**

Photo courtesy of Amy Willbanks, www.textilefabric.com.

■ **Besides the techniques used** to weave or interlace yarns, several other methods can be used to combine yarns into textile structures suitable for interior applications. Yarns can be interlooped, inserted or embedded, braided, or knotted and twisted. Techniques are also available that use no yarns, enabling producers to combine fibers directly into fabrics, and other techniques use neither yarns nor fibers, allowing producers to convert polymer solutions directly into film fabrics.

In recent years, existing fabrication techniques have been revised and combined, and entirely new processes have been invented, expanding the variety of fabric production methods available to the industry. While the primary goal of this expansion was to control or reduce production time and material costs, textile engineers also sought to enable manufacturers to control the aesthetic, functional, and structural features of their fabrics efficiently. The resulting operations have helped producers respond more quickly and accurately to changing product selection criteria among consumers.

Knitting

Three major interior textile fabrications use yarn interlooping operations to produce fabrics: the age-old techniques of knitting and crocheting, and the relatively new technique of chain-stitching.

Knitting operations are separated into two major categories, warp knitting and weft or filling knitting, according to the manner in which the yarns are interlooped. Although different stitches are used in these operations, all knitted fabrics have some common features.

Rows of yarn loops running lengthwise in a knitted fabric are known as **wales**, and those running crosswise are known as **courses**. The wales and courses should be at right angles to one another, in much the same way as warp and filling yarns should be perpendicular to one another in woven fabrics. Unlike woven fabric, in which the true bias offers the greatest elasticity, knitted fabrics are generally most stretchable in the crosswise direction, since the rounded loops expand and contract laterally.

The compactness of construction of knitted fabrics is determined by the gauge used. The **gauge** is the number of loops per inch or per bar inch (1½ inches) and is controlled by the size of the knitting needles. Along with the size of the yarns used, gauge helps to determine the transparency, porosity, and weight of the fabric.

Warp Knitting

In **warp knitting**, fabrics are produced by the simultaneous interlooping of adjacent yarns in a vertical direction. As shown in Figure 7.1, a portion of each yarn has a diagonal orientation but the wales are essentially parallel. Although courses can be identified, no filling yarns are used.

Warp knitting is an extremely fast operation, with large machines producing more than four million loops per minute. Warp knitting machines can construct fabrics up to 168 inches in width, but only in flat, rectangular shapes.

Stitches

Two warp knitting stitches, the tricot stitch and the raschel stitch, are commonly used for interior fabrics. The **tricot stitch** is produced using spring needles, illustrated in Figure 7.2a, and one or two **guide bars**, attachments that guide or shift yarns around the hooked or curved portion of the needles prior to interlooping.

Tricot fabrics are distinguished by the presence of herringbone-like wales on the face of the fabric and by a crosswise rib-like effect on the back of the fabric (Figure 7.3). Tricot-stitched fabrics have comparatively low stretchability. When these fabrics are made of thermoplastic fibers, heat setting can be used to improve their dimensional stability. Tricot fabrics are used for automobile interiors, upholstered furniture coverings, and wallcoverings.

The **raschel stitch** is executed on a machine that may be equipped with up to thirty guide bars, which select and position the various yarns in preparation for interlooping.

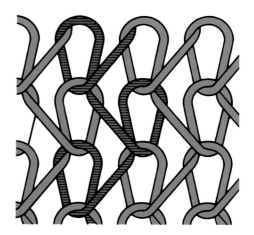

Figure 7.1 Interlooping of adjacent yarns in warp knitting. Illustration by Andrea Lau.

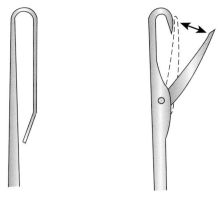

a) Head of spring needle.   b) Head of latch needle.

Figure 7.2 Head of needles used in tricot stitching.
Courtesy of Celanese Corporation.

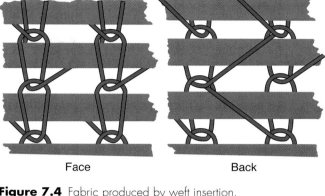

Face   Back

Figure 7.4 Fabric produced by weft insertion.
Illustration by Andrea Lau.

Increasing the number of guide bars is equivalent to increasing the number of harnesses on looms; thus, raschel machines are extremely versatile. As shown in Figure 7.2b, the needles used have a latch that opens and closes to secure the yarn, enabling the manufacturer to use virtually any fiber and any style of yarn.

Raschel-stitched fabrics often have a lace-like appearance and are used as window coverings (Figure 17.29a and b, p. 296). They are also often produced for use as tabletop accessories.

Weft Insertion

Warp knitting and weaving are combined in a fabrication technique known as **weft insertion**. In this operation, weft or filling yarns are inserted or "woven" through the

loops being formed in a tricot-stitching operation. One of the distinct advantages weft-inserted fabrics offer is readily apparent in Figure 7.4. Virtually all of the fabric weight and cover is provided by the weft yarns; thus, the need for larger and more expensive warp yarns is reduced. Because the transparency and covering power of the fabric can be controlled by the size and character of the weft yarns used, manufacturers are increasingly using weft insertion to produce window coverings (Figure 17.30, p. 297).

Weft or Filling Knitting

In **weft** or **filling knitting** (Figure 7.5), fabrics are produced by continuously interlooping one or more yarns from side to side, creating one course after another. No warp yarns are used.

Figure 7.3 Brushed tricot knit.
Courtesy of Amy Willbanks, www.textilefabric.com.

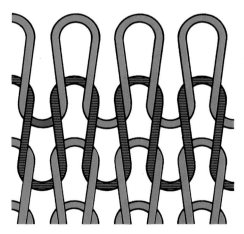

Figure 7.5 Continuous interlooping of one yarn in filling or weft knitting.
Illustration by Andrea Lau.

Filling knitting is slower than warp knitting. Approximately three million loops are formed per minute. While warp knitting machines can produce only flat, straight-sided fabrics, filling knitting machines can produce rectangular fabrics, fabrics with a circular or tubular form, and fabrics with a preplanned, angular shape. Knitting flat-to-shape, a procedure used extensively in the production of apparel items, is rarely if ever used in the production of interior textile items. Circular knitting produces the fabric used in the knit-de-knit yarn texturing method explained in Chapter 5.

Stitches

Among the filling knitting stitches used to manufacture interior fabrics are the jersey stitch and the interlock stitch. The **jersey stitch**, used in some bedsheets, creates herringbone-like wales on the face of the fabric and crescent-shaped loops on the back of the fabric (see Figure 7.5). Knitted pile fabrics, used to make simulated fur bedspreads, are formed by incorporating additional yarns or fibers into a jersey-stitched base fabric.

The **interlock stitch** is formed by continuously interlooping two yarns. The completed fabric appears to be two interknitted fabrics, as shown schematically in Figure 7.6. Interlock-stitched fabrics are resistant to running and snagging and have high dimensional stability when heat set. These characteristics support the selection of **doubleknit fabrics**—interlock-stitched fabrics with relatively large loops—for use as furniture and wallcoverings.

Figure 7.6 An interlock-stitched fabric. Illustration by Andrea Lau.

Crocheting

Crocheting can be described as knitting with one needle. The needle is continually manipulated to interloop one yarn into previously formed loops. Artisans use crocheting to make decorative borders for pillowcases and to create such accessories as afghans, doilies, and potholders.

Chain-Stitching

Over the past several years, advances in technology have enabled manufacturers to produce fabrics more rapidly than they could with conventional techniques. In two fast techniques, stitch-knitting and stitch-bonding, knitting stitches are used as stabilizing chain-stitches.

Stitch-Knitting

Stitch-knitting, which is also known as knit-sewing and by the patented name of Malimo, is an innovative fabrication technique. In this operation, webs of yarns are layered and chain-stitched together to produce a usable fabric structure. The chain-stitching is, in effect, "sewing" with knitting stitches, and the rate of fabric production is high. As no abrasive mechanisms (such as drop wires, heddles, or reeds) are used, highly decorative, complex yarns can be incorporated in either fabric direction. This yarn placement flexibility permits manufacturers to control the level of fabric transparency easily and produce fabrics that vary widely in their visual and textural features. A fabric produced by this technique is shown in Figure 17.31, p. 297.

Stitch-Bonding

Stitch-bonding operations involve chain-stitching across a fibrous batt, converting the layered webs of fibers into a usable textile structure.

Tufting and Fusion Bonding

Tufting and fusion bonding operations are used to introduce pile yarns to already-formed fabrics. Both techniques are fast and efficient.

Tufting

In **tufting** operations, pile yarns are threaded through needles that are mounted across the tufting machine and suspended vertically above the base fabric. As shown in Figure 7.7, the needles punch through the back of the fabric and loopers engage the yarns. As each needle is with-

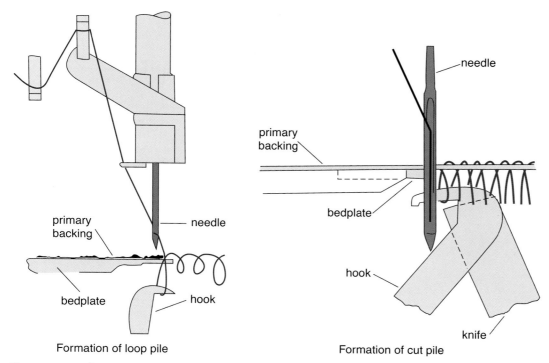

Formation of loop pile

Formation of cut pile

Figure 7.7 Tufting operations. Illustration by Andrea Lau.

drawn, a pile loop is formed. If a cut-pile texture is desired, the loopers are equipped with oscillating knives.

At this stage, the tufted pile yarns could easily be pulled out as they are only held in the base fabric mechanically. To provide better stability, a thin coating of an adhesive compound is applied to the fabric back.

Tufting has captured a modest portion of the upholstery fabrics market, but it has taken over the soft floor coverings market, accounting for more than 96 percent of all carpet and rugs produced. Readers may refer to Chapter 22 for an extensive discussion of tufting processes.

Fusion Bonding

In **fusion bonding** operations, pile yarns are inserted, or, more precisely, embedded, into an adhesive coating that has been applied to a base fabric. This technique, increasingly used in the production of soft floor coverings, is discussed and illustrated in Chapter 23.

Knotting and Twisting Yarns

Highly decorative lace and macramé fabrics are produced by knotting or twisting intersecting yarns. A major difference between these two kinds of fabric is the size of

the yarns used, with macramé items made up of heavier strands.

Producing Macramé

Macramé is usually a relatively heavy fabric constructed by knotting and twisting textile cords. Machine-made macramé is used in vertical blinds, and hand-made macramé panels are used as decorative hangings.

Lace Making

In the manufacture of lace fabrics, complex machinery is used to twist relatively fine yarns around one another. The yarns in lace fabrics are not parallel and perpendicular; they are instead oriented in various directions. Machine-made lace is used in window coverings, bed coverings, and tabletop accents. Hand-made lace, produced using small bobbins, is used as trimming for bedding products and is constructed into such items as dresser scarves and **doilies**.

Creating Bobbin Lace

Multiple pairs of bobbins are used to twist and cross yarns in the production of **bobbin lace**. The small wooden bobbins are wound with a length of yarn and hung below the work area to keep the yarns under slight tension.

With practice, skill, and patience, artisans manipulate the several bobbins in twisting and crossing motions. These motions are combined to execute various stitches.

Bobbin lace may be designed and constructed for such interior uses as open casements in window treatments. It may also be produced for use as coverings for decorative pillows.

Creating Tatted Lace

In **tatting**, the artisan deftly moves one small bobbin to twist fine yarns into open fabric structures. Tatting often produces such small items as doilies and other tabletop accessories.

Braiding Yarns

Braiding techniques are similar in some ways to basic weaving, triaxial weaving, and twisting operations. As in basic weaving, the yarn strands are interlaced; as in triaxial weaving, the yarns are interlaced at a less than a 90-degree angle; and as in twisting, the direction or orientation of the yarns is continually reversed as production progresses.

To produce **flat braids**, which are frequently used as trims or converted into rugs, three yarns or yarn-like structures are interlaced (Figure 23.14, p. 368). To produce the **circular braids** often used as accent tie-backs for draperies, several strands are interlaced around a textile cord or other round structure.

Combining Fibers

Textile machinery engineers and producers have devised new ways to produce fabric structures while bypassing the yarn stage. Techniques such as spunbonding and spunlacing have joined the age-old technique of felting and the efficient method of needlepunching as ways to combine fibers directly into fabrics.

Bonding Fibrous Batts

In one fabrication, **fibrous batts** are bonded into essentially flat structures with a paper-like quality. (These nonwoven structures must not be confused with the three-dimensional fibrous batts produced for use as fillings and paddings; see Chapter 12.) Webs of fibers are first layered to form a relatively thin batt. The webs may be layered parallel to each other, at right angles, or randomly (Figure 7.9a). An adhesive must be sprayed over the batt to cause

nonthermoplastic fibers to adhere to one another. Heat can be used to soften thermoplastic fibers and cause them to stick together.

Bonded-web or **nonwoven fabrics** are used as interfacing in upholstery skirts, adding body and weight. They are also used to interface the heading in curtains and draperies, providing support for such treatments as pleats and scallops (see Chapter 16).

Felting Fibrous Batts

In the production of **felt**, wool fibers are cleaned and carded into thin webs, which are then layered at right angles to form a batt. The batt is exposed to controlled heat, agitation, moisture, and pressure. These conditions cause the overlapping scales of the fibers to intermesh and entangle, compacting and shrinking the batt into felt.

Felt is widely used to prevent artifacts from scratching hard-surfaced tabletops. Felt can also be used for decorative wall hangings (Figure 7.9b). Thick felt is an effective insulation material. To reduce its cost, felt can be produced from a blend of wool and rayon fibers. A blended felt fabric must be at least 80 percent wool to achieve the interlocking of the scales.

Needlepunching Fibrous Batts

The technique of using barbed needles to create a mechanical chain-stitch within a fibrous batt has long been employed in the production of some carpet and blankets. More recently, the method has been refined and used in the production of some carpet, wallcoverings, and blankets (Figure 7.9c). For added stability, a loosely woven fabric,

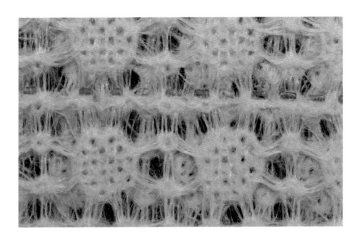

Figure 7.8 Spunlaced fabric.
Courtesy of Amy Willbanks, www.textilefabric.com.

a) Bonded fibrous batt.

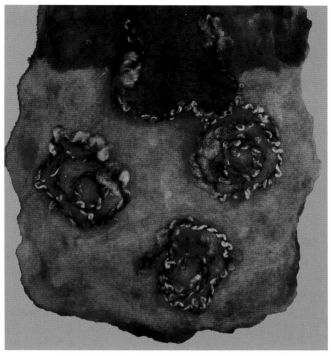

b) Felted wall hanging.

c) Needlepunched carpeting.

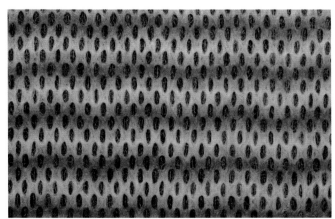

d) Spunlaced disposable wipe.

Figure 7.9 Fabric structures which bypass the yarn stage.
a) Courtesy of Amy Willbanks, www.textilefabric.com. b) Courtesy of Nancy Oxford. c) Courtesy of Amy Willbanks, www.textilefabric.com. d) Courtesy of Amy Willbanks, www.textilefabric.com.

called a **scrim**, or an adhesive may be enclosed within the batt prior to **needlepunching**.

Spunbonding Webs of Filaments

Spunbonding converts thermoplastic filaments directly into fabric structures. After the filaments are arranged into a thin web, they are stabilized with heat or chemical binders. For added strength, stability, weight, or reduced transparency, additional compounds can be sprayed over the fine web. Spunbonded fabrics are increasingly used as tablecloths, as coverings for bedding products, and as backings for wallcoverings and carpet.

Spunlacing Fibers

Textile fabrics produced by mechanically entangling fibers are referred to as **spunlaced** fabrics. While an adhesive or other type of binder is generally used with spunbonded and bonded-web fabrics, the fibers in spunlaced fabrics are stabilized solely by fiber-to-fiber friction (Figure 7.8). Today, spunlaced fabrics are used to back textile wallcoverings, simulated leather upholstery fabrics, mattress pads, and comforters, and they are also made into pillow coverings. Disposable towels and wipes are also produced by this method (Figure 7.9d).

Extruding Polymer Solutions

Polymer solutions can be converted directly into **film sheeting** fabrics. This is accomplished by extruding the solution through a spinneret that has a narrow slit rather than minute holes. As the polymer ribbon emerges, it is stretched into a thin film or sheet. The thickness of the film can be controlled by varying the extrusion pressure and the amount of stretching. Film sheetings are used for such interior products as simulated leather upholstery coverings, drapery linings, and shower curtains.

Summary

To manufacture the wide variety of interior textile components and fabrics required by end-product producers, a wide range of fabrication techniques is necessarily employed. Several of these techniques enable the fabric producer to interloop, insert, or otherwise combine yarns into greige goods, supplementing the methods used to interlace yarns. Other techniques enable the producer to combine fibers and convert solutions directly into usable structures, avoiding spinning, throwing, and fiber extruding operations. Many of the fabrications reviewed in this chapter are more efficient and less costly than weaving.

Following the sequence of production outlined in Chapter 1, the greige goods produced by weaving, knitting, tufting, spunbonding, and so on are forwarded to colorists or converters. These members of the industry work to make the goods more attractive and functional, helping to ensure their selection by consumers, contract designers, and architects.

Key Terms

bobbin lace
bonded-web fabric
circular braids
courses
crocheting
doilies
doubleknit fabric
felt
fibrous batts
filling knitting
film sheeting
flat braids

fusion bonding
gauge
guide bars
interlock stitch
jersey stitch
knitting
macramé
needlepunching
nonwoven fabric
raschel stitch
scrim
spunbonding

spunlaced
stitch-bonding
stitch-knitting
tatting
tricot stitch
tufting
wales
warp knitting
weft insertion
weft knitting

Review Questions

1. Why is the most stretchable position in knitted fabric generally the crosswise direction?

2. What is the function of the guide bars?

3. How can one distinguish between tricot and jersey fabrics?

4. Both warp knitting and filling knitting are extremely fast production techniques. Does this translate into savings for the ultimate consumer?

5. Why is stitch-knitting sometimes referred to as knit-sewing?

6. Differentiate between tufting and fusion bonding.

7. Why are bonded-web fabrics known as nonwoven fabrics?

8. Distinguish between spunbonded and spunlaced fabrics.

9. Describe the uses of spunlaced fabrics.

10. Differentiate between needle punching and felting.

CHAPTER EIGHT

Textile Colorants, Color Perception, and Color Application

Photo courtesy of Amy Willbanks,
www.textilefabric.com.

■ **Interior environments are** enhanced when the addition of colored textiles is carefully planned. The planning effort entails an examination of factors that alter the apparent characteristics of the textile colorants. Whatever characteristics are chosen, they will appear different when viewed under different conditions; an obvious example of such a condition is the lighting of a particular environment.

The importance of color-related variables to the selection of interior textile products is reflected in the availability of several methods for applying colorants. These methods may be divided into three major categories: dyeing, printing, and dyeing and printing combinations. Colorists select the method of application that can introduce the color styling features preferred by the contemporary consumer or specified by the contract designer or architect.

Carpet and rug fibers, yarns, and greige goods can be colored by the same basic techniques used with other textiles. However, different equipment and procedures are often required for handling these heavier, wider, and bulkier structures, and larger amounts of dyestuff and water are needed to produce an acceptable level of color intensity. In recent years, increased energy costs and heightened concern for water conservation have led to the development of new and innovative techniques for dye application.

Although most natural fibers have some color-producing substances, which may or may not be retained, and most textiles have color-producing substances added, no fibers or other textile structures have intrinsic color. Not until incident light waves are reflected, and interpreted by an observer, will color be perceived.

Colorants and Color Perception

For color to be perceived, incident light waves must first be reflected to the eye. In turn, these rays must stimulate the eye to transmit optical sensations to the brain for interpretation. Only then will the viewer see a particular "color." What the viewer is responding to, in fact, is a concentration of light waves of certain lengths. Because light waves play a critical role in color stimulus and sensation, a brief review of the nature of light will augment our discussion of textile colorants and color perceptions.

Nature of Light

Light is visible electromagnetic energy, which accounts for a relatively small portion of the **electromagnetic spec-**trum. This spectrum, schematized in Figure 8.1, includes waves of vastly different lengths, but all are very short. At one end are cosmic and gamma rays, which are quite short; at the opposite end are radio and electrical power waves, which are relatively long in comparison with cosmic waves. The actual length of most waves—the distance from the crest of one wave to the crest of the next—is measured and reported in minuscule units called **nanometers** (nm). One nanometer is equal to one billionth of a meter or to 0.000000039 inch.

In the central portion of the electromagnetic spectrum is an area known as the **visible spectrum**. The lengths of waves in this region range from some 400 nm to about 700 nm. When reflected to the eye, these radiations stimulate the eye to send messages to the brain, allowing us to interpret the sensation and see color. While the human eye is not sensitive to wavelengths outside of the visible spectrum, we are aware that some of the so-called invisible rays, for instance, ultraviolet and infrared rays, can have negative effects on colored textiles, altering the reflective characteristics of colorants and degrading the fibers.

Natural and artificial light sources emit all wavelengths within the boundaries of the visible spectrum. They do not, however, have equal mixtures of the various lengths: some have predominantly longer waves, others predominantly shorter waves. Colorants differ in their capacities to reflect the various wavelengths. The length of the waves emitted by the light source together with the length of the waves reflected by the colorant determine the particular color or hue perceived and affect other color characteristics as well.

Color Characteristics

Three color characteristics are determined by the emission, reflection, and interpretation of light waves. These are hue, value, and intensity.

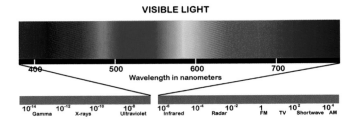

Figure 8.1 The electromagnetic spectrum.
Courtesy of Sharon Coleman.

Hue

Depending on the light source, larger quantities of certain wavelengths will be emitted, and, depending on the colorant, larger quantities of certain lengths will be reflected. The length of the waves that predominate in both emission and reflection will determine the particular **hue** or color perceived. When blue is perceived, for example, the illuminant is emitting a high concentration of waves around 465 nm in length and the colorant is reflecting a high concentration of these waves and absorbing other lengths. When green is perceived, a high concentration of waves around 520 nm is being emitted and reflected; when red is perceived, waves around 650 nm are being emitted and reflected; and so on.

Value

Value refers to the relative lightness or darkness of a color. When a compound known to reflect all wavelengths, creating white, is used with colorants, a **tint** is produced and value is increased. The coloration produced would be perceived as a lighter value of a hue such as pale blue. When a compound known to absorb all wavelengths, creating black, is used with colorants, a **shade** is produced and value is decreased. The coloration produced would be perceived as a darker value of a hue such as navy.

Intensity

Intensity and **chroma** are terms used to describe the purity or strength of a color. A blue hue, for example, may appear strong, bright, and clear, or weak, grayed, and dull. Changes in intensity generally produce concomitant changes in value.

The effects of various fiber- and fabric-related variables—such as the presence of delusterants, fiber cross-sectional shapes, and the use of floating yarns—on the luster and brightness of colored textiles were discussed in earlier chapters. The effects of certain finishing agents and processes on color dimensions are described in Chapter 9.

The challenge to the dye chemist is to select a colorant or a mixture of colorants and additives that can create the planned hue, value, and intensity. To accomplish this, the chemist must work cooperatively with fiber, yarn, and fabric producers, as well as with converters.

Colorants

Textile colorants may be dyes or pigments. **Dyes or dyestuffs** are color-producing compounds that are normally soluble in water. **Pigments** are also color-producing agents, but they are insoluble in water. The chemical structure of either type of colorant enables it selectively to absorb and reflect certain wavelengths. Pigments are held to the fabric surface with a binding agent that works like an adhesive. Dyes penetrate the fabric surface and chemically bond with the fiber. Because of this difference, dyes are usually more durable than pigments. Pigments are used to color textiles in the fabric stage, while dyestuffs are used to color textiles in the solution, fiber, yarn, fabric or finished textile stage.

Dyes are classified by their chemical composition. Because dyes involve a chemical reaction with the fiber, the dyestuff must be chemically compatible with the fiber (Figure 17.2a, p. 287). This is referred to as having an **affinity** to the fiber. If not compatible, the fabric will not accept the dye. No one dyestuff is colorfast to all fiber contents and color range varies within each dye classification. Each dyestuff is carefully chosen based on the chemical composition, fiber content, range of colors, and desired performance characteristics.

Because pigments are held to the surface by a binding or adhesive agent, any color can be used on any fiber content. Pigments, which resemble paint lying on the surface of the fabric, can lead to fabric problems such as stiffening and cracking (Figure 17.27, p. 295). Pigment printing is very fast and inexpensive. Colors are easier to match because of the surface treatment.

Colorants contain groups called auxochromes and groups called chromophores. **Auxochromes** are responsible for the selective absorption and reflection of light waves: these groups determine the hue. **Chromophores** control the quantity of waves reflected, influencing the value of the hue. The intensity is controlled by the mixture of colorants and the amount of dyestuff accepted by the fibers. Some highly amorphous fibers, such as wool, readily accept high amounts of dye; other fibers, especially those with highly crystallized interiors, do not readily accept dyestuffs, and high pressure and temperature or dye-carriers may be required during the dyeing operation. In some cases, the affinity between the fiber and the dyestuff can be improved by the use of special agents known as **mordants**.

Extensive formal study in the fields of dye chemistry and textile chemistry is necessary for a thorough understanding of colorants and their reaction with or attraction for different fibers. This high level of knowledge is mandatory for the dye chemist, but not for the interior designer, architect, and consumer. Textile chemists and colorists recognize that consumers will prefer fashionable colors to out-of-date ones, and they direct their work accordingly.

Whereas the dye chemist is responsible for the correct match of fiber and colorant, the precise application of the dyestuff or pigment is the responsibility of the dyers and printers. Dyers and printers recognize that adequate penetration of the colorant is needed to produce the planned intensity and to ensure an acceptable level of color retention. They also recognize that accurate placement or registration of all colors will make for better clarity and definition of printed designs.

Dyeing Fabrics and Fabric Components

Dye operations can be carried out at the fiber, yarn, or fabric stage. Most dyeing operations require immersion of the textile into **dye liquor**, an aqueous solution of dyestuff.

Dyeing in the Fiber Stage

Color-producing agents can be added in the fiber stage by one of two methods, solution dyeing and fiber or stock dyeing. Solution dyeing can be used only with manufactured fibers, but fiber dyeing may be used with both natural and manufactured fibers.

Solution Dyeing

Solution dyeing and **dope dyeing** are synonyms for an operation in which dye pigments are added to the polymer solution prior to extrusion. This produces manufactured filaments with coloring agents locked inside the fiber. The term **color-sealed** identifies solution-dyed fibers; because the manufactured fiber producer adds the color, the term **producer-colored** may also be used.

With the color-producing pigment incorporated as an integral part of the fiber, solution-dyed fibers have comparatively high color retention and stability. This supports the use of solution dyeing to color fibers that will be used in carpet produced for installation outdoors. Because such fibers must have little or no capacity to absorb moisture, they cannot absorb sufficient quantities of aqueous dye liquor. The relatively high cost of the pigments, however, precludes the routine use of this technique.

Fiber or Stock Dyeing

Immersing natural or manufactured fibers into dye liquor is known as **fiber or stock dyeing**. Because loose masses of the fibers are submerged, the dyestuff can be absorbed more readily and thoroughly than it can when yarns or fabrics are immersed. In yarn structures, fiber packing and twisting may physically restrict the level of dyeing; in fabrics, yarn crossings and structural compactness may present physical barriers. The old phrase **dyed-in-the-wool** meaning through and through, deeply ingrained, or staunchly dedicated, arose from the observation that wool fibers dyed prior to spinning had richer and deeper colors than those produced by dyeing yarns or fabrics.

Fiber dyeing is frequently used with manufactured staple fibers to produce carpet yarns that simulate the soft, mellow patina of wool. The wool-like appearance is further enhanced when the colored fibers are spun on the woolen system.

Fiber dyeing can be used in combination with yarn production to produce yarns having distinctive color styling. When two or more colors of fibers are uniformly distributed throughout a spun yarn, the term **heather** identifies the coloration. A heather appearance can also be produced by throwing different colors of filaments.

The term **marled** identifies the coloration produced by combining two differently colored rovings together in spinning. Although the resulting structure is a single yarn, its visual spiral resembles that produced by plying two differently colored yarns. A marled yarn is pictured in Figure 8.2.

Figure 8.2 A marled yarn.
Courtesy of Amy Willbanks, www.textilefabric.com.

Figure 8.3 Dyeing packages of yarn in a dye beck. Courtesy of Ascend Performance Materials.

Ombré, French for **shade**, describes color styling in which there is a gradual change in the value of a single hue, for instance, from pink to red to maroon. In yarns, this delicate color style is produced by carefully controlling the introduction of fibers of the appropriate shade or tint during yarn spinning. If the process is well executed, the location of a change is barely perceptible.

Dyeing in the Yarn Stage

Adding colorants to yarn structures before fabric formation is known as **yarn dyeing**. Certain techniques, collectively known as space dyeing, can be used to produce multicolored yarns; these techniques are described later in this chapter. Most yarn-dyeing operations, however, produce single-colored yarns, and these yarns cannot be distinguished from those constructed of one color of fiber.

Package Dyeing

The equipment used in **package dyeing** is shown in Figure 8.3. Yarns are first wound on perforated cylinders to

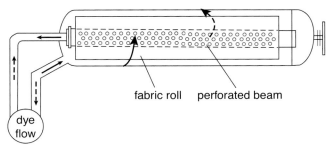

fabric roll   perforated beam

Beam Dyeing Machine

Figure 8.4 Beam dyeing. Courtesy of Celanese International Corporation.

form packages of yarn. Because carpet and rug yarns have relatively large diameters, smaller amounts of the strands are wound on the packages. Several packages are then mounted on posts and lowered into a pressure cooker-like vessel known as a **dye beck**. Dye liquor is then forcibly circulated throughout each package of yarn. To ensure adequate penetration of the dye, high levels of pressure and temperatures may be used in the operation; this may be necessary when manufactured fibers with low moisture regain values, such as polyester, nylon, and acrylic, are being dyed.

Beam Dyeing

Beam dyeing is a second way of dyeing yarns a single color. In preparation for the operation, warp yarns are wound on a perforated beam barrel. The beam is then loaded into a beam dyeing machine (Figure 8.4), and the dye liquor is circulated through the yarns, from the outside to the inside and from the inside to the outside, via the perforations. The beams of dyed warp yarns, when rinsed and dried, are ready to be placed on a loom, bypassing the unwinding and rewinding operations required after package dyeing. Beam dyeing may also be used for greige goods.

Skein Dyeing

Immersing long skeins of yarn into troughs filled with dye liquor is known as **skein dyeing** (Figure 8.5a and b). This procedure may be employed when the winding and compacting of yarns on cylinders or beam barrels could alter their textural features, or when a relatively small quantity of custom-colored yarn is required. The procedure is rarely used for dyeing large quantities of yarns, however, because it is a relatively slow and therefore costly operation.

Single-colored yarns, each dyed a different shade of the same hue or a different hue, are often plied. Such combinations produce a color style described as **moresque**.

a) Skein/yarn dyeing.

b) Skein/yarn dyeing.

Figure 8.5 Skein dyeing carpet pile yarns.
Courtesy of J&J/Invision.

Space Dyeing

Space-dyeing operations produce multicolored yarns. Unlike heather yarns in which the colors are uniformly distributed throughout the yarns, and unlike ombré yarns in which various values of one color are repeated, space-dyed yarns have differently colored segments along their lengths (Figure 8.6). The various hues may be related or contrasting; the segments may be equal or unequal in length; and the junctures between colors may be sharp or muted.

Although space-dyed yarns, also known as **variegated yarns**, have long been used in the hand and machine knitting of apparel items, their use in interior textiles, especially in upholstery fabrics and pile carpet, is increasing. The styling not only provides visual interest, but the mixture of colors also effectively camouflages the soil that accumulates in use.

Various techniques can produce this color styling. Although some of these techniques are printing rather than dyeing operations, they fall in the category of space dyeing because they create the characteristic coloration. When well-defined, sharp color junctures are planned, sheets of yarns will be printed. When muted junctures of the selected colors are desired, segments of the yarns will be dipped into dye liquor or **jet spraying** may be used. In the latter technique, pressurized dye jets spray dye liquor onto skeins of yarns. Another method uses dye-loaded needles, called **astrojets**, to give packages of yarn repeated, programmed "injections." This **package-injection technique** requires minimal handling of the yarns.

Knit-De-Knit Space Dyeing Yarn texturing and color application are combined in **knit-de-knit space dyeing**. Pile yarns, undyed or precolored, are rapidly knitted into a long, jersey-stitched tube. One or more colors are then printed onto the tubing with dye jets before heat setting. Finally, the tube is de-knit or unraveled, producing variegated, crinkled pile yarns (Figures 8.6 and 8.7a and b).

Dyeing Greige Goods

Unless colored fibers or yarns were used in fabrication, greige goods bear little resemblance to those offered to residential and commercial consumers. Except for any textural and visual interest contributed by complex yarns or decorative interlacings, such fabrics have virtually no aesthetic appeal. Lacking the critical fashion element of color, such coverings would be summarily rejected by most consumers. For greater consumer appeal, greige goods are virtually always colored.

Figure 8.6 Space dyeing.
Courtesy of J&J/Invision.

Dyeing operations once could produce only solid-colored surfaces, and printing techniques only patterned surfaces. Advances in dye chemistry and technology now enable colorists to use immersion processes for the production of multicolored designs and printing techniques for the production of solid-colored surfaces.

Piece Dyeing

Piece dyeing is carried out after fabrication by immersing the piece goods or greige goods into dye liquor. It produces single-colored fabrics with identical color characteristics on both sides.

In dyeing operations involving the immersion or circulation of tufted greige goods in dye liquor, the primary backing may be thinly coated with an adhesive to stabilize the pile tufts. A secondary backing is not applied. Any secondary backing would add bulk and weight, making handling of the long lengths more difficult. A secondary backing of jute would absorb a large amount of dye liquor, increasing the cost of the dyestuffs, as well as the time and expense of drying the floor covering. However, prior to printing greige goods, a secondary backing is normally applied to add dimensional stability and ensure good registration of the colors in the motifs.

Greige rollgoods and rugs may be dyed in a discontinuous or a continuous dyeing operation. Discontinuous operations are so named because the coloring process is interrupted when the wet carpet must be removed from the dyeing machine and dried elsewhere.

Discontinuous Dyeing   Because relatively small quantities or batches of carpet can be dyed in **discontinuous-dyeing** operations, they are often known as **batch-dyeing** operations. They are carried out in various vessels or becks, including a carpet winch, a jet beck, and a horizontal beam-dyeing machine.

In preparation for dyeing in a **carpet winch**, the ends of a batch of greige goods weighing approximately 2,000 pounds are sewn together and loaded into the beck. This weight roughly corresponds to 327 linear yards of goods. The full width of carpet is plaited or folded as it is fed into the dye liquor. If the plaiting operation is controlled so that it will produce folds from 8 to 16 inches deep and never creases the carpet in the same place twice, the development of crosswise surface markings will be minimized; avoiding these markings is especially important for velour and plush textures. The carpet is cycled through the dye

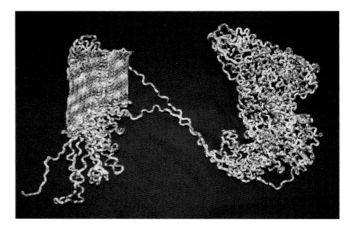

a) Space-dyed yarn.

b) Space-dyed carpet.

Figure 8.7 Colored yarns add consumer appeal.
a) Courtesy of Amy Willbanks, www.textilefabric.com.
b) Courtesy of J&J/Invision.

liquor, which is continually filtered, for an average of two to four hours, and it is then rinsed, unloaded, and dried.

In preparation for dyeing in a **jet beck**, a batch of carpet in rope form is loaded into a long vessel (Figure

Figure 8.8 Beck dyeing.
Courtesy of J&J/Invision.

8.8). The unit is nearly 40 feet long, and can accommodate some 2,800 pounds of goods. Jets introduce the dye, and the carpet is cycled through the liquor. For effective dyeing of polyester, temperature and pressure can be elevated.

Beam-dyeing operations begin with the winding of an open width of greige goods on a perforated beam. The beam can accommodate approximately 218 linear feet of carpet that has a total thickness of 0.32 inch and a maximum width of 17.5 feet. The batch is loaded into a horizontal dyeing machine and the dye liquor is forcibly circulated through the rolled goods. Because the carpet is rolled in beam dyeing, soft, deep pile textures would be severely deformed. This technique is therefore generally restricted to the dyeing of low pile, loop textures. A distinct advantage of the operation is that no crossmarks can develop because no folding is involved. When required, higher temperatures can also be used.

Two factors support the increased use of batch-dyeing operations. First, an increase in consumer demand for specialized colorations requires the use of equipment that can economically dye smaller amounts of greige goods. Second, the challenge of reducing the consumption of water and energy can be more effectively met with batch-dyeing operations than with continuous-dyeing methods. Specifically, the becks are designed to use comparatively low **liquor ratios** (pounds of liquor to pounds of carpet). Since water is the principal component in most dye liquors, this results in substantial savings in water cost and drying expenses.

Continuous Dyeing Continuous-dyeing operations are used when large quantities of greige goods are to be dyed one color. Because several lengths of greige goods or undyed carpet are generally sewn together, their construction and composition must be identical or quite similar if uniform color characteristics are to be reproduced. The dyeing systems, known as **ranges**, comprise units for wetting the carpet pile, applying the dyestuff, steaming, washing, drying, and rolling up the dyed and dried goods. These units are aligned so the carpet goes directly from one step to the next. Such operations do not require unloading of the greige goods and transporting them to other units for final processing, so they are said to be continuous.

When carpet is introduced into a continuous-dyeing range, it is wetted to increase dye absorption. In some systems, a squeegee-like blade transfers the dye liquor from a roller to the wet carpet surface. Steaming helps increase the movement or **migration** of the liquor through the pile layer, promoting uniform application of the dye and avoiding the problem of **tippiness**, the concentration of color on the tips of the pile yarns. As the carpet continues through the system, it is washed, dried, and rolled.

Formerly, continuous-dyeing operations required comparatively high liquor ratios. In recent years, these ratios have been reduced by applying the dye in forms that are not highly aqueous solutions. In some cases, the dye is applied as a spray, that is, a mixture of air and dye; in other cases, the dye is carried on the surface of bubbles. One method involves depositing dye on the carpet as foamed dye liquor. The foam is an unstable froth that collapses on the fiber and dyes it.

The spray, bubbles, or foam can be delivered through tubes, jets, or spray nozzles oriented toward the pile layer. They may also be delivered by blades and rollers, blowers, and rotary screens. In any case, the tremendous reduction in water usage in these new dye application methods has resulted in marked savings in processing costs.

Cross Dyeing

Cross dyeing, also called **differential dyeing**, is a color application process based on chemical variables. The process produces a multicolored fabric from a single immersion in one dyebath formulation. Two or more fibers that are chemically different—classified in different generic groups or variants of the same fiber—are strategically placed in yarns or in greige goods. Carpet and rug producers generally use a blend of nylon variants, rather than generically dissimilar fibers, in this coloring operation. For a heather appearance, different fibers are uniformly distributed in the yarns; for plaids or stripes, warp or filling yarns with different fiber contents are used in bands; and for multicolored design motifs, yarns of different fibers are selectively incorporated during fabrication (Figure 6.11a, p. 106).

A single dyebath is formulated. The dye chemist, often with the aid of a computer, may select specific dyestuffs, each of which will be accepted by one fiber and rejected by all other fibers, or use one dyestuff that will be absorbed in different amounts by related fiber variants. In the former case, each type of fiber or variant has a different hue, and, in the latter case, each variant has a different level of intensity of the same hue. The economic advantage of cross dyeing is readily apparent: "you only dye once."

A second major advantage of cross dyeing is that orders for specific colors can be filled accurately and quickly. Whatever the color mixture ordered, the stored greige goods are ready for immediate dyeing, finishing, and shipping. Without cross-dyeing technology, fibers or yarns would have to be dyed the necessary number of colors in separate dyebaths; the fibers would then have to be spun or thrown; and, finally, the colored yarns packaged or wound on beams and sent to the mill for preparation of the loom and for winding of the bobbins or cones used for the filling yarns. Shipment would be further delayed by the time required for fabrication and subsequent finishing. Producers who attempt to save time another way—by second guessing the fashion colors of the distant future and coloring fabrics in advance of orders—may find themselves with a sizable inventory of unpopular colors.

Union Dyeing

Like cross dyeing, **union dyeing** is based on chemical variables. Unlike cross dyeing, however, union dyeing is chosen when two or more different fibers are used in a fabric that is to become a single, uniform color. Again, a single dyebath is formulated but each fiber becomes the same color. The use of this method of color application has paralleled the increased use of fiber blends, especially cotton and polyester (Figure 17.7, p. 288).

Printing Greige Goods

High-speed mechanized operations are generally used to print greige goods when stylists or contract designers specify printed fabrics. Printing requires thicker dyestuffs than those used in dyeing operations. Whereas migration or movement of the dye is required to achieve a uniform level of color in dyed textile structures, such migration in printed goods would result in poor definition of the shapes and details of the motifs. Therefore, the dyestuff used in most printing operations is a **dye paste** rather than a highly aqueous dye liquor. After application of the dye paste, the textile is exposed to steam, heat, or chemicals to fix the dye in or on the fibers. Pigments may also be used to print greige goods.

In **pigment printing**, water-insoluble pigments are mixed with an adhesive compound or resin binders and applied to textiles surfaces. As the pigments are not absorbed by the fibers, the printed designs stand in slight relief. Frequently, white or metallic-colored pigments are printed on a previously dyed surface, and may be referred to as **overprinting**.

Fabric immersion can be used in combination with a printing procedure to produce interior fabrics having colored backgrounds and noncolored design motifs. Industrial methods involving such combinations include discharge printing and resist printing.

Direct Printing

In direct printing, color is applied directly to the fabric or yarns. Application can be done by hand or machine.

Block Printing

Using hand-carved blocks, artisans create distinctive prints. Because such hand-printing procedures are time-

Figure 8.9 Carved blocks used in block printing. Blocks courtesy of Nancy Oxford. Photo courtesy of Amy Willbanks, www.textilefabric.com.

a) Artisan presses dye onto fabric.

b) Carved block and printed fabric.

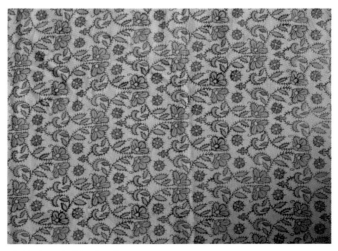

c) Authentic block print.

Figure 8.10 Block printing process.
Courtesy of Cheryl Kolander.

and labor-intensive, the prints would be expected to be comparatively expensive. They are generally made, however, by artisans in developing countries where labor costs are relatively low. In preparation for **block printing**, all shapes of the planned design that will be the same color are carved to stand in relief on the face of a block of wood. A separate block is prepared for each color to be printed. The blocks pictured in Figure 8.9 are curved instead of square or rectangular; they can be used to print medallion-like motifs.

During printing, the artisan dips the face of the carved design into the dyestuff and then presses it onto the fabric surface (Figure 8.10a and b). Since the printer may pick up different amounts of dye paste each time and exert different amounts of pressure with each printing action, various levels of intensity may be seen for the same hue, as in Figure 8.10c.

Roller Printing

Lighter weight, flat fabrics can be printed with engraved metal rollers. The shapes of those portions of the repeat that are to be the same color are etched into the surface of one roller. The number of colors planned thus dictates the number of rollers prepared. As schematized in Figure 8.12, small cylinders revolve through the dye paste and transfer the paste to the engraved rollers. A metal squeegee-like blade, called a **doctor blade**, then removes the excess dye paste from the smooth, nonengraved surface areas. As the rollers revolve against the fabric surface, the dye paste is transferred and the pattern repeat is completed. Here, the rollers and the fabric must be properly aligned to ensure that patterns, especially those having linear motifs, are printed on grain (Figure 8.11).

Large areas, whether in the ground or in the design, cannot be roller printed because the revolving motion of the rollers would create waves in the dye, causing poor registration and definition of the design. Coloring large areas of the ground is more readily accomplished by discharge printing, a technique discussed later in this chapter, and coloring large-scale motifs is more effectively accomplished by screen printing. Screen printing must also be used to print pattern repeats whose lengths exceed the circumference of the rollers.

Although **roller printing** is an extremely fast operation, its use has diminished because the cost of copper, the metal normally used to cover the rollers, and the cost of the

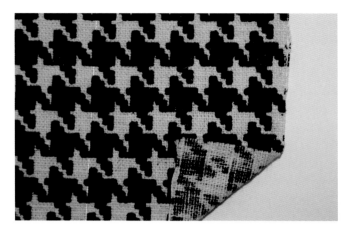

Figure 8.11 Roller print.
Courtesy of Amy Willbanks, www.textilefabric.com.

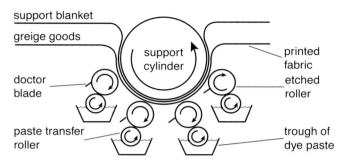

Figure 8.12 Roller printing.

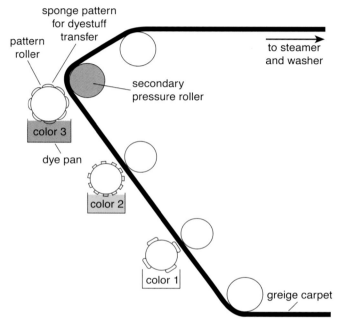

Figure 8.13 The Stalwart roller printing process.
Courtesy of Ascend Performance Materials.

labor needed to prepare the rollers have increased. Growing competition from screen printing has also had an effect.

Stalwart Roller Printing

Because carpet and rugs are comparatively heavy textile structures and their printed pattern repeats are typically large, they cannot be printed with engraved metal-covered rollers. They can, however, be roller printed with large cylinders covered with three-dimensional sponge forms. The sponges are cut according to the shapes planned for the designs. All the shapes that are to be one color are positioned on the surface of one cylinder; the shapes to be a second color are placed on a second cylinder, and so on.

Stalwart roller printing is illustrated schematically in Figure 8.13. As the sponge-covered rollers rotate against the moving greige goods, the dye paste is transferred to the pile yarns. The printed designs have muted, rather than sharply defined, edges. Use of this printing operation has decreased as more efficient units, especially jet-printing systems, are put into service.

Warp Printing

In warp printing, patterns are applied on the warp yarns by engraved rollers, flat-bed screens, or rotary screens prior to weaving. Fabrics printed by this method have a muted, hazy appearance.

To identify a warp print, ravel two adjacent sides of the fabric. The filling yarns are a solid color, while the warp yarns are printed with the design. Warp printing is a very time consuming and expensive process. A drapery fabric having a warp printed motif is shown in Figure 17.25, p. 295.

Resist Printing

In resist printing, color absorption is blocked using various techniques that prevent absorption or flow of the dyestuff. When the fabrics are subsequently piece dyed or printed, the dye is absorbed only in the areas that are free of the resist. Artisans use several different hand-resist printing operations to create distinctive interior fabrics. These fabrics include batik, tie-dye, and ikat. Industrial or mechanical resist-printing operations include screen and gum printing.

Although consumers may prefer an authentic batik, tie-dye, or ikat fabric, many are unable to find the yardage or they conclude that the costs of the imported goods exceed their interior furnishings budget. Recognizing this dilemma, manufacturers often simulate the hand-printed patterns with high-speed, commercial printing techniques. Professionals and consumers can readily distinguish authentic prints from most simulated ones by examining the back of the fabric. All authentic batik, tie-dye, and ikat fabrics have the same depth of color on both sides of the fabric.

Batik

Beeswax is the resist agent in traditional **batik fabrics**. It is melted and applied with a tjanting tool to all areas of the fabric that are to resist penetration of the dye liquor. The tjanting has a small copper cup and a tiny spout. In use, the tool functions somewhat like a fountain pen, and skilled artisans can apply fine lines of wax to create intricate details within the motifs.

After the wax hardens, the fabric is immersed into a dye bath; only the nonwaxed areas absorb the dye. The wax is then removed from the fabric by boiling. The artisan again applies melted wax, this time to all areas—including those that are to remain the first color—that are to resist the second dye liquor. If a **crackle effect** characterized by linear striations is planned, the artist randomly cracks the hardened wax at this time. Piece dyeing then results in absorption of the second color in all unwaxed areas, as well as in those areas below any cracks (Figure 8.14). This sequence of wax removal, wax application, and immersion is repeated until all planned colors have been applied.

Tie-Dye

In **tie-dyeing**, folds, gathers, and knots, which are introduced in the fabric and secured with waxed thread, function as the resist medium. These are selected and posi-

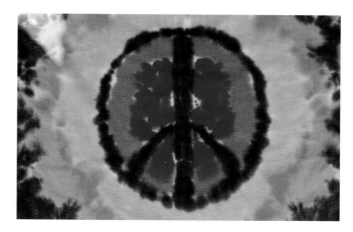

Figure 8.15 Authentic tie-dyed fabric. Courtesy of Amy Willbanks, www.textilefabric.com.

tioned according to the motifs and pattern scale planned. When the fabric is immersed into the dye bath, the tied-off areas resist penetration of the dye liquor. The fabric is then opened flat and again tied off and immersed in a second dye bath. The processes will be repeated in sequence until all planned colors and designs have been introduced. A tie-dyed fabric is pictured in Figure 8.15.

Ikat

In **ikat** (e-cot) **fabrics**, specific portions of bundles of warp and filling yarns, not fabric, are wrapped to resist dye penetration. The wrapping is carefully positioned to create the planned motifs. Subsequent dyeing results in absorption of the dye liquor by the unwrapped yarn portions only. Portions of the wrapping may be removed and

Figure 8.14 Authentic batik print with crackle effects. Courtesy of Amy Willbanks, www.textilefabric.com.

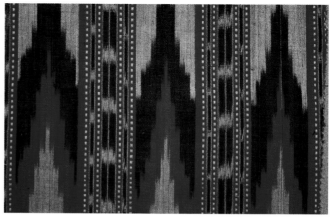

Figure 8.16 Authentic ikat print. Courtesy of Amy Willbanks, www.textilefabric.com.

additional colors applied. Because the aqueous dye liquor migrates through the yarns and varied levels of relaxation shrinkage may occur after weaving, ikat motifs have a striated appearance (Figure 8.16).

Screen Printing

Two methods of **screen printing**, flat-bed screen printing and rotary screen printing, are available for use with textile greige goods. Both methods can deliver large amounts of dyestuff, and both can facilitate the printing of large-scale motifs and pattern repeats. Since most upholstery fabrics are relatively heavy and require large amounts of dye, and since sheetings and curtain and drapery fabrics are often designed with large-scale motifs and pattern repeats, these interior fabrics are very frequently screen printed (Figure 8.18).

The apparatus and procedures used in flat-bed and rotary screen printing operations differ. Both techniques, however, are based on the principle of a stencil: portions of the printing equipment are blocked to resist the flow of dye.

Flat-bed Screen Printing

In preparation for **flat-bed screen printing**, large rectangular frames are covered with a fine, strong fabric. The compactness of the fabric determines the amount of dye paste allowed to flow through the fabric interstices. Today, nylon and polyester filaments have replaced silk filaments in these fabrics, mostly as a result of the higher cost of the natural fiber. The frames are as wide as the greige goods, generally 45 or 60 inches, and up to 80 inches in length.

Each screen will be used to print one color, so the number of planned colors determines the number of screens that must be prepared. Some areas of each screen are treated with a compound that can prevent or block the flow of the dye paste; other areas are left untreated to allow the paste to pass through the fabric. The untreated areas on each screen are in the shapes of the designs in the repeat that are to be the same color.

For printing, the screens are aligned and mounted horizontally above the fabric, as shown in Figure 8.17. The dye paste is spread over the screen surface from one side to the other, flowing through the untreated areas and printing the fabric below. The fabric is then advanced and the procedure is repeated. Because each screen adds one color, the fabric must advance under all the screens for the

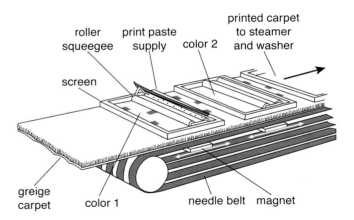

Figure 8.17 The Zimmer flat-bed screen printing machine. Courtesy of Ascend Performance Materials.

Figure 8.18 Screen print. Courtesy of Amy Willbanks, www.textilefabric.com.

coloration of the repeat to be completed. It is evident that the width of the pattern repeat and the width of the fabric govern the number of repeats that can be printed side by side; the length of the repeat and the height of the screen limit the number of repeats that can be simultaneously printed end to end.

Because large amounts of dyestuff can be passed through the screens, a good level of saturation can be obtained in screen printing heavier flat fabrics and pile structures. When working with pile structures, printers must carefully position the screens to avoid distortion of the pile yarns, and the dye paste must be drawn into the pile layer or the colored design will be carried only by the yarn tips.

Zimmer Flat-bed Screen Printing In the **Zimmer flat-bed screen printing** operation, the dye paste is drawn into the pile by an electromagnetic field. A needle belt advances the carpet one pattern repeat at a time. Other flatbed printing units use a vacuum system to pull the print paste into the pile yarns.

Rotary Screen Printing

Developed in the early 1960s, **rotary screen printing** has become the predominant method of printing textile structures. The technique is used to print flat fabrics as well as such three-dimensional structures as velveteen and velvet. It is also used to print sheets of warp yarns with motifs and with randomized, space-dyed effects. In addition, it is frequently used to print the paper used in transfer-printing operations, which are discussed in the following section.

Rotary screen printing is so widely used because several of its features make it economical. It is generally faster and more accurate than other printing techniques, and it produces a more uniform level of coloration when large quantities of goods are being run.

The cylindrical rollers used in rotary screen printing have microscopic openings in their nickel-coated surfaces. While earlier screens had some 120 holes per inch, newer screens have up to 215 holes per inch. The holes in the newer screens are more regular and well defined, and the surface is smoother. These improvements have facilitated more precise control of shaded effects and better definition of design details.

The planned pattern motifs are transferred to the surfaces of the cylinders. The holes in the areas to be printed are left open and those in the adjacent areas are blocked with water-insoluble lacquer. During printing, the dye paste is continually forced from the interior of the cylindrical screen through the minute openings.

One color of the repeat is applied by each rotating screen. After the fabric has passed under all screens, all colors and designs will have been added. Some rotary screen printing machines can accept up to 20 screens, so they can print up to 20 colors.

Rotary-screen printing is used infrequently to print soft floor coverings. In most cases, rotary screens have not been designed to supply the large amount of paste required for dyeing heavier pile layers. The recent introduction of a system that uses foam instead of paste, however, may increase the popularity of this high-speed printing technique.

Gum Printing

In **gum printing**, a gum compound known to resist dye absorption is applied to the tips of the pile yarns prior to dyeing. The gum will prevent dye absorption and migration, causing the upper portion of the pile layer to have a frosted appearance. **Frostiness** describes the absence of dye on the yarn tips. It is a planned color style, unlike tippiness, the unplanned and unwanted concentration of dye on the yarn tips that occurs when dye migration is not sufficient to produce uniform intensity. Gum printing for frostiness has the drawback of consuming additional utilities in removing the gum.

Discharge Printing

Discharge printing is an efficient way to color large areas of the ground and create a pattern. The fabric is first piece dyed, producing the same depth of color on both sides. It is then printed with a discharge paste that removes the color wherever the design motifs are planned. The agent reduces or discharges the dyestuff. Recent developments in discharge-printing equipment turn discharging and immediate color printing into one sequential operation.

Discharge prints can be identified by examining the fabric on both sides. The background will be the same color on both the face and back of the fabric. The design on the back of the fabric may show parts of the background color where the dye was not completely removed. A discharge print is shown in Figure 17.24, p. 295.

TAK Printing

TAK (from Textile Austustungs, a German carpet firm, and Kusters, the machinery supplier) printing units have been employed to add intense colors to precolored carpet surfaces. Because dye liquor, not dye paste, is used, some authorities refer to this operation as TAK dyeing. But because the application of the dye liquor is mechanically controlled, most colorists prefer to label the operation as **TAK printing**.

In TAK printing, dye is doctored from a revolving roller as a sheet of liquor. As the sheet flows downward, it is cut or interrupted by laterally oscillating chains. The liquor is thus sprinkled or deposited as randomly placed droplets on the moving carpet.

Use of TAK printing units has diminished as consumer preferences for color styling have changed and new equipment has been engineered. The Multi-TAK® unit developed by Kusters, for example, is somewhat more versatile than the conventional TAK apparatus. This unit can deposit liquor in simple geometric and wave-like patterns. The doctor blade has a notched or carved edge. During the printing operation, the blade oscillates laterally, and the liquor is removed from the roller only by the extended blade edges. Thus, the liquor flows in waves to the moving carpet. Attachments can be added to interrupt the descending streams and effect planned patterns.

Digital Printing (Inkjet)

Digital (inkjet) printing technologies are among the more recent and innovative developments for coloring soft floor coverings. In most cases, the same dye applicator units used to produce solid-colored surfaces in continuous-dyeing operations, including tubes, nozzles, blowers, and jets, are used in these operations. In jet printing, however, the delivery of the dye is precisely controlled to create detailed designs and pattern repeats.

The engineering is so sophisticated in some jet printing systems that the intricate color placement and elaborate patterns of authentic Oriental rugs can be replicated. The Foamcolor® unit developed by Kusters uses a computer to control jets that shoot air at streams of dye foam, deflecting them from their vertical path of descent. The Jet Foam Printer®, marketed by Otting, and the Colorburst® unit, manufactured by Greenwood, use photoelectric cells and solenoid systems to regulate the opening and closing of the valves controlling the flow of spray to print nozzles. In still another system, the Millitron® system, owned by Milliken Carpets, has hundreds of dye jets directed toward the moving carpet surface. Printing is electronically controlled by a computer that triggers the jets to "shoot" the surface with dye liquor in a programmed sequence.

Some jet-printing systems have applicator components placed only 0.10 inch apart. This helps to ensure full coverage of the surface. To ensure the production of sharp, well-defined designs, greige goods are generally sheared and vacuumed prior to printing. Because no equipment is in contact with the floor covering during printing, the potential problem of pile distortion is avoided.

Along with a high rate of production, the utilization of relatively little water, dye, and energy makes jet printing a comparatively inexpensive operation. The cost advantages of the operation, however, may be offset by the high capital investment initially required to purchase and install the various units.

Heat Transfer Printing

Heat transfer printing, also known as **sublistatic printing**, involves the use of heat to transfer dyestuff from paper to fabric. The difference between transfer printing and other methods of printing described in this chapter is that the surface of the fabric is not directly printed. Instead the pattern is first created on paper and is then transferred from the paper to the fabric (Figure 8.20). The technique has long been used to print the outlines of motifs in preparation for hand embroidering, and, more recently, colored motifs have been available as tear-out pages in popular magazines. The technique was adapted for the industrial-scale printing of textile fabric in the early 1970s.

In preparation for this operation, transfer paper is printed by one of four techniques, gravure, flexo, rotary screen printing (Figure 8.19), and computerized digital printing (Figure 8.21). "Gravure" identifies roller printing with engraved copper-covered rollers, "flexo" identifies roller printing with engraved rubber-covered rollers, and "rotary screen" identifies rotary screen transfer printing. The recent introduction of computerized heat transfer printing allows for greater customization in textile printing. Computerization also allows access to a wide variety of colors and gradient patterns at a more economical price. Customized bedding and team sportswear apparel are just a few of the many textiles that are increasing in popularity with this type of printing method. While the computerized printing equipment and inks are still slightly more expensive and slower to produce than more traditional methods, customers are willing to pay for the uniqueness of the customization gained through computerized heat transfer printing. As printing and ink technology advances, the printing speed will increase as well as the cost effectiveness of the process.

For printing, the colored paper is placed face down on the face of the greige goods. The dyestuffs used have a

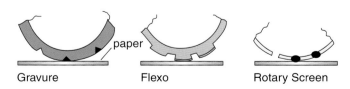

Figure 8.19 Techniques used for printing transfer paper.

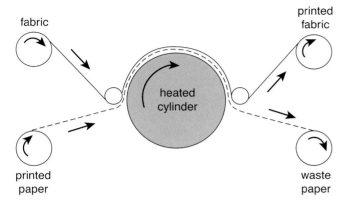

Figure 8.20 Heat transfer printing.
Courtesy of Celanese International Corporation.

Figure 8.21 Computerized digital printing.
Courtesy of US Sublimation.

higher affinity for the fibers than for the paper; when they are exposed to heat, they **sublime**, changing from a solid on the paper, to a gas, to a solid on the fabric. The procedure is fast and energy-efficient, and the fabric requires no afterwash because no excess dye-stuff remains.

The use of transfer printing as an industrial technique was initially encouraged by widespread consumer acceptance of polyester knits in the 1970s. The inherent elasticity of the fiber and the knitted structure resulted in relatively high relaxation shrinkage following release of the tension used in roller and screen printing operations. The shrinkage caused distortion of the printed patterns. In order to avoid this problem, manufacturers used transfer printing, which requires minimal fabric tensioning.

New classes of dyes have been produced that allow heat transfer printing on nylon fabrics in addition to polyester. The majority of fabrics printed with the heat trans-

fer method contain polyester, nylon, or blends with a high polyester content.

Acid Printing

Acid printing produces a color style known as a **burnt-out or etched-out print**. In this styling, the motifs and the ground have different levels of transparency. Because this technique is a chemically dependent process and one in which no colorants are added, some textile authorities prefer to classify the procedure as a finishing operation. On the other hand, because the technique produces a patterned effect, other authorities classify the procedure as a printing operation.

Fabrics used in an acid-printing operation must be composed of an acid-resistant fiber and an acid-degradable fiber; a blend of nylon and rayon is typically used. During printing, weak sulfuric acid (H_2SO_4) is printed on selected areas of the fabric, destroying or burning away the acid-degradable rayon. This chemical reaction changes the composition of these areas to 100 percent nylon, creating a higher level of transparency than is seen in the untreated areas. A burnt-out print is pictured in Figure 17.28, p. 296).

Fusion Printing

Fusion printing is a type of pigment printing used to secure colorants to the surface of fabrics composed of glass fiber. Colored acrylic resins are first printed on the surface of the fabric. Heat is then used to soften the thermoplastic compound and fuse it to the nonabsorbent glass. Like other pigment-printed designs, fusion-printed designs stand in slight relief.

Factors Affecting Apparent Color

Several factors have no direct effect on colorants but may alter perception of the original color of a product. Some of these factors, including changes in texture and soiling, relate to end-use activities; others, such as the source and quantity of light, are aspects of the interior environment. These variables alter the **apparent color** characteristics of interior textiles; the **actual color** characteristics are unchanged.

Following virtually every method of color application, the textile structures must be washed, rinsed, and dried. Dyed goods may be tentered, and some may be heat set. A secondary backing will be applied to tufted structures that were dyed. To restore distorted pile yarns to their upright position, the carpet will be passed against an angled blade that lifts the yarns. Cut pile textures may be sheared to create a uniform pile height and vacuumed to remove lint. A final inspection is made prior to shipment.

A colorant may be scientifically selected and precisely applied, but the immediate and long-term appearance of the color may nonetheless be affected by various environmental conditions and end-use activities. Some substances and conditions, such as cleaning agents and atmospheric contaminants, can produce changes in actual color characteristics. These variables, and test methods to measure their effects, are described in later units. The potential effects of various factors on apparent color characteristics are discussed below.

Light Source

Color may be the most important aesthetic variable in the selection of an interior textile product. Unfortunately, color choices are often made in a setting other than the one in which the product will be used. Inevitably, the lighting in the showroom or retail display area differs from that in the residential or commercial interior. Viewing a colored item in the separate locations, an observer may perceive marked differences in hue and value. Products to be used in an interior space should be color matched under lighting conditions that mimic those of the actual space to avoid the potential for mismatched colors once they are installed.

As mentioned earlier in this chapter, artificial light sources differ from each other and from natural light in the mixture of visible wavelengths they emit. While natural light emits almost equal quantities of all wavelengths, artificial sources emit unequal quantities. Incandescent lamps contain more of the warmer colors or longer wavelengths of red, orange, and yellow. Fluorescent lamps are available in a wide variety of colors and should be selected to enhance the colors of the space. Lamps are rated in two ways that will facilitate selection of the appropriate light to give the best appearance to a space. The first rating is the apparent color temperature, which describes the visual appearance of the light source and is expressed in degrees Kelvin (K). The lower the K value, the warmer the light will appear. Higher K values indicate a cooler or bluer appearance of the light. This measure does not indicate how accurately the light source will show color. The second rating is the color rendering index (CRI), which measures how well the lamp renders color. The CRI is expressed on a scale of 0 to 100, with 100 being the best color rendering. Incandescent lights have a CRI of 100, whereas fluorescents typically range from the 60s to the 90s. A CRI of 85 or higher is considered acceptable for fluorescent lamps in spaces where true colors are desirable. When comparing fluorescent light sources for color rendering, accurate comparisons can only be made when sources have the same color temperature. Both the apparent color temperature and the color rendering index should be provided by the manufacturer lamp specifications.

Quantity of Light

The quantity of light incident on a textile directly affects its color characteristics, especially its value: increases in the level of light produce apparent increases in the lightness of the surface. The amount of light emitted from artificial light sources can be controlled by dimmers and the wattages of lamps. The amount of natural light can be regulated by the compactness of the window coverings and the use of exterior awnings. Of course, the size of windows and skylights and their orientation to the seasonal angles of the sun are also very important.

In interior settings, the quantity of light is not limited to that radiating through the windows and emanating from artificial sources. A significant amount can be **indirect light** reflected from walls, ceilings, doors, and furnishings.

Natural light can appear cooler in the early part of the day and shift to a much warmer appearance as the day progresses; thus, colors may appear to change as the natural light illuminating them changes. This is especially apparent in the late afternoon. When coupled with the color variations available in artificial lighting, even minimal changes in the quantity of light affect the perception of an object's color value or intensity. Darker values may appear almost black in very low light levels, and much muted color intensity may appear gray. It is important to keep in mind that without light, there is no color; therefore, quantity of light can dramatically alter the perceived hue, value, and intensity.

Changes in Texture

The abrasive and crushing forces that textile structures may encounter during use produce changes in their original textural features. Such changes affect the apparent lightness and darkness of colored surfaces.

As people shift their seated positions and move their arms over upholstery fabrics, they can rupture the yarns and destroy prominent decorative effects. Such physical changes have no effect on the colorants, but the abraded areas appear darker because the pattern of light reflection is altered.

When fibers and yarns used in soft floor coverings are abraded by shoe soles, furniture casters, and the like, their surfaces may be roughened as dirt and sharp-edged grit particles grind severely against the fibers. Deterioration of the smoothness of the fibers and yarns results in deflection of incident light waves and a decrease in apparent value. A decrease in lightness is also apparent when abrasive forces rupture the loops of pile floor coverings and other pile fabrics, because the quantity of light reflected from the fiber ends is less than that reflected from the sides of the yarns in the intact loops.

Textural changes caused by crushing, especially of pile surfaces, may be less readily noticed or less objectionable if the compression is spread uniformly over the surface. But people tend to sit in the central portion of upholstered cushions, to repeatedly lean against the same region of back cushions, and to walk in established traffic patterns. These practices result in localized compression, which may gradually result in a nonuniform pile depth across the textile surface. This creates variations in the apparent value of the surface, with flattened areas appearing lighter and distorted areas appearing darker than undisturbed pile areas. Consumers and professionals can minimize the development of this unsightly effect by selecting pile fabrics made of resilient fibers and having high pile construction densities when a high level of use is expected.

Soil Accumulation

Residential and commercial consumers may be convinced that the original color of their textile product has changed when in fact it is merely masked by soil. As soil accumulates, especially on bright, solid-colored surfaces, the coloration appears duller. As is true for changes in texture, soiling is often localized, with heavier buildup occurring on the arms and seat cushions of furniture and in traffic lanes and entrance areas.

If soil accumulation is expected to be rapid, a multicolored surface that can mask the appearance of soil should be considered. Protective items, such as removable arm covers and walk-off mats, are also available.

Composition and Structural Variables

Different fibers have different color characteristics even when dyed the same color. This difference is the result of the chemical structures of the fibers and dyes used and the affinity the fibers have for the colorants. Increasing or decreasing yarn size causes accompanying changes in the intensity of the chosen hue. Similar effects appear with changes in pile construction density. Contract designers and architects must consider the potential impact on apparent color of specifying composition or construction features that differ from those characterizing the color samples.

Consumers and professionals must be aware that even yarns and fabrics intended to look identical generally have differences in color intensity when dyed or printed in different operations. To avoid this problem, the initial order should include sufficient yardage for the planned project.

Summary

For a particular hue to be perceived, the source of incident light must include a high concentration of wavelengths known to produce the hue, and the colorant used must reflect, not absorb, these waves. Although the dye chemist is responsible for selecting the correct colorant, consumers and professionals are responsible for examining the effects of the lighting conditions on the hue, value, and intensity of the colorant. Whenever possible, a swatch of fabric, a cushion, an arm cover, or a carpet sample should be examined in the end-use setting under a variety of lighting conditions. Consumers and professionals are also responsible for assessing the potential effects that such in-use variables as soil accumulation, abrasion, and crushing may have.

Dyers and printers are responsible for selecting and executing the appropriate method of color application. This method is largely determined by the features that the fabric stylist or contract designer specifies. Fiber dyeing is used when multicolored yarns are needed; yarn dyeing when plaid patterns or other types of woven-in motifs are to be produced; and screen printing when large-scale motifs and pattern repeats are specified. Ultimately, dye chemists, fabric stylists, and textile colorists must be guided by the color and styling preferences of the contemporary consumer.

Textile chemists, colorists, and engineers constantly strive to refine and improve methods of applying color to textile structures. The urgent need to conserve energy and reduce production costs encourages this effort. Moreover, the rapid shifting of consumer style preferences requires that colorists be capable of an equally speedy response to remain competitive.

Key Terms

acid printing
actual color
affinity
apparent color
apparent color temperature
astrojets
auxochromes
batch dyeing
batik fabric
beam dyeing
block printing
burnt-out or etched-out print
carpet winch
chroma
chromophores
color rendering index
color-sealed
continuous dyeing
crackle effect
cross dyeing
differential dyeing
digital (inkjet) printing
direct printing
discharge printing
discontinuous dyeing
doctor blade
dope dyeing
dye beck
dye liquor

dye migration
dye paste
dyed-in-the-wool
dyeing ranges
dyes or dyestuffs
electromagnetic spectrum
fiber or stock dyeing
flat-bed screen printing
frostiness
fusion printing
gum printing
heather
heat transfer printing
hue
ikat fabric
intensity
jet beck
jet printing
jet spraying
knit-de-knit space dyeing
liquor ratio
marled
mordant
moresque
nanometer
ombré
overprinting
package dyeing
package-injection technique

piece dyeing
pigment printing
pigments
producer-colored
resist printing
reused or indirect light
roller printing
rotary screen printing
screen printing
shade
skein dyeing
solution dyeing
space dyeing
Stalwart roller printing
sublime
sublistatic printing
TAK printing
tie-dyeing
tint
tippiness
transfer printing
union dyeing
value
variegated yarns
visible spectrum
warp printing
yarn dyeing
Zimmer flat-bed screen printing

Review Questions

1. Discuss the impact that increased energy costs and heightened concern for water conservation have had on the dyeing and printing industries.

2. Explain the difference between the electromagnetic spectrum and the visible spectrum.

3. What is meant by "wavelength?"

4. Explain how the combination of incident light waves and colorant present determine the hue we see.

5. Distinguish between tints and shades.

6. What is the role of a mordant?

7. Why are the terms color-sealed and producer-colored used as synonyms for solution dyed fibers?

8. What is a distinct advantage of solution dyeing? Why isn't it routinely used?

9. Explain how fiber or stock dyeing gave rise to the old adage "dyed-in-the-wool."

10. Differentiate among the following color styling terms: heather, marled, ombré, and moresque.

11. Why is the use of skein dyeing generally limited to smaller quantities of yarn?

12. Which operation is more efficient, discontinuous dyeing or continuous dyeing?

13. Why do dyers avoid creasing or sharply folding pile fabrics in dyeing operations?

14. Distinguish between tippiness and frostiness.

15. Explain the advantages of cross dyeing. What has led to the growth of both cross dyeing and union dyeing?

16. What are the resist media used in batik, tie-dye, and ikat fabrics?

17. Why can't large motifs and large pattern repeats be printed with rollers?

18. Discuss the advantages of rotary screen printing.

19. Why has the growth of heat transfer printing paralleled the growth of knitted fabric?

20. What do dyestuffs do when they sublime?

21. Could a blue fabric with white polka dots be made with either discharge printing or resist printing?

22. Explain the critical need to examine colored textiles in the setting in which they will be used or installed.

23. Cite examples where changes in texture occur and have concomitant changes in the apparent luster of a colored textile surface.

24. If different fibers and various sizes of yarns are dyed the same color, will they all look the same?

25. Explain the differences between pigments and dyestuffs.

Converting Interior Textile Greige Goods

Photo courtesy of Amy Willbanks, www.textilefabric.com.

■ **Colored goods** are more appealing than greige goods. However, until the goods are converted into finished fabrics, they may lack the aesthetic characteristics preferred by consumers of interior textile products. The fabrics may also lack structural stability, and they may not exhibit the service-related performance features sought by consumers or required by an agency with jurisdiction over their selection and installation.

In many cases, the finishing agents and processes to be used are specified by the fabric stylist, who has monitored consumer preferences for various aesthetic features, functional attributes, and care requirements. Sometimes they are dictated by the contract designer or architect, who may require an interior fabric with a unique appearance characteristic or a specific level of performance in end use. The appropriate selection and proper application of finishes greatly expands the variety of fabrics available to end-product producers and consumers.

Transforming Surface Appearance

With appropriate agents and processes, converters can transform the surface appearance of greige goods. When necessary they can remove or neutralize inherent color, and when specified they can control the level of surface luster, alter the fabric form, and embellish the fabric face.

Removing Inherent Color

The **inherent colors** of natural fibers are determined by nature. Unless the stylist specifies their retention, converters remove or neutralize them. When fashion colors are planned, the removal or neutralization precedes the addition of colorants, preventing the subsequent reflection of a mixture of light waves from two sources. When no colorants are to be added, the process precedes other conversion operations to prevent the natural colorants from interfering with the appearance of the finished fabrics.

Bleaching

Bleaching agents remove unwanted color from cellulosic fibers by oxidation. Hydrogen peroxide (H_2O_2) and sodium hypochlorite (NaCLO) are generally used.

Grassing

In **grassing**, sunlight removes inherent color from flax fibers spread over a grass field. Because grassing is slower than other bleaching methods, its use to prepare flax fibers for manufacture into fine tabletop products is quite rare today.

Controlling Surface Luster

Whereas manufactured fiber producers are responsible for controlling the **luster** of fabrics composed of their fibers—decreasing it by incorporating delusterant particles in the polymer solution—converters are generally charged with controlling the luster of fabrics composed of natural fibers. The conversion processes involved virtually always increase, rather than decrease, the quantity of light reflected from the fabric surface.

Friction Calendering

With the help of high levels of pressure and heat and a fast rate of revolution, highly polished metal cylinders, known as **calendering rollers** can be used to flatten the cross section of the yarns, thus increasing the amount of surface area available to reflect light. This change in the physical configuration of the yarns is illustrated in Figure 9.1. Friction calendering is frequently used to increase the reflection of sateen-woven drapery linings.

Beetling

Converters may use a process known as **beetling** to increase the surface luster of fabrics composed of flax. In the operation, heavy wooden planks hammer the fabric and flatten the cross section of the yarns, similar to the change shown in Figure 9.1. This process is often used on elaborately woven **damask** fabrics. The yarns in the varied interlacings reflect incident light in different directions and in different quantities; beetling augments the reflections and enables the viewer to see the distinctive patterns. The

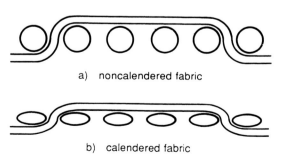

a) noncalendered fabric

b) calendered fabric

Figure 9.1 Effect of friction calendering on the cross section of yarns.

increased amount of light reflected from the floating yarns increases the visual distinction between the motifs and the ground (Figure 30.4, p. 464).

Glazing

In **glazing** operations, the surface of greige goods is impregnated with resin, shellac, or wax, and high-speed calendering rollers then buff and polish the surface. Glazing produces a smooth surface texture and a high level of surface luster. **Chintz** fabrics produced for use as upholstered furniture coverings and curtain fabrics are frequently glazed (Figure 17.3, p. 287).

Schreinering

The **schreinering** process creates fine hills and valleys on the surface of the fabric. In preparation for this mechanical treatment, calendering rollers are etched with fine, parallel lines that approximate the angle of yarn twist. The number of etched lines may range from 250 to 350 per inch. After schreinering, the modified surface develops a soft luster as light is reflected in different directions from the fine peaks and flattened valleys. The effect is not permanent unless heat or resin treatments are also performed. The use of these treatments is discussed below with embossing operations.

Moiréing

Moiréing is a special type of calendering used on filling-rib woven fabrics; frequently the fabric chosen is **taffeta**. Two fabrics are laid face to face and passed between paired calendering rollers. The pressure causes the mirrored ribs to impact on one another, slightly altering their form and changing the pattern of light reflection. Moiré fabrics are described as having a wood-grain appearance or a **water-marked effect** (Figure 9.2).

Introducing Three-dimensional Designs

Embossing, like schreinering and moiréing, involves the use of calendering rollers and alters the form of the greige goods. The changes produced by embossing are, however, greater than those produced by schreinering and moiréing. Embossing creates highly visible three-dimensional surface designs. Whether the changes are slight or marked, their preservation depends on the application of heat or resins.

Embossing

Embossing treatments convert flat, essentially two-dimensional fabrics into three-dimensional structures with convex and concave design forms. The planned designs are first etched into the surface of one calendering roller, which is then paired with a soft-surfaced roller. As the fabric passes between the two intermeshing rollers, it conforms to the etched forms. Greige goods are often embossed for use as decorative curtain fabrics.

Calendering rollers can be heated to emboss, schreiner, or moiré fabrics composed of thermoplastic fibers. In this way, the converter can introduce three-dimensional designs and heat set them in one operation. The heat loosens the strained lateral bonds of the distorted fibers, and the new lateral bonds that form as the fibers cool preserve the imposed configuration.

When fabrics composed of nonthermoplastic fibers, such as cotton and rayon, are processed, chemical cross-linking resins must be applied to preserve the imposed changes. The resins form lateral bonds, linking adjacent polymer chains and stabilizing the distorted configurations of the fibers. (This treatment, also used to improve resiliency, is schematized in Figure 9.20)

Changing the Orientation of Pile Yarns

Mechanical treatments are used to alter the upright positions of the pile yarns in virtually all pile fabrics. The realignment affects the reflective characteristics and tactile features of the pile layer.

Brushing, Smoothing, and Shearing

Brushing, smoothing, and shearing operations are used to align, smooth, and level the pile yarns in such fabrics as corduroy, velveteen, and velvet. In **brushing**, cylinders

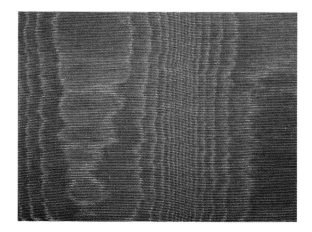

Figure 9.2 Moiré faille.
Courtesy of Amy Willbanks, www.textilefabric.com.

covered with straight wires revolve against the matted cut-pile surface, raising the pile yarns and aligning them parallel to one another. Brushing is followed by **smoothing**, laying the pile yarns in one direction. The results of these processes are essentially the same as those produced by combing and brushing hair. Because the angle at which the pile yarns are oriented to the base fabric is reduced, a surface feature known as **pile sweep**, **directional pile lay**, or **fabric nap** is introduced (Figure 9.3).

After the pile yarns have been brushed and smoothed, they undergo **shearing** to produce an even pile height. This is accomplished by passing the fabric against a rotating cylinder with a spiral blade. The shearing cylinder is similar to that in rotary lawn mowers.

Obviously, the tactile characteristics of a pile surface will be altered by these operations. The fabric will feel smooth when stroked in the direction of lay and rough when stroked in the opposite direction. And because the quantity of light waves reflected by the sides of the yarns will be significantly greater than that reflected by the cut tips, the level of luster observed will depend on the position of the viewer. The tactile and visual qualities of nap make it imperative that all fabric pieces cut for an item and all adjoining carpet lengths have the same direction of pile lay. Usually, for such items as upholstered furniture, pile yarns are oriented downward to help maintain the original appearance. The positioning of pile lay in carpet is discussed in Chapter 27.

Crushing

A mechanical finishing operation known as **crushing** is used on some velvet fabrics. In this operation, the pile yarns in some areas are crushed or flattened, while the pile yarns in the adjacent areas are oriented in various directions. Because each area reflects incident light waves in different quantities and in different directions, the surface has various levels of luster. A crushed velvet upholstery fabric is pictured in Figure 9.4.

Embellishing Fabric Surfaces

The appearance of greige goods, especially those to be used as curtain fabrics and tabletop accessories, is often embellished by the addition of fibers or yarns to their surfaces. Yarns are added in an embroidering operation, and fibers are added in a flocking operation.

Skilled artisans use textile yarns or fabrics to create such items as needlepoint pictures, crewel pillow coverings, quilts, doilies, throws, laces, and soft sculptures. They may hold onto completed projects for personal use or sell them in wholesale or retail markets. In some cases, an artist is commissioned to design and produce a needlework item for use as an accent in a specific interior, such as a corporate office, an airport lounge, or a bank.

Hand Needleworking

Fiber artists use various techniques to embellish fabric surfaces for use as accents in interiors. Among these are needlepoint stitching, embroidering, and appliquéing.

Needlepoint Stitching In **needlepoint stitching**, also referred to as **canvas embroidering**, yarns are used to cover all or part of the surface of a canvas fabric. Typically, the surface has a solid-colored ground surrounding

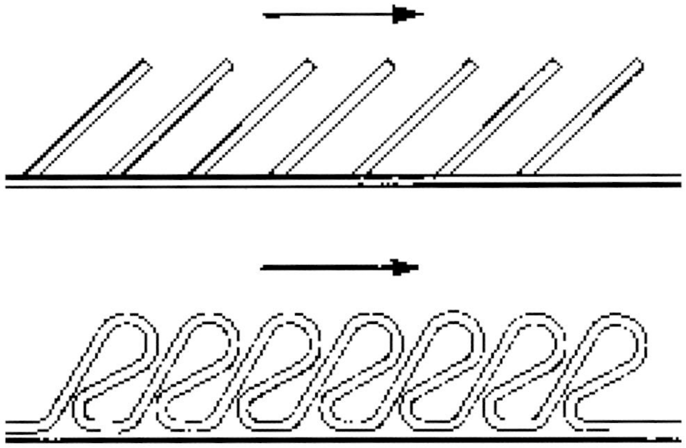

Figure 9.3 Directional pile lay, pile sweep, or fabric nap.

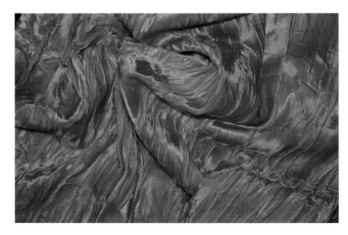

Figure 9.4 Crushed velvet.
Courtesy of Amy Willbanks, www.textilefabric.com.

a multicolored, detailed pattern (Figure 9.5), or the design repeats identical or mirror-image geometric motifs.

Needlepoint projects may be done with either **single-mesh canvas**, which is plain woven, or **double-mesh (penelope) canvas**, which has closely spaced pairs of warp and filling yarns. The term *mesh* refers to one intersection of the yarns used in the canvas; the compactness of construction of the fabric is designated by the number of **meshes per inch**. **Fine canvas**, with 18 or more meshes per inch, is used for petitpoint work. These projects usually have small motifs and are framed and hung as wall accents or placed on tabletops. **Medium canvas**, with 10 or 12 meshes per inch, is used in such needlepoint items as dining chair seat coverings, a rendition of a company logo, and backgammon and other game boards. **Coarse canvas**, with 3 to 7 meshes per inch, is used to construct rugs.

Figure 9.5 Needlepoint wallhanging. Needlepoint courtesy of Trudy Weldy.

Needlepoint work uses Persian yarns and tapestry yarns. **Persian yarns** are loosely twisted three-ply strands composed of wool. Frequently, the plied yarns are untwisted and a single strand is used in stitching. **Tapestry yarns** are highly twisted, four-ply yarns, which are used without being separated. Examples of frequently used needlepoint stitches are shown in Figure 9.6.

Hand Embroidering   **Hand embroidering** is the stitching of colored yarns in decorative patterns on a portion of a base fabric, leaving the other portion unadorned to serve as the ground and accentuate the slightly raised motifs. Embroidered fabrics are used as the outer coverings of decorative pillows and as cases for bed pillows. They are also framed and hung as wall accents, and cut and finished for use as tabletop accessories.

Crewel, floss, pearl, and candlewick yarns are used for embroidery work. **Crewel yarns** are fine, two-ply strands composed of wool; **floss yarns** are loosely twisted, six-ply strands composed of mercerized cotton; **pearl yarns** are fine cords formed by plying three two-ply yarns composed of mercerized cotton; and **candlewick yarns** are four-ply yarns composed of unmercerized cotton. Since these yarns vary in texture, size, and luster, they produce distinct appearances when used in any of the many embroidery stitches, examples of which are illustrated in Figure 9.7.

Embroidery techniques are primarily distinguished by the type of yarn used, not by differences in the stitches used. One exception is **candlewicking**, in which the design motifs are created by the extensive use of French knots. The knots are used singly, but collectively they create a recognizable pattern (Figure 9.8).

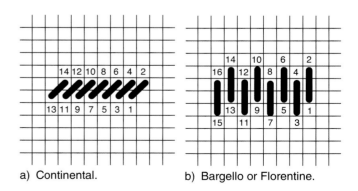

a) Continental.   b) Bargello or Florentine.

Figure 9.6 Frequently used needlepoint stitches.

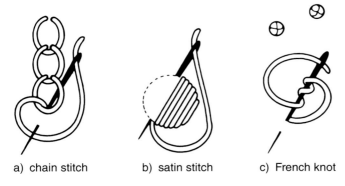

a) chain stitch   b) satin stitch   c) French knot

Figure 9.7 Common embroidery stitches.

Figure 9.8 Candlewicking embroidery used to embellish the outer covering of a decorative pillow. Courtesy of www.garyclarkedesigns.com.au.

Appliquéing In most **appliqué work**, shaped pieces of coordinating or contrasting fabric are placed over the face of a second fabric. The raw edges are turned under and blind stitches or embroidery stitches are used to secure the applique. Appliquéd fabrics are constructed into decorative pillow coverings, bedspreads, and tablecloths, and are used as the face fabric in quilts.

An intricate appliqué technique is employed by needlework artisans in South America to produce molas. **Molas** have multiple layers of fabric and are typically charac-terized by highly stylized animal motifs (Figure 9.9a,b). Various colors of fabrics are layered and a large, shaped area is cut from the top fabric. The raw edges are turned under, and the folded edge is stitched to the second fabric. A slightly smaller shape is then cut from the second fabric and the raw edges are turned and stitched to the third fabric; this **reverse appliqué** sequence is repeated until the base fabric is reached. Molas are prized as framed wall accents and decorative pillow coverings.

Machine Embroidering

Because hand embroidering, like hand printing, is labor- and time-intensive, **machine embroidering** is employed to embellish fabric surfaces with motifs resembling those created by artisans. Many machine-embroidered curtain and drapery fabrics are stitched on Schiffli machines. Each of these machines is equipped with more than a thousand needles that operate at right angles to the base fabric. For multicolored motifs, each needle is threaded with a specific color of yarn; control mechanisms similar to those used on the dobby loom are programmed with the planned design shapes and shift the position of the fabric during the embroidering operation.

Flocking

In **flocking** operations, extremely short fibers, known as **flock**, are embedded in an adhesive or resin compound. In curtain and drapery fabrics, the flock is generally used to create raised motifs and pattern repeats (Figure 9.10a and b.) In simulated suede upholstery fabrics (Figure 13.30, p. 230) and some blankets and floor mats, the flock is applied to the entire fabric surface. Both types of flock placement are used in textile wallcoverings.

In preparation for flocking, an adhesive or resin is printed on all areas of the greige goods to be flocked. In **mechanical flocking** processes, the flock is then sifted through a screen to the coated surface (Figure 9.11). Beater bars encourage the short fibers to orient themselves perpendicularly to the base fabric. In **electrostatic flocking** operations, an electrostatic field induces the flock to embed itself into the coating (Figure 13.28, p. 229).

Quilting

Commercial quilting may be done by sewing or by melding. The quilting operation serves to join the separate layers (Figure 9.14b) and sometimes to impart a surface pattern as well.

a)

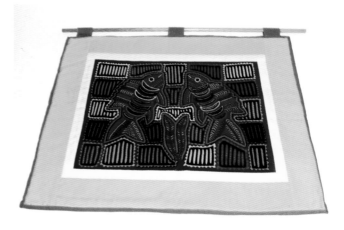

b)

Figure 9.9 *Mola, a textile accent produced by a reverse appliqué technique.*
a) Courtesy of Rita Smith, www.molaartandcrafts.com. b) Courtesy of Lainey Wilkins, www.fabricandwoodideas.com.

Machine stitching and pinsonic melding are used in commercial quilting operations. The equipment used in **machine stitching** operates in the same manner as a conventional sewing machine, except that many needles stitch at the same time. In **pinsonic melding**, a wide cylinder with raised designs is rolled over the multilayer structure while heat and sound waves meld the layers at the contact points. The meld points simulate the appearance of sewn quilting stitches (Figure 9.12).

Three patterns are typical of commercial quilting. In **channel quilting**, the stitches or meld points are aligned in parallel rows (Figure 9.13a). In **pattern quilting** (Figures 9.13b, c and 9.14a), the quilting lines develop a surface pattern with slightly three-dimensional motifs. Such quilting is frequently used on solid-covered fabrics. In **outline quilting** (Figure 9.13d), the stitches follow the outline of pattern motifs, making them stand in slight relief.

Hand Quilting With quilting stitches, artisans join three layers: a face fabric, a fibrous batting, and a backing or lining fabric. The face fabric may be an

a) Localized flocking pattern on vinyl.

Figure 9.10 Flocked vinyl.
Courtesy of Amy Willbanks, www.textilefabric.com.

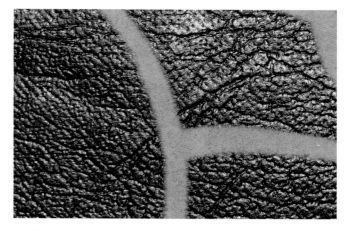

b) Close-up view of localized flocking.

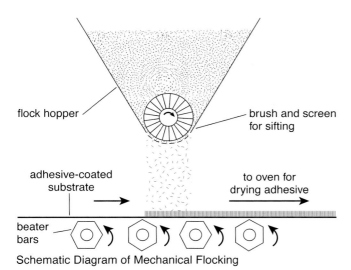

Schematic Diagram of Mechanical Flocking

Figure 9.11 Mechanical flocking.
Courtesy of Ascend Performance Materials.

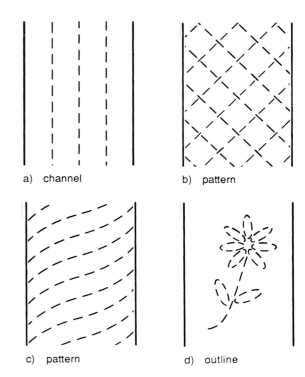

a) channel   b) pattern

c) pattern   d) outline

Figure 9.13 Quilting patterns.

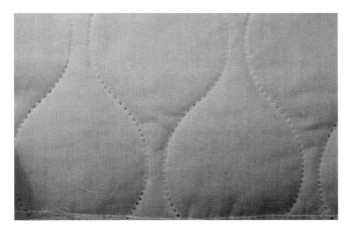

Figure 9.12 Pinsonic quilted.
Courtesy of Amy Willbanks, www.textilefabric.com.

appliquéd fabric, a solid-colored or printed fabric, or constructed of small pieces of coordinated fabrics. (Figure 29.13, p. 454.) Both commercial and hand-stitched quilts are discussed in Chapter 29.

Improving the Quality and Serviceability of Structural Features

Converters use finishing procedures to improve the quality and potential serviceability of the structural features of greige goods. They can, for example, use a mechanical process to improve the alignment of yarns in woven fabrics; a heat setting operation to stabilize the shape and form of fabrics composed of thermoplastic fibers; and small flames to minimize the formation of pills on fabrics composed of cellulosic fibers.

Correcting Fabric Grain

When all the warp yarns are not perpendicular to all the filling yarns in a biaxially woven fabric, the fabric is said to be **off-grain**. Off-grain fabrics have a negative effect on appearance when used in the construction of such end products as upholstered furniture, curtains, draperies, and tabletop accessories. For example, a drapery fabric with a **bowed yarn alignment** produces treatments that appear to sag, and, as illustrated in Figure 9.15a, an undulating or waving effect could develop if several widths are used. Fabrics with a **skewed yarn alignment** produce a lopsided appearance, as shown in Figure 9.15b, and attempts to align crosswise pattern repeats when seaming fabric widths only compound the problem. The negative effects of off-grain upholstery fabrics are illustrated in Figure 14.1, p. 235.

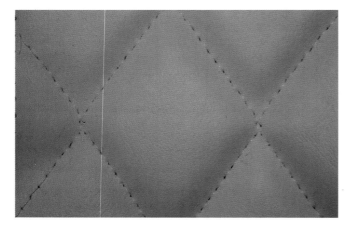

a) Stitched, quilted.

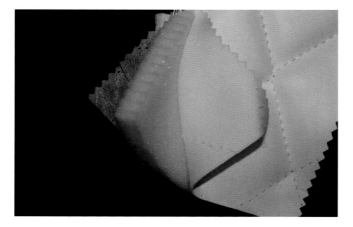

b) Layers of a quilted fabric.

Figure 9.14 Quilted vinyl and layers of a quilted fabric. Courtesy of Amy Willbanks, www.textilefabric.com.

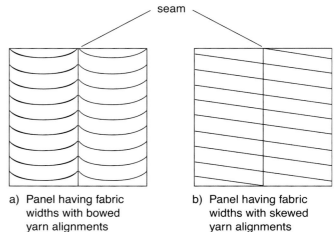

a) Panel having fabric widths with bowed yarn alignments

b) Panel having fabric widths with skewed yarn alignments

Figure 9.15 Effects of bowed and skewed yarn alignments on the appearance of window treatments.

Tentering

To minimize distortions resulting from bow and skew, converters use a mechanical finishing process known as **tentering**. In this operation, the fabric is mounted full-width on a tenter frame. Tension is applied to properly align the warp and filling yarns, and the fabric is then steamed and passed through a heated oven and dried. Today, computer-assisted mechanisms often monitor and control the alignment of the yarns during the operation. Small holes are visible in the selvage areas of tentered fabrics, indicating where the fabric was secured by pins or metal clips.

When greige goods are to be printed, tentering should precede the printing operation. Correcting the grain of printed fabrics would distort the shapes of the motifs and the positions of the pattern repeats.

Minimizing Yarn Slippage

If plain weave and other simple fabrics are produced from smooth, multifilament yarns in loose constructions, converters may apply an adhesive compound, such as polyurethane, polyacrylonitrile, or latex, to the fabric back. The coating helps to prevent yarn slippage and yarn raveling. **Yarn slippage** is the sliding or "traveling" of warp or filling yarns, shown in Figure 9.16. In patterned coverings, slippage distorts the shapes and details of the design motifs. Yarn slippage may also occur at seamlines, with the yarns moving away from the stitching and leaving a gap or opening; a testing procedure for evaluating slippage at seamlines is described in Chapter 14.

Yarn raveling occurs when yarns fall from cut edges of fabrics. This becomes a problem in upholstery when seam allowances have been closely trimmed to reduce bulk and the fabric has been pulled to fit smoothly over the frame and filling. The stress exerted on the seams with use may force the yarns in the narrow seam allowances to slide off the cut edge, weakening the seam and causing the stitching to rupture.

Stabilizing Fabric Shape

A textile structure that maintains its original size and shape after use and care is said to have **dimensional stability**. Dimensionally stable fabrics do not exhibit growth, bag-

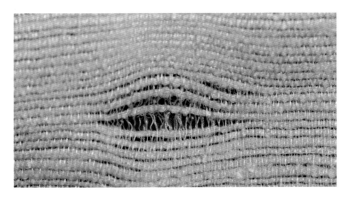

Figure 9.16 Yarn slippage.
Courtesy of Amy Willbanks, www.textilefabric.com.

ging or sagging from unrecovered stretch—nor do they exhibit shrinkage.

With most interior textile fabrics, there is great concern for the potential problems caused by relaxation shrinkage, and to a lesser extent for those caused by residual shrinkage. **Residual shrinkage** is shrinkage of the fibers; it generally occurs over time in such frequently laundered items as towels and table linens. **Relaxation shrinkage** occurs when strained components relax after the stress forces involved in various manufacturing processes are released.

Several processes subject fibers and yarns to stress, deforming and straining them. Extruding and drawing strain the polymer chains in manufactured filaments, while drawing out and spinning can strain spun yarns. During weaving, tension introduces strain to the warp yarns, and bobbin tensioning devices may impart strain to the filling yarns. The pulling and forcing of yarns and fabrics through dyeing or printing and finishing operations can add various amounts of strain.

The behavior of strained fabric components is similar to that of elastic bands that have been stretched, but there is a marked difference between the rates at which the two materials recover from imposed deformations. When the stretching force is released from an elastic band, it will generally exhibit immediate and complete relaxation shrinkage, returning to its original length. By contrast, when manufacturing stress forces are released, textile components relax only gradually and incompletely. Unless the imposed strain has been released or the fabric components have been intentionally stabilized prior to shipment to the end product producer or fabric retailer, full recovery may not occur until sometime during end use, destroying the appearance or fit of the fabric.

Converters encourage relaxation of strained components with heat setting, fulling, and compressive shrinkage operations. The technique used is determined by the fiber composition of the greige goods.

Heat Setting

Fabrics composed of thermoplastic fibers can be stabilized by **heat setting**. Unless textured yarns have been used, this procedure is normally carried out during tentering of the greige goods to ensure that the strains introduced during fabrication are released.

When heat setting is combined with tentering, converters must correctly align the warp and filling yarns in woven structures. Fabrics that have been heat set off-grain cannot be straightened.

Fulling

Fabrics composed of wool fibers are encouraged to relax by a finishing process known as **fulling**. The goods are exposed to controlled conditions of moisture, heat, and pressure, which cause the yarns to relax and shrink, resulting in a fuller, more compact fabric. Although this procedure reduces the potential for relaxation shrinkage of the fabrics in end use, it does not reduce the possibility of felting shrinkage.

Compressive Shrinkage Treatments

The dimensional stability of fabrics composed of cotton can be improved during tentering or with a **compressive shrinkage treatment**. In compressive shrinkage procedures, the greige goods are laid over a supporting fabric, moistened, and mechanically shifted to encourage relaxation of the yarns. Labeling practices that distinguish fabrics stabilized by such treatments are discussed in Chapter 10.

During tentering, cotton yard goods can be compressed lengthwise by feeding them onto the metal pins at a faster rate than the pins are moving forward. This technique encourages the warp yarns to relax; in some cases, a 10-yard length of fabric can shrink to 8 yards. Crosswise relaxation can be encouraged by reducing the distance between the parallel rows of tenter pins.

Heat-setting operations help to minimize bagging and sagging of fabrics composed of thermoplastic fibers; fulling and compressive shrinkage treatments have little or no effect on this performance feature. Wool fibers are highly elastic and fabrics composed of them recover well after being stressed. However, cellulosic fibers, including cotton, flax, and rayon, have comparatively low elasticity and may exhibit excessive growth.

Figure 9.17 Pilling on an acrylic afghan.
Courtesy of Hannah Willbanks.

Improving Texture Retention

As explained earlier in this chapter, smoothing and crushing operations are used to alter the positions of pile yarns, producing the depth, directional lay, and reflective features specified by the stylist and preferred by the consumer. The serviceability of pile fabrics depends on the extent to which these features are retained. For long-term retention, the pile yarns must be resilient. In fabrics composed of thermoplastic fibers, heat setting can be used to engineer this performance property. In fabrics composed of cotton, such as corduroy and velveteen, this feature can be improved by using a high pile construction density, a structural characteristic that of course is controlled by the fabric manufacturer, not by the converter. Texture retention can also be improved by blending a resilient fiber such as nylon or polyester with the cellulosic fiber.

Reducing Pilling

As discussed in Chapter 3, **pilling** occurs when abrasive forces cause free fibers and fiber ends to roll up into minute balls that tend to cling to the surface of the fabric (Figure 9.17). These pills can be reduced by singeing the greige goods. In **singeing**, small gas flames are used to burn away loose fibers, bits of lint, and fiber ends from fabrics composed of cotton, flax, rayon, hemp or lyocell. Fabrics made of thermoplastic fibers cannot be singed with flames because the intense heat would melt the base fabric; instead, hot, smooth metal plates are used to soften and carefully shrink the protruding fibers so that they can be sheared from the surface. Fabrics composed of wool or silk are not singed because these fibers decompose and form a crusty residue when exposed to flames.

Engineering Functional Performance

Converters use numerous finishing agents and treatments to develop specific functional properties—performance features that are not characteristic of the components and cannot be introduced by improving the structural features of the greige goods. These functional properties improve the service-related performance of textile fabrics; they include, for example, retarding the rate and level of soil accumulation, minimizing ironing, and so on. Such properties are primarily service-related, but are frequently important to consumer selection, and may lead to a preference for one firm's product over that of another.

Increasing Apparent Brightness

The use of **optical brighteners** to increase the **apparent whiteness and brightness** of manufactured fibers was discussed in Chapter 3. Brighteners also can be added by the converter as a surface application, or by the consumer who chooses a detergent containing brighteners. In any case, the effectiveness of the brighteners is dependent upon the nature of the light waves incident on the textile surface.

Reducing Fiber Flammability

Flame resistance is engineered in natural cellulosic fibers by adding **flame retardants** to the greige goods. These agents are normally based on phosphorous or nitrogen and include various amounts of such compounds as diammonium phosphate ($(NH_4)_2HPO_4$), ammonium sulfate ($(NH_4)_2SO_4$), and boric acid (H_3BO_3). These compounds inhibit or halt the combustion process at some stage in the cycle. Flame resistance is engineered in manufactured fibers by incorporating a compound based chlorine or bromine in the polymer solution prior to extrusion.

Increasing Insulative Value

The insulative value of textile structures can be increased by a mechanical process known as napping. It can also be increased by applying a cellular coating to the face or back of a fabric.

Napping

In **napping** operations, the ends of many fibers are raised to the surface; fabrics napped on both sides are called **flannel**, those napped on one side are called **flannelette**. In use, the raised fibers entrap air and provide thermal insulation, while also providing a soft hand and pleasing appearance.

Applying Coatings

Converters frequently apply foamed acrylic compounds to the back of drapery fabrics and drapery lining fabrics to increase their insulative value (Figure 17.32, p. 298). There is, however, a concomitant decrease in drapability of the fabric. The effectiveness of this treatment is discussed in Chapter 26.

Reducing Microbial Action

The growing awareness of antimicrobials in the textile industry has come from the demand to improve overall functionality of textiles. Hangtags and labels to get the customers' attention are a fairly recent marketing tool. Information regarding soft flooring microbial control can be found in Chapter 26 (Figure 9.18).

Increasing Moisture Absorption

To improve the ability of cellulosic fibers, especially cotton, to absorb moisture, converters use a process known as mercerization. This chemical treatment also increases the luster of the fibers and their ability to withstand stress loads and abrasive forces.

Mercerizing

In **mercerization**, threads, yarns, or fabrics are exposed to sodium hydroxide (NaOH) or liquid ammonia while they are held under tension to prevent excessive shrinkage. This treatment alters various internal and external structural features of the fibers, producing changes in their properties. The degree of orientation is increased, increasing the strength or tenacity of the fibers, and the level of crystallinity is reduced, increasing the moisture absorption. As shown in Figure 3.2b, p. 29, mercerized cotton has a more rounded cross-sectional shape and fewer longitudinal twists than unmercerized cotton. These external features may be compared with the flat shape and highly twisted configuration characterizing unmercerized cotton. Although flat cross sections typically reflect higher amounts of incident light than do round cross sections, removal of the twist results in increased luster.

Because mercerization improves the absorption, as well as the luster and strength, of cotton, the finish is routinely used on greige towelings and sheetings. Colorants are generally applied after mercerization, using the increased absorbency to develop deep, rich color characteristics.

Repelling Moths

Insects, most notably moth and carpet beetle larvae, thrive on wool fibers after they break the **disulfide cross links** (-S-S-) contained in the cystine monomer. Moths and beetles prefer to live and breed in dark places, where the larvae will be undisturbed and can sustain themselves on the nutrients obtained from the wool fibers. In unprotected wool carpet the damage is more likely to be seen under rarely moved furniture, and in wool blankets and wool upholstery the attack generally occurs during storage. Today, all domestic wool floor coverings are treated to repel these insects, but residential and commercial consumers must examine the labels of imported products to confirm the use of such treatments.

Converters render wool fiber durably moth resistant by chemically modifying the disulfide linkage, making the

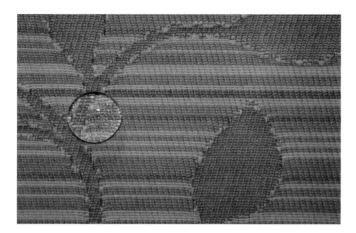

Figure 9.18 Crypton upholstery fabric is stain-, water-, and bacteria-resistant.
Courtesy of Amy Willbanks, www.textilefabric.com.

 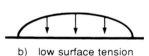

a) high surface tension   b) low surface tension

Figure 9.19 Surface tension and fabric wetting.

fiber indigestible. Several compounds can be used, including **permethrin**. Because mothproofing treatments are generally combined with dyeing or finishing operations to control processing costs, the protective agents become integral parts of the fibers.

Naphthalene compounds, available in such familiar forms as moth balls, crystals, blocks, and sprays, can be used in storage areas to protect wool products from attack by moth larvae. Naphthalene fumes do not kill moth adults or larvae; rather they repel them by giving the wool fibers and the immediate area a noxious odor, so unattractive to moths that they will seek other places for laying their eggs. A note should be added about safety: if internalized, naphthalene compounds are potentially hazardous to humans. To prevent their being ingested by young children or companion animals, moth balls and crystals may be knotted inside sheer hosiery; the porous construction of the hosiery will not hinder the effectiveness of the fumes.

Increasing Water Repellency

Converters can apply **silicone compounds** to reduce the rate at which textile structures absorb water. Because these compounds offer little or no protection from oily soiling and staining, their use is diminishing in favor of fluorocarbon compounds, which provide both water and soil resistance. Cryton upholstery fabric is stain, water, and bacteria resistant (Figure 9.18).

Imparting Soil and Stain Resistance

Many textile authorities differentiate "soil" and "stain" on the basis of how tenaciously the soil or dirt clings to the textile structure. When dirt or other foreign matter is mechanically held and comparatively easy to remove, it is known as **soil**; when the dirt becomes chemically bonded to the fiber surfaces and is comparatively difficult to remove, it is called a **stain**. Converters seek to prevent staining by using compounds that enable the fibers to repel or resist soil by increasing surface tension or by blocking sites where selected foreign matter could chemically bond.

Fluorocarbon compounds are used extensively to help textile fibers and fabrics repel or resist soil accumulation. These agents make the textile component more **oleophobic** or oil-hating, as well as more **hydrophobic**. Rather than spreading over the fabric surface, wetting it, and penetrating into the fibers and yarns, spilled water and oily compounds bead up, maintaining their surface tension. As schematized in Figure 9.19a, **high surface tension** means that the molecules in the foreign matter have a higher affinity for one another than for the fibers. Similar action can be observed when raindrops bead up on a waxed car surface.

Spilled liquids should be absorbed immediately from the surface because the protection is temporary; the rate of absorption is slowed, not halted. As the surface tension gradually lowers, the droplets will spread, as shown in Figure 9.19b, wetting and potentially staining the fabric.

Trade names identifying fluorocarbon finishing compounds include Scotchgard®, produced by the 3M Company, and Teflon® and ZePel®, produced by DuPont.

Colorless acid dyes are used to help carpet fibers resist staining. Here, the carpet is saturated with a dyestuff that attaches itself to acid-receptive sites on the fibers. As these compounds occupy sites to which foreign matter, especially such foods as acid-colored fruit drinks, could attach, staining is prevented. Trade names identifying carpet protected in this manner include StainMaster®, owned by DuPont; and Wear Dated®, owned by Monsanto.

Introducing Soil Release

Soil release compounds may be used to help fibers release food stains. These compounds are designed to function in unison with detergent molecules in the laundry solution. The detergent molecules will reduce the surface tension of the water; in effect, this makes the water "wetter" by causing it to spread rather than bead. At the same time, the fluorocarbon-based finishing agent will increase the surface energy of the fibers, making them more hydrophilic, so the water can more readily carry the detergent molecules into the fiber crevices and emulsify and remove the soil and stain material.

Improving Smoothness Retention

The extent to which textile fabrics retain their original smoothness in use and after care depends on their ability to recover from the strains and deformations imposed by such stress forces as bending, folding, twisting, and crushing. Fabrics exhibiting a high level of recovery are resilient; in effect, they "remember" their original configuration. **Resiliency** and "memory" can be engineered by applying heat or by incorporating resins in a durable press finishing operation.

Heat Setting

The application of heat to stabilize the dimensions of fabrics composed of thermoplastic fibers was discussed earlier in this chapter. Heat setting also can be used to help flat fabrics remain smooth and wrinkle-free, minimizing the need for ironing.

Durable Press Finishing

Smooth fabrics composed of cotton, flax, or rayon exhibit extremely poor recovery when crushed, folded, or wrinkled, and remain crumpled. To compensate for this poor resiliency, converters use **durable press finishing** treatments with the greige goods.

In these chemical finishing processes, the fabrics are impregnated with a **resin or reactant compound**, which has generally been a formaldehyde-based substance. Heat is then used to cure the compound, causing it to form strong cross links between the polymer chains within the cellulosic fibers. These bonds, schematized in Figure 9.20, function in the same manner as those found in wool and thermoplastic fibers. They stabilize the positions of the chains and introduce to the fibers the so-called "memory" for whatever shape and form they were in when heat-cured.

Relatively high amounts of resin must be applied to ensure no-iron performance. While the resin significantly improves the resiliency, it also decreases absorption and increases soil retention. There may be a temporary "fishy" odor that remains until any unreacted resin is washed away. The resin weakens the fibers, lowering their abrasion resistance and shortening their use-life. The loss in abrasion resistance also can result in a **frosted** appearance. This unsightly problem occurs when abrasive forces remove some of the resin-weakened cellulosic fibers: as the

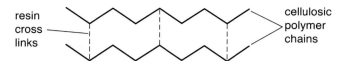

Figure 9.20 Resin cross links introduced into cellulosic fibers to improve their resiliency.

color carried by the fibers is also removed, the abraded area appears faded and lighter than the adjacent areas. Although frosting is a color-related problem, it is the result of fiber failure, not of colorant failure.

To compensate for the decreased strength and abrasion resistance suffered by the cellulosic fibers, manufacturers often blend them with polyester fiber. The polyester extends the wear-life of the fabric. It does not strengthen the cellulosic components. Together with the potential for loss of the cellulosic fiber, development of a frosted appearance remains a possibility in blends.

Currently, various federal agencies, scientific associations, chemical suppliers, and product manufacturers are investigating the possibility that health hazards may be associated with the use of formaldehyde compounds and their subsequent release from durable press fabrics. Some consumers have, in fact, reported an allergic reaction to such resins. Members of the textile industry are now supporting research activities focused on the development and perfection of new durable press finishing agents and procedures.

Summary

Finishing operations are important to the commercial success of all segments of the interior textile industry. They convert greige goods into finished fabrics exhibiting the appearance features, structural qualities, and functional performance properties preferred by contemporary consumers or mandated by regulatory agencies.

The final conversion process is inspection: trained personnel carefully examine the finished fabrics for flaws and defects, rejecting those that contain an unacceptable number of irreparable defects. Together, quality-control tests and visual examinations help to ensure acceptance of the fabrics by end product producers and residential and commercial consumers. These evaluations also help suppliers and producers to determine the advisability of labeling the product with their company name or a name owned by their company. If the qualities of the finished fabrics are unacceptable, their suppliers and producers may be denied the use of voluntary labeling, an effective marketing tool discussed in the following chapter.

Key Terms

antimicrobial chemicals
apparent whiteness and brightness
appliqué work
appliqué, reverse
bacteria
beetling
bleaching agents
bowed yarn alignment
brushing
calendering rollers
candlewicking
candlewick yarns
canvas embroidering
channel quilting
chintz
coarse canvas
commercial quilting
compressive shrinkage treatment
crewel yarns
crushing
damask
dimensional stability
directional pile lay
disulfide cross links
double-mesh (penelope) canvas
durable press finishing
electrostatic flocking
embossing
embroidering
fabric nap
fine canvas
flame resistance

flame retardant
flannel
flannelette
flock
flocking
floss yarns
fluorocarbon compounds
frosting
fulling
fungi
glazing
growth
grassing
hand embroidering
heat setting
high surface tension
hydrophobic
inherent color
luster
machine embroidering
machine stitching
mechanical flocking
medium canvas
mercerization
meshes per inch
microbes
moiréing
molas
naphthalene
napping
needlepoint stitching
off-grain

oleophobic
optical brighteners
outline quilting
pattern quilting
pearl yarns
permethrin
Persian yarns
pile sweep
pilling
pinsonic melding
relaxation shrinkage
residual shrinkage
resiliency
resin or reactant compounds
schreinering
shearing
silicone compounds
singeing
single-mesh canvas
skewed yarn alignment
smoothing
soil
soil release
spectrum
stain
taffeta
tapestry yarns
tentering
water-marked effect
yarn raveling
yarn slippage

Review Questions

1. Explain the physical changes to fibers and yarns imposed by friction calendering, beetling, schreinering, and moiréing. Are these changes permanent?

2. Virtually all moiré fabric is one color. How is it possible, then, to see a water-marked or wood-grain pattern on the fabric surface?

3. Discuss the effect of pile sweep, pile lay, or fabric nap on the luster of a fabric. Why is it critical to carefully position adjoining fabric pieces or carpet lengths having directional pile lay?

4. Cite examples or commercial locations of textile works created by artisans that you have seen.

5. Explain what is meant by "reverse" appliqué.

6. Differentiate between mechanical flocking processes and electrostatic flocking operations.

7. Sketch some applications of interior textile products, such as a window treatment or a piece of upholstered furniture. Then, add a bowed and a skewed fabric to each and note the appearance. Does this help you to appreciate the critical need for grain-straight fabrics, especially those having strong motifs, stripes, or plaids?

8. Why are production costs lowered when converters combine tentering and heat setting?

9. Sketch a simple motif, one representing part of a pattern repeat. Now, introduce yarn traveling. Does the design take on a stained appearance?

10. Why is it critically important to release imposed strain in textile fibers, yarns, and fabrics?

11. Identify ways to improve texture retention.

12. Why is singeing useful in reducing pilling? Does it reduce the number of pills or does it simply make them easier to remove?

13. Are the approaches for reducing the flammability of natural and manufactured fibers different?

14. In what end-use applications is it highly advisable to reduce microbial action?

15. How does mercerization increase the absorption and dyeability of cellulosic fibers? How does it extend the wear-life of the fibers? What effect does it have on the luster of cotton fibers?

16. How do naphthalene compounds protect wool fiber from moth damage? How do converters render wool fibers permanently mothproof?

17. Explain the type of protection offered by silicone compounds and by fluorocarbon compounds.

18. What role does surface tension play in water and soil repellency?

19. How do colorless acid dyes reduce staining? How would a consumer know whether this stain resistant method had been used?

20. Explain how "memory" is introduced to fabrics composed of thermoplastic fibers and to fabrics composed of cellulosic fibers.

21. Differentiate among tippiness, frostiness, and frosting.

22. Why is frosting said to be caused by failure of the fiber not the colorant?

Interior Textile Product Labeling

Photo courtesy of Christian Fischbacher, www.fischbacher.com.

■ **Textile markets are highly** competitive: companies must utilize effective marketing techniques to succeed at capturing an adequate share of the consumer market. Several corporations have concentrated their competitive efforts on developing distinctive methods of product labeling. Trade associations have also undertaken similar efforts on behalf of their member firms. Often, a name or symbol is added to the label to increase product recognition; sometimes information about such things as quality, care, reliability, and special performance features is put on the label. Such information assists the consumer and design professional in successfully choosing textile products which meet their private needs or which conform with specification requirements. The immediate goal of this voluntary, optional labeling is to secure the initial purchase of a firm's products; the long-term goal is to encourage repeated selection of products bearing the firm's label.

Use of voluntary product labeling is optional, but compliance with certain prescribed commercial practices is not. Textile companies must avoid unfair and deceptive marketing practices and activities that would weaken the competitive position of an industry member and restrain trade illegally. To ensure that consumers and members of the industry are protected from abusive practices, the United States Congress and the Federal Trade Commission have established labeling rules and guidelines, as well as antitrust regulations.

Federal Trade Commission

The **Federal Trade Commission (FTC)** was created by an act of Congress in 1914.[1] Initially, the Commission was empowered and directed to prevent "unfair methods of competition in commerce." The scope of the Commission's work was expanded by the Wheeler-Lea Act of 1938 also to include "unfair or deceptive acts or practices." An example of such a practice is the failure to disclose that a product or material is not what it appears to be; for instance, disclosure is necessary for a nonleather fabric resembling leather.

Responsibilities and Powers

Improvements in the Commission's operations and revisions of its jurisdiction, responsibilities, and powers have continued over the years. Today, the FTC has the responsibility to investigate commercial trade practices, to encourage voluntary corrective action and compliance, and to commence legal proceedings when necessary. The Commission also has the power to "prescribe interpretative rules and general statements of policy with respect to unfair or deceptive acts or practices in or affecting commerce." This provision has led the FTC to issue various rules and guidelines to be followed in labeling textile products.

The FTC has enforcement and administrative responsibilities for several practices pertaining to the marketing of interior textiles. Within the FTC, the Bureau of Consumer Protection has several major program divisions that gather and provide information, investigate practices reported to be deceptive, monitor marketplace activities, and enforce federal statutes assigned to them. The Energy and Product Information Division, for example, focuses its work principally on energy policy and conservation, enforcing such rules as the one governing the disclosure of the insulative value (R-value) of home insulation, much of which is glass fiber batting.

Of particular interest to interior textile consumers and producers is the work of the Product Reliability Division. This division is responsible for enforcement of the **Magnuson-Moss Warranty Act**, which sets forth the procedures to be followed when written warranties are offered. This act and the growing use of warranties for interior textiles are described later in this chapter. Also of critical interest is the work of the Regional Offices Division. The offices in this unit are located in major cities nationwide and have exclusive responsibility for enforcing the mandatory fiber product labeling acts passed by Congress, as well as the trade regulation rules prescribed and promulgated by the FTC.

Investigative and Rulemaking Procedures

As noted earlier, the FTC is empowered to investigate marketplace activities and to develop rules affecting the commercial practices of an entire industry. A review of the investigative and rulemaking procedures followed by the Commission will provide greater understanding of the role it assumes in halting unfair and deceptive marketing practices.

The FTC is not authorized to handle individual consumer complaints, but acts when it sees a pattern of marketplace abuse. Complaints from individual consumers may serve to provide the pattern plus the evidence necessary to begin an investigation.

Investigations can begin in many different ways. Complaint letters, scholarly articles on consumer or economic subjects, or congressional requests may trigger an investigation. Investigations are either "public" or "nonpublic." Generally, public announcements will be made of investigations of the practices of an entire industry. An investigation of an individual company will probably be "nonpublic" in order to protect that company's privacy until the agency is ready formally to make an allegation.

After an investigation, the staff may find reason to believe that a business has violated the law. If the case is not settled voluntarily by some official corrective action by the company (a "consent order"), the Commission could issue a "complaint." After that, and if no settlement is reached, a formal hearing is held before an administrative law judge. Members of the public can participate at this point if they have evidence relating to the case. The administrative law judge issues a decision. There may be an appeal to the FTC commissioners. The commissioners' decision may be appealed to the United States Court of Appeals and ultimately to the United States Supreme Court.

After an investigation, the FTC staff may find what it believes to be unfair or deceptive practices in an entire industry. The staff then could make a recommendation to the commissioners to begin rulemaking. If the recommendation is accepted, a presiding officer is appointed, and a notice is published in the *Federal Register*, setting out the proposed rule and what the commissioners believe are the central issues to be discussed. Members of the public can, at this point, comment or testify on the rule or suggest issues to be examined.

The presiding officer conducts public hearings, which include cross-examination on certain issues. After the hearings, the staff prepares a report on the issues. This is followed by the presiding officer's report. Then members of the public have another opportunity to comment on the entire rulemaking record.

The matter then goes before the commissioners who deliberate on the record (which includes the presiding officer's report, the FTC staff report, and the public comments) to decide whether to issue the rule. They can make changes in the provisions of the rule and issue a revised version as they judge appropriate. This procedure has been followed to establish labeling and marketing rules that apply to various segments of the interior textile industry. Some of these rules are mandatory; others are advisory.

Regulatory and Advisory Labeling Practices

Labeling rules and guidelines are intended to afford consumers protection, not from any hazardous product, but from such things as misrepresentation of the composition of textile products. There are regulations, such as flammability standards, that focus on safety concerns, but product labeling is not generally required with these laws. Mandatory labeling rules also serve to protect industry members by specifying acceptable and legal practices for them to follow when engaged in commercial activities.

Fiber Product Labeling Acts

The United States Congress has passed three acts specifically designed to protect consumers and producers from the unrevealed presence of substitutes and mixtures in fibrous products and from misrepresentation and false advertising of the fiber content of textile fiber products. The provisions of these acts are especially important today as fibers can be engineered successfully to simulate the appearance of other fibers: acrylic can resemble wool; rayon can imitate flax; and acetate, nylon, and polyester can look like silk.

Failure to accurately disclose fiber content is an unfair and deceptive act or practice in commerce. Such illegal misbranding can be avoided by strict adherence to the provisions set forth in each act and its accompanying set of rules and regulations. The latter are established and issued by the FTC to help producers, distributors, and consumers interpret the mandates of each act.[2]

Wool Products Labeling Act of 1939 (WPLA)

The **WPLA of 1939**, effective July 15, 1941, focuses on the labeling requirements for products containing any percentage of wool fiber. (The meaning of "wool" in this act is given below.) Interior textile products subject to the provisions of the WPLA include, for example, conventional blankets and underblankets that are composed in whole or in part of wool. Interior textile products that have been specifically exempted include carpets, rugs, mats, and upholsteries.

Products included within the scope of the WPLA must conspicuously display a label or hangtag disclosing the following information:

1. The percentages of all fibers present in amounts of 5 percent or more of the total fiber weight of the product. Those fibers present to the extent of less than 5 percent should be disclosed as "other fiber" or "other fibers." Constituent fibers are identified by the following terms:

   Wool means the fiber from the fleece of the sheep or lamb or hair of the Angora or Cashmere goat (and may include the so-called specialty fibers from the hair of the camel, alpaca, llama, and vicuna) that has never been reclaimed from any woven or felted wool product. In lieu of the word "wool," the specialty fiber name may be used; "mohair" may be used for naming the fibers from the Angora goat; and "cashmere" may be used for naming the fibers from the Cashmere goat.

   Recycled wool means the constituent fibers were obtained by reducing (shredding) a previously manufactured product to its original fibrous state and then again subjecting the fibers to the product manufacturing sequence. This includes wool that has been woven or felted into a wool product that, without ever having been used in any way by a consumer, subsequently has been returned to a fibrous state. It also includes wool that has been spun, woven, knitted, or felted into a wool product that, after having been used by a consumer, subsequently has been returned to a fibrous state.

   Virgin wool, **new wool**, and "wool" are synonymous terms. The use of these terms means the constituent fibers have undergone manufacturing only once; they have not been reclaimed from any spun, woven, knitted, felted, braided, bonded, or otherwise manufactured or used product.

2. The identifying name or registered number of the manufacturer of the product must be included.

3. The country of origin must be included. The FTC and the United States Customs Service have issued country-of-origin regulations. Under the FTC rules, all products entirely manufactured and made of materials manufactured in the United States must bear the label "Made in the U.S.A." For products substantially manufactured in the United States

using materials from another country, the label must read "Sewn in the U.S.A. of Imported Components" or words of equivalent meaning.

On October 31, 1984, new country-of-origin regulations established by the United States Customs Service, a unit of the Department of Treasury, went into effect and are used in determining the country of origin of imported goods for the purpose of product labeling. These rules apply to products fully processed in one or more foreign countries and subsequently imported into the United States under trade quotas. For quota purposes, the Customs Service designates the country in which there has been a substantial transformation (generally cutting and sewing) of the product as the country of origin; the product is then counted in that country's import quota. (The Customs Service believes these regulations also will curb the practice of exporting products to the United States via countries having an unfilled quota or no quota limitation.)

Fur Products Labeling Act (FPLA)

The **FPLA**, effective August 9, 1952, governs the labeling and advertising of furs and fur products. The term "fur product" means any article of apparel made in whole or in part of fur or used fur. The FPLA's provisions do not apply to products other than apparel products.

Textile Fiber Products Identification Act (TFPIA)

Before World War II, consumers, distributors, and producers had few types of fibers from which to choose in comparison to the number available today. There were the widely used natural fibers, including wool, silk, linen, and cotton, and the less widely used natural fibers, such as jute, hemp, sisal, and camel. Rayon and acetate, initially known as "artificial silk" fibers, were also available. While consumers were familiar with the appearance, general performance properties, and care requirements of most of these fibers, they were not familiar with the characteristics of the several types of synthesized fibers subsequently introduced.

The first fully synthesized manufactured fiber, nylon, was unceremoniously adopted for use in toothbrush bristles in 1938, and enthusiastically welcomed in sheer hosiery in 1939. It was available to consumers for only a brief time before World War II required its use to be redirected to the production of military textiles. The chemical knowledge gained in the development of nylon, together with advances in production technology, led to the postwar production of an expanding number of manufactured fibers.

As each new fiber was developed and manufactured by various companies, each of which assigned a different name to the fiber, the market became filled with what appeared to be many distinct and unrelated fibers. Consumers, distributors, and producers had no way of knowing the composition of the new fibers, what performance to expect, and what care might be appropriate. Ultimately, growing concern to minimize this confusion, as well as to prevent unfair and deceptive marketing practices (intentional or not), led to the passage of the **TFPIA** in 1958. The act became effective on March 3, 1960.

Provisions of the TFPIA apply to many textile fiber products, including articles of wearing apparel, bedding, curtains, casements, draperies, tablecloths, floor coverings, towels, furniture slipcovers, afghans and throws, and all fibers, yarns, and fabrics. Specifically exempted are such products as upholstery stuffing (unless it was previously used); outer coverings of furniture, mattresses, and boxsprings; and backings of, and paddings or cushions to be used under, floor coverings. Thus, although carpets, rugs, and mats are specifically exempted from the WPLA, the face or pile layers of these floor products are subject to the provisions of the TFPIA. Also, while upholsteries are exempted from the WPLA, they come under the TFPIA when they are marketed in fabric form, that is, when not permanently attached to the furniture frame.

Products included within the scope of the TFPIA must bear a conspicuous label or hangtag displaying the following information:

1. The constituent fiber or combination of fibers in the textile fiber product, designating with equal prominence each natural or manufactured fiber in the textile fiber product by its generic name and percentage in the order of predominance by weight, if the weight of such fiber is 5 percent or more of the total fiber weight of the product. Fibers present to the extent of less than 5 percent of the total fiber weight of the product are designated as "other fiber" or "other fibers," except when a definite functional

significance has clearly been established. In the latter case, the percentage by weight, the generic name, and the functional significance of the fiber should be set out, for example, 3 percent spandex for elasticity.

2. The identifying name or registered number of the manufacturer of the product.

3. The first time a trademark appears in the required information, it must appear in immediate conjunction with the generic name in equally sized type. Unlike the generic name, trademarks are not required information.

4. The country of origin, according to the rules established by the FTC and the United States Customs Service. These regulations were described in the discussion of the WPLA.

Nondeceptive and truthful terms are permitted with the generic name, for example, combed cotton, solution-dyed acetate, and antistatic nylon. The information voluntarily provided by this and other forms of permissive labeling is particularly helpful to consumers and design professionals selecting interior textile products.

When products are labeled in accordance with these acts, consumers are not challenged to recognize fibers by their appearance or to know the performance properties and care requirements of many individual fibers. Instead, they need only become familiar with the features generally characteristic of each generic class of chemically related fibers. We should note that care instructions are not required under the WPLA, the FPLA, or the TFPIA. The disclosure of safe care procedures for finished fabrics and apparel items is governed by a trade regulation rule.

Trade Regulation Rules Regarding Labeling

Trade regulation rules set out provisions for mandatory and acceptable practices considered to be in the public interest. Producers following the rules will avoid illegal and unacceptable marketing practices as defined in the FTC Act.

In the marketing of interior textile products, some of the rules apply to a specific market segment. There is, for example, the Trade Regulations Rule Relating to the Deceptive Advertising and Labeling as to Size of Tablecloths and Related Products (see Chapter 30). A second example illustrating specific orientation to one market sector is the Trade Regulation Rule Relating to Failure to Disclose that Skin Irritation May Result from Washing or Handling Glass Fiber Curtains and Draperies and Glass Fiber Curtain and Drapery Fabrics (see Chapter 17).

In April 1974, the FTC gathered comments concerning the advisability of expanding the scope of the Trade Regulation Rule Related to the Care Labeling of Textile Wearing Apparel, 16 CFR Part 423, which had gone into effect on July 3, 1972. After analyzing the comments, the Commission published, in June 1976, a proposed amended rule recommending the extension of the current rule's coverage to draperies, curtains, slipcovers, linens, piece goods sold for covering furniture or making slipcovers, leather and suede apparel, yarn, carpets and rugs, and upholstered furniture. Oral testimony and written comments were continuously received and analyzed until June 1982; based on these, the Commission did not approve the proposed extensions. The new title of the amended rule, Care Labeling of Textile Wearing Apparel and Certain Piece Goods, reflects this decision. The amended rule became effective on January 2, 1984. The amended rule also included a glossary of standard terms based on ASTM D 3136 Terminology Relating to Care Labeling for Apparel, Textile, and Leather Products Other Than Textile Floor Coverings and Upholstery.[3] With passage of the North American Free Trade Agreement that promotes free trade among Mexico, Canada, and the United States, it became necessary to provide care instructions that were not language dependent. Working through ASTM International, members of the industry developed a guide that provides a uniform system of care symbols (Figure 10.1).

Although textile floor coverings and textile upholstered furniture were not included in the 1984 Care Labeling amendment, there remained an interest by consumers for care instructions for carpet, rugs, and upholstery. In response, ASTM International continued its work on care instructions for these products and published ASTM D 5253 Standard Terminology Related to Floor Coverings and Textile Upholstered Furniture. This ASTM standard provides a uniform language for the writing of care instructions to be supplied with carpets, rugs, and uphol-

stered furniture, excluding leather. The terminology is recommended for use by sellers who voluntarily choose to provide care information to their consumers.

The role of the FTC should not be construed as strictly adversarial in nature. Although it has been assigned exclusive responsibility for enforcing specific congressional acts and for monitoring commerce in general, the Commission also continually strives to inform and educate both the consuming public and industry members concerning fair market practices. Trade practice rules and labeling guides have been helpful to this endeavor.

Trade Practice Rules and Guides Regarding Labeling

As generally set forth in the introduction of each **trade practice rule and guide**, the provisions are interpretive of laws administered by the Commission, and thus are advisory in nature. These rules are designed to foster and promote the maintenance of fair competitive conditions in the interest of protecting industry, trade, and the public. By complying with the stated provisions, industry members can avoid engaging in unfair and deceptive marketing practices that can lead to litigation.

The major difference between trade practice rules and guides lies in who initiated the proceedings. In the case of trade practice rules, a single industry segment has requested assistance from the FTC in an effort to clarify what trade practices are acceptable. Conferences are then held to provide a forum for all industry members; thereafter, proposed rules are published, responses considered, and final advisory rules published. Guides are the result of proceedings initiated by the Commission, and they supersede several trade practice rules.

Trade practice rules and guides, like trade regulation rules, have a specific and limited scope. There are, for example, guides for the household furniture industry and guides for the feather and down products industry. These guides are explained in Chapters 12 and 29, respectively.

To ensure that they are using fair and nondeceptive marketing practices, textile firms must label their products in accordance with all applicable acts, rules, and guides. In order to gain a competitive edge in the marketplace, they may also choose to label their products with a distinctive name or logo or to offer a warranty pertaining to in-use performance. The use of such labeling is permissible and strictly voluntary.

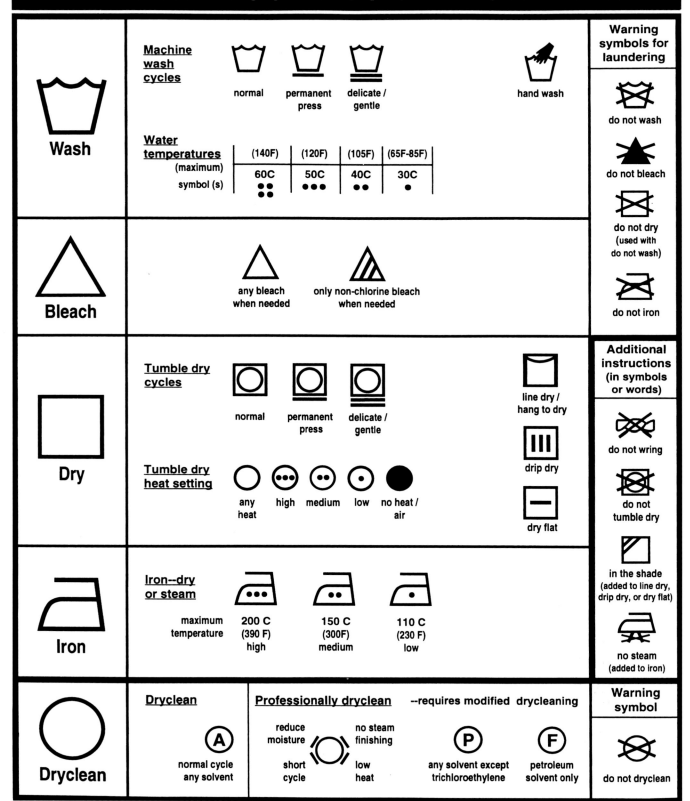

Figure 10.1 Commercial and home laundering and dry cleaning symbols.
Reprinted, with permission, from the 2005 Annual Book of ASTM Standards.

Voluntary Labeling Programs

Voluntary labeling programs are used extensively in the marketing of interior textile products. These programs are primarily intended to increase sales, assisting in the commercial success of all suppliers, producers, and distributors of the labeled product. At the same time, such labeling is helpful to contract designers, architects, and consumers who understand the intention or implication of the various kinds of labeling, such as those relating to nondescriptive fiber names, certification marks, licensing programs, and warranty programs. In virtually all programs, a trademark is a valuable promotional aid.

Use of TM and ®

Trademarks are distinctive names, words, phrases, and stylized logos (letters or symbols) that aim at capturing the attention of professionals and consumers. The ownership and use of trademarks is carefully guarded.

Producers and trade associations allocate significant amounts of money, time, and talent to coining names, designing graphic symbols, and writing eye-catching phrases that will be effective trademarks. Once this effort is completed, the chosen name, phrase, or logo appears on product labels and in promotional materials accompanied by the letters TM. This labeling constitutes basic ownership of the trademark, assuming the person or firm was the first to use the trademark in commerce. Frequently, the user elects to apply for registered ownership of the trademark with the United States Patent and Trademark Office. Following approval of the application, the symbol ® is used in lieu of TM to indicate registered ownership.

Trademarks are widely promoted to ensure recognition of the mark by the consumer. At the same time, the use of the mark is carefully controlled. Every effort is taken to protect the reputation of the trademark, as well as to ensure that the legal owner is the only one benefiting from the increased recognition and selection of products labeled with the mark. Unauthorized adoption of a trademark is illegal: in recent years, such piracy has resulted in several multimillion-dollar lawsuits and confiscation of illegally branded goods.

Fiber Trademarks

Fiber suppliers and producers use trade names and logos to distinguish their products from those of their competitors. Manufactured fiber producers use trade names extensively, and apparently their promotional efforts have been successful. Many consumers are more familiar with fiber trade names than with their generic names. A trademarked fiber may be considered unique when in fact several other chemically related fibers produced by other companies are also available. Appendix A lists generic fiber names.

Informed consumers and trained professionals can make valuable use of fiber trade names, especially those that designate a special property. They may, for example, know that solution dyeing has been used or that a fiber is self-extinguishing (i.e., stops burning when the source of ignition is removed) when special trade names are used.

Cotton Incorporated grants permission to qualifying retailers, manufacturers, and mills to use its registered trademark on packaging, hangtags, or in advertisements. The trademark is a stylized design, the Seal of Cotton Trademark, illustrated in Figure 10.2.

Some companies license or certify the use of their fiber trade names on end products. In this marketing, the fiber company tests fabrics or end products for quality and performance. Fiber trademark licensing and certifying should not be confused with other licensing and certification programs applying to textile products.

Certification Marks

Certification marks are coined names and stylized logos that may be used alone or in conjunction with other types of voluntary labeling. They may be used on the labels of end products that conform with fiber content specifications or performance specifications established by the owner of the mark.

Some fiber trade associations control or certify the use of their registered trademark logos. Australian Wool Innovation, for example, owns and controls the use of the Woolmark and the Woolmark Blend trademarks (Figure 10.3). End products carrying these symbols have been quality tested by The Woolmark Company for compliance with its performance and fiber content specifications. The Woolmark trademark is one of the most globally recognized symbols and represents the world's largest fiber quality assurance scheme.

For contract or commercial upholstery fabrics, members of the industry created the Association for Contract

Figure 10.2 The Seal of Cotton Trademark. Registered trademark of Cotton Incorporated.

WOOLMARK

WOOLMARK
BLEND

Figure 10.3 Registered trademark logos used by The Woolmark Company.
The Woolmark logo is reproduced with the permission of Australian Wool Innovation Limited, owner of The Woolmark Company.

Textiles (ACT) in 1985. The objective for this organization was to address issues concerning contract fabrics, including performance standards and industry education. Members of the association established performance guidelines for colorfastness to wet and dry crocking, colorfastness to light, resistance to pilling, strength, seam slippage, and abrasion resistance. (Standard methods of testing these performance variables are discussed in Chapter 14.) Recommendations were delineated for both general contract use and heavy duty contract use. Compliance with the recommended standards is denoted by corresponding symbols, each of which is shown in Figure 10.4.

Licensing Programs

Licensing companies sell the right to use their company-owned processes to producers and converters; they do not process any components or manufacture any end products. Licensing companies do, however, certify the use of their coined names in the labeling and marketing of products. The Sanforized Company, for example, licenses the use of its compressive shrinkage and durable press processes. Producers using these fabric conversion techniques may label and promote their end products with such names as Sanforized®, Sanfor®, and Sanforizota, trade names owned by the Sanforized Company.

Consumers, contract designers, and architects must recognize that certification and **licensing programs** provide assurances, not guarantees. The presence of a certi-

fied or licensed name or logo on a label may confirm a specific fiber content, the use of a particular process, or that the product has met standard performance specifications, but it does not guarantee any features.

Warranty Programs

Today, **warranty or guarantee programs** are used more frequently in textile marketing than they were in earlier, less economically challenging times. Budgetary pressures have increasingly encouraged designers, architects, and consumers to seek or even demand a legally binding agreement guaranteeing the long-term satisfactory performance of some interior textile products. They are, of course, seeking protection from defective or faulty merchandise and the expense of premature replacement.

In order to meet the demands of professionals and consumers, and thus to remain competitive, several producers of textile components and end products offer written warranties. Fiber companies may, for example, try to enhance their competitive position by voluntarily offering to stand behind products composed of their fiber but manufactured by a downstream firm. This is an especially frequent practice with soft floor coverings.

There are important differences among the various types of warranties. A review of the major types of warranties—spoken, implied, and written—can help to identify and clarify these differences.

Spoken Warranties

Spoken warranties are merely verbal promises, virtually impossible to enforce. Consumers and professionals should have spoken warranties put into writing.

Implied Warranties

Implied warranties are not written, and they are not voluntary; they are rights provided to consumers by state law.

ACT

Symbol	Function
🔥®	flammability
®	colorfastness to wet & dry crocking
✳️®	colorfastness to light
⭐®	physical properties
a®	abrasion
A®	abrasion

Figure 10.4 The marks are Registered Certification Marks at the US Patent and Trademark Office and are owned by the Association for Contract Textiles, Inc. Courtesy of the Association for Contract Textiles, Inc.

These rights include such things as the "warranty of merchantability," for instance, that an electric blanket will heat, and the "warranty of fitness for a particular purpose," for instance, that a carpet produced for installation around a swimming pool will not dissolve in water. In states having such laws, implied warranties are not voluntary; they come automatically with every sale unless the product is sold "as is."

Written Warranties

A **written warranty** constitutes a legally binding promise that the warrantor is insuring quality and performance and is willing to stand behind the warranted product, assuming it is neither misused nor abused by the warrantee. While written warranties are strictly voluntary, when they are offered they are subject to the provisions of the Magnuson-Moss Warranty Act, passed by the U.S. Congress in 1975. This act is under the jurisdiction of the FTC.

Like the textile labeling mandates discussed earlier, the Magnuson-Moss Warranty Act serves and protects both producers and consumers. By strictly adhering to the provisions of the act, producers can avoid unfair and deceptive marketing practices. By examining the features included in any warranty offered, and by exercising their rights under the act, consumers can protect themselves from defective products.

The act requires that written warranties offered on consumer products costing more than fifteen dollars must be made available to prospective consumers prior to the sale of the product. The warranty shall "fully and conspicuously disclose in simple and readily understood language the terms and conditions of such warranty." This provision prohibits the use of "legalese" and fine print. Specific information that must be set forth in written warranties includes, but is not limited to, the following items:

1. The clear identification of the names and addresses of the warrantors.
2. The identity of the party or parties to whom the warranty is extended; this is often stated as "original purchasers only."
3. The products or parts covered.
4. What the warrantor will do in the event of a defect, malfunction, or failure to conform with such written warranty, at whose expense, and for what period of time.
5. What the consumer must do and what expenses the consumer must bear.

6. The step-by-step procedure the consumer should take in order to obtain performance of any obligation under the warranty, including the identification of any person or class of persons authorized to perform the obligations set forth in the warranty.

7. The characteristics, properties, or parts of the product that are not covered by the warranty.

Written warranties are required also to carry the designation "full" or "limited." These designations indicate what the warrantor agrees to do for the purchaser, as well as what is expected of the purchaser. An examination of the meanings and implications of these designations will provide greater understanding of warranty labeling.

FULL WARRANTY: The title FULL on a warranty tells you that:

- A defective product will be repaired or replaced for free, including removal and reinstallation when necessary.

- The product will be repaired within a reasonable time period after you have told the company about the problem.

- You will not have to do anything unreasonable to get warranty service (such as return a heavy product to the store).

- The warranty is good for anyone who owns the product during the warranty period.

- If the product has not been repaired after a reasonable number of tries, you can get a replacement or a refund. (This is commonly known as the "lemon" provision.)

- You do not have to return a warranty card for a product with a FULL warranty. But, a company may give a registration card and suggest that it be returned, so long as it is clear that the return of the card is voluntary.

- Implied warranties cannot be disclaimed or denied or limited to any specific length of time.

  Warning: The title FULL does NOT mean:

- That the entire product is covered by the warranty.

- That the warranty has to last for one year or any other particular length of time.

- That the company must pay for "consequential or incidental damages" (such as towing, car rental, food spoilage, etc.).

- That the product is warranted in all geographic areas.

LIMITED WARRANTY: The title LIMITED on a warranty tells you that the warranty gives you less than what the FULL warranty gives you. You have to read your warranty to see what protection is missing. For example:

- You may have to pay for labor, reinstallation, or other charges.

- You may be required to bring a heavy product back to the store for service or do something else you may find difficult.

- Your warranty may be good only for the first purchaser (that is, a second owner would not be entitled to any warranty service).

- You may be promised a pro-rata refund or credit which means you will have to pay for the time you owned the product before the defect appeared.

- You may have to return your warranty registration card to get warranty coverage.

- Your implied warranties may expire when your written warranty expires. (For example, a one-year limited warranty can say that the implied warranties only last for one year.)

- The "lemon" provision does not apply to limited warranties, but even under a limited warranty you are entitled to what the warranty promises. If the company cannot do what it has promised to do, the company has to do something else comparable for you.

  Warning: The title LIMITED does NOT mean:

- That your product is inferior or will not work as promised.

- That only part of the product is covered. For example, you may have a LIMITED warranty that covers the entire product.

- That the warranty only covers the cost of repair parts. A LIMITED warranty can include labor, too.

- That the warranty will last for any particular length of time.
- That you can only have warranty service done in a few locations.

A product can carry more than one written warranty. For example, an automatic washer can have a FULL warranty on the entire product for one year and a LIMITED four-year warranty on the gear assembly.[4]

Sample Labeling

Another form of voluntary labeling used by interior textile product producers that should be highlighted is the use of style, color, and design names on product samples displayed in product showrooms and retail outlets. In most cases, these names are nondescriptive and provide no useful information, but they may have the effect of attracting and holding prospective purchasers' attention. For example, "blue-green" may identify a color accurately, but "sea foam" may sound more enticing; the terms "level, cutpile" may describe a carpet texture informatively, but "plateau" may seem more interesting; "polka dot" may be readily understandable, but "micro dot" may add contemporary flair; and so on.

It is apparent that the marketing strategy behind this type of sample labeling is the same as that behind the use of a well-known designer's name on product labels. Producers purchase the right to use the name, after confirming that it will be a persuasive and effective marketing aid.

Summary

Members of the interior textile industry must disclose the fiber composition and country of origin of most of their products, using the practices prescribed in the congressional fiber product labeling acts. Members of certain industry segments also must adhere to trade regulation rules, and some are advised also to comply with recommendations set forth in a trade practice rule or in guides. Compliance with these acts and guidelines helps to ensure that producers are not engaged in unfair or deceptive commercial activities related to product disclosures. It also helps to ensure that consumers and professionals have useful and accurate information, enabling them to make reliable decisions when they select textile products for interior applications.

To enhance the marketability of their products, many producers use voluntary labeling programs. They may distinguish their products with trade names or certification marks, or they may elect to guarantee their quality or performance. The use of such labeling offers reciprocal advantages for producers and consumers. Producers gain a competitive edge in the marketplace, and consumers are provided more information or protection than is legally required.

Key Terms

certification marks
Federal Trade Commission (FTC)
FPLA
full warranty
guides
implied warranties
licensing programs
limited warranty

Magnuson-Moss Warranty Act
new wool
recycled wool
reprocessed wool
reused wool
spoken warranties
TFPIA
trademarks

trade practice rules
trade regulation rules
virgin wool
warranty or guarantee programs
wool
WPLA of 1939
written warranties

Review Questions

1. Explain what is meant by "unfair or deceptive acts or practices" in commerce.

2. Describe the investigative and rulemaking procedures followed by the FTC.

3. What are the purposes of the fiber product labeling acts?

4. Differentiate between virgin wool and recycled wool as they apply to wool product labeling.

5. When a product is labeled "virgin wool," are there connotations of quality?

6. How is the country of origin determined for imported textile products? How are these regulations used in controlling textile imports to the United States?

7. Distinguish between the provisions of trade regulation rules and labeling acts and between the provisions of trade regulation rules and trade practice rules. Differentiate between trade practice rules and guidelines.

8. Are care instructions required for textile upholstered furniture, carpet, and rugs?

9. How have members of the industry responded to the desire and need for care instructions for these products?

10. Explain the use of TM and ®.

11. Discuss the importance of trademarks in textile marketing.

12. When an informed consumer or design professional sees an ACT certification symbol on contract upholstery, what is understood?

13. Are written warranties mandatory? When are warranties subject to the provisions of the Magnuson-Moss Warranty Act?

14. Identify some differences between full and limited warranties.

15. What is meant by the "lemon" provision?

16. Cite various types of sample labeling. What is the purpose of such labeling?

Notes

1. Copies of the Federal Trade Commission Act are available from the FTC, Distribution Branch, Room 270, Washington, DC 20580.

2. Copies of these acts and their accompanying rules and regulations are available from the FTC.

3. The full text of ASTM standards is available in the *Annual Book of ASTM Standards* Volume 07.01 or Volume 07.02.

4. "Warranties: There Ought to Be a Law," Federal Trade Commission, Washington, D.C., undated.

Interior Textile Products and Fire

CHAPTER **ELEVEN**

■ **Since the late 1960s**, consumers, industry members, and local, state, and federal government personnel have given increased attention to the fire-related behavior of interior textile products. This has resulted in the establishment of flammability codes and standards applying to interior products intended for use in certain occupancies; such codes are issued and enforced by various regulatory agencies, several of which were identified in Chapter 1. This attention has also resulted in the establishment of mandatory flammability standards with which specific interior textile products must comply prior to marketing. These standards were established in accordance with provisions of the Flammable Fabrics Act, a congressional act administered by the Consumer Product Safety Commission.

Residential and commercial consumers should be aware of the role interior textiles play in fires. Interior designers must understand fire-related terms and processes and test methods used in fire-safety. This knowledge enables the professional to specify products that widen the margin for consumer safety, minimize structural damage, and lessen economic losses in the event of fire, thus allowing the professional to specify products that conform to mandated selection criteria.

Consumer Product Safety Commission

The **Consumer Product Safety Commission (CPSC)** was established as an independent federal agency in late 1972. When the Commission began operation on May 14, 1973, administration and enforcement responsibilities for certain safety-oriented acts, including the **Flammable Fabrics Act (FFA)**, were transferred to it from other federal regulatory agencies. Prior to this transfer, the **FTC** and the **U.S. Department of Commerce (DOC)** administered the FFA.

In carrying out its responsibilities, the CPSC analyzes information and statistics regarding the frequency and severity of injury associated with interior textile and other consumer products. When products are found to pose an unreasonable risk to consumers, the Commission has the power to initiate the necessary proceedings that ultimately may lead to the establishment of a new or revised safety standard. When regulating interior textile products, the CPSC adheres to procedures set forth in the FFA.

Flammable Fabrics Act

The FFA was passed by the U.S. Congress in 1953 and became effective on July 1, 1954. This act prohibits the introduction and movement in interstate commerce of articles of wearing apparel and fabrics so highly flammable as to be dangerous when worn by individuals. Congress amended the act in 1967, expanding its scope to include interior furnishings and permitting the establishment of standards specific to these textile products.

The 1967 Amendment

In addition to expanding the scope of the FFA, the 1967 amendment directed the Secretary of Commerce and the Secretary of Health, Education, and Welfare (now Health and Human Services) to "conduct a continuing study and investigation of the deaths, injuries, and economic losses resulting from accidental burning of products, fabrics, or related materials." Much of the statistical information pertaining to fabric-related burning accidents is provided by the **National Electronic Injury Surveillance System (NEISS)**. The NEISS records personal injury data from scores of hospital emergency rooms throughout the United States and forwards it to the CPSC for analysis.

The 1967 amendment also authorized the Secretary of Commerce to carry out the following four activities:

1. Conduct research into the flammability of products, fabrics, and materials.

2. Conduct feasibility studies on reduction of flammability of products, fabrics, and materials.

3. Develop flammability test methods and testing devices.

4. Offer appropriate training on the use of flammability test methods and testing devices.

The federally funded **National Institute of Standards and Technology (NIST)** carries out much of the investigative work involved in the laboratories of its Center for Fire Research. The NIST does not promulgate standards, but it does provide information to the CPSC and other federal agencies.

When statistical injury data and laboratory test results support the possibility that a new or revised **safety standard** is needed, it is the responsibility of the CPSC to initiate and carry out the following procedures:

1. Publish the notice of a possible need and the proposed standard in the *Federal Register*. (Prior to April 23, 1976, the notice and proposed standard were published separately.)

2. Invite and consider response from affected and interested persons.

3. Publish the final version of the standard in the *Federal Register*.

4. Allow one year for firms affected by the standard to manufacture products meeting specified performance criteria. (The CPSC may set an earlier or later effective date if it finds good cause.)

5. Prohibit noncomplying products manufactured after the effective date from being introduced into commerce. (The CPSC may allow exceptions.)

Flammability Standards

Six standards have been promulgated and another proposed as a result of the provisions of the 1967 amendment. The standards are published with their **Code of Federal Regulations (CFR)** notation. Professionals and consumers should become familiar with the following standards, five of which apply to interior textile products:

16 CFR 1615	Children's Sleepwear, Sizes 0–6X
16 CFR 1616	Children's Sleepwear, Sizes, 7–14
16 CFR 1630	Large Carpets and Rugs
16 CFR 1631	Small Carpets and Rugs
16 CFR 1632	Mattresses and Mattress Pads— Smoldering Resistance
16 CFR 1633	Mattresses and Mattress Pads— Open Flame Resistance
16 CFR 1634	Upholstered Furniture (Proposed)

All of the above standards are mandatory except for 16 CFR 1634, which was proposed by the USPC in 2008.

UFAC Voluntary Action Program

PFF 6–81 *Draft* Proposed Standard for the Flammability (Cigarette Ignition Resistance) of Upholstered Furniture, did not move beyond the proposed stage. Instead, when the original draft proposal (PFF 6–74) was issued, members of the upholstered furniture industry consolidated their efforts concerning more cigarette-resistant upholstering methods. Through this organization, the industry sought to demonstrate that the majority of its member firms would voluntarily participate in a program designed to ensure the production of *safer* products.

Officially launched in April 1979, the **Upholstered Furniture Action Council (UFAC)** Voluntary Action Program was designed to improve the ability of upholstered furniture to resist catching fire from a burning cigarette, the most common source of furniture ignition. The program includes four aspects: fabric classification, which is determined by a prescribed test method; construction criteria, which are paired with test methods; a labeling plan; and a compliance procedure. The test methods used in the program are described later in this chapter.

By combining the ability of the outer covering to resist catching fire from a burning cigarette with construction method, members of the industry intended to assure the production of safer upholstered furniture while avoiding the limitation of a large number of upholstery fabrics traditionally available to consumers.

The labeling plan devised by the UFAC centers on a hangtag that identifies furniture meeting UFAC criteria. Prospective purchasers are informed that the labeled item has been made in accordance with UFAC methods designed to reduce the likelihood of furniture fire from cigarettes.

In 2001 UFAC introduced a new tag (Figure 11.1) that is designed to be simpler and easier for consumers to read. It contains an added precaution about small open flames, such as matches, candles, and lighters. The trifold tags are presented in English, French, and Spanish so that they can be easily understood. UFAC provides the tags at a nominal cost to the manufacturer. Revenues are used to finance the UFAC voluntary program, including compliance verification, to fund additional research, and to promote the program to the industry and consumers.

Participation in the UFAC program is strictly voluntary. The UFAC encourages furniture component suppliers and end-product manufacturers to participate and provides technical assistance to promote compliance. An independent laboratory verifies that materials used in making the items carrying the compliance hangtag meet the performance criteria set forth in the program.

Periodically, the results of the verification tests and the level of industry participation are reported to the CPSC. By such reporting, the UFAC seeks to demonstrate that members of the industry can and will produce

a) Front.

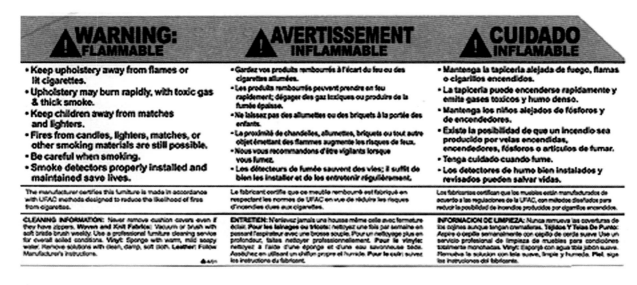

b) Back.

Figure 11.1 Upholstered Furniture Action Council Hangtag.
Courtesy of the Upholstered Furniture Action Council.

safer upholstered furniture items, eliminating the need for a federal flammability mandate. Currently there are no national codes that recognize or require UFAC flammability tests. However, because of the overwhelming number of upholstered furniture fires caused by smoldering cigarettes, in 2008 the U.S. Consumer Product Safety Commission (CPSC) again proposed a federal standard, **CFR 16 Part 1634**, for residential upholstered furniture under the Flammable Fabrics Act.

Combustion Processes and Byproducts

Combustion is a chemical process in which oxidation, the combination of oxygen with elements or compounds, produces heat energy. In some combustion reactions, light and such other byproducts as molten polymer compounds, smoke, and toxic gases are also produced.

Combustion Processes

Flaming combustion processes are initiated by **pyrolysis**, in which heat causes organic compounds to decompose, producing combustible materials. A burning match, a lit cigarette, glowing embers, or an electrical spark may supply heat. While a lighted match, which has a temperature of approximately 1,000 °F, is a common source of ignition heat for interior textile products, the most common source is a burning cigarette. When the **kindling or ignition temperature** is reached, the combustible materials combine with oxygen, ignite, and produce heat and light in the form of flames. The heat generated by this combustion can promote further decomposition of the textile substance, causing the cyclic process to continue until the structure is consumed.

Spontaneous combustion occurs when a textile substrate is heated to its kindling temperature without the involvement of a flaming ignition source. Although this is not common with fibers, it is a potential hazard with latex foam compounds, especially when they are being tumbled in a heated dryer. Because cellular latex is a good heat insulator, heat builds up, the relatively low ignition temperature of the material is quickly reached, and it bursts into flame.

In addition to flaming combustion, **flameless combustion** can also occur. One type of flameless combustion, **glowing**, is characteristic of cellulosic fibers: after a small area of flame has been extinguished, the fiber continues to be consumed without flames rising. **Smoldering** is another type of flameless combustion, which may occur with fibrous fillings and battings. This suppressed combustion often produces large volumes of dense smoke filled with deadly **toxicants**.

Byproducts of Combustion

Beside the heat energy and light produced during most combustion reactions, burning textiles and other interior materials generate various other products. Among these, toxic gases pose the greatest threat to life.

Molten Polymer Compounds

When thermoplastic fibers are heated to their melting points, the **molten polymer compounds** produced can play conflicting roles in interior fires. When window and wallcoverings contain these fibers, for example, the molten polymer may drip and carry the flames downward. This could be a positive event if the burning fabric **self-extinguished** and the flaming droplets fell on a noncombustible flooring material. It would be a negative event if the flaming droplets propagated the fire to a flammable floor covering.

Smoke

The amount and density of smoke generated by items undergoing flaming combustion or smoldering can have a major effect on safe exit procedures because smoke reduces visibility and obscures illuminated exit markers. A test method to evaluate **smoke density** is discussed and illustrated later in this chapter.

Smoke, not heat or flame, is the primary cause of all fire deaths.[1] Smoke is deadly because of the toxicants it contains.

Toxic Gases

Toxicity studies have shown that varied quantities of specific gases can be detected after the isolated combustion of commonly used fibers. The most toxic of these gases, carbon monoxide (CO), is present in all fires, whether textiles are involved or not; it causes death by preventing red blood cells from absorbing oxygen.

At the current time, no flammability regulations include specific requirements related to **toxic gases**, although it may be reasonable to expect such mandates in the future. Fire-safety researchers are, in fact, focusing their attentions on the development of a test method to measure the hazards of inhaled toxicants.

Stages of an Interior Fire

The principal concern of industry personnel, educators, government employees, and others engaged in fire-safety work is not for the damage sustained by textile products or other interior items—burned items can be repaired or replaced—but instead for the reduction of the hazard to life. They strive to minimize the likelihood of initial ignition and, in the event of fire, they seek to make the environment safer by preserving the means for quick and efficient **egress** from a burning area or structure.

The critical importance of preserving the possibility of safe egress is confirmed when the three distinct stages through which an interior fire progresses are examined. This examination will also confirm the value of early warning systems and automatic sprinkling systems.

Stage 1

A **Stage 1 fire** is schematized in Figure 11.2. Only the ignited item is burning. The overriding concern is that the fire remain localized. If, for example, a burning cigarette is carelessly dropped onto a carpet or an upholstered chair, the item should be designed to resist ignition. If ignition occurs, the item should not propagate or spread the flame throughout the room, making it more challenging to extinguish the fire and more difficult to exit safely.

When a fire is small and isolated, smoke detectors or other alarm systems serve to alert residents. The early warning may enable occupants to contain the fire, preventing its growth to Stage 2.

Stage 2

A **fire in Stage 2** is illustrated in Figure 11.3. Here, the fire has spread from the area of origin, igniting other items in its path. As the fire spreads and grows, more heat is generated and the air in the room becomes hotter and hotter. When sufficient heat has built up, all combustible items in the room burst into flames, producing a situation known as **flashover**.

Automatic sprinkling systems, which are usually heat activated, can halt **flame propagation**, thus minimizing heat buildup and preventing flashover. The Federal Management Agency has found that using smoke detectors and automatic sprinkling systems in all buildings and residences could reduce overall injuries, loss of life, and property damage by at least 50 percent.[2]

Stage 3

In **Stage 3 of an interior fire**, shown schematically in Figure 11.4, the flames spread beyond the burning room

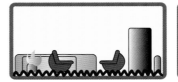 

Side Elevation (Room) Floor Plan (Room)

Figure 11.2 Stage 1 of an interior fire.
I.A. Benjamin and S. Davis, *Flammability Testing for Carpet*, NBSIR 78-1436, Center for Fire Research, Institute for Applied Technology, National Bureau of Standards, Washington, DC, April 1978.

Side Elevation (Room) Floor Plan (Room)

Figure 11.3 Stage 2 of an interior fire.
I.A. Benjamin and S. Davis, *Flammability Testing for Carpet*, NBSIR 78-1436, Center for Fire Research, Institute for Applied Technology, National Bureau of Standards, Washington, DC, April 1978.

into the corridor or passageway. In addition to the flames, a significant amount of heat may be radiating into the corridor as the fire spills out. If the fire spreads down the corridor, all exits may be blocked.

Fire researchers consider the three stages of fire growth when they design flammability test methods. Members of the Consumer Product Safety Commission

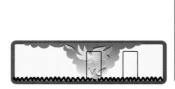 

Side Elevation (Corridor) Floor Plan (Building)

Figure 11.4 Stage 3 of an interior fire.
I.A. Benjamin and S. Davis, *Flammability Testing for Carpet*, NBSIR 78-1436, Center for Fire Research, Institute for Applied Technology, National Bureau of Standards, Washington, DC, April 1978.

and other regulatory agencies consider them when they establish flammability standards for selected interior textile products.

Flammability Testing

Various types of testing are used to measure the fire-related behavior of interior textile products and components. Currently, small-scale, large-scale, and full-scale procedures are used in this work.

Small-scale Test Methods

Small-scale test methods are used in the laboratory to measure specific flammability characteristics. Like other standard test methods, these are designed to simulate the conditions associated with real-life situations; in some test methods, for example, a lit cigarette is the source of heat for ignition (Figure 11.5, Figure 11.6, and Figure 11.7). Small-scale tests enable the producer to make reasonably accurate predictions concerning the behavior of the item being tested in a Stage 1 fire.

Methenamine Tablet (Pill) Test Method

This test method, designated ASTM D 2859, is designed to simulate a situation in which a textile floor covering is exposed to a small source of ignition, such as a burning match, an ignited cigarette, or a glowing ember. Structures that resist ignition and do not propagate the flame could reasonably be expected to contain a fire in Stage 1.

Test Specimens and Procedures Eight specimens, each one 9 inches square, are dried in an oven so that they will be free of moisture. Then, one at a time, the specimens are placed in a draft-protected burn chamber and covered by a steel flattening frame with an opening 8 inches in diameter. As shown in Figure 11.8, a **methenamine tablet**, which is formulated to burn for two minutes, is placed in the center of the specimen and ignited. Testing is complete when burning of the tablet or the carpet specimen ceases, whichever occurs last.

Analysis of Results A **char length** measurement is taken on each of the eight specimens. Measurements are made of the shortest distance between the edge of the hole in the ring and the charred area. Smoke and toxic gases are not considered.

Figure 11.5 Interior fire at 0 seconds.
Courtesy of the National Institute of Standards and Technology.

Figure 11.6 Interior fire at 90 seconds.
Courtesy of the National Institute of Standards and Technology.

Figure 11.7 Interior fire at 180 seconds.
Courtesy of the National Institute of Standards and Technology.

Performance Requirements A specimen meets either standard when the char area does not extend to within 1 inch of the hole in the ring. Seven out of the eight specimens

Figure 11.8 Methenamine tablet test.
Illustration by Andrea Lau.

must pass for the floor covering to pass. The provisions of 16 CFR 1631 permit rugs that fail the test to be marketed as long as they carry a label warning: flammable (fails U.S. Consumer Product Safety Commission Standard 16 CFR 1631: should not be used near source of fire).

Adoption of the Method This test has been adopted as the method to be used in 16 CFR 1630 and 16 CFR 1631. The **scope of 16 CFR 1630** is limited to large carpets and rugs, those having an area greater than 24 square feet and one dimension greater than 6 feet. Carpet modules, because they are installed to cover large areas, are also subject to the provisions of 16 CFR 1630. The **scope of 16 CFR 1631** includes floor coverings that are not large enough to fall within the scope of 16 CFR 1630. Such structures include scatter rugs, bathroom rugs, and smaller area rugs. These standards became effective in 1971, and virtually all imported and domestic soft floor

coverings offered for sale in the United States must conform to the provisions of the applicable standard.

Forty-five-degree Angle Test Method

Although ASTM D 1230 Standard Test Method for Flammability of Apparel Textiles was originally designed for use with apparel textiles, it may be selected to evaluate the flammability of towelings. This small-scale test is also known as the 45-degree angle test.

Test Specimens and Procedure In accordance with ASTM D 1230, exploratory testing is used to determine the direction in which the most rapid rate of flame spread occurs. With pile fabrics, flame spread is most rapid when progressing against the lay of the pile, so the long dimension of the specimens should parallel the lay of the pile. Four specimens are then cut 2 inches by 6 inches, oven dried, and placed in a specimen holder. One at a time, each specimen is placed in the flammability tester at a 45-degree angle. Automated mechanisms are then activated to apply a flame to the lower edge of the specimen for 1 second; timing begins upon application of the flame and ends when burning releases a stop cord.

Analysis of Results The arithmetic mean flame-spread time of the preliminary specimen and the four test specimens is calculated.

Performance Guidelines

Class 1 textiles do not have a raised fiber surface but had an average time of flame spread in the test of 3.5 seconds or more, or they have a **raised fiber surface**, including the pile loops of terry, and an average time of **flame spread** in the test of more than 7 seconds or burn with a surface flash (time of flame spread less than 7 seconds), provided the intensity of the flame is insufficient to ignite, char, or melt the base fabric. Class 2 textiles have a raised fiber surface and had an average time of flame spread in the test of 4 to 7 seconds, inclusive, and the base fabric was ignited, charred, or melted. Class 3 textiles have a raised fiber surface and had an average time of flame spread in the test of less than 4 seconds, and the base fabric was ignited, charred, or melted.

Adoption of Method If purchaser and supplier agree to have the flammability of toweling evaluated, they may use this test (see Chapter 28).

Flooring Radiant Panel Test Method

The National Institute of Standards and Technology maintains corridor-like testing facilities. Using these facilities, fire researchers have confirmed that the amount of heat radiating onto a floor covering directly affects the distance flames spread in a Stage 3 fire. Because such spreading may restrict or prevent safe egress, a small-scale test method including **radiant heat** as a condition is increasingly used to measure the flame spread of floor coverings intended for installation in corridors. The equipment and procedures used in this test are described here.

This test method has been designated as ASTM E 648 and NFPA 253. It accurately simulates real-life floor covering installation practices and the conditions characteristic of a Stage 3 interior fire. This test does assess the critical relationship between heat energy radiating from the ceiling and flame spread along a corridor floor covering. Because it has thus overcome the major shortcoming of the tunnel test, which is described below, the radiant panel test method is increasingly used by authorities who have jurisdiction over the selection of interior floor finishes for commercial interiors.

The **panel test apparatus** is much smaller than the other tunnel-shaped furnace devices but, like them, it has a corridor-like design (Figure 11.9). An inclined panel radiates heat energy to the surface of the specimen. Because the level of heat radiating onto a corridor carpet

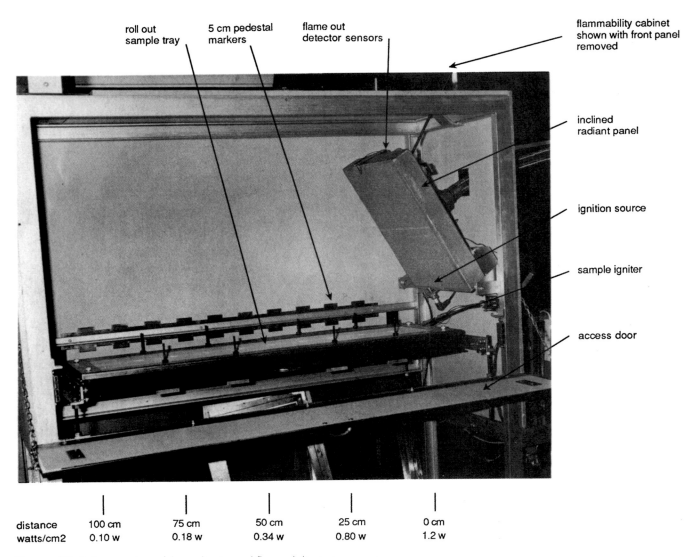

| distance | 100 cm | 75 cm | 50 cm | 25 cm | 0 cm |
| watts/cm2 | 0.10 w | 0.18 w | 0.34 w | 0.80 w | 1.2 w |

Figure 11.9 Interior view of the radiant panel flammability test apparatus.
Courtesy of Custom Scientific Instruments, Inc.

would be highest at the point of **spillover**, the panel is positioned at an angle of 30 degrees to the carpet specimen. The amount of heat energy radiating along the carpet during testing ranges from a maximum of 1.2 watts per square centimeter immediately below the panel to a minimum of 0.10 watt per square centimeter at the opposite end of the specimen.

Test Specimens and Procedures   A carpet specimen, with or without a separate or attached cushion, is cut 42 inches long and 10 inches wide and placed pile side up on the floor of the chamber. A gas flame is impinged on the surface of the specimen immediately below the preheated panel for 10 minutes. Air is allowed to flow through the chamber bottom and exit via a chimney-like opening. The test continues until the floor covering ceases to burn. Three replicate tests are normally required.

Analysis of Results   A numerical value, the **critical radiant flux (CRF)**, is determined by converting the distance of flame spread into watts per square centimeter. The CRF indicates the minimum heat energy that is necessary, or critical, to sustain burning of the floor covering and support flame propagation. According to Figure 11.9, a test sample that stops burning at a distance just short of 20 inches (50 centimeters) down its length would have a CRF of 0.34 watt per square centimeter, whereas a carpet that burned the entire distance would have a CRF of 0.10 watt per square centimeter. Higher CRF values thus indicate safer systems. The CRF value reported is the average of the three replicate tests. No analysis is made of smoke generation.

Performance Requirements   The levels of fire performance of soft floor coverings mandated by municipal, state, and federal agencies are frequently based on recommendations set forth in the **NFPA 101® Life Safety Code®**. Table 11.1 summarizes recommendations pertaining to interior finishes, such as carpet installed on walls, and to interior floor finishes. The materials used for interior finishes are classified in accordance with the tunnel test, and those used for interior floor finishes are classified in accordance with the radiant panel test. Because all large floor coverings must conform with 16 CFR 1630 (FF 1–70), the NFPA does not recommend additional testing for floor coverings other than those installed in exit ways and corridors in certain occupancies.

Adoption of the Method   Several local, state, and federal regulatory agencies have adopted the panel test in lieu of the tunnel test. Some also have established standards pertaining to smoke development. When these agencies have jurisdiction over an installation, smoke development must be measured in a separate test.

Smoke Chamber Test Method

This test method is assigned the designations ASTM E 662 and NFPA 258. It measures the **smoke generation** of solid materials under flaming and nonflaming (smoldering) conditions. The purpose of such testing is to identify materials that would generate large volumes of dense smoke, which would hinder quick and efficient egress by obscuring exit markers and would also hamper breathing.

Test Specimens and Procedures   A specimen, 3 inches square and up to 1 inch thick, is suspended vertically in an enclosed test chamber. Three replicate tests are conducted by exposing the specimen surface to an irradiance level of 2.5 watts per square centimeter; the individual tests are conducted by impinging six flamelets (small flames) across the lower edge of the specimen in combination with the radiant heat. A light beam is passed vertically through the smoke chamber. The test is completed when a minimum **light transmittance value** is reached or 20 minutes have elapsed, whichever occurs first.

Analysis of Results   A photometric system measures the continuous decrease in light transmission as smoke accumulates. These measurements are converted into specific **optical density values**.

Performance Requirements   Required values vary from a low of 50 to a maximum of 450. In some cases, an agency may specify an average of the flaming and nonflaming tests; in other cases, only the results of the flaming tests may be involved.

Adoption of the Method   Various city, state, and federal agencies have adopted this test method for materials in-

Table 11.1 NFPA 101® Life Safety Code® Interior Finish and Interior Floor Finish Recommendations

The following is a compilation of the interior finish requirements of the occupancy chapters of the Code.

Occupancy	Exits	Access to Exits	Other Spaces
Places of assembly—new*	A	A or B	A, B, or C
Places of assembly—existing*	A	A or B	A, B, or C
Educational–new	A	A or B	A, B, or C
	I or II	I or II	A, B, or C
Educational—existing	A	A or B	A, B, or C
Open plan and flexible plan*	A	A	A or B
			C on movable partitions not over 5 ft. (1.5 m) high
Child day-care centers—new	A	A or B	A or B
	I or II	I or II	
Child day-care centers—existing	A	A or B	A or B
	I or II	I or II	
Group day-care homes	A or B	A or B	A, B, or C
Family child day-care homes	A or B	A or B	A, B, or C
Health care—new	A	A	A
	I or II	I or II	B in individual room with capacity not more than four persons
	I	I	
Health care—existing	A or B	A or B	A or B
Detention & correctional—new	A	A	A, B, or C
	I or II	I or II	
Detention & correctional—existing	A or B	A or B	A, B, or C
	I or II	I or II	
Residential, hotels—new	A	A or B	A, B, or C
	I or II	I or II	
Residential, hotels—existing	A or B	A or B	A, B, or C
	I or II	I or II	
Residential, apartment buildings—new	A	A or B	A, B, or C
	I or II	I or II	
Residential, apartment buildings—existing	A or B	A or B	A, B, or C
	I or II	I or II	
Residential, dormitories—new	A	A or B	A, B, or C
	I or II	I or II	
Residential, dormitories—existing	A or B	A or B	A, B, or C
	I or II	I or II	
Residential, 1- and 2-family, small lodging or rooming houses		A, B, or C	
Residential, 1- and 2-family, large lodging or rooming houses	A	B	B
Mercantile—new*	I or II	I or II	A or B

(continued)

Table 11.1 NFPA 101® Life Safety Code® Interior Finish and Interior Floor Finish Recommendations *(continued)*

The following is a compilation of the interior finish requirements of the occupancy chapters of the Code.

Occupancy	Exits	Access to Exits	Other Spaces
Mercantile—existing Class A or B*	A or B	A or B	ceilings—A or B existing on walls—A ,B, or C
Mercantile—existing class C*	A, B, or C	A, B, or C	A, B, or C
Office—new and existing	A or B	A or B	A, B, or C
Industrial	I or II	I or II	A, B, or C
Storage	I or II	I or II	A, B, or C
Unusual structures*	A or B	A, B, or C	A, B, or C

*Exposed portions of structural members complying with the requirements for heavy timber construction may be permitted.

Notes:
Class A Interior Finish—flame spread 0–25, smoke developed 0–450.
Class B Interior Finish—flame spread 26–75, smoke developed 0–450.
Class C Interior Finish—flame spread 76–200, smoke developed 0–450.
Class I Interior Floor Finish—minimum 0.45 watt per sq. cm.
Class II Interior Floor Finish—minimum 0.22 watt per sq. cm.

Automatic Sprinklers—where a complete standard system of automatic sprinklers is installed, interior finish with spread rating not over Class C may be used in any location where Class B is normally specified and with rating of Class B in any location where Class A is normally specified; similarly, Class II interior floor finish may be used in any location where Class I is normally specified and no critical radiant flux rating is required where Class II is normally specified.

Reprinted with permission from NFPA 101–2009, Life Safety Code, Copyright 2009, National Fire Protection Association, Quincy, MA 02269. This reprinted material is not the complete and official position of the NFPA on the referenced subject, which is represented only by the standard in its entirety.

stalled in facilities they oversee. The General Services Administration, for example, has combined CRF and smoke development limits to establish two classifications, and defined a third through 16 CFR 1630. The three classes and the various GSA spaces to which they apply are listed below. These classes must not be confused with the A, B, and C classes that categorize the results of tunnel testing.

> Class A: a CRF of 0.50 watt per square centimeter or greater and a maximum specific optical density not over 450 flaming. Class A carpet is not needed in office buildings.
>
> Class B: a CRF of 0.25 watt per square centimeter or greater and a maximum specific optical density not over 450 flaming. Class B carpet is required in unsprinklered corridors exposed to office space having a controlled equivalent **fuel load** of 6 pounds per square foot or less.
>
> Class C: the face and back of the carpet and separate cushion pass 16 CFR 1630. Class C carpet may be installed in all office areas and in corridors protected with automatic sprinklers.

Motor Vehicle Safety Standard No. 302

The **Motor Vehicle Safety Standard No. 302 (MVSS 302)** became effective on September 1, 1972. This standard is designed to reduce deaths and injuries to motor vehicle occupants caused by vehicle fires, especially those originating in the interior of the vehicle from sources such as matches or cigarettes.

Test Specimens and Procedures   Whenever possible, each specimen of material to be tested is a rectangle 4 inches wide by 14 inches long. The specimens are conditioned for 24 hours at a temperature of 70 °F and a relative humidity of 50 percent and each is then clamped in a U-shaped frame, exposing an area that measures 2 inches wide by 13 inches long. A secured specimen is mounted horizontally in a test apparatus, such as that shown in Figure 11.10. A flame is impinged on the bottom edge of the open end of the specimen for 15 seconds.

Timing of the flame spread is begun when the flame from the burning specimen reaches a point 1½ inches from the open end of the specimen. The time elapsed for the flame to progress to a point 1½ inches from the clamped end of the specimen is measured.

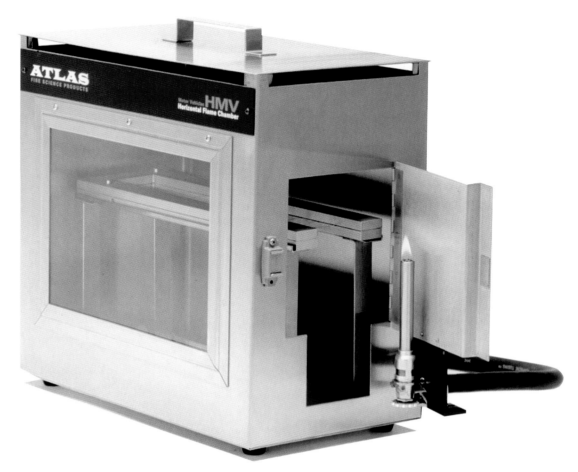

Figure 11.10 Horizontal flammability tester. Courtesy of SDL Atlas LLC.

Analysis of Results The burn rate for the specimen is calculated by the following formula:

$$B = 60 \times D/T$$

where B = burning rate inches/minute, D = length the flame travels in inches, and T = time in seconds to travel D inches.

Performance Requirements A material is considered to pass the test and be acceptable for use if the burn rate does not exceed 4 inches per minute. If a material stops burning before it has burned for 60 seconds from the start of timing and has not burned more than 2 inches from the point where timing was started, it also meets the requirements.

Adoption of the Method The National Highway Traffic Safety Administration (NHTSA) intends that the rate at which an interior material transmits flame across its surface should not be so rapid as to prevent the driver from stopping the vehicle and all occupants from leaving it before injury occurs as a result of fire. The provisions of MVSS 302 apply to seat cushions, seat backs, seat belts, interior roof lining, front and side panels, floor coverings, and other materials used in occupant compartments of passenger cars, multipurpose passenger vehicles, trucks, and buses.

FAA Paragraph 25.853 (b)

The Federal Aviation Administration (FAA) flammability regulation for textile items used in compartments occupied by the crew or passengers in airplanes is designated as **Paragraph 25.853 (b)**. Other paragraphs in the standard, which was issued on February 15, 1972, concern such items as landing-gear systems, escape routes, exit markers, and nontextile interior finishing materials. The general focus of the standard is to improve the crashworthiness and emergency evacuation equipment of airliners.

Test Specimens and Procedures   The specimens are cut 2¾ by 12½ inches, with the most critical flammability conditions corresponding to the long dimension. The specimens are conditioned for 24 hours at a temperature of 70 °F and a relative humidity of 50 percent; they are then clamped in a U-shaped frame. The secured specimen is vertically suspended in a draft-free test chamber, shown in Figure 11.11. A flame is impinged on the lower edge of the specimen for 12 seconds and then removed.

Analysis of Results   Three results are determined for each specimen:

1.   The **after flame time** is the time the specimen continues to flame after the burner flame is removed.

2.   The **afterglow time** is the time the specimen continues to glow after it stops flaming.

3.   The **char length** is measured by inserting the correct weight (determined by the weight of the fabric being tested) on one side of the charred area and gently raising the opposite side of the specimen. The length of the tear is measured and recorded.

Performance Requirements   Materials used in compartment interiors must be self-extinguishing. The average char length may not exceed 8 inches and the average after flame time may not exceed 15 seconds.

Adoption of the Method   The provisions of Paragraph 25.853 (b) apply to upholstery, draperies, floor coverings, seat cushions, padding, decorative and nondecorative coated fabrics, leather, trays, and galley furnishings. They also apply to such items as acoustical insulation.

NFPA 701 Small-scale Test Method I

NFPA 701 Standard Methods of Fire Tests for Flame Propagation of Textiles and Films may be used to evaluate the effectiveness of polymer additives and finishing compounds in reducing the flammability of textile window coverings. The small-scale test method can be used to evaluate the flame resistance of fabrics that do not exhibit excessive shrinkage or melting when exposed to a flame.

Test Specimens and Procedures.   Ten specimens of the covering are cut 5.9 inches by 15.8 inches, with the length parallel to the lengthwise direction of the material. The specimens are then conditioned in an oven at a temperature of 220 °F for 30 minutes or, if they would melt or distort in the oven, they are conditioned at 68 °F for a minimum of 24 hours. Each specimen is then placed in an open-ended specimen holder and suspended in a vertical flammability tester, similar to the apparatus in Figure 11.11. The flame from a burner is then applied to the lower edge for 45 seconds.

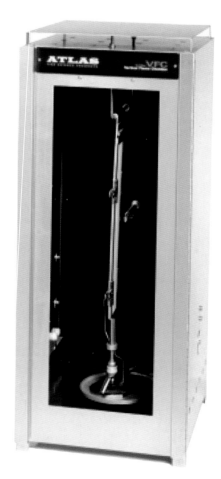

Figure 11.11 Vertical flammability tester. Courtesy of SDL Atlas LLC.

Flame Resistance Requirements   In order for the material to pass the small-scale test, the specimens must meet the following three requirements:

1. Fragments or residues of specimens that fall to the floor of the test chamber shall not continue to burn for more than an average of 2 seconds per specimen for the sample of 10 specimens.

2. The average weight loss of the 10 specimens in a sample shall be 40 percent or less.

3. No individual specimen's percent mass loss shall deviate more than 3 standard deviations from the mean for the 10 specimens.

Adoption of the Method   NFPA 701 is intended for use with textiles and films treated with flame-retardant agents or composed of flame-resistant manufactured fibers. Fabrics expected to retain their flame-resistant qualities through dry cleaning, laundering, weathering, or other exposures to water are subjected to accelerated exposure procedures prior to testing. Treated awning fabrics, for example, would be exposed to simulated weathering conditions and then tested.

UFAC Fabric Classification Test Method

The **UFAC Voluntary Action Program**, discussed earlier in this chapter, is designed to improve the ability of upholstered furniture to resist catching fire from a burning cigarette, the most common source of furniture ignition. At the outset, upholstery fabrics are divided into two categories of ignition propensity, based on their ability to resist ignition when exposed to a burning cigarette. The procedures used are outlined in the **UFAC Fabric Classification Test Method—1990**. This test is similar to NFPA 260, Standard Methods of Tests and Classification System for Cigarette Ignition Resistance of Components of Upholstered Furniture, and ASTM E 1353, Standard Test Methods for Cigarette Ignition Resistance of Components of Upholstered Furniture.

Test Specimens and Procedures   In this test method, vertical and horizontal panels are upholstered using the cover fabrics to be tested and 2-inch thick polyurethane foam filling materials. As schematized in Figure 11.12, the panels are placed in the test assembly, and a lighted nonfilter cigarette is placed in the crevice of the assembly and cov-

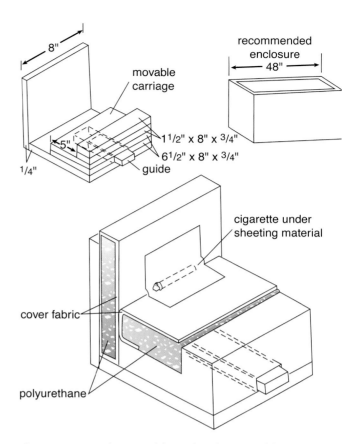

Figure 11.12 The assembly used in the UFAC fabric classification test.
Courtesy of the Upholstered Furniture Action Council, Inc.

ered with a piece of cotton bedsheeting fabric. The cigarette is allowed to burn its entire length unless an obvious ignition occurs. Three replicate tests are required for each fabric.

Test Criteria   If ignition occurs on any one of the three specimens, the fabric is Class II. If no ignition occurs, the vertical char length is measured from the crevice to the highest part of the destroyed or degraded cover fabric. If the char length is less than 1¾ inches, the fabric is Class I; if the char length is equal to or greater than 1¾ inches, the fabric is Class II. This classification determines which construction methods must be employed with the cover fabric to comply with UFAC construction criteria.

Adoption of the Method   In accordance with the UFAC Voluntary Action Program, Class I fabrics may be used directly over conventional polyurethane in the horizontal seating surfaces of upholstered furniture bearing the UFAC hangtag. Class II fabrics require an approved barrier between the cover fabric and conventional polyurethane foam in the horizontal seating surfaces.

UFAC Welt Cord Test Method

This test method is employed to identify welt cording that is suitable for use in seats, backs, and pillows in UFAC-approved constructions. The welt cords must meet the requirement of the **UFAC Welt Cord Test Method—1990**.

Test Specimens and Procedures   In this test, welt cording is placed in the center of a piece of UFAC Standard Type II cover fabric that is folded to make an unsewn welt. This cover fabric, a 100 percent bright, regular rayon in basket weave construction, is also used to cover the vertical and horizontal panels. The welt is placed in the crevice formed by the abutment of the horizontal and vertical panels in the test assembly, which is similar to that shown in Figure 11.12. As shown in Figure 11.13, a lighted cigarette is placed on the welt and covered with a piece of cotton bedsheeting. Three replicate tests are run.

Test Criteria   The welt cording is acceptable if no ignition occurs, or if the maximum height of the vertical char on each of the vertical panels does not equal or exceed 1½ inches.

If one specimen has a vertical char equal to or greater than 1½ inches, three additional specimens are tested. If one or more additional specimens have a vertical char equal to or greater than 1½ inches, the test material fails.

Adoption of the Method   In accordance with the UFAC Voluntary Action Program, welt cording used with furniture carrying the UFAC hangtag must meet the requirements of this test.

UFAC Decking Materials Test Method

As part of the UFAC Voluntary Action Program, deck padding materials used under loose cushions should resist ignition from smoldering cigarettes. The resistance of polyurethane foam, bonded fiber pads, treated cotton batting, and other padding materials intended for use in decking under loose cushions can be assessed by subjecting them to the **UFAC Decking Materials Test Method—1990**.

Test Specimens and Procedures   In preparation for this test, decking material is cut to size and placed on a plywood assembly base, shown schematically in Figure 11.14. The decking material is covered with UFAC Standard Type II fabric and the layered fabrics are held in place by a wooden retainer ring. Three lighted cigarettes are placed on the decking cover fabric and covered with 100 percent

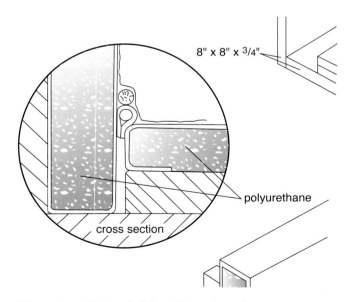

Figure 11.13 Detail of the UFAC welt cord test.
Courtesy of the Upholstered Furniture Action Council, Inc.

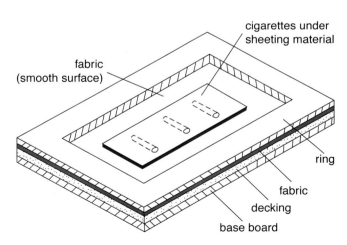

Figure 11.14 The assembly used in the UFAC decking materials test method.
Courtesy of the Upholstered Furniture Action Council, Inc.

cotton sheeting. The cigarettes are allowed to burn their full lengths and the maximum char lengths measured from the cigarettes are recorded.

Test Criteria   The decking material is acceptable if it meets the same criteria listed for the Welt Cord Test Method.

Adoption of the Method   In accordance with the UFAC Voluntary Action Program, decking material used with furniture carrying the UFAC hangtag must meet the requirements of this test.

UFAC Filling/Padding Component Test Method, Parts A and B

This test method, which has two parts, determines which filling or padding components intended for use in upholstered furniture exhibit sufficient resistance to smoldering cigarette ignition to merit use in items bearing the UFAC hangtag. Part A of this test method is used with slab or garnetted filling/padding components that include, but are not limited to, battings of natural and man-made (manufactured) fibers, foamed or cellular fillings or cushioning materials, and resilient pads of natural or man-made (manufactured) fibers. Part B of this test method is used with fibrous or particulate materials that include, but are not limited to, staple of natural and man-made (manufactured) fibers, shredded foamed or cellular filling materials, and composites of any of these, together with any protective interliners that may be necessary to meet the requirements of the test method.

Test Specimens and Procedures   The filling material to be tested is used in the vertical and horizontal panels of the test assembly shown in Figure 11.12, in place of the polyurethane. It is covered with UFAC Standard Type I mattress ticking, which is composed of 100 percent cotton and has been laundered and tumble-dried once in accordance with prescribed UFAC procedures. One at a time, three ignited cigarettes are placed in the crevice and covered with sheeting fabric.

Test Criteria   In Part A, the filling/padding material is acceptable if no ignition occurs, or if no vertical char equals or exceeds 1½ inches. If one specimen has a vertical char equal to or greater than 1½ inches, three additional specimens are tested. If one or more additional specimens have a vertical char equal to or greater than 1½ inches, the test

material fails. Part B has an additional criterion: no specimen can have evolvement of smoke or heat.

Adoption of the Method   In accordance with the UFAC Voluntary Action Program, filling/padding material used with furniture carrying the UFAC hangtag must meet the requirements of this test.

UFAC Interior Fabric Test Method

In order for upholstered furniture items to bear the UFAC hangtag, interior fabrics used in intimate contact with the outer fabrics must exhibit an acceptable level of performance with respect to cigarette ignition resistance. **UFAC Interior Fabric Test Method—1990** can be used to assess this performance.

Test Specimens and Procedures   The assembly used in the required three replicate tests is like that illustrated in Figure 11.12, except that an interior fabric test specimen is placed between the outer covering and the foam filling of the horizontal panels. For this test, the vertical and horizontal panels are covered with UFAC Standard Type I mattress ticking. The three lighted cigarettes are again placed one at a time in the crevice and covered.

Test Criteria.   The test criteria for this test are identical to those for the Welt Cord test.

Adoption of the Method   In accordance with the UFAC Voluntary Action Program, interior fabrics used with furniture carrying the UFAC hangtag must meet the requirements of this test.

UFAC Barrier Test Method

This test method is intended to define the minimum performance level for barrier materials to be placed between Class II fabrics and conventional polyurethane foam in horizontal seating surfaces. This will minimize the likelihood of ignition of the foam in the event a Class II fabric is generating considerable heat as it undergoes decomposition and combustion.

Test Specimens and Procedures   Three tests are run using the assembly illustrated in Figure 11.15. UFAC Standard Type II cover fabric is used as the covering. The barrier material to be tested is placed between the cover fabric and the polyurethane substrate in both vertical and hori-

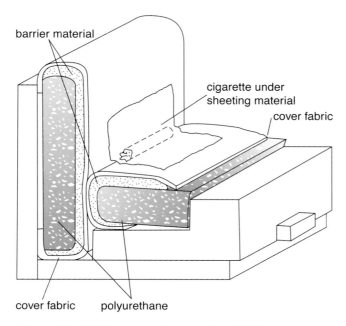

barrier material

cigarette under
sheeting material

cover fabric

cover fabric   polyurethane

Figure 11.15 The assembly used in the UFAC barrier test.
Courtesy of the Upholstered Furniture Action Council, Inc.

zontal panels. A lighted cigarette is placed in the crevice and covered with a piece of sheeting material.

Test Criteria The test criteria for this test are identical to those for the Welt Cord Test Method.

Adoption of the Method In accordance with the UFAC Voluntary Action Program, barrier materials used with furniture covered with Class II fabric and filled with polyurethane foam must meet the requirements of this test if the item is to bear the UFAC hangtag.

The importance of a suitable barrier is underscored by the full-scale fire tests shown in Figures 11.16 and 11.17. When conventional items, including a chair with no flame-resistant barrier, were used, the fire quickly spread, with flashover occurring within two and a half minutes after ignition.

For the test pictured in Figure 11.17, the model room was furnished with bedding, window treatments, and wall-coverings of glass fiber fabrics, and the chair had a flame-resistant barrier of specially coated glass fiber yarns. In this case, the nylon upholstery burned away, the protective barrier charred but did not burn, and the fire was contained in Stage 1.

A closeup photograph of the chairs used in the UFAC Barrier Test Method is shown in Figure 11.18. It is evident that the presence of the protective barrier in the chair on the right prevented ignition of the foam substrate. The charred area is substantial, but it should be noted that the ignition source was a paper-filled grocery bag, not an ignited cigarette.

UFAC Standard Test Methods for Decorative Trims, Edging, and Brush Fringes In a continuing effort to make upholstered furniture *safer* when exposed to an ignition source, members of the UFAC developed the UFAC Standard Test Methods for Decorative Trims, Edging, and Brush Fringes—1993.

Test Specimens and Procedures The test apparatus used in this test is similar to that used in the Welt Cord Test Method shown in Figure 11.13. Again, Type II cover fabric, polyurethane foam, and cotton sheeting are used. A lighted cigarette is placed on top of the trim, edging, or brush fringe being tested and covered with sheeting.

Test Criteria If all test specimens have no ignition, or if the vertical char of each is less than 1½ inches upward from the crevice, the test material passes. If one test specimen has a vertical char equal to or greater than 1½ inches, three additional specimens are tested. If all three additional specimens have a vertical char of less than 1½ inches, the test material passes. If one additional specimen has a vertical char equal to or greater than 1½ inches, the material fails. If two or more original test specimens have a vertical char of ½ inches or more, the material fails.

Adoption of the Method Trims meeting the above criteria will be classified as UFAC Type I decorative trim, edging, or brush fringe; providing the remainder of the upholstered furniture meets UFAC requirements, the UFAC hangtag may be used when Type I trim is present.

In the event the trim fails to conform to the above criteria, it should be retested, using a polyester fiber barrier and UFAC Standard Type II covering. If the trim then meets the above requirements, it is labeled UFAC Type II trimming. The furniture would then be eligible to bear the UFAC hangtag, as long as a garnetted polyester fiber barrier is used.

If the decorative trim, edging, or brush fringe fails with both the Type II fabric alone and the Type II fabric and polyester fiber barrier, the trimming is classified as

Figure 11.16 Full-scale fire test in mock hotel room furnished with conventional items, including a chair having no flame-resistant barrier.
Courtesy of Owens Corning.

Type III. UFAC hangtags are not permitted with uphol-stered furniture using Type III decorative trim, edging, or brush fringe.

California Technical Bulletins

California is one of only a few states that regulate seat-ing products through mandatory testing. These tests are described in what are known as California Bulletins. Cali-fornia Bulletin 117 (CAL 117) is a small-scale upholstery fabric flammability test developed by the California Bu-reau of Home Furnishings and Thermal Insulation. The test has a pass/fail rating system. California Bulletin 133 (CAL 133) is a full-scale upholstered seating flammability test used to evaluate seating for occupancies such as pris-ons, hospitals, nursing homes, and other high-risk public spaces. This test also utilizes a pass/fail rating system.[4]

Proposed Standard for Residential Upholstered Furniture, CFR Part 1634

The proposal, **Standard for the Flammability of Residential Upholstered Furniture CFR Part 1634,** would establish performance requirements and certifica-tion and labeling requirements for upholstered furniture. There has been much concern regarding the lack of an open flame standard for residential upholstered furniture. The goal of the proposed standard is to prevent ignition or slow the spread and intensity of upholstered furniture fires without requiring the use of fire-retardant chemicals. Under the proposal, manufacturers could meet the perfor-mance standard by using smolder-resistant cover fabrics or interior fire-resistant barriers to protect the furniture's internal filling material, which is the primary fuel in an upholstered furniture fire. The proposed standard applies

Figure 11.17 Full-scale fire test in a mock hotel room furnished with flame-resistant items, including a chair with a flame-resistant barrier between the outer covering and the foam filling.
Courtesy of Owens Corning.

to (1) residential seating products intended for indoor use and constructed with contiguous upholstered seats and backs, such as chairs and sofas; (2) upholstered furniture used in dormitories; and (3) some home office furniture sold through retailers for household use. The main focus of the new standard is smoldering resistance, minimal reliance on fire-retardant chemicals, and compliance options utilizing barrier materials that can be used with any cover fabrics that do not comply with the smoldering ignition requirements.

The upholstered furniture tests are conducted using seating mockups of fabric and filling materials. The proposed test contains a cigarette smoldering test for both the cover fabric and the barrier but has no provisions for an open flame test of the upholstery cover fabric. For fabrics that fail the smoldering test, a barrier is considered in the standard that includes both a smoldering test and an open flame test. Type I cover fabrics protect interior fillings from progressive smoldering and transition to flaming. Complying fabrics can be used with any material. Type II cover fabrics must contain interior barriers that protect the filling from progressive smoldering and from flaming by ignited cover fabrics. Complying barriers may be used with any cover fabrics and filling materials.

Test Specimens and Procedures The **cover fabric smoldering resistance test** requires testing of fabrics in combination with a standard polyurethane foam substrate. A

Figure 11.18 Close-up view of upholstered chairs used in full-scale tests. The chair on the right had a flame-resistant fabric of specially coated glass fiber installed as a protective barrier between the outer covering and the foam filling. Courtesy of Owens Corning.

lighted cigarette is placed in the seat/back crevice of the mockup and is allowed to burn its entire length.

Test Criteria   The mockup must not continue to smolder after the end of the 45-minute test or transition to flaming at any time during the test. Initially, 10 specimens are tested. If the 10 initial specimens meet these criteria, the cover fabric sample passes. If there is a failure in any one of the 10 initial specimens, the test must be repeated on an additional 20 specimens. At least 25 of the 30 must meet the criteria.

Test Specimens and Procedures   For the **interior fire barrier smoldering test**, the barrier is placed between

a standard foam substrate and a standard cotton velvet cover. A lighted cigarette is placed in the seat/back crevice of the mockup.

Test Criteria   The foam substrate must not exceed 1 percent mass loss by the end of the 45-minute test, and the mockup must not transition to open flaming at any time during the duration of the test. Initially, 10 specimens are tested. If all 10 initial samples meet these criteria, the barrier sample passes. If any one of the 10 samples fails, an additional 20 specimens must be tested, and at least 25 of 30 must meet the criteria.

Test Specimens and Procedures The proposed standard also contains provisions for the open flame resistance of barriers. In addition to providing protection from small flame ignition, the open flame performance test contributes to the protection of materials from the progression of smoldering to flaming combustion. The **fire barrier open flame test** requires the testing of barriers used in upholstered furniture interiors. In this test the barrier is placed between a standard rayon cover fabric and a standard foam substrate on a metal test frame. An open flame ignition source is applied to the seat/back crevice of the mockup.

Test Criteria The mockup must not exceed 20 percent mass loss by the end of the 45-minute test. Again, 10 initial samples are tested. If there is a failure with any of the 10 specimens, an additional 20 specimens are tested, and at least 25 of the 30 must meet the criteria for the sample barrier to pass.

Adaptation of the Test Method In addition to flammability performance requirements, the proposed standard contains provisions relating to certification and record-keeping, testing to support guaranties, and labeling of finished articles of upholstered furniture. The manufacturer is required to label the product either type I or type II, certifying that it meets the criteria. These requirements are intended to help manufacturers, importers, and suppliers ensure that their products comply and to help the CPSC staff enforce the proposed standard.

The CPSC is planning full-scale testing, lab testing, and the evaluation of reduced ignition-propensity cigarettes. It will also be responding to public comments on this issue. This federal flammability standard for residential upholstered furniture remains in the developmental phase. There has been much concern regarding the lack of an open-flame standard for residential upholstered furniture.

Large-scale Test Methods

Large-scale test methods are also laboratory procedures, but they use larger test specimens than do small-scale tests. A large-scale test method is used with textile window coverings, soft floor coverings, and mattresses.

NFPA 701 Large-scale Test Method

The **NFPA 701 large-scale test** may be selected for use with covering materials that show excessive melting or shrinkage when tested by the small-scale test. This method is also useful for evaluating the fire behavior of coverings hung in folds, as is typical in window treatments.

Test Specimens and Procedures Specimens of the covering material may be tested in single, flat sheets or they may be hung with folds. For flat testing, ten specimens, 5 inches by 7 feet, are cut. For testing with folds, four lengths of the covering, each cut 25 inches by 7 feet, are folded longitudinally to form four folds, each approximately 5 inches wide. In either case, half the specimens have their long dimension in the direction of the warp and half have their long dimension in the direction of the filling. The specimens are conditioned as described for the small-scale test.

The specimens, flat or folded, are suspended in the tester, which is a sheet-iron stack 12 inches square and 7 feet high. The lower edge of the specimen is 4 inches above the burner tip and an 11-inch flame is held under the specimen for 2 minutes.

Flame Resistance Requirements In order for the covering material to pass the large-scale test, the specimens must meet the following four requirements:

1. No specimen shall continue flaming for more than two seconds after the test flame is removed from contact with the specimen.

2. The vertical spread of burning on the material in single sheets shall not exceed 10 inches above the tip of the test flame. This vertical spread shall be measured as the distance from the tip of the test flame to a horizontal line above which all material is sound and in original condition, except for possible smoke deposits.

3. The vertical spread of burning on the folded specimens shall not exceed 35 inches above the tip of the test flame, but the afterglow may spread in the folds.

4. At no time during or after the application of the test flame shall portions or residues of textiles or films that break or drip from any test specimen continue to flame after they reach the floor of the tester.[3]

In the event of fire, fabrics meeting the flame resistance requirements included in the small- or large-scale test methods would not be likely to propagate the flames to the floor, wall, and ceiling. This reduces the threat of a Stage 1 fire growing into a Stage 2 fire.

Adoption of the Method

As with the NFPA 701 small-scale test method, the large-scale test method may be used to measure the ignition propensity of fabrics to be installed indoors or outdoors.

Tunnel Test Method

This test method, also known as the **Steiner Tunnel Test Method**, measures the surface burning characteristics of building materials. It has been designated as ASTM E 84, NFPA 255, and UL 723. The testing apparatus is structured to simulate a corridor, and the testing procedures and results are used to assess flame spread and smoke generation. The method is thus intended to evaluate the potential hazard of a textile floor covering in a Stage 3 fire.

Test Specimens and Procedures

A specimen, 25 feet by 1 foot 8 inches, is mounted on the ceiling of the tunnel chamber. The sample is then subjected to gas jet flames and heat for 10 minutes. Temperatures range from 1,600 to 1,800 7F. Testing is complete when 10 minutes have elapsed or the specimen has burned completely, whichever occurs first.

Analysis of Results

Time and flame spread distance values are plotted graphically and compared with those recorded for asbestos-cement board (assigned a flame spread rating of 0) and select-grade red oak flooring (assigned a flame spread rating of 100) to arrive at a flame spread classification. Class A includes flame spread ratings from 0 to 25, Class B from 26 to 75, and Class C from 76 to 200. Smoke density values are determined separately.

Performance Requirements

Flammability requirements for selected interior finishes, such as textile wallcoverings, are classified according to the tunnel test. The NFPA 101® Life Safety Code® includes recommendations that may be mandated by an agency having jurisdiction over an occupancy and the materials to be installed within the facility (see Table 11.1).

Adoption of the Method

In recent years, the use of the tunnel test as a method for evaluating the potential fire hazard of textile structures to be installed as floor coverings has been diminishing. Although the long, tunnel-shaped testing apparatus does indeed resemble a corridor, the method has two major shortcomings when correlated to end use. First, because the specimen is mounted on the ceiling, the test does not realistically portray real-life installations. Second, the method fails to incorporate the critical variable of the heat energy that will be radiating into a corridor in the event an interior fire progresses from Stage 2 to Stage 3. Nonetheless, testing by this method continues to be required for some installations, and is often recommended or required for carpet to be used as an interior finish on walls and ceilings (see Table 11.1).

Mattress and Mattress Pad Test Method

The Standard for the Flammability of Mattresses, **16 CFR Part 1632**, was established in 1974 to protect the public against unreasonable risk of mattress fires. The most common mode of bedding ignition, a burning cigarette, is used as the source of ignition in the test.

Test Specimens and Procedures

In testing, the bare sleeping surface of mattresses, including smooth, tape edge, and quilted or tufted locations, is exposed to as least nine ignited cigarettes that are 85 millimeters long and have no filter tips. These locations are also tested by placing nine additional burning cigarettes between two bed sheets that cover the mattress (Figure 11.19). The muslin or percale sheets used must be 100 percent cotton, have no durable press resins or flame-retardant agents, and be laundered one time prior to testing.

Mattress pads are tested in the same manner before they are laundered or dry cleaned and again after they have been cleaned in accordance with prescribed procedures. Pads treated with a flame-retardant agent must be labeled with precautionary care instructions to help prevent the use of agents or procedures that could impair the effectiveness of the finishing compound.

Analysis of Results

The char length of each test location is measured and reported in inches.

Performance Requirements

Individual cigarette test locations pass the test if the char length of the mattress or mattress pad surface is not more than 2 inches in any direction

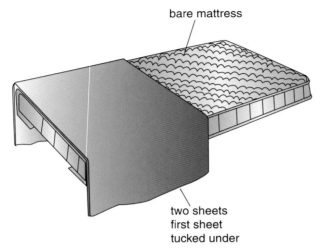

bare mattress

two sheets
first sheet
tucked under

a) mattress preparation

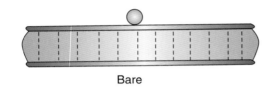

Bare

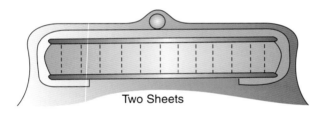

Two Sheets

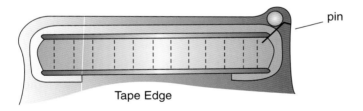

pin

Tape Edge

b) cigarette location

Figure 11.19 Mattress preparation and cigarette locations used in 16 CFR 1632.

from the nearest point of the cigarette. All eighteen cigarette locations must pass the test in order for the mattress or pad to be marketed.

Adoption of the Method The provisions of 16 CFR 1632 apply to domestic and imported mattresses. Included in the definition of mattresses are mattress pads; adult, youth,

crib, and portable crib mattresses; bunk bed mattresses; corner group and daybed mattresses; rollaway and convertible sofa bed mattresses; high risers; trundle bed mattresses; and **futons**—flexible mattresses filled with cotton batting. Items specifically excluded from 16 CFR 1632 are sleeping bags, pillows, mattress foundations such as box springs, water bed and air mattresses, and other items such as chaise lounges and sofa beds, which are distinct from convertible sofa beds. A **convertible sofa bed** is an upholstered sofa with a mattress concealed under the cushions; a **sofa bed** is an upholstered sofa with a hinged back that swings down flat with the seating cushions to form the sleeping surface.

16 CFR Part 1633

In 1996 the Sleep Product Safety Council (SPSC) and CPSC studied residential mattress fires set by open flames. Based on this research, the mattress industry began discussing a federal regulation for mattresses and resistance to open flame sources, such as candles, matches, and cigarette lighters. In 2001 the CPSC proposed a new federal regulation to address mattress flammability to open flame sources. The U.S. Product and Consumer Safety Commission approved **16 CFR Part 1633**, the new federal Standard for the Flammability (Open-Flame) of Mattress Sets, in 2006. The standard is the first new federal flammability regulation for mattresses in 35 years and became effective July 1, 2007.

The CPSC issued the flammability regulation to reduce deaths and injuries related to mattress fires, particularly those initially ignited by open flame sources. 16 CFR Part 1633 was developed with the active support of many members of the U.S. mattress industry, barrier suppliers, and the polyurethane foam industry and applies to residential mattresses and mattress sets manufactured in the United States.

The standard addresses stringent manufacturing, testing, and document retention requirements. The mattresses that comply with the requirements will generate a smaller-size fire with a slower growth rate, thus reducing the possibility of **flashover** occurring. Flashover is the point at which the entire contents of a room are ignited simultaneously by radiant heat, making conditions in the room untenable and safe exit from the room impossible. About two-thirds of all mattress fatalities are attributed to mattress fires that lead to flashover.

The new law is based on California's TB603, a mattress flammability standard adopted in 2005. The standard was based, in part, on research performed by the National

Figure 11.20 Full-scale fire test showing the growth of an interior fire from Stage 1 to Stage 2. The room was furnished with flammable items.
Courtesy of Owens Corning.

Figure 11.21 Full-scale test showing minimal flame propagation in a room furnished with some flame-resistant items. Courtesy of Owens Corning.

Institute of Standards and Technology (NIST). A key advantage of the new mattress standard is its flexibility. It requires composite performance and leaves it up to the manufacturer to find the best way to comply. Compliance is not optional, and the standard preempts individual states from setting different mattress flammability rules.

Test Specimens and Procedures 16 CFR Part 1633 is a full-scale test necessary to evaluate the fire performance of a mattress. The specimen, a mattress and foundation or mattress alone, is exposed to a pair of T-shaped propane gas burners. The specimen is to be no smaller than twin size, unless the largest size mattress or set produced of that type is smaller than twin size, in which case the largest size must be tested. The burners impose a speci-

fied heat simultaneously to the top and side of the mattress set for a specified period of time. The mattress is allowed to burn freely for 30 minutes. Measurements are taken of the heat release rate from the specimen and the energy generated from the fire.

Test Criteria The standard established two test criteria, both of which the mattress set must meet in order to comply with the standard: (1) the peak rate of heat release for the mattress set must not exceed 200 kilowatts at any time during the 30-minute test, and (2) the total heat release must not exceed 15 megajoules for the first 10 minutes of the test. Mattresses that meet the standard's criteria will make only a limited contribution to a fire, especially in the early stages of a fire. This will allow occupants to discover the fire and escape.

Adoption of the Method Each mattress set must bear a permanent label stating (1) the name of the manufacturer, (2) the complete physical address of the manufacturer, (3) the month and year of manufacture, (4) the model identification, (5) prototype identification, and (6) a certification that the mattress complies with the standard.

Most mattress manufacturers have initially complied with the new flammability standard by adding an ignition-resistant barrier material between the outside covering and the interior component material. Using this approach, manufacturers use better quality foam cushioning materials, which offer all the comfort, support, and lasting physical performance required of a good mattress product. These improved mattresses have resulted in significant reductions in deaths and injuries associated with the risk of mattress fires.

Specifically excluded from the definition of mattress are mattress pads, pillows, and other items used on top of a mattress, upholstered furniture that does not contain a mattress, and other product pads.

Full-scale Test Methods

Full-scale testing facilities may be constructed to replicate a room or a corridor. Room-size facilities make possible ob-servation of the progressive growth of an interior fire, and they are particularly useful in assessing the involvement of each of several items. Corridor-like facilities can be used to determine the effects various conditions have on a Stage 3 fire; results obtained with them underscore the importance of preserving a safe means of egress.

In the Life Safety Laboratory maintained by Owens Corning, a replica of a typical hotel room has been constructed. For the test shown in Figure 11.20, the room was furnished with conventional, as opposed to flame resistant, items. Flashover occurred within two and a half minutes after the newspaper-filled brown paper bag on the chair was ignited. For the test shown in Figure 11.21, beddings composed of specially coated Fiberglas® and flame-resistant carpet were used. Here, the fire did not spread beyond the immediate ignition site; the growth of the fire from Stage 1 to Stage 2 was prevented.

These investigations show that occupants of a room furnished with some flame-resistant items would have more time for safe egress. Both tests make apparent the value of early warning systems and automatic sprinklers.

Summary

In an effort to reduce the threat to life and property posed by flammable fabrics, the U.S. Congress passed the Flammable Fabrics Act and directed the Consumer Product Safety Commission to monitor the involvement of textile products in burn accidents. As a result, flammability performance standards have been established for carpet, rugs, and mattresses, and a standard has been proposed for upholstered furniture. The test methods adopted in these standards simulate the conditions of real-life situations, so that researchers and producers can make reliable predictions of in-use performance.

Although a flammability standard was considered for upholstered furniture in the 1970s, a mandatory standard did not follow. Instead, the CPSC monitored the fire-related hazards of upholstered furniture and the work of the UFAC. Because of the increase in upholstery fires related to smoldering cigarettes, the FTC published a proposed flammability standard for upholstered furniture in 2008. This standard test has been proposed to test upholstery cover fabrics and interior barriers and is currently in the development phase. The UFAC developed a program, including several test methods reviewed in this chapter, to improve the ability of upholstered furniture to resist ignition from a burning cigarette. A hangtag identifies items that comply with the UFAC program. Products so labeled are safer, but they are not fireproof, and consumers must exercise care in using smoking materials.

Several practices can widen the margin of fire safety beyond that provided by law. Residential and commercial consumers can select noncombustible fibers and fibers with inherent or engineered flame resistance. Smoke detectors can be installed to alert residents before a small fire spreads. When a fire extinguisher is readily available, the fire can then be extinguished, further property damage prevented, and personal injury avoided. Automatic sprinkling systems can be in place to halt the spreading of an uncontained fire, thus lessening the generation of smoke and lethal concentrations of toxic gases and preserving the means of egress to a safe area. Corridors leading to exits must be kept clear and the exits themselves clearly illuminated. Finally, of course, most textiles require an external source of heat for ignition. To reduce the frequency of ignition, consumers must handle the most common source of ignition, burning cigarettes, and other smoking materials carefully.

Key Terms

after flame time
afterglow time
char length
Code of Federal Regulations (CFR)
combustion
Consumer Product Safety Commission (CPSC)
convertible sofa bed
cover fabric smoldering resistance test
critical radiant flux (CRF)
egress
Federal Trade Commission (FTC)
fire barrier open flame test
flameless combustion
flame propagation
flame spread
flaming combustion
Flammable Fabrics Act (FFA)
flashover
fuel load
full-scale testing
futons
glowing
interior fire barrier smoldering test
kindling or ignition temperature
large-scale test methods

light transmittance value
methenamine tablet
molten polymer compounds
Motor Vehicle Safety Standard No. 302 (MVSS 302)
National Electronic Injury Surveillance System (NEISS)
National Institute of Standards and Technology (NIST)
NFPA 101® Life Safety Code®
NFPA 701 small-scale test
NFPA 701 large-scale test
optical density values
panel test apparatus
paragraph 25.853 (b)
pyrolysis
radiant heat
raised fiber surface
safety standard
self-extinguishing
16 CFR 1630
16 CFR 1631
16 CFR 1632
16 CFR 1633
16 CFR 1634 (proposed)
small-scale test methods

smoke density
smoke generation
smoldering
sofa bed
spillover
spontaneous combustion
Stage 1 fire
Stage 2 fire
Stage 3 fire
Steiner Tunnel Test Method
toxicants
toxic gases
Upholstered Furniture Action Council (UFAC)
UFAC Decking Materials Test Method—1990
UFAC Fabric Classification Test Method—1990
UFAC Interior Fabric Test Method—1990
UFAC Voluntary Action Program
UFAC Welt Cord Test Method—1990
U.S. Department of Commerce (DOC)

Review Questions

1. Discuss the responsibilities of the CPSC in fire safety work.

2. What prompts the CPSC to propose a new flammability standard?

3. Has the 1967 amendment to the FFA had far-reaching effects? Cite some of the developments in fire safety that followed this amendment.

4. Why is a one-year grace period allowed before a new flammability standard goes into effect?

5. Discuss the UFAC Voluntary Action Program. What is the purpose of fabric classification? How are construction methods incorporated into the program?

6. Discuss the proposed 16 CFR Part 1634.

7. When can upholstered furniture bear the UFAC hangtag?

8. Explain the cyclic combustion process.

9. Distinguish between combustion, spontaneous combustion, glowing, and smoldering.

10. Why do toxic gases pose the greatest threat to life in interior fires?

11. Discuss the influence of smoke density on egress.

12. In the event of fire, why is it critical to preserve the means for quick and efficient egress?

13. Differentiate among a Stage 1, a Stage 2, and a Stage 3 fire. Then, discuss the value of early warning systems and automatic sprinklers in each stage.

14. What is the unique value of small-scale test methods, large-scale test methods, and full-scale test methods to fire researchers?

15. How does the methenamine tablet test simulate real-life situations?

16. At which stage of an interior fire is radiant heat an important variable?

17. Cite two significant reasons the flooring radiant panel test method is replacing the tunnel test method in the evaluation of the flammability hazards of soft floor coverings.

18. Which carpet would be safer in the event of fire, one having a CRF of 0.14 watt per square centimeter or one having a CRF of 0.30 watt per square centimeter?

19. Are the standards set forth in the NFPA 101® Life Safety Code® recommended or mandatory?

20. What is the goal of the NHTSA with respect to rate of flame spread and automobile occupant safety?

21. When would the large-scale test method, rather than the small-scale test method, be used for evaluating the flame resistance of textiles and films?

22. Why are full-scale fire testing facilities especially useful in studying the phenomenon of flashover?

Notes

1. Federal Emergency Management Agency, "An Ounce of Prevention," U.S. Fire Administration, Washington, D.C., 3.

2. Ibid., p. 4.

3. Reprinted with permission of NFPA 701-2004, Standard Methods of Fire Tests for Flame Propagation of Textiles and Films, Copyright© 2008, National Fire Protection Association, Quincy, MA 02269. This reprinted material is not the complete and official position of the NFPA on the referenced subject, which is represented only by the standard in its entirety.

4. *Cal Technical Bulletin* 117, "Requirements, Test Procedure and Apparatus for Testing the Flame Retardance of Resilient Filling Materials Used in Upholstered Furniture," and *Cal Technical Bulletin* 133, "Flammability Test Procedure for Seating Furniture for Use in Public Occupancies."

Upholstered Furniture Coverings and Fillings

UNIT TWO focuses on upholstery coverings and fillings for commercial and residential furniture products. Chapter 12 discusses methods of applying outercovering to furniture framework and their various features. It also reviews the different materials used to fill furniture, along with their performance characteristics.

In Chapter 13, statistical profiles detail fiber and yarn usage in upholstery fabrics, including those channeled to transportation applications, and several textile upholstery fabrics are described. The production of other upholstery fabrics, including genuine leather, simulated leather and suede, and vinyl, is also reviewed.

Chapter 14 presents several performance standards developed by members of the upholstered furniture industry. These standards, which are voluntary, recommend test methods and levels of performance and are tended to serve as guidelines for evaluating the end-use serviceability of finished upholstery fabrics. The standards apply to physical attributes, such as breaking strength, yarn distortion, abrasion resistance, and dimensional change. Other standards are directed to cleanability and can help the consumer determine what are appropriate cleaning agents. These agents and the proper procedures to follow in maintaining upholstery fabrics also are discussed in this chapter. Other colorfast properties are also discussed, such as colorfastness to crocking, ozone, and light.

CHAPTER TWELVE

Construction Features of Upholstered Furniture

Photo courtesy of C.R. Laine Furniture, www.crlaine.com.

■ **Residential and commercial** consumers have an almost unlimited variety of upholstered furniture styles from which to choose. All these forms and decorative stylings have some components in common. By definition, an upholstered item has an outercovering that surrounds and conceals a filling or stuffing, and such other structural components as springs, fabric linings, and framework. The various construction techniques for applying outercoverings expand the range of styling features available to consumers.

Filling materials in upholstered furniture serve structural as well as functional purposes. Frequently, the in-use behavior of the filling material is more important than that of other components, including the outercovering.

Exterior Construction Features

In addition to the upholstery fabric used to cover the cushions, backs, arms, and sides of furniture items, other fabrics may be used to cover the deck and bottom areas. Bottom fabrics are rarely seen, but deck fabrics may be exposed if the furniture has loose pillows. Other construction features, including the styling of the skirt and any surface embellishments, also affect the appearance of an upholstered item.

Deck Fabrics and Bottom Fabrics

The **deck** of an upholstered item comprises the platform, springs, and filling structures that support the seat cushions. To conceal these units and to prevent dust and objects from falling into the deck, a fabric covers the uppermost filling layer. When the fabric is the same as the exposed outercovering, it is referred to as a **self-deck treatment**; it looks like the outercovering in the event cushions are separated from the furniture in use. If the outercovering is heavy or highly textured, a smoother, lighter weight, less expensive deck fabric may be used; the color of this fabric coordinates with that of the outercovering. When outercoverings have low porosity, as is true for simulated leather fabrics, a porous deck fabric must be used to permit air movement when the seat cushions are compressed.

Bottom fabrics are used underneath the deck to conceal the interior components and give a finished look to the upholstered item if the bottom should come into view (Figure 12.1a,b). The fabric must be dimensionally stable to prevent sagging. Today, spunbonded olefin fabrics are frequently used for bottom fabrics. These lightweight fabrics resist moisture and mildew, do not ravel, and are dimensionally stable.

Patterned Fabric Applications

Unless the fabric has an overall design of no particular orientation (as in Figure 12.5), precise fabric cutting and motif positioning are required for upholstery fabrics with woven-in or printed patterns. Attention must first be given to the directional features of the motifs and repeats. These visual characteristics determine whether a fabric should be cut **up-the-bolt** or **to railroad**; the meanings of these terms are schematically illustrated in Figure 12.2. The importance of pattern direction to subsequent placement can be appreciated by examining the floral motifs in the fabric covering the

a)

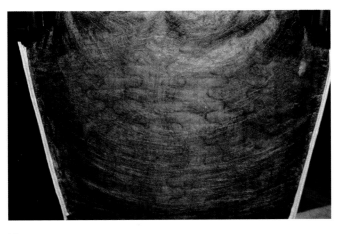

b)

Figure 12.1 Examples of spunbonded polypropylene olefin for bottom fabric applications.
Courtesy of Amy Willbanks, www.textilefabric.com.

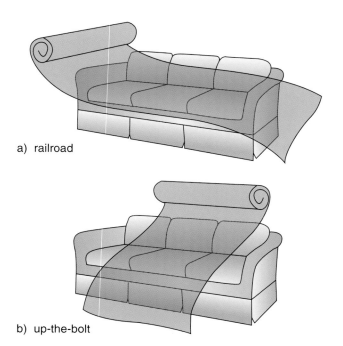

a) railroad

b) up-the-bolt

Figure 12.2 Illustrations of terms describing the directional cutting and placement of patterned upholstery fabric. Courtesy of Pennsylvania House.

sofa in Figure 12.3. Assuming the linear path of the flowers paralleled the selvages, the flowers would have appeared to grow sideways if the fabric had been cut to railroad.

When a fabric has a main motif, the motif must be centered on the back pillows, as well as on the seat cushions. For maximum aesthetic appeal, distinct patterns can also be cut and applied in a process known as **completion**. A completed pattern flows uninterrupted down the back pillows, the seat cushions, the seat boxing and the seat front. The completion method was used to place the patterned fabric on the sofa in Figure 12.3; the motifs in the fabric were also centered.

Cushion and Pillow Treatments

Three constructions of upholstery cushions and pillows are illustrated in Figure 12.4. The use of a plain seam to join the fabric pieces is called a **knife-edge treatment**. Inserting a fabric-covered cord into the seam is known as **welting**. The cords may be covered with the outercovering fabric, or, for greater emphasis, with a contrasting fabric. When welts are planned for items covered with highly textured fabrics, a smooth fabric may be used to cover the cords and increase

Figure 12.3 Sofa with large motif that aligns with the back and seat cushions. Courtesy of Pearson Company, www.pearsonco.com.

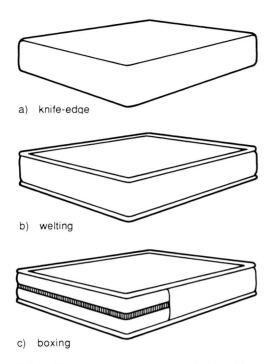

a) knife-edge

b) welting

c) boxing

Figure 12.4 Construction treatments for upholstered furniture cushions and pillows.

Figure 12.5 Overall pattern with no particular orientation on chaise with loose cushions.
Courtesy of C.R. Laine Furniture, www.crlaine.com.

their abrasion resistance. Wrapping a strip of fabric around the front and sides of cushions is known as **boxing**. This treatment (shown in Figure 12.4c) is generally combined with a zipper closure that enables manufacturers to insert the filling materials easily.

Upholstered cushions and pillows are treated two different ways in the construction of end products. In **tight-pillow construction styles**, the pillows are securely at-tached to the framework and cannot be shifted or removed. In **loose-pillow styles** (Figure 12.5), the pillows are not secured. Unless a different fabric has been used to cover the backs of the pillows, they can be frequently reversed to equalize wear patterns and soiling levels.

Skirt Options

Several options are available for the treatment of upholstered furniture **skirts**. Typical construction styles are illustrated in Figure 12.6. The skirt may be flat with single or double kick pleats; it may be shirred; it may have box pleats; or it may be shirred only at the corners in a princess style. Buttons may be added as decorative accents.

When a skirt is designed to hang straight and flat, a firm, bonded-web interfacing is generally employed to control the draping quality and to provide support. Skirts

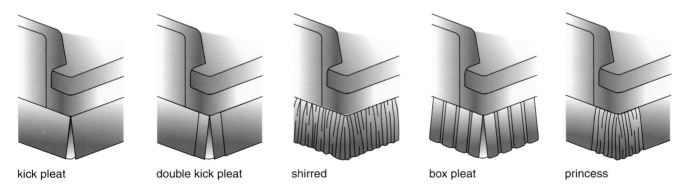

kick pleat   double kick pleat   shirred   box pleat   princess

Figure 12.6 Optional skirt treatments.
Courtesy of Pennsylvania House.

may be lined with a spunbonded fabric in order to reduce bulk and weight.

Slipcovers

Many consumers use **slipcovers** to protect the attached covering from excessive soil accumulation, as well as to change the appearance of the furniture from one season to another (Figure 12.7). Slipcovers are cut, seamed, and fitted over furniture. Some manufacturers offer upholstered furniture **in-the-muslin**: the items are covered in muslin, an undyed, plain-woven fabric composed of carded cotton yarns. Consumers can then order one or more sets of decorative slipcovers.

Arm Covers and Head Rests

Arm covers, also called **arm caps** and **armettes**, protect the arms of upholstered furniture from excessive abrasion and soiling. Frequently, these covers are offered optionally. **Head rests** or **head covers** protect the upholstery fabric from neck and hair oils and hair coloring. They may be cut from the outercoverings, be cut from a highly decorative lace or be richly embroidered, or as is the case in commercial airliners, buses, and trains, they may be cut from disposable fabric. Exposed wood arms can have padded arm rests or arm boards (Figures 12.8 and 12.9).

Figure 12.7 Slipcovers used to protect the permanent covering and to change the seasonal appearance of the furniture. Courtesy of LEE Industries.

Figure 12.8 Armpad.
Courtesy of C.R. Laine Furniture, www.crlaine.com.

Figure 12.10 Sofa embellished with button tufting.
Courtesy of C.R. Laine Furniture, www.crlaine.com.

Figure 12.11 Channel back tufting.
Courtesy of C.R. Laine Furniture, www.crlaine.com.

Figure 12.9 Wrapped arm board (Gregory armchair).
Courtesy of Drexel Heritage.

Surface Embellishments

The furniture manufacturer can use various treatments to embellish the surface of upholstery fabrics and finished products. These treatments are distinct from others, such as coloring and finishing, which also enrich the surface appearance but are performed on fabric prior to end-product construction.

Quilting is generally offered as an optional fabric treatment. The stitching may be done in parallel rows or on curved and angled lines to create slightly raised design motifs: on pattern fabrics, it may follow the outline of the design motifs. Channel back tufting can run parallel or vertical to the seat (Figure 12.11). When the surface is **tufted**, buttons secure the outercovering and filling tightly in a deeply indented three-dimensional pattern (Figure 12.10). Extensive buttoning should not be used on delicate fabrics with low levels of tear strength.

Nailhead trimming may be used to secure heavier coverings, such as genuine leather, to framework (Figure 12.12). The nails are generally aligned to emphasize the lines of the upholstered item.

To select a product that will retain its original appearance and the stability of its exterior construction features longer, residential and commercial consumers should consider its interior components and construction features. Some of these interior components are often textiles.

Figure 12.12 Chair and ottoman embellished with button tufting and nailhead trimming.
Courtesy of C.R. Laine Furniture, www.crlaine.com.

Interior Textile Components

Within an upholstered furniture item, several textile components, including fabric linings, filling structures, and cords, frequently appear. **Textile cords** are often used to hand tie or hand knot the several spring units together; the network of cords helps to stabilize the configuration of each spring and to minimize lateral shifting. A fabric lining, such as burlap or spunbonded olefin, is generally laid over the springs to prevent them from penetrating the filling materials. Two layers of filling, one for softness and one for firm support, may be used over the fabric linings. In most cases, the inside vertical walls and the extended portions of the frame will be padded with one or more layers of filling.

The framing material used in upholstered furniture may be hardwood, wood veneer, metal, or molded polymer. Although a discussion of these materials is not in the context of this book, consumers are encouraged to ascertain the soundness and stability of the frame prior to purchase. Special attention should be given to the quality and sturdiness of the framing joints. Consumers should also investigate the composition and structural features of the filling materials used. Often, consumers and interior designers can specify the use of a particular filling material.

Fillings Used in Upholstered Furniture

Three types of filling structures—fibrous battings, foam cushions, and loose particulate materials—are available to stuff or cushion upholstered furniture components and pillows. These structures differ in compressibility, loftiness, resiliency, and flammability. The Federal Trade Commission advises manufacturers to disclose the presence of such filling materials as goose down and feathers and requires disclosure of the presence of previously used filling materials.

Fibrous Battings

Battings are three-dimensional textile structures formed directly from fibers, bypassing the yarn stage. Natural or manufactured fibers may be employed.

Cotton Felt

Although batting structures composed of cotton fibers may be referred to as **cotton felt**, the term is descriptive of the felt-like appearance, not of the processing used. Layering thin webs of cotton fibers to form a batt of the desired thickness produces such structures. The natural convolutions of cotton fibers (Figure 3.2b, p. 29) help them to entwine and adhere to another, but for added stability the batt may be impregnated with an adhesive or resin.

The use of cotton, as well as kapok and jute, for upholstery fillings has diminished in recent years. These cellulosic fibers have comparatively low resiliency. Supply and delivery problems also hinder the selection of kapok and jute. Moreover, the results of flammability research have encouraged many manufacturers to restrict voluntarily the use of cotton batting that has not been treated to be flame resistant.

Curled Hair Batting

The use of curled **horsehair**, **cattlehair**, and **hoghair** for upholstered furniture filling has been declining. These three-dimensional hair forms can easily be entwined into **resilient battings**, but they are subject to such moisture- and microbe-related problems as odor and mildew, and, for some people, they can act as allergens. These natural materials, which are byproducts of the leather industry, have generally been replaced by manufactured fiber structures.

Bonded Polyester Batting

Most manufactured fiber batting is composed of staple-length polyester fibers. These fibers are produced by breaking or cutting the crimped filaments in a tow bundle.

When used in upholstered furniture, batting must not only provide comfort and superior resiliency, but also firm support, a feature not required of fillings for quilts and comforters. To engineer these features, manufacturers frequently combine two distinctly different layers of polyester fibers into one batt. The upper layer contains fine, low denier fibers that are easily flexed and soft, making for comfort; the lower layer contains coarser, stiffer fibers that provide firm support as they resist flexing and compression. For increased stability and greater resiliency, resin is sprayed throughout such dual denier batts, bonding the fibers into position.

Foam Cushions

Three-dimensional foam structures, frequently referred to as **slab cushions,** often fill upholstered furniture items to preserve their shape and form. Latex and urethane compounds are used to manufacture these cushions. For commercial projects it is important to specify combustion-modified (CM) foam to meet flammability requirements. Manufacturers of commercial seating will provide detailed information on the types of foams and other stuffing materials used in their products.

Latex Foam Structures

Latex foam may be produced from natural rubber or from synthesized rubber compounds. The compound is foamed, creating tiny, air-filled cells, and formed into a slab of the desired thickness. By controlling the quantity and size of the cells, manufacturers can engineer the **density** of the structure, which in turn determines the degree of firmness or the compression resistance offered by the cushion. Frequently, the latex is **vulcanized** or heated with sulfur to introduce strong chemical cross links that stabilize the shape and add strength. Latex foam cushions are resilient, but they may exhibit gradual aging and deterioration.

Polyurethane Foam Structures

Polyurethane foam is increasingly replacing latex foam in furniture applications. Unlike latex, polyurethane compounds do not exhibit aging, and they are resistant to both microbes and moisture.

During manufacturing, the urethane compound is expanded by heating, increasing the apparent volume and decreasing the density. Structures are produced with lower densities when softness and comfort are the performance features of principal importance, and with higher densities when greater support and resistance to crushing and compression are sought.

As illustrated in Figure 12.13, a latex or polyurethane foam structure may be carefully cut and used alone to fill

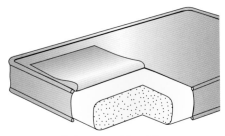

a) foam cushion filling

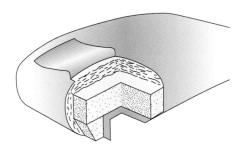

b) foam cushion core surrounded by polyester batting

Figure 12.13 Foam cushion fillings. Courtesy of Simmons Company.

and impart form to a furniture cushion, or it may form a core unit surrounded by polyester batting. In the latter case, support is provided principally by the foam structure and softness largely by the batting; both components provide resiliency and help the outercovering to maintain its dimensional stability and smoothness.

Loose Particulate Materials

Masses of loose particles are used to fill some upholstered furniture structures. Today, these particles include shredded or flaked latex or urethane foam, feathers, down, and fiberfill. The use of such materials as straw, sawdust, and newspapers has been discontinued because of cleaning and flammability problems. **Shredded foam particles** are less expensive than slab foam cushions, but they may clump with use. **Down,** the soft undercoat feathers retrieved from waterfowl, is soft, easily compressed, and lightweight, but the labor costs incurred in retrieving the necessary volume of the tiny feathers make the material comparatively expensive. **Feathers** from chickens, turkeys, ducks, and geese are soft and lofty filling materials, but many people are allergic to them. **Fiberfill,** usually composed of crimped polyester fibers, is lofty and resilient.

Polyester offers a cost advantage over down, and unlike down and feathers, manufactured fibers are not allergens.

Loose filling materials are frequently enclosed in an inner fabric structure before being inserted into the sewn outercoverings. Today, the inner fabric is often a spunbonded polypropylene olefin fabric.

Service-related Properties

Along with their fire-related behavior, the physical properties exhibited by filling materials greatly influence the serviceability of upholstered furniture items. If, for example, the filling material failed to recover after compression, the cushion would show a deep indentation that would destroy the original design of the item and the smooth appearance of the outercovering.

Compressibility

The ease with which a textile structure can be crushed or reduced in thickness is the measure of its **compressibility**. All filling structures must be somewhat compressible for comfort. An "overstuffed" chair is specifically designed to be easily compressed under the weight of the seated person; unless they are nursing back problems, people generally prefer these chairs over straight-backed, noncompressible wooden ones.

The degree of resistance a filling structure offers to being crushed or compressed can be measured in the laboratory. Structures that require a heavier load, in pounds per square inch, to produce a given deflection or reduction in thickness provide firmer support than those that reach this deflection with a lighter load.

Loftiness

Loftiness is bulk without heaviness. This feature is especially desirable for fillings used in furniture cushions and pillows. If identical cushion or pillow forms are filled, one with down, and one with polyurethane foam, they would have equal thickness and volume. The foam pillow, however, would be heavier, thus failing the loftiness test of bulkiness without undue weight. Down and feather filling materials are prized for their inherent loftiness. Even extremely large upholstered cushions filled with these natural materials are light in weight.

To increase the loftiness of fiberfill without increasing the weight, fiber chemists have engineered polyester fibers with hollow interiors. **Hollow fibers** are currently used extensively in bedding products, and their use in upholstered furniture items is increasing.

Compressional Resiliency

Compressional resiliency and **compressional loft** are synonyms that describe the ability of a textile structure to recover from compression deformations. Filling structures must be compressible, but their serviceability depends on their ability to spring back to their original thickness. Without compressional loft or resiliency, fillings would not recover from the force exerted by body weight, and the cushions would develop permanent depressions.

It was noted earlier in this chapter that spraying resin throughout a fibrous batt helps to reduce the compressibility of the structure. This treatment also helps to increase the springiness of a batt, which encourages it to recover after compression.

Flammability

The flammability characteristics of filling materials become very important variables when upholstered furniture catches fire. Because filling materials are always covered by an outercovering, however, their role in upholstery fires must be evaluated in combination with the outercovering and exterior construction features used in a particular item. These fire-related variables are discussed in Chapter 11.

Labeling Upholstery Fillings

The Textile Fiber Products Identification Act and the two FTC guides described below[1] have provisions that apply to the labeling of upholstered fillings. Manufacturers should comply with these provisions to avoid engaging in unfair or deceptive commercial practices.

Textile Fiber Products Identification Act

Although the provisions of the **TFPIA** do not apply to new upholstery stuffings and fillings, manufacturers may voluntarily identify the fiber used by its generic name, and distinguish it with a trade name to make the product more competitive. When the stuffing or filling has been used previously, the product is considered to be misbranded or unfairly and deceptively marketed unless it carries a label or hangtag clearly stating the presence of reused materials. The act does not, however, require the disclosure of the composition of the reused material.

Guides for the Household Furniture Industry

The FTC gives advice in the **Guides for the Household Furniture Industry** concerning the labeling practices manufacturers should use when they elect to provide information about fillings. To summarize these **advisory practices**, the information may not be false (e.g., labeling cotton felt as wool felt), nor may it be deceiving (e.g., labeling shredded or flaked latex or urethane foam merely as latex foam or as urethane foam). Furthermore, foam fillings must be specifically identified as latex or urethane foam, not merely as foam.

Interested readers may review the guides for information regarding the labeling of genuine wood, simulated wood, and wood veneer components of upholstered furniture and of such case goods as tables, cabinets, desks, and chests. Students planning careers as professional furniture designers, interior designers, or retailers should become familiar with the guidelines concerning the use of such terms as "Mediterranean," "French Provincial," and "Danish Modern" to describe furniture manufactured in the United States. Consumers and retailers should also understand the recommended use of such descriptive terms as "new," "used," "floor sample," and "discontinued model" in the marketing of upholstered furniture.

Guides for the Feather and Down Products Industry
The **Guides for the Feather and Down Products Industry** became effective on December 29, 1971. Included in these guides are definitions of the specific terms to be used in labeling feather and down fillings, such as **down**, **feathers**, **waterfowl feathers**, and **nonwaterfowl feathers**. Guidelines are also given for the use of such terms as **all down** and **pure down**. Other guidelines pertain to the use of damaged and crushed feathers and to the cleanliness of the filling materials. Since feather and down filling materials are used more extensively in bedding products than in upholstered furniture, these guides are reviewed in detail in Chapter 29.

We should note that no labeling provisions have been mandated or recommended for other textile components used in the interior of upholstered furniture. Therefore, the composition of textile cords and fabric linings is rarely, if ever, disclosed.

Summary

The fabric that covers the exterior of upholstered furniture may be textile or nontextile. Various construction treatments can be used to apply the outercovering, several of which add decorative features to the item. These treatments range from quilting the fabric surface to gathering the skirt to boxing the cushions and pillows.

Upholstered furniture contains various interior components including springs, framework, fabric linings, and fillings. The fillings may be cotton or bonded polyester batting, latex or urethane foam cushions, or such loose particles as down, feathers, and fiberfill. Manufacturers must disclose the presence of reused filling materials; they should also comply with the labeling practices set forth in guides provided by the Federal Trade Commission.

The end-use serviceability of a piece of upholstered furniture is strongly influenced by the performance characteristics of the filling materials employed. The degree of softness and comfort is primarily determined by the compressibility of the filling; the weight of the cushions is influenced by the loftiness of the filling component; and the long-term retention of the original form and fabric smoothness directly depends on the compressional resiliency of the filling structure.

Key Terms

advisory practices
all down
arm caps
arm covers
armettes
battings

bottom fabrics
boxing
box pleats
cattlehair
completion
compressibility

compressional loft
compressional resiliency
cotton felt
deck
density
down

feathers
fiberfill
Guides for the Feather and Down
    Products Industry
Guides for the Household Furniture
    Industry
head covers
head rests
hoghair
hollow fibers
horsehair
in-the-muslin

knife-edge treatment
latex foam
loftiness
loose-pillow styles
nailhead trimming
nonwaterfowl feathers
polyurethane foam
pure down
quilting
railroad
resilient battings
self-deck treatment

shredded foam particles
skirt
slab cushions
slipcovers
textile cords
TFPIA
tight-pillow styles
tufted trimming
up-the-bolt
vulcanized
waterfowl feathers
welting

Review Questions

1. Discuss the selection and functions of deck fabric.

2. What advantages are offered by spunbonded fabrics when used as bottom fabric?

3. Distinguish between "up-the-bolt" and "to railroad" applications. When is it critical to use the correct positioning of upholstery fabric on the furniture frame?

4. Sketch an example of "completion" as it relates to upholstery fabric application.

5. What is the purpose of zippers in boxed cushions?

6. Do slipcovers have both a functional and a decorative purpose?

7. Why is cotton "felt" a misnomer?

8. Why is the use of curled hair batting diminishing?

9. When two distinctly different layers of polyester fibers are combined into one batt, the structure is referred to as a dual denier batt. Why is this an appropriate descriptive name, and what advantages are offered by the fibers used?

10. What advantages does polyurethane foam offer over latex foam?

11. Distinguish between compressibility and compressional resiliency.

12. Explain the TFPIA requirements pertaining to the labeling of upholstery fabric and furniture fillings.

13. Are the labeling practices included in the Guides for the Household Furniture Industry and the Guides for the Feather and Down Products Industry advisory or mandatory?

Notes

1. Copies of these guides are available from the Federal Trade Commission, Washington, DC 20580

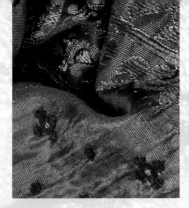

Upholstery Coverings

■ **Virtually every method of** fabrication used to construct apparel fabrics is also used to construct upholstery coverings. Thus, the variety of fabrics available for use on furniture is as extensive as that available for apparel applications. The assortment includes textile fabrics that are essentially two-dimensional and fabrics that are markedly three-dimensional. Nontextile furniture coverings are composed of elements other than textile fibers and yarns. Some of these coverings, including simulated leather fabrics, are produced directly from polymer solutions; others, specifically genuine leather fabrics, are converted from the raw skins and hides of animals.

Some fabrics are composed entirely of simple yarns in simple, compact constructions, making for relatively great durability and little aesthetic interest. Others incorporate complex yarns in simple, loose constructions, providing much visual and tactile interest but less durability. Fabric patterns range in complexity, from small, geometric figures to large and elaborately detailed motifs. Pile upholstery fabrics are available in various construction densities and surface textures. Some pile fabrics are woven, some tufted, and some knitted.

Although virtually every natural and manufactured fiber is used in textile upholstery fabric, current statistical profiles show that cotton and the noncellulosic fibers hold significant portions of the market. Disclosure of the fiber composition is particularly appropriate today, as the use of noncellulosic fibers to simulate natural fibers in upholstery applications increases.

Fiber and Yarn Usage

Currently, the upholstery fabric market is somewhat evenly divided between cotton and the manufactured fibers. At the same time, fabrics used in transportation applications are made principally of manufactured fibers. The dominance of spun yarns in upholstery underscores an apparent preference of consumers and design professionals for more decorative coverings.

Fiber Usage in Upholstery Fabrics

In the four year span shown in Table 13.1, the quantities of cotton decreased from 352.8 million pounds in 2001 (48 percent of the total market) to 180.8 million pounds in 2005 (40 percent of the total market). Concurrently, the market share held by the manufactured fibers increased from roughly 52 percent to 59 percent, while the market share captured by wool fell approximately 4 percent. While the natural beauty, resiliency, and inherent flame and stain resistance of wool fibers are valued characteristics, the relatively high cost of the fiber tends to limit its selection.

Fiber Usage in Transportation Applications

The end-use category of transportation fabrics includes automobile seat upholstery and slipcovers, sidewalls (the vertical portion of car seats), interior roof linings, and sheeting. The cotton quantities include the knit and woven fabric used as the backing for vinyl sheeting. The category also includes convertible automobile tops and replacement tops, as well as upholstery used in other

Table 13.1 Fiber Usage in U.S. Upholstery Fabric (millions of pounds).*								
		MANUFACTURED FIBERS**						
			Cellulosic		**Noncellulosic**			
Year	Total Fiber	Total	Yarn***	Staple	Yarn	Staple	Cotton	Wool
2001	742.7	382.7	--	19.4	232.1	131.1	352.8	7.2
2002	719.9	364.4	--	16.4	222.7	125.4	349.3	6.1
2003	590.1	308.7	--	12.8	192.1	103.8	276.1	5.3
2004	499.1	296.9	--	12.0	194.2	90.7	199.0	3.2
2005	447.3	263.3	--	11.1	172.3	79.9	180.8	3.1

 * Includes slipcovers and vinyl-coated cotton fabrics, excludes olefin and saran webbing for outdoor furniture.
** Manufactured fiber end use is divided between cellulosic (rayon + acetate) and noncellulosic (nylon, polyester, acrylic, olefin). Yarn includes multifilament, monofilament, and spunbonded. Olefin includes polypropylene and polyethylene staple and yarn. Olefin yarn also includes film fiber and spunbonded polypropylene. Staple includes tow and fiberfill.
*** Little or none of the fiber is used.
Source: Textiles Economics Bureau, *Fiber Organon*, "U.S. End Use Survey: 2001–2005," October 2006, page 192, Table 4.

modes of transportation, such as airplanes, railroad and subway cars, and buses. It does not include such things as seat padding, window channeling, and carpet and rugs.

The marked shift from cotton to the noncellulosic fibers in transportation fabrics (Table 13.2) can primarily be attributed to the advances made in manufactured fiber processing. Such properties as soil repellency, high resiliency, and flame resistance can be directly engineered into manufactured fibers, whereas finishing agents and treatments must be used to develop such features with cotton. Again, the relatively high cost of wool precludes its widespread selection, but its inherent flame resistance and resiliency make it an attractive choice when the budget is adequate.

The lack of a more marked increase from 2001 to 2005 in the total number of pounds of fiber used in the transportation market should not be interpreted as indicating a similar lack of growth in yardage production. The effect of fiber density must be considered. Noncellulosic fibers, which accounted for some 96 percent of the 2005 market, are not as dense as cotton fibers (see Table 3.9, p. 41). Thus, a greater amount of yardage can be produced from one pound of noncellulosic fibers than from one pound of cotton. Another factor responsible for this modest growth in fiber usage is the smaller size of many of today's automobiles.

Disclosure of Fiber Composition

Upholstery and transportation fabrics offered to consumers and professionals in piece good form must be labeled in accordance with the provisions of the **Textile Fiber Products Identification Act (TFPIA)**. As noted in Chapter 10, the **Wool Products Labeling Act (WPLA) of 1939** specifically exempts all upholsteries, and the TFPIA specifically exempts permanently incorporated outcovering fabrics.

The scope of the TFPIA also includes **slipcovers**, and **doilies** (decorative covers placed on the backs and arms of furniture), swatches, and samples. The required information may be listed on the end of a bolt of yardgoods and on a label or hangtag attached to a slipcover. With swatches less than two square inches in size, the information may appear in accompanying promotional matter. Other swatches and samples may be labeled with the required information or keyed to a catalog, indicating to prospective purchasers where the information can be obtained.

Dominance of Spun Yarns

The dominance of spun yarns in upholstery is evident from the data presented in Table 13.1. Together, natural and manufactured staple-length fibers accounted for more than 62 percent of the 2005 upholstery fabric market. More pronounced textural effects and design features, which consumers and designers apparently consider relatively important in selection, can be produced more readily by spinning and plying processes than by throwing operations.

Table 13.2 Fiber Usage in U.S. Transportation Fabric (millions of pounds).

| | | | **MANUFACTURED FIBERS*** | | | | | |
| | | | Cellulosic** | | Noncellulosic | | | |
Year	Total Fiber	Total	Yarn	Staple	Yarn	Staple	Cotton	Wool**
2001	175.2	170.2	--	--	122.7	47.5	5.0	--
2002	181.3	176.2	--	--	126.2	50.0	5.2	--
2003	170.8	165.6	--	--	118.8	46.8	5.2	--
2004	162.8	157.5	--	--	120.9	36.5	5.3	--
2005	149.8	144.1	--	--	109.1	35.0	5.8	--

* Manufactured fiber end use is divided between cellulosic (rayon + acetate) and noncellulosic (nylon, polyester, acrylic, olefin). Yarn includes multifilament, monofilament, and spunbonded. Olefin includes polypropylene and polyethylene staple and yarn. Olefin yarn also includes film fiber and spunbonded polypropylene. Staple includes tow and fiberfill.
** Little or none of the fiber is used.
Source: Textiles Economics Bureau, *Fiber Organon*, "U.S. End Use Survey: 2001–2005," October 2006, page 194, Table 6.

Noncellulosic staple-length fibers are used more extensively than are manufactured cellulosic staple-length fibers and wool. To a large extent, this is the result of the increased use of spun yarns of polyester in lieu of spun yarns of rayon and the increasing use of spun yarns of acrylic or polypropylene olefin fibers to replace more expensive woolen yarns.

While the loops, nubs, and other textural features characteristic of complex spun yarns add aesthetic interest to upholstered furniture, prospective purchasers and specifiers should consider the possible effects of end use abrasion on the raised areas. Consumers and interior designers should also evaluate the hand of the fabric to confirm that novelty yarn features are not too harsh or rough for their comfort or that of their clients.

Multifilament Yarn Usage

Today, filament-length fibers account for more than a fifth of the upholstery fabrics market. In order to produce a softer and warmer hand, increase covering power, and minimize the development of unsightly fuzz and pills, throwsters often introduce a three-dimensional form to the filaments by using one of the texturing processes illustrated in Figure 5.2 (p. 86). For economy, ease of care, and strength, multifilament yarns composed of nylon are increasingly replacing acetate as a substitute for expensive silk filaments.

When stretch characteristics are needed in a woven upholstery fabric, manufacturers may incorporate a few yarns whose spandex filament cores are covered by fibers identical in color to the other yarns in the fabric. As noted in Table 3.5 (p. 34), spandex fibers have 500 to 700 percent elongation at break and 98 percent recovery after 200 percent strain. The requisite fabric elasticity can often be obtained when the highly elastic fiber accounts for as little as 3 percent of the total fabric weight.

Multifilament yarns are especially important in the transportation market. Whereas noncellulosic staple fibers accounted for approximately 23 percent of the 2005 market, filament fibers captured some 73 percent. This increase may reflect the expanded use of textile fabrics in commercial transportation vehicles, installations that are subjected to a high level of use. The increase may also reflect the expanding use of textile upholstery in automobile interiors.

Flat Upholstery Fabrics

Greige goods producers, dyers, printers, stylists, and converters work together to manufacture an expansive variety of flat and pile structures. Several of these are identified by specific fabric names. Traditionally, fiber composition was an important variable in the descriptions of these fabrics. Today, however, the increased use of the noncellulosic fibers has made fiber content less valuable as a distinguishing characteristic, and more useful descriptions are based on structural and appearance features. This section describes and illustrates flat or nonpile upholstery fabrics.

Several relatively simple upholstery fabrics are produced with basic weaving patterns or a variation of these patterns, and a few are produced with a simple knitting operation. Several complex coverings are produced with a decorative dobby, surface-figure, or Jacquard interlacing pattern. These constructions are discussed and illustrated in Chapters 6 and 7.

Plain-woven Fabrics

Homespun, tweed, and hopsacking are plain-woven upholstery fabrics. **Homespun**, shown in Figure 13.1a, is made of heavy, coarse yarns that resemble hand-spun yarns. The use of **speck yarns**, as shown in Figure 13.1b, adds distinctive color styling to **tweed** upholstery fabrics. **Hopsacking** (hopsack), shown in Figure 13.1c, may be made with a plain or a basket weave. This fabric's name is derived from its coarse, irregular yarns, which resemble the rough jute yarns of the gunny sacks use to store hops.

Consumers and interior designers should carefully inspect **backcoated upholstery fabrics** to determine whether the compound is visible on the face of the fabric. This problem generally occurs only when the coating has been used to compensate for low-quality fabric construction. The coating on the fabric shown in Figure 13.2 is color coordinated with the face yarns to make it as inconspicuous as possible. Because coatings cost less than fibers and yarns, coated fabrics are relatively inexpensive, but may not be durable in use.

Glazed chintz is produced for upholstery applications in somewhat heavier weights than those produced for window treatments. Chintz typically has a floral or geometric pattern printed in bright colors, as well as high surface luster produced

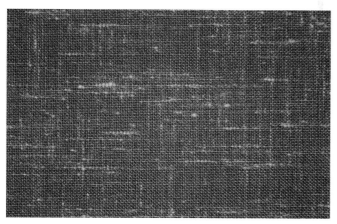

a) Homespun.

b) Tweed.

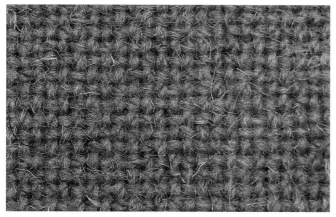

c) Hopsacking.

Figure 13.1 Plain-woven upholstery fabrics.
Courtesy of Amy Willbanks, www.textilefabric.com.

by the use of a glazing finishing process. The fabric is often used in removable, fitted slipcovers (Figure 17.3, p. 287).

Figure 13.2 Low yarn count, adhesive-backed upholstery fabric. Courtesy of Amy Willbanks, www.textilefabric.com.

Basket-woven Fabrics

A 4 × 4 basket pattern is often used to weave rope composed of sisal or other natural materials into chair seats and backs. Basket-woven upholstery fabrics often have warp and filling yarns of different colors. This styling is extensively used with upholstery designed and woven in Scandinavian countries. **Duck** is a basket-woven fabric often used in slipcovers for furniture, outdoor furniture, and boat covers (Figure 17.9, p. 289).

Filling-rib Woven Fabrics

Upholstery fabrics produced with a filling-rib weave, including rep, faille, bengaline, ottoman, and shantung, are shown in Figure 13.3. **Rep** (Figure 13.3a) has fine ribs, slightly larger than those characterizing taffeta. The ribs in **faille** (Figure 13.3b) are slightly larger and flatter still, numbering approximately 36 per inch. **Bengaline** (Figure 13.3c) has equally sized and spaced ribs, numbering about 24 per inch, and **ottoman** (Figure 13.3d) has large ribs that may be equally sized and spaced or varied in size and spacing. **Shantung** (Figure 13.3e) is a fabric with a slightly irregular surface due to thick and thin yarns in the filling direction.

Twill-woven Fabrics

Different colors or sizes of warp and filling yarns are often used to accentuate the visual diagonal of twill-woven upholstery fabrics. This kind of effect is evident in the **plaid** fabric in Figure 13.4. The twill interlacings and colored yarns in **houndstooth** vary to create broken checks or a unique star pattern (Figure 13.5). Similar

a) Rep

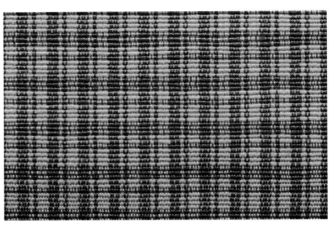

b) Faille

c) Bengaline

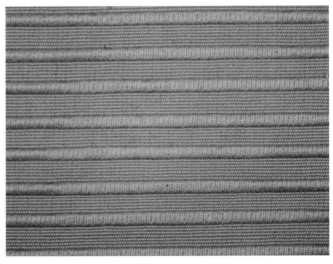

d) Ottoman

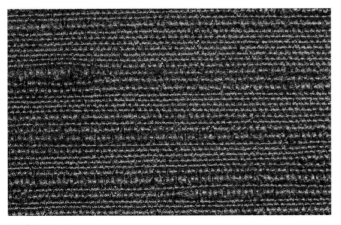

e) Shantung

Figure 13.3 Filling rib weaves.
Courtesy of Amy Willbanks, www.textilefabric.com.

fabrics are frequently selected for use on contemporary furniture, especially on items designed for casual residential interiors.

The reversed diagonals of **herringbone** make for a visual interest that may be enhanced by using different colors or sizes of warp and filling yarns (Figure 13.6). Because the yarn interlacings in twill weaves occur less frequently than they do in plain weaves, higher fabric counts can be used to produce strong, compactly constructed twill upholstery fabrics. Such fabrics are serviceable in high-use residential and commercial applications, including transportation installations; various color stylings can add visual interest.

Figure 13.4 Plaid twill upholstery fabric.
Courtesy of Amy Willbanks, www.textilefabric.com.

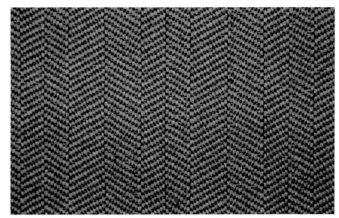

Figure 13.6 Herringbone upholstery fabric.
Courtesy of Amy Willbanks, www.textilefabric.com.

Figure 13.5 Houndstooth upholstery fabric.
Courtesy of Amy Willbanks, www.textilefabric.com.

Satin-woven Fabrics

Frequently, fine, bright acetate or nylon filaments are thrown into low-twist, multifilament yarns for the production of elegant **satin** upholstery fabrics (Figure 17.12, p. 290). Satin is a warp-faced sating weave, therefore the majority of warp yarns are on the face of the fabric. While such fabrics may have silk-like beauty, the low-twist yarns are relatively weak and the floating yarns may be easily snagged. Therefore, the application of these fabrics as furniture coverings should be limited to items that will not be subjected to high levels of use and abrasion. In most cases, upholstery fabric stylists use satin interlacings in combination with other, more du-

rable interlacings, especially in elaborately patterned Jacquard fabrics.

Sateen, a filling-faced satin weave, has the majority of filling yarns on the face of the fabric. The upholstery fabric pictured in Figure 13.7 has chenille filling yarns which appear on the face of the fabric.

Crepe-woven Fabrics

Crepe-woven fabrics have a random, or irregular, interlacing pattern. The floats are of unequal length in no distinct pattern. A crinkly, pebbly, or rough surface characterizes **crepe** fabrics. An advantage of crepe-woven fabrics over crepe fabrics made with high-twist yarns is that the crinkle is permanent. Crepe-woven fabrics also hold their shape and are one of the most wrinkle resistant of all the weaves. The irregular interlacing pattern is shown in Figure 13.8. Crepe-woven fabrics are also called **momie weaves**.

Dobby-woven Fabrics

Some dobby-woven upholstery fabrics use a single color and two distinctly different interlacing patterns, one for the designs and another for the background. The slight difference in height between the designs and the ground highlights the motifs, as does the difference in the quantity of light that the yarns in the two interlacings reflect. Other dobby fabrics have yarns of several colors, some appearing in the background and some appearing in the designs (Figure 13.9a and b).

The **goose-eye twill** shown in Figure 13.9c illustrates how a dobby weave can produce a woven-in design.

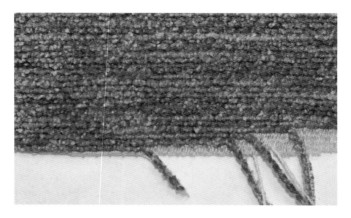

Figure 13.7 Chenille pile fabric.
Courtesy of Amy Willbanks, www.textilefabric.com.

a) Dobby leaves.

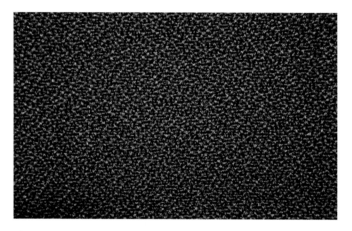

Figure 13.8 Crepe made from recycled polyester.
Courtesy of Amy Willbanks, www.textilefabric.com.

b) Dobby squares.

The motifs were formed by selectively reversing the direction of the visual diagonal, creating small diamond shapes said to resemble the eyes of a goose.

Surface-Figure Woven Fabrics

One type of surface-figure weave, the **dot or spot weave** (Figure 13.10a and b), is used to produce decorative upholstery fabrics. In this weave, extra yarns are interlaced to create small, geometric motifs. The visual impact of the motifs is augmented by the use of contrastingly colored base yarns. For stability and weight, the lengths of the extra yarns floating across the back between the motif interlacings are left unclipped.

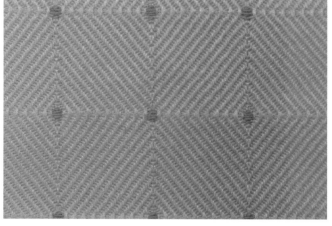

c) Goose-eye twill.

Figure 13.9 Dobby-woven upholstery fabrics.
Courtesy of Amy Willbanks, www.textilefabric.com.

Jacquard-woven Fabrics

Several distinctive Jacquard-woven fabrics are manufactured for use as furniture coverings. They may be produced with two, three, or four sets of yarns, but all have relatively elaborate motifs and multiple interlacing patterns.

Damask is woven from one set of warp yarns and one set of filling yarns. Removal of individual yarns would destroy the details of the motifs, as well as the fabric integrity. Damask fabrics are essentially two-dimensional and generally incorporate one or two colors. When a single color is used, the design motifs are highlighted because their interlacing pattern differs from that of the ground. They may be further accentuated by the use of yarns differing in brightness, level of twist, and degree of complexity from the yarns in the ground. The damask fabrics in Figure 13.11a and b contain both simple and complex yarns.

Frequently, the motifs in damask have a plain, filling-rib, or sateen weave while the ground has a satin, twill, or filling-rib weave. The visual interest of the ground areas in the damask fabric may be enhanced by weaving narrow bands of warp yarns that are various shades of the same hue. The term **strié** identifies this kind of coloration (Figure 13.11b).

Liseré fabrics are woven from two sets of warp yarns and one set of filling yarns (Figure 13.2). One set of warp yarns is generally identical in color to the filling yarns; together, these form the ground. The second set of warp

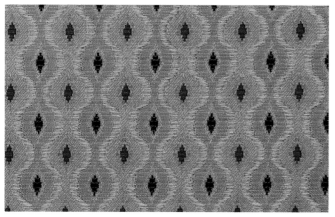

a) Front.

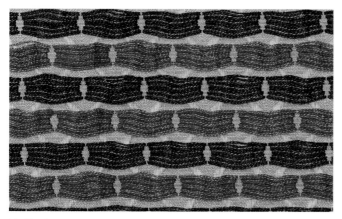

b) Back.

Figure 13.10 Surface-figure weave with unclipped extra filling yarns floating on the back of the fabric.
Courtesy of Amy Willbanks, www.textilefabric.com.

a) Chenille damask.

b) Strié damask.

Figure 13.11 Damask upholstery fabrics distinguished by the use of simple and complex yarns.
Courtesy of Amy Willbanks, www.textilefabric.com.

yarns is composed of a variety of single-colored yarns. In accordance with the planned pattern, different colors of these yarns are wound in bands of various widths on a separate loom beam. During weaving, the Jacquard mechanism raises these yarns and controls their interlacing to produce detailed motifs in lengthwise bands. In many liseré fabrics, the patterned bands are interspersed with satin-woven stripes.

Brocade is woven from more than one set of filling or weft yarns; the number of sets is governed by the number of colors that are to appear in the motifs. The extra yarns are generally woven in a filling-faced twill or sateen interlacing pattern, giving the design motifs a slightly raised effect (Figure 13.13a and b). The ground is compactly constructed in a plain, twill, satin, or filling-rib weave.

Brocatelle is often made from one set of fine warp yarns, one set of heavy warp yarns, and two sets of filling yarns. Brocatelle (Figure 13.14) is similar to brocade, but the pattern is raised and padded with stuffer yarns. The raised pattern (a distinctive puffed appearance) is generally formed by inserting filling stuffer yarns on the back of the fabric.

Jacquard-woven tapestry should not be confused with hand-woven tapestry. The two differ not only in their modes of production, but also in the manner in which the filling or weft yarns are handled. In machine-woven tapestry, these yarns are carried from one selvage to the other, interlacing into the face when needed. In hand-woven tapestry, they are interlaced within the perimeter of a design motif and then cut, leaving a short length of yarn hanging fringe-like on the back. Machine-woven tapestry may also be made of many sets of yarns.

a)

b)

Figure 13.13 Examples of brocade upholstery fabric. Courtesy of Amy Willbanks, www.textilefabric.com.

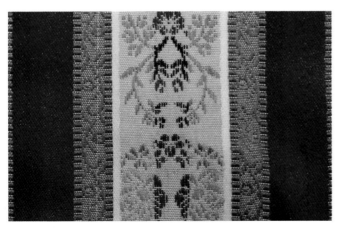

Figure 13.12 Liseré upholstery fabric. Courtesy of Amy Willbanks, www.textilefabric.com.

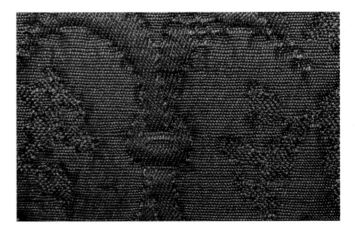

Figure 13.14 Brocatelle upholstery fabric. Courtesy of Amy Willbanks, www.textilefabric.com.

Like hand-woven tapestries, Jacquard-woven tapestries often have picture-like motifs. Yarns not used in the face of these fabrics are floated across the back, producing a mirror-image pattern of opposite colors (Figure 13.15). The fabric is not reversible, however, because the lengthy floats would be snagged and ruptured in use.

Because the motifs and pattern repeats of some machine-woven tapestries resemble those of hand-stitched needlepoint accents, they are commonly referred to as **needlepoint weave** fabrics. They cannot be woven on a dobby loom; a Jacquard mechanism is required to control the placement of the various colors and the interlacing of the many sets of yarns (Figure 13.16).

A distinguishing characteristic of Jacquard-woven tapestries is that the various colors are introduced in

Figure 13.16 Needlepoint-weave tapestry. Courtesy of Amy Willbanks, www.textilefabric.com.

a) Face.

a) Face.

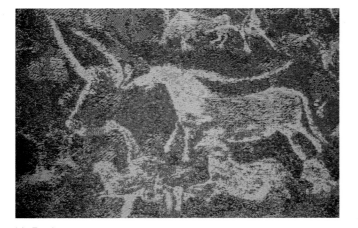

b) Back.

Figure 13.15 Jacquard-woven tapestry upholstery fabric. Courtesy of Amy Willbanks, www.textilefabric.com.

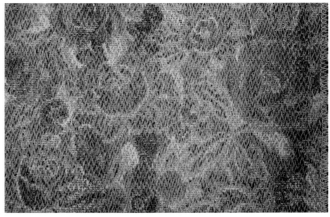

b) Back.

Figure 13.17 Jacquard-woven tapestry upholstery fabric. Courtesy of Amy Willbanks, www.textilefabric.com.

crosswise or lengthwise bands. When the colors in a band are not used in the face designs, they are interlaced in the back, creating colored bands or stripes on the back side of the fabric (Figure 13.17a and b).

Fabrics woven of three or more sets of yarns, including liseré, brocade, brocatelle, and tapestry, may be classified as **doublecloth** fabrics. Other Jacquard-woven fabrics, including some tapestries, are also doublecloths, but they are further distinguished by the formation of enclosed **pockets**, areas where there is no interlacing between two distinct fabric structures that face one another. As shown in Figure 13.18, the face of the pocket is composed of one set of warp yarns and one set of filling yarns, and the back of a second set of warp yarns and a second set of filling yarns. These pockets may show up in the motifs or in the ground; closure occurs where the positions of the face yarns and the back yarns are shifted at the juncture of the motifs and the ground. These fabrics are commonly referred to as **pocket cloth**.

In **matelassé**, the pockets are formed in the motifs. The mutual interlacing of the multiple sets of yarns is planned to produce the appearance of quilting stitches. When a third set of filling yarns is floated in the pockets, the designs stand out in relief, puffing the fabric and enhancing the quilt-like appearance (Figure 13.19a and b).

Cloque is another doublecloth fabric in which interlacings of the four sets of yarns are planned to simulate the appearance of quilting stitches. As shown in Figure 13.20a, the mutual interlacings, strategically positioned, create a pattern on the solid-colored surface. Unlike matelassé, cloque is an essentially flat fabric, since the pockets are not padded.

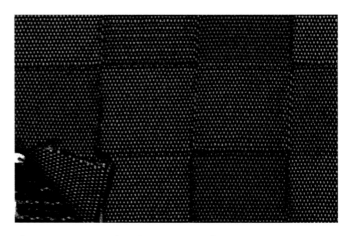

Figure 13.18 Pocket cloth upholstery fabric. Courtesy of Amy Willbanks, www.textilefabric.com.

Because Jacquard-woven upholstery fabrics have high production and materials costs, they may be comparatively expensive. Nevertheless, their richly patterned surfaces prompt many designers and consumers to give them priority in the furnishings budget.

Triaxially Woven Fabrics

Triaxially woven fabrics (Figure 6.18, p. 111) display uniform stretch in all directions and high strength in relation to their weight. Because they easily conform to curves and resist tearing, they are used to cover molded furniture frames and automobile seats.

Knitted Fabrics

Virtually all knitted upholstered furniture coverings are flat structures produced by interlooping simple yarns with an

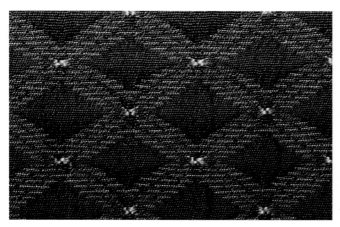

a) Front.

Figure 13.19 Matelassé. Courtesy of Amy Willbanks, www.textilefabric.com.

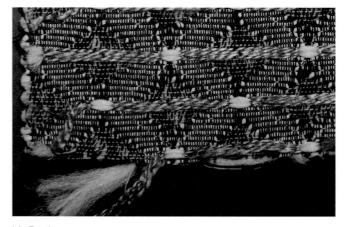

b) Back.

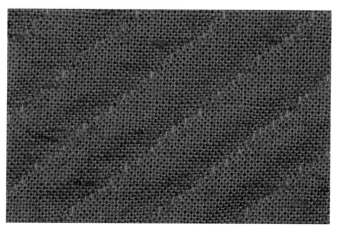

a) Front.

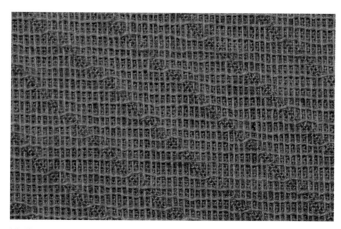

b) Back.

Figure 13.20 Cloque upholstery fabric.
Courtesy of Amy Willbanks, www.textilefabric.com.

interlock stitch (Figure 7.6, p. 116). This stitch helps ensure that the fabrics will be serviceable during use. These fabrics cannot be varied by incorporating complex yarns or by altering structural features, but textile stylists, often with the assistance of a computer, can provide variety by specifying the use of two colors of yarns, Jacquard patterns, printed patterns, heather colorations, or cross-dyed effects.

The elasticity and flexibility of knitted fabrics make them particularly suitable for use as coverings on curved furniture frames. The loops of the fabric open slightly under stress, allowing the fabric to fit smoothly over the filling and frame. Upholstery knits are generally composed of nylon fibers, which can be heat set to impart dimensional stability and resiliency. Moreover, unlike other weft knitting stitches, the interlock stitch is resistant to running and snagging.

Pile Upholstery Fabrics

The assortment of pile fabrics available for use as upholstered furniture coverings includes several whose pile yarns are uniformly distributed over the fabric surface, as well as several whose pile yarns are strategically placed to create a patterned layer. The techniques used to produce woven pile fabrics were described and illustrated in Chapter 6, and those used to produce knitted pile and tufted fabrics were discussed in Chapter 7.

Woven Pile Fabrics

Two filling pile fabrics, **corduroy** and **velveteen**, are used as furniture coverings. Both have a cut-pile surface texture

and are normally composed of cotton or cotton/polyester blends. The surface of most corduroy upholstery fabric is uniformly covered with relatively wide and densely constructed wales (Figure 6.14, p. 109).

Among the upholstery fabrics produced by interlacing extra warp yarns with base yarns are velvet, velour, friezé, and grospoint. With the exception of grospoint and some friezé fabrics, these coverings have cut-pile textures.

Velvet is normally woven to have a uniform pile surface. The pile is created by extra warp yarns interlacing with filling yarns (Figure 13.21a). Omitting selected pile yarns and thus exposing some portions of the base fabric produces a variation in velvet upholstery. These fabrics, called **voided velvets**, may have even greater aesthetic

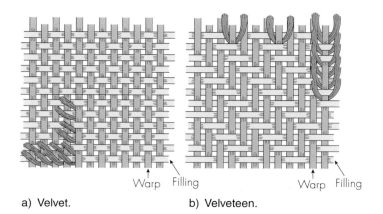

a) Velvet.   b) Velveteen.

Figure 13.21 Comparison of filling pile and warp pile.
Illustrations by Ron Carboni.

interest when a Jacquard mechanism has been employed to control the strategic placement of various colors of pile yarns. In the fabric pictured in Figure 13.22, the voided areas define the shapes of the design motifs forming the pile layer, while Jacquard patterning creates the colored details appearing within each motif. Jacquard patterning may also be used with level-surfaced velvet.

In most velvet upholstery fabrics, only a slight nap is introduced. In **panné velvet**, however, a pronounced nap augments the luster contributed by bright fibers, which are often rayon (see Figure 13.23). The effects of pile yarn orientation on surface reflection are readily seen in the **crushed velvet** in Figure 9.4, p. 145.

Velour, which is generally produced by the over-the-wire construction technique, has a slightly deeper pile and a more pronounced nap than velvet. Most velour is composed of cotton fibers, which give the fabric a soft, warm hand.

Velveteen also has a uniform pile surface and is created by interlacing an extra set of filling yarns with a single set of warp yarns (Figure 13.21b).

Friezé (frisé) upholstery fabrics normally have a level, uncut-pile surface made of multifilament yarns composed of stiff, strong nylon fibers. For variety, manufacturers may incorporate more than one color of pile yarns, expose areas of the base fabric (Figure 13.24), or selectively shear some pile loops to vary the level of surface luster.

Grospoint, pictured in Figure 13.25, has a level surface with pronounced loops larger than those characteristic of friezé. Multifilament nylon yarns are often used in the loops to augment their durability. Surface patterns

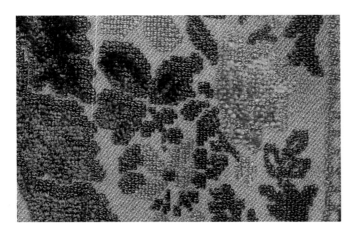

Figure 13.22 Voided velvet upholstery fabric. Courtesy of Amy Willbanks, www.textilefabric.com.

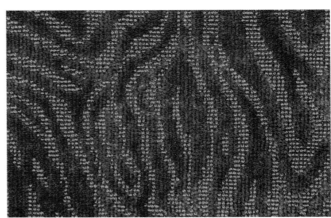

Figure 13.24 Friezé upholstery fabric. Courtesy of Amy Willbanks, www.textilefabric.com.

Figure 13.23 Panné velvet upholstery fabric. Courtesy of Amy Willbanks, www.textilefabric.com.

Figure 13.25 Grospoint upholstery fabric. Courtesy of Amy Willbanks, www.textilefabric.com.

may also be introduced by exposing areas of the base fabric and by combining two or more colors of pile yarns. Grospoint fabrics are frequently used for covering office chairs and the bottom and back cushions installed in transportation vehicles.

Knitted Pile Fabrics

A limited number of knitted upholstery fabrics have a pile layer. Generally, these structures are used more frequently as bedcoverings than as furniture coverings (see Chapter 29).

Tufted Fabrics

Tufting machines can produce the pile construction density desired in **tufted** upholstery fabrics. High density is necessary to prevent exposure of the base fabric, especially on curved areas of furniture. Today, some machines can insert some 400 pile yarns per square inch of base fabric. Together with the high rate of production characteristic of tufting, these developments result in increased use of this technique for upholstery fabric production.

Genuine Leather Upholstery

The basic structures used in manufacturing genuine leather coverings—raw skins and hides—are "fabricated" by various animals in assorted sizes, shapes, and thicknesses. **Skins**, retrieved from such small animals as lambs, goats, and calves, are thinner than hides and have an average size that does not normally exceed approximately 9 square feet. **Hides**, retrieved from such large animals as deer, horses, and cattle, on average reach a maximum size of about 25 square feet. Because heavier and larger pieces of leather are required for upholstery applications, hides are usually selected, and they are processed whole.

Composition and Structure of Raw Hides

The processes used in producing leather upholstery can be better understood if the composition and structural features of raw hide are first examined. Raw hide has three distinct sections: the epidermis, the corium, and the flesh layer.

The indentations in the top layer, the **epidermis**, are the hair follicles or pores. After the hair is removed, the exposed pores are seen as the **grain markings**, a surface feature found naturally only in coverings produced from the topmost layer of the hide. The central portion of the hide, the **corium**, is a network of interlaced bundles of tiny fibers composed of a protein called **collagen**. Gelatinous matter surrounds the fibrous bundles. The bottommost portion of the hide is **flesh tissue** (Figure 13.26). It should be noted that while leather is composed of a network of tiny fibers, these fibers are not classified as textile fibers.

The processing of raw skins and hides is an involved procedure that may be divided into four major operations: curing and cleaning, tanning, coloring, and finishing. A single firm in a vertical manufacturing operation usually carries out these operations.

Curing and Cleaning

Processing begins with **curing**—salting the raw hides. Curing retards bacterial action, helping prevent putrefaction or decomposition, and it also removes the gelatinous matter from the corium. The hides must be thoroughly cleaned, defleshed, and dehaired before further processing. If the hides are thick enough to be split into multiple layers, the splitting will also be done at this stage, prior to tanning.

Tanning

In earlier times, **tanning** solutions were often made from tannins extracted from such sources as tree bark. Because these vegetable tanning agents are slow-acting, they are rarely used in commercial tanning operations. Today, tanning solutions are composed of mineral substances, such as chromium-based salts, and oils. The cured and cleaned hides are immersed in the solution, where the tanning agents react with the collagen, rendering the fibers insoluble. The agents and oils fill the spaces that were formerly filled by the gelatinous materials. The hides are now soft, water- and mildew-resistant, pliable leathers.

Figure 13.26 Face and back of leather.
Courtesy of Amy Willbanks, www.textilefabric.com.

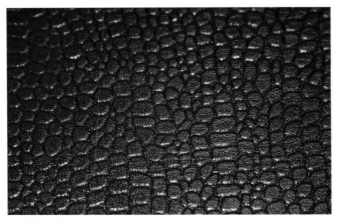

a) Glazed leather.

b) Top-grain leather.

Figure 13.27 *Genuine leather upholstery.*
Courtesy of Amy Willbanks, www.textilefabric.com.

Coloring

Coloring may be called for to camouflage an uneven natural color or to introduce currently popular fashion colors. The color may be applied by a piece-dyeing or a surface-dyeing operation.

In piece dyeing, referred to in the leather industry as **drum dyeing**, the tanned leather is rotated in large vessels filled with dye liquor. In **surface dyeing**, pigments are mixed with binding agents and spread or brushed over the surface of the leather; this technique is actually a type of staining and colors the surface portion only.

Finishing

Finishing operations may involve the application of lubricants and softening agents to increase the suppleness of the leather. Imperfect areas of grain may be corrected by gently abrading the surface or by shaving a thin film off the surface. If the natural grain is very imperfect, mechanical embossing operations may be employed to impart attractive markings. Resins, waxes, and lacquer-based compounds may be applied and polished for a glazed finish. The high gloss characteristic of **glazed leather** is shown in Figure 13.27a. Compounds used in glazing also increase the moisture resistance of the leather.

Finished leather fabrics are labeled with such terms as **full-grain leather**, top-grain leather, and split leather. The natural grain markings in full-grain leather have not been corrected or altered in any way. **Top-grain leather** (Figure 13.27b) has undergone minor corrections to its natural grain markings.

Split leather is produced from a central portion of the hide; since the top layer of the hide is not present in split leather coverings, no natural grain markings appear. Split leather may not be as durable as full- and top-grain leathers.

Genuine suede—leather fabric produced with the flesh side of the hide exposed—is rarely used in upholstery because of its habit of **crocking** or rubbing off color. Laboratory procedures to evaluate crocking are reviewed in the following chapter.

Vinyl and Simulated Leather and Suede Fabrics

Along with the relatively high cost of skins and hides, the lengthy and expensive processing required to convert them into finished coverings puts genuine leather upholstery beyond the financial reach of many residential and commercial consumers. Recognizing this, producers have developed some apparently successful techniques for manufacturing simulated leather coverings. When furniture manufacturers use these coverings, they should follow specific labeling guidelines.

Vinyl (vinyon in film form) and simulated leather fabrics are produced by extruding or expanding polymer solutions. Simulated suede fabrics are produced with selected finishing operations.

Extruding Film Sheeting

The compounds used most often to create **vinyl** and **simulated leather** (Figure 19.10, p. 318) fabrics include polyvinylchloride and polyurethane. Solutions of these compounds are extruded as film sheeting, using the process described in Chapter 7. To provide the dimensional stability required for upholstery applications, the sheeting is bonded to a supporting fabric, generally a conventional knitted, woven, bonded-web, or spunlaced fabric.

The grain markings that distinguish full- and top-grain leathers are introduced to simulated leathers by **embossing**. This is accomplished by pressing a metal-coated die that has been prepared with the desired markings into the surface of the film.

Incorporating air into the compounds will **expand polymer solutions**. The effect of this expansion is similar to that produced by whipping cream or egg whites: the apparent, but not the actual, volume is increased. The ex-

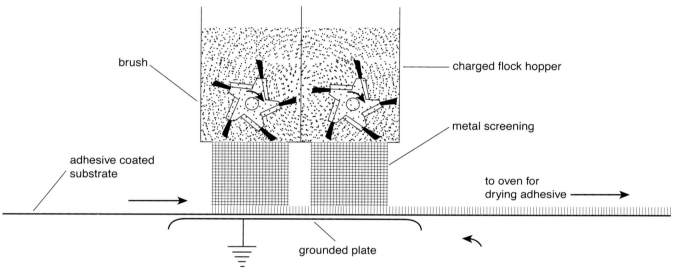

Schematic Diagram of Electrostatic Flocking

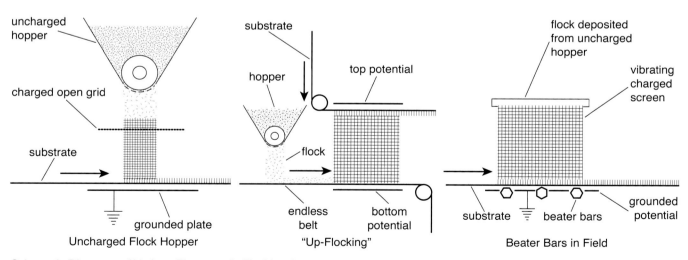

Schematic Diagrams of Various Electrostatic Flocking Arrangements

Figure 13.28 Various electrostatic flocking arrangements.
Courtesy of Ascend Performance Materials.

Figure 13.29 Vinyl with nonwoven backing.
Courtesy of Amy Willbanks, www.textilefabric.com.

Figure 13.30 Simulated suede upholstery.
Courtesy of Amy Willbanks, www.textilefabric.com.

panded polymer solution is then applied to a base fabric as a coating. This process increases the comfort characteristics. Again, embossing can be used to impart grain markings (Figure 13.29).

Polymer films and coatings have little or no porosity. Because of this lack of breathability, many people find these fabrics uncomfortable, especially in hot or humid weather.

Simulating Genuine Suede

Many upholstery coverings that appear to be genuine suede are actually simulated structures. Two operations, flocking and sueding, are used to produce these fabrics.

Flocking and Sueding

An **electrostatic flocking** operation is generally used to produce **simulated suede.** One of the arrangements illustrated in Figure 13.28 is used. Deposition of the flock is followed by sueding or emerizing (Figures 13.30 and 19.11, p. 318).

In **sueding** or **emerizing** operations, sandpaper-covered disks revolve against the flocked surface. Unlike brushing and smoothing finishes, which raise and orient pile yarns in one direction, and unlike napping finishes, which raise fiber ends, sueding roughens the surface, generally orienting the flock in every direction. However, in Ultrasuede®, a simulated suede marketed by Toray Ultrasuede (America), Inc. (TUA), the flock is given a directional lay or nap.

The durability of a flocked and sueded surface is determined by the cohesiveness of the substrate, resin, and flock. The surface must resist abrasive forces and the resin must be stable to cleaning agents.

Simulated leather and suede fabrics are used extensively to cover dining chairs and the seats, backs, and armrests in automobiles. Apart from any damage caused by cutting or puncturing, heavier vinyl and urethane fabrics can withstand the high levels of use in mass transit vehicles.

Summary

Both upholstery and transportation fabrics are predominantly composed of manufactured fibers, although a significant amount of upholstery fabric is made of cotton. The widespread use of noncellulosic fibers is largely the result of fiber engineering that enables manufacturers to introduce desirable properties during synthesis and production.

The extensive use of cotton and the growing use of staple-length noncellulosic fibers underscore the importance of complex spun yarns in upholstered furniture coverings. Such yarns contribute decorative interest, but may be ruptured and abraded more readily than simple, smooth yarns. Many flat and pile upholstery fabrics are produced by combining yarns in weaving, knitting, and tufting operations. The balance of the upholstery fabric assortment is produced by converting polymer solutions or raw animal skins into nontextile coverings.

Various techniques are used to convert raw hides and polymer solutions into furniture coverings. Hides un-dergo lengthy processing, including curing and cleaning, tanning, coloring, and finishing. Polymer solutions may be converted into film sheetings or expanded coatings. To simulate the surface appearance of full- and top-grain leathers, manufacturers emboss films and coatings with grain markings.

Key Terms

backcoated upholstery fabrics
bengaline
brocade
brocatelle
cloque
collagen
corduroy
corium
crepe
crocking
crushed velvet
curing
damask
doilies
dot or spot weave
doublecloth
drum dyeing
duck
electrostatic flocking
embossing
emerizing
epidermis
expanded polymer solutions
faille
flesh tissue
friezé

full-grain leather
genuine suede
glazed chintz
glazed leather
goose-eye twill
grain markings
grospoint
herringbone
hides
high twist
homespun
hopsacking
houndstooth checks
Jacquard-woven tapestry
liseré
matelassé
momie weave
needlepoint weave
ottoman
panné velvet
plaid
pocket cloth
pockets
rep
sateen
satin

shantung
simulated leather
simulated suede
skins
slipcovers
speck yarns
split leather
strié
sueding
surface dyeing
tanning
Textile Fiber Products Identification Act (TFPIA)
top-grain leather
triaxially woven fabric
tufted
tweed
velour
velvet
velveteen
vinyl
voided velvets
Wool Products Labeling Act (WPLA) of 1939

Review Questions

1. Noncellulosic fibers hold a significant portion of the upholstery market. What accounts for their growth, and why does their increased use underscore the importance of fiber content labeling?

2. Identify factors that have led to the shifting from cotton to the noncellulosic fibers for transportation applications.

3. Explain why spun yarns dominant the upholstery market.

4. What should the consumer and interior designer consider when selecting upholstery fabric having complex yarns?

5. Identify positive and potentially negative features of backcoated upholstery fabric.

6. Cite reasons why satin and sateen upholstery fabrics may have limited serviceability in end-use.

7. Distinguish between hand-woven and machine-woven tapestry.

8. Why are "needlepoint weave" fabrics so named?

9. Knitted fabric has limited use as upholstered furniture covering. What are the advantages and the limitations of these structures?

10. Grospoint fabrics have frequently been used for commercial upholstery applications. What supports their use in this market?

11. Differentiate among full-grain leather, top-grain leather, and split leather.

12. How are natural grain markings simulated?

Evaluation and Maintenance of Finished Upholstery Fabric

CHAPTER **FOURTEEN**

■ **The characteristics of the** components used and the quality of the manufacturing processes employed influence the appearance and serviceability of finished upholstery fabrics. Although quality finishing can improve the performance and enhance the visual features of fabrics, it cannot compensate for the use of inferior fibers and yarns, unstable colorants, poor pattern registration, or shoddy fabrication. Similarly, the use of high quality components and fabrication techniques cannot make up for poor fabric conversion. This interdependence encouraged representatives from segments of the industry to cooperate in establishing standards for finished upholstery fabrics. These standards are based on ASTM International and AATCC fabric tests. Residential and commercial upholstered furniture manufacturers (purchasers) communicate their specific fabric performance requirements to the fabric manufacturers (suppliers).

Use of the industry standards is strictly voluntary; minimum or maximum levels of performance are recommended, not required. These standards do, however, identify properties that should be considered when selecting woven upholstery fabrics, and they provide a basis for evaluating quality and predicting end-use serviceability. Code requirements pertaining to fabric flammability are covered in chapter 11.

ASTM D 3597, Performance Specification for Woven Upholstery Fabrics—Plain, Tufted or Flocked, includes specification requirements for such properties as breaking strength, tear strength, abrasion resistance, dimensional change, and yarn distortion. ASTM D 3597 also includes specification requirements for colorfast properties related to water, solvents, burnt-gas fumes, crocking, light, and ozone. These colorfast tests relate to the cleanability and serviceability of applied colorants when they are exposed to cleaning agents (Table 14.1).

ASTM D 4771, Standard Performance Specification for Knitted Upholstery Fabrics for Indoor Furniture, also includes physical and colorfastness tests relating to the serviceability of knitted upholstery furniture. This standard is not applicable to contract fabrics (Table 14.2).

The cleanability standard for upholstery fabric is based on the stability of applied colorants when they are exposed to water and to solvent according to prescribed testing procedures. Fabric manufacturers may use the results of such tests to help determine what agents should be used in the overall maintenance of a fabric. The need for overall cleaning can be delayed, however, if routine care and immediate stain removal are consistently used to maintain an outer covering.

Members of the Association for Contract Textiles established performance guidelines for upholstery fabric intended for contract applications. The ACT symbols (Table 14.3) placed on fabrics provide assurance to specifiers that the fabrics have performed to contract standards and pass all applicable testing. The performance properties included in the ACT program are included in this chapter.

Standards for Structural Qualities

Two standards concern the structural qualities of finished upholstery. One pertains to flaws and defects and the other to yarn alignment. The ACT standards do not include guidelines for these properties.

Flaws and Defects

Converters should carefully examine finished upholstery fabrics for the presence of unsightly **defects**, or flaws, which also could decrease the durability of the upholstered fabric. Assessment of quality can be made by examining the fabric with the eyes or an instrument to identify defects, or flaws. The increasing use of computer-aided-fabric evaluation systems (CAFE) not only increase the accuracy of the inspection, but greatly speed up the process of inspection.

Yarn Alignment

Problems caused by the use of **off-grain fabrics** are illustrated in Figure 14.1. Furniture items appear to be sagging when covered with a fabric exhibiting **bow** and crooked when covered with a fabric exhibiting **skew**. These problems are emphasized when colored yarns have been used to create such woven-in linear patterns as stripes and plaids.

In accordance with ASTM D 3882 Standard Test Method for Bow and Skew in Woven and Knitted Fabrics, measurements of bow are taken at the maximum point of distortion in three widely spaced places along the length of fabric (Figure 14.2). The measurements of maximum distortion produced by skew are taken parallel to and along a selvage, as shown in Figure 14.3. For each measurement, the maximum bow or skew is calculated as a percentage of fabric width. Together, the purchaser and supplier reach agreement on the acceptable level of yarn misalignment. ASTM International performance specifications recommend that the average of the three bow measurements (not percentages) not exceed 0.5 inch, and the average of the three skew measurements (not percentages) not exceed 1.0 inch.

Evaluations of Physical Performance Properties

Table 14.1 includes selected physical properties, the test methods used to measure these properties, and recom-

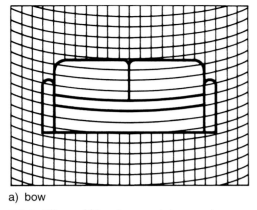

a) bow

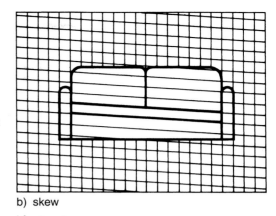

b) skew

Figure 14.1 Effects of filling bow and skew on the appearance of upholstered furniture items.

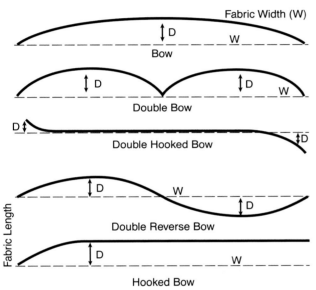

Figure 14.2 Typical bow conditions.
Adapted, with permission from D3882-08 Standard Test Method for Bow and Skew in Woven and Knitted Fabrics, copyright ASTM International, 100 Barr Harbor Drive, West Conshohocken, PA 19428, www.astm.org. A copy of the complete standard may be obtained from ASTM International.

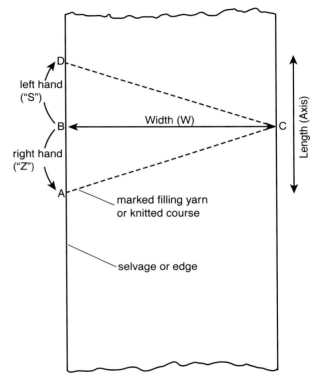

Figure 14.3 Typical skew conditions.
Adapted, with permission from D3882-08 Standard Test Method for Bow and Skew in Woven and Knitted Fabrics, copyright ASTM International, 100 Barr Harbor Drive, West Conshohocken, PA 19428, www.astm.org. A copy of the complete standard may be obtained from ASTM International.

mended performance levels noted in ASTM D 3597. Mutual agreement between purchaser and supplier determines which requirements must be met. In making these decisions, consideration must be given to any fashion or aesthetic preferences currently important to the ultimate consumer. Such variables may take precedence over performance requirements.

Tear Strength

ASTM D 2261 Standard Test Method for Tearing Strength of Woven Fabrics by the Tongue (Single Rip) Method

(Constant-Rate-of-Extension Tensile Testing Machine) may be used to evaluate the force required to continue or propagate a tear in a fabric under specified conditions. The test results can predict the likelihood that a small cut or puncture would become a large tear with continued use of the upholstered item.

Table 14.1 Standard Specification of Woven Upholstery Fabrics (Plain, Tufted or Flocked)

Characteristics	Test Method Number	Requirements
Breaking strength (load)	ASTM D 5034	222 N (50 lbf), min
Tongue tear strength	ASTM D 2261[f] (ASTM D 2262 discontinued)	27 N (6 lbf), min
Resistance to yarn distortion	ASTM D 1336[f] (ASTM D 0434 discontinued)	111 N (25 lbf), min
Surface abrasion[a]	ASTM D 4157[f] (ASTM D 1175 discontinued)	
Light-duty		3,000 cycles (double rubs), min
Medium-duty		9,000 cycles (double rubs), min
Heavy-duty		15,000 cycles (double rubs), min
Dimensional change:	ASTM D 3597	5.0% shrinkage, max to
Warp or filling		2.0% gain, max
Colorfastness to:[b]		
Water,[c] Color Change	AATCC 107	Class 4,[d] min
Solvent,[c] Color Change	AATCC 107	Class 4,[d] min
Burnt gas fumes—2 cycles	AATCC 23	Class 4,[d] min
Crocking:		
Dry	AATCC 8 or AATCC 116	Class 4,[e] min
Wet	AATCC 8 or AATCC 116	Class 3,[e] min
Light (40 AATCC Fading Units)	AATCC 16	Class 4,[d] min
Ozone 1 cycle	AATCC 129	Class 4,[d] min
Retention of hand, character, and appearance	ASTM D 3597, AATCC 107	no significant change
Durability of back coating	ASTM D 3597, AATCC 107	no significant change
Flammability	Code of Federal Registry, Part 1610	pass
FTC Requirements	TFPIA	pass

[a]For guideline purposes see 6.4.1.
[b]Class in the colorfastness requirements is based on a numerical scale of 5 for negligible for no color change or color transfer to 1 for very severe color change or color transfer.
[c]For guideline purposes see section 6.6.2.
[d]AATCC Gray Scale for Color Change.
[e]AATCC Chromatic Transference Scale.
[f]ASTM International has discontinued or withdrawn ASTM D 2262, ASTM D 0434, and ASTM D 1175. These test methods have been replaced by ASTM D 2261, ASTM D 1136, and ASTM D 4157.
Adapted, with permission from D3597-02(2008) Standard Specification for Woven Upholstery Fabrics—Plain, Tufted, or Flocked, copyright ASTM International, 100 Barr Harbor Drive, West Conshohocken, PA 19428, www.astm.org. A copy of the complete standard may be obtained from ASTM International.

Test Specimens and Procedures

Test specimens are cut to a size of 3 by 8 inches, with the short dimension corresponding to the direction to be tested. A 3-inch cut is made at the center of and perpendicular to the short side of each specimen, forming two "tongues" or "tails."

After conditioning the specimens for a minimum of 24 hours in a controlled atmosphere of 70 ± 2 °F and 65 ± 2 percent relative humidity, each is successively placed in paired clamps on a **constant-rate-of-extension (CRTE)** testing machine. One tongue is secured in the jaws of the upper clamp and one tongue is secured in the jaws of the lower clamp; thus, opposite sides of the specimen are exposed to the operator. As the machine operates, the lower clamp moves downward at a constant rate for a distance of 3 inches. The loads required to tear each specimen are automatically recorded.

Analysis of Results

The five peak loads recorded during tearing of a specimen are averaged. The **tear strength** values for all replicate specimens are then averaged and reported.

Performance Guidelines

ASTM D 3597 specifies a minimum of 6 pounds of force to propagate the tear. UFS guidelines include three levels of performance. The levels are based on differences in the construction and weight of upholstery fabrics. Category III fabrics, lightweight printed cotton structures, are generally rated "delicate"; therefore, these fabrics should not be buttoned excessively nor should furniture covered with these fabrics be placed where it will receive heavy use.

Breaking Strength and Elongation

The **apparent elongation** and **tensile strength** of upholstery fabrics can be determined in one testing procedure, ASTM D 5034 Standard Test Method for Breaking Strength and Elongation of Textile Fabrics (Grab Test).

Test Specimens and Procedures

In the **breaking force**-grab method, only a part of the specimen is gripped in the clamps. Each specimen is 4 inches wide and 6 inches long, and is held in the center by 1-inch wide clamps, as shown in Figure 14.4. (Using a larger back clamp is permissible and tends to reduce slippage.) To ensure accurate alignment when securing the specimen in the clamps, a line is drawn 1.5 inches from the long edge of the specimen. A **constant-rate-of-extension (CRE)** or a CRT testing machine may be used.

Analysis of Results

The **breaking force** in pounds is recorded for each replicate specimen tested, and the average of these values is calculated and reported. The apparent elongation is expressed as the percentage increase in length based on the distance between the clamps, which is normally 3 inches (% elongation at rupture = [length stretched/original length] × 100).

Performance Guidelines

As detailed in Table 14.1, the ASTM International guidelines for elongation differ for different categories of fabrics. ASTM specifies a minimum breaking force of 50 pounds for all fabrics, regardless of construction and weight.

ACT standards for contract upholstery breaking force are the same as the ASTM and UFS guidelines. A minimum of 50 pounds of breaking load is required in both the warp and filling or weft directions.

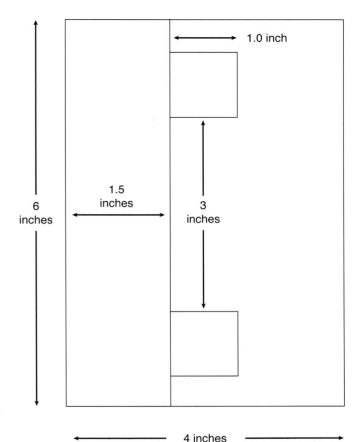

Figure 14.4 Preparation and placement of a specimen for measuring the breaking force and apparent elongation of fabrics by the grab method.

Bursting Strength

ASTM D 3787, Standard Test Method for Bursting Strength of Textiles—**Constant-Rate-of-Traverse (CRT)** Ball Burst Test, describes the measurement for bursting strength with a ball burst strength tester. This test is used for textiles that exhibit a high degree of ultimate of ultimate elongation.

Test Methods and Procedures

Five specimens are cut to at least 5 inches square or a circle 5 inches in diameter. The specimen is placed in the testing machine in the clamp ring without tension. The ball burst tester pushes the fabric at a speed of 12 inches per minute. This speed is continued until the specimen bursts.

Analysis of Results

After bursting, specimens are removed from the clamp and the average bursting strength is recorded to the nearest ½ inch.

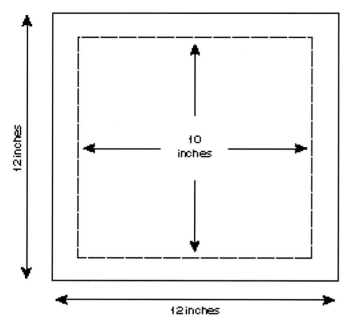

Figure 14.5 Specimen marked for measuring dimensional stability.

Dimensional Stability

Upholstery fabrics must maintain their original dimensions, within reasonable limitations. With permanently attached, as well as removable, furniture coverings, there should be no prolonged bagging and sagging of the fabric after a person rises from the item; nor should there

be excessive **growth** of the fabric in cleaning. Excessive **shrinkage** of the fabric in use or cleaning would cause the fabric to become smaller than the filling, distorting the three-dimensional form of the cushions. It would also place stress on the fabric seams and zipper closures, causing them to ripple or split.

Industry representatives recommend that procedures set out in ASTM D 3597 be followed in measuring the **dimensional stability** of upholstery fabrics. Measurements of the relaxation shrinkage or growth of the specimens are made after exposing them to water.

Test Specimens and Procedures

In preparation for testing, fabric specimens are cut 12 inches square and marked with sets of three 10-inch-gauge distances in both the warp direction and the filling directions, as illustrated in Figure 14.5. The marked specimens are submerged in distilled water for 10 ± 1 minutes. They are then placed on horizontal screens and allowed to dry for 24 hours.

Analysis of Results

The distance between the gauge marks is measured in each direction. Separate averages are then determined for the warp and the filling. The percentage of change is calculated as directed in the following equations:

$$\% \text{ shrinkage} = [(A - B)/A] \times 100$$
$$\% \text{ gain} = [(B - A)/A] \times 100$$

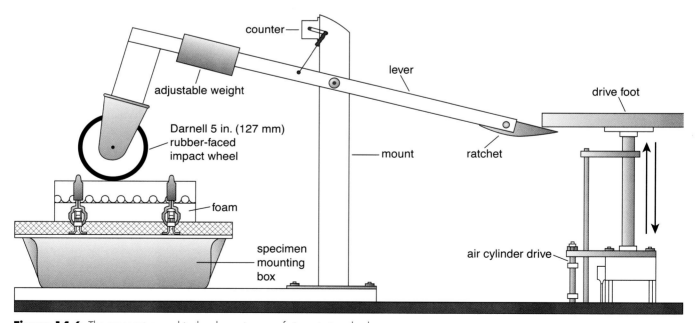

Figure 14.6 The apparatus used in the dynamic seam fatigue test method. Courtesy of the American Home Furnishings Alliance.

Table 14.2 Standard Performance Specification for Knitted Upholstery Fabrics for Indoor Furniture

Characteristics	Test Method Number	Requirements
Resistance to yarn slippage	ASTM D 1336 (ASTM D 0434 discontinued)[d]	⅛" max at 7,000 cycles
Dimensional change, wale or course	AATCC 135 (FCT Upholstered Standard Guidelines)**	5% shrinkage max, to 2% gain max
Colorfastness to:[a]		
Water, Color Change	AATCC 107	Grade 4[b] min
Solvent, Color Change	AATCC 107	Grade 4[b] min
Crocking:	AATCC 8 or AATCC 116	
Dry		Grade 4[c] min
Wet		Grade 3[c] min
Burnt gas fumes—2 cycles	AATCC 23	Grade 4[b] min
Light (40 AATCC Fading Units)	AATCC 16	Grade 4[b] min
Ozone 1 cycle	AATCC 129	Grade 4[b] min
Retention of hand, character, and appearance	AATCC 8, 107, 116	Shall not change more than limitations set by prior agreement between the buyer and the seller
Durability of back coating	AATCC 8, 107, 116	No peeling or cracking of the backcoating shall occur; durability shall be compatible with cleaning code
Flammability:		
	California Bulletin 117	pass
	UFAC Fabric Classification	Class I—vertical char length is equal to or less than 1.75 in.
		Class II—vertical char length is greater than 1.75 in.
FTC Requirements	TFPIA	pass

[a]The grade rating in the colorfastness requirements is based on a numerical scale of 5 for negligible for no color change or color transfer to 1 for very severe color change or color transfer.
[b]AATCC Gray Scale for Color Change.
[c]AATCC Chromatic Transference Scale.
[d]ASTM International withdrew ASTM D 0434. This method has been replaced by ASTM D 1336.
**Test Methods related to dimensional stability in the *Upholstery Standard Guidelines* have been rescinded by the FTC. Test Method AATCC 187 can be used for dimensional stability.
Adapted, with permission from D4771/D4771M-09 Standard Performance Specification for Knitted Upholstery Fabrics for Indoor Furniture, copyright ASTM International, 100 Barr Harbor Drive, West Conshohocken, PA 19428, www.astm.org. A copy of the complete standard may be obtained from ASTM International.

where A = distance between gauge marks before wetout, and B = distance between gauge marks after wetout and drying.

Performance Guidelines

Upholstery fabrics should not exhibit more than 5 percent shrinkage in either fabric direction. The guidelines also suggest a maximum gain of 2 percent in either direction. The reason for this differential is that upholstery fabric is usually under tension; therefore, shrinkage up to 5 percent is generally less objectionable than fabric gain, which produces bagging.

Yarn Distortion

ASTM D 1336, Standard Test Method for Distortion of Yarn in Woven Fabrics, is used as an indicator of the tendency of yarns to slip or distort, causing an unsightly appearance in woven upholstery fabrics. ASTMD covers the measurement of yarn distortion in woven cloth following the application of surface friction. This test method is especially applicable to low yarn count fabrics, such as netting, gauzes, chiffons, and marquisette. Distortion of yarn should also be examined in satin-woven fabrics made of smooth, filament yarns.

Figure 14.7 Oscillatory cylinder abrasive machine used to evaluate abrasion resistance.
Courtesy of College of Textiles at North Carolina State University.

Test Specimens and Procedures

Five specimens are cut with the longer dimension parallel to the set of yarns having the greater resistance to shifting as determined by a preliminary test. The preliminary test includes exerting a force on the fabric at opposite surfaces, noting the direction of least resistance to yarn slippage. Test specimens are placed vertically in the frame of the fabric shift tester and clamped. A friction drum provides the force specified in the product specifications (Figure 14.6). The rubber surfaces of the friction drum are turned in their clamps to present a new surface after every 40 rubbing cycles.

Analysis of Results

After the fabric is removed from the shift tester, the degree to which the force causes yarns to shift distorting the original symmetry of the weave is taken as a measurement of yarn distortion. A degree of distortion is reported in terms of the widest slippage or opening, measure in hundredths of an inch.

Performance Guidelines

As detailed in Table 14.1, ASTM International specifies a minimum of ⅛ inch maximum at 7,000 cycles. ACT specifies a 20 pound weight minimum in both warp and filling yarns.

Abrasion Resistance

The extensive use of complex yarns and decorative interlacings in upholstery fabric requires that consumers, interior designers, and architects consider the level of **abrasion** to which the covering will be subjected in end use. This will assist in the selection of a fabric that will be serviceable for a reasonable length of time, minimizing the potential need for premature replacement or recovering of the item.

For the evaluation of the abrasion resistance of upholstery fabrics, ASTM D 4157 Standard Test Method for Abrasion Resistance of Textile Fabrics **(Oscillatory Cylinder Method)** is used. This procedure, frequently referred to as the **Wyzenbeek test method**, was selected because it has traditionally been employed in the industry. The Oscillatory Cylinder Abrasive Machine (Figure 14.7) used is described in the following section.

Test Specimens and Procedures

Test specimens are cut 1⅞ inches by 9 inches. The long dimensions are cut parallel to the warp yarns to test warpwise abrasion resistance and parallel to the filling yarns to test fillingwise abrasion resistance. The specimens are secured in the clamps of the apparatus after conditioning. The specimen supports are then lowered over the curved cylinder, which is covered with No. 0 emery paper as the abradant. The cylinder oscillates at the rate of 90 cycles **(double rubs)** per minute, effecting unidirectional rubbing action on the specimens.

Analysis of Results

At the end of 3,000 cycles (double rubs), the specimens are examined for loose threads and wear; slight discoloration from the abradant on light-colored fabrics is disregarded. If no noticeable change is apparent, the test is continued for another 6,000 cycles and the specimens are again examined. If no noticeable change is apparent, the test is continued for another 6,000 cycles for a total of 15,000 cycles.

Performance Guidelines

As noted in Table 14.1, different levels of abrasion resistance are recommended for light duty, medium duty, and heavy duty applications, 3,000 cycles, 9,000 cycles, and 15,000

Table 14.3 ACT Voluntary Performance Guidelines

Flammability

The measurement of a fabric's performance when it is exposed to specific sources of ignition.

Upholstery
California Technical Bulletin #117 Section E – Class 1 (Pass)

Direct Glue Wallcoverings
ASTM E 84-03 (Adhered Mounting Method) – Class A or Class 1

Wrapped Panels and Upholstered Walls
ASTM E 84-03 (Unadhered Mounting Method) – Class A or Class 1

Drapery
NFPA 701-89 (Small Scale)* – Pass

* NFPA 701-99 Test #1 is being phased in at the time of this publication, but is not yet cited in all relevant codes. Therefore, the small-scale test remains the ACT standard until further notice.

Wet & Dry Crocking

Transfer of dye from the surface of a dyed or printed fabric onto another surface by rubbing.

Upholstery
AATCC 8-2001 · · · · · · · · Dry Crocking, Grade 4 minimum
· · · · · · · · · · · · · · · · · · Wet Crocking, Grade 3 minimum

Direct Glue Wallcoverings
AATCC 8-2001 · · · · · · · · Dry Crocking, Grade 3 minimum
· · · · · · · · · · · · · · · · · · Wet Crocking, Grade 3 minimum

Wrapped Panels and Upholstered Walls
AATCC 8-2001 · · · · · · · · Dry Crocking, Grade 3 minimum
· · · · · · · · · · · · · · · · · · Wet Crocking, Grade 3 minimum

Drapery
AATCC 8-2001 (Solids) · · · Dry Crocking, Grade 3 minimum
· · · · · · · · · · · · · · · · · · Wet Crocking, Grade 3 minimum
AATCC 116-2001 (Prints) · · Dry Crocking, Grade 3 minimum
· · · · · · · · · · · · · · · · · · Wet Crocking, Grade 3 minimum

Colorfastness to Light

A material's degree of resistance to the fading effect of light.

Upholstery
AATCC 16 Option 1 or 3-2003 · · · Grade 4 minimum at 40 hours

Direct Glue Wallcoverings
AATCC 16 Option 1 or 3-2003 · · · Grade 4 minimum at 40 hours

Wrapped Panels and Upholstered Walls
AATCC 16 Option 1 or 3-2003 · · · Grade 4 minimum at 40 hours

Drapery
AATCC 16 Option 1 or 3-2003 · · · Grade 4 minimum at 60 hours

Table 14.3 ACT Voluntary Performance Guidelines (continued)

Physical Properties

Pilling is the formation of fuzzy balls of fiber on the surface of a fabric that remain attached to the fabric. *Breaking strength* is the measurement of stress exerted to pull a fabric apart under tension. *Seam Slippage* is the movement of yarns in a fabric that occurs when it is pulled apart at a seam.

Upholstery
Brush pill ASTM D3511-02, Class 3 minimum

Breaking strength ASTM D5034-95 (2001) (Grab Test)
50 lbs. minimum in warp and weft

Seam slippage ASTM D4034*
25 lbs. minimum in warp and weft

Wrapped Panels and Upholstered Walls
Breaking strength ASTM D5034-95 (2001) (Grab Test)
35 lbs. minimum in warp and weft

Drapery
Seam slippage ASTM D3597-02-D434-95 for fabrics over 6 oz./sq. yard
25 lbs. minimum in warp and weft

Abrasion

The surface wear of a fabric caused by rubbing and contact with another fabric.

General Contract Upholstery

General Contract Upholstery
ASTM D4157-02 (ACT approved #10 Cotton Duck)
15,000 double rubs Wyzenbeek method

ASTM D4966-98 (12 KPa pressure)
20,000 cycles Martindale method

Heavy Duty Upholstery

Heavy Duty Upholstery
ASTM D4157-02 (ACT approved #10 Cotton Duck)
30,000 double rubs Wyzenbeek method

ASTM D4966-98 (12 KPa pressure)
40,000 cycles Martindale method

Source: Association for Contract Textiles.
*ASTM International withdrew D5034 in 2001. This test method has been replaced by D1336, Standard Test Method for Distortion of Yarns in Woven Fabrics.

cycles, respectively. As detailed in Table 14.3, these in-use applications are defined in terms of frequency of use.

ACT Standards The ACT guidelines require that general contract upholstery fabric tested by the Wyzenbeek method withstand 15,000 cycles. Heavy duty upholstery should withstand 30,000 cycles. (Table 14.3)

The ACT guidelines also include abrasion resistance standards for fabric tested by ASTM D 4966 Standard Test Method for Abrasion Resistance of Textile Fabrics

(Martindale Abrasion Test Method). In this testing, the fabric is mounted flat and abraded in a figure-eight fashion by a worsted wool fabric. General contract upholstery should withstand 20,000 rubs and heavy duty upholstery should withstand 40,000 rubs before showing an objectionable change in appearance.

Resistance to Pilling

Small balls or pills on the surface of fabrics are unsightly, especially when fibers of contrasting colors are present. To assess the extent of **pilling**, ACT recommends that contract fabrics be subjected to the procedures in ASTM D 3511 Standard Test Method for Pilling Resistance and Other Related Surface Changes of Textile Fabrics: Brush Pilling Tester. The fabric specimens are first brushed with nylon bristles to free fiber ends that form fuzz on the surface of the fabric. Subsequently, the face sides of two specimens are rubbed together in a circular motion to roll the fiber ends into pills.

Contract upholstery fabrics that meet or exceed the recommended performance levels in pilling resistance, breaking strength, and yarn slippage at seams may be marketed with an ACT symbol (Table 14.3).

Examination of Color Consistency and Retention

Colorfastness refers to the ability of colorants to retain their original properties when they are exposed to various environmental conditions, cleaning agents, and end-use activities. Residential consumers, contract designers, and architects should be aware of sources of potential harm to colorants and avoid them, if possible. Manufacturers should ascertain the stability of colorants applied to upholstery fabrics and discontinue the use of those failing to exhibit acceptable levels of fastness.

As part of their quality-control work, dyers and printers should examine the uniformity of color characteristics and look for any variability in pattern repeats. End-product producers and consumers may reject upholstery fabrics exhibiting inconsistent color or pattern placements.

Sophisticated electronic color meters can be used to detect differences in the color characteristics of fabrics. Colors of a fabric should not vary within any single piece or roll, and streaks are unacceptable.

Because changes in the texture of pile fabrics may produce changes in the **apparent brightness** of the fabric, members of the industry recommend that packaging, storing, and handling of these fabrics be controlled to avoid distortion of the original pile yarn orientation. Care during processing and shipping can minimize the development of apparent shading problems.

The variation of **pattern repeats** should be measured from center point to center point of any contiguous repeats, and a minimum of four measurements should be taken in a continuous length of 50 yards. When pattern repeats are 13 inches or more in length, the variation should not exceed 0.5 inch; when pattern repeats are less than 13 inches in length, the variation should not exceed 0.25 inch.

Changes in **color characteristics** may be described in relative terms—"barely perceptible," "quite noticeable,"

and so on—but the degree of change can be measured and rated in numerical terms by using standard test methods. Manufacturers of upholstery fabrics may elect to compare the results of such tests with the levels of fastness recommended by representatives of the industry. These standards are listed in Table 14.1.

Colorfastness to Crocking

Rubbing may cause unstable colorants to exhibit a problem known as **crocking**, the transfer of color from one surface to another area of the same fabric or from one material to another. The loss or transfer can occur under dry or wet conditions. Crocking may occur in upholstery fabric when, for example, apparel fabric rubs against the colored seat of a chair.

The **Crockmeter**, shown in Figure 14.8, is the instrument used in AAATC 8 Colorfastness to Crocking (Rubbing): AATCC Crockmeter Method. During testing, the upholstery fabric is cyclically rubbed by a rod covered with white fabric. Transfer of color from the upholstery surface to the white fabric is evidence of crocking.

The degree of transference is evaluated visually, and a numerical fastness value is determined by comparing the white fabric that covered the rod during testing with pairs of chips on the **International Geometric Gray Scale for Evaluating Staining**.[2] As shown in Figure 14.9, there is no difference between the members of the first pair of chips, and the rating is 5; a perceptible difference appears in the second pair, a combination of the white reference chip and a slightly grayed chip, and the rating is 4.5. The last pair includes a white reference chip and the strongest gray chip: a marked contrast appears, representing a significant level of color transfer.

If no color was transferred from the upholstery fabric surface to the white test fabric, a rating of 5 would be recorded. If transfer occurred, the degree of contrast observed between the unstained and stained areas on the test fabric would be compared with that observed between the paired chips on the scale, and the appropriate number would be assigned. Thus, the higher the reported value, the more stable the colorant and the better the resistance to crocking.

The **AATCC Chromatic Transference Scale**, (shown in Figure 18.6, p. 308), is specified for evaluation of both dry and wet crocking in ASTM 3597. The numerical ratings are equivalent to the Gray Scale ratings.

The ACT standard requires a Class 4 minimum for dry crocking, and a Class 3 minimum for wet crocking. Contract fabrics meeting or exceeding these minimums may be marked with the ACT symbol, an artist's palette (Table 14.3), to denote compliance.

Figure 14.8 The Crockmeter testing apparatus.
Courtesy of SDL Atlas.

Colorfastness to Light

AATCC 16 Colorfastness to Light sets out several procedures that can be used to evaluate the **lightfastness** of colored fabrics. There are procedures for accelerated laboratory testing and for extended outdoor exposure testing. Various light sources and testing conditions are specified in each test procedure. Because lightfastness is especially critical for draperies, curtains, and awnings, these test methods are explained in Unit Three, Chapter 18.

After completion of the selected lightfastness testing procedure, producers visually evaluate and rate the level of color retention in essentially the same manner as crocking evaluations are made. In this case, however, the **International Geometric Gray Scale for Color Change** is used. As shown in Figure 14.10, the reference chip is a saturated gray color, and it is successively paired with lighter gray chips.

Numerical ratings are determined by comparing the difference observed between an original and an exposed fabric specimen with that observed between the members of a pair of chips on the scale. Again, the higher the reported value, the more stable the colorant. A rating of Class 4 or higher after 40 hours of exposure to light is required to meet the standard. Class 5 indi-

cates no fading, while Class 1 indicates a high degree of fading.

Colorfastness to Burnt Gas Fumes

Atmospheric contaminant fading, ozone or O-fading, fume fading, and **gas fading** are terms describing the destructive effects of various gases on colored textiles. Gases that commonly cause problems include oxides of sulfur, oxides of nitrogen, and ozone. Exposing colored textiles to various concentrations of these gases may result in weakening or fading of the original color or an actual change in hue. Either type of change in the color characteristics of interior textile products is a twofold disaster: the harmony among several items in an interior setting is destroyed, and the cost of replacement must be paid.

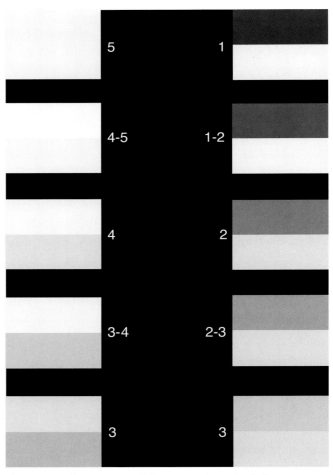

Figure 14.9 International Geometric Gray Scale for Evaluating Staining.
Courtesy of the American Association of Textile Chemists and Colorists.

Greater numbers of fume fading incidents occur in industrial centers, geographic regions where coal and fuel oil are major heating sources, and densely populated areas where personal automobiles are widely relied on. Automobile exhaust can contain as much as fifty thousand times more nitric oxide than a normal atmosphere. While emission control devices on automobiles and clean air standards are reducing the concentrations of some atmospheric pollutants, the increasing use of fireplaces and wood-burning stoves for home heating is generating greater concentrations of others.

Fume fading is a particular problem in acetate fibers dyed with disperse dyestuffs. After prolonged exposure to oxides of nitrogen or sulfur, certain colors gradually and permanently change hue. Blues turn pink, greens turn brownish yellow, and browns turn red. Solution dyeing is necessary to avoid such changes, and trade names may be used to distinguish the solution-dyed fibers.

AATCC 23 Colorfastness to Burnt Gas Fumes can be used for analyzing the negative effects of various gases, but it is generally used to determine the effects of nitrogen dioxide. The test is conducted in an enclosed chamber, such as the one in Figure 14.11, with controlled concentrations of the gas. After completion of two cycles of testing, the level of color change is determined in the same manner as lightfastness ratings are determined, using the Gray Scale for Color Change. AATCC 129 Colorfastness to Ozone in the Atmosphere Under High Humidities is used to measure the deleterious effects of ozone on colored textiles.

Colorfastness to Cleaning Agents

The fastness of the colorants determines the cleanability of upholstery fabrics when they are exposed to water and to solvents, the agents that are typically used to clean upholstery. Manufacturers are specifically concerned with the potential for color bleeding and migration (movement of the dyestuff through the fabric components). **Bleeding**, either to the interior of the covering or onto cleaning cloths, would weaken the surface color. **Migration** would create various levels of intensity over the surface and could transfer color from one area to another area of a different color.

Colorfastness to Water

AATCC 107 Colorfastness to Water is recommended for evaluating the fastness of colored upholstery fabric to water. In preparation for testing, a multifiber fabric, a structure that has narrow bands of six different fibers, backs the fabric specimen. The paired fabrics are immersed in distilled water and then removed, pressed between glass plates, and heated in an oven at 100 ±2 °F for 18 hours. After air drying, the fabric specimen is visually evaluated and rated for color change using the Gray Scale for Color Change. The multifiber fabric backing is visually evaluated for staining using the Gray Scale for Staining.

Colorfastness to Solvents

AATCC 107 is also used to evaluate the fastness of colored upholstery fabrics to solvents. In this procedure, however, the paired fabrics are immersed in a solvent, perchloroeth-

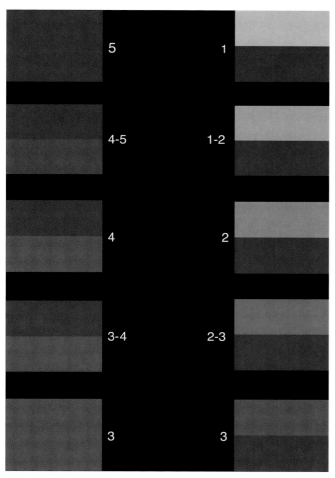

Figure 14.10 International Geometric Gray Scale for Color Change.
Courtesy of the American Association of Textile Chemists and Colorists.

Figure 14.11 Gas fume chamber. Courtesy of SDL Atlas.

ylene, instead of in water. The exposed fabrics are again evaluated for color change and staining.

It should be noted that these colorfastness test methods give reliable information on the stability of colorants to water and to solvent only. They do not take into account the rubbing or blotting action usually involved in a cleaning process. Therefore, fastness to water or solvent does not necessarily guarantee a satisfactory outcome to actual soil and stain removal efforts.

Upholstery fabrics meeting or exceeding the standards recommended for the several properties discussed in this chapter should perform well in end use. However, proper maintenance is required to ensure that the original appearance features are retained at an acceptable level for an extended period of time.

Colorfastness to Ozone

AATCC 129 Colorfast to Ozone in the Atmosphere under High Humidities is recommended for evaluation of the colorfastness of upholstered furniture to ozone. As in other colorfastness tests, a multifiber test fabric backs the test specimens. They are simultaneously exposed to ozone in

a testing chamber until the control sample shows a color change. After drying, a fabric specimen is rated for color change using the Gray Scale for Color Change. The multifiber backing is rated for staining using the Gray Scale for Staining.

Maintenance of Upholstery Fabrics

Residential and commercial consumers do not expect an upholstery fabric to retain its new, fresh, clean appearance forever. On the other hand, they do not anticipate that soil accumulation will be so rapid that an unreasonable maintenance program will be required. Consumers also expect that the removal of stains will not be an impossible challenge.

Preventive Maintenance

As a preventive maintenance measure, contract designers and other specifiers may request that the surface of upholstery fabrics be laminated with clear or translucent vinyl film sheeting. Although **vinylized fabrics** can be washed with mild detergent and warm water, they are not waterproof; they are not intended for installation outdoors. Because this treatment produces some variation in color and luster, converters suggest that the client examine a treated sample of the fabric before the vinyl application is ordered.

With routine care and immediate stain removal, residential and commercial consumers can assist in the long-term retention of the original appearance of upholstery fabrics. As long as the appearance is satisfactory to the consumer, the need for an overall or restorative cleaning procedure is postponed.

Routine Care

Upholstered furniture products should be frequently and thoroughly vacuumed to remove airborne dust and lint. If possible, loose cushions should be turned and rotated to equalize wear and soiling levels. Protective arm covers and head rests should be cleaned to minimize differences between the appearance of these items and that of other exposed areas.

Simulated leather fabrics with a polyvinylchloride or polyurethane surface may be washed with warm water and a mild soap (not a detergent), and then rinsed with a dampened cloth and dried. As a protective measure, a hard wax can be applied to the surface. However, waxes, oils, and furniture polishes must not be applied to genuine leather coverings as they may damage the finish.

Emergency Action

Prompt action must be taken in the event of spillage or deposition of other foreign matter. Fluids must be immediately absorbed from the surface to confine the area of spillage and to prevent them from penetrating into the fibers and fabric backing. Solid materials, such as candle wax and crayon, should be broken up, scraped, and vacuumed to remove as much of the substance as possible before stain removal agents are used.

When stain removal agents are required, they should first be applied as directed to an inconspicuous area of the outer covering. After the agent has been removed and the fabric has dried, the area should be examined for evidence of change in the original color characteristics. If necessary, different agents should be tried until one causing no change in color can be identified.

In order to avoid spreading the stain and overwetting the fabric, stain removal compounds should be applied in small amounts from the outside edges toward the center of the stain. To avoid distortion of the surface texture, the agent should be blotted on, not rubbed into, the foreign matter and fabric. After the stain has been completely removed, the cleaning agent residue must also be removed by rinsing the fabric and blotting it dry.

Waterborne stains can be removed from most textile upholstery fabrics with a mild detergent diluted with warm water, using one teaspoon of detergent per cup of water. **Oilborne stains** can be removed with a solvent-type dry cleaning fluid, such as K2r®, produced by Texize.

Table 14.4 lists the stain removal agents and procedures recommended for use with wool. Additional stain removal agents and procedures are listed in Tables 27.3, 27.4, and 27.5 (pp. 414, 415, and 416, respectively). Although these are specifically applicable to soft floor coverings, they may also be used with upholstery fabrics. In all cases, however, a pretest should be performed to confirm that the agent would not alter the color of the fabric or the integrity of the fabric structure.

If warm, soapy water does not remove soil from simulated leather coverings, the surface can be cleaned with a cloth dampened with kerosene or naphtha. These compounds are flammable and should be used with caution in a well-ventilated area to avoid inhalation of the fumes. Ballpoint ink can usually be removed by spraying the stain with hair spray and immediately wiping the surface.

Procedures used to remove stains will also remove accumulated soil. This may result in a localized clean area that can readily be distinguished from adjacent soiled areas. When such differences are apparent, or when large areas are soiled, the entire surface should be cleaned.

Restorative Maintenance

The original appearance of upholstery fabrics can usually be restored by carefully cleaning the fabric surface. Consumers may elect to do the restoration themselves, to send the item to a professional cleaner, or to have a professional cleaner restore the item on-site.

Frequently, upholstery manufacturers voluntarily label their products with a **cleaning code**. The code to be used is determined by measuring the level of color migration and bleeding caused by water and by solvent, using the standard test methods described earlier in this chapter. Industry representatives recommend that all upholstered furniture be identified as to its cleanability code, using the letter codes defined as follows:

W—use water base upholstery cleaner only.

S—use solvent base upholstery cleaner only.

WS—can use water base or solvent base cleaners.

X—do not clean with water base or solvent base cleaners; use vacuuming or light brushing only.

Water-based cleaning agents are commonly labeled upholstery shampoo. These agents are commercially available as foams, concentrated liquids, and dry compounds.

It should be emphasized that these cleaning codes apply to the outer covering fabric only; it is imperative that overwetting of the fabric be avoided to prevent contact with the filling materials. It must also be noted that zippered covers should not be removed for cleaning or excessive shrinkage may occur and the backing compound may be damaged. Zippers are used to facilitate filling the cushions, not to facilitate cleaning.

Genuine leather coverings may be cleaned with cheesecloth soaked in a solution of warm water and any mild soap. The surface should then be wiped with a slightly damp cloth and dried with a soft cloth.

Table 14.4 Removal of Spots and Stains From Wool Upholstery

Stain	Detergent or Vinegar	Cleaning Fluid	Other	Stain	Detergent or Vinegar	Cleaning Fluid	Other
Acids			Detergent	Iodine	•		Alcohol
Alcoholic beverages	•	•		Lipstick	•	•	
Ammonia or alkali	•			Metal polish	•	•	
Beer	•			Milk	•	•	
Bleach	•			Mud	•		
Blood	•			Mustard	•		
Butter		•		Nail Polish			Polish remover
Candy	•		Scrape and vacuum	Oils		•	
Chewing gum	•	•		Paint	•	•	
Chocolate	•	•		Perfume	•	•	
Coffee	•			Salad dressing	•	•	
Cosmetics	•	•		Sauces	•	•	
Crayon	•	•	Scrape and vacuum	Shoe polish	•	•	Scrape and vacuum
Egg	•			Soft drinks	•		
Excrement	•			Tar		•	
Fruit and juices	•			Tea	•		
Furniture polish	•	•		Urine	•		
Glue			Alcohol	Vomit	•	•	
Grease		•	Scrape and vacuum	Washable ink	•		
Household cement	•	•		Wax		•	Scrape and vacuum
Ice cream	•	•					

Courtesy of Australian Wool Innovation Limited.

Salvage Maintenance

In the event that an upholstered furniture covering no longer has an acceptable appearance, even after overall cleaning, consumers may elect to have the item reupholstered. Because such projects involve materials costs, skilled labor charges, and, often, transportation expenses, they may be relatively expensive. For this reason, reupholstering is often restricted to well-constructed items and antique pieces.

Summary

Fiber, yarn, and fabric manufacturers, colorists, converters, and end-product producers have established standards for various physical and color-related properties of finished upholstery fabrics. These standards include suggested methods for testing the fabrics in the laboratory and recommended levels of performance. The test methods were chosen because they provide a reasonable simulation of end-use conditions; fabrics meeting the standards based on these methods should therefore display an acceptable level of in-use serviceability.

The original appearance of upholstery coverings can be retained for a longer period of time if vacuuming is routine and removal of stains is prompt. For overall cleaning, informed consumers can interpret the cleaning code that is frequently, albeit voluntarily, listed on upholstered furniture labels or hangtags. Manufacturers whose fabric has been examined for color migration and bleeding after being exposed to water and to solvent use these letter codes.

Key Terms

AATCC 9-Step Chromatic Transference Scale
ASTM 3597
abrasion
ACT standards
ACT symbols
apparent brightness
apparent elongation
Association for Contract Textiles (ACT)
atmospheric contaminant fading
bleeding
bow
breaking force
bursting strength
cleaning code
color characteristics
colorfastness
constant-rate-of-extension (CRE)
constant-rate-of-traverse (CRT)

crocking
Crockmeter
dimensional stability
double rubs
electronic color meter
flaws and defects
fume fading
gas fading
growth
International Geometric Gray Scale for Color Change
International Geometric Gray Scale for Evaluating Staining
lightfastness
Martindale abrasion test method
migration
off-grain fabrics
oilborne stains
oscillatory cylinder abrasion test method

ozone or O-fading
pattern repeats
Performance Specification for Knitted Upholstery Fabric (ASTM D 4771)
Performance Specification for Woven Upholstery Fabric (ASTM D 3597)
pilling
resistance to yarn slippage
shrinkage
skew
tear strength
tensile strength
vinylized fabric
waterborne stains
Wyzenbeck test method
yarn distortion

Review Questions

1. Are the recommended levels of flaws and defects in upholstery fabrics reasonable?

2. Distinguish between filling bow and filling skew. What causes these yarn alignment problems, and how do they affect the appearance of such things as upholstered furniture and window coverings?

3. Explain the differences in operations of a CRE and a CRT testing machine.

4. How would fabric shrinkage affect the appearance of upholstered furniture? Would fabric growth present problems with an upholstered item?

5. Describe the problems caused with yarn slippage at seamlines.

6. How is seam failure measured? Explain the relationship between the various levels of seam failure and use of the seams in end-use items.

7. Why is frequency of use a reasonable measure to use in defining in-use applications terms for upholstered furniture (i.e., light duty, medium duty, and heavy duty)?

8. Explain the membership and work of ACT. What symbols are used by this group, and what connotations are associated with each symbol?

9. Differentiate between brightness and apparent brightness. What causes changes in the apparent brightness of fabrics, especially pile fabrics?

10. Explain how the Gray Scales and the AATCC Chromatic Transference Scale are used in fabric evaluations.

11. Identify the problems that atmospheric contaminants cause with colored textiles.

12. Identify the cleanability codes voluntarily used with upholstery fabric. What does each indicate? How do manufacturers determine which code to include on a label?

Notes

1. The full text of ASTM International standards pertaining to textiles may be reviewed in the *Annual Book of ASTM Standards*, Vol. 07.01 and Vol. 07.02.

2. The AATCC Chromatic Transference Scale (Figure 18.6, p. 308) could also be used. The numerical ratings are equivalent to the Gray Scale ratings.

3. The full text of AATCC Standards may be reviewed in the *AATCC Technical Manual*, published annually.

UNIT TWO CASE STUDY

Project Type: Assisted Living Chains

Statement of the Project:

Karrington Communities, based in Columbus, Ohio, is one of the assisted living chains in the United States. They want to achieve a high-end residential look that is appealing to current residents and people looking to reside in these types of communities.

Statement of the Problem:

Assisted living communities need a durable, easily maintained, cost-effective upholstery creating a high-end residential appearance. In dealing with incontinence and soiling, the upholstery also needs to be antibacterial, antifungal, antimicrobial and maintain its original appearance qualities. The aesthetics and maintenance were more important to the client than cost.

Selection Criteria:

The upholstery was chosen because of its proven performance and aesthetic value. Crypton® is a chemically treated upholstery covered with the appearance of a fabric yet the durability of a vinyl. It upholsters very well, giving the lounge and dining pieces a very tailored look. From approximately 15 feet away, a chair upholstered in Crypton® looks like a chair upholstered in fabric. Karrington did not want to use vinyl because they felt that it looked low end. Vinylized fabrics, on the other hand, tend to delaminate and turn yellow, which also does not make them good solutions for maintaining the desired appearance. In the 20+ facilities that we have done with Karrington, the Crypton® has performed miraculously in both durability and aesthetics.

Product Specifications:

Crypton®

- Resists staining of blood, urine, and betadine
- Passes the Tensile Strength test of 284 lbs.
- Passes the Tongue Tear Strength test of 15.4 lbs.
- Resists yard slippage of 100 lbs.
- Resists the Wyzenbeek test of 100,000 double rubs
- Classified in UFAC Class 1
- Passes the State of California Bulletin 117, Section E
- Is antibacterial, antifungal, and antimicrobial

Maintenance and Cost:

In laboratory settings, all stains were easily removed with mild soap and water. Solvent based cleaners are not used to clean Crypton®. Although Crypton® is more expensive than vinylized fabrics and vinyl, the durability of Crypton® makes it a very viable solution. Lower long-term cost is achieved because of its durability over time. Standard maintenance products and simple maintenance procedures also reduce long-term cost.

Discussion Questions

1. Identify two of the client's requirements for the design project.

2. Identify an aesthetic feature of the product which meets the client's requirements.

3. Distinguish functional features of the product which meet the client's requirements.

4. Discuss the implications of the tactile qualities versus the visual qualities.

5. List the performance advantages of Crypton®.

6. Compare and contrast long-term appearance retention of Crypton® with vinylized fabrics.

7. Research another product that is appropriate for this application. Next compare and contrast the cost effectiveness, availability, durability, and maintenance of the new product with the one used in the casestudy.

8. If cost was a factor, what other fabrics would be appropriate for assisted living facility applications?

Window and Wallcoverings

UNIT THREE focuses on textiles produced for use in window treatments and as wallcoverings. Chapter 15 discusses the influence of appearance features, functional values, cost variables, and performance requirements on the selection of window treatment styles and coverings. Styles of curtain and drapery treatments, blinds, shades, shutters, and awnings are described and illustrated in Chapter 16. The chapter covers measurements and calculations for determining rod length and placement and the amount of yardage required for constructing lined, two-way draw panels. The fibers, yarns, and nontextile elements used in window coverings are identified in Chapter 17. Also described in this chapter are the curtain, drapery, and lining fabrics produced with these components.

Along with the performance guidelines recommended by members of the industry, test methods for measuring various service-related properties of textile window covering fabrics are summarized in Chapter 18. This chapter also reviews procedures for proper maintenance of finished curtain, drapery, and lining fabrics. The last chapter in this unit, Chapter 19, focuses on textile wall and panel coverings. Attention is given to the selection and installation of these coverings, and to their effectiveness in reducing noise and energy consumption.

CHAPTER FIFTEEN

Selection Criteria for Window Treatments

Appearance Factors
Aesthetic Preferences
Structural Factors
Color-related Variables

Functional Values
Reduction of Glare
Restriction of Inward Vision
Modification of Outward
    Vision
Reduction of Interior Noise
Conservation of Energy
Protection of Other Interior
    Furnishings
Microbe Resistance

Cost Factors
Initial Costs
Replacement Costs
Maintenance Costs

Photo courtesy of Christian Fischbacher, www.fischbacher.com.

■ **The selection of window** treatments and window coverings is influenced by several variables. At the outset, the **fenestration**—the design, arrangement, and proportioning of the windows and doors—may limit the range of styles that can be considered. Designers need to consider what the window treatment will look like from the outside, window by window, and in relationship to the entire façade. Structural defects needing to be camouflaged impose additional limitations, and so do desires for such functional properties as privacy enhancement and noise or glare reduction. The range of colored covering choices may be narrowed by such conditions as the source and quantity of light and the presence of atmospheric contaminants. Legal standards or codes may also apply to the covering choices made for certain commercial interiors. In all cases, the selections must be affordable; it must be considered whether multiple fabric components, elaborate hardware fixtures, or extensive trimming will escalate the cost beyond the limit of the furnishings budget. For some treatments, however, future savings in energy could help to compensate for the initial cost.

Fiber, yarn, and fabric features have a great impact on the appearance and serviceability of window treatments. Professionals and consumers should consider these characteristics, as well as those of nontextile materials, when they are specifying or selecting window coverings. As for all product choices, the final selection of window treatment style and materials should be based on considerations involving more than aesthetics.

Appearance Factors

Window treatment styles and coverings cannot always be selected on the basis of personal preference alone. The fenestration and any structural defects must be considered first if the setting is to appear attractive. The effects of various factors on color must be examined to assure the realization and retention of the planned appearance. Attention must also be paid to the visual and textural features of the yarns and fabrics being considered.

Aesthetic Preferences

At least initially, consumers' personal preferences limit the range of window treatment styles and coverings they will consider. Interior designers typically use design elements and principles to create a treatment that dominates the in-

terior setting or one that attracts little attention and serves as a backdrop for distinctive upholstered items and soft floor coverings. Other solutions may include symmetrically versus asymmetrically balanced designs or informal versus formal treatments. Whatever the design, it should offer the most appropriate solution for the client's need.

For coverings planned to have minimal textural interest, manufacturers use simple yarns in the fabrication operation. Fine monofilament or multifilament yarns are used, for example, to produce the smooth surfaces characterizing ninon, a plain-woven fabric shown in Figure 15.1.

Complex yarns are frequently employed to add visual and textural interest to curtain and drapery fabrics. Seed yarns, for example, appear in the novelty Raschel curtain fabric shown in Figure 15.2a, and bouclé yarns in the drapery fabric in Figure 15.2b.

Relatively coarse and irregular yarns can be made to simulate the appearance of hand-spun yarns. This is typically seen in such curtain and drapery fabrics as osnaburg and monk's cloth (Figures 17.6 and 17.8, p. 288).

All window coverings intended to be used as free-hanging panels must be drapable, but those fabrics intended for such overhead and side treatments as swags, jabots, and cascades must be exceptionally so. The importance of drapability in these applications is readily apparent in the treatments in Figure 16.7, p. 271. Fabric manufacturers generally use fine, low-twist, multifilament yarns in a satin weave to produce good drapability.

Fabrics produced for curtains, especially ruffled curtains, often are made from fine, high-twist yarns that

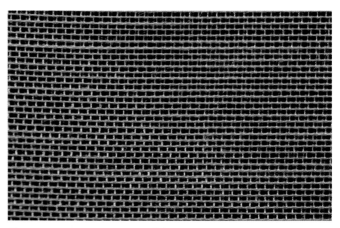

Figure 15.1 Ninon curtain fabric.
Courtesy of Amy Willbanks, www.textilefabric.com.

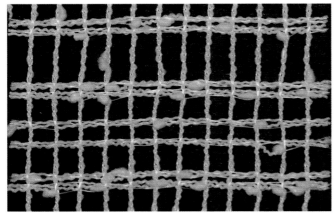

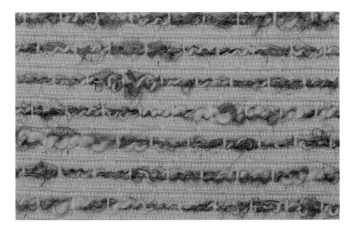

a) Raschel knit with seed yarns.

b) Drapery fabric with bouclé yarns.

Figure 15.2 Complex yarns add visual and textural interest to curtain and drapery fabrics. Courtesy of Amy Willbanks, www.textilefabric.com.

introduce a crisp hand and provide the body needed to support the folds of the ruffles and the tie-back panels. Fine, soft yarns are selected for fabrics intended to be used in such window treatments as sash curtains and Austrian shades; these yarns produce soft, rounded folds that enhance the shirred effect while preserving the preferred level of transparency. Fabrics intended for awnings or other exterior treatments are often composed of relatively large, high-twist yarns strong enough to resist rupturing when the fabric is stretched over the framework and when it is repeatedly stressed by wind gusts.

Woven wood coverings may be constructed with simple ply or cord yarns contrasting with or matching the color of the wooden slats. They may also be constructed with a variety of highly decorative, complex yarns that are variously colored to coordinate with other interior furnishings. In these coverings, the yarns are often incorporated in lengthwise bands to create stripes that augment the visual and textural interest of the shade.

Structural Factors

Within an interior space, the fenestration may require that two windows be covered with a single treatment, that treatments on neighboring windows be mounted to equalize differences in height, or that the coverings draw one way or not at all. A small, isolated window may require a large-scale treatment with fabric identical to that used for other windows in the interior to make it appear larger and integrated. Certain types of windows preclude the use of certain treatment styles. Bow windows, for example, cannot be covered with Roman shades or with accordion-pleated shades. Windows that open inward cannot be covered with stationary panels unless the panels and rods are attached to the window sashes.

The large expanses of glass that typify contemporary homes and office buildings may require coverings to control light and heat transmission during the day and to provide privacy and avoid a "black wall" effect at night. Walls in need of repair and windows in need of replacement can be camouflaged by covering them with stationary treatments.

Color-related Variables

Various factors that may affect the **apparent color** of textile structures were discussed in Chapter 8. These factors, and those affecting **actual color**, should be considered so that the colors chosen appear the same in the interior and will go on appearing so for a reasonable period of time. Careful consideration will also help assure that the coordination planned between the window treatments and other interior furnishings and wallcoverings is realized.

Factors Affecting Apparent Color

It is critically important to confirm the acceptability of any changes in the apparent color of a window covering produced by the lighting conditions in an interior. Professionals and consumers are advised to hang sample lengths of their possible covering choices at their windows, along with any planned shades or linings. If the quantity of incident natural light is judged too high, the consumer may consider adding sheers or exterior awnings.

Because window coverings are normally not subject to the great amounts of abrasion often inflicted on upholstery fabrics and soft floor coverings, changes in texture, and therefore in luster, may be minimal. Because of this, fabrics having prominent relief effects, like those provided by complex yarns, are often appropriate for window treatments. The rate and level of soiling may also be lower with window coverings than with other interior textile applications. However, repeatedly opening and closing panels by pulling on their side hems or headings may lead to rapid soil accumulation; and, especially in stationary treatments, airborne dust, smoke, and oily cooking fumes may settle on the fabrics and gradually alter the apparent colors.

Factors Affecting Actual Color

When window covering fabrics are to be installed indoors, concerns arise for lightfastness, gasfastness, and fastness to cleaning agents. When coverings are to be installed outdoors, concern arises as well for the stability of the colorants to weather elements and changing ambient temperature. The accelerated and long-term testing procedures used to ascertain the colorfastness of interior and exterior window coverings exposed to these conditions and substances are discussed in Chapter 18.

Window coverings are continually subjected to solar rays. Sun-related alterations in the structure of dyes produce concomitant changes in the structure of the fibers. To help minimize the degradation of the colorants and the fibers used in decorative panels, the use of permanently attached or separately hung lining materials, and possibly exterior awnings, is advisable.

Functional Values

Consumers, interior designers, and architects may elect to restrict their style and covering choices to those that can provide specific functional benefits, such as light control, privacy, insulation, and noise reduction. **Fabric openness**, the ratio of the open areas between the yarns to the total area of the fabric, has a major influence on these functional values. Manufacturers often consult with interior designers and architects to identify the functional properties needed or desired by their clients and then determine the appropriate degree of openness for a particular fabric.

Reduction of Glare

The degree of brightness control that window coverings should provide depends on the solar exposure conditions, the type of glass in the window, and the preferences and needs of the people who use the interior space. Windows with a northern exposure are subject to less direct sunlight than those with a southern exposure. Windows with an eastern exposure receive more direct light in the morning, and those with a western exposure more in the afternoon hours. Installing tinted or reflective-coated vision glass in lieu of clear glass will reduce the level of light transmission, but this reduction may or may not be adequate.

When the degree of transmission fails to coincide with the preferences and needs of the people using the interior, it can be balanced by interior and exterior window treatments. Often, the treatment should be designed to provide varied levels of control throughout the day, ranging from full transmission to total blackout.

The brightness control provided by window treatments is influenced by the color characteristics of the coverings, the number of layers used, the fullness of the panels, the addition of fiber delusterants and fabric coatings, and the fabric openness. It is apparent from Figure 15.3a that an open fabric would permit more light to pass through than would a semi-open (Figure 15.3b) or semi-closed fabric (Figure 15.3c). Openness is not, however, the only variable of fabric composition that affects light transmission. A portion of the light waves striking a fiber are reflected, another portion absorbed, and the remaining portion transmitted. Light-colored fibers, especially those containing no delusterants, permit more light waves to be transmitted to the interior. Increasing the fullness of the panels reduces this transmission, since more fibers reflect and absorb more waves.

In textile coverings, balancing the size of the yarns and the compactness of construction used can readily produce the requisite openness. Manufacturers of semi-open window coverings often use loop or curl yarns to engineer the desired degree of fabric openness. The airy projections of these complex yarns effectively cover the surface area and increase the opacity (Figure 15.4).

Because the quantity of direct and reflected light varies with the exposure and the hour of the day, consumers

a) Open.

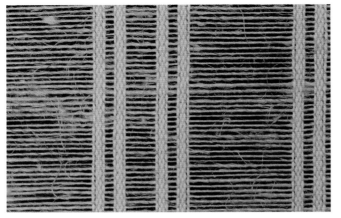

b) Semi-open.

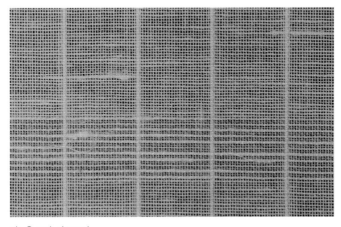

c) Semi-closed.

Figure 15.3 Levels of fabric openness.
Courtesy of Amy Willbanks, www.textilefabric.com.

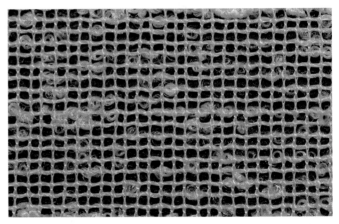

Figure 15.4 Loop yarns reduce openness but add little weight to this leno casement.
Courtesy of Amy Willbanks, www.textilefabric.com.

may elect to use multiple layers of window coverings to widen the range of brightness control options. For maximum flexibility, various combinations of shades, curtains, draperies, and awnings may be used. For total blackout in such interiors as motel rooms, shades or fabrics with opaque coatings may be installed; an example of such fabrics is given in Figure 17.32 (p. 298).

Controlling the level of brightness may be desirable for aesthetic purposes, but it may be critical to reduce the glare when persons with impaired vision reside or work in the interior. As the human eye ages, it becomes more sensitive to excessive brightness or glare. Uncontrolled levels of brightness can contribute to discomfort or safety issues, such as falls. It may also be necessary to reduce the glare for the visual comfort of employees stationed near windows. Electronic devices (computer monitors and televisions) are particularly susceptible to glare from bright windows, creating veiling reflections that obscure the image on the screen. Both computer monitors and TV screens have significantly increased in size and should be considered when determining the need for window treatments.

Restriction of Inward Vision

Providing privacy has long been a basic function of window coverings. For windows placed so that inward vision must be continually restricted, full, stationary curtains may be selected. Most coverings will reduce the view inward during daylight hours, but a lining or separate curtains may be needed to ensure privacy at night when artificial illuminants brighten the interior. Moreover, when a window faces a private outdoor area, some covering may be considered to relieve any sense of being open to observation.

Modification of Outward Vision

A covering with the appropriate degree of openness can modify an exterior view. As the size of the yarns and the compactness of construction increase, outward vision is decreased. In some settings, complete blockage of an unsightly view may be required; this can be accomplished by combining relatively heavy closed fabrics with opaque linings in stationary mountings.

Reduction of Interior Noise

Three types of sounds may be heard within interiors. **Airborne sounds** radiate directly into the air from people talking and typing, photocopiers and printers producing copies, telephones ringing, video machines, radios, and the like. **Surface sounds** are produced as people traverse across the floor or push and pull items along it. **Impact or structurally borne sounds** result from impacts on a structural surface that cause it to vibrate, for instance, walking, jumping, dancing, bouncing balls, knocking on doors, and hammering nails. Of course, several activities, such as walking and vacuuming, create more than one type of sound. Also, most sounds can be transmitted to areas well beyond their origin. From the exterior come sounds from lawn mowers, cars, trucks, buses, airplanes, and the neighbor's dog.

Sounds that we want to hear can be entertaining and enlightening; but if we don't want to hear the sounds, they become noise, which can be annoying and disruptive. Thus, residential and commercial consumers often seek ways to control sounds and prevent them from becoming unwanted noise.

Figure 15.5a illustrates how interior sound can be prolonged and magnified as it is reflected from the floor to the ceiling and from a bare wall to a bare window. Figure 15.5b illustrates how ceiling materials and soft floor coverings will absorb sound that is traveling vertically; window and wallcoverings can be installed to absorb sound that is traveling horizontally. (The sound absorption qualities of wallcoverings are discussed in Chapter 19.)

The sound absorption quality of draperies varies with the density of the weave and whether the drapery panel construction consists of a single layer or multiple layers of fabric. The degree to which materials such as ceiling tiles, carpeting, wallcoverings, and window treatments will absorb noise is indicated in terms of its **noise reduction coefficient (NRC)**. The higher the NRC, the more noise is absorbed.

In multibed hospital rooms, fabric partitions are hung primarily to provide privacy; in large, open interiors they are used principally for decoration and to divide space. However, these interior partitions will also lessen horizontally reflected sound if they are constructed of closed, compactly constructed fabrics.

Conservation of Energy

Along with concern for the depletion of energy sources, especially the limited supply of fossil fuels, the pressures of rising heating and cooling costs have impelled consumers and manufacturers to search for ways to reduce energy consumption. Substantial improvements in the design of

Hard Surface Classroom

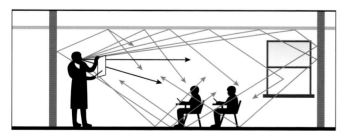

Black arrows represent direct sound, with a clear path from teacher to student. Red arrows represent reflected sound. Note the many red arrows which indicate the longer, more indirect path taken to reach the student.

a) Without sound absorbing materials.

Figure 15.5 Interior sound travel.
Illustrations by Ron Carboni.

Acoustically Treated Classroom

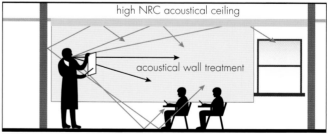

The addition of sound absorbing materials reduces late arriving reflected sound, lowers reverberation time, and improves speech intelligibility.

b) With sound absorbing materials.

windows has reduced the role of window treatments as the primary control of the amount of light and glare coming in and the amount of heat gain or loss through windows. The selection of appropriate window treatments can further contribute to the maintenance of interior temperatures. Since 2005, windows have been consistently evaluated and labeled to indicate ratings for several characteristics. The National Fenestration Rating Council (NFRC) energy performance label is shown in Figure 15.6.

The thermal performance criteria for window treatments change as the seasons change. In winter, insulation is necessary to reduce heat loss, and in summer rejection of radiant energy is necessary to reduce heat gain. Reviewing the mechanisms by which heat is lost and gained is good preparation for making the appropriate selections of window treatments and components.

Air movement, including wind and forced circulation, causes heat transfer by **convection**. As wind circulates against exterior surfaces, it will convect heat away; the loss will be more pronounced with higher air speeds and greater differences between inside and outside temperatures.

(Convection is the mechanism that causes a bridge surface to freeze before the rest of the road's surface does.) In an interior, warm air may be drawn between the window coverings and the window glass, where it is cooled, becomes heavier, and flows under the lower edges of free-hanging coverings and back into the room. Air movement is also responsible for drafts, the infiltration of cold air through structural openings such as cracks between window and wall frames and wall joints.

Conduction is the movement of thermal energy through solids, liquids, and gases. Insulation resists thermal transfer and stems conduction. In residential and commercial structures, heat energy will be conducted through the walls, doors, floors, and roof areas as well as the windows. However, from 25 to 50 percent of the heat generated in residences may be lost through the windows alone.[1]

The extent to which windows and window treatments retard heat loss in the winter and heat gain in the summer can be measured and the results reported numerically in terms of U-values. **U-values** indicate how much heat actually does pass outward in winter and inward in summer. To become familiar with U-values, we can examine the values for various types of windows; these values are approximate and vary with construction, thickness of the glass, and the presence of tints or coatings. Single-pane window glass has a U-value of 1.13, double panes with $\frac{3}{16}$ inch of insulating air space between them have a U-value of 0.41, and triple panes with a total of $\frac{5}{8}$ inch of insulating air space have a U-value of 0.35. A U-value of 1.13 BTU/ft^2-hr-°F means that 1.13 British thermal units of heat pass through each square foot of window configuration every hour for each Fahrenheit degree of difference between inside and outside temperatures.

Because air is a poor heat conductor and a good heat insulator, window coverings intended to significantly contribute to the reduction of energy loss in winter should be installed to provide a tight enclosure that will entrap dead air between the fabric and the glass, similar to the enclosure between the panes in double- and triple-pane windows. The dead air will retard conduction, and the sealed covering also helps to prevent warm air from being drawn against the window. The installation of a free-hanging, traversing drapery treatment has been found to be minimally effective. The use of tight-fitting closed draperies may reduce heat loss up to 25 percent.[2] To reduce air flow be-

Figure 15.6 Example of an NFRC label. Courtesy of NFRC.

tween drapery panels and the glass, the top of the window treatment should go all the way to the ceiling or be topped with a cornice. The sides of the panels should be sealed along the wall or facing, and the panels should overlap where they meet in the center. The bottom hem should be long enough to allow fabric to stack on the floor, preventing cool air from escaping into the room along the floor. Similarly, the use of a tight-fitting lining, sealed around the perimeter of the window, has been found to be more effective than a free-hanging lining.

Multilayered roller shades, many of which are not unlike the familiar mattress pad, can be used for their insulative value. Dead air is trapped between the layers; again, thermal efficiency improves when the edges of the shade are sealed to restrict air flow.[3]

With Roman shades constructed of woven wood, an increase in the quantity of complex yarns was found to increase the insulative quality.[4] Cellular shades incorporate dead air spaces within their construction to provide more insulation. Conventional Venetian blinds and vertical blinds, especially those made of metal, are comparatively ineffective in reducing winter heat loss, because of the small gaps remaining between the closed louvers and the high conductivity of the metal components. On the other hand, their louvers can easily be angled to let in sunlight and increase heat gain during daylight hours in winter.

Interior shutters without louvers can contribute significantly to energy conservation, provided they fit tightly and are used consistently. Like blinds, louvered shutters provide little value in preventing heat loss in winter. They can, however, be effective in blocking intense summer sunlight.

Radiation is the transfer of heat in the form of waves or rays. Waves radiating against the exterior surfaces of windows include those emanating directly from the sun, as well as those reflected from the sky and such other surfaces as the facades of neighboring buildings, paved parking areas, streets, and sidewalks. As schematized in Figure 15.7, some of the incident waves are rejected, some absorbed, and some transmitted. Of the rays transmitted through the outdoor glass, various portions will be rejected, absorbed, and transmitted by the indoor glass in double pane windows. Finally, various portions of the rays transmitted through the indoor glass will be rejected, absorbed, and transmitted by the draperies.

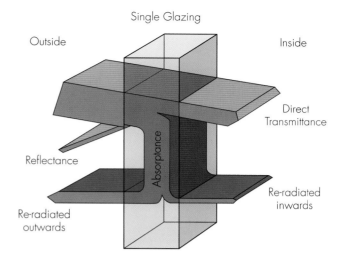

Figure 15.7 Glass transmission properties. Illustration by Ron Carboni.

Clearly, window treatments that can be opened and closed provide the flexibility needed to control seasonal solar heat gain. On sunny winter days, the coverings can be opened to increase the level of heat transmission; on sunny summer days, they can be closed to increase the level of heat rejection. Solar heat gain in the summer, of course, warms the interior and increases the air conditioning load.

The effectiveness of windows and window coverings in reducing the level of radiant energy transmitted into the interior can be measured and the results reported numerically in terms of the **shading coefficient (S/C)**. To calculate the S/C, the total amount of heat transmitted by a window glass and covering combination is divided by the total amount of heat transmitted by a single pane of clear $\frac{1}{8}$-inch-thick glass. S/C values (ranging from 0 to 1) indicate how well a window and covering reduce heat gain, with lower values indicating more effective control. The actual amount of heat gain is reported in terms of the U-value.

Although drapery treatments produce insignificant reductions in the S/C value of insulated reflective glass, they produce significant decreases in the values of clear and tinted vision glass. Closed, light-colored draperies produce the most significant reductions in these cases.

Conventional Venetian blinds and vertical blinds are relatively ineffective in retarding winter heat loss, but they are quite effective in reducing summer heat gain. Various types and colors of roller shades are also highly effective in reducing heat gain. The color of both blinds and shades will affect the amount of light reflected and the light energy absorbed. White and light colors will reflect higher amounts of light, whereas black and dark colors will reflect less light, absorbing the heat energy of the light not reflected. In turn, this absorbed heat will be transferred into the room, a negative effect in the summer but a positive effect in the winter.

Exterior shutters and awnings can be highly effective in reducing solar heat gain. Light colors should be used for both types of coverings for high reflection and low absorption of radiant energy. Heat absorbed by these coverings can be transferred through the windows to the interior: for maximum effectiveness, awnings must be correctly angled over the windows to reflect all direct rays and vented to avoid trapping heat. During summer, correctly sized and placed awnings on south-facing windows can reduce solar heat gain by as much as 65 percent and for west-facing windows, by as much as 77 percent.[5]

Protection of Other Interior Furnishings

The radiant energy of the sun not only warms and brightens interior space; it also weakens textile fibers and, as discussed earlier in this chapter, changes their apparent and actual color characteristics. To protect other textile and nontextile furnishings, window coverings can be drawn to minimize light transmission. This will, of course, subject the window coverings themselves to higher levels of radiant energy. The replacement cost of the window treatments, however, is normally less than that of other furnishings, and relatively inexpensive curtains and linings can be used to protect more expensive overdraperies.

Microbe Resistance

Window treatments may occupy a significant amount of wall area and are subject to handling by many users. Hard surface treatments such as blinds can be washed down to reduce the presence of bacteria but textile treatments are more time-consuming and expensive to clean. Therefore, textile window treatments can benefit from antimicrobial properties, especially in applications where users may be more susceptible to adverse effects caused by these microbes (healthcare or senior care facilities) or where large numbers of users may be present (educational and daycare facilities). Trade names such as BioCote® or AEGIS Microbe Shield® identify drapery fabrics and blinds as having microbe resistant characteristics.

Cost Factors

Various cost-related factors must be considered prior to final selection of window treatments. Together with the initial costs of the materials, labor, and accessories required, residential and commercial consumers should consider financial variables related to replacement and maintenance.

Initial Costs

The initial cost of a window treatment is not limited to the cost of the outercovering; it also includes the cost of any linings, curtains, shades, and shutters to be used. The choice of a relatively narrow fabric with a comparatively high price per yard, elaborate styling, and fuller panels will escalate the materials cost. The cost is higher still when solution-dyed fibers and such treatments as flame-resistant finishes and reflective coatings are specified. Custom projects involve separate charges for consultations with the designer and for measuring, cutting, sewing, trimming, and installing. Whether consumers choose readymade coverings, elect to have a custom-designed treatment, or plan to construct the treatment themselves, added costs include those for the rods and any tie-backs, hold-backs, or overhead treatments.

Residential and commercial consumers should ascertain whether their new treatment qualifies for an energy tax credit. Through various tax credits, Congress has offered incentives to consumers to reduce their energy consumption voluntarily by selecting materials known to be effective insulators. These incentives have time limits and may be extended or allowed to expire. They may also balance the initial cost of the treatment against any energy savings that will be realized during the use-life of the treatment. Regardless of potential savings, however, the total cost and terms of payment—whether due in full on delivery or made in installments with interest charges—must coincide with the ability of the purchaser to pay. Financial institutions may permit the cost of some window treatment projects to be included in long-term mortgage obligations.

Replacement Costs

When selecting window treatment styles and coverings, consumers should consider the initial cost in relationship to the expected use-life. Fiber and fabric variables, styling features, exposure conditions, and care affect the use-life of textile coverings; the average use-life generally ranges from three to five years. Because linings can extend the service-life of drapery fabrics for a year or more, consumers may determine that linings are especially cost-effective. Solution dyeing, although a comparatively expensive color application technique, should be used whenever coverings composed of acetate are installed in areas having high concentrations of atmospheric pollutants. This will avoid the expense and disruption associated with the premature replacement of a covering that has changed hue.

Unless new hardware is required, replacement costs are normally limited to the cost of the new materials and the labor costs incurred for construction and installation. In some cases, charges may also be assessed for removing the existing treatments.

Maintenance Costs

Several variables related to fabric composition, such as the type of fiber used, the dimensional stability of the fabric, the use of durable press resins, the stability of the colorants, and the structural characteristics of the coverings, are the main determinants of what cleaning method should be used to maintain a window treatment. By considering these variables, consumers can determine whether laundering or dry cleaning is required; if the more expensive dry cleaning is called for, consumers may elect to reconsider their covering options.

Elaborate styling and multiple components, such as shades, curtains, draperies, and swags, will increase maintenance cost, since charges are incurred for the commercial laundering or dry cleaning of each covering and component. Wide, long panels are also more expensive to clean than are narrow, short panels. Separate charges may be assessed for removing and transporting the coverings to the cleaning plant, for ironing and reforming the folds, and for returning and rehanging the treatment. Of course, the anticipated frequency of cleaning—determined to a large extent by the appearance required by the owner—must be considered when estimating long-term maintenance costs.

Summary

To ensure reliable judgments and sound decisions in selecting window treatment styles and coverings, residential and commercial consumers should consider several factors, some of which may limit their choices. They should examine the fenestration to determine which styles can be considered and which would be unworkable. They should consider the immediate and long-term effects of various color-related variables to verify that the planned appearance will be realized and retained. They should determine the need for such functional qualities as glare reduction, energy conservation, privacy enhancement, and view modification. They should also investigate the properties of the fibers and yarns used, the characteristics of the fabric structure, and the effects of the various finishing agents and processes employed. Then they should limit their choices to styles and coverings that are capable of providing the necessary or desirable characteristics.

Professionals must ascertain whether the coverings they select for a commercial interior have to comply with any performance standards and/or codes. All consumers must have sufficient funds to cover the cost of the project; for some projects, the initial cost may be partially offset by energy tax credits and energy savings.

Key Terms

actual color	fabric openness	shading coefficient (S/C)
airborne sounds	fenestration	surface sounds
apparent color	impact or structurally borne sounds	U-values
conduction	noise reduction coefficient (NRC)	
convection	radiation	

Review Questions

1. Identify complex yarns that give maximum visual and textural interest to window coverings. Why can these yarns be used in window coverings but not in upholstery fabric?

2. Cite examples of how a window treatment can be effectively used in meeting challenges presented by the fenestration in an interior.

3. Identify window styles that severely limit treatment choices.

4. Differentiate between apparent and actual color.

5. Why is it critically important to examine colored textiles in the end-use setting?

6. Discuss the factors that affect the level of light transmission.

7. Explain the roles of yarn size and compactness of construction in determining fabric openness.

8. Discuss factors affecting the apparent color and those that affect the actual color.

9. Explain how window treatments can support energy conservation efforts.

10. Identify all variables affecting the cost of window treatments.

Notes

1. G. Cukierski and Dr. D. R. Buchanan, "Effectiveness of Conventional, Modified, and New Interior Window Treatments in Reducing Heat Transfer Losses," *Proceedings of the Fourth National Passive Solar Conference*, American Section of the International Solar Energy Society, University of Delaware, Newark, DE, 402–406.

2. Energy Efficiency and Renewable Energy (EERE), Department of Energy, "A Consumer's Guide to Energy Efficiency and Renewable Energy: Your Home," http://apps1.eere.energy.gov/consumer/your_home/.

3. Cukierski, op. cit., 404.

4. Ibid., 403.

5. EERE, op cit.

Window Treatment Styles

■ **Window treatments include** curtains, draperies, blinds, shades, shutters, and awnings, used alone or in combinations. These treatments are decorated with such items as rods, cornices, hold-backs, tie-backs, and valances. The styling features of window treatments call for special consideration by consumers and professionals. Some need a highly drapable textile fabric; some require a stiffened fabric; and some, especially those having multiple layers, may demand an unaffordable amount of yardage. Attention should also be given to whether there is a need for hand drawing, the type and number of rods a particular treatment requires, and the like.

Window treatment styles do not change, but their popularity does. For example, priscilla curtains, illustrated in Figure 16.1e, are always distinguished by ruffles and criss-crossed panels, but they may not be fashionable at all times. With each subsequent adoption, however, designers and consumers select from a wide variety of contemporary fabrics, colors, motifs, and components to execute it; thus, identical styles may have dramatically different appearances.

Curtain and Drapery Treatments

In general, **curtains** describes relatively sheer, lightweight coverings that are hung without linings, while **draperies** describes heavy, often opaque coverings usually hung with linings. The term casement may be assigned to numerous fabrics of medium weight and some degree of transparency. Casement fabrics may be hung as unlined curtains or as lined draperies. Curtains and draperies are normally textile fabrics, but some novel treatments involve such components as strands of glass and polymer film fabrics.

The coverings in some curtain and drapery treatments are hung as stationary, nontraversing panels. Other coverings are hung as traversing panels that can be opened and closed as desired. Additional styling features may be

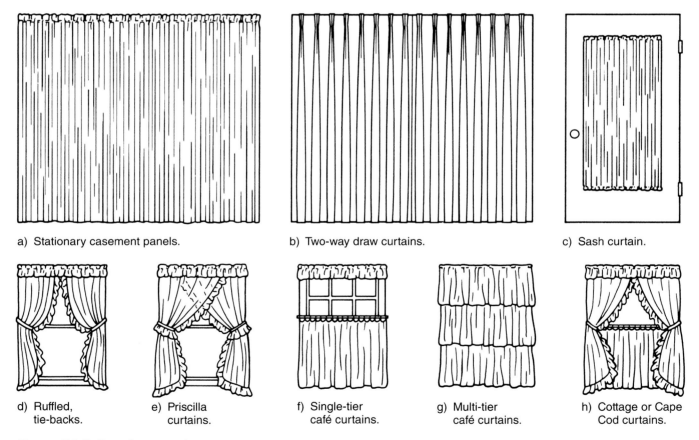

a) Stationary casement panels.

b) Two-way draw curtains.

c) Sash curtain.

d) Ruffled, tie-backs.

e) Priscilla curtains.

f) Single-tier café curtains.

g) Multi-tier café curtains.

h) Cottage or Cape Cod curtains.

Figure 16.1 Typical curtain styles.

added with the judicious use of decorative headings and side treatments, trimmings, and hardware fixtures.

Curtain Treatments

Figure 16.1 shows some typical styles of curtain treatments. **Stationary casement panels** (Figure 16.1a) are approximately two and one-half times wider than the window. The panels are supported by a conventional, nontraversing curtain rod inserted through a **casing** sewn into the upper edge of the fabric. The casing may be plain or constructed with a **heading** (Figure 16.6a and b).

Some contemporary treatments have fabric panels with limited fullness to accentuate the window and highlight the rod. Frequently, the panel headings have tabs that are formed into two- or three-inch-long loops (Figure 16.2), knots, or bows for great visual interest. The top may have deep scallops, resulting in a drooping but dramatic effect, or it may have large buttonholes for a more tailored look. While the rods are nontraversing, a yard-long wooden rod, known as a **curtain tender**, may be used to open and close the panels.

A traditional panel treatment involves the use of tambour-embroidered curtain panels. The rich embroidery on such transparent fabrics as organdy, bobbinet, and voile is shown best by having limited fullness.

A heading, such as pinched pleats, and a traversing rod convert stationary panels into **draw curtains** (Figure 16.1b). Panels anchored at their upper and lower edges are known as **sash curtains**, and are typically used on French doors (Figure 16.1c). As the width of the fabric is increased with respect to the width of the window, the shirred effect becomes more pronounced, increasing privacy and reducing the degree of light transmission.

Whereas the panels in **ruffled, tie-back curtains** (Figure 16.1d) do not cross at their upper edges, the panels in **priscilla curtains** overlap; priscilla treatments always involve ruffled tie-backs, as well (Figure 16.1e). Ruffled curtain treatments must be carefully chosen to avoid an overdressed appearance. The use of such crisp, transparent fabrics as organdy, voile, and dotted swiss (described in Chapter 17) can help to minimize the visual weight of these treatments, as well as provide the body required for attractive ruffles.

Café curtains (Figure 16.1f and g) may be used alone or in combination with draperies. They are frequently

Figure 16.2 Tab-top fabric panels.
Courtesy of Country Curtains, www.countrycurtains.com.

constructed with scalloped headings and hung by rings looped over a rod. **Multi-tier café curtains**, with each tier normally overlapping the lower tier by about three inches, may be hung by rings or by rods run through fabric casings. When **single-tier café curtains** are combined with ruffled, tied-back panels, the treatment is labeled a **cottage or Cape Cod curtain** style (Figure 16.1h).

Drapery Treatments

Typical drapery treatments are illustrated in Figure 16.3. **One-way draw draperies** are drawn in one direction, stacking on one side of the window; **two-way draperies** are drawn to stack on both sides.

Cords, chains, medallions, hooks, and the like secure the panels in **tied-back** and **held-back** styles (Figure 16.4), but the panels may be released, if desired. **Pinned-up** styles are held by two-piece, stylized magnets or by decorative pins that function like large tie-tacks. These allow the designer or consumer to be more creative with such things as asymmetrical draping as the pins or magnets are not anchored to the wall or window frame. **Pouf or**

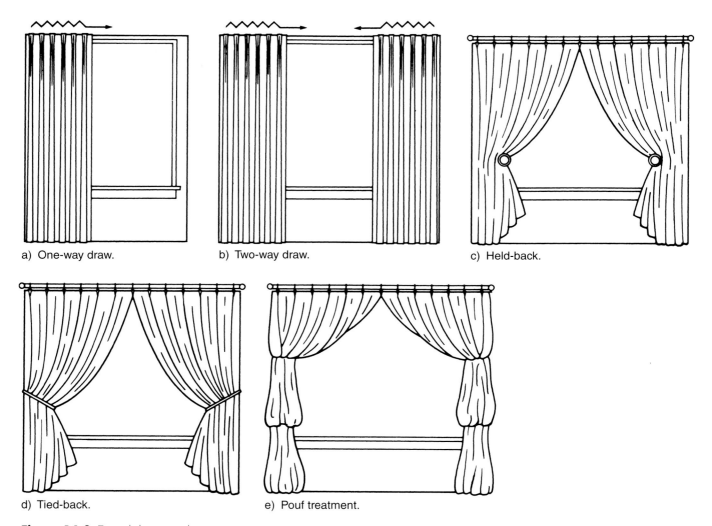

a) One-way draw.   b) Two-way draw.   c) Held-back.

d) Tied-back.   e) Pouf treatment.

Figure 16.3 Typical drapery styles.

bishop's sleeve treatments (Figure 16.3e) have tiers of bouffant or billowed-out areas created by periodically gathering the fabric panels.

When draperies are combined with sheer curtains, they are called **overdraperies**, and the curtains are called **sheers** or **glass curtains**. Here, the term "glass" indicates that the curtains hang next to the window glass; it is not describing the use of glass fiber. Combining draperies and curtains increases the cost of a window treatment, but it may also improve interior insulation and acoustics.

Headings

Headings appear at the top of curtain and drapery panels. These treatments finish the upper edge and distribute fullness evenly across the finished width. Figure 16.6 illustrates various styles of headings. Headings may be hand measured and sewn or produced with commercial tape. Pleats produced with tape are slightly rounded instead of sharply creased, but the hooks can be removed for cleaning.

Sewn headings, in contrast to those formed with tape, should be interfaced with a fabric such as buckram or crinoline. These plain-woven fabrics are stiffened with sizing, starch, or resin and can provide support for the heading treatment. The stability of the stiffening agent to cleaning agents should be ascertained prior to use.

Trimmings

Curtain and drapery treatments may be enriched by the use of ornamental **trimmings**, such as cord, tasseled or looped fringe, gimp, piping, rickrack, lace, beading, galloons (narrow lengths of braid, embroidered fabric, or lace), or ribbon (Figure 16.5). Some trimmings may be

a)

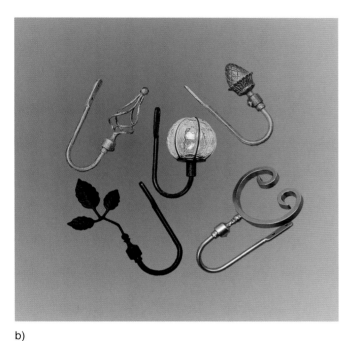

b)

Figure 16.4 Various styles of curtain and drapery holdbacks. Courtesy of Country Curtains, www.countrycurtains.com.

Figure 16.5 Various styles of trimmings are used on these draperies to add visual interest.
Les Marquises Collection is courtesy of www.houles.com.

sewn directly to the covering fabric, while others may be used as tie-backs.

Overhead and Side Treatments

Overhead treatments cover and conceal panel headings and hardware and enrich window treatments. Valances and swags are overhead treatments executed in fabric and are generally used in combination with such side treatments as cascades and jabots; other overhead treatments employ wood or metal.

In effect, **valances** are short draperies and may have any of the headings shown in Figure 16.6. Relatively simple valances may have lower edges that are pointed, curved,

or crescent shaped, or finished with trimming or a simple, straight hem (Figure 16.7a). Those in sheer fabric may have the added feature of a French tuck hem. More elaborate valance treatments include Austrian, tapered, puffed, balloon, or festoon styling.

Unlike the structured styling of valances, **swags** are softly draping lengths of fabrics (Figure 16.7b). Swags may be paired with cascades or jabots as in Figure 16.7c. **Cascades** are side treatments that are gathered and designed to fall in folds of graduated length; they are used with or without a valance. **Jabots** are pleated side treatments. Their lower edges may be level, or they may be angled as in Figure 16.7d. Swags are normally designed to hang behind any valance or festoon, while jabots may be hung in front of or behind the ends of an overhead

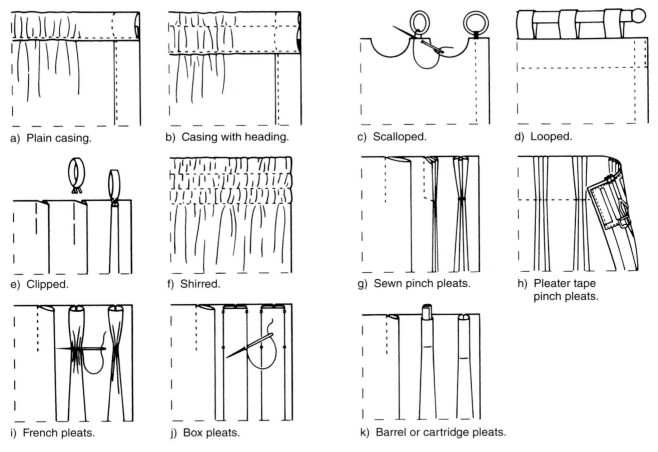

a) Plain casing. b) Casing with heading. c) Scalloped. d) Looped.

e) Clipped. f) Shirred. g) Sewn pinch pleats. h) Pleater tape pinch pleats.

i) French pleats. j) Box pleats. k) Barrel or cartridge pleats.

Figure 16.6 Various styles of curtain and drapery headings.

treatment. However they are hung, the length of the side treatments should be at least one-third that of the window treatment.

Cornices, cantonnières, and lambrequins are rigid overhead treatments constructed of wood or metal. They can be covered with the panel fabric or coordinating fabric, or painted, stained, or left as natural wood. A **cornice** (Figure 16.10a) is mounted to cover the drapery heading and hardware. Typically, cornices project 4 to 6 inches from the wall and cover one-seventh of the treatment length. Adding straight sides and shaped front panels to a cornice board converts it into a **lambrequin** (Figure 16.10b). A **cantonnière** fits flush to the wall and has a shaped overhead panel and sides that extend to the floor. Although the cantonnière is frequently fabric covered, it can also be stenciled directly to the wall surface, coordinating with the fabric panels, blinds, or shades used (Figure 16.10c).

Hardware

The assortment of hardware used with curtains and draperies includes rods, mounting screws and bolts, batons, curtain tenders, and fabric weights. **Batons** and curtain tenders are used manually to open and close the panels; **fabric weights**, placed in the lower hem area, improve the draping quality of the fabric. The assortment also includes such decorative accessories as café rings and clips, chains, medallions, pin-ups, and two-piece magnets. Medallions are permanently attached to the window frame for use as hold-backs, as shown in Figure 16.4, while pin-ups and magnets are used selectively to hold the panels in distinctive folds or configurations.

Conventional Rods

A variety of conventional, nondecorative curtain and drapery rods is available today. Conventional rods are

a) Valance on a continental rod.

b) Swag held up by holdbacks.

c) Swag with cascades.

d) Jabots combined with a horizontally pleated valance and festoon.

Figure 16.7 Overhead and side treatments.
a, b, c) Courtesy of Country Curtains, www.countrycurtains.com. d) Courtesy of Horizons by B & W Window Fashions.

Figure 16.8 Continental combo rod set.
Courtesy of Country Curtains, www.countrycurtains.com.

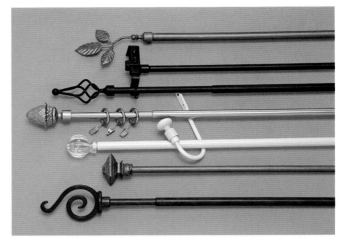

Figure 16.9 Various types of decorative rods.
Courtesy of Country Curtains, www.countrycurtains.com.

comparatively inexpensive, but consumers and interior designers should consider the aesthetic impact of these rods when not covered by the headings. Conventional traversing rods are usually equipped with a system of cords to control opening and closing. A note of safety should be added. Numerous cases of young children being seriously injured by closed cord systems have been reported, and the problem is currently under study by the U.S. Consumer Product Safety Commission. Systems without a closed cord or cordless systems are recommended. Cords may be wrapped on a cord cleat attached to the wall to keep them out of the reach of children or pets.

For window treatments that require a closed cord system to function, a tie down device can be mounted on the wall or floor to keep the cord pulled tight.

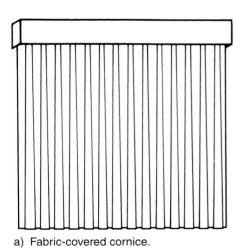

a) Fabric-covered cornice.

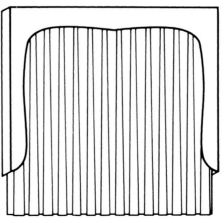

b) Lambrequin.

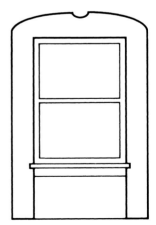

c) Fabric-covered cantonnière.

Figure 16.10 Rigid overhead and side treatments.

The **continental rod** is another style of conventional rod having a height of 2½ inches or 4½ inches (Figure 16.8). The added depth creates the look of a valence when casings, with or without headings, are shirred over the rod.

Decorative Rods

Decorative curtain and drapery rods are made of wood, metal, or plastic finished to resemble, for example, brass, pewter, gold, or natural wood (Figure 16.9). Coordinating rings (Figure 17.33, p. 298) secure the panels. Grommets inserted in the drapery heading eliminate the need for rings to attach panels to the rod (Figure 16.11). In many cases, matching tieback chains, hold-back medallions, and various styles of finials (the decorative pieces attached to the ends of rods) are available (Figures 16.4 and 16.9). Decorative traversing rods may be controlled electrically, by a system of cords, or by batons.

Nontraversing decorative rods are especially useful for supporting stationary panels. These panels are hung from wooden or metallic rings or fabric tabs looped over the rod. If the panels are to be opened and closed, they should be shifted by a baton or curtain tender and not by pulling on the side hems, which could deform the edge and lead to excessive soiling and wear.

Calculating Yardage Required

The successful execution of a window treatment depends on the accuracy of the measurements taken when determining the amount of fabric required for the project. As is true for any project involving colored textiles, the amount of fabric initially ordered must be sufficient to complete the treatment. As noted in Chapter 8, separate orders generally result in the delivery of fabrics with slightly differing color characteristics; even slight differences may prove to be unacceptable.

The following sections summarize the variables that generally should be considered when measuring for curtains and draperies. Other publications, readily available from Cooperative Extension Services, product manufacturers, and interior furnishings retailers, may be reviewed for instructions pertinent to specific styles and various overhead treatments. Usually, these materials also include detailed sewing and hanging instructions.

Determining Rod Length and Placement

A yardstick or steel tape should be used for taking all measurements, beginning with those needed to determine the rod length and placement. Before determining the length

Figure 16.11 Drapery panels with built-in grommets. Courtesy of Ado Corporation USA.

of the rod, a decision must be made concerning the extent of the outward view desired when the panels are open. For maximum outward vision, it should be possible to stack the panels back beyond the window glass. The values listed in Table 16.1 will help to determine the length of the rod needed when full clearance of the glass is preferred. The distances can be adjusted when the panels must camouflage a structural defect and when a portion of the glass is to be used for **stackback space**.

Rods should be mounted so that the drapery headings will not be visible to the outside. Headings are normally 4 inches in height; thus, the rod should normally be located 4 inches above the top edge of the window glass. Again, if structural defects, such as unequal frame heights, must be camouflaged, the location of the rod can be adjusted. The rod should be installed prior to taking the measurements needed for determining the yardage required.

Table 16.1 Rod Lengths Needed for Various Widths of Windows and Stackback Spaces		
If the Glass is	The stackback* should be	Your rod length and drapery coverage should be (add for overlaps and returns)
38"	26"	64"
44"	28"	72"
50"	30"	80"
56"	32"	88"
62"	34"	96"
68"	36"	104"
75"	37"	112"
81"	39"	120"
87"	41"	128"
94"	42"	136"
100"	44"	144"
106"	46"	152"
112"	48"	160"
119"	49"	168"
125"	51"	176"
131"	53"	184"
137"	55"	192"
144"	56"	200"
150"	58"	208"
156"	60"	216"
162"	62"	224"
169"	63"	232"
175"	65"	240"
181"	67"	248"
187"	69"	256"

Figures are based on average pleating and medium weight fabric. For extra bulky fabrics, add to stackback to compensate for the additional space they require.
*For one-way draws, deduct 7" from stackback.
Courtesy of Kirsch Window Fashions, a Newell Rubbermaid Company.

Determining Panel Length

Lengthwise measurements are taken from the top of conventional rods and from the bottom of the rings on decorative rods. The panels may extend to the window sill, to the apron (the horizontal board below the sill), or to the floor. One inch should be subtracted from the measurement taken to the floor to allow for clearance, especially when soft floor coverings are in place. For distinctive styling and reduced air infiltration, consumers and designers may elect to have the panels stack or mound on the floor, in which case extra yardage must be allowed. For the purpose of this discussion, assume the finished panel will be 85 inches in length.

If patterned fabrics are chosen, extra yardage must be added for matching repeats. The lengthwise measurement must be evenly divisible by the length of the repeat. Thus, assuming the length of the repeat is 18 inches, 5 inches must be added to the measured 85 inches so that it will be divisible by 18. Normally, a full repeat is placed at the lower hem of sill- and apron-length panels, and at the top hem of floor-length panels.

Yardage must now be added for the hem allowances. For unlined panels, a doubled, 4-inch top hem is planned, and for lined panels, 0.5 inch is allowed for top turnover. The lower hem allowance is generally 4 inches, but as a precaution against potential relaxation and residual shrinkage, this figure should be doubled. In the event that in-use shrinkage shortens the panels, the fabric needed for lengthening is readily available. The hem allowance must always be doubled when such fabrics as taffeta, faille, and bengaline are to be used. The numerous fibers in the crosswise ribs of these fabrics, especially if they are cotton or rayon, may swell during cleaning; this increase in the diameter of the ribs would draw up the warp yarns, causing lengthwise shrinkage. Whatever its fiber content, any fabric may exhibit from 1 to 3 percent residual shrinkage, even if it was preshrunk to encourage relaxation shrinkage.

The total cut length of the panel fabric may now be calculated as follows:

finished length of panel	85	inches
+ allowance for pattern matching	5	inches
+ allowance for top hem	0.5	inch
+ allowance for bottom hem	8	inches
= total cut length of panel	98.5	inches

For the lining fabric, no yardage is needed for pattern matching; the bottom hem is generally single and 2 inches deep, and the lower edge is 1 inch above the lower edge of the drapery panel. Again, an allowance may be made for potential in-use shrinkage. The total cut length of the lining fabric may now be calculated as follows:

finished length of panel	85	inches
− lining shorter than panel	1	inch
+ allowance for top hem	0.5	inch
+ allowance for bottom hem	2	inches
= total cut length of lining	88.5	inches

Determining Panel Width

Fabric panel is not synonymous with **fabric width**. A fabric panel (Figure 16.12) is formed by seaming a number of fabric widths and, if necessary, a partial width together. Pleated panel coverage, pleat coverage, and coverage are synonyms that refer to the horizontal distance covered by the pleated area of the panel. Coverage does not include the portion of the panel that covers the overlap at the center, or the portion that covers the return, the bracket extending perpendicularly from the wall at each end of the rod.

For the purposes of discussion, we will assume that the length of the installed rod is 56 inches. For a one-way draw treatment, the panel coverage would be 56 inches, with no allowance required for overlap. For a two-way draw treatment, the coverage for each panel would be 28 inches, and the allowance for overlap is normally 3.5 inches. Yardage must now be added for **fullness**, a requirement that generally doubles the yardage but may triple it when sheer fabrics are used. The allowance for the return is equal to the bracket projection distance, typically 3.5 inches. Each of the two side hems requires an allowance of 2 inches. Of this, 0.5 inch will be used as an allowance when seaming the lining, and 1.5 inches will be turned to show at the side of the lining. The total width of one flat, unhemmed panel for a two-way draw treatment may now be calculated as follows:

coverage	28	inches
+ allowance for fullness	28	inches
+ allowance for overlap	3.5	inches
+ allowance for return	3.5	inches
+ allowance for side hems	4	inches
= total width of one flat panel	67	inches

The values listed in Table 16.2 were calculated in this manner and can be used after coverage is determined. The table also contains guidelines for spacing pleats to control the fullness.

One inch must be allowed for seaming the sides of the lining to the drapery panel. The flat, unhemmed lining is

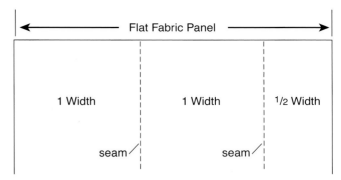

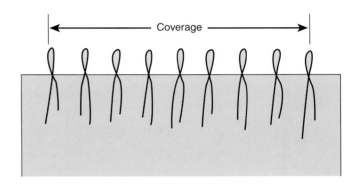

"Flat fabric" refers to the seamed panel before the pleats are put in.

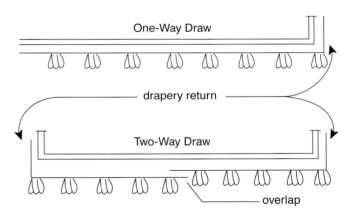

Figure 16.12 Illustrations of terms that describe the measurements taken to determine panel width. Courtesy of Kirsch Window Fashions, a Newell Rubbermaid Company.

thus cut 3 inches narrower than the flat, unhemmed drapery panel that will be turned 1.5 inches inward on each side.

Determining Yardage Total

If, for example, the width of the covering fabric is 45 inches, one full fabric width and one partial width would be seamed to produce the 67-inch-wide panel. Since a second panel is needed for the two-way draw treatment,

Table 16.2 Fabric Panel Widths and Pleating Guidelines

Desired Pleated Panel Coverage	Flat Fabric Without Hems	Hemmed Flat Fabric	Number of 4" Flat Spaces Between Pleats	Number of Pleats	Width of Fabric in Each Pleat
16"	43"	39"	4	5	3 1/8"
20"	51"	47"	5	6	3 1/4"
24"	59"	55"	6	7	3 3/8"
28"	67"	63"	7	8	3 1/2"
32"	75"	71"	8	9	3 1/2"
36"	83"	79"	9	10	3 9/16"
40"	91"	87"	10	11	3 5/8"
44"	99"	95"	11	12	3 5/8"
48"	107"	103"	12	13	3 5/8"
52"	115"	111"	13	14	3 5/8"
56"	123"	119"	14	15	3 3/4"
60"	131"	127"	15	16	3 3/4"
64"	139"	135"	16	17	3 3/4"
68"	147"	143"	17	18	3 3/4"
72"	155"	151"	18	19	3 3/4"
76"	163"	159"	19	20	3 3/4"
80"	171"	167"	20	21	3 3/4"
84"	179"	175"	21	22	3 3/4"
88"	187"	183"	22	23	3 3/4"
92"	195"	191"	23	24	3 3/4"
96"	203"	199"	24	25	3 3/4"
100"	211"	207"	25	26	3 3/4"
104"	219"	215"	26	27	3 3/4"
108"	227"	223"	27	28	3 3/4"
112"	235"	231"	28	29	3 3/4"
116"	243"	239"	29	30	3 3/4"
120"	251"	247"	30	31	3 7/8"
124"	259"	254"	31	32	3 7/8"
128"	267"	263"	32	33	3 7/8"

Courtesy of Kirsch Window Fashions, a Newell Rubbermaid Company.

we may at first assume four fabric widths are required. In this particular case, half the divided fabric width could be used for each of the two panels and thus, only three fabric widths are required. Such an economical use of fabric is not always possible, especially when allowances must be made for matching crosswise repeats and for seam allowances, but we should be alert to the possibility. For some projects, especially those involving expensive fabric, it may even be desirable to slightly reduce the width of the fabric included in each pleat.

The total amount of fabric to be ordered can be determined by multiplying the total length of the unhemmed panel by the number of fabric widths needed. The amount of lining fabric is calculated in the same manner.

Blinds and Shades

In contrast to curtains and draperies, which are drawn horizontally, almost all blinds and shades are drawn vertically. Some styles of blinds and shades are executed with textile fabric, others with metal or wood, and still others employ textile and nontextile components.

Austrian Shades

Austrian shades (Figure 16.13) are constructed of textile fabric that is vertically shirred to create lengthwise bands of horizontally draping folds. The level of transparency is determined by the compactness of construction of the fabric and the amount of fabric taken up in the gathering.

Balloon Shades

Balloon shades, like Austrian shades, are composed of textile fabric and are vertically drawn. Their name derives from the balloon-like puffs they form when raised. The fullness of the panels may be distributed by shirring the top casing over a rod or by using inverted pleats. In inverted-pleat styling, the panels are essentially flat until raised, a feature that makes possible full visual appreciation of the fabric.

Accordion-pleated Shades

Accordion-pleated shades are constructed of woven or knitted fabric that has been stiffened and set in a three-dimensional, folded configuration (Figure 16.14). As the shades are raised and lowered, the folds open and close, the same way the folds in an accordion's bellows open and close when the instrument is played. A 24-inch-long shade takes up only 2¼ inches stackup space when raised, measuring from the top of the headrail to the bottom of the bottom rail; a 96-inch-long shade takes up 3¾ inches. The textural characteristics of these shades vary readily with the style of yarn used; the compactness of construction and the selective application of back coatings control their transparency. Metallic coatings may be used for insulation, and also for static reduction, which reduces the attraction for dust. These window coverings are frequently used in commercial interiors, generally in combination with drapery panels.

Honeycomb Cellular Shades

Another type of accordion-pleated shade is the **honeycomb or cellular shade** (Figure 16.15a). In these coverings, spun-

Figure 16.13 Austrian shade.
Courtesy of Country Curtains, www.countrycurtains.com.

bonded polyester fabrics are permanently pleated and paired to create a single or double-cell structure (Figure 16.15b) with an insulating layer of air that significantly reduces heat transfer. The fabric facing outward is always white to provide high heat reflection and present a uniform exterior appearance. Because the pleats are smaller than those in conventional accordion-pleated shades, a 24-inch-long honeycomb shade requires only 2 inches of stackup space; a 96-inch-long shade requires only 3⅛ inches. With these shades, hardware may be chosen to facilitate lowering the shade from the top or raising it from the bottom; the shades can also be positioned anywhere within the window opening.

Cascade Loop Shades

A **cascade loop shade** is shown in Figure 16.17. Horizontal tucks in the fabric panel add visual interest; soft

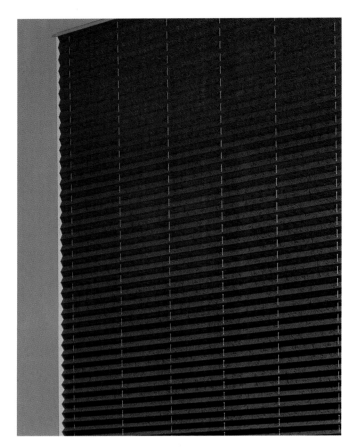

Figure 16.14 Accordion-pleated shade.
Courtesy of Comfortex.

a) Duette® honeycomb shades.

b) Duette® Architella™ honeycomb shades.

Figure 16.15 Honeycomb cellular shades.
a) Duette® honeycomb shade is a registered trademark of Hunter Douglas Inc. b) Duette® Architella™ honeycomb shade is a registered trademark of Hunter Douglas Inc.

loops, often called architectural folds, form when the shade is raised.

Roman Shades

Roman shades hang flat at the window until raised; then, horizontal pleats form. These window coverings may be made exclusively of textile fabric, but frequently they are constructed of woven wood, a combination of wooden slats and textile yarns. The yarns used may vary in color, luster, size, and complexity. To permit the necessary folding, the wooden slats always lie across the covering. Fabric linings or coatings are generally necessary for full privacy, especially at night.

Some Roman shades are hand woven, from grasses, cane, or wheat straws crosswise and textile yarns lengthwise. These shades are relatively transparent, but they nonetheless diminish the view into the interior and provide a natural look heightened by the irregularity of the materials and the hand weaving.

A variation of the conventional Roman shade styling is the use of two shades, normally constructed from textile fabric or cellular fabric. In these coverings, known as **athey shades**, one shade is lowered and one shade is raised for full closure.

Roller Shades

A **roller shade** may be plain or patterned, constructed of a textile fabric or a sheet of polymer film. It may mount at the bottom of the window and unroll upward or mount at the top of the window and unroll down-

Figure 16.16 Silhouette® window shade.
Silhouette® is a registered trademark of Hunter Douglas Inc.

a) Installed.

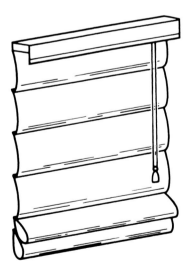

Figure 16.17 Cascade loop shade.

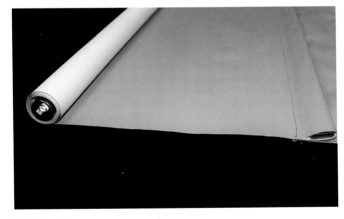

b) Side view.

Figure 16.18 Roller shades.
a) Courtesy of Comfortex. b) Courtesy of Amy Willbanks,
www.textilefabric.com.

ward (Figure 16.18a and b). Decorative hems and pulls, including rings, carved wood, molded plastic, and tassels, augment the visual interest of contemporary shades.

Solar shades are roller shades of synthetic mesh fabric that filter light while allowing a view out. The degree of openness of the mesh determines the percentage of light filtration.

Venetian Blinds

Venetian blinds are made up of horizontal slats, or louvers, laced together with textile cords (Figure 16.19). Slats are typically made of enamel-coated aluminum, painted or stained wood, wood composite, or vinyl (PVC). Off-gassing of PVC materials and the danger of inhaling PVC dust when sizing vinyl blinds is of concern to environmentally conscious consumers. Louvers vary in width from ⅝ inch (micro) to 1 inch (mini) to 2 inches. The wider variety is available with decorative cloth tapes for a more decorative look or with only the textile cords that minimize interference with views when blinds are open. Cords and wands allow blinds to be raised and lowered or tilted to the desired level of privacy or openness.

Softer variations of the hard-surfaced louvers use fabric vanes rather than wood or aluminum slats (Figure 16.16). Sheer fabric front and back panels on some models add to the softness and light-filtering capabilities. Both the traditional Venetian blinds and the newer fabric blinds can be stacked at the upper portion of the window.

Vertical Blinds

In **vertical blinds**, which may also be referred to as vertical Venetian blinds, the louvers or vanes are suspended

Figure 16.19 Venetian blinds.
Courtesy of Comfortex.

vertically from traversing or nontraversing rods (Figure 16.20). They may be rotated 180 degrees to balance privacy and inward light transmission. Traversing styles may have a one- or two-way draw.

The louvers or vanes used in vertical blinds may be as narrow as 2 inches or as wide as 6 inches. They may be constructed of vinyl, stable fabric, metal, or wood. Fabric vanes may be inserted into ivory or white vinyl backings to give greater light blockage and present a uniform streetside appearance. New variations of the traditional vertical blinds include soft-vane vertical systems and wide panels that operate on a wheel track system. The wider panels are especially good for large expanses of glass or as room dividers.

Initially, vertical blinds were almost exclusively used in commercial interior applications. Today, they can also be found in residential interiors, especially in settings having a contemporary design concept.

Figure 16.20 Vertical blinds.
Courtesy of Comfortex.

Awnings and Shutters

Awnings and shutters may be constructed from rigid materials only or from a combination of rigid materials and drapable textile fabrics. These structures can be used as interior and exterior window treatments.

Awnings

Awnings are basically rigid structures that may be composed of metal or molded polymer sheeting or of textile fabric stretched and held over a rigid frame. Awnings are occasionally used for novel interior applications, but primarily as exterior window treatments. Outside windows, they reduce solar heat transmission and provide protection from weather elements.

Textile awning fabric may be used in outdoor applications other than window treatments, for instance, as screens for privacy, windbreaks, and canopies over patios, gazebos, and carports. For all outdoor applications, fabrics must be composed of fibers resistant to sunlight, mildew, insects, water, wind, and atmospheric contaminants. Acrylic, saran, and olefin fibers are often employed, generally solution dyed for superior colorfastness.

Shutters

Decorative, stationary **shutters** have long framed windows on the exterior of homes and other structures. These panels cannot be unfolded to cover the window glass. Today, folding shutters are increasingly being mounted to unfold over the glass, reducing solar heat gain in the summer and interior heat loss in the winter. This current application of shutters is a revival of the practice of using folding shutters on colonial homes for protection from the elements.

Shutters are usually constructed of pine or oak, which is stained or painted the desired color. Stiles are shifted vertically to open and close the crosswise louvers in each rectangular section, and hinges permit the units to be folded and unfolded to control inward and outward vision, the level of light transmission, and heat gain and loss.

Textile fabrics are sometimes used to soften the appearance of wooden shutters. Shirred fabric may be inserted in some sections, or used in lieu of the wooden louvers.

Summary

Window treatment styles range from the relatively simple, with a single component, to the extremely complex, involving multiple layers, an overhead treatment, and decorative accessories. Some treatments are executed with textiles, some with nontextiles, and some with a combination of components.

The style of window treatment and the components needed to execute it should be chosen with the priority aesthetic, functional, and cost selection variables in mind. When consumers examine these variables before committing themselves—making a purchase or signing a contractual agreement—they will make more informed decisions and be better able to select treatments and components that provide the appearance and functional features they need at a price they can afford.

Key Terms

accordion-pleated shade
athey shade
Austrian shade
awnings
balloon shade
batons
café curtains
cantonnière
cascade loop shade
cascades
casement
casing
continental rod
cornice
cottage or Cape Cod curtains
curtain tender
curtains

draperies
draw curtains
fabric panel
fabric weights
fabric width
fullness
glass curtains
headings
held-back panels
honeycomb or cellular shade
jabots
lambrequin
multi-tier café curtains
one-way draw draperies
overdraperies
pinned-up panels
pouf or bishop's sleeve treatment

priscilla curtains
roller shade
Roman shade
ruffled, tie-back curtains
sash curtains
sheers
shutters
single-tier café curtains
stackback space
stationary casement panels
swags
tied-back panels
trimmings
two-way draperies
valances
Venetian blinds
vertical blinds

Review Questions

1. Explain what is meant by this statement: "Window treatment styles do not change, but their popularity does." Could the same be said for clothing styles?

2. What is meant by the terms "visual weight?" Why is this an important consideration when choosing ruffled curtain styles or using such fabrics as velvet in overdraperies?

3. Describe how overhead and side treatments can be used alone or in combinations.

4. Design a window treatment having multiple layers (e.g., overdraperies with separate lining and sheers, decorative rods and tie-backs, valance, etc.) Calculate the yardage required and its cost, together with the cost of the hardware. You may want to vary the styling features and fabrics used in two or three treatments and calculate the total cost of each.

5. What advantages are offered by honeycomb or cellular shades?

Window Coverings and Linings

Photo courtesy of Amy Willbanks, www.textilefabric.com.

■ **With the increased use of** such nontextile materials as wood, and with the expanded color styling of metal components, the variety of window covering structures offered to today's residential and commercial consumers has been greatly expanded. The major portion of the assortment, however, continues to be composed of textile fibers and yarns. Cotton and the noncellulosic fibers split the major portion of the market almost equally, with modest amounts of rayon and acetate also used. Both spun and filament yarns are available, ranging from fine, simple, single structures to coarse, complex, multi-unit structures.

Several techniques used to fabricate upholstery coverings are also used to fabricate textile window coverings. Because window coverings are normally subjected to less abrasion than upholstery coverings, however, additional techniques are available for fabricating a greater variety of window coverings. Some of these methods enable manufacturers to incorporate decorative surface features more economically; others facilitate the production of fabrics with maximum openness as well as high-dimensional stability; still others expedite production and thus reduce product cost.

Working together, fabric manufacturers and converters produce drapery fabrics with permanently attached linings. They also produce a vast amount of textile fabric for use in separately hung lining panels. Both types of material help to protect the decorative drapery panels from sunlight and degradation; some materials also help to reduce noise, heat transfer, and light transmission.

Components Used in Curtains and Draperies

Although their importance varies greatly, virtually all of the major groups of fibers are used in textile window coverings. Fortunately, mandatory rules require that information pertaining to fiber composition be available to prospective purchasers. These disclosures enable informed consumers and professionals to assess the properties of the fiber or fibers and select the fiber or blend that offers the best balance of features for their interior or exterior window treatments.

Statistical Profile of Fiber Usage

The data presented in Table 17.1 reveal the growing use of the noncellulosic fibers, as well as the extensive use of cotton fiber, in curtain and drapery fabrics. The cotton poundage listed in the table also includes the cotton fiber used in the production of drapery linings.

In 2005, at 82.3 million pounds, cotton held 44 percent of the contemporary curtain and drapery market. At the same time, the usage of noncellulosic fibers in curtains and draperies was 86.8 million pounds, 46 percent of the total market. Technological advances in fiber engineering and yarn processing and the increased use of polyester fibers to compensate for the poor resiliency of cellulosic fibers are largely responsible for the continued growth in usage of synthesized fibers.

Although the quantity of wool used in curtain and drapery fabrics is not sufficient to warrant listing in statistical re-

Table 17.1 Fiber Usage in U.S. Curtains and Draperies (in millions of pounds)

| | | Manufactured Fibers* | | | | | | |
| | | | Cellulosic | | Noncellulosic | | | |
Year	Total Fiber	Total	Yarn	Staple	Yarn	Staple	Cotton	Wool**
2001	328.0	160.6	2.6	22.7	46.9	88.4	167.4	–
2002	311.1	148.5	2.8	21.7	41.7	82.3	162.6	–
2003	254.9	130.4	3.6	19.3	35.4	72.1	124.5	–
2004	200.5	110.0	2.3	18.1	29.2	60.4	90.5	–
2005	187.2	104.9	2.1	16.0	25.2	61.6	82.3	–

* Manufactured fiber end use is divided between cellulosic (rayon + acetate) and noncellulosic (nylon, polyester, acrylic, olefin). Yarn includes multifilament, monofilament, and spunbonded. Olefin includes polypropylene and polyethylene staple and yarn. Olefin yarn also includes film fiber and spunbonded polypropylene. Staple includes tow and fiberfill.
** Little or none of the fiber is used.
Source: Textiles Economics Bureau, *Fiber Organon*, "U.S. End Use Survey: 2001–2005," October 2006, page 192, Table 4.

ports, its use should be noted. Currently, a limited number of casement fabrics composed of wool are designed and produced for commercial applications, principally in order to capitalize on the inherent flame resistance of the fiber.

The quantity of glass fiber used in curtains and draperies has steadily declined, and usage data is no longer reported. Although glass fiber is noncombustible, it may cause skin irritation. It also has extremely low flex abrasion resistance and relatively high density.

Fiber Labeling Laws

Currently, two labeling laws include provisions that apply to textile fibers used in window covering fabrics. One mandate pertains to fiber composition; the other concerns the potential skin irritation that may result from glass fiber fibrillations.

Disclosure of Fiber Composition

The provisions of the **Textile Fiber Products Identification Act** apply to all curtain, casement, and drapery fabrics and the products made from them. All curtains, casements, and draperies, or any portions of these items that would otherwise be subject to the act, made principally of slats, rods, or strips composed of wood, metal, plastic, or leather, are excluded. Thus, the fiber composition of certain textile components, such as the yarns used in woven wood shades, is not required to be disclosed.

Cautionary Labeling with Glass Fiber Products

Recognizing the problem of **fibrillation** with higher denier glass fibers, the FTC issued a trade regulation rule that requires the use of special labeling with glass fiber window coverings. The provisions of the rule, which became effective on January 2, 1968, apply to glass fiber curtains, draperies, and fabrics. These products must carry a tag or label cautioning purchasers that skin irritation may result: (1) to the exposed skin of persons handling such glass fiber products; and (2) from body contact with clothing or other articles, such as bed sheets, which have been washed (a) with such glass fiber products, or (b) in a container previously used for washing such glass fiber products unless the glass particles have been removed from such container by cleaning.

Dominance of Spun Yarns

The yarns used in curtains, draperies, and other window coverings are as varied as those used in upholstery fabric.

Spun yarns dominate the market, but a number of filament structures are used in curtain fabrics.

The data listed in Table 17.1 reveal that some 85 percent of the fibers used in curtain and drapery fabrics have been spun into yarns. (Relatively few of the staple-length fibers included in the data are used directly in the production of stitch-bonded and spunlaced curtain fabrics.) Filaments are used most often in curtain fabrics as a result of the demand for sheer, yet strong and stable, panels.

Nontextile Materials Used in Window Coverings

The assortment of nontextile window coverings in earlier years was basically limited to structures composed of wood or metal. More recently, the assortment has been expanded to include structures composed of molded polymer compounds and natural grasses.

Metals and Polymer Materials

Formerly, only cream-colored, enamel-coated aluminum slats were used for Venetian blinds. The aluminum slats now come in a wide variety of fashion colors, which makes these blinds more appealing to designers and consumers. A contemporary flair has also been introduced to some of these blinds by constructing them of slats composed of molded polymer compounds.

Metal, glass, and plastic beads are occasionally strung into chains and hung vertically as stationary, panel-like treatments. Metals, generally aluminum, are also frequently used for exterior shutters, awnings, and canopies.

Polymer compounds, such as polyvinylchloride (PVC), are extruded as film sheeting for use in manufacturing conventional roller shades. In a contemporary application, the polymer films are pressed onto window panes to simulate frosted/etched glass and to increase privacy. Increasingly, these "window wall papers" and roller shades are printed to coordinate with textile window and wallcoverings.

Woods

The slats of Roman shades, Venetian and vertical blinds, and shutters are frequently made of pine, but more expensive structures may be constructed of oak. The wood is first kiln dried to minimize the potential for cracking and splitting; it is then sanded and stained, or painted a fashion color.

Woven Woods and Grasses

Traditionally, Roman shades of woven wood, bamboo, and yarn have been bulky. Recent additions of shades made from reeds, jute, hemp, flax, and grasses produce a softer, more delicate look that is suitable for contemporary or traditional spaces. Interest in environmentally sustainable products has created new popularity for these window treatments of natural, renewable materials.

Woven Curtain and Drapery Fabrics

The aesthetic features of some textile window covering fabrics take precedence over their functional attributes; the converse is also sometimes true. In the production of most fabrics, however, manufacturers seek to strike a balance between appearance and function while also producing a stable structure. A wide variety of interlacing patterns is necessarily used in the production of curtain and drapery fabrics. Various surface embellishment techniques further expand the assortment.

Fabrics with Basic Interlacings

The basic interlacing patterns and their variations were explained in Chapter 6. This section describes and illustrates the several curtain and drapery fabrics constructed using these weaves. These fabrics are defined by such characteristics as yarn structure, interlacing pattern, color styling, finish, and hand. Shifts in fiber usage have diminished the value of fiber composition as a distinguishing characteristic for curtain and drapery fabrics, as is also true for upholstery fabrics.

Plain-woven Fabrics

The plain weave is used to produce several curtain and drapery fabrics that have distinct differences in their appearance features, tactile characteristics, and performance attributes. These variations derive from yarns that differ in size, design features, level of twist, or color styling; from different fabric counts; and from coloring methods and finishing procedures.

When composed of fine, combed cotton yarns, **batiste** (Figure 17.1) has a soft hand, is translucent, and is normally solid colored. Resins and preshrinking treatments may be employed to introduce resiliency and dimensional stability to fabrics made of these natural fibers. Batiste that is woven of yarns composed of polyester has a crisp hand, is transparent, and is often white

in color. Heat setting may be used to impart dimensional stability and resiliency to these fabrics. Batiste fabrics are effectively used in all styles of curtain treatments (Figure 16.1, p. 266) and in Austrian shades (Figure 16.13, p. 277). Polyester batiste is increasingly replacing cotton batiste in the production of tambour-embroidered curtain panels.

Calico, formerly made exclusively from cotton fiber, is now generally composed of cotton and polyester for improved resiliency and dimensional stability. The fabric has a balanced fabric count (approximately 78 × 78) and small, colorful, printed design motifs on a solid-colored ground (Figure 17.2). Calico is particularly appropriate for multi-tier café curtains, because the short panels require short pattern repeats and the extensive gathering would camouflage large design motifs.

Chintz (Figure 17.3) is glazed to add body and high surface luster. Most chintz fabrics have colorful, printed designs, but some are solid colored. The fabric, which has relatively low drapability, is frequently used in single- and multi-tier café curtains.

Cretonne, a drapery fabric infrequently used in recent years, is produced from coarse yarns. Large, printed motifs, relatively high stiffness, and a dull surface characterize it.

Gauze or theatrical gauze (Figure 17.4) has a slightly higher fabric count than cheesecloth; stiffening agents are used to impart body. Originally produced for use in stage settings, the transparent fabric may be dyed and used for stationary or traversing curtain panels in residential and commercial interiors.

Figure 17.1 Batiste.
Courtesy of Amy Willbanks, www.textilefabric.com.

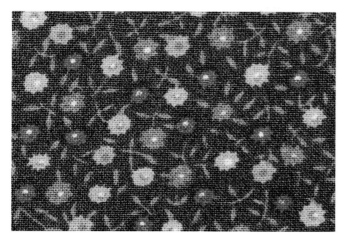

a) Face.

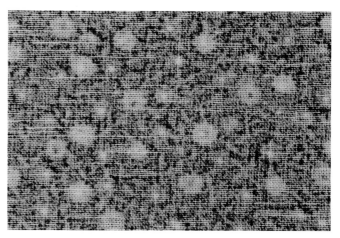

b) Back.

Figure 17.2 Calico.
Courtesy of Amy Willbanks, www.textilefabric.com.

Ninon (Figure 17.5) is used for sheer draw or stationary curtains, generally in combination with overdraperies. Close examination of the fabric shows that every third warp yarn has been omitted to increase the transparency of the fabric. The interlacing pattern in ninon is 1×1, not 2×1, which the paired spacing of the warp yarns may first suggest.

Transparency and a parchment-like hand characterize **organdy**, produced when an all-cotton fabric is exposed to a weak solution of sulfuric acid. In order to partially offset the weakening effect of the acid, the fabric is first mercerized to increase the strength of the fibers. Organdy is now also made of monofilament nylon, which requires no acid treatment. The sheer cotton or nylon fabrics are effective in most styles of curtain treatments.

Osnaburg is composed of coarse, carded cotton yarns. These are bleached only a little, if at all, to preserve the natural off-white color of the yarns, which are interspersed with bits of dark-colored fibers. Osnaburg was originally produced for use as grain and cement sack fabric; its unrefined look is apparent in Figure 17.6.

Voile is a transparent fabric woven of highly twisted yarns composed of cotton or a blend of cotton and polyester fibers (Figure 17.7). The fabric has a crisp hand and is generally white in ruffled curtains and printed in other styles. Voile may be flocked with small dots that convert the fabric into **dotted swiss** (Figure 17.21).

Basket-woven Fabrics

Two basket-woven fabrics, namely monk's cloth and duck, are commonly used for window treatments. **Monk's cloth**

Figure 17.3 Glazed chintz.
Courtesy of Amy Willbanks, www.textilefabric.com.

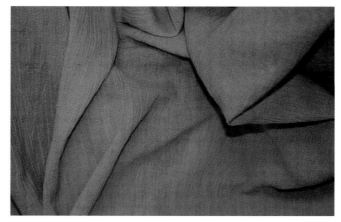

Figure 17.4 Gauze.
Courtesy of Amy Willbanks, www.textilefabric.com.

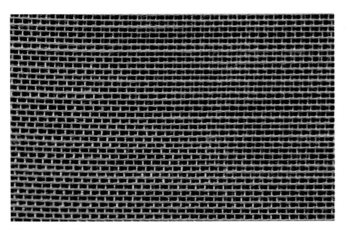

Figure 17.5 Ninon.
Courtesy of Amy Willbanks, www.textilefabric.com.

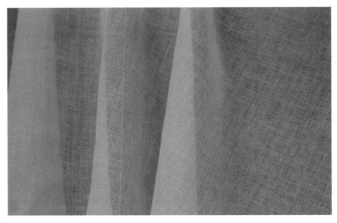

Figure 17.7 Voile.
Courtesy of Amy Willbanks, www.textilefabric.com.

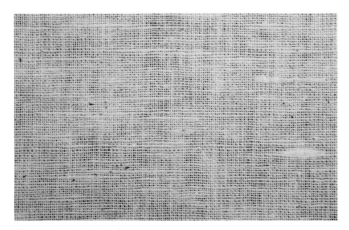

Figure 17.6 Osnaburg.
Courtesy of Amy Willbanks, www.textilefabric.com.

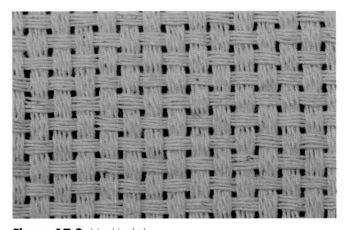

Figure 17.8 Monk's cloth.
Courtesy of Amy Willbanks, www.textilefabric.com.

(Figure 17.8) is usually produced in a 4 × 4 interlacing pattern, but a 2 × 2 pattern may be used. The yarns are spun to simulate those found in the fabric traditionally used for monk's robes. For use in window coverings, the fabric is generally bleached and occasionally dyed to create a refined, contemporary appearance.

Duck, also known as **canvas**, is typically constructed in a 2 × 1 basket weave (Figure 17.9). The fabric is often made from strong, two-ply yarns for use in exterior awning treatments. To make duck and other textile awning fabrics waterproof, converters coat them with vinyl solutions, rubber-based materials, or other synthesized compounds. These agents fill the yarn and fabric interstices, making the structures nonporous.

Filling-Rib Woven Fabrics. Taffeta, faille, and bengaline are produced for use in window treatments. **Faille** and **bengaline** (Figure 13.3b and c, p. 218) have slightly larger ribs than those in **taffeta**. Taffeta's smooth yarns are usually composed of bright acetate fibers; often a wood-grain or water-marked surface pattern is introduced by moiréing (Figure 9.2, p. 144).

Shantung (Figure 13.3e, p. 218) has an irregular ribbed surface in the crosswise direction, owing to the uneven surface of the filling yarns. Silk shantung is used in window treatments because of its luxury, luster, and durability.

Warp-Rib Woven Fabrics In dimity, a sheer fabric used for curtains, a lengthwise rib effect may be produced by

Figure 17.9 Duck/Canvas.
Courtesy of Amy Willbanks, www.textilefabric.com.

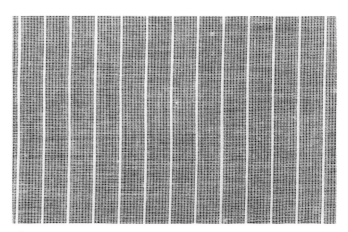

Figure 17.10 Dimity.
Courtesy of Amy Willbanks, www.textilefabric.com.

periodically placing one large warp among fine yarns, or, as shown in Figure 17.10, by periodically placing a group of warp yarns among fine yarns. Fine, combed cotton yarns produce a smooth surface; they are generally mercerized to increase luster and fiber strength. The degree of fabric openness is similar to that of organdy and voile.

The roller shade fabric shown in Figure 17.11 has a lengthwise rib effect produced by combining fine and coarse yarns. Called **ribcord**, the fabric may be coated on the back with a vinyl compound to increase its opacity.

Other curtain fabrics, such as piqué and Bedford cord, also have lengthwise ribs, but their interlacing patterns are too complicated to be executed on a two-harness loom. To make these fabrics, a dobby loom with multiple harnesses for increased shedding variations is a necessity.

Twill-woven Fabrics

Twill interlacing patterns are rarely used alone in the construction of curtain and drapery fabrics. Instead, they are generally combined with other interlacing patterns in decorative weaving procedures, including dobby and Jacquard operations.

Satin- and Sateen-woven Fabrics

Multifilament yarns composed of bright acetate fibers are often woven in a satin interlacing to produce highly drapable, lustrous drapery fabrics (Figure 17.12). Such fabrics are especially suitable for swags, jabots, and cascades (see Figure 16.7, p. 271).

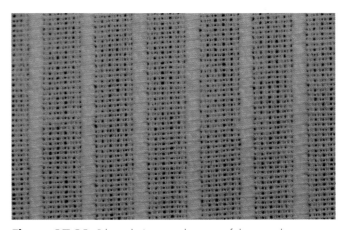

Figure 17.11 Ribcord. A warp-rib weave fabric used in roller shades.
Courtesy of Amy Willbanks, www.textilefabric.com.

Antique satin (Figure 17.13) has simple warp yarns and slub filling yarns. The slub yarns float over the face of the fabric in a sateen interlacing. When high luster is desired, the fabric is composed of bright acetate, and, for low luster, cotton is used. Antique satin enjoys great popularity among contemporary designers and consumers.

Simple interlacing patterns are also used in the production of woven wood and woven grass window coverings. These structures simply employ wood slats or grass strands, rather than textile yarns, as their crosswise elements.

Fabrics with Decorative Interlacings

Several decorative interlacing patterns, including the dobby, dot or spot, and Jacquard weaves, produce fabrics suitable for use in window treatments as well as in upholstery

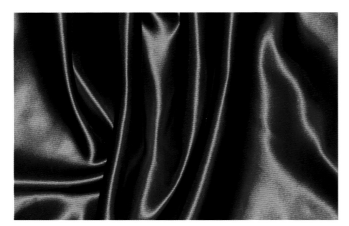

Figure 17.12 Satin.
Courtesy of Amy Willbanks, www.textilefabric.com.

applications. Additional complex interlacing patterns, including the leno, swivel, and lappet weaves, are used in curtain and drapery fabrics; the relatively low abrasion resistance or low covering power characterizing these weaves precludes their use in upholstery coverings.

Dobby-woven Fabrics

The multiple harnesses and control mechanisms on a dobby loom facilitate the production of novelty curtain fabrics with geometric features woven into the base fabric. Fine lengthwise ribs are found in **plain** or **pinwale piqué**; larger ribs are found in **Bedford cord**; small, diamond-shaped patterns are characteristic of **birdseye piqué**; and the grid of a waffle iron is replicated in **waffle piqué**. Examples of the piqué fabrics are given in Figure 17.14a,b, and c.

As shown in the cross-sectional sketch of pinwale piqué presented in Figure 17.15, extra warp yarns, called **stuffer yarns**, can be used to support the tunnel-like ribs or **wales**. Stuffer warp yarns may also appear in Bedford cord, and stuffer filling yarns in birdseye piqué.

The low drapability of these fabrics makes them more suitable for tailored curtain panels than for ruffled and shirred styles. Scalloped headings are especially effective with these fabrics.

Surface-figure woven Fabrics

Special attachments can be added to dobby looms to facilitate surface-figure weaving. Surface-figure woven fabrics have raised figures or motifs produced by incorporating extra yarns in various ways.

Dot- or Spot-woven Fabrics

In dot or spot weaving, extra yarns are periodically interlaced with the base yarns to create a small dot or figured spot (Figure 17.16). Between the decorative figures or dots, the extra yarns are floated on the back of the fabric. When the floating yarns are left in place, the fabric is known as an **unclipped dot or spot fabric** (Figure 13.10, p. 221); when the floating yarns are cut away, the fabric is known as a **clipped dot or spot** fabric. When the base fabric is sheer, the floats should be clipped to avoid linear shadows, especially when the fabric is intended for use as a window covering. Either side of a clipped dot or spot fabric can be used as the face side. The floating yarns should be left unclipped in opaque fabrics to minimize the pos-

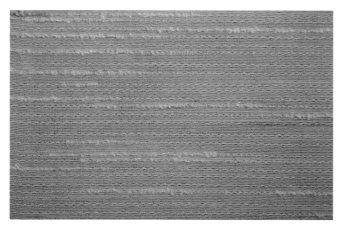

a) Face.

Figure 17.13 Antique satin.
Courtesy of Amy Willbanks, www.textilefabric.com.

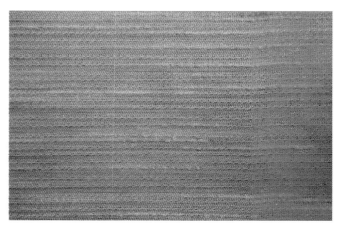

b) Back.

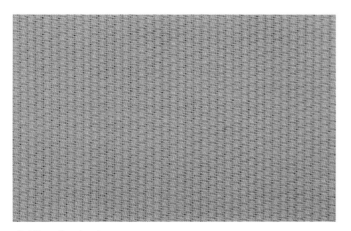

a) Pinwale piqué.

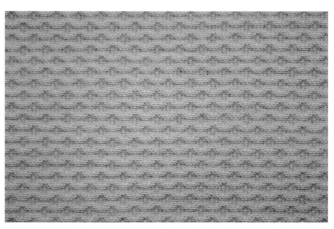

b) Birdseye piqué.

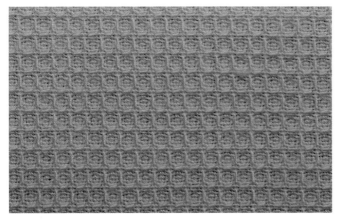

c) Waffle piqué.

Figure 17.14 Dobby-woven curtain fabrics.
Courtesy of Amy Willbanks, www.textilefabric.com.

sibility that the dots or spots will be removed by in-use abrasion and cleaning.

Swivel-woven Fabrics In **swivel weaving**, extra yarns periodically swivel around or encircle the base yarns to create small, secure dots. Some imported dotted swiss is produced with this interlacing technique, but the relatively slow rate of production precludes its widespread use.

Lappet-woven Fabrics In **lappet weaving**, hundreds of needles are used to interlace extra warp yarns. The needles are shifted laterally to create a zigzag surface pattern that resembles hand embroidery. Lappet fabrics, like swivel fabrics, are woven at comparatively slow rates.

Leno-woven Fabrics

Because the crossed warp yarns effectively lock the filling yarns into position and minimize yarn slippage, the leno weave is particularly useful for interlacing fine, smooth yarns into stable window covering fabrics. **Marquisette** (Figure 17.17) is a transparent leno-woven fabric composed of fine filament yarns; the lightweight fabric is used extensively in stationary or traversing curtain panels. **Mosquito netting** is also transparent but compactly constructed; it is used as a curtain-like bed canopy in tropical climates, forming a barrier against mosquitoes.

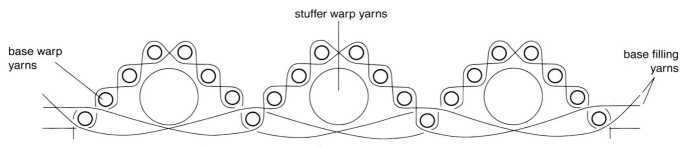

Figure 17.15 Cross-sectional view of pinwale piqué with stuffer warp yarns..

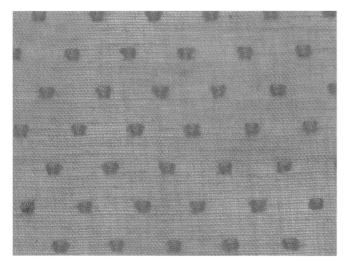

Figure 17.16 Dotted swiss—clipped dot curtain fabric. Courtesy of Amy Willbanks, www.textilefabric.com.

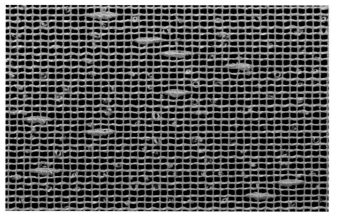

Figure 17.17 Marquisette. Courtesy of Amy Willbanks, www.textilefabric.com.

Figure 17.18 Leno-woven casement fabric. Courtesy of Amy Willbanks, www.textilefabric.com.

The stability and novel appearance of leno interlacing enables manufacturers to produce a wide variety of highly decorative, leno-woven fabrics. The visual interest of the casement shown in Figure 17.18 is enhanced by the use of monofilament and ply yarns, and that of the casement shown in Figure 17.17 is enriched by the use of splash yarns.

Jacquard-woven Fabrics

Such Jacquard-woven fabrics as **damask**, **brocade**, and **tapestry** are produced for use in drapery treatments as well as in upholstery. The damask drapery fabric in Figure 17.19 has linear motifs that are complemented by the strié color styling of the ground.

Another distinctive Jacquard-woven drapery and upholstery fabric is called **lampas**. The fabric is characterized by elaborate woven-in designs typical of the seventeenth

a) Strié damask.

b) Close-up view.

Figure 17.19 Strié damask drapery fabric. Courtesy of Amy Willbanks, www.textilefabric.com.

and eighteenth centuries. The detailed motifs are created by combining satin and sateen interlacings (Figure 17.20). In many lampases, two sets of identically colored warp yarns are combined with one or more sets of variously colored filling yarns.

Fabrics with Pile Interlacings

Such pile-woven fabrics as **corduroy**, **velveteen**, and **velvet**, which were described in Chapter 13, may be used for interior window treatments. Corduroy works well in single-tier café curtains and casual draperies, and velveteen and velvet are effective in formal drapery treatments. When considering these fabrics for use in any style of treatment, designers and consumers should make good use of design elements and principles when assessing whether the three-dimensional texture will be appropriate or too

a)

b)

Figure 17.20 Lampas.
Courtesy of Amy Willbanks, www.textilefabric.com.

imposing. They should also determine whether extra-strong rods and additional brackets would be required to support the panels constructed from these comparatively heavy fabrics.

Fabrics with Surface Embellishments

Converters can embellish the surfaces of already-woven fabrics to produce distinctive coverings for curtain treatments. They may use a flocking or an embroidering operation.

Flocked Fabrics

Flocked dotted swiss fabric (Figure 17.21) is less expensive than that produced by spot or swivel weaving. Frequently, the base fabric is voile.

Embroidered Fabrics

Embroidered curtain fabric is distinguished by chain-stitched, lace-like designs. The stitching (shown in detail in Figure 17.22a and b) resembles that created by artisans using a variety of embroidery stitches. Frequently, mirror-image panels with finished edges are produced from such fabrics as batiste and organdy.

Eyelet is produced with an embroidery machine used to stitch around holes created in the greige goods. Formerly, destroying cotton fibers with sulfuric acid produced these holes; today, knives are used. The eyelet shown in Figure 17.23 has a scalloped edge, a decorative feature often selected for single-tier café curtain treatments.

Fabrics Distinguished by Color Styling

Many textile window covering fabrics are distinguished by the decorative features of their yarns or the structural features introduced during fabrication; others are distinguished by their color styling. Among the latter group of fabrics are blotch prints, warp prints, toile de Jouy prints, pigment prints, and burnt-out prints.

Roller printing has traditionally been employed to create a color style known as a **blotch print** (Figure 17.2), in which the ground of the fabric is printed; the motifs may be left as undyed, white designs or they may also be printed. In contrast to **discharge prints** (Figure 17.24), blotch prints do not exhibit the same level of color intensity on both sides of the fabric (Figure 17.2).

A **warp print** color style is produced by first screen printing a web of warp yarns; the colors are applied in precise, well-defined motifs and pattern repeats. The

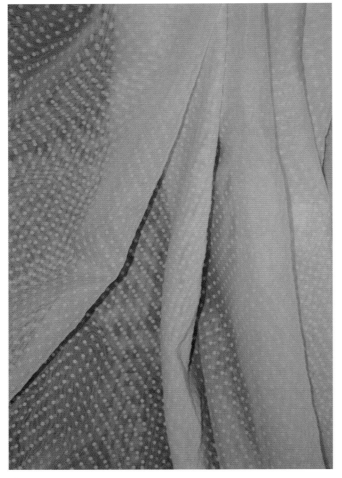

a)

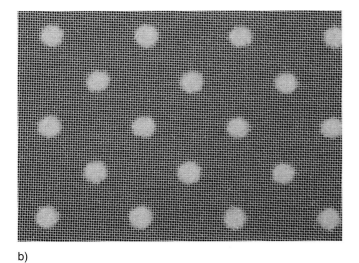

b)

Figure 17.21 Flocked dotted swiss.
Courtesy of Amy Willbanks, www.textilefabric.com.

a)

b)

Figure 17.22 Embroidered drapery fabric.
Courtesy of Amy Willbanks, www.textilefabric.com.

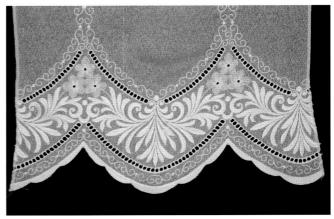

Figure 17.23 Eyelet embroidered sheer curtain panel.
Courtesy of Amy Willbanks, www.textilefabric.com.

subsequent interlacing of the printed warp yarns with neutral-colored filling yarns will develop a striated appearance (Figure 17.25) similar to that seen in ikat prints.

Toile de Jouy (*twal duh jzoo-weê*) **prints** have monochromatic color styling. The motifs have a picture-like quality, and designers must be cognizant of the unidirectional orientation of the motifs (Figure 17.26).

Thick pigment mixtures, typically white or gold, are used to produce **pigment print** curtain fabrics (Figure 17.27). These opaque compounds add visual interest and reduce fabric openness.

Different levels of transparency in the same fabric distinguish **etched-out or burnt-out prints**. After acid has been used to burn away the acid-degradable fibers (frequently, rayon), only the acid-resistant fiber (often nylon) remains in the highly transparent areas of the fabric (Figure 17.28).

Knitted Window Covering Fabrics

Knitting is a relatively fast and economical method of combining yarns into fabric structures that is increasingly employed in the fabrication of window coverings. Balancing the gauge and type of yarns used can produce specific levels of fabric openness. Raschel stitching provides high-dimensional stability, non-run performance, and design flexibility; many curtain and casement fabrics are produced with this interlooping technique. Two variations of conventional knitting procedures, weft insertion and stitch-knitting, are also used.

Figure 17.24 Discharge print.
Courtesy of Amy Willbanks, www.textilefabric.com.

Figure 17.26 Toile de Jouy prints with monochromatic color styling and picture-like motifs.
Courtesy of Amy Willbanks, www.textilefabric.com.

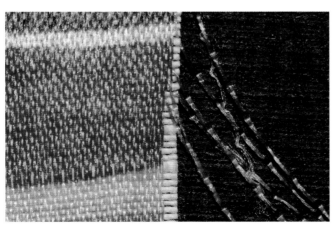

Figure 17.25 Warp print.
Courtesy of Amy Willbanks, www.textilefabric.com.

Figure 17.27 Pigment print.
Courtesy of Amy Willbanks, www.textilefabric.com.

Raschel-stitched Fabrics

The multiple guide bars and latch needles (Figure 7.2, p. 115) on the **raschel** machine facilitate the production of a variety of window covering fabrics, ranging from delicate, lacy curtain structures to heavy, elaborately interlooped casements. Raschel-stitched fabrics are shown in Figure 17.29a and b.

Fabrics Produced by Weft Insertion

Because the size and character of the weft or filling yarns effectively control the transparency and covering power of a fabric, manufacturers are increasingly using **weft insertion** to produce window coverings. In the casement fabric shown in Figure 17.30, the manufacturer has inserted various lengths of weft yarns to develop an integral pattern with different levels of fabric openness. Opaque pigments are frequently printed on the surface of such fabrics to reduce their transparency and enhance visual interest.

Stitch-knitted Casements

In Chapter 7, the use of knitting stitches to anchor webs of yarns in **stitch-knitting** operations was explained. An example of casement fabric produced this way is shown in Figure 17.31.

Because the stability and integrity of stitch-knitted fabrics can be lost when loops of the chain-stitching are ruptured, they should not be selected for panels that will be subject to abrasion. Panels of these fabrics must not be opened and closed by hand, and they must be cleaned with care.

a) Burnt-out.

Figure 17.28 Burnt-out print. Courtesy of Amy Willbanks, www.textilefabric.com.

b) Close-up view of burnt-out.

a) All over lace design.

Figure 17.29 Raschel stitched casement fabrics. Courtesy of Amy Willbanks, www.textilefabric.com.

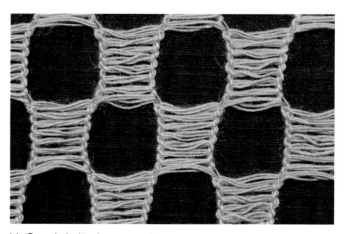

b) Openly knitted casement.

Figure 17.30 Weft-insertion casement fabric. Courtesy of Amy Willbanks, www.textilefabric.com.

Figure 17.31 Stitched-knitted malimo casement. Courtesy of Amy Willbanks, www.textilefabric.com.

Knotted and Twisted Window Coverings

Lace and net window coverings are fabricated with knotting and twisting operations. Designers and consumers desiring an airy, delicate, and highly ornamental **lace fabric** for a window treatment must be aware that the panels are likely to sag. Their stability can be improved when the fabric is made from thermoplastic fibers and properly heat set. Appliqués may increase the visual interest of **net curtain fabrics**.

Coverings Formed from Fibrous Webs

The stitch-bonding and spunlacing techniques explained in Chapter 7 enable manufacturers to produce window

coverings directly from fibers. Because these techniques bypass spinning operations, such coverings may be less expensive than those fabricated from yarns.

Manufacturers can produce **spunlaced** curtain fabrics with open, airy constructions by manipulating the positions of the fibers. Such fabrics may be treated as disposable, especially in care-type facilities where maintenance expenses are higher than replacement costs (Figure 7.8, p. 118).

Drapery Lining Materials

Two types of lining materials, coatings and film sheetings, may be permanently attached to the back of drapery fabric. These multicomponent fabrics, known as self-lined drapery fabrics, often display specific functional attributes. Other types of linings, virtually all of which are textile fabrics, are hung separately, behind the drapery panels.

Permanently Attached Lining Materials

The application of foamed acrylic compounds to the back of drapery fabric to increase its **insulative value** was introduced in Chapter 9. The air-filled cells of these coatings retard heat loss by convection as the compound restricts the flow of air through the yarn and fabric interstices. The insulative value of window treatments using these fabrics largely depends, however, on how tightly the panels are mounted (see Chapter 15). Acrylic polymers, which have high resistance to sunlight, provide the added benefit of slowing the rate at which the radiant energy of the sun degrades the fibers and colorants in treated fabric.

The amount of light transmitted through a window covering fabric is inversely related to its **opacity** or **level of openness**: increasing the opacity of the structure decreases the **level of light transmission**. In certain interiors, such as hospitals and similar facilities, coverings may need to be highly opaque to block most of the incident rays and provide **partial blackout**. In other interiors, such as rooms used for viewing films, the coverings must be fully closed or fully opaque, blocking all incident rays and providing **total blackout** (Figure 17.32).

Converters can increase the opacity of greige drapery fabrics with coatings and film sheetings. For total blackout, layers of acrylic foam coating may be spread over the surface or vinyl film sheeting may be bonded to a base

Figure 17.32 Blackout drapery lining.
Courtesy of Amy Willbanks, www.textilefabric.com.

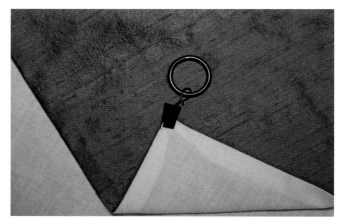

Figure 17.33 Roc-lon® lining sewn to the drapery fabric.
Courtesy of Nancy Oxford.

fabric. The vinyl component is frequently fashionably colored for greater aesthetic appeal. In many motel and hotel rooms, especially those operated by national chains, these multicomponent structures are the only window covering, functioning as both covering and lining and providing the necessary privacy and blackout.

Lining Fabrics

Lining fabrics may be sewn into draperies or hung as separate panels. Virtually all of these fabrics have a plain- or sateen-interlacing pattern, but a variety of surface appearance features and service-related properties are introduced by the use of finishing agents and processes.

Plain-woven Lining Fabrics

A great deal of lining fabric is produced from simple, single yarns of cotton combined in a plain-weave interlacing pattern. The greige goods are then finished in various operations, the first of which is bleaching. Silicone compounds may be applied for water-repellent performance. The silicone slows the rate of moisture absorption, minimizing the wetting of the fabric from moisture condensed on panes and frames and from rain that blows in when windows are inadvertently left open. It may also help to minimize the staining and streaking that can occur when moisture combines with smoke and oily cooking residues that have settled on the fabric; more effective protection against soiling and staining can be provided, however, by fluorocarbon compounds. Compressive shrinkage treatments may be employed to encourage relaxation shrinkage; chemical cross-linking resins may be used to improve appearance retention. Greige lining fabrics finished with some or all of these conversion processes are often mar-

keted with a registered trade name: an example is Roc-lon®, owned by the Roc-lon Corporation, Inc. (Figure 17.33).

Challis (*challie*) is a soft, drapable lining fabric produced from spun yarns of rayon or cotton fibers (Figure 17.34). During conversion, chemical cross-linking resins may be applied for improved resiliency, and fluorocarbon compounds may be added for water and soil repellency. Frequently, the manufactured cellulosic fibers are engineered to be flame resistant.

Sateen-woven Lining Fabric

Much of the fabric in separately hung drapery lining panels has been produced with the sateen weave. These **sateen linings** are composed of fine, combed cotton yarns, bleached to whiteness or piece dyed. Friction calender-

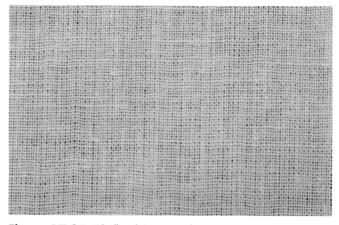

Figure 17.34 Challis plain-weave lining.
Courtesy of Amy Willbanks, www.textilefabric.com.

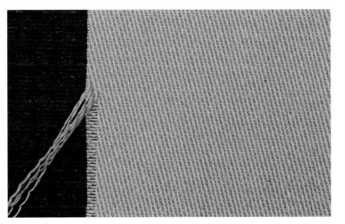

Figure 17.35 Warp sateen drapery.
Courtesy of Amy Willbanks, www.textilefabric.com.

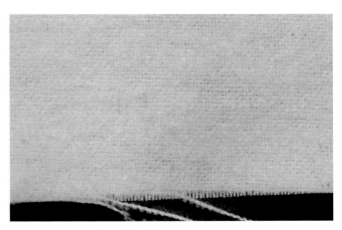

Figure 17.36 Flannel interlining.
Courtesy of Amy Willbanks, www.textilefabric.com.

ing or schreinering (see Chapter 9) may augment the soft luster produced by the floating yarns (Figure 17.35). At first glance, schreinered sateen lining may appear to have a fine twill interlacing: the "hills" suggest a visual diagonal. Close inspection, however, confirms the presence of floating filling yarns and proves the apparent diagonals to be three-dimensional protrusions of the fabric.

The luster that the floating filling yarns contribute to sateen will last until the yarns are ruptured. Cleaning processes, however, will eventually alter the reflective characteristics introduced by calendering and schreinering operations.

Interlining

Interlining is sandwiched between two fabrics of the window treatment. Placement can be between the face fabric and the lining or between two layers of face fabric. Cotton flannel interlining (Figure 17.36) will provide additional thermal and acoustical properties as well as fullness to the treatment.

English Bump is thicker than flannel interlining, adding more fullness and insulation to the window treatment.

Summary

Cotton fiber dominates the textile window coverings market; however, the market share of all manufactured fibers combined is almost equal to that of cotton. The fiber composition of curtains, draperies, and fabrics must be disclosed. This disclosure enables informed consumers and professionals to consider fiber properties in relationship to the planned end use. Besides textile yarns, such nontextile materials as wood, natural grasses, and plastic expand the assortment of window coverings available to today's residential and commercial consumer.

Primarily because window coverings do not have to withstand the same high level of abrasion as upholstered furniture coverings, window covering fabrics are manufactured using a more extensive variety of fabrication techniques. Some fabrics, especially those produced in stitch-knitting, stitch-bonding, weft insertion, and spunlacing operations, are relatively inexpensive, and their transparency and covering power is readily controlled.

Other curtain and drapery fabrics, including those produced by knotting, twisting, and surface figure weaving, display distinctive design features. Still other fabrics, such as those made in leno weaving and raschel stitching operations, exhibit a high degree of openness and dimensional stability and virtually no yarn slippage.

Drapery lining materials, whether permanently attached or separately hung, present a uniform appearance to outside viewers and reduce the negative effects of radiant energy on the fibers and colorants used in the decorative panels. They can also provide such functional benefits as insulation, noise reduction, and greater control of light transmission.

Key Terms

antique satin
batiste
Bedford cord
bengaline
birdseye piqué
blotch print
brocade
calico
canvas
challis
chintz
clipped dot or spot
corduroy
cretonne
damask
discharge print
dotted swiss
duck
Embroidered fabrics
etched-out or burnt-out print
eyelet
faille

fibrillation
gauze or theatrical gauze
insulative value
interlining
lace fabric
lampas
lappet weave
level of light transmission
level of openness
marquisette
monk's cloth
mosquito netting
net fabric
ninon
opacity
organdy
osnaburg
partial blackout
pigment print
plain or pinwale piqué
raschel stitching
ribcord

sateen linings
shantung
spunlacing
stitch-bonding
stitch-knitting
stuffer yarns
swivel weave
taffeta
tapestry
Textile Fiber Products Identification
   Act (TFPIA)
toile de Jouy prints
total blackout
unclipped dot or spot
velvet
velveteen
voile
waffle piqué
wales
warp print
weft insertion

Review Questions

1. What properties support the growing dominance of the noncellulosic fibers in the curtain and drapery markets?

2. Why has the use of glass fiber in curtains and draperies virtually ceased?

3. Explain the problems associated with the fibrillation of glass fibers.

4. What is "window wall paper"? Why is it used?

5. Why has the fiber content of such fabrics as batiste been shifted from 100 percent cotton to a blend of cotton and polyester?

6. Distinguish between voile and dotted swiss.

7. Examine examples of pinwale piqué, birdseye piqué, and waffle piqué. What are their similarities? Which one is reversible?

8. When should the floats be cut in dot or spot fabrics? When should they be left uncut?

9. Name three ways to manufacture dotted swiss. Which one is the least expensive technique? Which one is the most expensive?

10. Describe the features associated with lampases. Why would these fabrics be relatively expensive?

11. What is meant by "visual weight"? Why should it be considered with corduroy, velveteen, and velvet window coverings?

12. Distinguish between a blotch print and a discharge print.

13. What advantages does raschel stitching offer?

14. Explain the role of the filling or weft yarns in fabrics produced with weft insertion.

15. Differentiate between stitch-knitting and stitch-bonding.

16. Identify the advantages of foamed acrylic compounds applied to the back of drapery fabric.

17. Differentiate between total blackout and partial blackout.

18. Identify finishes commonly used with textile linings.

Evaluation and Maintenance of Finished Window Covering Fabrics

CHAPTER **EIGHTEEN**

■ **Laboratory tests conducted** on greige goods help to evaluate the potential quality of textile curtain, drapery, and lining fabrics. Reliable assessments of actual quality, however, must be based on tests conducted on the finished fabrics themselves. Results of these tests reflect the effects of the agents and processes used to transform the surface appearance of greige goods, improve performance, and minimize care requirements. Even though producers can make textile window coverings easier to care for, it is up to residential and commercial consumers to use a three-part maintenance program that will prolong the use-life of the fabric.

Manufacturers and converters evaluating the flame resistance of finished window covering fabrics often employ test methods developed by members of the National Fire Protection Association. When evaluating other performance characteristics, they often use the test methods and performance guidelines recommended by representatives of all segments of the window covering industry, as contained in ASTM D 3691 Standard Performance Specifications for Woven, Lace, and Knit Household Curtain and Drapery Fabrics. (See Table 18.1).

Standards for Physical Performance Properties

Because the satisfactory end-use performance of textile window covering fabrics depends on their physical performance, members of the industry set out performance guidelines for such characteristics as dimensional stability, distortion of yarn, and fabric strength in their recommended standard. Guidelines also concern the level of appearance retention that durable press curtain and drapery fabrics should exhibit.

Dimensional Stability
Dimensional stability is a critical performance property for textile window covering fabrics. Sagging and shrinking must be minimized to preserve the appearance and the usefulness of the treatments they compose. In swagged valances and such treatment styles as priscilla curtains and Austrian shades, sagging would destroy the balance of the laterally draping folds. In straight, free-hanging panels, sagging could cause the lower part of the fabric to stack on the floor. Sagging is more likely to occur in fabrics composed of conventional rayon (see Chapter 4), and in

fabrics of loose construction, especially when low-twist, spun yarns are involved or the yarns are variously angled, as in lace fabrics.

Shrinkage of the overdraperies in treatments having multiple layers could expose the lower edge of the curtains to the interior, and shrinkage of the lining panels could expose a portion of the overdraperies to the exterior. If the panels shrank, fabric transparency would be reduced and the tight closure that maintains an insulating layer of dead air between the covering and the glass might be destroyed.

Converters can use **compressive shrinkage processes** and **heat setting** operations to stabilize curtain and drapery greige goods. Laboratory tests can be used to evaluate the effectiveness of these treatments. Specimens of the stabilized fabric are prepared as illustrated in Figure 14.5 (p. 238), except they are larger and the inner markings are 18 inches apart. The specimens are laundered in accordance with AATCC 135 Dimensional Changes of Fabrics After Home Laundering, then they are dry cleaned in accordance with ASTM D 2724 Test Methods for Bonded, Fused, and Laminated Apparel Fabrics. As shown in Table 18.1, the performance guideline in ASTM D 3691 states that the fabrics should not change more than 3 percent in their lengthwise and crosswise dimensions after being laundered five times or dry cleaned three times.

Distortion of Yarn
Evaluating the propensity of yarns to shift or distort in such open curtain fabrics as voile, ninon, and marquisette is important. **Distortion of yarn** should also be examined in satin-woven fabrics with smooth yarns. The shifting or slipping of one set of yarns over the other produces areas having different levels of transparency (Figure 9.16, p. 151); in patterned coverings, a stain-like appearance may develop. ASTM D 1336 Test Method for Distortion of Yarn in Woven Fabrics measures the extent to which this unsightly characteristic occurs in woven curtain and drapery fabrics.

Test Specimens and Procedures
As directed in ASTM D 1336, five specimens are cut slightly larger than 4 inches by 8 inches, with their longer dimension parallel to the set of yarns having the greater resistance to shifting. The operator determines this direction by exerting a shearing motion on the fabric with the thumb and forefinger. After conditioning, a specimen is

Table 18.1 Performance Requirements for Woven, Lace, and Knit Household Curtain and Drapery Fabrics

Characteristic	Test Method Number	Requirements		
		Knit and Lace	**Sheer (woven)**	**Foam Back, Stitch Bonded, and Conventional Weights (woven)**
Breaking strength (load), CRT method, in both directions[e]	ASTM D5034	. . .	67 N (15 lbf), min	89 N (20 lbf), min
Bursting strength (ball burst)[a]	ASTM D3787	138 kPa (20 ibf/in.²), min	. . .	. . .
Tear strength (tongue tear), in both directions[e]	D2261	. . .	4.4 N (1 ibf), min	6.7 N (1.5 ibf), min
Dimensional change: After 5 launderings in both directions — After 3 dry cleanings in both directions	AATCC 135 or ASTM D2724	3.0% max 3.0% max	3.0% max 3.0% max	3.0% max 3.0% max
Distortion of yarn: 1-lbf load 2-lbf load	ASTM D1336	NA NA	2.54 mm (0.1 in.), max . . .	NA 2.54 mm(0.1 in.), max
Colorfastness	AATCC 61			
Laundering:				
Shade change		Class 4[c] min	Class 4[c] min	Class 4[c] min
Staining		Class 3[d] min	Class 3[d] min	Class 3[d] min
Dry Cleaning: Alteration in shade	AATCC 132	Class 4[c] min	Class 4[c] min	Class 4[c] min
Burnt gas fumes, 2 cycles: Alteration in shade After 1 refurbishing	AATCC 23	Class 4[c] min Class 4[c] min	Class 4[c] min Class 4[c] min	Class 4[c] min Class 4[c] min
Crocking: Dry Wet	AATCC 16	Class 4[e] min Class 3[e] min	Class 4[e] min Class 3[e] min	Class 4[e] min Class 3[e] min
Light (60 AATCC FU), xexon[e]	AATCC 16	Step 4[c] min	Step 4[c] min	Step 4[c] min
Ozone, 1 cycle	AATCC 129	Class 4[c] min	Class 4[c] min	Class 4[b] min
Fabric appearance	AATCC 124	DP 3.5[f] min	DP 3.0 min	DP 3.5 min
Retention of hand, character, and appearance	---*	No significant change	No significant change	No significant change
Durability of back coating	---**	No significant change	No significant change	No significant change
Flammability	---***		pass	pass

[a] There is more than one standard test method that can be used to measure breaking strength, bursting strength, tear strength, and lightfastness. These test methods cannot be used interchangeably since there may be no overall correlation between them.

[b] Class in colorfastness and 5A rating is based on a numerical scale of 5.0 for negligible color change, color transfer, or wrinkling to 1.0 for very severe color change, color transfer, or wrinkling. The numerical rating in Table 18.1 or higher is acceptable.

[c] AATCC Gray Scale for Color Change.

[d] AATCC Gray Scale for Staining.

[e] AATCC Chromatic Transference Scale.

[f] For durable-press fabrics only.

*No significant change in after laundering or dry cleaning.

**No evidence of cracking or peeling of back coating after laundering or dry cleaning.

***Shall be regulated by applicable government standards.

****No standard method available for determination.

Adapted, with permission from D3691/D3691M-09 Standard Performance Specification for Woven, Lace, and Knit Household Curtain and Drapery Fabrics, copyright ASTM International, 100 Barr Harbor Drive, West Conshohocken, PA 19428, www.astm.org. A copy of the complete standard may be obtained from ASTM International.

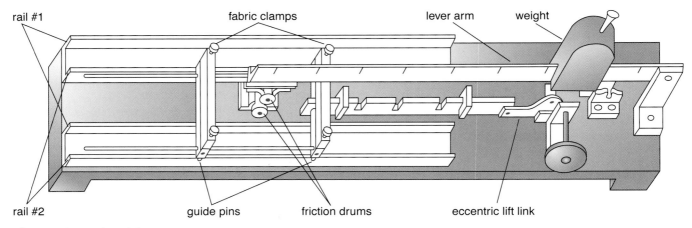

Figure 18.1 Fabric shift tester.
Reprinted, with permission, copyright American Society for Testing and Materials.

clamped into a rectangular carriage frame and placed between two frictional drums on the testing device (Figure 18.1). The weight of the upper drum is adjusted to provide a total force of one pound when sheer curtain fabrics are being tested and a total force of two pounds when conventional-weight woven fabrics are being tested. The carriage is then shifted so that the drums produce a shearing action on the specimen.

Analysis of Results

After the specimen has been removed from the carriage and allowed to relax for 15 minutes, the widest opening of each **shift mark,** or distorted yarn group, is measured

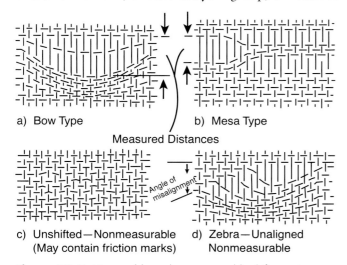

a) Bow Type   b) Mesa Type

Measured Distances

c) Unshifted—Nonmeasurable   d) Zebra—Unaligned
(May contain friction marks)   Nonmeasurable

Figure 18.2 Measurable and nonmeasurable shift openings. Adapted, with permission from D1336-07 Standard Test Method for Distortion of Yarn in Woven Fabrics, copyright ASTM International, 100 Barr Harbor Drive, West Conshohocken, PA 19428, www.astm.org. A copy of the complete standard may be obtained from ASTM International.

as shown in Figure 18.2a and b, Nonmeasurable openings, illustrated in Figure 18.2c and d, are described and reported. The average of the five measurements is calculated and reported.

Performance Guidelines

According to the performance specifications included in ASTM D 3691, sheer woven window coverings should exhibit a maximum distortion of 0.1 inch under a one-pound load, and conventional-weight woven coverings should exhibit the same maximum distortion, but under a two-pound load.

Fabric Strength

Performance guidelines for three types of fabric strength measurements are included in ASTM D 3691. Breaking strength and tear strength measurements are made with woven curtain and drapery fabrics; bursting strength measurements are made with knitted and knotted and twisted fabrics.

Breaking Strength

The **breaking strength (load)** of woven curtain and drapery fabrics may be evaluated in accordance with the procedures outlined in ASTM D 5034 Standard Test Method for Breaking and Elongation. This test method was described in Chapter 14. Sheer fabrics, such as batiste, dimity, ninon, and voile, should withstand a minimum load of 15 pounds before rupturing, and conventional-weight woven coverings should withstand a minimum load of 20 pounds.

Tear Strength

The **tear strength** of woven curtain and drapery fabrics may be evaluated as directed in ASTM D 2261 Test Method for Tearing Strength of Woven Fabrics by the Tongue (Single Rip) Method (Constant-Rate-of-Traverse Tensile Testing Machine). This procedure measures the force required to continue a tear in the specimens (see Chapter 14). Sheer curtain fabrics should require a force of at least 1 pound to propagate the tear, and conventional-weight woven fabrics should require at least 1.5 pounds.

Bursting Strength

Bursting strength measurements are made on woven or knitted fabrics. ASTM D 3787 Standard Test Method for Bursting Strength of Fabrics Constant-Rate-of-Traverse (CRT) Ball Burst Test is the specified test method.

In this test, a condition sample is secured under an O-shaped plate, one having an opening in the center. A force is exerted against the specimen by a hard steel ball. The test is completed when the ball bursts through the specimen. The maximum force required to burst each specimen is recorded. Knit fabrics should resist a minimum force of 20 pounds per square inch.

Durability of Back Coatings

A performance requirement for back coatings used on drapery fabrics is included in ASTM D 3691 Standard Performance Specifications for Woven, Lace, and Knit Household Curtain and Drapery Fabrics. The coating should exhibit no evidence of cracking or peeling when the fabric is subjected to prescribed laundering and dry cleaning tests.

Appearance Retention

Textile window coverings are repeatedly folded and bent as panels are opened and closed. They also are folded, bent, twisted, and crushed during cleaning. To help cur-

Figure 18.3 Three-dimensional plastic fabric replicas used to evaluate the appearance retention of durable press fabrics. Courtesy of the American Association of Textile Chemists and Colorists, photo courtesy of Amy Willbanks, www.textilefabric.com.

tain and drapery fabrics composed of cotton, linen, or rayon to recover from such treatment, converters apply chemical cross-linking or **durable press resins.** As long as treated fabrics retain their smooth appearance in use and care, ironing can be avoided.

Members of the industry have established recommended levels of performance for fabrics with a durable press finish. After specimens of the fabric have been laundered five times as directed in AATCC 124 Appearance of Fabrics After Repeated Home Laundering, their appearance is compared with that of three-dimensional plastic replicas (Figure 18.3). Smoothness progressively increases from the first to the fifth replica; each specimen is assigned the number of the replica it most closely resembles. Knit, lace, foam back, stitch bonded, and conventional-weight woven curtain and drapery fabrics should have an average minimum rating of 3.5, and woven sheer fabrics should have an average minimum rating of 3.0.

Evaluations of Colorfastness

Manufacturers and textile colorists use various testing procedures to ensure that colored interior and exterior window covering fabrics exhibit acceptable levels of fastness when exposed to potentially destructive conditions and substances. The test methods in ASTM D 3691 are used with textile coverings intended for use in residential interiors. The fastness guidelines set forth in the performance standard apply to household fabrics, but contract designers, architects, and other specifiers may refer to the recommended performance values when making decisions about fastness requirements in their commercial projects. Test methods other than those in ASTM D 3691 may be employed on textile fabrics for outdoor applications. Colorists should always discontinue the use of **fugitive colorants,** those found to exhibit an unacceptable level of fastness.

Colorfastness to Light

Although the **radiant energy** of all spectral rays—visible and invisible—can have a negative effect on textile colorants, ultraviolet waves have been shown to be particularly destructive. Because natural light has a higher quantity of these short waves than do artificial illuminants, concern for color retention is generally focused on the stability of textile colorants to sunlight. Such stability is critical in

colorants used in curtains and draperies, and in all textiles installed outdoors, in passive solar residences, and in commercial buildings with large expanses of glass. It is especially important in colorants for textile products installed in a southern exposure.

When solar rays strike a colored textile surface, the heat energy excites the dye molecules and gradually changes their chemical structure. Continued alteration of the molecular structure reduces the ability of the dyestuff to produce its original color characteristics. The textile develops a faded appearance: strong, bright, and pure hues become weak, dull, and grayed.

Several test methods have been developed for evaluating the effects of radiant energy, alone or in combination with moisture and heat, on the colorants used in textile products. Some methods are accelerated laboratory procedures; others are long-term outdoor tests.

Lightfastness of Interior Fabrics

Accelerated testing for **lightfastness** can be performed with the **Fade-Ometer®** (Figure 18.4), using one of two different lamps. A glass-enclosed carbon-arc lamp produces light energy throughout the visible spectrum and is a light source specified in AATCC 16 Colorfastness to

Figure 18.4 Interior view of the Fade-Ometer®.
The Atlas Ci3000+ Fade-Ometer® is courtesy of www.atlas-smts.com.

Light. Because this lamp is somewhat deficient in ultraviolet rays below 350 nm, its use is diminishing, and it is not recommended for use in evaluating textiles to be installed outdoors. A xenon-arc lamp more closely simulates natural light and gives a more accurate evaluation when correlating to end-use performance. This lamp is also specified in AATCC 16 Colorfastness to Light. This method is increasingly used for determining the lightfastness of window coverings intended for interior installation.

For testing with either light source, fabric specimens are mounted in holders, which are suspended in the apparatus and rotated for several hours. The number of hours of exposure (calculated as the **standard fading hours [SFH]**, or **standard fading units [SFU or FU]**) recommended for window coverings is 60.

After completion of an accelerated test, the color retention of the specimens is visually evaluated and numerically rated. The number is determined by comparing the difference observed between an original and exposed specimen with that observed between a pair of standard gray chips on the AATCC Gray Scale for Color Change, pictured in Figure 14.10 (p. 245). A minimum lightfastness rating of Step 4 is recommended for dyed and printed curtain and drapery fabrics produced for installation in residential interiors.

Lightfastness of Exterior Fabrics

A **Weather-Ometer®**, manufactured by Atlas Material Testing Technology, is used for the accelerated laboratory testing of textile fabrics to be installed outdoors. This unit effectively simulates the natural outdoor environment, since it facilitates temperature and humidity changes.

For extended outdoor testing, specimens may be fully exposed, or they may be mounted behind glass (Figure 18.5). Depending on the conditions anticipated in the end-use setting, the fabrics may be exposed continuously for 24 hours a day, placed in an enclosed cabinet to permit testing at elevated temperatures, or tested near the ocean for an analysis of the effects of salt atmosphere on the colorants.

Figure 18.5 Outdoor testing facility used to evaluate the effects of natural light on textile colorants. Courtesy of Atlas Material Testing Technology.

The level of color retention exhibited by exterior fabrics tested in the laboratory or outdoors may be rated on the basis of the AATCC Gray Scale for Color Change (Figure 14.10, p. 245). Because the exposure conditions may have degraded the fibers as well as the colorants, measurements are also often made to determine changes in such properties as strength and dimensional stability.

Colorfastness to Atmospheric Gases

The fastness of colored window coverings to controlled concentrations of gases, such as nitrogen dioxide (NO_2) and sulfur dioxide (SO_2), can be evaluated by following the procedures in AATCC 23 Colorfastness to Burnt Gas Fumes. This test method was described in Chapter 14. The apparatus used to expose the specimens is shown in Figure 14.11 (p. 246). Curtain and drapery specimens are exposed to **burnt gas fumes** and evaluated before and after one laundering or dry cleaning. The AATCC Gray Scale for Color Change is used to evaluate the amount of fading or color change, and a minimum Class 4 rating is recommended for acceptable performance.

The negative effects of ozone (O_3), a strong oxidizing agent, on colored window fabrics can be assessed through the procedures outlined in AATCC 129 Colorfastness to Ozone in the Atmosphere Under High Humidities. After one cycle of exposure, the specimens should have a minimum Class 4 rating when compared to the paired chips on the AATCC Gray Scale for Color Change.

Colorfastness to Crocking

Although **crocking**—the transfer of color from one material to another—is a more serious problem in upholstery fabrics, certain situations may lead to crocking problems in colored curtain and drapery fabrics. Color transfer may occur when fabrics rub together or are handled during shipping, sewing, hanging, opening, and closing.

The colorfastness of solid colors to dry and wet crocking is evaluated by the AATCC 8 Colorfastness to Crocking (Rubbing): AATCC Crockmeter Method. This method was described in Chapter 14; the apparatus used to rub the specimens is shown in Figure 14.8 (p. 244). For printed fabrics, the procedures in AATCC 116 Colorfastness to Crocking (Rubbing): Rotary Vertical Crockmeter Method should be followed.

After the test is completed, the **AATCC Chromatic Transference Scale** (Figure 18.6) is used to evaluate the

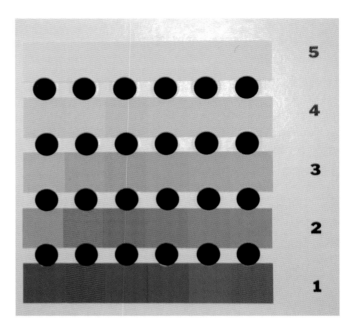

Figure 18.6 AATCC Chromatic Transference Scale. Courtesy of the American Association of Textile Chemists and Colorists. Photo courtesy of SDL Atlas.

amount of color transferred. The scale is a card with six colors (neutral gray, red, yellow, green, blue, and purple) mounted in each of four horizontal rows. In each of six vertical rows, the chroma or intensity of each hue is varied, beginning with an extremely light tint and ending with a moderately deep shade. The vertically aligned chips are separated by holes in the card.

For evaluation, the stained fabric is placed behind the card and visually examined through the holes. The observer shifts the card until the chroma or intensity of the stain is judged to be similar to that of a color chip, and the number of the row in which this chip is located is assigned to the fabric. Dry tests should yield a minimum rating of Class 4, wet tests a minimum rating of Class 3.

Colorfastness to Laundering and Dry Cleaning

When dyed and printed curtain and drapery fabrics are laundered or dry cleaned, the colorants should not exhibit unacceptable levels of **fading, bleeding,** or **migration.** A faded appearance may result when bleaching agents oxidize the colorants or when the dyestuff bleeds from the fabric. Excessive bleeding of the dyestuff into the cleaning solution may stain (in effect, dye) other articles in the load.

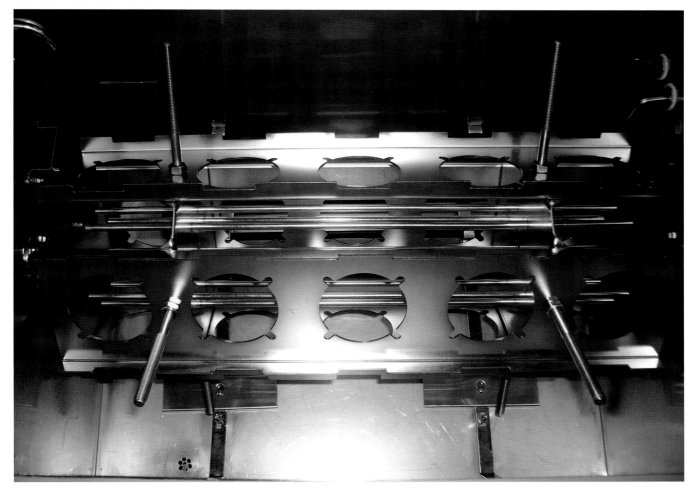

Figure 18.7 Interior view of the Launder-Ometer®.
Courtesy of SDL Atlas.

A stained appearance may also result when the dyestuff migrates or moves through the fabric. Product manufacturers and textile colorists use laboratory test methods to evaluate the potential for excessive fading and staining and to determine what type of cleaning agents should be used.

Accelerated testing for colorfastness to laundry and dry cleaning agents can be conducted with a **Launder-Ometer®** (Figure 18.7). This apparatus contains stainless steel jars to hold the specimens and the specified cleaning solution. During testing, the jars are rotated to simulate agitation. **Washfastness** evaluations are made following the procedures described in Test II A of AATCC 61 Colorfastness to Laundering: Accelerated. In this test, multifiber test fabric is paired with some specimens to facilitate evaluation of staining.

The effect of repeated dry cleaning is assessed by following the testing procedures outlined in AATCC 132 Colorfastness to Dry Cleaning. Unless otherwise noted on the label, launderable fabrics are assumed to be dry cleanable; thus, staining is not evaluated because migration and bleeding are not expected.

After completion of either testing procedure, the fabrics are evaluated for color change using the AATCC Gray Scale for Color Change; a rating of Class 4 is recommended for acceptable performance in end use. The multifiber test fabrics are evaluated for staining using the AATCC Gray Scale for Staining. A minimum rating of Class 3 is recommended.

Evaluations of Flame Resistance

Industry representatives included flammability guidelines in ASTM D 3691 Performance Specifications for Woven, Lace, and Knit Household Curtain and Drapery Fabric, but the Consumer Product Safety Commission has not established a flammability standard with which curtains and draperies must comply prior to their introduction into commerce. However, various regulatory agencies have set forth mandatory flammability standards for window coverings selected for use in certain commercial interiors. In many cases, these mandates are based on recommendations included in the NPFA 101® Life Safety Code® (Table 11.1, pp. 181, 182).[1]

NFPA 701 Standard Methods of Fire Tests for Flame Resistant Textiles and Films may be used to evaluate the effectiveness of polymer additives and finishing compounds in reducing the flammability of textile window coverings. Two test methods, both of which may be used to measure the ignition propensity of fabrics to be installed indoors or outdoors, are set out. These test methods, a small-scale and a large-scale procedure, are explained in detail in Chapter 11.

Maintenance of Window Covering Structures

By planning and following an appropriate maintenance program that includes **preventive, routine,** and **restorative** practices, residential and commercial consumers can effectively prolong the use-life of window treatments, especially those containing textile components. Manufacturers are not required to provide care instructions, but several voluntarily include them on their product labels. Such instructions are often based on the results of the colorfastness to laundering and dry cleaning tests described earlier in this chapter.

Preventive Maintenance Measures

Preventive maintenance techniques not only preserve the original appearance of window coverings, but may also reduce the weakening suffered by the fibers. Care should be taken to avoid allowing rainwater to blow in on linings and other fabric layers and to prevent panels from hanging in contact with framework on which water condenses. Water, including vapor-phase moisture, may combine

with soil present on the fibers and cause staining of the fabric. Water may also combine with pollutants and oily cooking fumes to form weak acids that attack and weaken the fibers (see Chapter 3). When gases and cooking fumes are present, especially in high concentrations, the coverings should be frequently cleaned to prevent accumulation of these acids.

An effort should be made to keep the level of relative humidity around coverings composed of conventional rayon fibers as constant as possible. This will avoid or minimize the development of the elevator effect, the sagging and shrinking problem described in Chapter 3.

Neither textile nor nontextile panels should be allowed to flap in the wind. This could result in tearing and abrading of textile fabrics, splitting and cracking of wood components, and bending of aluminum louvers.

Routine Care Practices

Textile fabric panels, especially those that are stationary or laterally draped, should be vacuumed or tumbled in an automatic dryer, using low heat or none at all, to remove airborne soil. This is especially important for coverings composed of hydrophobic fibers, whose tendency to build up electrical charges increases the fibers' attraction for airborne soil. The louvers and vanes in blinds and shutters and the surfaces of roller shades should be routinely vacuumed to remove accumulated dust.

Restorative Maintenance Procedures

Curtains and draperies are not included in the scope of the FTC trade regulation rule related to care labeling, but many producers elect to provide a cleaning code. Usually, the cleaning code letters for upholstery fabrics are used for curtains and draperies as well. These letters and their meanings were described in Chapter 14.

Unless specifically stated on the label or in literature accompanying glass fiber curtains, draperies, and fabrics, those products must not be dry cleaned or laundered in an automatic washer because the agitation promotes fibrillation. Because soil is held only on fiber surfaces and in yarn and fabric interstices, it may be removed by immersing the coverings in a bathtub or in a commercial cleaning tank filled with a detergent solution. After rinsing, the nearly dry panels should be rehung to dry.

Fabrics with a durable press finish may be laundered in an automatic washer. Strong oxidizing bleaches, such as chlorine compounds, should not be used. In high concentrations, these agents may be retained by the fibers, turning the fabric yellow and further weakening the cellulosic components. The laundered panels should be tumbled with low heat in an automatic dryer until dry, followed by a cool-down cycle and prompt removal.

Excessively high heat should not be used on any fiber. Recommended ironing temperatures are listed in Table 3.12 (p. 44). Unfortunately, consumers often find that iron dials are divided by fiber type or by finish, not by specific temperatures. Moreover, the same setting on different irons may produce quite different temperatures. Consumers and professional cleaners should be alert for signs of fiber and fabric damage. For fabrics composed of thermoplastic fibers, the slightest amount of fabric shrinkage and the slightest resistance of the soleplate to gliding are indications that the ironing temperature is too high.

Commercial and residential consumers may consider having their textile window coverings cleaned by a professional cleaner. This is advisable when long, heavy panels with multiple folds require large cleaning tanks and special pressing equipment. Frequently, laundry and dry cleaning firms offer removal and rehanging as optional services. Consumers can determine for themselves whether the value of these services overrides the burden of the additional charges.

Summary

As part of their quality-control work, producers and converters may subject curtain and drapery fabrics to prescribed laboratory test methods, measuring such properties as bursting strength, flame resistance, and appearance retention. The results of these tests can be compared with the performance guidelines established by members of the industry or the performance mandates of a regulatory agency. Different standards of performance have been set for fabrics with different construction features. If necessary, manufacturers may alter their choice of components or construction methods to improve the quality of their products.

Textile colorists may elect to evaluate the fastness of colorants used in interior and exterior window covering fabrics, following the procedures outlined in an accelerated or a long-term test method. Tests expose the colored fabrics to such conditions and substances as artificial light, natural light, atmospheric contaminants, and cleaning agents. The use of dyes and pigments that exhibit unacceptable levels of color retention in appropriate tests should be discontinued.

The original appearance and condition of curtain and drapery fabrics and other window covering structures can be well maintained by following a planned program. The program should include preventive measures, routine practices, and the use of appropriate procedures when restorative cleaning is needed. Frequently, producers voluntarily provide care instructions with textile window coverings.

Key Terms

AATCC Chromatic Transference Scale
bleeding
breaking strength (load)
burnt gas fumes
bursting strength
compressive shrinkage process
crocking
dimensional stability
distortion of yarn

durable press resins
Fade-Ometer®
fading
fugitive colorants
heat setting
Launder-Ometer®
lightfastness
migration
NFPA 701
preventive maintenance

radiant energy
restorative maintenance
routine maintenance
shift mark
standard fading hours (SFH)
standard fading units (SFU)
tear strength
washfastness
Weather-Ometer®

Review Questions

1. Identify dimensional stability problems that may occur with textile window coverings. Which conversion operations can minimize or prevent them?

2. Why should back coatings on textile fabrics be durable?

3. Identify conditions and substances that are harmful to colored textiles. Explain the changes that may occur in the color characteristics of the dyes or pigments.

4. Why has the use of carbon-arc lamps in lightfastness testing declined in recent years?

Note

1. Life Safety Code® and 101® are registered trademarks of the National Fire Protection Association, Inc., Quincy, Mass.

Textile and Nontextile Coverings for Walls and Panels

CHAPTER **NINETEEN**

■ **The walls of any interior** provide a large surface for interior designers to apply design elements and principles that are essential for successful completion of a design solution. Textiles and nontextiles are used in interiors to cover walls and panels to provide visual and tactile interest. In large, open interiors, textile fabrics often cover panels or partitions to absorb sound and define work areas (Figure 19.1). In some cases, acoustical panels may be wall mounted or suspended to baffle sound (Figure 19.2).

A variety of textile structures is produced exclusively for use on vertical surfaces. Many fabrics produced for use as window and upholstered furniture coverings, and several pile structures produced for use as soft floor coverings, can also be used as wall and panel coverings. Frequently, contract designers and consumers elect to coordinate similar fabrics to cover the walls, windows, and upholstered furniture in an interior.

Selection and Serviceability

Textile wallcoverings often serve primarily aesthetic or primarily functional purposes in an interior, but both purposes may be furthered if attention is given to certain selection and serviceability factors. In certain interiors, attention to the fire performance of the covering is regulated by codes. In other interiors, levels of sound transmission are suggested by standards to increase productivity.

Interior Enrichment

The coverings pictured in this chapter show how widely textile wallcoverings can differ in color styling, textural features, tactile characteristics, construction, and weight.

This wide assortment permits consumers and designers to select a covering that provides the ambiance and decorative impact they seek.

Because dyestuffs applied to different types of substrates inevitably show differences in color characteristics, a precise color match between fabric and paper is normally impossible to obtain. Consumers and designers can avoid a mismatch by having their upholstery or window fabric backed for application as a wallcovering, rather than installing coordinated wallpaper.

Functional Values

Textile wallcoverings may be selected to fulfill specific functional needs. They may, for example, provide some measure of acoustical control or of insulation.

Noise Reduction

Bare walls can reflect sound waves and prolong duration of noise (Figure 15.5, p. 259). Textile-covered interior panels or partitions placed throughout open areas interrupt the horizontal travel of sound waves; some of the sound generated within each enclosure can be contained this way. Textile coverings on permanent walls help reduce the amount of waves reflected back into the interior, as well as the amount transferred through the walls to adjoining rooms.

The acoustical benefits of textile structures used on vertical surfaces should be analyzed with testing equipment that can simulate the construction characteristics of the wall or partition and the technique for installing the covering. In one series of tests sponsored by the Carpet and Rug Institute, for example, various carpet specimens were

Figure 19.1 Office cubicle with fabric-covered panels. Courtesy of Cube Solutions®, www.cubesolutions.com.

Figure 19.2 Sound-absorbing vertical office panels. Courtesy of RUCKSTUHL AG, www.ruckstuhl.com.

mounted on standard wall constructions. One mounting system (Figure 19.3) places the face of the carpet approximately 2 inches from the structural wall, and accommodates approximately 1¼ inches of filler. The effectiveness of the coverings in reducing noise is numerically reported in terms of a **noise reduction coefficient (NRC)**; higher values indicate greater sound absorption.

When a loop pile carpet with a pile weight of 23 ounces per square yard and no backcoating was tested in this mounting, an NRC of 0.90 was recorded; when a cut-pile carpet having a pile weight of 44 ounces per square yard and having a backcoating was tested, an NRC of 0.70 was recorded. These results show that the structural features of textile coverings directly influence their acoustical properties. Thus, residential and commercial consumers should request actual test results from product manufacturers when selecting wall and panel coverings primarily for noise control.

Energy Conservation

Increasingly, residential and commercial consumers control heat transfer and reduce air infiltration by installing textile structures as interior wall finishes. As is true for acoustical evaluations, assessments of the insulative value of textile coverings must be conducted using a mounting that simulates the construction features of the structural walls and the techniques used to install the covering.

One technique that increases the insulative value of textile wallcovering installations is the application of a padding behind the fabric. The cost of the materials and labor incurred in installing these "upholstered walls" may be balanced against potential savings in energy charges.

Interior designers, architects, and specifiers must consult with representatives of the agency that has jurisdiction over a facility to ascertain whether the materials selected for the interior must meet noise or insulation criteria. They must also determine whether the materials are covered by flammability regulations.

Flammability Requirements

City, state, and federal agencies require that materials used inside certain occupancies conform to the requirements of the NFPA 101® Life Safety Code®. As detailed in Table 11.1 (pp. 181 and 182), material installed as an interior finish (in contrast to an interior floor finish) on building surfaces must exhibit a Class A, B, or C rating, depending upon the type of occupancy and area of installation. The ratings are determined by testing the coverings in accordance with the procedures outlined in ASTM E-84, which is equivalent to NFPA 255. This test method is described in Chapter 11.

Components and Constructions

Residential and light commercial textile wallcoverings are primarily expected to provide visual and tactile interest, and are subjected to few stresses in use. Thus, distinctive components and construction techniques are appropriate for them. Virtually all fabrics chosen for wall and panel coverings, however, carry some backing applied to impart dimensional stability and facilitate installation. Because wallcoverings in contract interiors are exposed to increased levels of abrasion, they are expected to be more durable and serviceable.

Fibers and Yarns

Natural fibers, including wool, silk, flax, jute, sisal, hemp, and cotton, are extensively and effectively used in wall and panel fabrics. Often, the inherent color variations of these fibers help stylists to design yarns and coverings with a warm and rich appearance. Stylists also capitalize on the natural surface irregularities of these fibers to produce distinctive textural characteristics. Such color and textural variations appear in the flax blend covering in Figure 19.4.

The high stiffness and low elasticity of flax limit its use in certain textile furnishings, but these properties contribute high dimensional stability to wallcoverings, helping to minimize sagging. When flame resistance is required by codes for contract interiors or desired in residential spaces, designers and architects can specify the application of flame-retardant compounds to fabrics composed

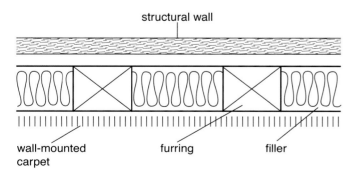

Figure 19.3 A wall sound absorption test.
Courtesy of the Carpet and Rug Institute.

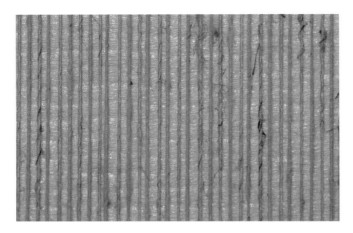

Figure 19.4 Laminated wallcovering enriched by the natural color and texture of cotton and flax yarns. Courtesy of Amy Willbanks, www.textilefabric.com.

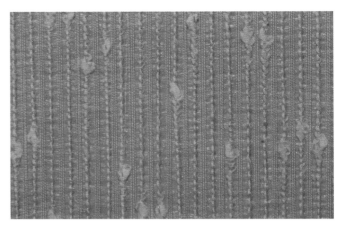

Figure 19.5 Novelty yarns increase the visual and textural interest of this wallcovering. Courtesy of Amy Willbanks, www.textilefabric.com.

of flax, cotton, or rayon, or they may elect to use wool or glass fibers.

To reduce the cost of coverings composed of some natural fibers, producers frequently blend them with viscose rayon. Although viscose rayon has poor dimensional stability, the use of a backing or coating can overcome the problem, and some coverings are composed entirely of this relatively inexpensive cellulose-based fiber.

Of the noncellulosic fibers, polypropylene (olefin) fibers have an extremely low specific gravity. They may be used to produce lightweight coverings resembling those composed of wool, flax, and silk. Recycled olefin and polyester textile wallcoverings are also available. Contract wallcovering manufacturers provide textile wallcoverings that meet indoor air quality and antimicrobial recommendations as well as flammability code requirements. Major contract textile wallcovering manufacturers include DesignTex, Maharam, Knoll, Carnegie, Eurotex, Wolf Gordon, and Ozite.

Simple and complex yarns are used alone or in combination. Placing the yarns individually in a parallel arrangement on a backing fabric often emphasizes the decorative effects of complex yarns. This technique highlights the varied features of the yarns (Figure 19.5).

Eye-catching reflections appear in wallcoverings when they incorporate bright manufactured fibers, silk, metal filaments, and metallic yarns. In some coverings, spiral yarns containing metallic strands are plied with simple yarns strategically positioned to create reflective highlights as viewers pass the wall.

Construction Techniques

Because wall and panel coverings are not subjected to significant levels of abrasion or repeated flexing, a great variety of coverings is available. The assortment of coverings offered to contemporary consumers includes a number of distinctively constructed fabrics, as well as fabrics produced by conventional weaving and knitting procedures. Wallcoverings for contract interiors are constructed to provide the increased durability and serviceability that are essential in high-use areas. Typically, vinyl coverings are chosen for contract interiors.

Weaving

Flat-woven wallcovering fabrics range from those produced with a simple biaxial interlacing pattern to those produced with a decorative dobby or Jacquard weave. The visual and tactile interest of these fabrics is often enhanced with flocking or embroidering (Figure 19.6). Woven pile fabrics, such as corduroy and velvet, and woven or tufted carpet are also available.

Frequently, fabric stylists design woven coverings with relatively low compactness of construction, so that the backings are visible. Figure 19.7 shows a plain-weave jute covering in which the backing can be viewed through the face fabric, and the visual interest of the surface is augmented. Figure 19.8 shows a jacquard-weave wallcovering.

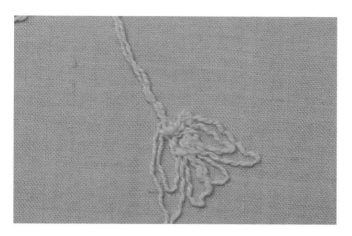

Figure 19.6 Embroidered wallcovering.
Courtesy of Amy Willbanks, www.textilefabric.com.

Figure 19.8 Jacquard-weave wallcovering.
Courtesy of Amy Willbanks, www.textilefabric.com.

Figure 19.7 Jute plain-weave wallcovering.
Courtesy of Amy Willbanks, www.textilefabric.com.

Figure 19.9 Woven wallcovering.
Courtesy of Amy Willbanks, www.textilefabric.com.

Knitting

For high-dimensional stability, most knitted wallcoverings are produced with a tricot or interlock stitch. Such fabrics readily conform to curved surfaces.

Needlepunching

Webs of fibers may be layered into a batt and stabilized by needlepunching (Figure 19.9). For increased visual and textural interest, the level surface may be punched or embossed to create a three-dimensional, patterned configuration. This alteration in fabric form may produce an appearance resembling that of more expensive woven pile fabrics. Such structural changes may also improve the acoustical value of the coverings, making them especially suitable for covering panels in open office interiors. Mea-

surement of the acoustical benefits of wall and panel coverings was discussed earlier in this chapter.

Laminating

Frequently, a single web or layer of textile yarns is laminated or glued directly to a paper base. In such structures, the parallel yarns may be closely or widely spaced, and the yarns may be fine or coarse, as in the laminated coverings in Figures 19.4 and 19.5.

Extruding

Vinyl wallcoverings are manufactured by extrusion. In many cases, they are subsequently embossed to simulate the textural effects of woven fabrics. There are three classes of vinyl wallcoverings. Type I vinyl wallcovering has a total face weight of 7 to 13 ounces per square yard and is used in residential or light-commercial interiors. Type II vinyl wallcovering has a total face weight of 15 to 22 ounces per square yard and is installed in medium-use contract applications. Type III vinyl wallcovering has a total face weight greater than 22 ounces per square yard and is used in high-service applications.

Backings and Finishes

Various backings and finishing agents are used with textile wall and panel fabrics. Some of these serve both functional and aesthetic purposes.

Sueding

Genuine suede and leather could be used to cover walls and panels, but such applications would be expensive. Manufacturers do, however, offer simulated coverings (Figure 19.10 and Figure 19.11). Not only is the materials cost of the simulated covering lower, but so is the potential for crocking when people inadvertently rub against the surfaces.

Backings

Acrylic foam, vinyl spray, paper, gypsum, or a spunlaced or spunbonded fabric must be applied to the back of most textile fabric coverings to prevent the application adhesive from striking through and producing a stained appearance and to provide dimensional stability. Spunbonded backings, normally composed of polypropylene olefin fibers, are designed to be strippable, a feature attractive to residents anticipating a change in coverings.

Gypsum, a high-density, uncrystallized plaster, may be used to coat the back of open-weave burlap wallcovering. When applied, the compound is soft, permitting the coverings to be rolled for shipment. After contact with the special adhesive that secures the fabric to the wall, the coating crystallizes and sets into a hard backing. The compound, available in numerous colors, fills fabric interstices and hides any surface defects.

Backings for vinyl wallcoverings are necessary for dimensional stability. The three backings used with vinyl wallcoverings are **scrim**, **osnaburg**, and **drill**. Scrim backings weigh an average of 1.2 ounces per square yard and are used with Type I wallcoverings. Osnaburg backings, which weigh an average of 2.0 ounces per square yard, are used with Type II wallcoverings. Drill fabrics weigh an average of 3.6 ounces per square yard and are used with Type III vinyl wallcoverings.

Functional Finishes

For increased safety in the event of fire, textile wall and panel coverings may be treated with a flame-retardant compound. The design professional is advised that these treatments may change such physical properties of the fabric as colorfastness, strength, dimensional stability, and hand. Additionally, the fabric may give off noxious fumes. To reduce the rate of soil accumulation and to protect the coverings from unsightly staining, fluorocarbon compounds may be applied. For maximum protection against soil accumulation, fingerprints, atmospheric contaminants, and general abuse, and to make the surface washable, textile wallcoverings may be laminated with a clear or translucent vinyl film. Over time, laminated fabrics may tend to yellow. This treatment, also used on upholstery fabric, was described in Chapter 14.

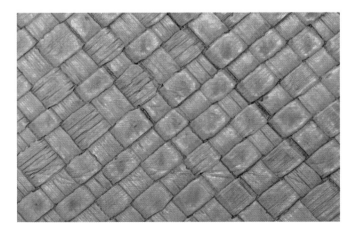

Figure 19.10 Simulated leather vinyl wallcovering.
Courtesy of Amy Willbanks, www.textilefabric.com.

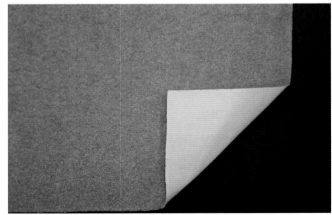

Figure 19.11 Simulated suede wallcovering.
Courtesy of Amy Willbanks, www.textilefabric.com.

Installation Techniques

Textile coverings are generally installed over structural wall surfaces with one of four techniques: shirring, stapling, adhesives, or premounted supports. Proper preparation of the substrate is important for the installation of both textile and nontextile wallcoverings to eliminate surface flaws from being seen.

Shirring

Shirring is a simple and inexpensive technique for covering walls with nonbacked textile fabrics. After yardage has been allowed for fullness and pattern matching, if necessary, the fabric widths are seamed and the top and bottom edges are finished with a casing. The casing may be plain or constructed with a heading (Figure 16.6a and b, p. 270). Conventional curtain rods are then inserted through the casings and positioned on the walls to support the shirred fabric.

Stapling

When the wall surface is smooth, the edges of textile fabric coverings may be stapled directly to the structural material. Seaming can be avoided by covering the joins with decorative tape or braid or with rigid molding. When the wall is rough and damaged, lath strips must be nailed first to the top, bottom, and sides of the wall and next to the framework of the doors and windows. After the fabric is stapled to the laths, decorative tape or braid may be glued over the edges to conceal the staples. Because the lath strips support the fabric a small distance from the wall surface, surface irregularities are concealed.

Using an Adhesive

Textile structures having a paper or foam backing may be handled in essentially the same manner as wallpaper is handled in the hanging procedure. With paper-backed textile structures, the adhesive is generally applied to the paper; with foam-backed structures, the adhesive is generally applied to the wall. With vinyl wallcoverings, the adhesive is generally applied to the vinyl prior to installation. Some lightweight vinyl wallcoverings are prepasted. The wallcovering is soaked in water for a few minutes to activate the adhesive.

Using Premounted Supports

As the use of textile structures on walls has increased, specialized mechanisms have been developed to add tension and support to the coverings. In one such system, the fabric is held in wall-mounted channels by locking clips. Another features loop and hook fasteners. The covering is backed with a soft fabric with tiny loops over its surface; the mounting strips have tiny hooks on their surfaces. Contact between the loops and hooks secures the fabric to the wall, and the raw edges are tucked into channels in the strips. Sewn seams are avoided by tucking the fabric edges into parallel panels built into double strips.

Summary

Webs of textile yarns and textile fabrics may be used as interior wall finishes for decorative purposes, noise reduction, and energy conservation. Professionals must confirm the acoustical and insulation values of the textiles prior to installation. Some coverings are composed of natural fibers with their inherent color characteristics; some are composed of manufactured fibers; and some contain metal filaments and metallic yarns. Most textile coverings for use on walls and panels are woven, knitted, needlepunched, or laminated. Paper or foam backings are applied to prevent strikethrough of an application adhesive and to provide dimensional stability. Vinyl structures are chosen for wall applications when durability and serviceability are of paramount importance.

A consumer may successfully execute some wallcovering installations, such as shirring and stapling. Other installations, however, should generally be left to a skilled professional.

Key Terms

drill	noise reduction coefficient (NRC)	scrim
gypsum	osnaburg	shirring

Review Questions

1. Discuss design elements and principles that are achieved with the use of textile wallcoverings.

2. List two functional characteristics of textile wallcoverings.

3. List the advantages of natural fibers for use in wallcoverings.

4. What is the purpose of backings for fabrics to be used as wallcoverings?

5. How is a three-dimensional patterned configuration achieved in needlepunching?

6. What are the three types of vinyl wallcovering?

7. What are the disadvantages of applying a flame-retardant finish to fabrics?

8. Over time, what tends to happen to fabrics that are laminated?

9. Discuss the three backings used on vinyl wallcoverings.

10. List four methods of installing textile wallcoverings.

UNIT THREE CASE STUDY

Project Type: Residence

Statement of the Project:

The newly constructed "garden house" needed textile accessories to complete the "romantic garden feel" that the client wanted. In order to soften the exposed wood of the house, textile window treatments and patio furniture with upholstered seat cushions were suggested.

The garden house is constructed like a gazebo; it has a roof that will provide some shelter from the elements. There are no walls, only a trellis panel to suggest a wall on one side, and three open sides. The house will be used for outside dinner parties, and for larger entertainments it may house a band or buffet table. The house that it complements is Tudor in design, probably constructed in the 1920s. The garden includes a reflecting pool with Japanese goldfish, and many types of English foliage, complete with a creek running through it. The new garden house needed to blend with the garden and be as comfortable as possible for the clients.

Statement of the Problem:

The fabric needed to withstand the elements year round, and be colorfast and mildew resistant. The furnishings also needed to maintain their original appearance for at least five years. Other considerations were the type of thread used to sew the hem in the drapery panels. The thread needed to be colorfast and not support mildew, like the fabric. The hem also had to be approximately 30 inches above finished floor (a.f.f.) in order to allow for possible flooding during the spring months. The drapery panels needed to be mounted on boards with stainless steel screws in order to prevent rusting.

Selection Criteria:

The recommendation was to use tailored drapery panels in each of the four corners of the space that would be tied back with a decorative tassel. The fabric recommended was an acrylic solid in a neutral shade of taupe. Chair cushions and settee cushions were recommended to complement the window treatments in a subtle print of taupe on créme. The cushions would then be snapped and tied to the chair seats. The style of chair was also chosen to replicate the trellis motif forming the back "wall."

Product Specifications:

SUNBRELLA®

- #8300 (solid taupe) and SUNBRELLA® #9305-01 (print)
- 100% solution-dyed acrylic fabric
- Width—54″
- Guarantee against mildew and fading
- Warranted for 5 years

Maintenance and Cost:

To reduce maintenance and accommodate the exterior application, the textile needed to resist mildew and fading. The manufacturer's recommended maintenance guidelines include spot washing with a sponge and warm, soapy water. Washing is to be followed by a thorough rinsing with clean water until soap is removed. After the fabric is rinsed, it should be air dried. Fabric spot remover is recommended for stubborn stains. While solution-dyed acrylic does not promote the growth of mildew, mildew may grow on other substances that are attached to the fabric. A solution of one cup bleach plus two capsfull of soap per gallon of water can be used to clean mildew. This solution should be sprayed on the entire area and allowed to penetrate. The fabric should be rinsed thoroughly and allowed to air dry. SUNBRELLA® is a midrange, affordable fabric with a five-year warranty that ensures a lower long-term cost for the product (Figure 4.45, p. 77). With proper maintenance and use the life-cycle of the fabric could extend to ten or fifteen years.

Discussion Questions

1. Identify two of the client's requirements for the design project.

2. Describe one of the aesthetic features that the client requires.

3. Distinguish one of the functional features of the product that meet the client's requirments.

4. Discuss specific features used to accommodate seasonal weather changes.

5. Discuss the importance of the solution-dyed fiber.

6. Research another product that is appropriate for this application. Next compare and contrast the cost effectiveness, availability, durability, and maintenance of the new product with the one used in the casestudy.

7. Assume you have found another fabric that is guaranteed for three years but is one-fifth the cost of the SUNBRELLA® fabric. Which one is more economical?

Soft Floor Coverings and Cushions

U NIT FOUR focuses on soft floor coverings and cushions. Chapter 20 offers a review of several variables affecting the selection of carpet, rugs, and cushions for residential and commercial interiors. In Chapter 21, statistical profiles detail fiber usage in today's soft floor coverings, and several fiber and yarn properties influencing floor covering performance are discussed. Chapter 22 explains tufting, the dominant carpet construction technique. Weaving and other machine techniques are examined in Chapter 23, and hand techniques are reviewed in Chapter 24.

The composition, construction, and performance properties of carpet and cushions are considered in Chapter 25. Chapter 26 summarizes procedures to measure functional characteristics and performance properties of carpet and cushion assemblies; it also identifies items included in carpet specification lists. Finally, the installation and maintenance of soft floor coverings is reviewed in Chapter 27.

CHAPTER TWENTY

Selection Criteria for Soft Floor Coverings

Appearance Features
Sizes and Shapes
Surface Texture
Surface Coloration

Serviceability Expectations
Functional Properties
Use-life Characteristics

Design and Performance Regulations

Cost Factors
Initial Purchase Price
Installation Charges
Maintenance Expenses
Life-cycle Costing

Environmental Considerations

Photo courtesy of InterfaceFlor® Commercial.

■ **Several of the selection** criteria discussed in Chapter 2 apply to the selection of soft floor coverings. Personal preference, professional recommendation, and anticipated in-use conditions and activities determine the nature and importance of these qualities. In some cases, certain design and performance characteristics are prescribed by regulatory agencies.

Soft floor coverings cannot be selected on the basis of appearance features alone. The built environment should be attractive, but it also must be safe and functional. Because the features of the combined carpet and cushion assembly influence the functional and safety characteristics of floor coverings, attention must be given to the structure and properties of both layers. Special attention should be given to the selection and installation of floor covering assemblies in locations frequented by people with physical or visual limitations. Interior floor finishes should not be hazardous barriers; they should help, not hinder, mobility.

As is true for any other consumer purchase, the total cost of a planned floor covering project must be affordable. The initial materials costs, the installation charges, and the long-term maintenance expenses must all be considered. In many cases, use-cost analyses, which reflect these financial variables, may show carpet and cushion assemblies to be more economical than other flooring materials.

The **Carpet and Rug Institute (CRI)** is the national trade association representing the carpet and rug industry. Membership consists of carpet manufacturers and suppliers to the industry of raw materials and services.

CRI provides information on:

- aesthetic, functional, and financial benefits of carpet
- carpet or rug selection process
- installation guidelines
- characteristics of fibers
- carpet construction
- carpet's role in indoor air quality and the environment
- daily maintenance and long-term care
- technical information
- health-related carpet issues
- sustainability issues

Appearance Features

Residential and commercial consumers have widely varying and constantly changing tastes in the size, shape, color, and texture of soft floor coverings. The visual impact and tactile interest of these features are primary concerns, but consideration must also be given to variables such as end-use lighting and yarn size if the planned appearance is to be realized, and to soiling if the appearance is to be retained. Anticipated traffic levels and safety concerns may preclude the choice of certain appearance features.

Sizes and Shapes

Some soft floor covering products, including rollgoods and modules, are designed to cover all of the floor space within an interior. Other products are designed to define a limited area, such as an entrance foyer or the space under a furniture grouping. The particular style chosen determines the method of installation. Generally speaking, a securely fastened or anchored floor covering is referred to as **carpet**, and a loosely laid structure is called a **rug**. The term **broadloom** is frequently used to identify rollgoods that are more than 54 inches wide. The term does not describe the method of construction, and it carries no implication about quality. In addition to standard 12-foot widths, some broadloom carpets are also available in 6-, 9-, and 15-foot widths.

Wall-to-Wall Carpet

Wall-to-wall carpet covers the entire floor space, baseboard to baseboard (Figure 20.1). As is true for other consumer purchases, certain compromises are inevitable when one style of floor covering is selected over another.

A wall-to-wall installation has some negative features:

- The initial cost is higher as more square yardage is required.
- Costs are incurred for installation.
- It must be cleaned in place.
- Repair of large damaged areas is difficult.
- It cannot be shifted to equalize traffic patterns and soiling.
- Extra yardage may be required for matching patterns.
- It is difficult to remove for relocation.

Figure 20.1 Wall-to-wall installation of rollgoods.
Courtesy of J&J/Invision.

On the other hand, a wall-to-wall installation has these positive features:

- It is securely anchored to prevent shifting.

- There are no loose edges to cause tripping.

- There is no "curb" effect for wheelchairs if low level pile is used.

- Potential for energy conservation is maximized.

- The room may appear larger.

- It can camouflage slightly worn or uneven floors.

- No special preparation of the floor is usually required.

- It may improve the resale value of a building.

Some manufacturers offer broadloom rollgoods with rug-like designs strategically placed. Such goods provide the appearance of a loose-laid rug, but can be securely attached to the floor, an advantage in high-traffic areas in commercial interiors.

Carpet Modules

Carpet modules are also known as squares or tiles, and are generally 18 or 36 inches square. Their use has been increasing, especially in commercial installations. Some are designed to be glued directly to the floor with a permanent or a releasable adhesive; others are manufactured to be extra heavy and stiff so that when they are free-laid, gravity holds them in place. When correctly installed, the surface has many of the same features as wall-to-wall carpet since the squares are laid across the entire floor space. The installation in Figure 20.2 illustrates the design flexibility offered by carpet modules.

Carpet modules have some limiting characteristics:

- Initial materials costs are high.
- Edge curl can occur with low-quality tiles.
- Butted joints can separate with improper installation.

They also offer some distinct advantages, especially when releasable or no adhesive is used:

- Loss of materials during installation is minimal.
- They are easily rotated to equalize traffic and soiling patterns.
- They may be replaced if damaged.
- They may be lifted for access to underfloor service trenches.

Room-Size Rugs

Room-size rugs are intended to be loose-laid, coming within 12 inches of each wall. **Room-fit rugs** are designed or cut to come to or within one or two inches of the walls. Either of these rugs can be cut to follow the contours of a room, with their raw edges finished by serging (machine overcasting), fringing, binding with twill-woven tape, or with a seam-sealing cement. Because these floor coverings can easily be rolled up for moving, they are especially attractive to people who rent and to those who anticipate frequent relocation.

Room-size rugs are often available in such standard sizes as 9 feet by 12 feet and 12 feet by 15 feet. Rugs have some negative features:

- They may have to be cut to fit an unconventional perimeter.

Figure 20.2 Carpet module installation
Courtesy of Bentley Prince Street.

- Cut edges require finishing.
- Unsecured edges may cause tripping.
- A "curb" effect may be presented to wheelchair drivers.

They also have some positive features:

- They are available in standard room sizes.
- No installation is required if standard size fits room contour.
- They are easily moved to a new location.
- They are highly decorative.

Runners

A **runner** is a long, narrow form of a room-fit rug installed in hallways and on stairs. Runners are normally 27 inches wide, cut to any length, and serged or fringed on the cut ends. On stairs, runners can be held in place with brass rods securely anchored at the back of the treads (Figure 27.6, p. 404).

A special form of runner is the **walk-off mat** used in entrance areas subjected to high traffic levels. These mats are intended to capture tracked-in dirt and grit, protecting the carpet from abrasion and apparent changes in color caused by such materials. For safety, walk-off mats should be heavy and stiff enough to prevent edge curl, which could cause tripping.

Area Rugs

The extensive range of sizes and shapes available in to-day's market can partly explain the rising popularity of **area rugs.** Whatever the spatial need, an area rug can be chosen to fill it (Figure 20.3). These floor coverings are available in such sizes as 27 inches by 54 inches, 4 feet by 6 feet, and 6 feet by 9 feet. There are square, round, oval, rectangular, octagonal, and free-form shapes; the rug may or may not have fringe. Coupled with the wide variety of constructions, fiber contents, textures, and colorations, these features can make for much design appeal. Some consumers and designers lay area rugs directly on smooth floors, especially on fine hardwood; others lay them over wall-to-wall carpet to define a furniture grouping or ac-centuate a living area; and still others hang them as deco-rative wall accents.

The selection of an area rug involves considering their drawbacks:

- They are hazardous to persons having limited vision or mobility.

Figure 20.3 Area rug used to define a furniture grouping. Photo courtesy of C.R. Laine Furniture, www.crlaine.com.

- They may shift or slide on smooth floors.
- They tend to "walk" off thick cushions and move on carpet.

However, area rugs are attractive:

- They come in an extensive variety of sizes, shapes, designs, and textures.
- No installation is required.
- They are easily moved.

Scatter Rugs

Scatter rugs are small rugs, often 2 feet by 3 feet or small-er. They are used in the home where traffic and soiling are concentrated, such as inside the entrance area and in front of sinks. Novelty scatter rugs serve as decorative ac-cents and are available in imaginative shapes ranging from a dog's paw print to an orange slice. These floor coverings are also relatively inexpensive. However, they are easily tripped over and they slide on smooth surfaces. Their use should be limited, especially when persons with visual or physical limitations use the interior.

Surface Texture

Besides their length and width, most textile floor cover-ings have a noticeable third dimension, that of depth, pro-duced by a pile or wear layer. Variations in the visual and tactile characteristics of pile layers depend on differences in pile sweep, pile height, pile thickness, pile construction density, and yarn twist, as well as whether the pile tufts have been cut.

Pile Sweep

Pile sweep is shown schematically in Figure 9.3 (p. 145). The greater the slant of the pile yarns, the more prominent the nap or lay of the pile layer. This feature determines the quantity of light a floor covering reflects, which increases as the angle decreases. Therefore, when pile floor cover-ings are installed, care must be taken that the nap goes in the same direction (see Chapter 27).

Pile Height

Pile height is the length of the pile tufts above the back-ing; the length of that part of the pile yarn incorporated in the backing is excluded. Pile height is normally report-ed in decimal form, and is routinely supplied to contract designers, architects, and others specifying floor covering variables. Pile heights typically range from 0.187 to 1.250 inches.

Pile Thickness

Pile thickness is the average thickness of the pile material above the backing. Because thickness measurements are made on finished floor coverings, they reflect any pile sweep introduced during conversion operations.

Pile Construction Density

Pile construction density is determined by the closeness of the pile tufts in the wear layer. A dense construction has closely spaced tufts; a sparse construction has widely spaced tufts (Figure 20.4). Density has a major influence on the surface appearance, texture retention, and wear-life of pile structures.

Consumers and professionals can make an eyeball evaluation of construction density by flexing a carpet or rug and judging how much backing is exposed, that is, how much the structure "grins" (Figure 20.5); lower densities produce broader smiles. Pile construction density and potential exposure of the backing are especially critical factors to examine when selecting carpet for installation on stairs.

Cut and Uncut Pile

The yarn loops in some soft floor coverings are cut, producing independent tufts. In other coverings, the loops are left uncut (Figure 20.4).

Yarn Twist

The level of twist used in pile yarns has a major influence on the appearance of soft floor coverings. Higher levels create well-defined yarn ends, and lower levels create flared tips (Figure 20.6). Differences in twist level are largely responsible for the appearance differences observed among one level cut pile surface textures (Figure 20.7a through f).

A brief outline will help to sort out the wide variety of textures available in pile floor coverings today. Differences among these surfaces are a result of variations in the textural characteristics described above.

I. One Level Cut Pile Styles
    A. Velour
    B. Plush
    C. Saxony

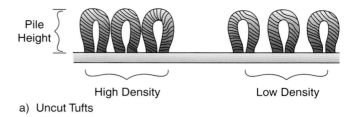

a) Uncut Tufts

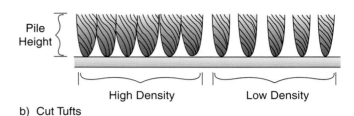

b) Cut Tufts

Figure 20.4 High and low pile construction densities. Illustration by Andrea Lau.

    D. Friezé
    E. Shag
    F. Tip Shear
  II. One Level Loop Pile Styles
 III. Multilevel Loop Pile Styles
 IV. Multilevel Cut and Loop Pile Styles
    A. Sculptured
    B. High-low
    C. Random Shear

One Level Cut Pile Styles

Several cut pile styles have a uniform level across their surfaces. These styles differ among themselves in pile height, pile density, and yarn construction, however.

Velour surfaces are fine, short, dense constructions for soft floor coverings (Figure 20.7a). Their production has been made possible by the development of machinery and fabrication processes that can yield high pile construction densities, for example, fusion bonding. High density allows pile height to be decreased without diminishing the important variable of pile yarn weight (see Chapter 22). Velour surfaces normally have a pile height of 0.25 inch.

The pile yarns in **plush**, also called **velvet** and **velvet plush**, surfaces (Figure 20.7b) range in height from 0.625 to 0.750 inch. The pile yarns have relatively low levels of

a) 20-ounce carpet

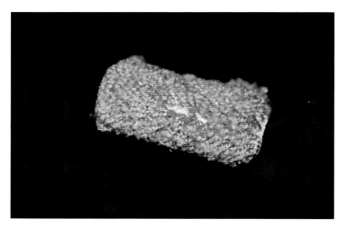

b) 30-ounce carpet

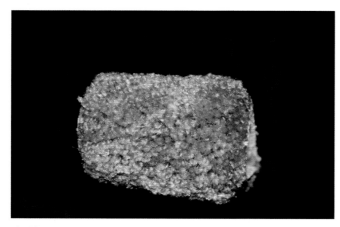

c) 51-ounce carpet

Figure 20.5 Eyeball evaluation of pile construction. Courtesy of Amy Willbanks, www.textilefabric.com.

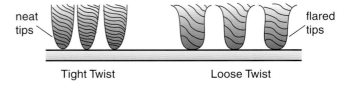

Figure 20.6 Effect of twist level on the appearance of pile yarns. Illustration by Andrea Lau.

twist: the cut yarn ends blend together for a luxurious, velvet-like look and feel. In use, these textures exhibit shading effects when the orientation of the pile yarns is physically changed. When occasional foot traffic or vacuum cleaning alters the direction of the pile yarns, the effect is normally temporary; the yarns gradually recover their original positions. In areas where directional traffic patterns cross or where pivoting action is common, the pile layer will be repeatedly crushed in opposing directions, and the effect may be permanent. In such areas, a darker area may appear as an irregularly shaped circle, somewhat like a large stain: the pile yarns are oriented in one direction inside and outside of the circle, and in the reverse direction along the outline. This appearance problem is variously described as **pile reversal, watermarking, shading,** and **pooling.**

Saxony textures (Figure 20.7c) have approximately the same pile height and density as that seen in plush. However, saxony yarns have a higher twist level that is heat-stabilized to reduce the amount of flaring at the tips of the cut yarns. Rather than blending together in a continuous surface, each yarn end is well defined, and the set twist minimizes splaying and improves thickness retention. Apparently, the improved yarn stability and resiliency exhibited by saxony textures have increased their popularity.

Friezé textures, also known as twist textures, are constructed of yarns having maximum twist for high stability and wear-life. Each yarn is clearly visible, since the high twist defines each yarn and encourages it to seek its own direction of orientation in the lower density pile (Figure 20.7d).

The height of pile yarns in **shag** surface (Figure 20.7e) goes up to approximately 1.250 inches. The pile density is lower than that in plush and saxony textures; the longer pile yarns are responsible for covering the backing.

Tip shear surfaces are produced by selectively shearing the uppermost portion of some yarn loops (Figure 20.7f). Subtle differences in luster appear because more light is reflected from the smooth loops than from the sheared fibers. Frequently, low pile, densely constructed floor coverings are sheared to camouflage future soil accumulation.

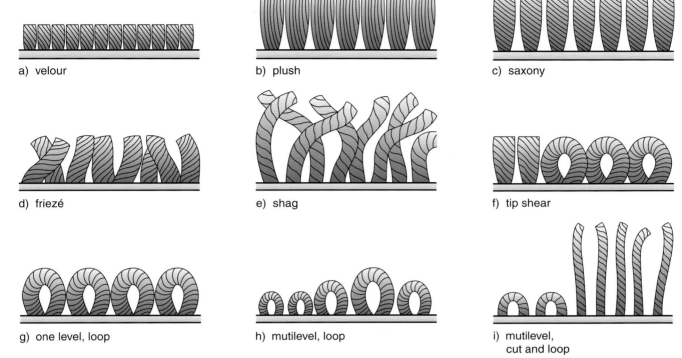

a) velour

b) plush

c) saxony

d) friezé

e) shag

f) tip shear

g) one level, loop

h) mutilevel, loop

i) mutilevel, cut and loop

Figure 20.7 Surface textures of contemporary pile floor coverings. Illustration by Andrea Lau.

One Level Loop Pile Styles

In the past, carpet with a short, level loop pile (Figure 20.7g) was normally seen only in such commercial settings as restaurants, airport terminals, and hospitals. Many professionals and consumers thought this surface had an "institutional" appearance. Today, improved color styling and yarn texturing have helped to make the uniform surface more appealing (Figure 20.8), and residential use of this durable, wear-resistant surface has increased.

Multilevel Loop Pile Styles

Multilevel loop pile styles show noticeable differences in the height of their pile yarns (Figure 20.7h). The variations may be random or planned to create a pattern. These surfaces are quite durable if density is reasonably high (Figure 20.9).

Multilevel Cut and Loop Pile Styles

Combining cut loops, uncut loops, and multiple pile heights (Figure 20.7i) produces various surface constructions (Figure 20.10). These include sculptured, high-low, and random shear textures.

Sculptured pile surfaces (Figure 20.11) have a definite three-dimensional appearance. In most cases, the higher loops are all cut and the lower loops all uncut for an embossed effect. Normally, the cut pile areas are dominant, and the visual impact is strong and formal. The exquisite texture of some custom floor coverings is produced by hand or machine carving dense, cut pile surfaces. Designs are created by using shears that cut (carve) the pile on a bevel to produce variations in the carpet pile height. Inlaid carved designs utilize two or more pieces of carpet, textures, and sizes, into a desired pattern (Figure 20.12). Bas relief is a carving process where entire areas of fiber are removed or lowered from the carpet face to produce designs that exhibit dramatic shadows.

High-low is the name given to some multilevel cut and loop styles with an informal appearance. Sometimes, the higher tufts have the appearance of shag textures.

Random shear textures differ from tip shear textures because they contain multiple levels of pile yarns instead of a single level. They differ from sculptured surfaces in that the uppermost portions of some of the higher yarn tufts are sheared, not all of them as in sculptured coverings.

Surface Coloration

Soft floor coverings may or may not dominate the aesthetics of an interior. A carpet or rug may have a subdued, solid-colored surface and serve as a backdrop for other more

Figure 20.8 Level-loop pile.
Courtesy of Amy Willbanks, www.textilefabric.com.

Figure 20.9 Multilevel-loop pile.
Courtesy of Amy Willbanks, www.textilefabric.com.

Figure 20.10 Cut and uncut pile.
Courtesy of Amy Willbanks, www.textilefabric.com.

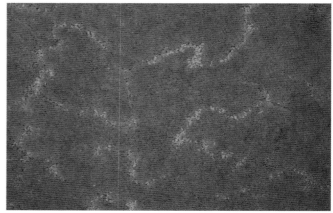

Figure 20.11 Sculptured pile.
Courtesy of Amy Willbanks, www.textilefabric.com.

distinctive furnishings; or it may have detailed designs or bold graphic colorations whose strong visual impact attracts attention. Residential consumers are generally free to choose color stylings that please them; contract designers and architects may be limited by the preferences of their clients, but they are able to use their professional training to recommend colorations. Whoever chooses the color styling, the possible effects of end-use conditions and activities on the color must be anticipated.

Color Styling

The color styling of soft floor coverings ranges from solid-colored surfaces in dark, deep hues to finely detailed designs in light, intense hues. Preferences for various color characteristics and styles in carpet and rugs fluctuate in the same cycles that hold for other fashion merchandise, such as apparel and cars.

Solid-colored surfaces can be produced in any combination of color characteristics preferred by the professional or consumer. Distinctive multicolored stylings are produced with heather, Berber, space-dyed, and moresque yarns. Authentic **Berber yarns,** a type of speck yarn hand spun by peoples of northern Africa, contain the deep, rich browns and grays of the wool retrieved from the sheep. Simulated Berber yarns (Figure 20.13) are produced by blending dyed, staple-length acrylic, olefin, and/or nylon fibers.

Carpets composed of space-dyed pile yarns are shown in Figures 20.14 and Figure 8.7b, p. 128. The varied coloration adds visual interest; its potential effectiveness for masking the appearance of soil and stains is apparent. Other multicolored effects can be produced with operations such as TAK and gum printing, described in Chapter 8.

Figure 20.12 Carved pile.
Courtesy of Amy Willbanks, www.textilefabric.com.

Figure 20.13 Simulated Berber yarn.
Courtesy of Amy Willbanks, www.textilefabric.com.

Patterned floor coverings may have designs created with colored fibers and yarns during construction or printed on the greige rollgoods. The almost infinite variety of patterns and colors available in stock lines can be expanded by custom design and color work. Some commercial carpet producers, in fact, maintain an inventory of floor coverings in a range of neutral colors, so that contract designers and architects can order the addition of distinctive motifs in specific colors.

Factors Affecting Apparent Color
The various conditions and activities that may affect the surface color should affect the choice of a soft floor covering. (Factors affecting apparent color were discussed in Chapter 8; those affecting actual color are identified in Chapter 26.) Special attention should be given to the potential effects of soiling on the apparent surface color. For interiors where there will be low traffic and minimal spillage, such as formal living rooms and executive conference rooms, relatively light, solid colored carpet may be serviceable. For locations where the covering will undergo much spillage and tracked-in dirt, a darker, multicolored surface may be called for to mask the appearance of soil. Tweeds, space-dyed yarns, and small, repetitive motifs may be effective. In some locations, it may even be advisable to coordinate the carpet color with the color of the soil in the area.

When heavy traffic is anticipated, consumers and professionals should select floor coverings whose components and construction features will encourage pile retention and provide abrasion resistance. This can help to minimize the development of a patchy surface luster in use.

Figure 20.14 Level-loop pile with space-dyed color styling.
Courtesy of Amy Willbanks, www.textilefabric.com.

Serviceability Expectations

Service-related considerations influence the selection of soft floor coverings. Some of these concern the functional benefits carpet and rugs can contribute, and others, their use-life characteristics.

Functional Properties
Many residential and commercial consumers seek to camouflage structural defects, reduce noise, or conserve energy with soft floor coverings. They may also be looking for improved safety and mobility for people with visual or physical limitations.

Camouflage Worn and Uneven Floors
An increase in building materials costs, and, at times, mortgage interest rates, has encouraged many people to

renovate and refurbish older structures. Such structures may be sound but have worn or uneven floors. Installing a carpet and cushion assembly can help to fill uneven spaces and hide damaged floor areas. This approach may be particularly effective when a multilevel loop surface texture is chosen. This property of soft floor coverings is both functional and aesthetic.

Add Comfort and Reduce Fatigue

The comfort provided by soft floor coverings might also be deemed an aesthetic and functional quality. The tactile pleasure of stepping onto a deep pile, cushioned surface is clear in contrast to the lack of give characteristic of such smooth, hard, nonresilient surfaces as slate and quarry tiles.

The compressibility of textile floor coverings enables them to absorb and cushion the impact forces of walking. For people who spend the major portion of the working day on their feet—homemakers, nurses, production managers and technicians, waiters and waitresses, bank tellers, and sales personnel—the cushioning effect of carpet can be critically important. It may lessen orthopedic problems, reduce fatigue, and increase productivity.

Increase Safety

The compressibility of soft floor coverings contributes comfort; it also is responsible for increasing the margin of safety. When falls are cushioned, the severity of injury may be reduced. This criterion is especially important to the selection of carpet and rugs for use in interiors where older persons work or reside.

Textile floor coverings may reduce the frequency of falling. They provide a slip-resistant surface for better footing, and they do not have the "slippery when wet" problem characteristic of some hard, polished floorings.

Improve Interiors for People with Disabilities

Textile floor coverings can be useful for people with mobility and sight impairments while enriching the interior space with their warmth and beauty of color and texture. Careful attention must be given to their selection and installation, however, to ensure that they do not become barriers. The Veterans' Administration has made recommendations for the design of residences for use by veterans with physical disabilities: "Low pile, high density carpet may be installed in any appropriate location. In addition to its aesthetic qualities, carpet greatly reduces sound transmission and serves to cushion accidental falls."[1]

Soft floor coverings can provide a slip-resistant surface for persons using canes and crutches. Slip resistance is especially critical for swing-through movement, when body weight is transferred to the crutches. All carpet and rug edges must be securely attached to the floor to prevent tripping and to minimize the movement of the carpet surface under force.

Recommendations regarding textile flooring for the elderly are similar to those listed by the Veteran's Administration. The tendency to shuffle their feet rather that lift them when walking make the elderly more susceptible to falls where thick, plush carpeting installed over thick padding is used. The sensation is similar to that of walking in wet sand and can intensify balance difficulties. The presence of rug edges also poses a potential tripping hazard for this group of users.

Wheelchair users need soft floor coverings with a low pile so that no curb effect is created. Pile should be dense and minimally compressible, allowing for easy movement of the chair over the surface. Shaggy, loose constructions tend to entrap the wheels and restrict forward movement. Cushions may be separate and thin, permanently attached to the carpet back, or not used. Shearing, the movement of the carpet and cushion in opposite directions, can occur when the chair is driven over the surface. Shearing can be avoided, and warping or rippling can be minimized, by gluing the carpet directly to the floor.

For people who are blind or have limited sight, certain carpet and rug features can provide cues for increased orientation and mobility. Orientation skills and cues help persons with diminished sight to identify their location within an environment; mobility skills and cues enable them to travel through the space. Total or partial loss of vision does not result in a more acute sense of smell or touch, or more sensitive hearing; but persons with impaired vision become more aware of their other senses and more perceptive with them. Patterns of variance in the texture underfoot may aid in orientation, helping the person to feel where he or she is within the interior. The surfaces must have marked textural differences if they are to be detected; an example would be carpet alternated with a smooth flooring such as tile or linoleum. Different surfaces can also provide auditory cues. The edges of carpet and rugs can serve as a physical guide for the visually impaired.

Carpet and rug surfaces lack any capacity for the glare and bright reflections characteristic of highly polished smooth surfaces, which are troublesome to persons with a visual limitation. With the visually impaired, depth perception can be problematic, particularly in discerning the tread and risers of stairs. The texture and color of soft flooring, coupled with strong directional lighting, should show marked value differences between the horizontal surface of the tread and the vertical surface of the riser. Patterned carpeting may be disorienting to the visually impaired.

Before modifying any environment for use by people of limited sight or mobility, their advice and counsel should be sought.

Reduce Noise

Noise abatement is often one of the more important functions of floor coverings and cushions. This is especially useful in such interiors as classrooms and conference rooms, music recording studios, open offices, and healthcare facilities. Along with the tests used to measure the acoustical values of carpet, alone and in combination with cushions, various factors influencing this property are identified in Chapter 26.

Conserve Energy

Extensive research has shown that certain structural features of carpet and cushions increase thermal resistance (see Chapter 26). Research has also shown that certain appearance features can increase light reflectance, decreasing the quantity of light needed from artificial illuminants. Studies have also shown than people may "feel" warmer in a room having carpet than in one without, thus enabling the temperature to be lowered without affecting comfort.

Use-life Characteristics

When selecting one of today's textile floor coverings, consumers and professionals should focus their attention on the variables that govern appearance or newness retention, retention of the original color and texture. Fortunately, minimal attention can be given to questions of wear caused by abrasion: the loss of significant amounts of fiber as a result of abrasive wear has largely been overcome by the use of nylon and improved processing.

If rapid changes in appearance are to be avoided or minimized, the fiber properties, yarn characteristics, and construction features of soft floor coverings must be chosen in light of anticipated end-use conditions. Traffic conditions, for example, vary for different interior locations. High levels of traffic are normally expected in such areas as

corridors and lobbies, and low levels in such spaces as executive offices and rooms within apartments (Table 20.1).

In most cases, a soft covering intended for use in areas of little traffic would not be serviceable where traffic is heavy. Early replacement, accompanied by annoying dislocation, interruption of normal activities, and a second outlay of money and time, would be necessary. Conversely, selecting a carpet engineered for use in a commercial corridor for installation in a residential interior may entail a higher initial investment than necessary. It may also require postponement of the inevitable redecorating desired when tastes and styling preferences change. Quality control and performance evaluations, a routine part of the production efforts of industry firms, provide assistance in making suitability decisions. Testing enables producers to label their products with specific performance data and recommendations pertaining to installations, for instance, whether the products are suitable for low-traffic, residential interiors or for high traffic, commercial interiors (see Chapter 26).

Multicolored surfaces may camouflage accumulated soil. But if large amounts of soil are anticipated, consideration should also be given to the selection of fibers engineered to hide, repel, or shed soil (see Chapter 4) and finishes designed to repel soil and minimize staining (see Chapter 9).

Design and Performance Regulations

Various local, state, and federal regulatory agencies have established regulations pertaining to the design and performance of textile floor coverings selected for use in certain commercial interiors (see Chapter 2). Laws pertain to such structural characteristics as pile height and pile construction density and such functional properties as noise reduction, as well as to flammability.

Specific regulations must be followed when selecting and installing carpet and rugs in interiors mandated by congressional action to be accessible and usable by persons with disabilities. The Architectural Barriers Act of 1968 requires certain federally owned, leased, or funded buildings and facilities to be accessible to people of limited mobility. Coming under the scope of the act are such structures as U.S. post offices, federally assisted housing units, several military facilities, and federal government

Table 20.1 Traffic Ratings for Selected Interior Spaces

L-M denotes light-medium traffic; H denotes heavy traffic.

Area (by Major Category)	Traffic Rating	Area (by Major Category)	Traffic Rating
Educational		**Commercial**	
Schools and colleges		*Banks*	
administration	L-M	executive	L-M
classroom	H	lobby	H
dormitory	H	teller windows	H
corridor	H*	corridors	H*
cafeteria	H	*Retail establishments*	
libraries	L-M	aisle	H*
Museums and art galleries		check-out	H
display room	H	sales counter	H
executive	L-M	smaller boutiques, etc.	H
lobby	H	window and display area	L-M
		Office buildings	
Medical		executive	L-M
Health care		clerical	H
executive	L-M	corridor	H*
patient's room	H	cafeteria	H
lounge	H	*Supermarkets*	H
nurses station	H	*Food services*	H
corridor	H*		
lobby	H	**Recreational**	
		Recreational areas	
Multi-residential		clubhouse	H
Apartments, hotels and motels		locker room	H
lobby/public areas	H*	swimming pool	H
corridors	H	recreational vehicles	H
rooms	L-M	boats	H
		Theaters and stadiums	H
Religious		*(indoors)*	H
Churches/temples		*Convention Centers*	
worship	L-M	auditorium	H
meeting room	H	corridor	H*
lobby	H	lobby	H

*If objects are to be rolled over an area of carpet, the carpet should be of maximum density to provide minimum resistance to rollers. For safety, select only level loop or low, level dense cut pile.

buildings. Enforcement of the standards set forth in the act is under the jurisdiction of the Architectural and Transportation Barriers Compliance Board (ATBCB). This board was created under section 502 of the Rehabili-

tation Act of 1973; subsequent amendments expanded its work to include responsibility for establishing minimum guidelines and requirements for accessible designs. The Department of Defense, the Department of Housing and

Urban Development, the U.S. Postal Service, and the General Services Administration must establish guidelines consistent with those prescribed by the ATBCB.

A revised edition of the ATBCB Minimum Guidelines for Accessible Design, which became effective on September 3, 1982, includes specific provisions governing the selection and installation of carpet and carpet tiles. Several of these provisions are based on the specifications developed by the American National Standards Institute. Among other things, ATBCB requires that carpet tile used on an accessible ground or floor surface have a maximum combined thickness of pile, cushion, and backing height of 0.5 inch. If carpet is used, then it should also meet this requirement, but in no case shall the pile height exceed 0.5 inch.[2] (Recall that pile sweep can reduce the thickness of a pile layer without affecting pile height.)

The 1990 Americans with Disabilities Act (ADA) contains accessibility design guidelines for new and existing construction. Issued by the Department of Justice, these ADA Standards for Accessible Design may be found in Title III Regulations: Code of Federal Regulations 28 CFR Part 36.

Cost Factors

Three basic elements of cost must be considered when selecting and specifying soft floor covering assemblies: the initial purchase price, installation charges (including floor preparation and removal of any existing carpet), and maintenance expenses. For the purpose of comparing various types of carpet, cushions, and hard-surfaced floorings, the total use-cost or life-cycle cost of each should be amortized according to its life expectancy. In this way, the important impact of maintenance expenses and the length of the product's use-life are taken into account.

Initial Purchase Price

The purchase price of carpet and cushion materials is normally given in dollars per square yard, although square foot prices are becoming popular. Residential and commercial consumers must confirm whether the quoted price is for the carpet only, the cushion only, or for the assembly. Labor costs must also be considered. Of course, the dollar figure must be multiplied by the number of square yards required, including any extra amount that may be needed for matching pattern repeats and for fitting and trimming (see Chapter 27).

Installation Charges

A number of cost variables are involved in installation. The cost of site preparation should be detailed: there may be per-square-yard charges assessed for removing the existing floor covering, for filling cracks and smoothing rough areas, and for reducing the amount of moisture and alkaline concentration, if necessary. Charges for installing the new carpet may be separate from those for installing the new cushion.

Maintenance Expenses

The cost of maintaining a flooring material at an attractive level of appearance is a critical factor in commercial installations. The major cleaning expense is generally the cost of labor; thus, the more time required for maintaining a flooring material, the greater will be maintenance costs. Other maintenance expenses include the purchase and repair of equipment and the continual replacement costs of expendable cleaning supplies.

The results of an investigative project sponsored by the Carpet and Rug Institute showed that the annual amortized cost (initial cost per square foot of the material divided by years of life expectancy) of purchasing and installing reinforced vinyl tile is significantly less than that of carpet, sheet vinyl, and terrazzo. When maintenance expenses were considered, however, the annual amortized life cycle or use-cost of carpet was significantly less than that of other flooring materials.[3]

Life-cycle Costing

Several producers of commercial carpet have established **life-cycle costing** programs. A life-cycle cost analysis compiles materials, installation, and maintenance costs. Such figures are prepared for each flooring material being considered by the designer or architect, and then form the basis for making use-cost comparisons.

Lending institutions may permit the cost of the soft floor covering assembly in certain new constructions to become part of the mortgage obligation. In such cases, the tax savings on the portion of interest attributable to the carpet and cushion may be considered in the life-cycle analysis. Depreciation and capital investment credits may be additional factors to analyze in the costing of a project. Similar tax-related assessments can be made when replacement installations involve interest charges.

Environmental Considerations

In the late 1990s, because of growing concerns about the environment, the carpet industry began working on programs designed to reduce negative ecological impact. Concerted efforts were begun to reduce air, water, and land pollution; to reduce energy consumption, waste generation, and water usage; to utilize manufacturing techniques and processes that would support environmental sustainability; and to promote responsible ecological stewardship industry-wide. In addition, human health issues such as indoor air quality were included in efforts to improve the interior environment.

In 2002, members of the carpet industry, representatives of federal, state, and local government, and industry-related organizations signed a **Memorandum of Understanding for Carpet Stewardship (MOU)**. This document established a ten-year plan to increase the amount of recycling and reuse of post-consumer carpet and to reduce the amount of waste carpet going into landfills, the goal being that by the year 2012, 40 percent of post-consumer carpet be diverted from landfills. It is estimated that by 2012, approximately 7 billion pounds of waste carpet will be generated. A 40 percent reduction would mean 2.8 billion pounds of carpet will be recycled or reused. To carry out the plan, the nonprofit **Carpet America Recovery Effort (CARE)** was formed to supervise efforts leading to completion of the MOU goals.[4]

Many carpet manufacturers are addressing post-consumer carpet recycling. Some of the larger carpet mills, such as Interface; Shaw; The Mohawk Group; Beaulieu of America; Collins and Aikman; Invista; J&J Industries; Mannington Carpets, Inc; and Milliken, have programs in place to help designers and end-users with carpet waste recycling. New products made from recycled carpet include fibers for new carpet, carpet backings, pads and cushions, furniture battings and cushions, paneling, backer boards, synthetic hay bales, filters, sound barriers and landscape wall systems, automotive parts, additives for concrete, asphalt, and plastic products. In addition to post-consumer recycling, carpet and fiber manufacturers have systems in place to recycle or reuse production wastes. Depending on the type of waste produced, approximately 2 percent to 25 percent of recycled materials are used in carpet fiber production and carpet manufacturing. Certain residential polyester carpets are made from post-consumer plastic bottles. Carpet padding and backings are being produced with recycled content ranging from 50 percent to 100 percent. Nylon and polypropylene (olefin) are the most often recycled carpet fibers.[5]

In 2007, the American National Standards Institute (ANSI) approved Standard ANSI/NSF 140-2007, Sustainable Carpet Assessment Standard for environmentally preferable building materials. This standard provides criteria for recycled content, reclamation, and end-of-life management.

The goal of ANSI/NSF 140-2007 is to provide measurable criteria for sustainable carpet and to establish performance and environmental requirements for public health, energy efficiency, recycled content, manufacturing, reclamation, and end-of-life management.

Summary

Several variables affect the selection of soft floor coverings. Decisions must be made about appearance features such as size, shape, surface coloration, and surface texture. Consideration must be given to various factors influencing apparent color of the surface. Prospective purchasers may seek floor covering assemblies providing such functional benefits as noise control, insulation, and usefulness to persons with limited mobility or impaired sight. Professionals must confirm that their selections conform with any applicable design and performance mandates. Ultimately, residential and commercial consumers must be sure that initial costs and long-term maintenance expenses do not outstrip their budgets.

Today, the satisfactory in-use performance of textile floor coverings depends on the level of appearance or newness retention exhibited by the surface; fiber and floor coverings producers have successfully engineered abrasion resistance. Consumers and professionals should therefore investigate composition and construction qualities that will maintain an acceptable appearance and texture, and they should select those best suited to end-use conditions.

Key Terms

area rugs
Berber yarns
broadloom
carpet
Carpet America Recovery Effort
  (CARE)
carpet modules
friezé
high-low
life cycle costing
Memorandum of Understanding for
  Carpet Stewardship (MOU)

pile construction density
pile height
pile reversal
pile sweep
pile thickness
plush
pooling
random shear
room-fit rugs
room-size rugs
rug
runner

saxony
scatter rugs
sculptured
shading
shag
tip shear
velour
velvet
velvet plush
walk-off mat
watermarking

Review Questions

1. Identify some advantages that carpet modules offer over wall-to-wall installations.

2. Distinguish between room-size and room-fit rugs.

3. Consider some of the aesthetic values offered by area rugs.

4. Why is pile sweep a critical consideration when soft floor coverings are installed?

5. Why is pile height likely to be greater than pile thickness?

6. Identify ways in which the carpet industry is promoting environmental sustainability.

7. What causes watermarking to occur with soft floor coverings?

8. Identify surface textures and colorations that help to camouflage soil.

9. Describe the color styling seen with Berber yarns.

10. Identify factors to be considered when selecting and installing soft floor coverings in an interior used by a person with mobility limitations. Which of these variables are positive?

11. How can soft floor coverings be chosen to help blind and partially sighted persons?

12. What is the purpose of life-cycle costing?

Notes

1. Department of Veterans' Benefits, Veterans' Administration, *Handbook for Design: Specially Adapted Housing, VA Pamphlet 26–13*, Washington, D.C., March 20, 2008.

2. The full text of the ATBCB Minimum Guidelines for Accessible Design may be reviewed in the *Federal Register*, Vol. 47, Wednesday, August 4, 1982, 33873–33875.

3. A description of this investigative project is available from the Carpet and Rug Institute.

4. The Carpet and Rug Institute, "The Carpet Industry's Sustainability Report 2003."

5. Ibid.

CHAPTER TWENTY-ONE

Fibers, Yarns, and Constructions Used in Textile Floor Coverings

Photo courtesy of Amy Willbanks, www.textilefabric.com.

■ Current statistical profiles show that noncellulosic fibers have captured the major portion of the soft floor coverings market. The growing consumption of these fibers began in the early 1950s when producers began shifting from weaving with wool to tufting with nylon. The more economical production operation and the less expensive fiber made textile floor coverings more affordable, enabling increased numbers of homeowners, builders, and commercial firms to choose them in lieu of linoleum, tile, and oak flooring. While tufting has become the dominant construction method today, weaving, knitting, and such other techniques as fusion bonding and needlepunching remain important.

The performance of a textile floor covering will not be totally determined by a single feature, but certain performance properties are strongly influenced by one component. A fiber characteristic or a yarn feature has the primary influence on some service-related properties. The development of fuzz on the surface of pile floor coverings, for example, depends on the ability of the yarns to maintain their original level of twist. This chapter discusses this and other yarn properties having a strong effect on floor covering serviceability.

Fibers Used in Carpet and Rugs

Carpet and rug producers used more than 4.5 billion pounds of textile fibers in 2005.[1] Of this large amount of fiber, approximately 86 percent was incorporated into face or pile yarns, and the balance was used in the backings (Table 21.1). The fiber composition of face yarns and backing structures is markedly different. The manufactured fibers most often used in carpet production are nylon, olefin, and polyester. Of these, nylon dominates the assortment of fibers used in face yarns, with some 2.172 million pounds (60.6 percent) used in 2005. That same year, more than 899 million pounds (25.1 percent) of olefin and 513 million pounds (14.3 percent) of polyester were incorporated into carpet face yarns.[1] Of the natural fibers, 22.2 million pounds of cotton and 16.3 million pounds of wool were used in face yarns[2] (see Table 21.2 for fiber yarn types and characteristics).

Fiber Usage in Face Yarns

The relative importance of cotton, wool, and manufactured fibers in **face yarns** is shown in Table 21.1. The changing patterns of fiber consumption in recent decades are apparent from these data.

Table 21.1 Fiber Consumed in U.S. Floor Coverings Production: 2001–2005 (millions of pounds)

End Use & Year		Total Fiber	Noncellulosic Fibers	Cotton	Wool
Face Yarns	2001	3,290.3	3,242.3	23.4	24.6
	2002	3,528.5	3,485.0	23.4	20.1
	2003	3,559.4	3,522.3	23.4	13.7
	2004	3,593.0	3,555.6	23.4	14.1
	2005	3,646.0	3,607.5	22.2	16.3
Backing					
	2001	798.6	791.6	7.0	------*
	2002	844.4	837.8	6.6	------
	2003	854.6	846.2	8.4	------
	2004	897.0	888.6	8.4	------
	2005	878.4	871.9	6.5	------
Total					
	2001	4,088.9	3,242.3	30.4	24.6
	2002	4,372.9	4,322.8	30.0	20.1
	2003	4.414.0	4,368.5	31.8	13.7
	2004	4,490.0	4,444.2	31.8	14.1
	2005	4,524.4	4,479.4	28.7	16.3

* Little or no fiber used.
Source: Fiber Organon, "U.S. End Survey: 2001–2005," October 2006, page 193, Table 5.

Table 21.2 Fiber/Yarn Types and Characteristics

Fiber	Definition and Characteristics	Characteristics in Carpet
NYLON	• Fiber-forming substance of any long-chain synthetic polyamide having recurring amide groups as an integral part of the polymer chain. Available as Nylon 6 or Nylon 6,6 • Offered as BCF or staple, both used for residential and commercial applications • Can be a solution-dyed fiber or yarn • Extensively used for commercial carpet and accounts for 60% of all carpet face fibers	• Durable, resilient • Abrasion-resistant • Versatile in coloration possibilities • Wet-cleaning friendly • Excellent colorfastness • Excellent color clarity
OLEFIN (Polypropylene)	• Fiber-forming substance of any long-chain, synthetic polymer composed of at least 85% by weight of ethylene, propylene, or other olefin units • Offered as BCF (or staple for needlepunch carpet) • Solution-dyed fiber or yarn • Can be engineered for outdoor applications • Accounts for 33% of all carpet face fibers	• Resists fading • Generates low levels of static electricity • Chemical, moisture and stain-resistant • Favorably priced
ACRYLIC	• Fiber-forming substance of any long-chain, synthetic polymer composed of at least 85% by weight of acrylonitrile units • One of the first synthetic fibers used in carpet • Used in bath mats, rugs • Sometimes used in blends with other fibers in carpet • Always used in staple yarn form	• Wool-like characteristics • Excellent bulk and cover • Seldom used in commercial carpet
POLYESTER	• Made from terephthalic acid and ethylene glycol • Offered in BCF, but mainly in staple form • Used in residential and some low traffic commercial applications	• Excellent color clarity • Excellent colorfastness • Resistant to water-soluble stains • Noted for luxurious "hand"
WOOL	• Natural fiber from sheep • Inherent resilient property	• Luxurious "hand" • Durable • Scaly character of fiber scatters light and reduces visible soil • Largely self-extinguishing when burned; will char rather than melt or drip
COTTON	• Natural fiber from cotton plant • Used in various area rugs, such as bath mats	• Soft "hand" • Seldom used in broadloom

The rate of growth exhibited by the noncellulosic fibers has been phenomenal. In 1966, noncellulosic fibers controlled roughly 65 percent of the domestic carpet and rug face yarn market, leaving approximately 16 percent to the manufactured cellulosic fibers, 15 percent to wool, and 4 percent to cotton. Today, noncellulosic fibers account for 99 percent of the market; wool and cotton share the remaining 1 percent.

Importance of BCF Nylon and BCF Olefin

BCF nylon dominates the assortment of fibers used in face yarns, with domestic consumption of 1619.5 million pounds used in 2005, up 21 percent from that used in 1990.[1] Domestic consumption of BCF olefin went from 833.8 million pounds in 1996 to 853.0 million pounds in 2005, an increase of 2 percent.[1] Fiber engineering continues to ensure the serviceability of these manufactured fibers in soft floor coverings.

Wool Usage in Carpet and Rugs

Long considered to be the finest and most luxurious of the face fibers, wool dominated the floor coverings market for centuries. In recent decades, however, the domestic mill consumption of wool has steadily declined. In 2001, 24.6 million pounds of carpet wool were consumed in the United States. Four years later, in 2005, 16.3 million pounds of wool were consumed (see Table 21.1).[2] This decline has been accompanied by an increase in the price of foreign carpet wool: all wool fiber used in carpet and rugs is imported because domestic wool is too fine for these products. It also reflects a continuing decline in worldwide sheep population.

The decrease in the use of wool has not come about because of any serious deficiencies in the properties or processing of the fiber. The initial challenge was on the basis of cost; the continuing challenge is from the lower cost and improved quality of manufactured fibers. If cost is no consideration, many people believe that the beauty, durability, inherent soil and flame resistance, and excellent resiliency of wool support its choice.

Fiber Usage in Backing Structures

Most of the fiber produced for carpet and rug backing structures is directed to fabrics for backing tufted goods. A smaller amount of fiber is used for the yarns in the backing layers of other constructions.

In 1985, some 432.5 million pounds of fiber (426 million pounds of manufactured fibers and 6.5 million pounds of cotton) were used in backing structures. Polypropylene (olefin) was dominant, but minor amounts of nylon and polyester were also used.[3] Some cotton yarn appears in the back of woven constructions and in fabrics used to back small, tufted rugs and mats, but none is used for tufted rollgoods. Other backing materials include foam rubber, fiberglass, kraftcord, vinyl, latex, and jute. Fabrics of jute are dimensionally stable unless they are overwetted during cleaning or flooding. Because they retain moisture and may rot and mildew, they should not be used with floor coverings installed below-grade where ground moisture can move through the floor to the carpet back. Because jute is imported from tropical areas, supply and delivery problems have often plagued producers using jute. Jute is no longer used as a backing for commercial tufted carpet.

By 2005 this market had grown to 4,524.4 million pounds of fiber used; 871.9 million pounds of manufactured fiber and 6.5 million pounds of cotton were used as backing structures. Polypropylene olefin was dominant, but minor amounts of nylon and polyester were also used[2] (see Table 21.3). Any quantity of jute used today is minor and not included.

Disclosure of Fiber Composition

The fiber composition of the pile layer of soft floor covering must be disclosed in accordance with the provisions of the Textile Fiber Products Identification Act. Backing fibers and yarns are exempt (see Chapter 10).

Fiber Properties Affecting Floor Performance

The selection of carpet and rug fibers should be based on an evaluation of both engineered and inherent properties. Virtually every inherent property can be engineered or altered for improved performance. Unless a particular feature is required by law, residential and commercial consumers may weigh appearance and performance benefits against any added cost. Such features as abrasion resistance, optical characteristics, static propensity, and soil-related properties are discussed in Chapter 4. Other properties such as microbe resistance and moth resistance are discussed in Chapter 9.

Yarn Features Affecting Serviceability

The appearance and floor performance of carpet and rugs relate to several yarn features, including some structural characteristics and the stability of the yarn twist. Often,

Table 21.3 Carpet Backing Systems

Construction Method	Typical Backing Fabrics and/or Backing Components	Typical Backcoating Chemical Compounds

Tufted	Primary:
	  woven polypropylene slit film
	  non-woven, polypropylene or polyester
	Secondary:
	  woven leno weave polypropylene
	  non-woven polypropylene, or polyester
	  woven jute, seldom used now
	  fiberglass reinforcement
		• synthetic SBR latex
		• polyurethane
		• polyvinyl acetate
		• ethylene vinyl acetate
		• polyvinyl chloride
		• amorphous resins or thermoplastic polyolefin

Woven	Construction yarns may include:
	  cotton
	  jute
	  polypropylene
	  polyester
	  viscose rayon
	  blends or combinations
		• Similar materials as tufted, but usually thinner coatings

Bonded	Fiberglass matting	• polyvinyl chloride
Needlepunched	(None typically used)	• SBR latex • acrylics • ethylene vinyl acetate • SBR latex foam

Source: Courtesy of the Carpet and Rug Institute.

spinners and throwsters can produce the desired appearance and expected service-related properties by manipulating these features.

Structural Characteristics

Virtually all carpet and rug yarns are constructed as simple, relatively coarse structures. Spun yarns were dominant until the late 1980s when they peaked at a 40 percent market share. Today, bulked continuous filament (BCF) yarns have captured approximately 72 percent of the market.[1]

Design Features

Complex yarns, except for speck yarns, are not used in floor coverings because loops, curls, and other irregular textural effects would readily be abraded and snagged. Decorative appeal, however, can be introduced by other variables, including color styling, pile height, and yarn twist.

Form

As noted above, spun yarns account for approximately 27 percent of the face yarn market.[1] For good floor performance, two- or three-ply spun yarns are produced from staple fibers 4, 6, or 8 inches long. Longer lengths help to reduce the number of protruding fiber ends and to in-

crease yarn strength, and thus to minimize the problems of shedding, fuzzing, and pilling induced by abrasion during use.

Most multifilament carpet yarns are textured, using the false-twist coiling or knit-de-knit crinkling techniques. Again, as noted above, there has been shifting from spun to BCF yarns. Because most of the filament ends are buried in the yarn bundle, BCF yarns, like longer staple spun yarns, exhibit less pill formation. In combination with heather color styling, BCF yarns often have a wool-like appearance (Figure 21.1).

Size and Weight

The average **denier** of filament carpet yarns composed of nylon, the dominant carpet fiber, has been decreasing over the past several years. The reduction in diameter has largely resulted from changes in fashion styling preferences—most notably a shift toward the finer velour surface texture—but rising raw material costs have had a major impact as well.

Although the average denier of filament nylon yarns has been decreasing, some carpet yarns and some carpet fibers are being manufactured with extra high denier counts. These extra large yarns, which have denier counts

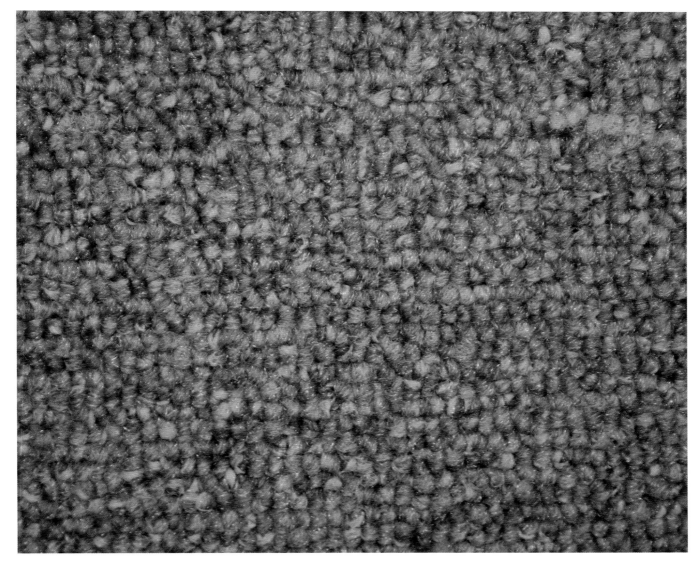

Figure 21.1 Level-loop pile made of BCF yarn.
Courtesy of Amy Willbanks, www.textilefabric.com.

as high as 7,000, are used in floor coverings intended for installation in commercial interiors that undergo heavy traffic. Most commercial carpet will have an average pile yarn density between 4,500 and 6,000.

Pile Yarn Integrity

Pile yarn integrity refers to the ability of the face yarns to maintain their stability and resist the effects of abrasion. Loop pile yarns should not rupture, and cut pile yarns should not splay or untwist. Such abrasion-induced changes would be accompanied by changes in the apparent luster, wrongly suggestive of colorant failure. Con-

comitant changes would be observed in the original textural characteristics: for example, fuzziness would replace smoothness.

When cut pile yarns fail to maintain their original level of twist, they are said to **splay**, flare, or "blossom," as shown in Figure 21.2. Because incident light waves are reflected from the small tips of the multiple, disoriented fibers, areas of splayed yarns appear duller than surrounding areas. Surface luster will also vary when fibers that are part of loop pile yarns are snagged and ruptured.

Pile yarn integrity can be improved with the use of abrasion-resistant fibers, BCF yarns, and more highly

Figure 21.2 Yarn splaying.

twisted and heat-stabilized yarns. Higher pile construction densities also exert a positive influence on the integrity of the yarns in a covering over time.

Constructions Used in Soft Floor Coverings

The division of body construction techniques on the basis of usage and economic importance is useful and meaningful. This separates the dominant technique, tufting, from other industrial techniques and from hand operations. An overview of carpet construction types is shown in Table 21.6. As shown in Table 21.5 shipments of tufted carpet and rugs increased from $10,996.4 million in 2000, to $13,095.9 million in 2005.

Dominance of Tufting

Tufting accounts for more than 90 percent of the floor coverings market. This is largely the result of the economic advantages offered by high-speed, wide-width tufting machines, and by the use of nylon instead of nonresilient cotton and expensive wool fibers. It has also resulted from improvements made in the quality of tufted carpet that have enabled designers and architects increasingly to specify tufted floor coverings for commercial interiors, including areas of heavy traffic.

Together with woven constructions and hand techniques, tufting is discussed in detail in the following chapters.

Table 21.4 Fiber Usage in Face Yarns—Shipments of Carpet and Rugs: 2005 and 2004 (quantity in thousands of square yards; value in thousands of dollars)

	2005		2004	
	Quantity	Value	Quantity	Value
Nylon	1,083,835	9,086,969	1,066,630	8,667,567
Polyester	218,692	1,310,489	r/ 192,403	r/ 1,002,338
Polypropylene	508,306	2,320,585	506,627	2,171,637
All other	51,244	377,831	53,912	383,025

r/Revised by 5 percent or more from previously published data.
Source: U.S. Department of Commerce, "MA314Q(05)-1."

Table 21.5 Carpet and Rug Shipments: 2000 to 2005 (millions of dollars)

Year	Rugs, Carpet, and Carpeting	Woven Carpet and Rugs	Tufted Carpet and Rugs	Other Carpet and Rugs
2005	13,994.3	594.9	13,095.9	303.5
2004	r/ 13,179.3	r/ 589.8	12,224.6	r/ 364.9
2003	r/ 11,785.3	r/ 422.9	10,958.7	403.7
2002	r/ 11,747.0	r/ 416.9	10,936.1	394.0
2001	12,175.5	645.6	11,104.7	425.2
2000	11,983.2	464.5	10,996.4	522.3

r/ Revised by 5 percent or more from previously published data.
Source: U.S. Department of Commerce, "MA314Q(05)-1."

Table 21.6 Carpet Construction

Type/Description	Special Characteristics
Tufting	
600–2,000 rows of pile yarn simultaneously stitched through carrier fabric (primary backing)	• Most prevalent method for carpet fabric production (over 90%) • Textural flexibility achieved with varying colors, surface textures, using various types of yarns, etc.
Cut Pile — Carpet pile surface with all of the yarn tufts of the same height	• Custom tufting available for specially designed carpet orders • Patterned effects created in the cut pile constructions by using different colors of yarns • Geometric designs created with a pattern attachment called a shifting needle bar
Loop Pile — Level loop / Multilevel loop	• All loops same height from row to row • A patterning attachment is used to achieve different pile heights in a pattern repeat
Cut and Loop — A combination of cut and loop pile	• Varying levels of pile height and pile textures create surface interest
Weaving	
Colored pile yarns and backing yarns woven simultaneously into finished product	• Primarily used in commercial installations • Heavy, firm hand; high strength • Often used in hospitality settings
Velvet Carpet — Carpet made on velvet loom; is cut or loop, level or multilevel pile	• Simplest loom of the three • Dominated by solid colors, but multicolor and multi-texture effects are becoming more widespread • Service quality is achieved with pile density (high pile density is achieved by specifying high pitch or a heavy yarn weight)
Wilton Carpet — Carpet made on Wilton loom; can have various pile heights (level or multilevel) and can have loop or cut pile	• Capable of intricate patterning, styling and coloration versatility • Withstands heavy traffic; used mostly in commercial applications and area rugs • Weaving process contributes to durability, strength, firmness, and flexibility (bends all ways)
Axminster Carpet — Carpet made on Axminster loom; cut pile only; most are single-level cut pile, but can be multilevel as well	• Offers wide range of patterns and colors • Withstands heavy traffic; used mostly in commercial applications and area rugs • Weaving process contributes to durability, strength, firmness, and flexibility (bends only horizontally)
Knitting	
Warp-knitted yarn fabricated on face and back simultaneously. Pile, backing and stitching yarns are looped together by three sets of needles	• Similar to woven carpet, but less stiff; bends horizontally only • Most is solid colored or tweed • Quality depends on the amount of pile yarn and strength of attachment of the face, chain, and backing yarns; quantity of yarn depends on the gauge and stitches per inch warpwise, which are related to the yarn size
Needlepunching	
Web of fibers moves through machine. Barbed felting needles penetrate and entangle fibers into durable felt-like fabrics	• Usually made with a solution-dyed polypropylene • Diverse range of designs-ribs, sculptured designs, and patterns • Only used in glue-down installations
Bonding	
Yarns are implanted into vinyl or thermoplastic coated backing	• Often die-cut for modules (tiles) • Cut pile produced by slitting two parallel sheets of face-to-face carpet

Source: Carpet and Rug Institute.

Summary

Today's soft floor coverings market is dominated by tufted constructions having either nylon BCF or olefin BCF face yarns. Olefin has also captured the greatest portion of the carpet and rug backings market. The increasing popularity of these noncellulosic fibers has been accompanied by a concomitant decrease in the use of wool. Like fibers, yarns can have specific structural features chosen for appearance and performance. Yarns can be textured, for example, to reduce pilling, and heat set to minimize splaying and increase appearance retention.

The choice of inherent and engineered fiber and yarn properties should be made in anticipation of traffic conditions and in the light of budgetary limits. It should also entail consideration of construction variables that affect floor performance; these variables are discussed in the following chapters.

Key Terms

denier
face yarns

pile yarn integrity
tufting

yarn splay

Review Questions

1. Identify two fibers that dominate the soft floor coverings face yarn market. What accounts for their prominence?

2. Review the usage of wool in soft floor coverings. What variables have influenced the significant shift in the consumption of this natural fiber for textile floor coverings? In what type of floor coverings does wool usage remain strong?

3. Identify the dominant fiber in the carpet and rug backings market. Why has the usage of jute declined?

4. Discuss the relative importance of spun yarns and BCF yarns in the face or wear layer of soft floor coverings. What advantages are offered by BCF yarns?

5. Explain the shift in the average denier of nylon carpet filament in the past two decades. How has this shift influenced surface texture design?

6. When did tufting begin to enjoy widespread usage as a construction technique? What advantages does it offer over weaving techniques?

Notes

1. Fiber Economics Bureau, *Fiber Organon*, "Carpet Face Fiber Analysis: 1996–2005," Vol. 77, No. 9, September 2006, 171.

2. Fiber Economics Bureau, *Fiber Organon*, "U.S. End Use Survey: 2001–2005," October 2006, 193.

3. Ibid., Vol. 57, No. 9, September 1985, 216.

Construction of Floor Coverings: Tufting

CHAPTER **TWENTY-TWO**

Photo courtesy of InterfaceFlor®.

■ **Body construction techniques** employed with textile floor coverings may be divided into two broad categories: those that create pile structures and those that create nonpile structures. Nonpile structures are produced by such methods as braiding, weaving, and needlepunching. Weaving can also be used to produce pile structures, as well. Other pile structures are produced by such methods as tufting, knitting, and fusion bonding. For pile structures, surface textures or constructions do not go hand in hand with body constructions; identical textures can be produced by any of several techniques.

Because tufted floor coverings are used so extensively, residential consumers, interior designers, and architects should understand their structural qualities. This will prepare them to make informed decisions and reliable judgments concerning the suitability of tufted structures for various installations. It will also enable the professional to interpret structural data supplied by producers.

Basic Components of Tufted Floor Coverings

Whether a carpet or rug is machine tufted or hand tufted, the principal components are the same. Tufted constructions include **pile or face yarns**, a **primary backing**, a layer of adhesive, and a **secondary backing** (Figure 22.1 and Figure 22.2).

Pile or Face Yarns

The composition and structural characteristics of face yarns used in pile floor coverings were discussed in Chapter 21. BCF yarns of nylon and olefin fibers dominate.

Primary Backing Fabrics

Typical primary backing fabrics are shown in Figure 22.3. Although jute (Figure 22.3a) formerly dominated the market, it has largely been replaced by olefin.

Plain-woven fabrics of yarn-like (fibrillated) tapes or ribbons of olefin (Figure 22.3b) have high stability unless heated above 338 °F. These fabrics are impervious to moisture; they resist mildew and the development of odors. To minimize raveling, a thin butyl coating is frequently applied to bond the warp and filling strands.

When low pile construction densities are planned, producers can use a plain-woven olefin backing with a "nylon cap," produced by needlepunching a thin nylon batt into the backing. Because nylon fibers accept dye more readily than olefin fibers, the needlepunched fibers can be colored to coordinate with the face yarns. In the event the backing is exposed in use, any difference in color between the face fibers and the backing is masked.

Spunbonded olefin fabric (Figure 22.3c) exhibits no fraying or raveling and is not susceptible to problems from moisture. During tufting, the filaments are pushed aside; thus, the needle is only minimally deflected, which helps ensure uniform pile height and tuft placement.

Secondary Backing Fabrics

Secondary backing fabrics, also referred to as **scrims**, must adhere well and provide high dimensional stability. Fabrics composed of jute are naturally rough and adhere well; spunbonded fabrics are smooth and have poor adhesion.

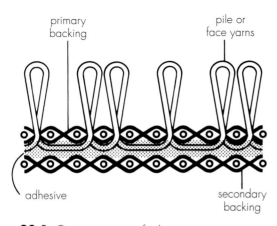

Figure 22.1 Components in tufted constructions.

Figure 22.2 Illustration of construction layers in tufted carpet. Courtesy of Brintons.

a) Plain woven jute.

b) Plain woven olefin.

c) Spunbonded olefin.

Figure 22.3 Typical primary backing fabrics.
Courtesy of Amy Willbanks, www.textilefabric.com.

A leno-woven fabric composed of olefin fibers is specifically manufactured for use as a secondary backing. The leno interlacing minimizes yarn raveling at the fabric edges, and the spun filling yarns provide the necessary roughness for adhesion of the fabric (Figure 22.4).

Some manufacturers use a glass fiber scrim to reinforce a vinyl secondary backing. This combination has high dimensional stability and virtually no moisture-related problems.

Permanently attached foam rubber or polyurethane cushions may be used as secondary backings, eliminating the need for a separate cushion. Secondary backings may or may not be used with commercially produced, hand-tufted carpet and rugs. Hard-backed polyvinyl chloride (PVC) is used as a backing for modular carpet tiles. Unitary backings are used primarily with tufted loop pile carpet and consist of either a rubber or latex used without an additional secondary backing. They are suitable only for direct glue-down installations.

Adhesives

The most frequently used adhesive is synthetic latex; approximately 12 ounces per square yard are applied to most tufted floor coverings. Some carpet producers are replacing latex adhesives with molten thermoplastic compounds.

To control electrical charge buildup, tufted carpet producers may incorporate a conductive compound into the adhesive used to secure the secondary backing, or they may sandwich an antistatic coating between the primary backing and the adhesive. Some carpet producers combine a conductive compound in the adhesive or backing fab-

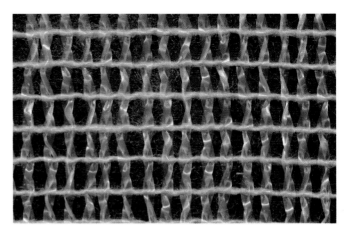

Figure 22.4 A leno-woven olefin secondary backing uses spun filling yarns for improved adhesion.
Courtesy of Amy Willbanks, www.textilefabric.com.

ric with an antistatic component in the pile layer. Tufted carpet producers may also incorporate a flame-retardant compound into the adhesive. To be effective, the coating must penetrate the primary backing.

Tufting Operations

Unlike most weaving operations, tufting is a relatively simple and uncomplicated process. Pile yarns are inserted into an already-formed primary backing fabric, and surface textures and construction densities can easily be varied.

Forming the Pile Layer

Pile yarns are supplied in one of two ways: either from cones mounted on a creel frame or from large spools re-ferred to as beams, erected in back of the tufting machine. So that they will not tangle, the yarns are fed through thin plastic tubes, visible in the upper portion of the photograph in Figure 22.5, to tension control devices and the tufting needles. The tension controls determine the quantity of yarn supplied to the needles, helping to ensure the production of the planned pile height.

Many needles are aligned crosswise on the machine. The number of needles required depends on the width and the planned crosswise density or gauge. **Gauge** is the fractional distance between adjacent needles; it can be converted to a **needle count**, which is the number of needles per crosswise inch on the machine. A gauge of ⅛ inch is equivalent to a needle count of eight; a gauge of ¹⁄₁₀ inch is equivalent to a needle count of ten. To prepare a tufting

Figure 22.5 Commercial tufting machine.
Courtesy of CTS Group Pty Ltd.

machine to produce carpet 12 feet wide, with a gauge of $\frac{1}{10}$ inch, 1,440 needles must be aligned and threaded with pile yarns (12 feet × 12 inches = 144 inches; 144 inches × 10 needles = 1,440 needles).

The sequence used to form loop pile floor coverings is schematized in Figure 7.7 (p. 117). Threaded with pile yarns, the needles descend through the back of the primary fabric. Working in a timed relationship with the descending needles, loop pile hooks rock forward, catching and holding the yarn loops while the needles ascend. The pile layer is then formed on the face of the primary fabric. One crosswise row of tufts is produced in each tufting cycle.

When a cut pile surface is planned, a knife blade is attached to the pile hook, which cuts the loops, forming one U-shaped tuft from each loop (Figure 7.7, p. 117). For either loop or cut pile coverings, the descend and ascend tufting cycle is followed by the advancement of the primary backing a predetermined distance and the repetition of the cycle.

The number of tufts or stitches per inch determines the distance the primary backing is advanced after each tufting cycle, and thus governs the lengthwise density. Typically, the number of stitches per inch ranges from 4 to 11. If, for example, a stitch of 8 is selected, the crosswise bank of needles would punch into the fabric 8 times in each lengthwise inch, and there would be $\frac{1}{8}$ inch between each crosswise row of tufts.

Modern tufting machines are capable of completing more than 500 tufting cycles per minute. Depending upon width, density, and surface texture, this capability can translate into the production of more than 1,000 square yards of cut pile carpet per day, and about twice that amount of loop pile carpet.

In comparison to machine tufting, hand tufting is an extremely slow and expensive process. It is used only for custom orders requiring a relatively small amount of yardage. Hand tufting is done with a hand-held, electrically powered tufting gun (Figure 22.6).

Creating Multilevel Surface Textures

Various attachments are available for tufting multilevel surfaces in random and patterned shapes. Differences in pile height are achieved by controlling the quantity of yarn supplied to the needles prior to their descent. The needles and loop hooks continue to operate in the conventional manner.

In some systems, the amount of yarn feeding to the needles is constant, and a level surface will be produced. When the speed is slowed, the amount of yarn feeding to the needles is reduced; then, as the hooks hold the loops while the needles ascend, the "missing" quantity of yarn is robbed mechanically by tension from the previously formed loops. In other systems, photoelectric cells control the amount of yarn fed to each needle. In yet a third technique, pile yarns are fed over slats having notched and uncut areas. When a pile yarn encounters a notched area,

a) Highly skilled artisans hand tufting a large rug.

b) Clipping stray yarns during the finishing stage of production.

Figure 22.6 Custom tufting.
Soroush Custom Rugs & Axminster Carpet, www.soroush.us

it is subjected to less tension and will form higher loops; when a pile yarn encounters an uncut area, its flow is restricted, and it will form a shorter loop. In recent years, the use of these techniques has diminished as manufacturers have adopted computerized programming to control pile height variations.

When tufting of the pile yarns is completed, several operations are required to convert the greige carpet into finished carpet. Among these, tip shearing, random shearing, and hand carving create even more variety in surface texture.

Applying an Adhesive and Scrim

Unless the tufted pile yarns are permanently anchored in the primary backing, they could easily be pulled out when snagged. In cut pile styles, this would show up as an empty space the size of the space once occupied by the removed tufts. In loop pile styles, pulling the continuous length of yarn would expose a lengthwise line of backing void of tufts, as illustrated in Figure 22.7.

In preparation for application of the adhesive, the back of the primary fabric is beaten to drive the pile yarn segments tightly against the fabric base. The coating is then applied uniformly across the back, securely binding the yarns into their positions. The secondary backing is then rolled onto the adhesive coating.

Most tufted broadloom carpet is manufactured in 12-foot widths. Some manufacturers also offer 6-foot and 15-foot widths to meet special needs. The yardage may be in **rollgoods** form or cut into small rugs and mats. The products are converted and then subjected to quality testing.

Structural Qualities of Tufted Constructions

As part of their quality-control programs, tufted carpet producers evaluate such structural features as the strength of the bond between the primary and secondary backings and the pile construction density. Several also measure various weight-related characteristics, for use in selection guidelines that coordinate minimum weight values with anticipated traffic levels.

Bundle Penetration

Visual examination enables carpet producers to estimate how thoroughly the adhesive penetrates the pile yarn bundle. A high degree of **bundle penetration** helps to prevent individual staple or filament fibers from being pulled out of the yarns and rubbed into fuzz and pills on the carpet surface.

Delamination Strength

Another crucial function of the adhesive coating is to develop a strong bond with the secondary backing. Good adhesion is especially important to prevent **delamination** or separation of the backings when they are subjected to heavy stress forces. The movement of heavy equipment or the flow of much traffic across a carpet surface can have a "snowplow" effect, crushing and pushing the structure, which in turn can cause shearing, the movement of the primary and secondary backings in opposite directions. Unless the bond between the two fabrics is strong, shearing can cause delamination. Delamination could result in bubbling, rippling, and straining at the seams.

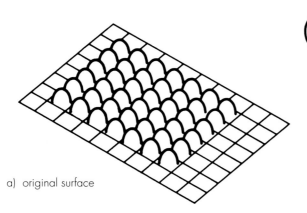

a) original surface

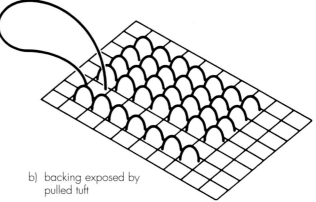

b) backing exposed by pulled tuft

Figure 22.7 Potential problem with poorly anchored pile yarns.

The strength of the bond between the backings may be measured in accordance with the procedures outlined in ASTM D 3936 Standard Test Method for Delamination Strength of Secondary Backing of Pile Floor Coverings. In Figure 22.8, stress is exerted on the specimen clamped in the jaws of the test apparatus. The force required to separate the components is measured for each of three specimens; the average is then reported in pounds per inch of specimen width. Values frequently range from 2.5 to 8.33 pounds per inch.

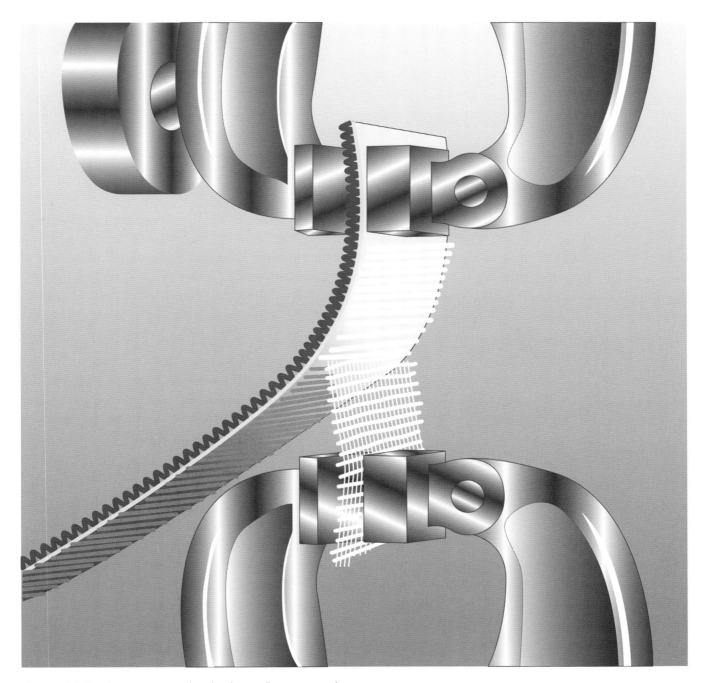

Figure 22.8 Measuring secondary backing adhesion strength.

Tuft Bind

Tuft bind testing may be carried out in accordance with the procedures outlined in ASTM D 1335 Standard Test Method for Tuft Bind of Pile Floor Coverings. The force required to pull one loop of pile tuft from a floor covering is measured by first anchoring the structure in clamps, as shown in Figure 22.9. A hook is inserted into the test loop, and the loops on either side of the test loop are cut. Raising the hook then exerts force. Three replicate tests are run, and the average force required to remove the tufts is reported in pounds-force. Values typically range from 4.5 to 20 pounds. For loop pile carpet, the recommended minimum value is 10 pounds of force per loop. This procedure can also be used on cut pile structures: a tweezer-like device is clamped onto one side or leg of a cut loop.

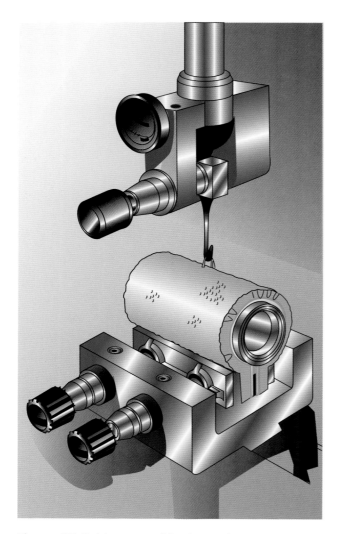

Figure 22.9 Measuring tuft bind strength.

Tufts per Square Inch

Although the "eyeball" method illustrated in Figure 20.5 (p. 330) can be used to roughly evaluate pile construction density, a more reliable technique is to determine the actual number of **tufts per square inch**. ASTM D 5793 Test Method for Binding Sites per Unit Length or Width of Pile Yarn Floor Coverings provides instructions on how to count binding sites per unit length and width. Producers measure and report the necessary lengthwise and crosswise values separately on data and specification sheets.

Gauge, needle count, and number of tufts or stitches per inch were explained earlier in this chapter. The number of tufts per square inch may be calculated by multiplying the needle count by the number of stitches per inch. If other construction features are equal, carpet and rugs with higher construction density values should exhibit better durability and texture retention.

The important influence of construction density on thickness retention can be appreciated by reviewing a simple principle of physics. When a stress load is distributed over a large, rather than a small, number of supports, the force or load each must bear is minimized. The same idea is behind the "magic" we see when a performer lies on a bed of nails without injury to the skin: each one of many nails supports an extremely small portion of the body weight, so the skin is not punctured. To pursue the analogy, each tuft in a pile floor covering may be considered equivalent to one nail; as the number of tufts is increased, the load each must support is reduced. Denser construction also helps to reduce yarn flexing within the pile because adjacent tufts support one another.

Pile construction density values are important, but they should not be used alone to predict thickness retention. For example, each square in Figure 22.10 has the same number of pile tufts, but the size and thus the weight of the yarns in each is significantly different. Evidently, accurate predictions of serviceability must also include weight factors.

Weight-related Factors

In general, as the weight of a textile floor covering increases, so does its quality, its potential texture retention, and its wear-life. For this reason, producers of tufted carpet and other soft floor coverings generally report vari-

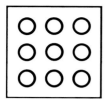 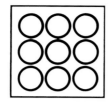

Figure 22.10 Equal pile construction densities having different sizes of yarns.

ous weight-related measurements. These include pile yarn weight, effective face weight, total weight, density factor, weight density, and HUD/FHA density. The challenge to students and practicing professionals is to understand the differences among these measurements. Professionals must also be aware that minimum weight values are often part of design standards established for certain commercial interiors.

Pile Yarn Weight

Pile yarn weight is the weight of the yarns used in the wear layer and those portions of the pile yarn that extend into the backing layer. Pile yarn weight values are expressed in ounces per square yard or in grams per square meter.

Several construction variables are reflected in pile weight values, including fiber density, yarn weight, pile height, and pile construction density. Pile yarn weight values are among the better references for judging the potential serviceability of similarly constructed floor coverings. To compare floor coverings of different constructions, however, consideration should be given to the proportional distribution of the pile yarns between the wear layer and the backing layer.

Effective Face Yarn Weight

The **effective face yarn weight** is a way to express the weight of the pile yarns in the wear layer, excluding those in the backing. Because fusion-bonded structures (discussed in Chapter 23) contain a relatively small amount of their pile yarns in the backing layer, producers of these carpets often report the effective face yarn weight.

Total Weight

The **total weight** of a floor covering includes the weight of the pile yarns as well as the weight of the backing yarns, backing fabrics, and backcoatings. Weight measurements

and other construction variables should be coordinated with traffic conditions for good performance. (Traffic classifications for various areas within several commercial interiors are listed in Table 20.1, p. 336.) Since the weight values listed are minimums, increasing them should provide increased floor performance; but such increases should always be balanced against concomitant increases in cost.

Density Factor

The **density factor** or **density index** is a calculation that reflects both pile construction density and yarn size (denier). The following formula is used to calculate this factor:

$$\text{Density factor} = \text{yarn size} \times \text{needle count} \times \text{stitches per inch}$$

Increasing the density factor will increase floor performance, up to a point.

The usefulness of pile yarn weight, effective face yarn weight, and total weight measurements is limited in that they do not reflect the true pile density (mass or amount of matter per unit of volume). Consider, for example, two carpets that have the same pile yarn and identical pile construction densities, but different pile heights. The carpet with the higher pile would weigh more, but would have lower true density. On the other hand, if two carpets differed only in their yarn size, the carpet containing the heavier yarns would not only weigh more but would also have a higher true density. The density factor also does not reflect true density because it does not consider pile height. It would seem that structures with equal construction densities and yarn sizes, but different pile heights, will have identical density factors; but increasing the pile height will in fact reduce the true density. Therefore, measurements that reflect the true density are often reported.

Average Density and Weight Density

Average density and **weight density** measurements take pile height (finished thickness) into consideration and thus can indicate the true density of floor covering structures. Minimum density values may be recommended or required in some settings. Required minimum values are set out, for example, in the HUD/FHA Use of Materials Bulletin 44d (see Chapter 2). Commercial specifiers must select a floor covering that has been certified to meet or exceed the minimum requirements in effect at the time of the project work. Certification must be carried out by an independent laboratory administrator approved by HUD/FHA. The bulletin offers these formulas for calculating average density and weight density:

$$(D) = \text{average density} = \frac{36\,(W)}{(t)}, \text{ where}$$

(W) = average pile weight in ounces per square yard, and (t) = average pile thickness in inches. (WD) = weight density = $W(D)$

Weight-related features not only affect texture retention, but also such functional values as noise control and insulation. Test methods for evaluating these and other service-related properties are discussed in Chapter 26.

Summary

Constructing pile floor coverings through tufting operations is relatively fast and economical. The economic advantages of machine tufting, of course, may be overridden by the selection of more expensive fibers, yarns, and finishes and by the use of higher pile construction densities. Costs can also escalate when production runs are small and specialized, as is generally the case with custom work made to order. The costs will also be higher for small, unique orders that must be hand tufted, a comparatively slow, labor-intensive process.

In their quality-control programs, tufting firms generally measure and evaluate such structural qualities as the strength of the bond between the primary and secondary backing fabrics, the pile construction density, and the weight and density of the pile layer. Tufting firms use the results of these evaluations to help secure the widespread selection of their floor coverings.

Key Terms

average density
bundle penetration
delamination
density factor
density index
effective face yarn weight

gauge
needle count
pile or face yarns
pile yarn weight
primary backing
rollgoods

scrims
secondary backing
total weight
tuft bind
tufts per square inch
weight density

Review Questions

1. Draw and label a cross-sectional illustration of a tufted floor covering.

2. Identify the advantages and limitations of the three types of primary backings.

3. How is a "nylon cap" produced and what positive features does it offer in use?

4. Distinguish between gauge and needle count.

5. Discuss the problems that could occur when pile yarn is not securely anchored in the primary backing.

6. Explain the importance of having the adhesive penetrate the pile yarn bundles.

7. Explain the meaning of "snowplow" effect and shearing.

8. Differentiate between pile yarn weight and effective face yarn weight.

CHAPTER TWENTY-THREE

Construction of Floor Coverings: Weaving and Other Machine Techniques

■ **Commercial weaving of** textile floor coverings began in the United States in the late 1700s. The principal product was a flat, yarn-dyed, reversible structure called ingrain. Gradually, this rug began to replace the braided and hand-woven rugs made in the home. Pile carpet was imported until the mid-1800s, when the power loom was adapted for the domestic production of a patterned, loop pile carpet known as Brussels. Over the years, other techniques and looms augmented the production capabilities of domestic manufacturers. In addition to ingrain and Brussels carpet, cut pile constructions, such as Wilton, Axminster, velvet, and chenille, also became available. Together, woven floor coverings dominated markets until the mid-1950s, when large-scale tufting operations were widely adopted.

In addition to tufting and weaving operations, other machine techniques, including fusion bonding, flocking, and needlepunching, are used to produce contemporary carpet and rugs. Although machine techniques other than tufting produce only a relatively small portion of today's residential and commercial floor coverings, even small percentages translate into millions of dollars (see Table 21.5, p. 346).

Weaving Pile Floor Coverings

Several methods of weaving are employed in the manufacture of pile floor coverings. Among these, major differences exist in the structure and operation of the

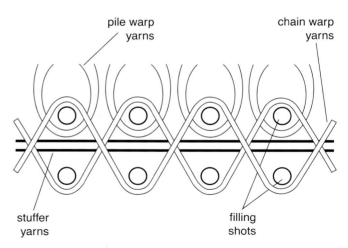

Figure 23.1 Basic components of woven pile carpet and rugs.

looms, the nature of the surface patterns formed, and the degree of interlacing complexity involved. Some yarn components are, however, common to all forms of woven pile structures.

Basic Components

Most woven pile floor coverings contain warp yarns, stuffer yarns, filling shots (yarns), and pile yarns. These yarns are illustrated schematically in Figure 23.1.

Filling or weft shots (yarns) are crosswise yarns used to anchor the **pile warp yarns**. The shots are generally of polypropylene olefin, jute, or cotton, and the pile yarns may be spun or multifilament yarns of any fiber. For added body and weight, extra warp yarns, called **stuffer yarns**, are

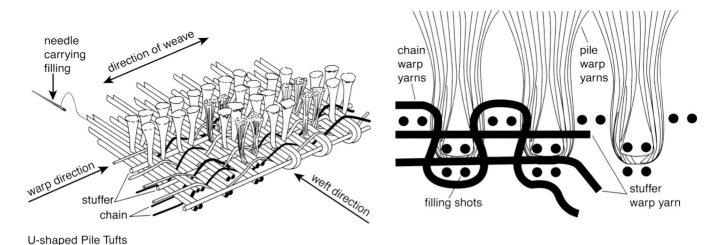

U-shaped Pile Tufts

Figure 23.2 Cross-sectional sketches of Axminster carpet with paired filling shots.
Courtesy of Mohawk Carpet.

inserted in a plane in the back layer. Stuffers are normally kraftcord or stiff jute yarns. **Chain warp yarns** pass over and under the shots, securing all components of the structure tightly together. The zigzag configuration of these yarns in most woven floor coverings makes them easy to recognize. Today, chains are generally composed of polyester, not cotton.

Unlike tufting, in which the pile layer is added to an already-formed base fabric, weaving operations form the pile and backing layers simultaneously. Some methods, such as velvet weaving, are relatively simple procedures that have only limited design capabilities; others, including

Axminster and Wilton, are quite complicated and virtually unlimited in the range of designs they can produce. Weaving operations are comparatively slow and labor-intensive, however, so they are used less frequently than tufting by domestic producers.

Axminster Weaving

Two schematic illustrations of Axminster carpet are shown in Figures 23.2 and 23.4. A distinctive feature is the use of paired filling shots, with either two pairs used per tuft row, as shown in the left sketch, or three pairs per tuft row, as shown in the right sketch. This makes the crosswise direction of the carpet somewhat rigid and inflexible, a distinguishing characteristic of Axminster floor coverings.

Preparation for Axminster weaving is lengthy and involved; the more intricate and complex the design and pattern repeat to be woven, the more complicated preparation becomes. First, a colored **print design** displaying the full length and width of one pattern repeat is prepared. A portion of the design prepared for weaving an intricate Oriental pattern is shown in Figure 23.3. Each small block represents one pile tuft. Clearly, the colored tufts must be woven precisely in their planned positions, as shown in Figure 23.5b, or the motifs will be irregular and flawed (Figure 23.5b).

When the print design is ready, skilled technicians assemble cones of yarns colored according to its specifications. They then wind the various colors of yarns onto 3-foot-long **spools**, following the sequence printed on

Project: Oyster Point Marriott

A	B	C	D	E	F	G	H	I	J
H22 S-690	H19 S-687	T2 S-886	T7 S-891	S10 S-870	N6 S-770	N11 S-775	D14 S-586	A17 S-517	A13 S-513

SOROUSH
Custom Rugs & Axminster Carpet

301-929-5000 1-800-483-9955 Fax 301-929-5960 www.soroush.us

a) Print design for a portion of Axminster pattern.

Figure 23.3 Axminster pattern.
Courtesy of Soroush Custom Rugs & Axminster Carpet, www.soroush.us.

b) Axminster pattern made from design.

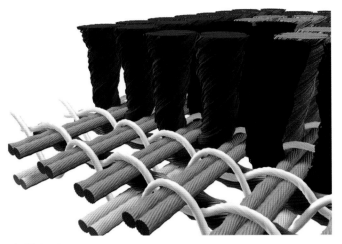

a) Side view.

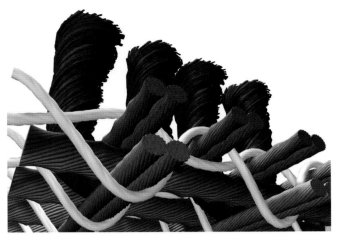

b) Back view.

Figure 23.4 Illustrations of Axminster weaving pattern.
Courtesy of Brintons.

one crosswise row of the point design. For a repeat 18 inches in width, the sequence would be used twice on each spool. Spools are linked end to end to form a **bracket**. If the carpet is to be woven 12 feet wide, four spools are used, and the sequence would be repeated eight times across the bracket.

The pitch determines the number of yarns wound on each spool. **Pitch** is the number of pile units (loops or cut, U-shaped tufts) per 27 inches of width; it commonly ranges from 162 to 216. The pitch method of reporting crosswise density in woven carpet has persisted from earlier times when looms were narrower: carpet was woven in 27-inch widths and seamed as often as necessary. If a carpet is to be 12 feet wide and have a pitch of 189, a total of 1,008 tufts will form each crosswise row. This is calculated as follows: 12 feet × 12 inches = 144 inches; 144 inches divided by 27 inches = 5.33; that is, there are five and a third of the 27-inch segments in the carpet width; and $5\frac{1}{3}$ × 189 tufts = 1,008 total tufts. Each bracket thus carries 1,008 yarns, and each 3-foot-long spool carries one-third of the total, or 336 yarns.

After the first bracket is completed, spools are wound with yarns according to the sequence shown in the second row of squares on the print design. The process continues until one bracket has been prepared for each crosswise row in the pattern repeat. The length of the repeat and the planned lengthwise density governs the number of brackets required.

The number of **rows per inch**—the number of crosswise rows of tufts per lengthwise inch—in an Axminster carpet is commonly within the range of seven to ten. If, for example, a count of eight rows per inch is selected, eight brackets would be prepared for weaving one lengthwise inch of carpet. A repeat 25 inches long would then require 200 brackets.

In preparation for weaving, the multiple brackets are positioned in proper order on the loom (Figure 23.5a). Yarn from the first bracket is rolled off, lowered into position, and the stuffers, chain warp yarns, and pairs of weft shots are integrated with the pile yarns, locking them into the structure. The amount of yarn reeled off is determined by the planned pile height. The pile yarn is cut, the bracket is moved away, and the second bracket is lowered. A complete cycle of all the brackets would produce the length of one repeat; a second cycle would produce another length, and so on.

Wilton Weaving

Formerly, loop pile carpet woven on a Jacquard loom was called **Brussels**, and cut pile carpet was called **Wilton**. Today, all pile floor covering woven on a Jacquard loom is called Wilton.

The number of colors of pile yarns used in the pattern is denoted by the number of **frames**; for instance, a three-frame Wilton has three colors, a six-frame Wilton has six colors, and so on. When the variously colored yarns are not required to form part of the surface design, they are carried in a plane in the backing layer (Figure 23.6). The

a) Weaving the design on an Axminster loom.

b) Axminster carpet.

Figure 23.5 Axminster weaving.
Courtesy of Soroush Custom Rugs & Axminster Carpet, www.soroush.us.

presence of such **dead and buried yarns**, also called floats, distinguishes Wilton constructions. Although the hidden lengths contribute weight, cushioning, and resiliency, they also add to the materials cost.

An enlarged section of a print design for a three-frame Wilton carpet is shown in Figure 23.7. The shed for weaving the first crosswise row would be formed by raising a red, a blue, and a green yarn. A blue and a green yarn would be lowered below the red yarn; a green yarn and a red yarn would be lowered below the blue yarn; and a red and a blue yarn would be lowered below the green yarn. The shed for weaving the second crosswise

row would be formed by raising a blue, a green, and a red yarn. A red and a green yarn would be lowered behind the blue yarn, and so on. One cone of yarn must be supplied for each color appearing in each lengthwise row of pile tufts. Weaving the three rows of carpet represented in the draft would require nine cones of yarn, one of each color for each row.

The total number of cones of yarn required for Wilton weaving is determined by the carpet width, the pitch, and the number of colors planned. If, for example, a three-frame Wilton is to be woven 12 feet wide with a pitch of 189, a total of 3,024 cones would be required, assuming each color is used in each lengthwise row. Since there are 1,008 pile units in each crosswise row, the total is calculated by multiplying 1,008 by 3, which equals 3,024.

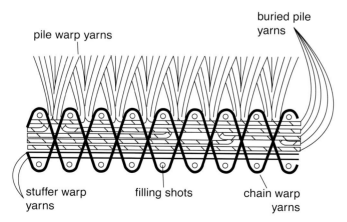

Figure 23.6 Cross-sectional sketch of a Wilton carpet.
Courtesy of Mohawk Carpet.

green	red	blue
blue	green	red
red	blue	green

Figure 23.7 Enlarged portion of a print design for a Wilton carpet.

To reduce yarn costs, a system of **planting** colored pile yarns may be employed: an added color of yarn is periodically substituted ("planted") for one of the basic pile colors. Planting can cause a three-frame Wilton carpet to appear to be a four-frame structure; an investigation of the backing, however, would uncover only two buried pile yarns behind each tuft (Figure 23.8a and b).

Jacquard carpet weaving is similar to other Jacquard weaving operations (see Chapter 6 and Figure 6.13, p. 108). In carpet weaving, however, the Jacquard attachment controls the pile yarns, not the base yarns; additional harnesses are used to control the chain warp yarns; and additional loom beams are used to hold the chain and stuffer yarns. As shown schematically in Figure 23.9, wires are inserted into the shed formed by the pile yarns, and weft shots are inserted into the separate shed formed by the chain warp yarns. The reed moves forward, pushing the wire and shot against the already-woven carpet. The heddle-like cords holding the raised pile yarns then descend, lowering the pile yarn over the wires. A weft shot is carried across the carpet, above the pile yarns and below the chain warp yarns. Then, a new pile yarn shed is formed, the harnesses reverse their positions, and the sequence is repeated.

The pile loops are formed over wires whose height determines the pile height. If a cut pile is planned, the wires are equipped with knives on one end; as the wires are withdrawn, they cut the loops. If a looped pile texture is planned, the wires will have rounded ends.

Since one wire is used for each crosswise row of pile tufts, the lengthwise density of Wilton carpet is reported as the number of **wires per inch**. Typically, this number is within the range of seven to ten. The crosswise density commonly ranges from a pitch of 189 to 252, but it may be as high as 270 or 346.

Velvet Carpet Weaving

Velvet carpet weaving is an over-the-wire construction technique used to produce velvet carpet. This use of "velvet" must not be confused with its use to name a surface texture nor with its use as a name for an upholstery fabric.

Velvet weaving is one of the least complicated methods of producing pile carpet. As in Wilton construction, the wire height determines the pile height. Again, the wires may or may not have knives on their ends. Use of the term *tapestry* to distinguish loop pile velvet carpet has been discontinued. Unlike Wilton weaving, however, no Jacquard attachment is used, so intricate details and elaborate patterns are not possible. Appearance variations may be created by combining cut and loop textures, by incorporating different colors of pile yarns in bands of various widths, or by employing pile yarns with distinctive color styling.

a) Side view.

b) Back view.

Figure 23.8 Illustration of Wilton carpet.
Courtesy of Brintons.

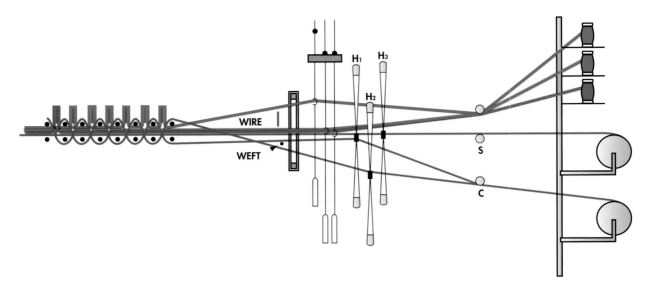

Figure 23.9 Diagram of Jacquard carpet weaving.

The cross sections in Figure 23.10 show two structural forms of velvet carpet. In Figure 23.10a, the pile yarns are anchored by the upper filling shots only. In Figure 23.10b, they are held by both the upper and lower filling shots: the carpet constructed this way would be described as a **woven-through-the-back** velvet. If other construction variables are the same, a woven-through-the-back velvet is more serviceable because the pile tufts are more securely bound and the total weight is greater. The carpet back in either type of velvet weave may be coated with latex or a thermoplastic compound for greater stability.

The pitch of velvet carpet ranges from 165 to 270. The number of wires per inch ranges from a low of seven to a high of ten.

Chenille Carpet Production

Two completely separate weaving operations are required to manufacture **chenille carpet**. The producer must first manufacture chenille "yarns," using the leno-weaving and fabric-cutting processes described in Chapter 5. The

Figure 23.10 Cross-sectional sketches of velvet carpets.

a) Conventional velvet construction
b) Woven-through-the-back construction

pile warp yarns

filling shots stuffer yarn chain warp yarns

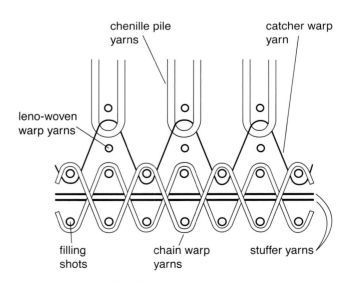

Figure 23.11 A chenille carpet.

chenille pile yarns catcher warp yarn

leno-woven warp yarns

filling shots chain warp yarns stuffer yarns

chenille strips are folded for use as pile yarns; the leno-entwined warp yarns form a base and the extended filling yarns form a V shape.

Figure 23.11 details the structural components of a chenille carpet. In addition to the stuffer, chain warp, and filling shots normally found in woven pile carpet, chenille carpet also has catcher or binder warp yarns to secure the chenille pile yarns to the base components.

Chenille carpet is comparatively expensive: the production sequence is involved and time-consuming, and an additional yarn component is required. Because of its cost, this construction technique is rarely used today, and not at all by domestic producers.

Pile Construction Density

The number of tufts per square inch in woven floor coverings can easily be calculated by first dividing the pitch value by 27. The resulting figure, the number of pile units per crosswise inch, is equivalent to the needle count with tufted constructions.

After pitch has been converted, the resulting value is multiplied by the number of rows or wires per inch. Direct comparisons can then be made with tufted constructions.

Other Machine Operations

Machine operations other than tufting and weaving are also used to produce soft floor coverings. Among these are fusion bonding, braiding, flocking, and needlepunching.

Fusion Bonding Operations

A significant portion of the recent research efforts of some commercial carpet producers has been channeled to the improvement of **fusion bonding** operations. Some operations are used for the production of rollgoods, which will be installed wall-to-wall; others are used for the production of carpet, which will subsequently be die-cut into modules.

Basic Components

Fusion-bonded structures have a minimum of three components: pile yarns, adhesive, and a primary backing (Figure 23.12). The adhesive, which is generally a vinyl compound such as polyvinylchloride (PVC), is placed on the face of the backing, which may be woven jute or a nonwoven glass fiber fabric. The pile yarns are embedded or implanted into the vinyl; they are not woven or tufted through the primary backing.

Fusion-bonded carpet has approximately 5 to 8 percent of the total pile yarn weight embedded in the adhesive; tufted structures may have 15 to 30 percent of the pile yarn weight enclosed in the primary backing; and woven constructions may have 20 to 50 percent of the total pile yarn weight interlaced in the backing layers. Thus, fusion-bonded carpet and modules can have more of the yarn available to the wearing face. Together with denser gauge fusing capabilities, this feature helps producers to engineer fusion-bonded floor coverings, even those having fine velour textures, to withstand the high levels of traffic encountered in commercial installations. The processing is slower than tufting, however, and the vinyl compound is more expensive than tufting substrates.

A special use of fusion bonding is the production of entrance mats made of coir fibers. Figure 23.13 provides a close-up view of the implantation of the ends of the fibers in PVC. The superior stiffness of these fibers helps them function like hundreds of miniature brushes, efficiently cleaning shoe soles and protecting the interior carpet from excessive amounts of tracked-in dirt. Coir mats generally range in total thickness from 0.68 to 1.2 inches. Some producers offer coir rollgoods and carpet modules, as well as mats.

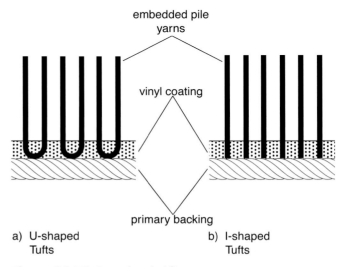

Figure 23.12 Fusion-bonded floor coverings.

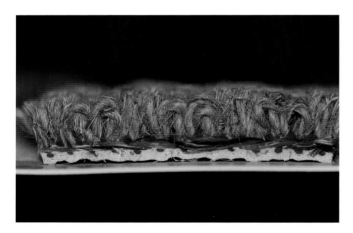

Figure 23.13 Cross-sectional view of rug containing implanted coir yarns.
Courtesy of Amy Willbanks, www.textilefabric.com.

Braiding

Braided rugs are constructed of braided components; the rugs themselves are not braided. The braids in the rug in Figure 23.14a were formed by interlacing groups of filament yarns; the braids in the rug in Figure 23.14b were formed by interlacing chenille yarns. In both rugs, core yarns composed of waste fibers were incorporated for weight, body, and cushioning. It is also possible to enclose yarn-like strands of sponge rubber for these purposes.

Braided strands are assembled side by side in a round or oval shape; machine zigzag stitching links adjacent braids. In a few rugs, flat braids are handled as conventional yarns and interlaced in a plain-weave pattern.

Flocking

Fibers with relatively high denier counts, ranging from 30 to 60, are used for flocked floor coverings. The fibers must be straight and nontextured so that they may be embedded in the adhesive coating in very large quantities. In preparation for the **flocking** operation, the fibers are cut into uniform lengths, ranging from 0.08 to 0.25 inch, and placed in a charged hopper. As shown in Figure 13.28 (p. 229), the flock is drawn into the adhesive coating on a substrate as it passes over a grounded plate. Often, the substrate is heavy-gauge vinyl sheeting.

Because electrostatic flocking draws the fibers vertically into the adhesive, the quantity of fibers per square inch can be greater than that in mechanical flocking. This high density provides better abrasion resistance and durability, performance features that are especially important when the structures are to be used as walk-off mats and automotive floor coverings. The accelerated laboratory tests used to assess the abrasion resistance of floor coverings are detailed in Chapter 26.

Needlepunching

Needlepunched floor coverings are often referred to as indoor-outdoor carpet. These structures are manufac-

a) Braided rug filled with many recycled yarns for dimensional stability.

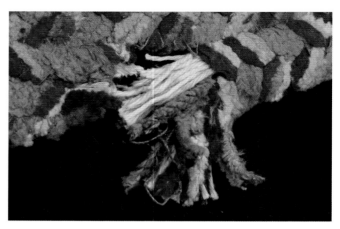

b) Braided rug containing chenille yarns braided around many ply yarns.

Figure 23.14 Braided rugs.
Courtesy of Amy Willbanks, www.textilefabric.com

a) Nonpile texture.

Figure 23.15 Needlepunched floor coverings.
Courtesy of Amy Willbanks, www.textilefabric.com

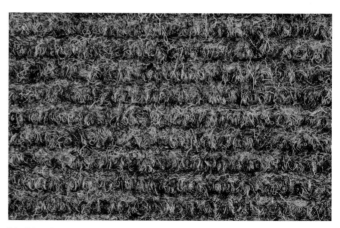

b) Simulated loop pile textures.

tured in the following sequence. Various colors of 3- to 4-inch fibers are blended to achieve uniform distribution of the colors. Long webs, as wide as the needle loom and weighing approximately 0.5 to 1.0 ounce per square yard, are formed by laying the fibers flat. Layering the webs at 45- or 90-degree angles to one another forms a thick batt of the desired weight, which typically ranges from 16 to 32 ounces per square yard. For strength and dimensional stability, an adhesive-coated jute or nylon scrim may be centered in the batt or placed behind it. The batt is then tacked or prepunched to reduce its thickness and fed into a needle loom. Here, hundreds of barbed needles punch into the batt some 800 to 1,200 times per square inch, creating a mechanical chain-stitch among the fibers and locking them into the scrim and adhesive.

The barbed needles used in the punching operation produce flat carpet with a felt-like appearance (Figure 23.15a). Carpet having loop-like protrusions (Figure 23.15b) can be produced by using needles with crescent-shaped points for the final punches.

When needlepunched structures are to be installed outdoors, on patios and golf greens and around pools, their composition is chosen to withstand the ravages of sunlight, rain, and insects. They are permeable, so they can be hosed to flush away dirt. If these structures are installed wall-to-wall indoors, their permeability presents obvious problems when liquids are spilled on them.

Summary

Machine techniques other than tufting used to produce soft floor coverings include weaving, fusion bonding, braiding, flocking, and needlepunching. Axminster, Wilton, and chenille weaving operations are relatively slow and expensive, but Axminster and Wilton weaving can produce patterns of intricate detail and many colors. Fusion bonding is increasingly used to produce rollgoods and carpet modules with fine, velour surface textures.

Key Terms

bracket	Brussels	chenille carpet
braiding	chain warp yarns	dead and buried yarns

filling yarns
filling or weft shots
floats
flocking
frames
fusion bonding
ingrain

needlepunching
pile warp yarns
pitch
planting
print design
rows per inch
spools

stuffer yarns
velvet carpet weaving
warp yarns
Wilton
wires per inch
woven-through-the-back

Review Questions

1. Draw and label a cross-sectional sketch of a woven carpet.

2. What is the purpose of stuffer yarns?

3. How can one identify chain warps?

4. What construction feature tends to make the crosswise direction of Axminster floor coverings inflexible?

5. Explain the use of print designs, spools, and brackets in the preparation of Axminster weaving.

6. Identify the positive and negative features of having "dead and buried" pile yarns in Wilton carpet.

7. How does the Jacquard loom used for weaving floor coverings differ from that used for weaving apparel fabric?

8. Why is the lengthwise density of Wilton carpet reported as wires per inch?

9. Why is chenille carpet construction comparatively expensive?

10. How does one use pitch and needle count to compare the crosswise densities of a woven carpet and a tufted carpet?

11. Fusion-bonded floor coverings are said to have more effective face weight; that is, they have more of the yarn available to the wearing face. How does this help such floor coverings to withstand high levels of traffic?

12. What, in fact, is braided in braided floor coverings?

Construction of Floor Coverings: Hand Techniques

■ **Hand operations produce** rugs, not rollgoods. Some of these operations are carried out by highly organized, commercial organizations. In such cases, the quality of the products is carefully controlled and the marketing strategies that promote them are sophisticated. This is typical of the production and promotion of authentic Oriental rugs and rugs woven by Native Americans.

The distinctive styling of many hand constructed rugs leads many people to use them as ornamental wall accents, perhaps as often as they use them as floor coverings. Whether placed on the floor or on the wall, most of these rugs are produced by weaving, but some are constructed in braiding, hooking, and felting operations. Hand weaving and hand knotting are generally combined to produce pile structures, and plain- or tapestry-interlacing patterns are used to produce many flat structures.

Hand-woven Pile Rugs

Two types of hand-woven rugs, Oriental rugs and rya rugs, contain hand-knotted pile yarns. Another type, the Flokati rug, has a hand-pulled pile layer.

Oriental Rugs

Intricate motifs and many colors are found in the pile layers of **Oriental rugs**. Typical are geometric shapes, stylized dragons, rosettes, medallions, trees, flowers, vines, and many styles of borders. Historically, weavers executed only their own ancestral designs or those first produced in their geographic regions; the designs reflected the cultural heritage and life of the weavers. The origin of these rugs could be identified by their pattern, and they were known by such names as Persian, Turkoman, Chinese, Caucasian, and Indian. Today, weavers throughout the world have adapted most of the traditional patterns, and it is no longer possible to accurately identify the origin of a rug by its design.

Savonnerie rugs, which were first produced in France, present an example of pattern dispersion. The name derives from savon, French for "soap," because these rugs were first woven in a factory that earlier had been used for the production of soap. Today, the classic designs and soft pastel colors characteristic of these rugs, and of the fine, loop pile French **Aubusson rugs**, have been liberally copied by rug weavers in other countries. A Savonnerie rug woven in India is pictured in Figure 24.1.

The design of Aubusson and Savonnerie rugs is often emphasized by hand carving.

The distinguishing feature of all authentic Oriental rugs is that each pile tuft is hand knotted. The **Sehna (Senna)** or **Persian knot** (Figure 24.2a) or the **Ghiordes** or **Turkish knot** (Figure 24.2b) is used. The Sehna knot can be tied to slant to the left or right, but must be tied the same way throughout a project. The Sehna knot completely encircles one warp yarn and passes under the adjacent warp yarn; as a result, one pile tuft projects from every space between the warp yarns. When the Ghiordes knot is tied, both ends of the pile yarn extend from the same space; no pile tufts fill the alternate spaces. If other construction features are identical, a Sehna-knotted rug is finer than a Ghiordes-knotted rug, and the pattern is more sharply defined.

During the hand weaving operation, several weavers may work simultaneously on the same project, knotting the pile yarns in horizontal rows. Normally, one or two filling or weft yarns are used in plain-weave interlacing patterns between each crosswise row of pile knots. Increasing the number of filling yarns decreases the pile construction density.

Figure 24.1 Savonnerie rug.
Courtesy of www.rugswithflair.com (supplies to the trade only).

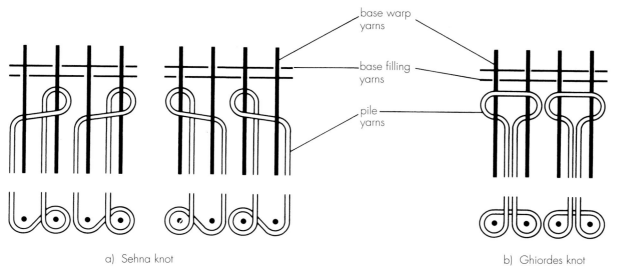

base warp yarns

base filling yarns

pile yarns

a) Sehna knot

b) Ghiordes knot

Figure 24.2 Knots used to form the pile layers in authentic Oriental rugs.

The quality of Oriental rugs depends on the number of knots per square inch. Whereas the number of warp yarns per inch and the frequency of knot placement determine the crosswise density, the skill of the weavers, the size of the pile yarns, and the number of filling yarns per tuft row determine the lengthwise density. **Antique Oriental rugs**, those produced prior to the mid-1800s, often had as many as 500 knots per square inch. The famous Ardebil Mosque Carpet, produced in 1539–1540 and now housed in London, England, was woven with some 380 knots per square inch. Old or **semi-antique rugs**, those woven during the latter part of the nineteenth century, and **modern rugs**, those produced during this century, generally have 100 to 225 knots per square inch, but some have as many as 324 knots per square inch.

Other important quality-related factors are pile height, fiber content, and level of luster. The use of natural dyestuffs for antique Oriental rugs resulted in a subdued, mellow luster. Synthetic dyestuffs developed in the mid-1850s simplified dyeing operations and were adopted by weavers. Because these colorants produce brighter colors than the natural dyestuffs, many of today's Oriental rugs are treated with chlorine or acetic acid and glycerin to simulate the prized sheen and soft luster of the older rugs: this processing is variously described as **chemical washing**, **culturing**, and **luster washing**. This treatment may weaken the fibers, but many producers and consumers consider the beauty of the rug more important than its wear-life.

Economic considerations have largely been responsible for the diminished use of silk in Oriental rug pile yarns. Today, most of these rugs have pile yarns composed of wool and base yarns of cotton.

The labor-intensive, tedious, and slow production of hand-knotted Oriental rugs makes them relatively expensive, beyond the reach of many consumers. To lower the cost, manufacturers have increasingly produced rugs with traditional Oriental patterns on power looms, principally on Axminster looms. Machine-woven rugs, known as **Oriental design rugs**, generally have a sewn-on fringe, which may differ from the base warp yarns; in hand-knotted rugs, the base warp yarns extending from the ends of the rug form the fringe. Recently, computerized printing systems have been employed to increase the availability and affordability of these prized designs.

Rya Rugs

Rya rugs originated in Scandinavian countries where weavers hand knotted long pile yarns. Today, authentic rya rugs are still hand knotted, but machine-made rya rugs are also available; both are prized worldwide for their decorative value. Typically, yarns in related colors form the pile layer, and the designs are gently flowing and curved (Figure 24.3).

In rya rug construction, the pile yarns are knotted with the Ghiordes knot (Figure 24.2b) as in Oriental rugs. Rya rugs differ from Oriental rugs, however, in two

a)

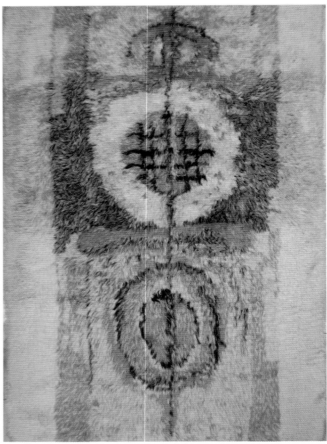

b)

Figure 24.3 Rya rugs.
NAZMIYAL, Inc., www.nazmiyalantiquerugs.com.

principal ways. First, the pile height in rya rugs is considerably longer, ranging from 1 to 3 inches. As the pile height increases, the spacing between the pile rows can also increase, since the longer pile yarns will readily cover the base fabric. Second, more filling or weft yarns are used between each crosswise row of knotted pile yarns in rya constructions. These are interlaced with the base warp yarns in a plain- or tapestry-weave pattern.

So that the pile loops will be uniform in height, the yarn is continuously looped over a **rya** or **flossa stick**. The depth of the stick determines the pile height in the same way the wire height determines the pile height in Wilton and velvet carpet constructions. The stick is grooved to facilitate cutting the loops after a row has been knotted on it.

Pile yarns in authentic rya rugs are normally composed of wool. Along with the large amount of yarn used, the relatively high cost of the fiber makes the rugs comparatively expensive.

Flokati Rugs

Flokati (Flocati) rugs (Figure 24.4) are long pile wool structures woven in Greece. The weaver who pulls a wooden rod inserted under the yarns controls the pile yarn length. The loops are then cut by hand. After weaving, every authentic Flokati rug is immersed in a deep vat in a pool beyond a natural waterfall. Here, the swirling water causes the wool fibers to felt, converting the yarns into pointed strands. Like authentic rya rugs, these rugs

Figure 24.4 Flokati rug.
Courtesy of www.rugswithflair.com (supplies to the trade only).

use large amounts of wool and labor-intensive processing, making them comparatively expensive.

Hand-constructed Flat Rugs

Most hand-constructed flat rugs are woven in a plain or tapestry-based interlacing pattern. The motifs of these floor coverings, like those of Oriental rugs, often reflect the cultural heritage of the weavers.

Khilim Rugs

Khilim (Kelim, Kilim) rugs are woven in eastern European countries. These colorful floor coverings have graceful, stylized designs depicting flowers, animals, and other natural things (Figure 24.5).

The construction of Khilim rugs is similar to tapestry weaving: the filling yarns are woven in sections according to color. Unlike those in tapestry structures, however, the ends of all filling yarns in Khilim rugs are woven in, so the structure is reversible. In some cases, the weaving may produce slits or openings where the colors change in the design motif. These openings are finished and will not ravel (Figure 24.6). The slits may be retained as part of the design or they may be sewn together by hand.

Figure 24.5 Khilim rug.
Courtesy of www.kilim.com.

Rugs Woven by Native Americans

Rugs produced by Native Americans, primarily the Navajo, Cheyenne, and Hopi peoples, are hand woven with a tapestry-related interlacing. Because the end of each filling yarn is woven in at the juncture of color changes, these rugs, like Khilims, are reversible. In contrast to the Khilim rug technique, however, the filling yarns are woven to avoid slits, with a dovetailing or interlocking technique (Figure 24.7).

The designs used in these rugs are bold graphic symbols (Figure 24.8) or detailed patterns representing tribal life and culture. Weavers throughout the world frequently adapt them. Today, these rugs are often chosen to act as wall accents.

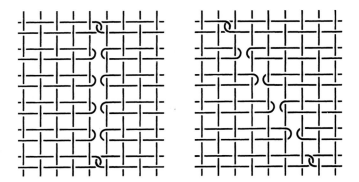

Figure 24.6 Slits found in Khilim rugs.

According to the rules and regulations issued by the FTC pursuant to the Textile Fiber Products Identification Act, all hand-woven rugs made by Navajo Indians that carry the "Certificate of Genuineness" supplied by the Indian Arts and Crafts Board of the U.S. Department of Interior are exempt from the provisions of the TFPIA. Here, the term "Navajo Indian" means any Indian listed on the register of the Navajo Indian tribe or eligible for listing thereon.

Dhurrie Rugs

Dhurrie (durrie, durry) rugs are flat, hand-woven rugs made in India. They have a plain, twill, or tapestry interlacing. These rugs may display crosswise striations, produced by interspersing various colors of heavy, hand-spun cotton filling yarns, or stylized designs executed with wool filling yarns (Figures 24.9 and 24.10).

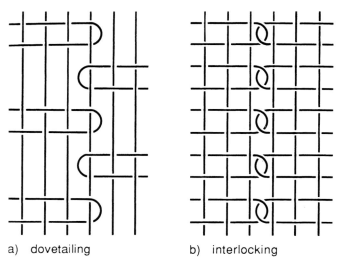

a) dovetailing   b) interlocking

Figure 24.7 Techniques used to avoid the formation of slits in tapestry.

Figure 24.8 Navajo rug.
Courtesy of www.indianterritory.com.

Floor Mats

Floor mats composed of various grasses, coir, sisal, linen, hemp, or jute fibers are available in an extensive variety of sizes, shapes, and interlacings. Frequently, twill interlacing is used to create diamond, herringbone, and other geometric patterns over the surface. For larger floor coverings, several small mats can be sewn together.

Other Rugs and Mats

Rag rugs are hand woven in plain-weave interlacing. The filling component is formed by rolling and twisting new or previously used fabric into yarn-like structures. Braiding and felting operations produce other small rugs and mats. Some felted rugs are embellished with surface embroidery.

Figure 24.9 Dhurrie rug.
Courtesy of Shreevaas Exports.

Figure 24.10 Dhurrie rug production.
Courtesy of Shreevaas Exports.

Summary

Among the pile floor coverings produced by hand techniques are Oriental rugs, rya rugs, and Flokati rugs. Khilim, Navajo, and dhurrie rugs are examples of hand-woven, flat rugs. While Flokati and rya rugs are distinguished by the use of relatively long pile yarns, traditional motifs and colorations generally distinguish other hand-constructed rugs. Color styling is important to selection of these as well as machine-constructed floor coverings.

Key Terms

antique Oriental rugs

Aubusson rugs

chemical washing

culturing

dhurrie (durrie, durry) rugs

Flokati (Flocati) rugs

flossa stick

Ghiordes knot

Khilim (Kelim, Kilim) rugs

luster washing

modern rugs

Oriental design rugs

Oriental rugs
Persian knot
rya rugs

rya stick
Savonnerie rugs
Sehna (Senna) knot

semi-antique rugs
Turkish knot

Review Questions

1. Why is it difficult today to identify the origin of Oriental rugs by their motifs?

2. What is the derivation of the name "Savonnerie" for rugs?

3. Identify differences between the Sehna and Ghiordes knots.

4. Differentiate among the following: antique Oriental rugs, old or semi-antique Oriental rugs, and modern Oriental rugs.

5. Identify differences in the construction of the pile portion of Oriental and rya rugs.

6. How is the pile height controlled in rya rugs and Flokati rugs?

7. Discuss similarities and differences between Khilim rugs and rugs woven by Native Americans.

Carpet and Rug Cushions

CHAPTER **TWENTY-FIVE**

Photo courtesy of Tesri, www.tesri.fr.

■ **Many names—cushion, pad,** padding, lining, foundation, underlayment—identify the structure placed between a carpet or rug and the floor. Today, members of the industry prefer to use the term cushion or carpet cushion, although many continue to use the term padding. Carpet cushions vary in chemical composition, thickness, compressibility, resiliency, resistance to moisture, resistance to microbes, and cost. They also differ in acoustical value, insulative benefit, and the contributions they make toward extending the wear-life of the soft floor covering. Table 25.3 supplies information regarding type of pad and density required based on moderate, heavy, and extra heavy traffic. Some cushions can only be used separately; others can be separate or permanently attached to the carpet back. Cushion-related variables should be considered in light of the carpet or rug selected, the kind of "feel" preferred underfoot, the environmental and traffic conditions anticipated in end use, and the floor covering budget. Moisture barrier backing systems usually combine cushioning with a barrier to prevent spills from penetrating the backing and soaking into the subfloor. The backing is typically made of PVC or other hard backing and can be applied on either broadloom or modular carpet tiles.

Professionals must understand the evaluation of carpet cushions, so that they can interpret the data provided by producers and understand requirements set forth by an authority with jurisdiction over certain installations. Professionals must be able to supply accurate data for custom projects. The information required depends on the type of cushion selected. The cushions available on today's market fall into three major categories: fibrous cushions, cellular rubber cushions, and urethane foam cushions.

Fibrous Cushion Structures

Fibrous cushions are produced by needlepunching hair or jute fibers into felt-like structures. Four types of fibrous cushions are on the market: all hair, all jute, blends of hair and jute, and hair or jute fibers or both bonded between sheets of latex.

All-hair structures are normally made of cleaned, stiff cattle hair (Figure 25.1). Like all-jute cushions, all-hair cushions are relatively inexpensive, but both types tend to shift, bunch, and clump under heavy traffic conditions. For added stability, a loosely woven jute scrim may be centered in the batt prior to needlepunching. Antimicro-bial agents are recommended to retard the growth of mildew and fungi and the odor and deterioration they cause. These cushions tend to exhibit aging; they can crumble and disintegrate after prolonged use. Because these fibers are subject to moisture damage, the use of latex sheets as protective barriers is recommended when below-grade installation is planned. For skid resistance, as well as to compensate for the somewhat low compressibility and resiliency, the surfaces of the fibrous batts and latex sheets are generally embossed.

Fibrous cushions are available in rolls up to 12 feet wide. Their weights range from 32 to 86 ounces per square yard.

Cellular Rubber Cushions

Cellular rubber cushions can be either foam rubber or sponge rubber. Both types can be made from natural or synthesized rubber compounds. For some people, these rubber or latex compounds may be allergens.

Sponge Rubber Structures

Sponge rubber cushions frequently contain chemicals, oils, and fillers that were added to the rubber compound for weight. The mixture is pulverized and then expanded into continuous flat sheets or into three-dimensional forms. The three-dimensional cushions are variously referred to as waffle, ripple, or bubble sponge cushions; a typical profile is in Figure 25.2. The flat form is available in uniform thicknesses that range from 0.125 to 0.3125 inch.

Sponge rubber has larger cells and thicker cell walls than foam rubber; sponge structures are therefore more porous and less likely to retain odors. The cellular quali-

Figure 25.1 Fibrous cushions made of hair.
Courtesy of Amy Willbanks, www.textilefabric.com.

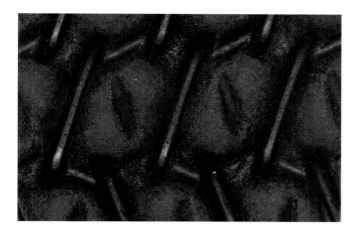

Figure 25.2 Bubble sponge rubber cushion.
Courtesy of Amy Willbanks, www.textilefabric.com.

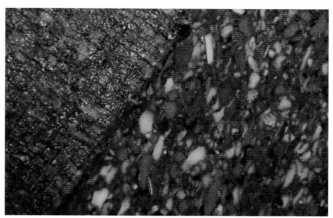

Figure 25.3 Bonded foam cushion.
Courtesy of Amy Willbanks, www.textilefabric.com.

ties also contribute buoyancy and softness, characteristics further enhanced when the cushion is three-dimensional. Sponge cushions are highly compressible and produce the plushness often sought in residential interiors and executive offices. Under heavy commercial traffic, however, the waffle forms do not provide uniform support: repeated deformation and flexing of the carpet backing can produce uneven surfaces. Moreover, the clay or ash fillers may grind against other components and crumbling may occur. Flat sponge rubber cushions can provide more uniform support for carpet used in areas of medium and heavy traffic, and better skid resistance for area rugs.

Sponge rubber cushions are available in rolls up to 12 feet wide. Their weights range from 41 to 120 ounces per square yard.

Foam Rubber Structures

Foam rubber cushions are manufactured by converting liquid latex and fillers into flat, continuous sheets. The sheets may be as thin as 0.125 inch or as thick as 0.625 inch. A spunbonded fabric is normally applied to the top of sponge and foam rubber cushions. The fabric facilitates handling during installation since it permits the carpet back to slide over the fabric without stretching and distorting the cushion. The bonded foam cushion in Figure 25.3 has been reinforced with a woven scrim.

Because foam rubber has smaller cells than sponge rubber, foam cushions provide firmer, more uniform support, but they may exhibit more odor retention. Foam rubber cushions are available in rolls up to 12 feet wide, and in weights ranging from 28 to 65 ounces per square yard.

In thinner forms, foam rubber cushions can be permanently bonded to the back of carpet structures (Figure 25.4). The assembly can then be laid on the floor without installing a separate cushion; for maximum stability, it can be glued to the floor.

Minimum standards have been established for attached foam cushions in an effort to promote consistent quality. These standards are listed in Table 25.1. In this table, **density** refers to the amount of rubber per unit of volume; increasing the density would increase the weight of the cushion and the level of support provided.

Table 25.1 Recommended Minimum Specifications for Attached Latex Foam Cushions	
Weight	38 oz./sq. yd.
Thickness	$\frac{1}{8}$ in.
Density	17 lb./cu. ft.
Compression loss	Maximum of 15% loss
Compression deflection	Not less than 5 psi
Delamination strength	2 lb./in.
Accelerated aging	(a) Heat aging: 24 hrs at 275 °F; after flexing, should remain flexible and serviceable. (b) Fade-Ometer® aging: 20 hrs. exposure; sample should show only slight crazing.
Ash content	Maximum of 50%

Courtesy of the Carpet and Rug Institute.

Figure 25.4 Polyurethane foam cushion. Courtesy of Amy Willbanks, www.textilefabric.com.

Compression loss, also known as *compression set*, is the extent to which the structure fails to recover its original thickness after being compressed 50 percent under a static load. **Compression deflection** is the extent (reported as psi or pounds per square inch) to which the structure resists compression force. **Delamination strength** is the force per inch of width required to separate the cushion from the carpet; it is measured as described in Chapter 22, using the test apparatus clamps shown in Figure 22.8 (p. 355). Procedures for measuring other properties are discussed later in this chapter.

Several of the recommended specifications for attached foam cushions have been adopted as required standards by a number of federal agencies, including the Office of Housing and Urban Development, the General Services Administration, and the Veterans' Administration. These authorities have also set forth additional requirements pertaining to fire performance. The test methods used to evaluate flammability are explained in Chapter 11.

Urethane Foam Cushions

Three types of urethane foam cushions are generally available for residential and commercial use: prime or conventional foam, densified prime foam, and bonded or rebond foam. The chemical composition of these cushions is basically the same, but they are manufactured by different processes, and their cellular structures differ.

Prime Urethane Foam Structures

Prime urethane foam cushions are manufactured by foaming the urethane polymer units into a continuous sheet, generally 6 feet wide. "Prime" distinguishes this kind of cushion from the bonded or rebond type.

Prime urethane foam has comparatively large cells shaped somewhat like ellipses, and the foam struts or columns among the cells are vertically oriented. This cellular form provides various degrees of compressibility, depending on density. Under load, these structures may "bottom out": the cushion suddenly flattens under force. Prime foams may contain powdered fillers for weight and polymer additives for increased stability.

Densified Prime Urethane Foam Structures

Densified foam cushions have a higher density than prime foam. The higher density is produced from a finer, elongated cellular structure and somewhat horizontal struts. No fillers are used. These cushions are said to be odorless, resilient, mildew-resistant, and resistant to bottoming out.

Bonded Urethane Foam Structures

Bonded urethane foam cushions are made by bonding and compressing together granulated pieces of prime urethane trim; the term "rebond" is sometimes used to identify these cushions. The strength of these structures largely depends on the strength of the prime urethane foam material used in the trim pieces.

All three types of urethane foam cushions are manufactured in several thicknesses, generally ranging from 0.375 to 0.750 inch, and all generally have a spun-bonded facing to facilitate installation. In their thinner forms, these cushions can provide skid resistance to area rugs and runners. As do other types of cushions used for this purpose, the thin form minimizes the problem known as "rug walking" or "rug crawling," the tendency for rugs to shift or move off cushions under the stress of traffic.

The density of urethane cushions is usually within the range of 2.4 to 5.0 pounds per cubic foot. Cushions with higher densities have higher compression deflection values; they provide firmer support underfoot.

Listing Specification Data for Carpet Cushions

Specification listings detail the composition, construction, and performance features of a textile structure.

Specification data may be prepared by the producer, or by the trained and experienced professional. The data reported by the producer include values obtained from the accelerated laboratory testing of their products. Professionals list the characteristics and properties they or their clients prefer, or those mandated for textile products used in a particular project. For certain installations, the professional must specify test methods and levels of performance to ensure that the structure conforms to standards established by the authority that has jurisdiction.

Specification listings for cushions are less extensive than those prepared for carpet and rugs (see Table 26.2, p. 390). The data required will depend on the type of cushion selected, the anticipated traffic conditions, the carpet selected, and any mandated features. The recommended minimum specifications for attached foam cushions are listed in Table 25.1; Table 25.2 exemplifies the various features that may be specified for a densified prime urethane foam cushion.

The first item in Table 25.2 states the composition of the cushion; the second item states that a spunbonded fabric is to be applied to the top side of the structure; the next two items describe structural characteristics; and the remaining items detail performance features and levels. The values used are for illustrative purposes only. Laboratory testing confirms that a cushion exhibits specified characteristics.

Table 25.2 Sample Cushion Specification/Data List

Cushion compound: densified prime, unfilled polyurethane foam; clean and free of defects
Coating: spunbonded polypropylene olefin
Density: 5.0 lb./cu. ft.
Thickness: 0.265 in.

Compressive load deflection:
  25% deflection   1.5 psi minimum
  65% deflection   6.5 psi minimum
  75% deflection   11.0 psi minimum

Compression set: maximum of 15% at 50% deflection
Tensile strength: 25 psi minimum
Elongation: 50% minimum

Flammability: (a) CFR 1630 (FF 1-70/tablet test): passes
           (b) Flooring radiant panel test: greater
                than 0.25 watt/sq. cm.

Evaluating the Performance of Cushions

Some performance features, including compression loss and compression set, are important to all cushion materials. One performance variable, aging, is important only in cellular rubber cushions, and, as noted earlier in this chapter, delamination strength is a concern only with permanently attached cushions. Refer to Chapter 26 for information on cushions and indoor air quality (IAQ).

Accelerated Aging

In prolonged use, rubber cushion compounds may be affected by heat and exhibit aging in the form of cracking, crumbling, and sticking. To assure that the cushion will not show **accelerated aging**, the structure can be evaluated in accelerated laboratory testing. In one procedure, latex cushion material may be exposed for 24 hours to a temperature of 275 °F in a circulating air oven prior to evaluation. In a second accelerated procedure, a specimen may be placed in a Fade-Ometer® (Figure 18.4, p. 306) for 20 hours in accordance with Federal Test Method Standard 191A, Method 5660. As stated in Table 25.1, foam latex samples should withstand these exposures with no more than slight discoloration or surface degradation. Upon flexing, a slight cracking or crazing is acceptable.

Compressibility

Compressibility evaluations measure the degree of resistance a cushion offers to being crushed or deflected under a static load. The measurements are made by following the procedures outlined in ASTM D 3574. In preparation for evaluating this performance quality, cushion specimens are cut into small squares (often 2 inches square) and layered to a thickness of 1 inch. The plied structure is then placed on the platform of a testing unit (Figure 25.5). The support platform has perforations to allow for rapid escape of air during the test. A flat, circular foot is used to indent or deflect the layered specimens.

The force required to deflect or compress the specimen assembly a given percentage of its original thickness is measured for each of two replicate tests. Together with the percentage of deflection used, the average number of pounds per square inch required to compress the cushion

Figure 25.5 Compression deflection testing apparatus. Courtesy of SDL Atlas.

are layered to a thickness of 1 inch and deflected 50 percent. The compressed structure is then placed in an oven at 158 °F for 22 hours. At the end of this period, the load is removed and the thickness is measured after a 30-minute recovery period. The compression set is calculated with the following formula:

compression set = [(original thickness − thickness after compression)/original thickness] × 100. The average of two replicate tests is reported.

A high recovery of cushion thickness is desirable, and a minimum recovery level of 85 percent (maximum loss of 15 percent) is frequently recommended or mandated. As a cushion recovers from compression, it exerts an upward pressure that encourages the carpet also to recover. The actual level of recovery depends upon the particular combination of carpet and cushion.

Tensile Strength

The **tensile strength** of cushion structures is measured in the laboratory according to prescribed test methods, such as FTMS 191A, Method 5100. The value reported is the average of five replicate tests and is the force per unit of cross-sectional area necessary to cause rupture. Required minimum tensile strength values may range from 8 to 20 psi.

Elongation

Elongation values describe how far a cushion structure extends before rupturing. The performance is evaluated as part of the procedure for evaluating tensile strength. The value reported is the average of five readings, each calculated by the following formula: % elongation at break = (length stretched/original length) × 100.

Because cushions are always used in combination with a carpet or rug, some performance evaluations are more meaningful when they are made on the floor covering assembly. This is especially true when such functional values as noise reduction and insulation benefits are being considered. In some cases the functional benefits of an assembly will be more strongly influenced by the cushion than by the carpet; in many cases, carpet and cushion both contribute to a functional value. Evaluations of floor covering assemblies are described in the following chapter.

material is reported to the nearest pound. Several federal agencies have mandated specific levels of **compression load deflection (CLD)**; these vary with the type of cushion and the interior facility.

The compressibility of a cushion correlates with the degree of softness felt underfoot. Cushions having low CLD values are soft and easily compressed; cushions having high values are firmer, less compressible structures. Firmer cushions should be selected for interior floor space subjected to rolling equipment or wheelchairs.

Compression Set

Compression set is synonymous with **compression loss**. It describes the extent to which a structure fails to recover its original thickness after static compression. In most evaluation procedures, cushion specimens

Table 25.3 Recommended Pad Densities			
Types of Cushion	Class I Moderate Traffic	Class II Heavy Traffic	Class III Extra Heavy Traffic
Commercial Application	**Office Buildings:** Executive or private offices, conference rooms **Health Care:** Executive, administration **Schools:** Administration **Airports:** Administration **Retail:** Windows and display areas **Banks:** Executive areas **Hotels/Motels:** Sleeping rooms **Libraries/Museums:** Administration	**Office Buildings:** Clerical areas, corridors (moderate traffic) **Health Care:** Patients' rooms, lounges **Schools:** Dormitories and classrooms **Retail:** Minor aisles, boutiques, specialty **Banks:** Lobbies, corridors (moderate traffic) **Hotels/Motels:** Corridors **Libraries/Museums:** Public areas, moderate traffic **Convention Center:** Auditoriums	**Office Buildings:** Corridors (heavy traffic), cafeterias **Health Care:** Lobbies, corridors, nurses' stations **Schools:** Corridors, cafeterias **Retail:** Major aisles, checkouts, supermarkets **Banks:** corridors (moderate traffic), teller windows **Hotels/Motels:** Corridors and public areas **Libraries/Museums:** Public areas **Country Clubs:** Locker rooms, pro shops, dining areas **Convention Center:** Corridors and lobbies **Restaurants:** Dining area and lobbies
Fiber, oz/sq. yd.			
Natural (Hair, jute, etc.)	Wt. 32 oz. Th: $1/4''$ + 5% max.	Wt. 40 oz. Th: $5/16''$ + 5% max.	Wt. 50 oz. Th: $3/8''$ + 5% max.
Synthetic, Needled	Wt. 20 oz. Th: $5/16''$ + 5% max.	Wt. 28 oz. Th: $3/8''$ + 5% max.	Wt. 36 oz. Th: $3/8''$ + 5% max.
SPONGE RUBBER, oz/sq. yd.			
Flat Sponge	Wt. 56 oz. Th: .225'' + 5% CLD@25% .75 psi	Wt. 64 oz. Th: .250'' + 5% CLD@25% 1.0 psi	Wt. 80 oz. Th: .250'' + 5% CLD@25% 1.5 psi
Ripple Sponge	Wt. 64 oz. Th: .350'' + 5% CLD@25% .75 psi	Wt. 80 oz. Th: .400'' + 5% CLD@25% 1.0 psi	
Reinforced Foam Rubber	Wt. 56 oz. Th: .225'' + 5% CLD@25% .75 psi	Wt. 64 oz. Th: .235'' + 5% CLD@25% 1.0 psi	Wt. 80 oz. Th: .235'' + 5% CLD@25% 1.5 psi
POLYURETHANE FOAM, lbs/cu. ft. (pcf)	Polyester foam content not to exceed 50% Particle size not to exceed $1/2''$	Polyester foam content not to exceed 50% Particle size not to exceed $1/2''$	Polyester foam content not to exceed 50% Particle size not to exceed $1/2''$
Bonded Urethane	D: 5.0 pcf ± 5% Th: $3/8'' \pm 1/32''$ CLD @ 25% 4.0 psi	D: 6.5 pcf ± 5% Th: $5/16'' \pm 1/32''$ CLD @ 65% ($3/8''$): 5.0 psi	D: 8.0 pcf ± 5% Th: $1/4''$ + ; $1/32''$ CLD @ 65% (1'') 7.0 psi
Modified Prime Urethane	D: 2.5 pcf ± 5% Th: $1/4'' \pm 1/32''$ ILD @ 25%: 100 lb ± 10%	D: 2.7 pcf ± 5% Th: $1/4'' \pm 1/32''$ ILD @ 25%: 100 lb ± 10%	D: 3.2 pcf ± 5% Th: $3/16'' + 1/32''$ ILD @ 25%: 120 lb ± 10%
Densified Prime Urethane	D: 2.1 pcf ± 5% Th: .350'' $\pm 1/32''$ CLD @ 65%: .85 psi	D: 3.5 pcf ± 5% Th: .265'' − .015'' + .031'' CLD @ 65%: 1.8 psi	D: 4.5 pcf Th: .265'' − .015'' + .031'' CLD @ 65%: .2.3 psi

Courtesy of Ascend Performance Materials.

Summary

Most of the cushions available today can be classified in one of three major categories: fibrous felt cushions, cellular rubber cushions, and urethane cushions. Numerous variations exist within each category, in thickness; weight; density; compressibility; resiliency; resistance to moisture, heat, and microbes; and cost. The choice of a cushion involves an assessment of these features, as well as an analysis of the traffic levels and activities anticipated in the interior area to be carpeted. In light-traffic areas, a thick, low-density structure could be selected for greater buoyancy and softness underfoot. In areas where traffic is heavy, a thin, high-density structure should be used. The cost of installing a separate cushion will normally be higher than using an attached cushion or no cushion, but certain performance benefits may partially offset the additional materials and installation charges. In all installations, the quality of the cushion should be consistent with that of the carpet: a high-quality cushion cannot compensate for a low-quality carpet, and a skimpy cushion cannot support a heavy, high-quality carpet or rug.

Key Terms

accelerated aging

acoustical value

bonded urethane foam

cellular rubber cushions

compressibility

compression deflection

compression load deflection (CLD)

compression loss

compression set

delamination strength

densified foam

density

elongation

fibrous cushions

prime urethane foam

tensile strength

Review Questions

1. Identify the types of fibrous cushions produced and cite the positive and negative features of each.

2. Distinguish between sponge rubber and foam rubber cushions.

3. Why is one form of urethane foam cushions less susceptible to "bottoming out?"

4. How can the consumer minimize "rug walking" or "rug crawling?"

5. What is the purpose of using a spunbonded facing fabric with rubber and urethane cushions?

6. What are the advantages of having minimum compression loss?

Evaluations and Specifications for Soft Floor Coverings

CHAPTER **TWENTY-SIX**

Photo courtesy of Amy Willbanks, www.textilefabric.com

■ **For suppliers, producers,** colorists, and converters of textile floor coverings and components, standard test methods and performance specifications are an important part of manufacturing and marketing efforts. Data gathered from this quality-control work help industry members identify the need for changes in the composition, manufacturing, or conversion of their products. The data also provide the basis for claims about performance made in promotional materials, whether targeted at the trade or at the consumer (Table 26.1).

Interior designers, architects, commercial specifiers, and retailers must understand the test methods used to measure structural and performance qualities of carpet and cushions and the implications of the reported data. Such an understanding makes it possible for professionals to interpret data supplied by producers and determine the suitability of a carpet or an assembly for relevant traffic and other end-use conditions. The informed professional also can prepare specification listings that cover specific features and levels of performance required by end-use conditions or a regulatory agency.

Listing Specification Data for Carpet

Because tufting is the dominant floor covering construction technique, the sample **specification listing** presented in Table 26.2 is written for a tufted structure. Several of the items would, however, also be listed for woven and fusion-bonded carpet. Virtually all of the test methods listed in the table and discussed in this chapter apply to all textile floor coverings, regardless of their construction. The specific values listed in the table are for illustrative purposes only.

The first several items listed in Table 26.2 describe the appearance, composition, and construction features of the carpet. The following standard test methods and practices may be used to determine the data reported for these features:

- ASTM D 629 Standard Test Methods for Quantitative Analysis of Textiles
- ASTM D 861 Standard Practice for Use of the Tex System to Designate Linear Density of Fibers, Yarn Intermediates, and Yarns
- ASTM D 1244 Standard Practice for Designation of Yarn Construction

- ASTM D 2260 Standard Tables of Conversion Factors and Equivalent Yarn Numbers Measured in Various Numbering Systems
- ASTM D 2646 Standard Test Methods for Backing Fabric Characteristics of Pile Yarn Floor Coverings
- ASTM D 5684 Standard Terminology Relating to Pile Floor Coverings
- ASTM D 5793 Standard Test Method for Binding Sites per Unit Length or Width of Pile Yarn Floor Coverings
- ASTM D 5823 Standard Test Method for Tuft Height of Pile Floor Coverings
- ASTM D 6859 Standard Test Method for Pile Thickness of Finished Level Pile Yarn Floor Coverings

As discussed in Chapter 10, trade names frequently distinguish fibers, especially those engineered to exhibit special properties. When a trade name is used to advertise a carpet, the fiber composition of the pile layer must be disclosed in accordance with the provisions of the Textile Fiber Products Identification Act.

Pile construction density, pile height, weight-related factors, and structural variables are specified to ensure that a floor covering will withstand the traffic conditions in the end-use location, and will conform to design codes if applicable. These construction features were reviewed in Chapter 22.

The remaining data in Table 26.2 detail the functional benefits and performance properties of a carpet. Test methods for determining the values reported for these characteristics are frequently identified in specification lists.

Evaluating Functional Features

Carpet and cushion assemblies may be designed and selected to provide such functional benefits as noise control and insulation. Carpet may also be selected to reduce energy consumption by contributing to the efficient management of interior light and by helping to lower the rate of heat exchange.

Acoustical Ratings

One of the more important functional benefits of floor covering assemblies is their **acoustical value**, the extent to which they prevent sound from becoming un-

Table 26.1 Common Test Methods Used for Finished Commercial Carpet

Characteristic	Test Method/Explanation	Suggested Requirement
Average Pile Yarn Weight (ounces/square yard)	ASTM* D5848 METHOD OF TESTING MASS PER UNIT AREA: Chemically dissolves parts of the finished carpet sample to determine the pile mass or weight. Pile mass or weight includes the pile yarn, both above the primary backing and the amount hidden or buried below the backing.	As specified
Tufts Per Square Inch	Determine the gauge and multiply by the stitches per inch (SPI). ASTM D-5793 offers instructions on counting the binding sites per unit length or width.	As specified
Pile Thickness/Tuft Height	ASTM D 6859 METHOD OF TESTING PILE YARN FLOOR COVERING CONSTRUCTION: Determine pile thickness for level-loop carpet. Tuft height for cut pile carpet should be determined by ASTM D-5823, Tuft Height for Pile Floor Coverings. Accurate laboratory determination of height is important for the average pile yarn density determinations.	As specified
Average Pile Yarn Density	CALCULATION: Measures the amount of pile fiber by weight in a given area of carpet space. Typically calculated in ounces per cubic yard. Important element in equating quality of carpet to wearability, resilience, and appearance retention.	As specified
Tuft Bind	ASTM D-1335 TEST METHOD FOR TUFT BIND OF PILE FLOOR COVERINGS: The amount of force required to pull a single carpet from its primary backing. Determines the ability of the tufted carpet to withstand zippering and snags.	10.0 lbs. of force for loop pile only [minimum average value]
Delamination Strength of Secondary Backing	ASTM D-3936 TEST METHOD FOR DELAMINATION STRENGTH OF SECONDARY BACKING OF PILE FLOOR COVERINGS: Measures the amount of force required to strip the secondary backing from the primary carpet structure. Measured in pounds of force per inch width. Its importance is to predict the secondary delaminating due to flexing caused by traffic or heavy rolling objects.	2.5 pounds of force per inch is the minimum average value
Colorfastness to Crocking	COLORFASTNESS TO CROCKING: CARPET - AATCC-165 CROCKMETER METHOD: Transfer of colorant from the surface of a carpet to another surface by rubbing. The transference of color is graded against a standardized scale ranging from 5 (no color transference) to 1 (severe transference).	Rating of 4 minimum, wet and dry, using AATCC color transference scale
Colorfastness to Light	COLORFASTNESS TO LIGHT: WATER - COOLED XENON - ARC LAMP, CONTINUOUS LIGHT AATCC-16, OPTION E: Accelerated fading test using a xenon light source. After specified exposure, the specimen is graded for color loss using a 5 (no color change) to 1 (severe change) scale.	Rating of 4 minimum after 40 AATCC fading units using AATCC gray scale for color change
Electrostatic Propensity	AATCC-134 ELECTROSTATIC PROPENSITY OF CARPETS: Assesses the static-generating propensity of carpets developed when a person walks across them by laboratory simulation of conditions that may be met in practice. Static generation is dependent upon humidity condition; therefore, testing is performed at 20 percent relative humidity. Results are expressed as kilovolts (kV). The threshold of human sensitivity is 3.5 kV, but sensitive areas may require that a lower kV product be specified.	Less than 3.5 kV for general commercial areas

(continued)

Table 26.1 Common Test Methods Used for Finished Commercial Carpet *(continued)*

Flammability		
Surface Flammability	16 CFR 1630 AND ALSO ASTM D-2859: This small-scale ignition test is required of all carpet for sale in the U.S. Methenamine tablet is used as an ignition source.	All carpet must meet this standard, per federal regulation
Critical Radiant Flux	ASTM E-648, CRITICAL RADIANT FLUX OF FLOOR COVERING SYSTEMS USING A RADIANT HEAT ENERGY SOURCE: Depending upon occupancy use and local, state, or other building or fire codes, carpets for commercial use may require flooring radiant panel test classification (class I or II). Class I is considered to be a minimum rating of 0.45 watts per sq. cm or greater. Most codes require flooring radiant panel testing only for carpet to be installed in corridors and exit-way areas.	Applicable local, state, and federal requirements
Additional Requirements for Modular Carpet		
Tile Size and Thickness	Physical Measurement	Typical tolerances are in the range of five thousandths of an inch (5 mils, 0.0005 inch) Within 1/32 inch of stated dimensional specifications
Dimensional Stability	Machine-made Textile Floor Coverings - Determination of Dimensional Changes in Varying Moisture Conditions ISO 2551 (Aachen Test)	+/− 0.2% maximum
Requirement for Indoor Air Quality		
CRI IAQ Testing Program Label	CRI IAQ Testing Program Label: Assesses emission rates of carpet product types to meet program criteria. When using carpet cushion or adhesive, include CRI IAQ label.	Total volatile organic compounds criteria not to exceed 0.5 mg/m2*hr

*ASTM standard test methods are available from the American Society for Testing and Materials, 1916 Race Street, Philadelphia, PA 19103, Telephone: 215-299-5400.
Source: Courtesy of the Carpet and Rug Institute.

wanted noise. The noise reduction benefits of carpet installed on walls and panels were discussed in Chapter 19; those of carpet and carpet and cushion assemblies are discussed here.

Sound Absorption

Residential interiors are often filled with many electrical appliances and pieces of entertainment equipment, each one of which generates sound. Contemporary office designs frequently call for large open areas that will permit maximum flexibility in space utilization: such areas can contain numerous people, telephones, computers, and printers, all of which, again, generate sound. Commercial structures are often built to serve several firms and many employees and executives; places where people assemble, such as theaters, often house thousands; schools accommodate hundreds of students. In these interiors, the constant movement of equipment and people, continual verbal exchange, and the like create sound. Lowering the level of **airborne and surface sounds** in these environments is highly desirable; in some cases it is mandatory.

Table 26.3 presents the results of controlled testing for the sound absorption of various carpets with and without an all-hair cushion. The results are reported numerically as the **noise reduction coefficient (NRC)**. Higher NRC values indicate greater sound absorption. The values reported in Table 26.3 reveal the effects of various structural features. Cut pile textures are somewhat more efficient in absorbing sound than loop pile textures. Increasing the weight of the pile layer or the height of the pile yarns in cut pile structures will increase the sound absorption capabilities. In loop textures, pile height apparently has a greater positive influence than does pile weight. The Carpet and Rug Institute has reported that

Table 26.2 Sample Carpet Specification/Data List
Style: Kamiakin
Surface texture: one level loop
Coloration: jet printed
Face fiber: 99% Super® XYZ nylon; 1% Stat-Redux® stainless steel for static control
Face fiber size: 20 dpf
Yarn size: 2.00/2cc (equivalent denier 5315)

Body construction: tufted
    gauge: 1/10
    stitches per inch: 8
    primary backing: 100% woven polypropylene olefin
    secondary backing: 100% woven jute

Pile height: 0.250 in.
Pile yarn weight: 40.0 oz/sq. yd.
Total weight: 65 oz./sq. yd.
Density factor: 425,200
Average density: 4383
Weight density: 122,713

Structural stability:
    bundle penetration: 80%
    delamination strength: 2.5 lbs./in.
    tuft bind: 6.25 lbs.

Acoustical ratings:
    NRC .45 over 40 oz. hair pad; IIC 73 over 40 oz. hair
    pad (INR +22)

Insulative value: R-2 over concrete slab
Light reflectance factor: 15

Colorfastness
    crocking: 4.0 (AATCC 8)
    gas fade: 4.0 (AATCC 23)
    ozone fade: 3.0 (AATCC 129): 4.0 (AATCC 109)
    shampoo: 4.0 (AATCC 138)
    lightfastness: Class 4 (AATCC 16E)

Flammability
    tablet test (ASTM D 2859, 16CFR 1630): passes
    tunnel test (ASTM E 84): Class A
    flooring radiant panel test (ASTM E 648): CRF greater
    than 0.25 watts/sq. cm.

Static generation: 3,500 static volts at 70 °F and 20% RH (AATCC 134)

Wear resistance
    textural change: min. 30,000 foot traffic units
    pilling: 3.0
    abrasion (Taber): not worn through to backing after
    10,000 cycles

such structural variations produce similar effects when the carpet is glued directly to the floor. Regardless of the method of installation, the fiber content of the pile yarns has virtually no effect on sound absorption.

From the results listed in Table 26.3, a **permeability principle** can be established: the more permeable the structure, the more efficiently it will absorb sound.

As shown in Table 26.4, the more permeable hair and hair-jute cushions were more effective acoustically than the less permeable sponge rubber cushions of similar weight. Attaching the cushion reduces the permeability and thus the level of sound absorption.

Within an interior, surface noise is created by the routine activities of walking, running, and shuffling, and by the shifting of furniture and equipment. Experimental testing has indicated that carpet is significantly more effective in reducing **surface noise radiation** than is vinyl tile.[1]

Noise Transmission

Controlling **impact and structurally borne sounds** is especially important in multilevel structures, where impact sounds can be transmitted as noise to the interior spaces below. Evaluations of the acoustical role of carpet and cushions in such a situation are made in a chamber with 100 square feet of either concrete or wood joist flooring. The ISO R 140 Tapping Machine is used to impact the surface, and the noise transmitted to the room-like chamber below is picked up by a microphone (Figure 26.1).

The ability of a floor, carpet, or cushion to minimize **noise transmission** is evaluated and reported numerically as an **impact noise rating (INR)** or as an **impact insulation class (IIC)**. Higher values indicate greater noise control, that is, a reduced level of transmission. IIC values are roughly equal to the INR value plus 51.

The values reported in Table 26.5 show the effectiveness of various carpet and cushion features in reducing the level of noise transmission. In this series of tests, a concrete floor was used in the test facility. Concrete floors are generally used in commercial structures, and they are less effective in controlling impact sounds than the wood joist floors commonly used in residential construction as shown in Table 26.6. When tested without floor coverings, a concrete slab had an INR of −17 and a wood joist floor had an INR of −19.

The ratings in Table 26.5 show that increases in the weight of the pile layers of the test carpets improved

Table 26.3 Sound Absorption of Hair Cushions

		Test A-2 Carpet over 40 oz/sy Hair Cushion		
Pile Weight oz/sy	Pile Height inches	Surface	NRC Without Cushion	NRC With Cushion
44	.25	loop 1	.30	.40
32	.56	cut2	.50	.70
43	.50	cut3	.55	.70

Note: 40 oz/sy hair cushion, NRC 0.25 - 1woven wool -2tufted nylon - 3tufted wool
Source: Courtesy of the Carpet and Rug Institute.

Table 26.4 Sound Absorption of Various Cushion Types

	Test A-3 40 oz/sy Carpet with Various Cushion Types	
Cushion Weight oz/sy	Cushion Material	NRC
32	hair	.50
40	hair	.55
54	hair	.55
86	hair	.60
32	hair jute	.55
40	hair jute	.60
86	hair jute	.65
31	3/8 inch foam rubber	.60
44	sponge rubber	.45
86	3/8 inch sponge rubber	.50

Note: 40 oz/sy tufted wool, 0.39 inch pile height, loop pile control carpet on bare floor. NRC = .35
Source: Courtesy of the Carpet and Rug Institute.

their performance. All of the carpet and cushion assemblies tested were more effective than any of the test carpets alone. The rubber cushion specimens were more effective when used separately under the carpet than when permanently attached. Here, increased permeability had a negative influence, permitting more sound to be transmitted.

Insulative Value

Heat conductivity and **heat resistivity** are reciprocal terms referring to the rate at which a material conducts or transfers heat. The rate of heat transmittance is given numerically as the **K-value or K-factor**. Materials such as copper conduct heat rapidly and have relatively high K-values. Materials, including textile fibers, that have low K-values are poor heat conductors and can contribute insulative value.

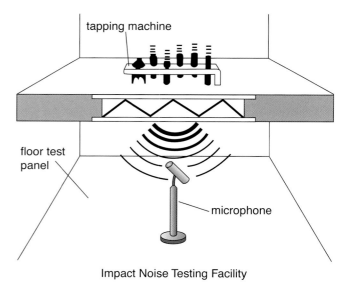

Figure 26.1 Impact noise testing facility.
Courtesy of the Carpet and Rug Institute.

Table 26.5 Noise Reduction Coefficients of Various Carpets and Cushions on a Concrete Slab

Test Variables	Pile Weight oz/sy	Pile Height inches	Surface	NRC
Test A-1 Commercial Carpet Laid Directly on Concrete				
Identical construction, different manufacturers	44	.25	loop	.30
	44	.25	loop	.30
	44	.25	loop	.30
Identical construction, different pile surfaces	35	.175	loop	.30
	35	.175	cut	.35
Pile weight/height relationships in cut pile carpet	32	.562	cut-nylon	.50
	36	.43	cut-acrylic	.50
	43	.50	cut-wool	.55
Increasing pile weight/height relationships in woven wool, loop pile carpet	44	.25	loop	.30
	66	.375	loop	.40
	88	.50	loop	.40
Increasing pile weight (pile height constant) in tufted loop pile carpet	15	.25	loop-nylon	.25
	40	.25	loop-wool	.35
	60	.25	loop-wool	.30
Varying pile height (pile weight constant) loop pile with regular back		.125	loop	.15
		.187	loop	.20
		.250	loop	.25
Varying pile height (pile weight constant) loop pile with foam back		.437	loop	.35
		.187	loop	.25
		.250	loop	.30
		.312	loop	.35
		.437	loop	.40

Source: Courtesy of the Carpet and Rug Institute.

R-values or R-factors numerically describe how effectively structures resist heat flow, that is, how effectively they insulate and prevent heat exchange. The following formula determines R-value: R-value = thickness/K-value. From the formula, it is apparent that resistance to heat flow is determined not only by the rate of conduction, the K-value, but also by the thickness of the structure. Increasing the thickness of a material does not increase its K-value, but does increase its R-factor, making it a more effective insulator.

Several trade associations jointly sponsored a research project to assess the effectiveness of carpet and cushions in reducing heat flow and subsequent heat loss by convection, the transmission of heat energy by air movement. Various carpet construction variables and types of cushions were tested over uninsulated wood floors over a vented crawl space and over a 6-inch-thick concrete slab. Heat was radiated downward from a hot plate to the surface of the carpet; the heat that flowed through the carpet or cushion or both was measured by a cold plate behind the assembly. Computer simulation was used to analyze the energy savings in residential and commercial structures of various sizes and shapes and located in different geographic areas.[2]

As a result of this work, the Carpet and Rug Institute published the following findings:

1. The carpet samples tested, typical of those available during the time of the study, had R-values ranging from .55 to 2.46.

2. The contribution of any component of the carpet or cushion test specimens to the total R-value depended more on the thickness of the component than on the fiber or yarn type.

3. R-values varied in direct proportion to thickness and pile density.

4. R-values were additive (R-value of carpet + R-value of cushion = R-value of assembly) for any combination of carpet and cushion.

5. Carpet installed on an uninsulated concrete slab provided greater savings than carpet installed on an insulated wood floor of the same area.

6. Energy savings varied substantially, depending on the R-value of the carpet and cushion assembly. For example, an assembly with an R-value of 4.0 provided

Table 26.6 Impact Insulation Class

Test B-1 Concrete Slab Floor-Ceiling Assembly			
Carpet	Cushion	INR (Impact Noise Rating)	IIC (Impact Insulation Class)
Bare Floor		−17	34
1	none	+2	53
2	none	+4	55
3	none	+6	57
4	none	+8	59
5	none	+9	65
6	none	+14	68
7	none	+18	70
8	attached ³/₁₆ inch sponge rubber	+17	69
6	40 oz/sy yd hair-jute	+22	73
6	polyurethane foam	+24	76
6	44 oz/sy yd sponge rubber	+25	79
6	31 oz/sy yd ³/₈ inch foam rubber	+28	79
6	80 oz/sy yd sponge rubber	+29	80

Test B-2 Wood Joist Floor-Ceiling Assembly			
Carpet	Cushion	INR (Impact Noise Rating)	IIC (Impact Insulation Class)
Bare Floor		−19	32
8	attached ³/₁₆ inch sponge rubber	+3	54
6	40 oz/sy yd hair-jute	+10	61
6	polyurethane foam	+12	63
6	44 oz/sy yd sponge rubber	+14	65
6	31 oz/sy yd ³/₈ inch foam rubber	+16	67
6	80 oz/sy yd sponge rubber	+17	68

Carpet Key					
Carpet	Type	Surface	Pile Wt. oz/sq yd	Pile Ht. inches	Fiber Content
1	tufted	H-L loop	20	.15-.35	wool
2	tufted	loop	27	.20	olefin
3	tufted	cut	32	.56	nylon
4	tufted	cut	36	.44	acrylic
5	tufted	loop	40	.25	wool
6	woven	loop	44	.25	wool
7	tufted	loop	60	.25	wool
8*	woven	loop	44	.25	wool

*with attached ³/₁₆ inch sponge rubber cushion
Source: Courtesy of the Carpet and Rug Institute.

estimated energy savings greater than two times the savings estimated for carpet with an R-value of 1.0.

Dollar savings varied according to local fuel charges and length of heating and cooling periods.

Indoor Air Quality (IAQ)

With improvements in the quality of building materials and construction methods over the years, newer residential and commercial structures have become almost airtight. Although this helps conserve energy used for heating and cooling, it limits the amount of fresh air available to the occupants. In particular, commercial buildings have few operable windows that allow fresh airflow. In both residential and commercial buildings, fresh air is pumped into the interior environment through the heating, ventilation, and air conditioning (HVAC) system. Indoor air is filtered, mixed with a small amount of outdoor air, and recirculated throughout interior spaces. The ability of HVAC systems to adequately clean the air varies, depending on equipment size, quality of filters, and the amount of indoor and outdoor air pollution. Health problems related to poor air quality continue to rise. Sensitivities to airborne chemicals can cause problems ranging from eye, sinus, and lung irritation to severe allergic reactions. Many airborne chemicals have the potential to cause cancer and other disabling diseases. Considering that we spend the majority of our time indoors, IAQ is an important health consideration.

The CRI, in collaboration with the EPA and ASTM International, developed the Green Label and Green Label Plus programs to identify carpet, cushions, and adhesives that produce very low emissions of VOCs. When installed according to CRI-recommended standards, the low-level VOC emissions from new carpet typically dissipate within 48 to 72 hours after installation. Manufacturers are permitted to display the CRI green-and-white logo on products that meet the low-VOC standards.

The ASTM D 5116 Guide for Small-Scale Environmental Chamber Determinations of Organic Emissions from Indoor Materials/Products test identifies maximum allowable levels of VOCs for carpet, cushions, and adhesives. Measurements are given in mg/m2·hr.[3]

Maximum allowable emissions for carpet:
total volatile organic compounds 0.50
4-PC (4-phenylcyclohexene) 0.05
formaldehyde 0.05
styrene 0.40

Maximum allowable emissions for adhesives:
total volatile organic compounds 10.0 mg/m2·hr
formaldehyde 0.05 mg/m2·hr
2-ethyl-1-hexanol 3.0 mg/m2·hr

Maximum allowable emissions for cushions and pads:
total volatile organic compounds 1.00
4-phenylcyclohexene (4-PC) 0.05
formaldehyde 0.05
butylated hydroxytoluene (BHT) 0.30

Evaluating Performance Properties

Besides the functional properties discussed in the preceding section, other properties, including colorfastness, flammability, static generation, and wear resistance, also help to determine the in-use performance of textile floor coverings. Such properties should be evaluated prior to selection; again, professionals may be required to specify or select floor coverings exhibiting a mandated level of performance.

Colorfastness

Standard laboratory test methods are available to evaluate the stability of the colorants in most colored floor coverings. Generally, fastness to crocking, atmospheric gases, light, and cleaning agents are measured.

Fastness to Crocking, Gases, and Light

The standard test methods used to measure crocking, the transfer of dye from one surface to another, and gasfastness were discussed and illustrated in Chapter 14; standard test methods used to measure lightfastness were discussed in Chapter 18. The designations of these test methods may be listed with the appropriate fastness ratings, as in Table 26.2.

Fastness to Shampoo and Water

Textile floor coverings are frequently tested for their fastness to water and to shampoo using the methods in AATCC 107 Colorfastness to Water and AATCC 138 Cleaning: Washing of Textile Floor Coverings. Either test method allows for analysis of the test results in terms of bleeding and staining, as well as in terms of color change. Test specimens are compared with the appropriate Gray Scale (Figures 14.9 and 14.10, pp. 244, 245), and the numerical values recorded.

Microbe Resistance

Protecting soft floor coverings from the deterioration, discoloration, and odor development caused by microorganisms is an area of ongoing research in the floor coverings industry. For floor coverings installed in damp areas, the growth of odor-causing mildew and bacteria should be inhibited; for carpet and rugs exposed to pets, the retention of odors in the structure should be prevented. Carpet installed in hospitals, nursing homes, and similar facilities should be resistant to a variety of bacteria and fungi, so that the structures will remain odor free and will not harbor microbes that could spread disease and slow patient recovery.

Biological resistance has been engineered into nylon carpet fibers by incorporating **antimicrobial agents** into the polymer solution or by adding them early in the production sequence. Examples of trade names indicating that microbe resistance has been introduced include AlphaSan, owned by Milliken and Company; Intersept, owned by Interface Inc.; Zeftron, owned by BASF Corporation; ProSept, owned by J & J/Invision; Chitosan, owned by Mitsubishi Rayon Company, Ltd.; and Aegis, owned by Dow Corning.

According to antimicrobial textile consultants, the "sleeping giant" of a new market for antimicrobials is residential carpeting. Just as antimicrobials are routinely used in commercial carpeting, especially in schools and health-care facilities, these treatments are rapidly expanding into the residential carpet market.[4]

Flammability

As is true of other laboratory testing procedures, test methods that assess the potential flammability of soft floor coverings have been designed to simulate real-life conditions. Prior to marketing most carpet and large rugs, producers must subject them to the methenamine tablet test to confirm that they conform to the performance standards enforced by the Consumer Product Safety Commission. For use in commercial interiors, carpet and rugs are required to conform to additional flammability codes. In such cases, the floor coverings are often tested in accordance with the procedures outlined in the flooring radiant panel test.

All domestic and imported carpets and rugs sold in the United States must pass the methenamine pill test. There are two Code of Federal Regulations standards that pertain to this test: 16 CFR 1630 (carpet) and 16 CFR 1631 (small rugs); the rating system is either pass or fail. Carpet for use in commercial spaces must meet certain flame spread and smoke development requirements based on building code occupancies, also known as use groups. The flame spread test for commercial carpet is the radiant panel test. The test method is accepted by the American Society for Testing and Materials (ASTM) and the National Fire Protection Association (NFPA) and is identified as ASTM E 648 and NFPA 253. The rating system is divided into two categories: Class I, with a minimum critical radiant flux of 0.45 watts per square centimeter, and Class II, with a minimum critical radiant flux of 0.22 watts per square centimeter. Carpeting with a Class I rating is more fire resistant than that with a Class II rating. These and other flammability tests are described and illustrated in Chapter 11, and fire performance recommendations are presented in Table 11.1 (pp. 181–82).

Static Generation

The test method generally accepted in the industry for evaluating the static propensity of floor covering assemblies is AATCC 134 Electrostatic Propensity of Carpets. The test procedure, designed to closely simulate actual end-use conditions, is conducted in an atmosphere having 20 percent relative humidity and a temperature of 70 °F. During the testing, a person wearing clean, neolite-soled shoes walks across a carpet while linked to an electrometer. This device measures the voltage building up on the body, and the recorded level is then reported in static volts. Generally, acceptable maximum voltage ratings are 5.0 kilovolts for residential carpet and 3.5 kilovolts for commercial carpet. For environments with sensitive electronic equipment, 2.0 kilovolts is an acceptable upper limit. In highly critical areas, such as the handling of semiconductors, the typical antistatic carpet may not provide sufficient static protection.[5] (The mechanisms of static voltage buildup and the threshold of human sensitivity to static discharge were explained in Chapter 4.)

Frequently, regulations and/or specifications state that the control of static generation must be durable. In such cases, the agency having jurisdiction may require that floor coverings be cleaned in accordance with the procedures outlined in AATCC 138 Cleaning: Washing of Textile Floor Coverings prior to testing with AATCC 134.

Wear Resistance

The extent to which a carpet or rug exhibits satisfactory in-service performance with respect to appearance retention and durability is determined by several factors. The

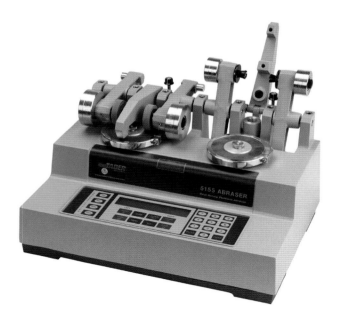

Figure 26.2 Taber Abraser with double heads. Courtesy of Taber Industries.

abrasion resistance of the floor covering will affect the extent to which fuzzing, pilling, and fiber loss occur. The resiliency of the structure will affect the degree to which the original thickness and luster are retained when the assembly is subjected to the static pressure of furniture legs, repeated loads of foot traffic, and the rolling stresses of moving equipment. If the original texture is lost, the consumer may regard the structure as "worn out," even though fiber loss may be negligible. Therefore, service performance analyses related to wear cannot be limited to abrasion-related performance; they must also include evaluations of textural changes.

Textural Changes

ASTM D 6119 Standard Practice for Creating Surface Appearance Changes in Pile Yarn Floor Covering from Foot Traffic may be used in evaluations of textural changes. The practice is directed to appearance changes, such as matting, flattening, or the loss of tuft definition, that do not necessarily involve fiber loss by abrasion or the development of a threadbare appearance. It does not simulate surface appearance changes resulting from soiling, pivoting, or rolling traffic. Carpet specimens are securely placed in a floor layout having an odd number of traffic lanes that require walkers to automatically reverse their direction with each pass through the course. Counting devices accurately count **foot traffic units**, the number of passes by human walkers (not the number of times each specimen is stepped on). A traffic level high enough to cause noticeable change is used. The cumulative change in surface appearance is analyzed by comparing unexposed and exposed specimens. Purchasers and suppliers may mutually agree on the minimum number of foot traffic units a floor covering should withstand before the textural change is unacceptable.

ASTM D 5251 Standard Practice for the Operation of the Tetrapod Walker Drum Tester may be used to produce changes in texture on the surface of pile floor covering caused by mechanical action. Test carpet is installed as the lining of a rotatable cylindrical chamber with the pile surface exposed. During testing, the plastic-tipped "feet" of the **tetrapod walker** tumble against the carpet surface as the drum revolves, simulating foot traffic. The change in texture may be assessed visually and by measuring the change in pile thickness. The resistance to abrasion may be assessed by measuring the loss in pile weight.

Abrasion Resistance

ASTM D 3884 Standard Test Method for Abrasion Resistance of Textile Fabrics (Rotary Platform, Double Head Method) is used in the carpet and rug industry for the accelerated laboratory testing of the abrasion resistance of floor coverings. The apparatus used in the test has two flat platforms, or turntables, each supporting and rotating one specimen under two abradant wheels (Figure 26.2). The pressure of the wheels on the specimens can be controlled during the testing operation, and a vacuum unit may be employed to remove abraded particles continually. During testing, the abradant wheels rotate in opposite directions (Figure 26.3).

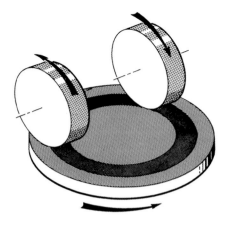

Figure 26.3 Directions of rotation of the abradant wheels and support platform during abrasion resistance testing. Courtesy of Taber Industries.

This results in abrasion marks that form a pattern of crossed, slightly curved, herringbone-like arcs over an area of approximately 4.5 inches. Some producers evaluate the results in terms of the number of cycles (revolutions of the turntable carrying the specimen) required to cause exposure of the backing. Other producers measure the percent of pile weight loss or the percent loss of breaking load. The value reported is the average of five replicate tests.

As noted in Chapter 22, manufacturers of tufted carpet seek to reduce the number of loose, individual fibers that travel to the surface and form pills through the proper application of adhesive coatings. Part of their quality control effort involves ascertaining how thoroughly the adhesive has penetrated the pile yarn bundle, to lock the fibers side by side.

Some manufacturers have adapted a floor tread test for use in evaluating the service performance of carpet installed on stairs. Commonly referred to as the **stair tread test**, the method is directed to assessing the extent to which the carpet withstands abrasion, especially at the nosing of stairs. This is a long-term, service exposure test: carpet specimens are installed without a cushion on heavily trafficked stairs. Producers may evaluate the level of abrasion resistance visually; they may measure the pile weight loss; or they may record the traffic count required to expose the backing and create a threadbare appearance.

Summary

Soft floor covering manufacturers use prescribed test methods, as well as some adapted procedures, to evaluate the quality of their products and to predict their in-service performance. In turn, they frequently use the results of these tests to promote the selection of their carpet and rugs.

For commercial interiors, selection prerequisites include not only an assessment of the traffic conditions and activities anticipated in the end-use setting, but also an investigation of performance codes and structural requirements. Special requirements may exist regarding, for example, static generation, flammability, weight-related factors, and colorfastness. The interior designer and architect can use the test data provided by the producer to determine whether a stock product meets or exceeds requirements. When working on a custom project, the professional can specify the composition, construction features, and levels of performance desired or required.

Key Terms

acoustical value

airborne and surface sounds

antimicrobial agents

foot traffic units

heat conductivity

heat resistivity

impact and structurally borne sounds

impact insulation class (IIC)

impact noise rating (INR)

indoor air quality (IAQ)

K-values or K-factors

permeability principle

noise reduction coefficient (NRC)

noise transmission

R-values or R-factors

specification listing

stair tread test

surface noise radiation

tetrapod walker

Review Questions

1. Discuss the value standard test methods and performance specifications have for members of the industry.

2. Explain the usefulness of product performance data for the design professional.

3. Discuss the influence pile construction density, pile height, and pile weight have on the end-use of carpet and rugs.

4. Identify the textural characteristics and weight factors of soft floor coverings that aid in sound absorption.

5. Does any fiber have significantly greater value in absorbing sound?

6. Explain the "permeability principle" as it relates to noise reduction within an interior by carpet and cushions. How does this principle relate to noise transmission?

7. Are textile fibers relatively good heat conductors or relatively good heat insulators?

8. If one wants to improve the insulative value of a carpet and cushion assembly, which is changed, the R-value or the K-value?

9. When specifying products and materials for a carpet installation, what factors should be considered that pertain to indoor air quality?

10. Does a soft floor covering have to have measurable fiber loss to be perceived as "worn out?"

Notes

1. *Acoustical Benefits: Sound Conditioning with Carpet*, Carpet and Rug Institute, Dalton, Ga., 2008.

2. *The Carpet Primer*, Dalton, Ga: Carpet and Rug Institute, 2003.

3. Carpet and Rug Institute, "Technical Bulletin: Carpet and Indoor Air Quality," 2001, 395.

4. Maria C. Thiry, "Unsung Heroes: Antimicrobials Save the Day," *AATCC Review*, Vol. 9, No. 5, May 2009, 20.

5. Carpet and Rug Institute, "Technical Bulletin: Static Control," 2000.

CHAPTER TWENTY-SEVEN

Installation and Maintenance of Floor Covering Assemblies

Installing Soft Floor Coverings and Cushions

Wall-to-Wall Installation
    Methods
Loose Laid Rug Installations
Factors Affecting Choice of
    Installation Method
Determining Yardage
    Required

Maintaining Textile Floor Coverings

Initial Care
Preventive Maintenance
Interim Maintenance
Restorative Maintenance
Salvage Maintenance

Photo courtesy of Tesri, www.tesri.fr.

■ **To ensure long-term** serviceability in their textile floor coverings and cushions, residential and commercial consumers should consider installation and maintenance factors as thoroughly as they do appearance and performance variables. Unless the floor covering assembly is carefully installed by qualified persons, ripples, bubbles, prominent seams, and mismatched patterns may appear. An insecure installation could be hazardous, as well as result in undue stress on the structure itself.

Cleaning and stain removal procedures, if part of a planned maintenance program, should not cause marked changes in texture, nor should they alter the original color of a product. The installation to be used and the maintenance program to be followed should be investigated prior to the final selection of the floor covering assembly.

Installing Soft Floor Coverings and Cushions

Residential consumers, contract designers, and architects should be familiar with the basic procedures used in wall-to-wall installations. This will prepare them for an accurate analysis of whatever factors will influence their choice of method of installation. They should be familiar also with such features as pile lay and types of pattern repeats and with the principles governing seam placement and floor space measurements. Such familiarity is the foundation for correctly planning the carpet layout, determining the yardage required, and estimating the cost of the project.

Proper installation procedures are also critical to carpet performance and will help protect the quality of the indoor air. The installer must follow the installation guidelines set forth by the manufacturer and/or the minimum guidelines in CRI's 104 and 105—Standards for the Installation of Commercial/Residential Textile Floorcovering Materials. (See Table 27.2.)

Wall-to-Wall Installation Methods

Three methods may be considered for the **wall-to-wall installation** of textile floor coverings. These include stretch-in, glue-down, and free-lay techniques. Before proceeding with any installation, the site must be properly prepared. Often, skilled persons fully experienced in the procedures should do this preliminary work and installation.

Site Preparation

An important part of site preparation is the removal of the previously installed floor covering assembly. Old carpet, if left in place, would prevent the new cushion from sliding smoothly into place during installation, causing it to become distorted and thus preventing the proper stretching and smooth installation of the replacement carpet. Moreover, loading of a multilayered installation that included the old floor covering would result in severe and repeated flexing of the new assembly, promoting deterioration of the backing and the development of an uneven wear layer. For glue-down installations, sheet vinyl and linoleum must be removed for the new structure to adhere well.

Although the subfloor should be dry for all installations, dryness is especially critical for glue-down installations. New concrete floors, which may require up to four months to dry, should be checked carefully for dryness; so should subfloors that are close to or in contact with the ground, either on-grade (ground level) or below-grade. Ground moisture may be transported upward through the slab, facilitating the migration of alkaline compounds at the same time. The moisture can prevent good adhesion of the floor covering and foster microbe-related problems. The alkaline substance may react with the adhesive compounds that stabilize the carpet and with those that secure it to the floor, causing degradation and loosening of the carpet. In order to avoid such problems, the moisture condition must be resolved and the alkaline must be neutralized prior to installation.

The interior floor space to be covered should be smooth and free of cracks, crevices, and holes, for a more pleasing appearance and uniform support for the assembly. Rough areas should be sanded, and openings should be filled. Finally, the floor should be free of dust, lint, and grit.

Stretch-in Installations

Stretch-in installations involve stretching rollgoods and fastening them over pin-holding strips that have been secured to the perimeter of the floor space. These plywood strips, also known as **tackless strips**, are approximately 1.5 inches wide, and have rows of rust-resistant metal pins protruding upward at an angle of 60 degrees (Figure 27.1). The strips are up to 0.375 inch thick; the thickness of the strip is coordinated with the thickness of the cushion to be installed. When carpet lengths greater than 30 feet are

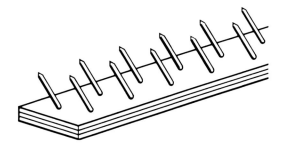

Figure 27.1 Pin-holding strip used in stretch-in tackless installation projects.

a) telescoping power stretcher

b) knee kicker

Figure 27.2 Tools used to install rollgoods in stretch-in tackless projects.
a) Courtesy of Kraft Tool®; b) Courtesy of ORCON products.

being installed or when heavy traffic loads are anticipated, three rows of pins should be used; for residential installations and smaller commercial installations, two rows of pins should be sufficient.

The strips are nailed or glued to the floor, with the pins angled toward the wall. A gully or space slightly narrower than the thickness of the carpet is left between the wall and the strip. If a separate cushion is used, it is laid within the perimeter of the strips and stapled or glued to the floor.

When seams and pattern matching are required, the parallel edges of the floor covering must be carefully aligned and trimmed to fit tightly. Butting of factory edges is not recommended since they may be slightly irregular; there may be a slight excess of printed pattern repeats provided for trimming to an accurate match. After the rollgoods are cut, a thin bead of an adhesive should be applied to prevent edge raveling and fraying during subsequent handling, seaming, and use.

Seams may be formed by hand sewing or by applying various types of tape. Crosswise seams are often sewn. Hot melt tape is often used for lengthwise seams. This tape has a thermoplastic coating that becomes tacky when heated with a special iron. The carpet edges are sealed together by the adhesive when it cools. In lieu of hot melt tape, a strip of pressure-sensitive or adhesive tape may be placed behind the parallel carpet edges and a latex bead applied along the seam line to secure the join.

After the seaming is completed, the carpet is stretched, generally 1 to 1.5 percent in length and width, and anchored over the pins in the wooden strips. A **power stretcher** is used to place uniform stretch over the surface of the carpet, and a **knee kicker** is used to grip and anchor the edges over the pins (Figure 27.2a and b).

The procedures recommended for stretching tufted carpet are shown in Figure 27.3. The power stretcher is anchored at the base of the walls and telescoped as needed.

Stairway carpet may be installed with a stretch-in technique, using pin-holding strips and a knee kicker. It may also be glued down.

Glue-down Installations

Glue-down installations involve securing floor covering structures to the floor with an adhesive. When no cushion is used, the procedure may be referred to as direct-glue down; when an attached cushion is involved, the procedure is called double glue-down. The same procedures are

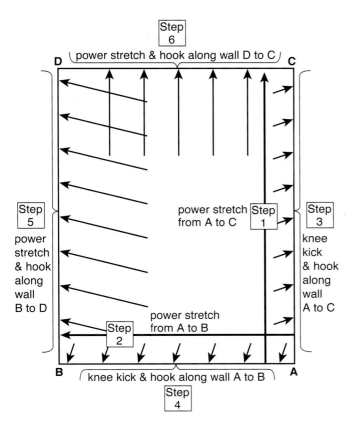

Figure 27.3 Stretching tufted structures.
Courtesy of the Carpet and Rug Institute.

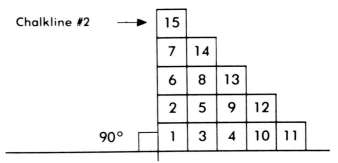

Figure 27.4 Pyramid technique recommended for positioning carpet modules.
Courtesy of Milliken and Company.

used in both operations, except that structures without a cushion are rolled onto the adhesive and structures with a cushion are pressed into the adhesive.

When installing rollgoods, the layout and seam placement must be carefully planned, and the floor measurements must be exact. If the carpet is too large, buckles and ripples may develop; if the carpet is too small, separation of the seams may occur. The cut edges of the carpet must be precisely marked, trimmed, and secured with a bead of latex. The selected adhesive is then spread over the floor with a notched trowel and the carpet is bonded to the adhesive.

When working with carpet modules, the installer should locate a starting point that will maximize the cut size of the perimeter modules. From this point, a grid is established and the selected adhesive is spread over the area. Each module is then slid into position, taking care to avoid catching any pile tufts in the joint. Successive tiles should be laid in a pyramid or stairstep manner (Figure 27.4). Perimeter modules can be precisely cut to fit the floor space.

The adhesive used to bond rollgoods and modules may be a nonreleasable (permanent) or a releasable type. Releasable adhesives may permit the floor covering structure to be repeatedly lifted and rebonded into position. This permits some degree of access to underfloor service trenches or to flatwire cable systems installed directly on the floor. It may also permit the rotation or removal of carpet modules.

Free-lay Installations

Free-lay installations may be considered for carpet modules when consumers wish to maximize the flexibility of the carpet tile, as long as heavy rolling traffic is not expected. Rolling casters on office chairs would have an insignificant effect, but such heavy items as hospital gurneys wheeled down corridors and automobiles driven into showrooms could have a "snowplow" effect, raising the edges of the modules.

Modules must have superior dimensional stability for free-lay use. This feature is often achieved with the application of a heavy secondary backing. Some free-lay tiles alternate layers of heavy-gauge vinyl and glass fiber scrims for the necessary stability (Figure 27.5).

In preparation for installation, a control grid is again planned to maximize the cut size of the perimeter modules. Within this grid, specific crosswise and lengthwise rows of modules should be secured to the floor with adhesive or double-face tape to minimize shifting. Selective glue-down leaves approximately 80 to 90 percent of the modules in the free-lay mode; tape, which is removed after installation, leaves all of the tiles held by gravity.

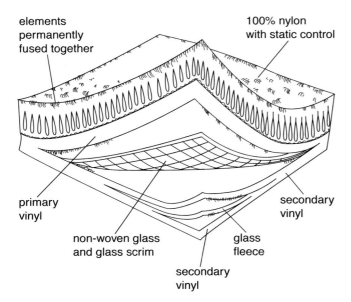

Figure 27.5 Fusion-bonded, free-lay tile with GlasBac™ secondary backing.
Courtesy of InterfaceFlor®.

elements permanently fused together

100% nylon with static control

primary vinyl

secondary vinyl

non-woven glass and glass scrim

glass fleece

secondary vinyl

secondary vinyl

Like installations with releasable adhesives, free-lay installations permit easy access to floor and underfloor utility systems. Free-lay also offers maximum convenience in shifting modules.

Loose Laid Rug Installations

Cut edges of rugs and runners must be bound by sewing twill-woven tape over the raw edges or by serging (machine overcasting). Cushions used with loose-laid rugs and runners should be thin and about 1 or 2 inches narrower and shorter than the floor coverings. This allows the rug or runner to lie close to the floor and minimizes the tendency for the soft floor covering to advance off the cushion. On stairs, runners may be securely installed with brass rods (Figure 27.6).

Factors Affecting Choice of Installation Method

Besides the site-related considerations identified in the previous section, other factors may limit the type of installation chosen for soft floor coverings. These include traffic conditions, planned space utilization, and concern for noise reduction and energy conservation.

Traffic Conditions

The traffic conditions in the area to be carpeted include a number of variables. First, the anticipated number of

Figure 27.6 Stair runner.
Courtesy of Tesri, www.tesri.fr.

persons who will walk over the floor covering should be estimated (see Table 20.1, p. 336). At low and medium levels, 500 to 1,000 traffic counts per day, the carpet may be stretched-in over most types of cushions; at higher levels, the carpet may be stretched-in over a thin, high-density cushion or over no cushion, or it may be glued down.

Second, it is important to consider what type of traffic will be usual. If people with canes, crutches, or limited vision will use the interior, area and room-size rugs and runners should be avoided, or their edges should be securely attached to the floor. When rolling traffic, such as wheelchairs and equipment, will impact the floor covering, strong consideration should be given to gluing the carpet structure directly to the subfloor. This installation technique will help to minimize shearing and seam separation.

A third traffic-related factor to consider is the amount of dirt and grit that will be tracked in. If a rapid rate of accumulation is expected, the specifier may elect to install carpet modules with a releasable adhesive or in a free-lay mode. The modules could then be rotated to minimize apparent and actual differences in appearance and texture throughout the interior. Soiled modules could be removed for off-site cleaning, and damaged modules lifted out and replaced.

Planned Space Utilization

Frequently, modern commercial offices have an open design; movable wall partitions define work stations. As personnel and activities change, the partitions can be moved to define new spaces consistent with current needs. For such interiors, the specifier may investigate the use of carpet modules instead of rollgoods. If rollgoods are installed to the base of each movable wall, shifting the wall would leave a bare strip of subfloor, which would have to be patched with carpet. If wall panels are placed over a carpet, eventual wall shifting may reveal unsightly lines, requiring a large amount of replacement carpet. These problems may be avoided through use of carpet modules.

As shown in Figure 27.7a, a common grid can be planned for the placement of the modules. When a square falls on a wall, it can be cut to fit on either side of the wall (Figure 27.7b). Later, when the wall panels are shifted, the cut modules can be lifted and a row of full-size modules laid in place (Figure 27.7c).

Acoustical and Insulative Control

The need for noise control and insulation may call for the installation of a carpet and cushion assembly, rather than a carpet glued to the floor. As noted in Chapter 26, a separate cushion increases the level of sound absorption, and any combination of a carpet and cushion provides greater reduction of impact noise transmission than does the carpet alone. Chapter 26 also discussed the finding that the insulative values of a carpet and cushion are additive, and are higher when the two structures are used separately. If traffic conditions dictate the selection of a direct glue-down installation, less effective control over noise and energy consumption may be partially offset by increasing the pile yarn weight and pile height of the carpet.

Cost-related Factors

As discussed in Chapter 20, there may be per square yard charges assessed for site preparation, for installation of the new cushion, and for installation of the new carpet. Normally, the cost of installing a separate cushion and car-

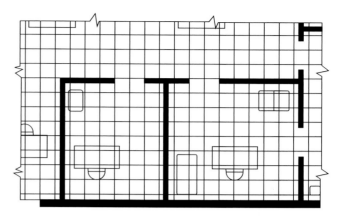

a) Common grid for module placement.

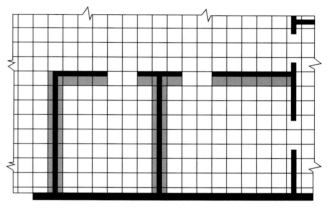

b) Modules cut to fit base of wall panels.

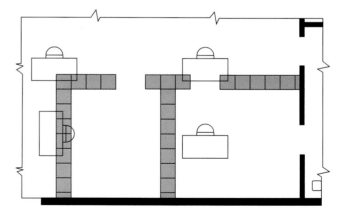

c) Full size replacement modules.

Figure 27.7 Use of carpet modules in interior space with movable walls.
Courtesy of InterfaceFlor®.

pet will be higher than that of installing a carpet with no cushion or a cushion attached. When selecting a type of installation, however, the consumer may consider acoustical benefits and energy savings that separate structures help realize. If the value of these benefits outweighs the additional installation costs, a separate cushion should be chosen, provided budgetary limitations are not exceeded. Of course, it is advisable to investigate the comparative life-cycle costs of all floor covering options.

Determining Yardage Required

The number of square yards of carpet required for a project must be accurately calculated. If the initial order was insufficient, the additional yardage of a second order inevitably has slightly different color characteristics as a result of being dyed or printed in a separate operation. Of course, if the initial order is excessive, unnecessary materials costs will be incurred.

Careful planning and correct measuring can ensure that the yardage order is accurate. Attention must be given to the direction of pile lay, the placement of seams, and the size and nature of pattern repeats.

Measuring Floor Space

The following lists the important rules to observe when measuring floor space for carpet:

1. Between opposite walls, each of which is uninterrupted, measure the distance from baseboard to baseboard and record the information on a sketch of the floor plan.

2. Between opposite walls, one of which is interrupted by an opening, measure from the baseboard to the mid-point of an archway or to a point halfway under the bottom edge of the closed door (Figure 27.8). Record the measurement on the floor plan sketch.

3. Measure stairs as illustrated in Figure 27.9. Landings are treated as if they were large steps. From 2 to 4 inches must be added to each of the recorded lengthwise and crosswise measurements. This will provide the yardage required for fitting and trimming.

Positioning the Pile Lay

The directional lay of pile yarns (Figure 9.3, p. 145) must be uniform for all adjoining pieces of carpet. The layout should be planned so that the lay parallels the longest dimension of

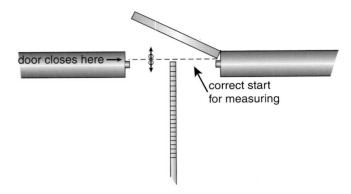

Figure 27.8 Measuring for carpet at a door jamb.

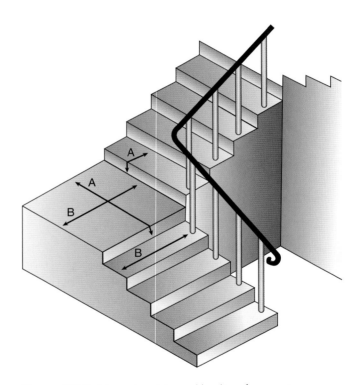

Figure 27.9 Measuring stairs and landings for carpet.

the largest room to be carpeted, as shown in Figure 27.10a. Unless pattern orientation or a similar feature must be considered, the pile lay direction should be away from the strongest source of light and toward entrance areas.

Figure 27.10b illustrates an incorrect layout. One length has been reversed and one length has been given a quarter turn. Because the quantity of light reflected by each section would be different, there would be marked

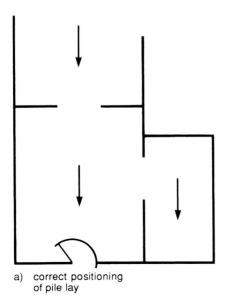

a) correct positioning
   of pile lay

b) incorrect positioning
   of pile lay

Figure 27.10 Planning pile lay direction.

differences in their apparent color. The carpet would appear darkest when the viewer is looking at the tips of the pile tufts and lightest when the viewer is looking at the sides of the yarns. Therefore, once the correct positioning of the pile lay direction has been established, all adjoining lengths of carpet of the same color and quality must be laid with their pile lay in the same direction.

Some interior designers and architects may purposely vary the pile direction of adjoining units in order to create marked differences in their apparent brightness. Examples of possible patterns for the placement of carpet modules are shown in Figure 27.11. In each of these four patterns, shading variations would alter the aesthetic characteristics of the installation.

When pile carpet is installed on stairs, the width of the carpet must parallel the width of the stairs so that carpet **grin** (Figure 20.5, p. 330), the exposure of the backing on the nose edges, will be minimized. With angled stairways, this will necessitate installation of the carpet with quarter turns of the pile lay (Figure 27.12). In such cases, the critical importance of avoiding exposure of the backing overrides concern for shade variations.

Planning Seam Placement

Several principles should govern the placement of seams. Whenever possible, seams should run lengthwise, parallel with the pile lay, not crosswise. Crosswise seams interrupt the pile sweep and are highlighted when the quantity of incident light is high. Seams should not run perpendicular to a doorway, although they may run across the opening (Figure 27.13b). A seam condition known as a **saddle**, with parallel seams on each side of a doorway, (Figure 27.13a) should be avoided by shifting the carpet and seaming it in a different location. For stability and safety, seams must not be located in traffic pivot areas and on stair treads.

Allowing Yardage for Matching Patterns

Patterned floor coverings have either a set-match or drop-match pattern repeat. The type of match and the lengthwise and crosswise dimensions of the repeat affect the yardage required.

Set-match patterns repeat themselves across the width of the carpet. Depending on the width of the repeat and the width of the carpet, the crosswise repeats may be fully completed or partially completed (Figure 27.14). In the latter case, the pattern is generally scaled so that the complement of the incomplete design is at the opposite edge.

Set-match patterned carpet should be cut at the next highest multiple of the pattern repeat length beyond the amount actually required. Thus, if the repeat is 12 inches long and 17 feet 6 inches are required, the carpet would be cut 18 feet long (18 is the next highest multiple of the 1-foot length); if the repeat is 36 inches long and 21 feet 6 inches are required, the carpet would be cut 24 feet long

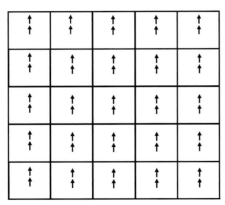

MONOLITHIC INSTALLATION
--ALL ARROWS IN SAME DIRECTION--
50CM AND 1 METER

a) Monolithic—corner to corner.

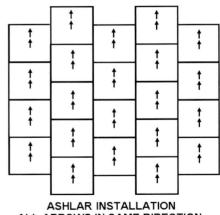

ASHLAR INSTALLATION
--ALL ARROWS IN SAME DIRECTION--
EVERY OTHER ROW HAS DROP STAGGER
50CM AND 1 METER

b) Monolithic—ashlar.

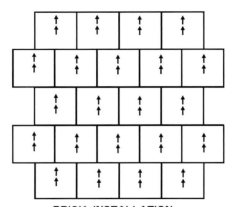

BRICK INSTALLATION
--ALL ARROWS IN SAME DIRECTION--
ROWS STAGGERED DIAGONAL
50CM AND 1 METER

c) Brick.

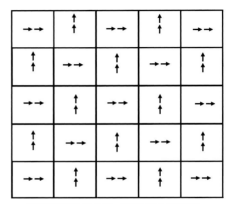

QUARTER-TURN INSTALLATION
--ALTERNATING CLOCKWISE TURN--
50CM AND 1METER

d) Quarter turn.

Figure 27.11 Four patterns for installing carpet modules.
Courtesy of Bentley Prince Street, Inc.

(24 is the next highest multiple of the 3-foot dimension). This cutting plan would provide the additional yardage needed for side matching. The installer would shift the long edges of the parallel carpet lengths, matching the pattern. The waste would then be cut away, but not necessarily from one end of each length (Figure 27.15).

Drop-match patterns repeat themselves diagonally across the width of the carpet. In **half-drop-match** patterns, the complementing portion of a design is located at a point up or down one-half the length of the repeat, as shown in the draft in Figure 27.16a and b.

Two methods may be used to cut carpet having half-drop match patterns. The first method is to cut on multiples of the repeat. If three 9-foot widths of carpet that has a 36-inch-long repeat are being installed in a room that measures 20 feet 6 inches in length, the first and third cuts would be cut on seven multiples or 21 feet. The second strip would then be cut 22 feet 6 inches, minimizing waste.

The second method is to cut on multiples of the repeat plus half a repeat. This method utilizes a half repeat to advantage. For example, a 12-inch pattern can be cut in lengths of 1 foot 6 inches, 2 feet 6 inches, 3 feet 6 inches,

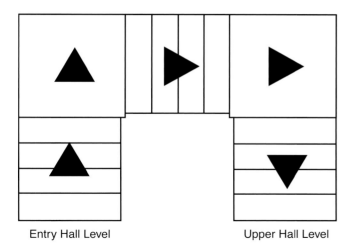

Entry Hall Level   Upper Hall Level

Figure 27.12 Direction of pile lay on angled stairs.
Courtesy of J.P. Stevens.

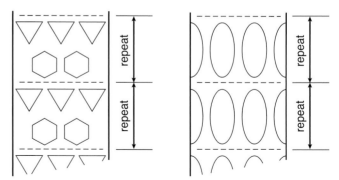

Figure 27.14 Set-match patterns.

and so on. If three widths of carpet with a 36-inch repeat are being installed in a room that measures 22 feet 6 inches in length, all lengths can be cut seven and a half repeats, or 22 feet 6 inches long.

A second type of drop-match pattern is the quarter-drop pattern. This type of repeat is frequently seen in colonial patterns; it has four blocks to a repeat. The figures match one quarter of the repeat on the opposite edge (Figure 27.17). It is apparent that successive pieces of carpet must be shifted and aligned to preserve the diagonal pattern. According to the length required and the length of the repeat, quarter-drop patterns can be cut in multiples of

the repeat plus one, two, or three blocks. Side matching can then be achieved by dropping one, two, or three blocks.

For all planned installations, it is advisable to sketch the layout of the carpet lengths on graph paper, noting the direction of pile lay, the placement of seams, and the orientation of patterns. The floor measurement and the calculations of the extra yardage needed for pattern matching should be rechecked. This plan will help ensure that the tally of the total number of linear feet and inches of carpet required is accurate; later it will serve as the cutting guide.

Linear measurements must be converted into square yards for ordering. Because most carpet is produced 12

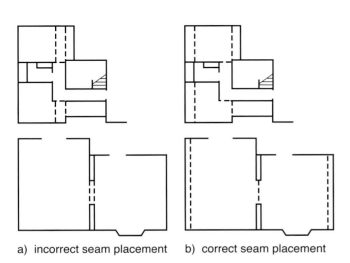

a) incorrect seam placement   b) correct seam placement

Figure 27.13 Planning carpet seam placement.
Courtesy of J.P. Stevens.

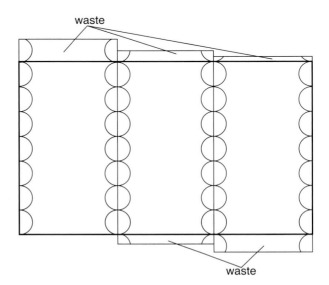

Figure 27.15 Matching set-match patterns.

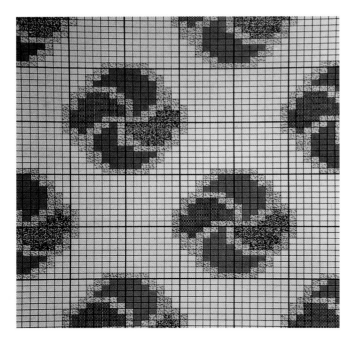

a) Draft of half-drop-match pattern.
Courtesy of Mohawk Carpet.

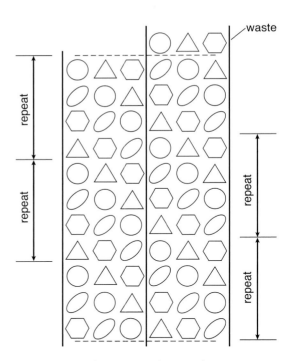

Figure 27.17 Matching quarter-drop-match pattern.

b) Example of installed half-drop-match pattern.

Figure 27.16 Half-drop-match pattern.
Courtesy of Tesri, www.tesri.fr.

feet wide, the conversions presented in Table 27.1 are based on this width. This conversion also facilitates an estimate of materials costs, since these charges are normally quoted on a per square yard basis.

When floor covering is received, it should be inspected to confirm that the quantity ordered was delivered and that the structure is free of unacceptable flaws and color variations. Most manufacturers will not assume responsibility for such defects after carpet has been cut.

After the carpet or carpet and cushion assembly has been installed, a planned maintenance program should be initiated. Without proper care, a carpet that has been carefully selected, correctly specified, and skillfully installed may **ugly out** (show wearing, soiling, matting, loss of color) long before it is worn out.

Maintaining Textile Floor Coverings

To ensure that they retain a high level of appearance, textile floor coverings installed in residential and commercial interiors should be maintained through a planned program. Scheduled maintenance can keep the appearance from changing noticeably, in contrast to sporadic maintenance, in which cleaning is undertaken as a last resort after excessive soil has already accumulated and visibly altered the look of the surface.

The primary objective of planned maintenance programs is to prevent soil, ordinarily captured in approximately 20 to 30 percent of the carpet area, from being spread throughout the interior. A second equally important objective is to reduce the amount of grit that becomes

Table 27.1 Conversion of Feet and Inches to Square Yards of 12-Foot-Wide Carpet

Example
74'5" of 12' width
74' = 98.67 sq. yds.
5" = .55 sq. yd.
Total = 99.22 sq. yds.

Inches		Feet									
Linear in.	Sq. yds.	Linear ft.	Sq. yds.	Linear ft.	Sq. yds.	Linear ft.	Sq. yds.	Linear ft.	Sq. yds.	Linear ft.	Sq. yds.
1	11	7	9.33	26	34.67	45	60.00	64	85.33	83	110.67
2	22	8	10.67	27	36.00	46	61.33	65	86.67	84	112.00
3	33	9	12.00	28	37.33	47	62.67	66	88.00	85	113.33
4	44	10	13.33	29	38.67	48	64.00	67	89.33	86	114.67
5	55	11	14.67	30	40.00	49	65.33	68	90.67	87	116.00
6	67	12	16.00	31	41.33	50	66.67	69	92.00	88	117.33
7	78	13	17.33	32	42.67	51	68.00	70	93.33	89	118.67
8	89	14	18.67	33	44.00	52	69.33	71	94.67	90	120.00
9	1.00	15	20.00	34	45.33	53	70.67	72	96.00	91	121.33
10	1.11	16	21.33	35	46.67	54	72.00	73	97.33	92	122.67
11	1.22	17	22.67	36	48.00	55	73.00	74	98.67	93	124.00
Feet		18	24.00	37	49.33	56	74.67	75	100.00	94	125.33
Linear ft.	Sq. yds.	19	25.33	38	50.67	57	76.00	76	101.33	95	126.67
1	1.33	20	26.67	39	52.00	58	77.33	77	102.67	96	128.00
2	2.67	21	28.00	40	53.33	59	78.67	78	104.00	97	129.33
3	4.00	22	29.33	41	54.67	60	80.00	79	105.33	98	130.67
4	5.33	23	30.67	42	56.00	61	81.33	80	106.67	99	132.00
5	6.67	24	32.00	43	57.33	62	82.67	81	108.00	100	133.33
6	8.00	25	33.33	44	58.67	63	84.00	82	109.33		

Courtesy of Milliken and Company.

embedded in the surface yarns. These objectives are met by strictly adhering to a schedule of regular, frequent vacuuming and cleaning, and, for localized areas that become highly soiled, stain removal. In addition to preserving carpet appearance, prolonging carpet life through proper maintenance will improve indoor air quality by reducing the accumulation of allergens, provide cost savings attributed to premature replacement, and reduce the amount of carpet going to landfills and recycling centers. Commercial cleaning programs are available, but professionals and consumers may design appropriate plans themselves. A planned maintenance program delays or prevents the development of apparent changes in color caused by excessive soil accumulation; it also reduces changes in texture and luster caused when traffic grinds gritty soil against fiber surfaces.

Initially, some corrective measures may be required to mend an occasional flaw or to remove loose fibers. Thereafter, specific preventive, interim, and restorative procedures should be followed, with salvage procedures used as necessary. Each of these activities is scheduled after consideration of the level of appearance preferred by the carpet owner, the anticipated traffic load, and the rate and type of soiling expected.

Table 27.2 Installation Checklist—Proper Procedures to Ensure Good IAQ

Pre-installation

- Choose a carpet with the CRI IAQ Testing Program logo.
- Store carpet at room temperature (between 65°F and 95°F) for at least 24 hours prior to installation in order for it to relax. Ideally, it should be unrolled, to allow it to condition to the ambient temperatures.
- If replacement carpet, vacuum the old carpet prior to removal, and vacuum the subfloor to minimize the amount of airborne dust.
- Carefully plan the carpet installation, using manufacturer's guidelines and/or the CRI 104 Standard for Installation of Commercial Textile Floor Covering Materials or CRI 105 Standard for Installation of Residential Textile Floor Covering Materials.

During Installation

- Use low-emitting (nonsolvent) adhesives for glue-down installations.
- Use low-emitting carpet cushion (for installations in which cushion is specified).
- Use low-emitting accessories (moldings, baseboards, seam sealers and tapes, etc.).
- Maintain fresh air ventilation for 48 to 72 hours.
- Open windows and doors, use exhaust fans, or both.
- Operate ventilation systems at full capacity.
- Segregate the air circulation of the renovation area from the remainder of the building.

Post-installation

- Vacuum new carpet to remove excess fibers loosened during installation.
- Continue fresh air ventilation for 48 to 72 hours at normal room temperatures to help dissipate any possible odors.
- Implement efficient carpet maintenance program to protect your investment.

For more detailed installation information, refer to the CRI 104 Standard for Installation of Commercial Textile Floorcovering Materials and the CRI 105 Standard for Installation of Residential Textile Floorcovering Materials.
Courtesy of Ascend Performance Materials.

Initial Care

Inspection of a newly installed carpet may reveal such problems as shedding, sprouting, missing tufts, and small dots of latex. Simple measures can correct these irregularities.

Shedding occurs when short lengths of fibers that have accumulated during manufacturing work to the surface. It is particularly characteristic of cut pile textures and will soon be corrected by regular vacuuming. The fiber loss will not be significant. **Sprouting** refers to the protrusion of a tuft above the surface of the wear layer. This may result from the release of a small fold of pile yarn that was caught during manufacturing. The extended tuft should simply be clipped to the proper pile height; it must never be pulled. The floor covering dealer, in a procedure known as burling, can replace a missing tuft. During manufacturing, a small dot of latex is frequently used to join or splice ends of pile yarns. All visible bits of latex are removed by the factory inspector. If, however, some were hidden and appear in the new carpet, the installer or consumer can simply cut them out, removing any residue with a small amount of dry-cleaning fluid.

Another activity to be carried out after installation of a new carpet is the placement of chair pads under wheeled desk chairs and casters or rests under furniture. These will protect the pile layer from excessive abrasion, shearing, and crushing, prolonging the wear-life and helping to retain the original texture of the carpet.

Preventive Maintenance

Preventive maintenance procedures are protective procedures, employed to capture soil and grit in track-off, funnel, and concentrated traffic areas. If soil and grit particles are continually removed from the sites where they were initially deposited, the amount spread throughout a facility can be significantly reduced. Preventive measures can also help minimize spotting and staining.

Using Protective Mats

Because over 80 percent of carpet soil is tracked-in, preventive maintenance must begin with walk-off mats or runners placed outside and inside of entrance areas. Walk-off mats should also be placed where foot traffic may transfer wax and dust from hard-surfaced floors to carpet surfaces. In areas where commercial traffic is concentrated or channeled, such as lobbies, elevators, in front of vending machines and file cabinets, down corridors, and at doorways, protective mats should be strategically located to capture soil.

In all cases, walk-off mats and runners must be cleaned so they do not themselves become sources of soil and grit. In elevators, removable rugs or carpet modules can facilitate off-site cleaning and rotation. In all commercial environments, carpets and mats should meet the Americans with Disabilities Act Design Guidelines for construction and installation methods.

Vacuuming

In most planned maintenance programs, a thorough vacuuming (five to seven passes of the sweeper over the surface) with an upright, rather than a canister, vacuum is recommended for track-off areas and primary traffic lanes every one or two days. For areas subjected to lower levels of traffic, vacuuming may be light (three passes of the sweeper) and as infrequent as every seven to ten days. Such light maintenance is reasonable for many areas: approximately 70 to 80 percent of all interior floor space is rarely walked on.

An example of a planned maintenance schedule for a commercial interior is presented in Figure 27.18. Vacuuming, stain removal, and interim cleaning activities are listed. Track-off and funnel areas are scheduled for dry cleaning once every twenty days; stain removal and dry cleaning procedures are discussed later in this chapter.

To assist consumers in identifying the best vacuum cleaners for use on carpeting, in 2000 the Carpet and Rug Institute launched the Green Label Vacuum Testing Program, which is now part of its Seal of Approval (SOA) programs. In addition to outstanding cleaning qualities, CRI-approved vacuums also reduce the amount of dust put back into the air. End users can identify these machines by looking for the CRI Seal of Approval "Green Label" on approved machines and packaging.

Pretesting Cleaning Products

Pretesting stain removal and carpet cleaning products is an important preventive activity, because it minimizes the chance that products will damage the fibers, cause color transfer, produce color changes, or leave sticky residues. The Carpet and Rug Institute recommends the

Recommended Cleaning Schedule				
Monday	Tuesday	Wednesday	Thursday	Friday
1 HT vacuum MT vacuum Rotate mats	2 HT vacuum Spot cleaning	3 HT vacuum MT vacuum	4 HT vacuum MT vacuum Spot cleaning	5 HT vacuum MT vacuum
8 HT vacuum MT vacuum Rotate mats	9 HT vacuum Spot cleaning	10 HT vacuum MT vacuum	11 HT vacuum MT vacuum Spot cleaning	12 HT vacuum MT vacuum
15 HT vacuum MT vacuum Rotate mats	16 HT vacuum Spot cleaning	17 HT vacuum MT vacuum	18 HT vacuum MT vacuum Spot cleaning	19 HT vacuum MT vacuum
22 HT vacuum MT vacuum Rotate mats	23 HT vacuum Spot cleaning	24 HT vacuum MT vacuum	25 HT vacuum MT vacuum Spot cleaning	26 HT vacuum MT vacuum
29 HT vacuum MT vacuum Rotate mats	30 HT vacuum Spot cleaning	31 HT vacuum MT vacuum	1 HT vacuum MT vacuum Spot cleaning	2 HT vacuum MT vacuum LT cleaning

HT = high traffic areas, MT = medium traffic areas, LT = low traffic areas: vacuum as needed. TF = traffic lane cleaning: overall cleaning performed periodically; increase during inclement weather. Schedule assumes no maintenance operations on Saturday or Sunday.

Figure 27.18 Commercial carpet cleaning frequency chart. Courtesy of Ascend Performance Materials.

use of two types of pretests. In one test, approximately one teaspoon of the prepared product is worked into the fibers in an inconspicuous area of the floor covering. The fibers are then pressed between a clean, white tissue for about ten seconds. The tissue is examined for evidence of bleeding, and the fibers are examined for evidence of damage. The procedure should be repeated until a safe agent is identified.

In the second test, a half cup of the prepared product is poured into a clear glass dish. After the liquid portion of the product has evaporated, the residue is examined. If a dry, powdery residue is found, it would be reasonable to expect that vacuuming could remove such deposits from the carpet. If a sticky or waxy residue is found, it is evident that such deposits would remain in the carpet after cleaning, causing the fibers to adhere to one another and promoting rapid resoiling.

The Seal of Approval (SOA) Carpet Cleaning Products Testing Program was introduced by the Carpet and Rug Institute in 2007. This program evaluates carpet cleaning products for their cleaning effectiveness without damage to carpet fibers and backings. An important aspect to cleaning products is that they not strip the carpet of its stain-resistant properties, thus allowing dirt to adhere easily to the carpet in the future. Products tested include prespray and in-tank cleaning detergents and extraction equipment.

Minimizing and Removing Stains

Another important preventive activity is the prompt and efficient removal of solid and liquid substances deposited or spilled on the carpet. This will help to prevent spotting and staining. A few basic rules should be observed in this practice.

1. Act promptly. Foreign substances are more difficult to remove after they have aged.

2. Vacuum dry substances, scoop up excess thick substances, and absorb as much spilled liquid as possible before proceeding with further removal procedures. To avoid diluting and spreading spilled liquids, do not wet at this time. Immediately place absorbent towels over the spill and apply pressure with the hands or heels to promote transfer of the moisture from the carpet to the towels. Use a blotting action: rubbing could cause distortion of

the pile. Continue blotting until no more of the spot shows on the towels. Next, cover the area with a half-inch thick layer of absorbent tissues topped by a sheet of foil and place a heavy object (for example, a big-city telephone directory) on the foil covered towels. Wait patiently overnight while the liquid wicks into the towels. If some of the spill remains, proceed with the appropriate removal technique listed in Table 27.4 or Table 27.5.

3. Be prepared. Have a kit of cleaning agents and materials assembled for immediate use. A list of common stain removal supplies is provided in Table 27.3. It does not include carbon tetrachloride, gasoline, or lighter fluid, which are flammable and hazardous to human health. Label the containers and store them in a locked cabinet out of the reach of children.

Common stains and the procedures recommended for removing them from nylon fibers are listed in Table 27.4. Procedures recommended for removing stains from wool carpet fibers are listed in Table 27.5. Residential and commercial consumers may obtain

Table 27.3 Spot and Stain Removal Supplies
Absorbent dry powders—examples include Hostt and Capture®
Abundant supply of absorbent white tissues and towels for blotting
Acetic acid or white vinegar solution ($\frac{1}{3}$ cup of vinegar to 1 cup of water)
Acetone or fingernail polish remover, non-oily type
Aerosol cleaners—commercial type available from floor covering dealers and in grocery stores
Alcohol, denatured or rubbing type
Ammonia solution (1 tablespoon to $\frac{3}{4}$ cup of water)
Detergent (use 1 teaspoon of mild hand dishwashing type without oily conditioners to 1 cup of warm water or 1 tablespoon of dry powdered laundry type to 1 cup of water)
Dry-cleaning fluid—examples include Carbona®, Renuzit®, and Energine®
POGR (paint, oil, and grease remover)—examples include Pyratex® and Buckeye®
Pre-soak laundry product (enzyme digester)
Squeeze bottles, medicine droppers, wooden scrapers

Table 27.4 Removal of Spots and Stains from Nylon Fibers

Stain/Procedure		Stain/Procedure		Procedure A	Procedure D	Procedure H
Asphalt	A	Lard	A	Apply solvent	Detergent	Apply solvent
Beer	E	Linseed Oil	A	*POGR	Blot	Wait several minutes
Berries	E	Machine Oil	A	Blot	Acetic acid	Blot
Blood	B	Mascara	A	Apply solvent	Blot	Detergent
Butter	A	Mayonnaise	B	Detergent	Rust remover	Blot
Candle Wax	G	Mercurochrome	E	Blot	Blot	Water
Candy (Sugar)	D	Merthiolate	E	Ammonia	Detergent	Blot
Carbon Black	A	Milk	B	Blot	Blot	
Catsup	B	Mimeo Correction Fluid	C	Detergent	Water	**Procedure I**
Charcoal	A	Mixed Drinks	E	Blot	Blot	Denatured alcohol
Cheese	B	Model Cement	L	Water		Blot
Chewing Gum	G	Mustard	E	Blot	**Procedure E**	Repeat, if necessary
Chocolate	B	Nail Polish	L		Detergent	Note: pretest as for
Coffee	E	Paint—Latex	A	**Procedure B**	Blot	other solutions
Cooking Oil	A	Paint—Oil	A	Detergent	Ammonia	
Crayon	A	Rubber Cement	A	Enzyme digestor	Blot	**Procedure J**
Créme de Menthe	F	Rust	D	Soak	Acetic acid	Detergent
Dye—Blue, Black, Green	F	Shellac	I	Ammonia	Blot	Blot
Dye—Red	E	Shoe Polish	A	Blot	Detergent	Vinegar
Earth	B	Shortening	A	Detergent	Blot	Blot
Egg	B	Soft Drinks	E	Blot	Water	Ammonia
Excrement	B	Soy Sauce	B	Water	Blot	Blot
Fish Slime	B	Starch	B	Blot		Detergent
Foundation Makeup	A	Tar	A		**Procedure F**	Blot
Fruit Juice	E	Tea	E	**Procedure C**	Detergent	Water
Furniture Polish	A	Tooth Paste	B	Apply solvent	Blot	Blot
Furniture Polish with Stain	H	Typewriter Ribbon	A	*POGR	Detergent	
Gravy	A	Urine—Dry	J	Blot	Blot	**Procedure K**
Hair Oil	A	Urine—Fresh	K	Apply solvent	Ammonia	Blot
Hair Spray	A	Varnish	C	Blot	Blot	Water
Hand Lotion	A	Vaseline	A	Detergent	Water	Blot
Ice Cream	B	Wax—Paste	A	Blot	Blot	Ammonia
Ink—Ball Point	A	White Glue	B	Water		Blot
Ink—Fountain Pen	F	Wine	E	Blot	**Procedure G**	Detergent
Ink—India	A				Freeze with ice cube	Blot
Ink—Marking Pen	A				Shatter w/blunt object	Water
Ink—Mimeo	A				Vacuum out chips	Blot
Lacquer	C				Apply solvent	
					Wait several minutes	**Procedure L**
					Blot	Polish remover
					Repeat, if necessary	(non-oily)
						Blot
						Repeat

*Paint, oil, and grease remover.
Courtesy of Shaw Industries.

Table 27.5 Removal of Spots and Stains from Wool Carpet Fibers

This table includes advice on methods of treating stains and the order in which they should be tried. For instance, if clean water does not remove all traces of a beverage, try a solution of washing powder next. Most of the agents mentioned are easy to obtain; however, if you cannot get a dye stripper or hydrochloric acid, call a professional cleaner instead. A freezing agent is available in aerosol sprays, but you can use ice instead to harden chewing gum in order to remove it. CAUTION: Before proceeding to treat a stain, pretest your treatments on an inconspicuous part of the carpet to check for possible color change. Some recommended treatments may be toxic; therefore all precautions should be taken when handling these products.

Types of treatments

1. Carpet shampoo solution. It is important to use a neutral shampoo on wool carpets, not one that is alkaline. Never use carpet shampoos that smell of ammonia.	10. Turpentine or white spirits.
2. Evaporating spot remover or dry-cleaning fluid.	11. Vacuum.
3. Warm water.	12. Starch paste.
4. Cold water.	13. Scrape lightly with fingers or a coin.
5. Laundry detergent (one teaspoon in one pint warm water).	14. Rub gently with coarse sandpaper.
6. Absorbent paper and hot iron.	15. Scrape and vacuum.
7. White vinegar.	16. Glycerine.
8. Rubbing alcohol.	17. Call a professional cleaner.
9. Nail polish remover or acetone.	

Stains

Acids 1, 5, or 7	Floor wax 2	Paint (oil) 10, 2, or 1
Alcoholic beverages 1, 2, 5, or 7	Fruit and juices 1, 2, 5, or 7	Perfume 1, 2, 5, or 7
Beer 1, 5, or 7	Furniture polish 1, 2, 5, or 7	Permanent ink 17
Bleach 1, 5, or 7	Glue 8	Rust 17
Blood 1, 5, 7, or 12	Grass 1, 2, 5, or 7	Salad dressing 1, 2, 5, or 7
Burn or scorch mark 13 or 14	Gravy 1, 2, 5, or 7	Sauces 1, 2, 5, or 7
Butter 1 or 2	Grease 2 or 15	Shoe polish 1, 2, 5, 7, or 15
Candy 1, 5, 7, or 15	Household cement 1, 2, 5, or 7	Soot 11, 1, 2, or 17
Chewing gum 1, 2, 5, or 7	Ice cream 1, 2, 5, or 7	Tar 2
Chocolate 1, 2, 5, or 7	Ink (fountain pen) 4 or 5	Tea 1, 5, or 7
Coffee 16	Ink (ball point pen) 1 or 8	Urine (human) 1, 5, or 7 (remove at once—
Coffee with cream 16 followed by 5	Iodine 8	chemicals in urine attack dyestuffs)
Colas 1 or 4	Jam 3	Urine (pet) 17
Cosmetics 1, 2, 5, or 7	Lipstick 1, 2, 5, or 7	Urine (old stain) 17
Crayon 1, 2, 5, 7, or 15	Medicine 17	Vomit 1, 2, 5, or 7
Cream 1 or 2	Metal polish 1	Wax 2 or 15
Egg 1, 5, or 7	Mildew 17	Wine 4, 5, 7, or 2
Excrement (human) 1, 5, or 7	Milk 1 or 3	
(remove at once—chemicals in	Mud 5 or 7	
excrement attack dyestuffs)	Mustard 1, 5, or 7	
Excrement (pet) 17	Nail polish 2 or 9	
Fat and oil 6 then 2	Oils 2 or 1	
(do not use iron after solvent)	Paint (emulsion) 4 or 1	

Note: While this advice is offered in good faith, no responsibility is accepted for claims arising from the treatments proposed. If stains fail to respond to treatments listed, call a professional carpet cleaner immediately.
Courtesy of the Australian Wool Innovation Limited.

additional stain removal guides and care instructions from retailers, fiber and carpet producers, and trade associations.

Pretests, described above, should precede the application of any stain removal agent.

When small bits of carpet fibers have been melted or singed, they can be carefully clipped and removed. If the damaged area is large, it must be cut out and replaced with a piece reserved at the time of installation.

Interim Maintenance

Interim maintenance activities are designed primarily to assure a high level of appearance retention for an extended period of time and to delay the need for restorative procedures. Interim maintenance is, specifically, the use of a restorative cleaning procedure in a localized area, such as a track-off area, every twenty or thirty-one days. A planned schedule will prevent soil accumulation in areas of heavy traffic from developing an appearance noticeably different from that of adjacent areas.

Interim cleaning may be done with a dry or a wet cleaning system. Frequently, dry cleaning is recommended so that no drying time is required and the area being cleaned can extend beyond the soiled area to prevent marked differences in appearance between the cleaned site and the adjacent areas. Some examples of dry-cleaning compounds are Capture®, produced by Milliken Chemical, Host,® produced by Racine Industries, Inc., and Blue Lustre® Dry, produced by Earl Grissmer Company. 3M Brand Carpet Protector Maintainer/Shampoo, produced for interim wet cleaning, deposits a fluorochemical stain repellent compound on the carpet during the cleaning process.

Other interim maintenance activities should be performed as needed. These may include the removal of pills, fuzz, and snags. Fuzziness may occur with loop pile textures when abrasion causes some fibers to rupture, leaving one end in the base of the yarn and one end protruding. The protruding length should be clipped away; it should not be pulled. Unsightly pills should be clipped away, although this is a tedious job. Snagged tufts are treated in the same manner as sprouting tufts. If rippling or seam separation is evident, the installer should be called to restretch or reglue the structure and to secure the seams. Area and room-size rugs and runners should be reversed and modules rotated to even the level of wear and soiling. Furniture may be shifted a few inches to allow crushed areas to recover: recovery may be assisted by steaming the areas with an iron held approximately 4 inches above the surface. An occasional raking can help to keep the pile tufts in shag floor coverings erect.

Restorative Maintenance

Restorative maintenance involves an overall or wall-to-wall cleaning procedure. The frequency with which such cleaning operations should be undertaken depends on the rate of soil accumulation and the effectiveness of interim maintenance procedures. Of course, the owner's opinion about the acceptability of the surface appearance is usually decisive. Four major restorative maintenance procedures can be considered: dry extraction, dry foam, wet shampoo, and hot water extraction.

Dry Extraction

Dry extraction cleaning is also referred to as absorbent powder or absorbent compound cleaning. The soil-extracting particles are generally composed of water-based cleaning fluids or detergents and a small amount of solvent. Their minute size results in an extremely high surface-area-to-volume ratio that increases their capacity for absorption.

The particles are sprinkled over the carpet structure and vigorously brushed by hand or machine into the pile layer. There, the solvent releases the soil and the porous particles act like tiny sponges, absorbing the soil. Subsequent vacuuming removes the soil-holding particles. Examples of several dry extraction products were listed in the earlier discussion of interim cleaning.

The advantage of dry extraction cleaning is that the fibers are not wetted. This avoids not only the need for drying, but also the problem of overwetting the structure, which could lead to shrinkage and microbe-related problems. When a jute backing is present, overwetting could also cause a problem known as **browning**, staining of the pile as the water wicks from the backing upward. Caution should be exercised when brushing the particles into the pile layer to avoid distortion of cut pile yarns.

Dry Foam

Dry foam cleaning is also called aerosol cleaning. The cleaning agent is generally a water-based shampoo that has been converted into foam. The foam is sprayed onto the carpet surface and worked into the pile layer with a hand-held sponge or with mechanically operated brushes.

After the compound dries, the surface must be thoroughly vacuumed or rinsed with a damp sponge to remove the soil-foam residue. Some electrically powered units apply the foam and vacuum the carpet in a one-step operation.

Cleaning with dry foam may not be as thorough as other methods, especially if a large amount of soil is deeply embedded in the pile layer. The risk of overwetting the carpet is minimal.

Wet Shampooing

The **wet shampoo method** of carpet restoration is commonly referred to as the rotary brush method. The properly diluted detergent solution or foam is driven into the pile with one or two rotating brushes. A thorough vacuuming, preferably with a wet vacuum, must follow. Wet vacuums, unlike conventional vacuums, are engineered to suction fluids, as well as dry matter, from surfaces safely and efficiently.

While the mechanical action of the rotating brushes works the detergent solution into the carpet, it may also cause pile distortion, especially of cut surfaces. Care must be taken in applying the solution or foam to avoid overwetting the structure. Vacuuming of the soil-shampoo compound must be thorough, since any residue will accelerate resoiling.

Hot Water Extraction

Hot water or spray extraction cleaning is commonly called steam extraction, although extremely hot water is used, not steam. The properly diluted shampoo is driven into the pile as a spray by high-pressure jets; it is then immediately extracted by the vacuum component of the machine.

Because no mechanical brushing is used in this extraction method, pile yarns are minimally distorted. Spots and stains must be removed before the cleaning operation is begun so that the hot water will not set them. As in wet shampooing, the detergent must be thoroughly removed to retard rapid resoiling.

Salvage Maintenance

Salvage maintenance procedures may be required for extremely soiled carpet or for removing built-up residue. When such problems are evident, it may be advisable to use a combination of wet shampooing and hot water extraction. The mechanical action of the rotary brushes will help to loosen the soil, and the extraction will make for better removal.

Summary

Carpet rollgoods may be installed with a stretch-in or glue-down technique. Modules may be glued to the floor, using a permanent or releasable adhesive; some may be free-laid. For all projects, yardage calculations must be accurate. Skilled personnel should generally carry out installation procedures.

Effective procedures and adherence to a planned maintenance schedule can maintain the original appearance of textile floor coverings at a higher level for a longer period of time. Wear-life can also be extended this way, and the need for premature replacement avoided.

Key Terms

browning

drop-match patterns

dry extraction cleaning

dry foam cleaning

free-lay installation

glue-down installation

grin

half-drop

hot water or spray extraction cleaning

interim maintenance

knee kicker

power stretcher

preventive maintenance

restorative maintenance

saddle

salvage maintenance

set-match patterns

shedding

sprouting

stretch-in installation

tackless strips

ugly out

wall-to-wall installation

wet shampoo cleaning

Review Questions

1. Identify several tasks that may have to be completed on site before a new floor covering assembly is installed.

2. Explain the techniques used in stretch-in installations. How is the stretching accomplished? How is the carpet secured?

3. Distinguish between double glue-down and direct glue-down installations. What advantages are offered by these modes of installation when rolling traffic is anticipated?

4. Identify some advantages of using releasable adhesives with carpet modules.

5. What factors limit the use of free-lay installations with carpet modules? What advantages are offered by this mode of installation?

6. Illustrate and discuss the important influence that the directional lay of pile yarns has on the quantity of light reflected from the carpet surface.

7. Differentiate among set-match, drop-match, half-drop-match, and quarter-drop-match patterns.

8. Cite the objectives of planned maintenance programs.

9. Confirm the importance of pretesting cleaning products.

10. What are the advantages and disadvantages of each of the restorative cleaning procedures?

UNIT FOUR CASE STUDY

Project Type: Long Term Care Unit

Statement of the Project:

The objective was to create a new, updated long-term care unit for the hospital that was comparable to similar units in the region with a goal of providing a truly pleasing environment for the elderly of the community. The textile consideration for this casestudy was the use of carpet down the central corridor.

Statement of the Problem:

The hospital needed a floorcovering that controlled glare and acoustics and established a residential feeling. It was also imperative that it be easily cleaned because of cases of incontinence. The existing vinyl was inadequate in addressing the aesthetics.

Selection Criteria:

Carpet was chosen to replace vinyl for several reasons. Aesthetically, the carpet provided a warmer, softer, more residential and familiar atmosphere for the residents. The residential feeling provides psychological comfort, which is significant to the health and well-being of the user. Extensive research reports and summaries were compiled from such agencies as the Alzheimer's Association and the American Institute of Architects/American Collegiate Schools of Architecture (AIA/ACSA) along with articles from industry publications such as *Facility Care* and *Hospitality Design* to explain the psychological advantages and wellness issues. The carpet was a neutral background with a variety of colored flecks to permit the designer to use more colors on other interior finishes. No pattern is evident to eliminate confusion for the residents. For safety, the carpet offered more traction, reduced glare, and is slightly softer in case of falls. The carpet was installed using a direct glue-down in-

stallation without a carpet pad. A carpet pad would have increased the difficulty for all roller traffic to move across the floor. The carpet also offered an acoustical advantage as the carpet reduces the noise from foot traffic and other everyday hospital occurrences. The quiet atmosphere increases the positive psychological affect of the residents, staff, and visitors because it reduces stress and encourages mobility and activity in the residents.

Product Specifications:

Patcraft Carpet

- Pattern: Endeavor #816-038 Progress
- 100% Dupont Antron Lumena® solution dyed
- Continuous filament nylon
- With antimicrobial properties

Maintenance and Cost:

Stains need to be spot cleaned immediately. A list of stains and appropriate cleaning methods for each specific stain was provided by the manufacturer. For moderate traffic (less than 500 walk-ons per day), vacuum 1–2 times per week with a heavy-duty commercial grade vacuum with cylinder brush and bar. Carpet should be cleaned using a dry extraction method (such as Host® or Ban Clene®) twice yearly. If the traffic increased to more than 500 walk-ons per day (heavy traffic), the vacuuming would increase to every 2–3 days and cleaning to quarterly. Over 1,000 walk-ons (extra-heavy traffic) would mean daily vacuuming and monthly cleaning. While the carpet is more expensive than vinyl floorcovering, the psychological advantages justified the additional expense.

Discussion Questions

1. Identify two of the client's requirements for the design project.

2. Distinguish one aesthetic feature of the product that meets the client's requirements.

3. Distinguish one functional feature of the product that meets the client's requirements.

4. Discuss the psychological impact of the textile on the user of the space.

5. Research another product that is appropriate for this application. Compare and contrast the cost effectiveness, availability, durability, and maintenance of the new product with the one used in the case study.

Household and Institutional Textiles

UNIT FIVE focuses on household and institutional textile products, several of which fulfill both decorative and functional needs. Chapter 28 examines the composition and construction of textile bath products. It also reviews performance and flammability standards. Chapter 29 covers the wide assortment of textile fabrics manufactured for use in bedding products, as well as the natural and synthesized fillings used in beddings. Performance and flammability requirements are also included. Chapter 30 presents various tabletop accessories, including tablecloths, napkins, table runners, and doilies.

CHAPTER TWENTY-EIGHT

Textile Products
for the Bath

Towels and Toweling

Bath Rugs and Mats

Shower Curtains

Photo courtesy of Nancy Oxford.

■ **Fabric stylists and end-product** designers have created many decorative variations of such textile bath products as towels, rugs, mats, and shower curtains, so that these items are often as ornamental as they are functional. While the primary function of towels is absorbency, they nonetheless contribute also to the aesthetics of the near environment. Manufacturers have expanded the size range of towels, increased the types of materials used in shower curtains, and varied the shapes and constructions of small bath rugs and mats. Frequently, contemporary bath products are offered in coordinated ensembles, and sometimes they are part of elaborate collections that include bedding products as well.

Today, bath products are produced and marketed for both household and institutional use. Standard performance specifications, such as those published by ASTM International, may be used between purchaser and supplier to establish required structural features and performance levels. With the exception of nontextile shower curtains, these products are subject to the provisions of the Textile Fiber Products Identification Act (see Chapter 10). Small rugs and bath mats are also subject to a federal flammability standard.

Towels and Toweling

Various fabrication techniques, including weaving, stitch-knitting, and bonding webs of fibers, are used to produce toweling. In contrast to many other interior products, which are composed primarily of manufactured fibers, towels and toweling are composed primarily of cotton. Manufacturers often produce cotton and polyester blended toweling to save on costs. However, this decreases the softness of the hand, the comfort, and the absorbency.

Statistical Profile of Fiber Usage

Fiber usage in towels and toweling is detailed in Table 28.1. The poundage listed includes the fiber used in the production of woven dish towels, but does not include the fiber used to produce bonded-web toweling.

Predominance of Cotton

The towel and towelings market has been and continues to be dominated by cotton. This natural fiber held more than 98 percent of the 2001 market, and although its use has decreased since 2001, it nonetheless holds more than 97 percent of the current market. Cotton is highly absorbent and soft, features that make it attractive and efficient for toweling. Flax, which has slightly higher moisture absorption and produces less lint than cotton, is also used but in small amounts. The harsh hand and low abrasion resistance characteristic of flax preclude its use in bath towels, and the comparatively high cost of the fiber limits its use in dish towels.

Manufactured cellulosic fibers, including rayon made from bamboo and lyocell, are now being used for bath products. Towels containing Seacell® active, which contains both seaweed and silver, are being marketed for their natural antimicrobial properties. Rayon (made from bamboo) towels and bath mats are soft, absorbent, and also have natural antimicrobial properties. Manufactured cellulosic fibers are discussed in Chapter 4.

The manufactured staple fibers consumed in towels are generally made into spun yarns that are incorporated in the base of pile toweling for strength and dimensional

Table 28.1 Fiber Usage in Towels and Toweling											
		Manufactured Fibers*									
			Cellulosic		Noncellulosic						
Year	Total Fiber	Total	Yarn	Staple	Yarn	%	Staple	%	Cotton	%	Wool**
2001	326.0	7.4	0.3	0.1	2.2	.007	4.8	.014	318.6	98.0	--
2002	281.4	7.4	0.4	0.1	1.9		5.0		274.1		--
2003	241.4	6.4	0.6	--**	1.4		4.4		235.0		--
2004	198.1	4.7	0.4	--	1.0		3.3		193.4		--
2005	181.4	5.7	0.4	--	1.2	.007	4.1	.023	175.7	96.86	--

* Manufactured fiber end-use is divided between cellulosic (rayon + acetate) and noncellulosic (nylon, polyester, acrylic, olefin). Yarn includes multifilament, monofilament, and spunbonded. Olefin includes polypropylene and polyethylene staple and yarn. Olefin yarn also includes film fiber and spunbonded polypropylene. Staple includes tow and fiberfill.
** Little or none of the fiber is used.
Source: Textiles Economics Bureau, *Fiber Organon*, "U.S. End Use Survey: 2001–2005," October 2006, page 192, Table 4.

stability. Although these fibers can be spun into yarns that simulate the appearance and hand of yarns composed of cotton, and they have recently shown improved hydrophilic properties, they continue to hold a very small part of the towel and toweling market. Manufacturers often produce cotton and polyester-blended towels to save on costs. However, this decreases the softness of the hand, the comfort, and the absorbency.

Manufacturing Toweling

Manufacturers use a variety of fabrication techniques to produce flat or nonpile toweling. They use a warp pile weaving operation to produce pile toweling.

Constructing Pile Toweling

Pile or **terry toweling** is also known as **Turkish toweling**. The components of this toweling are illustrated in Figure 28.1. One set of filling or weft yarns is interlaced with one set of base or ground warp yarns and two sets of pile warp yarns. If loops are planned for only one side of the fabric, only one set of pile warp yarns is used. Fabrics with loops on both sides have more fiber surface area for absorbing moisture, but they are also more expensive if the construction density is not reduced. For visual interest, the pile yarns appearing on each side can be of different colors.

Terry toweling is manufactured by the **slack tension technique** (see Chapter 6). For economical production, terry looms are generally threaded for full-width weaving. When hemmed edges and ends are planned, the dimensions of individual towels are demarcated by the omission of pile yarns in narrow lengthwise and crosswise bands; when fringed ends are planned, the crosswise bands are also void of filling picks. A dobby mechanism may be used to produce woven border designs.

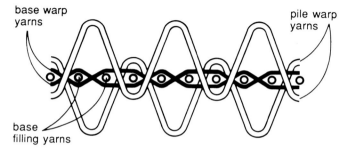

Figure 28.1 Cross-sectional sketch of terry toweling that has three filling picks per crosswise row of pile loops.

a) Loom engineered to weave multiple widths of terry toweling.

b) Terry toweling on loom.

Figure 28.2 Loom engineered to weave multiple widths of terry toweling.
a) Courtesy of Picanol; b) Courtesy of ITEMA Weaving, www.sultex.com.

For increased efficiency and economy in both weaving and finishing, textile machinery engineers have developed extra-wide looms capable of simultaneously weaving multiple widths of toweling. Looms of the type shown in Figure 28.2a and b can weave several widths of toweling during one operation. The several widths of toweling have tucked-in selvages (Figure 6.2b, p. 100). Rayon (made from bamboo) terry towels are shown in Figure 28.3. The Jacquard terry toweling in Figure 28.4a and b has been woven in a visually appealing geometric pattern.

Terry velour toweling (Figure 28.5) has a conventional looped pile surface on one side, and a dense, cut pile surface on the other side. The sheared velour surface has a thick and luxurious appearance and hand, but the level of moisture absorption is relatively low since only the small tips of the yarns are exposed.

Figure 28.3 Terry toweling rayon made from bamboo.
Courtesy of www.turkishtowels.com.

A small amount of terry is produced by a stitch-knitting operation known by the patent name **Malipol**. In this procedure, an expansion of the stitch-knitting technique described in Chapter 7, pile yarns are incorporated into webs of yarns that are layered and stitched.

Fabricating Flat Toweling

Flat or non-terry toweling is generally produced by weaving yarns in a basic biaxial or dobby interlacing pattern or by bonding webs of fibers. **Crash**, shown in Figure 28.6, is a plain-woven fabric composed of coarse, irregular yarns spun from flax. The fabric is constructed into dish towels intended for the lint free drying of glassware. Twill-woven toweling, often referred to as **institutional toweling**, is generally produced with brightly colored stripes on each long side and constructed into towels used in restaurants. **Huck toweling (huckaback)** is woven on a dobby loom and has small filling floats. These slightly raised floats, visible in the closeup photograph in Figure 28.7, improve the drying efficiency of the towel.

Disposable toweling is produced by bonding webs of fibers with heat or an adhesive. Some items are intended to be used once; others are for repeated use (Figure 28.8). For increased strength, a scrim of fine yarns may be anchored between the layered webs.

a) Various colors of jacquard toweling.

b) Close-up view of toweling.

Figure 28.4 Jacquard terry toweling.
Courtesy of www.turkishtowels.com.

Figure 28.5 Terry velour toweling.
Courtesy of Amy Willbanks, www.textilefabric.com.

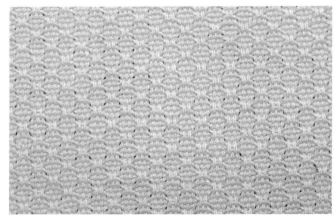

Figure 28.7 Huck toweling.
Courtesy of Amy Willbanks, www.textilefabric.com.

Constructing Towels

Towels come in a variety of sizes and with a variety of edge and end finishes. Trims and embroidery embellish their surfaces.

Types and Sizes

Several types of towels are included in today's market assortment. The approximate size ranges of the various types are listed in Table 28.2. If the toweling was not preshrunk, the towels may be oversized to compensate for relaxation shrinkage in laundering.

Edge Finishes and Decorative Treatments

Terry toweling is cut along the flat lengthwise and crosswise bands spaced throughout the pile greige goods. Cutting produces unfinished towels of various sizes. The sides may be finished with a small, machine-stitched hem or with machine serging. The ends may be hemmed or left with a yarn fringe. Squares of pile fabric are cut for washcloths, and the four raw edges are serged. For decorative interest, bands of embroidered fabric or trim may be sewn across towels and washcloths, or the surface may be embellished with a Schiffli-embroidered monogram or motif (Figure 28.9).

Coordinated Items

Yarn-dyed, solid-colored, or printed toweling used to construct dish towels may also be used to produce such coordinated items as oven mitts, pot holders, small appliance covers, and aprons. The color styling and decorative treatment of bath towels may be replicated in bedding products; the several bath and bedding products are then offered and promoted as a coordinated ensemble.

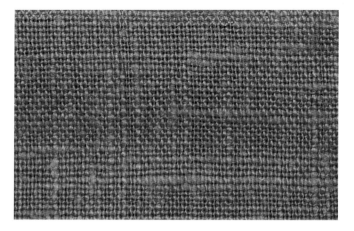

Figure 28.6 Crash.
Courtesy of Amy Willbanks, www.textilefabric.com.

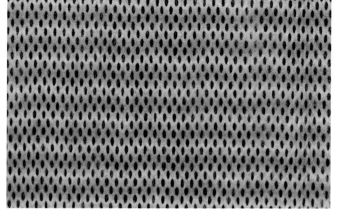

Figure 28.8 Disposable toweling.
Courtesy of Amy Willbanks, www.textilefabric.com.

Table 28.2 Types and Sizes of Towels

Type	Inches (width × length)
Dish towel	12 × 24 to 16 × 30
Fingertip/guest	9 × 14 to 11 × 20
Washcloth	12 × 12 to 14 × 14
Face/hand towel	15 × 25 to 20 × 36
Bath towel	20 × 40 to 27 × 50
Bath sheet	35 × 66 to 45 × 75

Evaluating the Physical Performance Properties of Towels

In order to assure satisfactory performance in use, manufacturers may elect to evaluate the properties of their towels in conjunction with recommendations set forth in ASTM D 5433 Standard Performance Specification for Towel Products for Institutional and Household Use. Specifications for woven terry items, including kitchen towels, dishcloths, bath and hand towels, washcloths, and bath sheets, are listed in Table 28.3; those for non-terry fabrics, including dishcloths, huck toweling, and crash, are shown in Table 28.4.

Breaking Force (Load)

The **breaking force (load)** of woven terry and non-terry towelings may be measured in accordance with the grab test procedure of ASTM D 5034 Standard Test Method for Breaking Strength and Elongation of Textile Fabrics (Grab Test). This procedure was discussed in Chapter 14, and the placement of the clamps on the specimen illustrated in Figure 14.4 (p. 237). As shown in Tables 28.3 and 28.4, the minimum force for towelings ranges from 30 to 40 to 50 pounds, depending on the fabric construction and the product.

Dimensional Change

Because towelings are used for absorption, and they are frequently laundered, it is critical that they exhibit relatively high **dimensional stability**. The fabrics may be tested after five launderings following prescribed care instructions, or in accordance with directions in AATCC Method 135 Dimensional Changes of Fabrics After Home Laundering or AATCC Method 96 Dimensional Changes in Commercial Laundering of Woven and Knitted Fabrics Except Wool. As shown in Tables 28.3 and 28.4, recommendations range from a maximum of 4 percent shrinkage for bath and hand towels in the crosswise direction to a maximum of 10 or 15 percent shrinkage for the lengthwise direction for both terry and non-terry towelings.

Figure 28.9 Embroidered toweling. Courtesy of www.turkishtowels.com.

Bow and Skew

The yarn alignment of towelings may be assessed in accordance with the procedures set forth in ASTM D 3882 Standard Test Method for Bow and Skew in Woven and Knitted Fabrics. This standard was discussed in Chapter 14, with illustrations of the measurement locations shown schematically in Figures 14.2 and 14.3 (p. 235). While the recommended level of **bow** and **skew** is 6 percent, purchaser and supplier may agree upon acceptable performance levels.

Appearance

The appearance of the construction features of towelings (e.g., selvages, hems, seams, and dobby borders) may be evaluated before and after laundering. Purchasers and suppliers should reach mutual appearance requirements.

Microbe Resistance

The humid conditions present in bathrooms are an inviting breeding ground for unwanted microbes. Manufacturers are responding to the growing concern of professionals

Table 28.3 Woven or Knitted Terry Fabric Specification Requirements for Institutional and Household Use

Characteristic	Test Method Number	Requirement		
		Kitchen Towels	Dishcloths	Bath, Hand, Wash-cloths, Bath Sheets
Breaking force (load):	ASTM D 5034			
Length		178 N (40 lbf) min	220 N (50 lbf) min	178 N (40 lbf) min
Width		133 N (30 lbf) min	178 N (40 lbf) min	133 N (30 lbf) min
Bursting force (knits only):	ASTM D 3787			
Diaphragm		222 N (50 lbf) min	222 N (50 lbf) min	222 N (50 lbf) min
Nonfibrous material	AATCC 97	3% max	5% max	3% max
Dimensional change:	AATCC 96 or AATOC 135			
Length		10% max	10% max	10% max
Width		5% max	5% max	4% max
Bow and skew	ASTM D 3882	6% max	6% max	6% max
Colorfastness:[a]				
Laundering	AATCC 61			
Shade change		Class 4[b] min	Class 4[b] min	Class 4[b] min
Staining		Class 3[c] min	Class 3[c] min	Class 3[c] min
Crocking:	AATCC 8 or AATOC 116			
Dry		Class 4[d] min	Class 4[d] min	Class 4[d] min
Wet		Class 3[d] min	Class 3[d] min	Class 3[d] min
Light (20 AATCC FU)	AATCC 16	Class 4[b] min	Class 4[b] min	Class 4[b] min
Absorbency	ASTM D 4772	Pass	Pass	Pass
Flammability	ASTM D 1230	Class I	Class I	Class I
Laundered appearance	---*	Acceptable	Acceptable	Acceptable

[a]Class for color change and color transfer is based on a numerical scale of 5 for negligible or no color change or color transfer to 1 for severe color change or color transfer. The numerical rating in Table 28.3 or higher is acceptable.
[b]AATCC Gray Scale for Color Change
[c]AATCC Gray Scale for Staining
[d]AATCC Chromatic Transference Scale
*As agreed by purchaser and seller
Adapted, with permission from D5433-00 Standard Performance Specification for Towel Products for Institutional and Household Use, copyright ASTM International, 100 Barr Harbor Drive, West Conshohocken, PA 19428, www.astm.org. A copy of the complete standard may be obtained from ASTM International.

in the healthcare, hospitality, and educational fields, as well as homeowners, regarding bacteria and fungi and the problems associated with them—illness, odors, mold and mildew. Toweling and bath rugs are now available with microbe resistant properties and are labeled with trade names including AEGIS Microbe Shield® by AEGIS Environments, Microban®, and Cupron™.

Evaluating Colorfastness

ASTM D 5433 Performance Specification for Towel Products for Institutional and Household Use includes recommendations for the acceptable levels of colorfastness of towelings. These recommendations focus on fastness to laundering, crocking (rubbing), and light.

Colorfastness to Laundering

The colorfastness of towelings to laundering is critical for both household and institutional uses. Because towels are frequently part of coordinated ensembles, marked fading or **shade changes** would be unacceptable. **Bleeding** could lead to **staining** of the body, dishes, swimwear, and so on.

The colorfastness of toweling to laundering may be evaluated in accordance with procedures set forth in AATCC Method 61 Colorfastness to Laundering: Accelerated. The general nature of this method is described in Chapter 18, and the apparatus used, the **Launder-Om-eter®**, is shown in Figure 18.7 (p. 309). Shade changes are evaluated using the **AATCC Gray Scale for Color Change** (Figure 14.10, p. 245); staining is evaluated using the **AATCC Gray Scale for Evaluating Staining** (Figure 14.9, p. 244). The recommended Class ratings are presented in Tables 28.3 and 28.4.

Colorfastness to Crocking

It is readily apparent that towels exhibiting color transfer when rubbed against the body or other fabrics would

Table 28.4 Specification Requirements for Non-Terry Towel Products for Institutional and Household Use

Characteristic	Test Method Number	Requirements	
		Huck and Crash Towels	Dishcloths
Breaking force (load):	ASTM D 5034		
Length		178 N (40 lbf) min	220 N (50 lbf) min
Width		133 N (30 lbf) min	178 N (40 lbf) min
Bursting force (knits only):	ASTM D 3787		
Diaphragm		222 N (50 lbf) min	222 N (50 lbf) min
Nonfibrous material	AATCC 97	5% max	5% max
Dimensional change:	AATCC 96 or AATCC 135		
Length		10% max	10% max
Width		5% max	5% max
Bow and skew	ASTM D 3882	6% Acceptable	6% Acceptable
Colorfastness:[a]			
Laundering:	AATCC 61		
Shade change		Class 4[b] min	Class 4[b] min
Staining		Class 3[c] min	Class 3[c] min
Crocking:	AATCC 8 or AATCC 116		
Dry		Class 4[d] min	Class 4[d] min
Wet		Class 3[d] min	Class 3[d] min
Light (20 AATCC FU)	AATCC 16	Class 4[b] min	Class 4[b] min
Absorbency	ASTM D 4772	Pass	Pass
Flammability	ASTM D 1230	Class I	Class I
Laundered appearance	---*	Acceptable	Acceptable

[a]Class for color change and color transfer is based on a numerical scale of 5 for negligible or no color change or color transfer to 1 for severe color change or color transfer. The numerical rating in Table 28.4 or higher is acceptable.
[b]AATCC Gray Scale for Color Change
[c]AATCC Gray Scale for Staining
[d]AATCC Chromatic Transference Scale
*As agreed by purchaser and seller
Adapted, with permission from D5433-00 Standard Performance Specification for Towel Products for Institutional and Household Use, copyright ASTM International, 100 Barr Harbor Drive, West Conshohocken, PA 19428, www.astm.org. A copy of the complete standard may be obtained from ASTM International.

be unacceptable. The **crocking** of solid-colored towelings may be assessed by following procedures set forth in AATCC Method 8 Colorfastness to Crocking: AATCC Crockmeter Method; this method was described in Chapter 14; the apparatus used to rub the specimens is presented in Figure 14.8 (p. 244). For printed toweling fabrics, the procedures in AATCC Method 116 Color-fastness to Crocking: Rotary Vertical Crock-meter Method should be followed.

Evaluations are done with the **AATCC Color Transference Scale**, shown in Figure 18.6 (p. 308). Dry tests should yield a minimum rating of Class 4, wet tests a minimum of Class 3.

Colorfastness to Light

With the exception of beach towels, towels and dishcloths are not normally subjected to extended exposure to light.

Nonetheless, their lightfastness may be assessed with AATCC Method 16 Colorfastness to Light (see Chapter 18). The apparatus used in these tests, the **Fade-Ome-ter®**, is presented in Figure 18.4 (p. 306).

Both terry and nonterry toweling should exhibit a Class 4 rating on the AATCC Gray Scale for Color Change after 20 hours of AATCC fading units of exposure.

Evaluating Absorbency

How efficiently toweling can absorb liquid water from such surfaces as human skin and dishware is a critical concern for both household and institutional applications. By following the procedures outlined in ASTM D 4772 Standard Test Method for Surface Water Absorption of Terry Fabrics (Water Flow), manufacturers can numerically assess the absorbency of terry toweling.

Test Specimens and Procedures

As directed in ASTM D 4772, three face and three back specimens are secured, one at a time, in an embroidery hoop. The hoop is then mounted at a 60-degree angle to a table surface and a pan is placed below the hoop assembly. Fifty milliliters of distilled water are then allowed to flow onto the surface of the specimen, some being absorbed and some flowing as runoff water into the pan.

Analysis of Results

The difference between the original 50 milliliters of water and the number of milliliters of water in the runoff pan gives the quantity of water absorbed. An average is determined for the three face specimens and for the three back specimens.

Performance Guidelines

The purchaser and the supplier shall agree on an acceptable level of absorbency.

Evaluating Flammability

The purchaser and the supplier shall agree on the flammability requirements of towelings. If flammability is to be tested, ASTM D 1230 Standard Test Method for Flammability of Apparel Textiles may be used. This small scale test method was described in Chapter 11.

Performance Guidelines

As shown in Table 28.3, a Class 1 rating is recommended for terry fabrics.

Caring for Towels

Although care labeling is voluntary, virtually all towels carry instructions for machine washing using warm water and machine drying. Towels with fancy borders and highly decorative trims may carry extra cautionary care instructions, such as hand wash in cool water and line dry. To avoid excessive fiber damage, white items should be bleached with chlorine compounds only when necessary, not routinely in each successive laundering, and an extra rinse should be used to ensure the complete removal of any residual chlorine. To avoid potential bleeding and staining problems, towels with intense, deep-toned colors should be laundered separately. To avoid excessive deposition of softening agents, which reduces moisture absorption, some liquid fabric softeners should be omitted every third or fourth time the items are laundered.

Bath Rugs and Mats

Soft floor coverings are produced in various sizes and shapes for use in bathroom interiors. **Bath rugs** (Figure 28.10) are larger and normally heavier than **bath mats**, and are used continuously for decoration, softness underfoot, or insulation. Bath mats are used temporarily to protect the floor from moisture and to prevent bathers from slipping. Both floor covering products are subject to a federal flammability mandate.

Constructing and Finishing Bath Rugs and Mats

Bath rugs are generally cut from tufted or knitted carpet that has a lower pile construction density and a greater pile height than carpet produced for other interior applications. For economy and ease of handling in use and care, no secondary backing is applied but an adhesive is used to secure the tufts. For skid resistance, the adhesive compound is normally embossed. End product producers cut various sizes of round, square, oval, and rectangular shapes from the wide carpet and finish the raw edges by hemming, serging, or binding with firmly woven tape. Frequently, rugs cut from solid colored greige goods are tufted a second time to introduce a distinctive design to the surface; no additional back-coating is applied to these items to secure the added pile yarns. Other rugs may be embellished with various types of trim, including rhinestone tape, braid, and fringe.

Pile fabric produced for use as a bath rug may also be used to construct such other items as toilet lid and tank covers. Lid covers have an elasticized edge or a drawstring run through a casing to secure them in use and permit their easy removal for laundering.

Bath mats may be woven in narrow widths, with the selvages as the side edges and small hems finishing the ends, or they may be cut from wide fabric and hemmed on all edges. Two different colors of warp pile yarns may be used to produce mats with different colors of loops on each side, or several colors of pile yarns may be used to produce richly patterned, Jacquard woven mats.

Evaluating Flammability

16 CFR 1631 Standard for the Surface Flammability of Small Carpets and Rugs became effective in December 1971. The scope of 16 CFR 1631 includes soft floor covering items that have an area not greater than 24 square feet and no dimension greater than 6 feet; such structures include scatter rugs, bath rugs, bath mats, and smaller area rugs.

a)

Figure 28.10 Bath rugs.
Courtesy of www.turkishtowels.com.

Test Method and Acceptance Criteria

Items within the scope of 16 CFR 1631 are tested in accordance with the procedures outlined in the **methenamine tablet test**. This test method is also specified in the flammability standard established for large carpets and rugs, **16 CFR 1630** (see Chapter 11). The acceptance criteria, which are based on **char length**, are the same in both standards.

Labeling Requirement

Small rugs and mats that fail the tablet test may be marketed. They must, however, carry a permanently attached label bearing the following statement: flammable (fails U.S. Consumer Product Safety Commission Standard 16 CFR 1631, should not be used near sources of ignition).

Shower Curtains

Shower curtains may be constructed of textile fabric or polymer film sheeting. Both types are often produced (Figure 28.11) as part of a coordinated bath ensemble.

b)

Polymer Film Shower Curtains

Various types of **polymer film sheeting** are used to produce nontextile shower curtains. The sheetings differ in gauge or thickness, in the level of transparency, and in color styling. Some films are relatively thin, others relatively thick; some are opaque, others transparent; some are solid colored, while others have contemporary designs printed with opaque pigments.

Textile Shower Curtains

With the exception of heavy, stiff structures, virtually any textile fabric may be used for a shower curtain (Figure 28.12). To protect the fabric from water and soap residue, converters may coat the interior surface with a waterproofing compound, or the consumer may hang a thin film as a separate curtain lining.

Evaluating Physical Performance Properties

ASTM D 5378 Standard Performance Specification for Woven and Knitted Shower Curtains for Institutional and Household Use may be used by purchaser and supplier to establish specification requirements. The physical and structural property evaluations used with towelings are also those used with shower curtains as shown in Table 28.5.

Breaking Force (Load)

The grab test procedure in ASTM D 5034, described above with towelings and earlier in Chapter 14, is used to mea-

Figure 28.11 Fabric shower curtain.
Courtesy of Ado Corporation USA, www.ado-usa.com.

Figure 28.12 Fabric shower curtain with liner.
Courtesy of Amy Willbanks, www.textilefabric.com.

sure the **breaking force (load)** of household and institutional shower curtains. A minimum of 40 pounds of force is recommended for dry fabric strength; a minimum of 20 pounds of force is recommended for wet fabric strength.

Dimensional Change
When measuring the dimensional stability of shower curtains, AATCC Method 135 may be used for household products and AATCC Method 96 may be used for institutional products. A maximum of 3 percent change is recommended.

Bow and Skew
ASTM D 3882, discussed above and in Chapter 14, is recommended for use in assessing the yarn alignment of shower curtains. ASTM D 5378 includes a recommended maximum of 4 percent skew.

Appearance Retention
The appearance of the construction features of shower curtains (e.g., hems, ruffles, or other embellishments) may be evaluated before and after laundering. Purchaser and supplier should reach mutual appearance requirements.

Evaluating Colorfastness
ASTM D 5378 specifies the same test methods for evaluating the colorfastness of shower curtains as used with towelings. These include fastness to laundering, to rubbing, and to light.

Colorfastness to Laundering
The colorfastness of household and institutional shower curtains to laundering may be measured in accordance with AATCC Method 61 (see Chapter 18). As with tow-

Table 28.5 Performance Specification for Woven and Knitted Shower Curtains for Institutional and Household Use

Characteristic	Test Method Number	Requirement
Breaking Force (load)	ASTM D 5034	
Dry		178 N (40 lbf), minimum
Wet		89 N (20 lbf), minimum
Bursting Force (knits only)	ASTM D 3786 or D 3787	178 N (40 lbf), minimum
Nonfibrous Material	AATCC 97	3.0% maximum
Dimensional Change (L × W)	AATCC 135 or AATCC 96	3.0% maximum
Fabric Appearance		5A 3.0 minimum
Bow and Skew	ASTM D 3882	4.0% maximum
Colorfastness:		
Laundering	AATCC 61	
Shade change		Class 4[a] minimum
Staining		Class 3[b] minimum
Crocking	AATCC 8 or AATCC 116	
Dry		Class 4[c] minimum
Wet		Class 4[c] minimum
Light (20 AATCC FU)	AATCC 16	Class 4[a] minimum
Water Resistance	AATCC 35	
Categories based on minimum time for		
1-g weight		
2 ft (600 mm)		30 s shower
2 ft (600 mm)		2 minute rain
3 ft (915 mm)		5 minute storm
Flammability	---*	Pass
Appearance Retention	---*	Acceptable

[a]AATCC Gray Scale for Color Change.
[b]AATCC Gray Scale for Staining.
[c]AATCC Chromatic Transference Scale.
*As agreed by purchaser and supplier.
Adapted, with permission from D5378-93(2000) Standard Performance Specification for Woven and Knitted Shower Curtains for Institutional and Household Use, copyright ASTM International, 100 Barr Harbor Drive, West Conshohocken, PA 19428, www.astm.org. A copy of the complete standard may be obtained from ASTM International.

eling, shade change of shower curtains is evaluated with the AATCC Gray Scale for Color Change, and bleeding is evaluated with the AATCC Gray Scale for Staining. Recommended minimum performance is Class 4 for shade change and Class 3 for staining.

Colorfastness to Crocking

AATCC Method 8 may be used to evaluate the fastness to crocking of solid-colored shower curtains, and AATCC Method 116 may be used for printed curtains. These methods were discussed briefly above and in depth in Chapter 14. Evaluations are done with the AATCC Color Transference Scale; recommended minimum performance is Class 4 for both dry and wet tests.

Colorfastness to Light

AATCC Method 16 (see Chapter 18) may be used to evaluate the fastness of household and institutional shower curtains to light. Evaluations are done with the AATCC Gray Scale for Color Change; recommended minimum performance is Class 4.

Evaluating Water Resistance

The **water resistance** of household and institutional shower curtains can be evaluated as directed in AATCC Method 35 Water Resistance: Rain Test. The performance recommendations listed may be agreed upon between purchaser and seller, or they may be required by an agency having jurisdiction over an interior where shower curtains may be used.

Evaluating Flammability

The purchaser and supplier shall agree on the flammability requirements of shower curtains. Any applicable codes would override such agreements.

Summary

Unlike other interior furnishings, which are primarily composed of manufactured fibers, towels are primarily composed of cotton because it provides softness, wickability, and good moisture absorption. Towels are available in a wide range of sizes and with a variety of decorative features and side and end finishes.

Bath rugs and mats are available in various sizes, shapes, colors, and textures. Like other soft floor coverings, bath rugs and bath mats are subject to a federal flammability mandate.

Shower curtains may be constructed of textile or non-textile fabrics. Along with towels and bath rugs and mats, shower curtains are frequently offered as part of a coordinated group of bath products.

Standard methods of testing, such as tests for fabric strength, colorfastness, skew (bias), and appearance, may be used to evaluate household and institutional towels and shower curtains. In turn, standard specifications are published to provide recommended levels of performance. In some cases, purchaser and supplier may reach a mutual agreement on the level of performance required.

Key Terms

16 CFR 1630
16 CFR 1631
AATCC Color Transference Scale
AATCC Gray Scale for Color
   Change
AATCC Gray Scale for Staining
bath mats
bath rugs
bleeding
bow
breaking force (load)

char length
crash
crocking
dimensional stability
disposable toweling
Fade-Ometer®
huck toweling
huckaback
institutional toweling
Launder-Ometer®
Malipol

methenamine tablet test
polymer film sheeting
shade changes
skew
slack tension technique
staining
terry toweling
terry velour toweling
Turkish toweling
water resistance
wickability

Review Questions

1. Explain the dominance of cotton in the toweling market.

2. Given that linen has higher moisture absorbency than cotton, why hasn't linen captured a larger portion of the towelings market?

3. Describe the slack tension technique used for manufacturing terry toweling.

4. Why is the level of absorbency lower on the cut side of terry velour?

5. Why are stable colorants important to have with textile bath products?

6. Describe the procedures and calculations used in evaluating the absorbency of toweling.

7. Explain the cautionary labeling used with 16 CFR 1631.

Textile Bedding Products

■ **The bedding products industry** is an important segment of the interior textile industry: approximately forty percent of the total fiber used for home textiles production (excluding soft floor coverings) is channeled to the production of beddings.[1] While the primary function of bedcoverings is to provide warmth and comfort for sleeping, **bedding** products, like towelings, have high visual impact as well.

The assortment of textile bedding products includes mattresses and box springs, mattress pads and mattress covers, sheets and pillowcases, quilts, throws, comforters, sleeping bags, blankets, bedspreads, and pillows. All of these are produced in different sizes, and some have styling features as distinctive and varied as those typical of fashion apparel. Many of these items are multicomponent structures. Most beddings are composed entirely of textile fibers, but some products, including mattresses, box springs, and sleeping bags, contain some nontextile components.

Fiber and Yarn Usage in Beddings

A statistical profile of the types of fibers used in residential and institutional bedding products is given in Table 29.1. Data cover the use of each item not only in homes, but also in such commercial settings as motels and hotels and in such institutional settings as health care facilities. The poundages listed in the first category, bedspreads and quilts, include the fiber used for producing the outer shells of comforters; the poundages listed in the second category, blankets and blanketing, include the fiber used for producing the bindings applied to the ends of the coverings; and the poundages listed in the last category, sheets and other bedding, include the fiber used to produce the outside cover of quilted pads, mattress pads, mattresses and innersprings, civilian cots, and sleeping bags. None of the poundages tabulated include any quantities of fiber used in fillings.

Since 2001, the total quantity of fiber used in bedding products has decreased from 791.9 million pounds to 618.5 million pounds in 2005.[2] While there has been a reapportionment of the market, cotton remains dominant.

Predominance of Cotton

In 2005 approximately 62 percent of the bedding products market was held by cotton, 37 percent by noncellulosic fiber, and the remaining 1 percent by wool. In today's mar-

ket, Modal® and rayon made from bamboo is increasing in use; however, the noncellulosic fibers and cotton still dominate the market.

Disclosure of Fiber Composition

Most textile bedding products are subject to the labeling mandates set forth in the Textile Fiber Products Identification Act and its accompanying set of rules and regulations. Specifically, the scope of the TFPIA includes all beddings, which, by definition, includes sheets, covers, blankets, comforters, pillows, pillowcases, quilts, bedspreads, pads, and all other textile fiber products used or intended to be used on or about a bed, not including furniture, mattresses, or box springs, or the outer coverings on these items. Fillings incorporated in bedding products primarily for warmth rather than for structural purposes are also included.

As explained in Chapter 10, products within the scope of the TFPIA must carry a label or hangtag that discloses the fiber composition, the name or registered number of the manufacturer, and the country of origin. Products having down or feather fillings should also be labeled in accordance with guidelines specifically established by the FTC for these materials; these guidelines are discussed in the next section.

Microbe Resistance

Problems associated with the presence of unwanted microbial organisms in bedding such as odors and illnesses, coupled with the fact that most bedding is used multiple times between launderings, has become a point of much interest for the hospitality and healthcare industries as well as the consumer. Bedding products with antimicrobial properties, such as mattresses and mattress covers, pillows, sheeting, and outer coverings such as bedspreads and comforters are becoming more prevalent. Interior designers, facility managers, and end users seeking bedding with antimicrobial qualities can look for trade names such as Nanocide® Antimicrobial from CMI Enterprises, AEGIS Microbe Shield® by AEGIS Environments, Cupron™, and Trevira® Bioactive.

Predominance of Spun Yarns

Staple fibers are used more extensively than filament fibers in bedding products, accounting for some 93 percent of today's market. All staple length fibers, natural as well as manufactured, must be spun to produce usable yarn structures; therefore, spun yarns predominate. In comparison with filament yarns, spun yarns are often

Table 29.1 Fiber Usage in Bedding Products (millions of pounds)

End Use	Year	Total Fiber	Manufactured Fibers* Total	Cellulosic** Yarn	Staple	Noncellulosic Yarn	Staple	Cotton	Wool
Bedspreads	2001	129.6	72.0	--	--	30.7	41.3	57.6	--**
and Quilts	2002	149.9	67.9	--	--	30.5	37.4	82.0	--
	2003	146.2	65.7	--	--	26.7	39.0	80.5	--
	2004	90.1	53.3	--	--	21.3	32.0	36.8	--
	2005	82.1	48.7	--	--	18.7	30.0	33.4	--
Blankets	2001	196.2	85.3	--	--	--**	85.3	105.4	5.5
and	2002	174.8	74.8	--	--	--	74.8	95.9	4.1
Blanketing	2003	172.3	70.8	--	--	--	70.8	95.0	6.5
	2004	145.7	62.6	--	--	--	62.6	76.0	7.2
	2005	128.7	53.4	--	--	--	53.4	69.0	6.2
Sheets and	2001	646.1	234.7	--	--	21.9	212.8	411.3	--
Other	2002	579.1	206.8	--	--	24.6	182.1	372.3	--
Bedding	2003	509.7	174.1	--	--	20.6	153.5	335.6	--
	2004	467.3	155.5	--	--	18.6	136.9	311.8	--
	2005	407.7	124.4	--	--	17.4	107.0	283.3	--

* Manufactured fiber end-use is divided between cellulosic (rayon + acetate) and noncellulosic (nylon, polyester, acrylic, olefin). Yarn includes multifilament, monofilament, and spunbonded. Olefin includes polypropylene and polyethylene staple and yarn. Olefin yarn also includes film fiber and spunbonded polypropylene. Staple includes tow and fiberfill.

** Little or none of the fiber is used.

Source: Fiber Economics Bureau, *Fiber Organon*, "U.S. End Use Survey: 2001–2005," October 2006, page 192, Table 4.

judged to have a more attractive appearance and a softer, more comfortable hand, qualities many consumers prefer in their bedding products.

Mattresses, Mattress Foundations, and Mattress Protectors

Beds, and such dual-purpose sleeping equipment as **sofa beds**, **convertible sofa beds**, **futons**, and studio couches, have two basic units, a mattress and a mattress foundation. Because mattresses, especially when used with a companion set of box springs, are comparatively expensive, covers and pads are often employed to protect them and prolong their use-life. Unlike other bedding products, mattresses and mattress pads are subject to a federal flammability standard. This information is discussed in Chapter 11.

Mattress Foundations

With the exception of air-filled mattresses, intended to be placed on the floor or ground, and water-filled mattresses, which are placed within a plastic-lined, boxlike frame, all mattresses are used with a resilient foundation. These foundations may be flat or three-dimensional units.

Flat Bedspring Units

In some flat bedspring units, flexible metal bands are anchored to the ends of the bed frame by tightly coiled springs. Additional springs, placed crosswise, stabilize the parallel bands. In other flat bedspring units, metal bands are interlaced and held to the sides and ends of the frame with spring units. While these nontextile foundations are relatively inexpensive, they do not provide adequate support for everyday use and are normally used only with items intended for occasional use, such as cots and roll-away beds.

Box Spring Units

In box spring units, hundreds of coiled springs are anchored to wooden slats and framing boards and to each other. Because box springs and mattresses are offered as a coordinated set, the fabric that decorates the mattress also covers the exposed surfaces of the foundation. For economy, a fine, lightweight fabric such as batiste or spunbonded olefin serves as a dustcover on the back of the springs unit. Various types and amounts of filling are used for top cushioning, and an insulator fabric is placed over the springs to prevent them from penetrating into the filling materials.

While the gauge of the wire used for the support springs in box springs is generally higher than that used

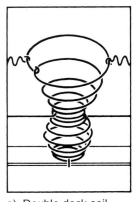

a) Double deck coil.

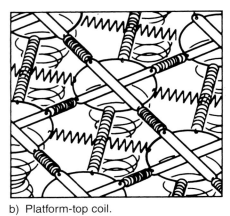

b) Platform-top coil.

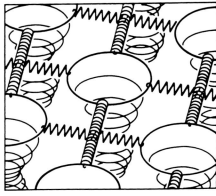

c) Convoluted coil.

Figure 29.1 Configurations of springs used in box springs and mattresses.

for the support springs in mattresses, the configuration of the coils in the units may be identical. In double-deck springs, the tighter coiling of the lower portion is designed to provide firm support and the looser coiling of the upper portion is for resiliency (Figure 29.1a). The flat metal bands anchored over platform top springs (Figure 29.1b) provide a more uniform surface than that created by open-top springs. The extra coils placed at the top of convoluted springs provide increased support when the foundation is depressed by the weight of the body (Figure 29.1c).

The quality of box springs and innerspring mattresses depends on the gauge of the wires and the level of spring coiling. These features are the main determinants of the use-life of the units; they also help to determine the length of any warranty offered by the manufacturer.

Mattresses

Mattresses are available with different interior components and construction features. They are produced in several sizes and covered with a variety of textile fabrics.

Interior Components

Mattresses are available in two constructions: innerspring and foam-core. The components in **innerspring units** are illustrated in Figure 29.3. The spring units may be anchored to one another by coiled wires, metal clips, or flexible metal bands, or each spring may be encased within a fabric pocket and all pockets sewn together to minimize side sway. An insulator fabric like that on box springs prevents the springs from penetrating the upper filling layers. The degree of firmness can be increased by using a high gauge of wire for the spring units and by using resinated

batting. Small holes should be built into the sides of mattresses to provide ventilation and preserve the freshness of the interior components.

Foam core mattresses have a single interior component, a slab of rubber or urethane foam (Figure 29.2). In these units, the level of support varies with the density of the foam. **Visco-elastic polyurethane foam** is often marketed at "memory foam" because it is slow to return to its original shape once weight is removed. Because they react to heat, they conform to the shape of the body more easily while remaining very supportive without pressure on the hips, head, elbows, and heels. This quality makes it especially desirable for users required to spend long periods of time in bed. In addition to mattresses, visco-elastic polyurethane foam is widely used for pillows and mattress pads. Some mattresses have air chambers enclosed by foam and padding. These chambers are accompanied by an inflating/deflating device that allows the firmness to be adjusted on each side of the mattress.

Exterior Coverings

Ticking is a generic term for any fabric used to cover the exterior of mattresses, box springs, and pillows. Tickings may be plain or highly decorative. To capture the attention of the contemporary consumer, such elaborately patterned fabrics as damask are mainly used today (Figure 29.4a) in place of the familiar twill-woven ticking with its blue or black stripes (Figure 29.4b).

For long-term serviceability, tickings should be firmly woven of strong, smooth yarns. Less durable and less expensive coverings generally are made of coarse yarns and contain low fabric counts.

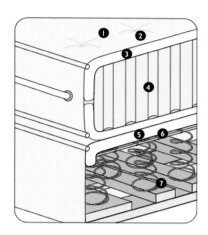

Figure 29.2 Cross-sectional sketch of natural latex core mattress. (1) cotton ticking, (2) hand tufting, (3) cotton padding, (4) natural latex, (5) cotton padding, (6) insulator pad, (7) box springs. Courtesy of Royal Pedic Mattress, www.royal-pedic.com.

Figure 29.3 Cross-sectional sketch of an innerspring mattress. (1) cotton ticking, (2) French wool cushioning, (3) polyester fiber padding, (4) natural latex cushioning, (5) cotton padding, (6) inner spring system, (7) side supports, (8) box spring. Courtesy of Royal Pedic Mattress, www.royal-pedic.com.

Sizes

Mattresses are produced in a variety of sizes, with each size designated by name, not by dimensions. The names and characteristic dimensions of the more common mattresses are listed in Table 29.2.

Larger mattresses should have permanently attached side handles to facilitate the turning of the unit. As a precaution, consumers should measure their mattresses prior to purchasing bed coverings.

Mattress Covers and Pads

Mattress covers protect mattresses from dust, moisture, and abrasion. Mattress pads provide these features and increased cushioning as well.

Covers

Mattress covers may be designed and constructed to completely encase the mattress or to cover only the exposed surfaces. Zippers or elasticized edges ensure a smooth fit. When maximum protection against moisture is needed, a polyurethane (olefin) film sheeting bonded to a cotton may be used as the covering fabric.

The American College of Allergy, Asthma and Immunology cites dust mites as the most common trigger for patients suffering from allergy to household dust. Dust mites thrive in pillows, mattresses, carpet, and upholstery fabrics found in most homes. Fully encasing pillow and mattress covers of tightly woven cotton or cotton blend fabrics with zipper closings helps control exposure to dust mites. American Textile Company (ATC) uses Dupont Hybrid Membrane Technology (HMT) in its Aller-Ease line of bedding products to achieve filtration efficiency of 95 percent of particles as small as 1 micron.[3] This would include allergens such as pollen, dust mites, and mold.

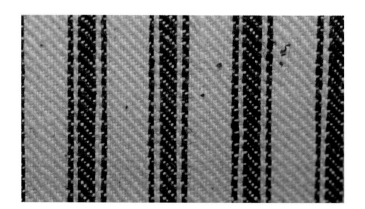

a) Patterned damask mattress covering.

b) Twill-woven ticking characterized by lengthwise stripes.

Figure 29.4 Twill-woven ticking characterized by lengthwise stripes. Courtesy of Amy Willbanks, www.textilefabric.com.

Table 29.2 Mattress Sizes and Names

Name	Inches (width × length)
Rollaway bed or cot	30 × 75
Studio couch or daybed	28 × 74
Single bed	33 × 75
Twin bed	39 × 75
Twin bed, extra long	39 × 80
Three-quarter bed	48 × 75
Double bed	54 × 75
Double bed, extra long	54 × 80
Queen-size bed	60 × 80
King-size bed	78 × 80
California bed	72 × 80

a) Fitted to cover top and sides.

Pads

Mattress pads are multicomponent structures that cushion and soften while they cover and protect the mattress. Most pads have a batting of polyester quilted between two woven or spunbonded fabrics. Some pads cover the sleeping surface only; others cover the sleeping surface and the vertical sides; and others completely encase the mattress (Figure 29.5).

Mattress pads of wool have been used in hospitals and health care facilities for some time, but have only recently been promoted for residential use. These structures are produced by locking slivers of lambswool into a knitted base fabric composed of polyester. The fleece-like fabric is placed, pile up, under the bottom sheet, providing softness, warmth, and moisture absorption. The wool used in some of these **underblankets** has been treated with agents that minimize felting shrinkage, permitting the pad to be laundered. Care tag instructions indicate appropriate cleaning methods and should be carefully followed.

Mattress covers and pads produced for use in hospitals and other health care facilities may be treated with agents that effectively reduce the action of such microbes as bacteria and fungi. Such antimicrobial chemicals can be applied during finishing (see Chapter 9) and are becoming increasingly important as the population ages and incontinence becomes a concern.

Flammability Standard

The Standard for the Flammability of Mattresses, 16 CFR 1632, was established in an effort to protect the public against unreasonable risk of mattress fires leading to death, personal injury, or significant property damage. The most

b) Mattress pad covering top only.

Figure 29.5 Mattress pads.
Courtesy of DOWNLITE, www.downlite.com.

common mode of bedding ignition, a burning cigarette, is used as the ignition source in the test procedure.

In 2007 the Consumer Product Safety Commission established another test method: 16 CFR Part 1633, Standard Test Method for the Flammability (Open-Flame) of Mattress Sets. Both of these standards are discussed in Chapter 11.

Fillings Used in Bedding Products

Filling components in bedding products may be composed of natural or synthesized materials. Some materials are used in loose, lofty masses; others, in stabilized battings; and still others, in well-defined, three-dimensional forms.

Natural Filling Materials

Natural filling materials include down, feathers, wool, and cotton. The low resiliency of cotton has prompted manufacturers to blend it with polyester. Although the use of wool as a filling material is limited, primarily because of its cost, some longer-staple wool fibers are occasionally used to produce lofty, three-dimensional battings for use in comforters.

Down and feathers are virtually always used loose in lofty masses. Bedding products filled with these materials should be labeled in accordance with the provisions of the USA 2000 Labeling Standards—Down and Feather Products. Because of consumer demand for purely natural filling materials in bedding, some manufacturers have returned to using all cotton and wool.

Standards for the Feather and Down Products Industry

Labeling standards developed by the International Association of Bedding and Furniture Law Officials (ABFLO) are required on products that include the use of down or feathers and are intended to avoid unfair or deceptive practices as defined under the Federal Trade Commissions Act. The **USA 2000 Labeling Standards–Down and Feather Products**, promulgated on September 1, 2000, are definitions of terms and recommended procedures for labeling products filled with theses natural materials. The only accepted test methods are those established by the **International Down and Feather Laboratory and Institute (IDFL)**. Both the USA 2000 label standards and the IDFB test methods are accepted by ASTM. Some of the terms and their definitions are listed below:

Down: The plumage forming the undercoating of waterfowl, consisting of tufts of light, fluffy filaments (e.g., barbs) growing from one quill point, but without any quill shaft.

Down cluster: Down cluster is the group of components: down, nestling down, and plumule. (Down fiber and other components are specifically excluded.)

Quill: The stem or central shaft of feathers.

Plumules: A plumule is a feather-like structure with characteristics of down. Plumules are three-dimensional with a soft, underdeveloped quill. The majority of barbs are down fibers and the plumule tip is open, transparent, and soft.

Feathers: The plumage or outgrowth forming the contour and external covering of fowl consisting of quills and barbs. Includes only material which has not been processed in any manner other than by washing, dusting, and sterilizing.

Waterfowl feathers: Feathers from ducks or geese, or both.

Landfowl feathers: Feathers derived from chickens, turkeys, or other landfowl.

Quill feathers: Feathers which are over 100 mm in length or which have a quill point exceeding 9.5 mm in length.

Down fiber: Detached barbs from down plumules and detached barbs from the basal ends of waterfowl feather quill shafts that are indistinguishable from the barbs of down.

Feather fiber: Detached barbs of feathers which are not joined or attached to each other.

Crushed/chopped/broken feathers: A feather is broken when more than 40 percent of the shaft is missing. A bare shaft is also classified as a broken feather. A feather whose shaft has been "fractured" in the middle is also classified as a broken feather. Schleiss or stripped feather pieces are classified as broken feathers.

Damaged feathers: A feather is damaged when more than 25 percent of the feather surface is missing but at least 60 percent of the shaft remains.

Residue: Quill pith, quill fragments, trash, or foreign matter.[3]

According to the provisions of the standards, industry products should be labeled as to the kind or type of filling material used. When the filling material consists of a mixture of more than one kind or type, then the proportion of each should be disclosed in the order of predominance, the largest proportion first. If the term "nonwaterfowl" or "land fowl" is used, it should be accompanied by the name of the fowl from which the products were obtained, for instance, chicken or turkey.

A certain leeway is permitted in the use of the terms down and waterfowl feathers. "Down" may be used to designate any industry product containing the following filling material:

Down cluster............................minimum 95 percent
Land fowl feathers...................maximum 2 percent
Damaged feathers.....................maximum 2 percent
Residue......................................maximum 2 percent
Down fiber...............................maximum 5 percent
Feather fiber ....maximum 5 percent

A product should not be designated "100 percent down," **all down**, **pure down**, or by other terms of similar import unless it in fact contains only down, without regard to the tolerance detailed above.

"Waterfowl feathers" may be used to designate any plumage product containing the following filling material, free of quill and crushed feathers:

Waterfowl feathers ....minimum 66 percent

Land fowl feathers....................maximum 5 percent

Damaged feathers.....................maximum 2 percent

Residue......................................maximum 2 percent

Down fiber...............................maximum 5 percent

Feather fiber ....maximum 5 percent[4]

Synthesized Filling Materials

Synthesized fillings include such materials as noncellulosic fibers, synthetic rubber, and polyurethane. Noncellulosic fi-

bers are virtually always in staple or tow forms for use as filling material. They may be used in loose, lofty masses, known as **fiberfill**, or organized into battings of various thicknesses. Today, fiberfill is almost exclusively composed of noncellulosic fibers.[5] **Batting** structures composed of polyester, as well as those composed of polyester and cotton, may be stabilized by spraying resin throughout the layered fibers. Synthesized rubber and urethane (olefin) compounds are generally foamed and formed into three-dimensional structures for use in pillows, into thick **slabs** for use in mattresses, and into thin slabs for use in quilts.

Functions and Properties of Filling Materials

In mattresses, fillings provide support for the body; in bed pillows, they cushion the head; in decorative pillows, they impart and maintain a distinctive form. In most other bedding products, fillings are primarily intended for **thermal insulation**. Ideally, filling materials should be lofty or bulky without being heavy. They must be resilient to regain their original **loftiness** after being compressed, and they must be affordable.

To improve the loftiness and insulative value of fiberfill without increasing the weight, textile fiber chemists have engineered fibers with hollow interiors (Figure 29.6).

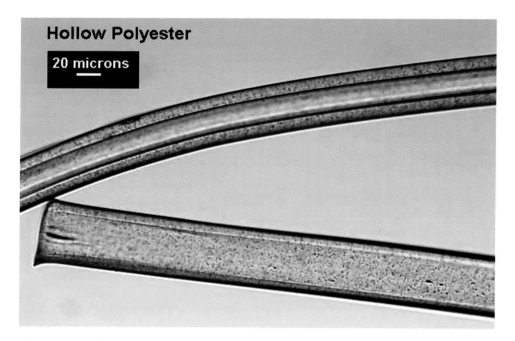

Figure 29.6 Photomicrographs of hollow polyester fibers. Courtesy of Wellman, Inc.

The open interiors of the fibers and the air pockets surrounding them provide a great deal of insulation.

The insulative values of down, wool, polyester, and olefin are all effective, each having advantages and disadvantages. Down and feathers offer the advantage of being inherently lofty and lightweight, but their limited supply in comparison to demand and the labor involved in their retrieval make them comparatively expensive. Wool has excellent resiliency, but the fibers are comparatively heavy and expensive. Fiberfill is lofty, lightweight, and economical; unlike the natural filling materials, it is also nonallergenic.

Comforel® is an example of a fiberfill developed to imitate the feel of down without the potential allergens.

Care of Fillings

Bedding products filled with wool batting must be dry cleaned to avoid the agitation that can cause felting shrinkage. Some manufacturers recommend that down, feather, and polyester fillings be dry cleaned to minimize shifting and clumping of the materials. Others recommend that the fillings be laundered and then tumble dried to encourage the materials to regain their original loftiness. In every case, the care procedures performed on the filling must be appropriate for the outer covering and vice versa. To prevent care practices that could cause unnecessary product failure—a problem generally accompanied by the consumer losing confidence in the producer's name—many manufacturers voluntarily label their goods with care instructions.

Pillows

Two categories of pillows, namely bed pillows and decorative pillows, are available on today's bedding products market. The same filling materials and ticking fabrics may be used in both types of pillows, but decorative pillows are produced in a wider variety of sizes and forms and their outer coverings have more elaborate styling features.

Sizes and Forms

Bed pillows are basically rectangular in shape, and most are 20 to 21 inches wide. Their length varies according to the width of the mattress with which they are intended to be paired. **Standard pillows**, intended to be used with a twin or double mattress, are 26 to 27 inches long; **queen-size pillows** are 30 to 31 inches long; and **king-size pillows** are 37 to 38 inches long.

Decorative pillows are available in various sizes and forms. **Neckroll pillows** are cylindrical forms 6 inches by 14 inches or a larger 7 inches by 17 inches; **boudoir pillows**, also called **breakfast pillows**, are 12 inches by 16 inches; **bolster pillows** are cylindrical or lozenge-shaped pillows that may be from 40 to 50 inches in length; **Turkish pillows**, which have gathered corners, are 16 inches square; **European pillows** are 26 inches square; **round pillows** are normally 12 inches in diameter; and a **bedrest pillow** has a back and arms. See Figure 29.7 for examples of pillow sizes and forms.

Fillings and Tickings

Bed pillows and decorative pillows may be filled with fiberfill, down, feathers, or foam. In many items, the filling material is enclosed in a nonremovable casing that is then protected by a zippered casing. The interior casing fabric should have an extremely high fabric count, around 220 when fine down filling materials are used, and the fabrics used for the pillow protectors must be machine washable. Commonly used fabrics include muslin, percale, twill-woven ticking, cotton damask, and more recently, spunbonded ticking composed of polypropylene olefin. The spunbonded ticking in Figure 29.8 is hypoallergenic.

Decorative Coverings for Pillows

For nighttime use, bed pillows are inserted into the familiar pillowcases. These may be plain or have decorative hem treatments. For daytime display, bed pillows may be inserted into a **pillow sham**, a decorative casing, which often has contrasting piping and ruffles. Shams are generally styled to match decorative pillows placed on the bed.

Today, consumers are frequently offered an assortment of decorative pillows covered and trimmed to coordinate with a variety of products included in an ensemble. The pillows are covered with the fabric used in other items in the grouping, and they are finished with identical trimmings. The trimming may include such embellishments as monograms, contrasting piping or fabric banding, Schiffli embroidered appliqués, ribbons, and ruffles.

Besides decorative pillows, a coordinated ensemble may include a quilt, a bedspread or comforter, sheets, and pillowcases. It may also include round and square tablecloths, towels, curtain and drapery panels, and valances for windows and canopy beds.

Sheets and Pillowcases

The assortment of sheets and pillowcases offered to contemporary consumers includes items ranging from those of minimal aesthetic appeal to those with distinctive color styling and decorative border embellishments. Much of today's sheeting is stabilized and given a resin finish to improve end-use serviceability.

Manufacturing Sheeting

Fabric manufacturers produce the major portion of sheeting fabric for both residential and institutional use in a plain-weave interlacing. For the residential market, however, the assortment has been expanded to include satin, jacquard, and knitted sheetings. Generally, they use spun yarns composed of cotton and polyester.

Fiber and Yarn Usage

As detailed in Table 29.1, 411.3 million pounds of cotton were used in sheets and other beddings in 2001, thus accounting for nearly 64 percent of the market. By 2005 the consumption of cotton in these items fell to 283.3 million pounds yet managed to garner 70 percent of the total market. Over the same period the market share captured by the noncellulosic fibers dropped from 36 percent to slightly more than 31 percent. As explained in Chapter 9, durable press resins improve the resiliency of cotton fibers but also weaken them and reduce their abrasion resistance. In

Figure 29.7 Examples of pillow sizes and forms. Courtesy of DOWNLITE, www.downlite.com.

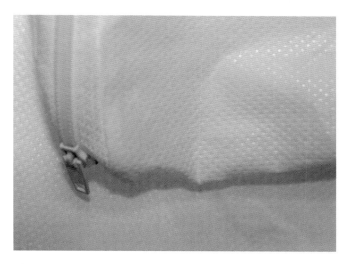

Figure 29.8 Spunbonded hypoallergenic polypropylene (olefin) pillow ticking.
Courtesy of Amy Willbanks, www.textilefabric.com.

a) Unbleached.

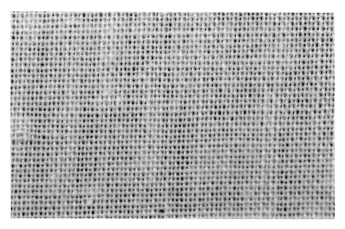

b) Bleached.

Figure 29.9 Muslin sheeting.
Courtesy of Amy Willbanks, www.textilefabric.com.

order to prolong the use-life of resin-treated sheeting, manufacturers altered the composition of the fabric, increasing the polyester content and decreasing the cotton content.

In recent years, consumers have expressed a preference for **reverse blends** of polyester and cotton (i.e., decreasing the polyester content and increasing the cotton content). In 2005, cotton accounted for some 70 percent of the sheeting market (Table 29.1).

Increasing interest in sustainable and environmental issues has resulted in the demand for organic sheeting fabrics. Modal® and bamboo are being marketed to environmentally conscious consumers as natural fibers. However, this information is incorrect and against TFPIA guidelines. Modal® and bamboo are both manufactured rayon fibers made from birch trees and bamboo. Even though they are made from natural materials, they first have to be chemically processed to be fibers in usable form. Tencel® lyocell sheets, also touted by sellers as an eco-friendly textile, are silky soft, durable and resist wrinkling. In this case, sustainability claims are more accurate. Each of these fibers is discussed in Chapter 4.

The predominance of spun yarns in all textile bedding products was mentioned earlier. In sheets and other bedding, more than 96 percent of all fibers used in 2005, natural and manufactured, are in staple lengths (Table 29.1). These fibers are converted into carded or combed yarns by spinning on the cotton system.

Fabricating Sheetings

Most sheeting fabrics have plain-woven interlacing, but they may have different yarns and different fabric counts. In general, finer yarns and higher fabric counts are characteristic of higher quality sheets. **Muslin** sheeting (Figure 29.9a and b) contains carded yarns and its fabric count may be as low as 112 or as high as 140, although 128 is most common. A large amount of sizing is generally used on muslin that has a very low fabric count. This increases fabric weight but not its durability, and few of these sized or **backfilled** fabrics are produced today. **Percale** sheeting's fabric count may be as low as 168 or as high as 220; 180 is common. Most percale sheeting (Figure 29.10) is woven from fine, combed yarns.

Advertising of higher thread count in sheets, which is equated with luxury and smoothness, has led the consumer

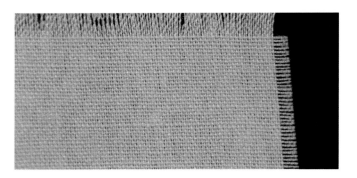

a) Plain weave percale sheeting.

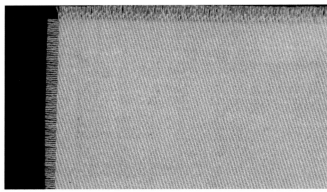

b) High thread count satin weave sheeting.

Figure 29.10 Low and high count sheetings.
Courtesy of Amy Willbanks, www.textilefabric.com.

to base purchases primarily on thread count. No distinction is made between counting individual threads or the plies of multi-ply threads; thus, a sheet with a thread count of 600 may actually have 300 two-ply threads per inch.[6]

Woven sheeting produced with a sateen weave is increasing in use. The floating warp yarns produce a smooth, luxurious sleeping surface, but they may be snagged and ruptured, interrupting the pattern of light reflection, producing a stain-like appearance, and shortening the use-life of the sheets. Most sateen sheets are 100% cotton.

Weft knitting is used to produce knitted sheets in a jersey fabric similar to tee-shirt fabric. The inherent stretchability offered by the interlooped yarns helps to keep the sheets fitting smoothly. A broken loop in a jersey-stitched product initiates the development of the unsightly, ladder-like effect known as a run.

Coloring and Finishing Sheetings

Rotary screen printing, explained in detail in Chapter 8, is the predominant technique for printing sheeting. Patterns range from those whose tiny motifs cover virtually the entire surface to those whose large motifs combine with sizable areas of white or solid colored ground. Frequently, producers seek to enhance their position in the market by enlisting the assistance of well known fashion fabric and apparel designers to create patterns and select the coloration.

Sheeting greige goods may be preshrunk to relax the yarns, minimizing later relaxation shrinkage. Woven goods processed through the compressive shrinkage operation generally exhibit no more than 1 or 2 percent residual shrinkage, unless dried in a dryer. A significant portion of sheeting greige goods is treated with durable press resins to avoid the need for ironing after laundering (durable press processing was explained in Chapter 9).

Converters have responded to the demands of energy conscious consumers by increased use of napping treatments on sheeting. In use, the raised fibers entrap air and provide thermal insulation. **Flannel** sheets are generally composed of 100 percent cotton or cotton blends, providing the comfort sought by consumers.

Constructing Sheets and Pillowcases

Sheets and pillowcases have few construction details, but are produced in a variety of sizes and types. Decorative trimmings may embellish their hems.

Types and Sizes

Three styles of sheets are produced: flat, semi-fitted, and fitted. **Flat sheets** are hemmed at both ends and may be used as top or bottom sheets. **Fitted or contour sheets** have four contour corners and can be used only as bottom sheets. The sheeting selvages provide a finished edge on the sides of all sheets; tape binding or elastic banding finishes the lower edges of contour corners.

For the construction of cases for bed pillows, sheeting fabric is cut into rectangular shapes of specific dimensions. The fabric is folded lengthwise, right sides together, stitched across one end and the side having raw edges, and then turned. The hem treatment used for the top hem of the coordinating flat sheet is also used to finish the open end of the cases.

Sheets and pillowcases are constructed in various sizes for use with various sizes of mattresses and pillows. Typical dimensions are listed in Table 29.3; actual dimensions vary among producers. It should be noted that the size of flat sheets that producers report is measured prior to hemming.

Hems and Border Embellishments

The hems that finish flat sheets and pillowcases may be simple or highly decorative. A simple hem is normally 1 inch deep at the bottom of sheets and 3 to 4 inches deep at the top of sheets and the end of cases. Decorative hems have such border embellishments as delicate lace, scalloped eyelet trim, and contrasting piping.

Coordinated Items

The sheeting fabric produced and used for a set of sheets and pillowcases frequently also appears in other items offered with the sheets and pillowcases in a coordinated ensemble, such as curtains, draperies, valences, tablecloths, sheet casings, and dust ruffles. **Dust ruffles**, also known as bedskirts, bed petticoats, and platform skirts, are fabric panels that drape from the top of the foundation to the floor; the panels are normally pleated or gathered. **Sheet casings** are covers that protect comforters and duvets from soil accumulation and abrasion; their releasable closures permit their easy removal for laundering.

Evaluating Sheeting Products

ASTM D 5431 Standard Performance Specification for Woven and Knitted Sheeting Products for Institutional and Household Use may be reviewed for recommended levels of performance. The specifications include requirements for nonflannel sheeting of 100 percent cotton or polyester and cotton blends, for flannel sheeting, and for knitted sheeting (see Table 29.4).

Blankets

Blankets are primarily used for warmth. Conventional structures provide warmth by reducing the transfer of body heat to the interior; electric blankets provide warmth by generating heat. The blanketing fabrics used to produce these coverings may be produced from yarns or, bypassing the yarn stage, directly from fibers.

Manufacturing Blanketing

Blanketing may be manufactured from yarn structures, using simple and decorative biaxial weaves, knitting, and tufting. It may also be manufactured directly from fibers, through a flocking or needlepunching operation. Like most other bedding products, blankets are composed of cotton fibers or of staple manufactured noncellulosic fibers. Unlike other bedding products, however, some blankets are composed of wool fiber, and a limited number of contemporary blankets are composed of specialty wools.

Fibers and Yarns Used

Since 2001 the use of the noncellulosic fibers in blanketing has steadily decreased; collectively, these fibers now hold about 41 percent of the market. The growth of the manufactured noncellulosic fiber usage in bedspreads and quilts has been at the expense of cotton. The reverse can be said for the blanket market. Manufactured noncellulosic fiber usage dropped from 43 percent in 2001 to 41 percent in 2005. At the same time, cotton remained steady at 54 percent and wool increased from 3 percent to 5 percent (Table 29.1, p. 439). Rayon is relatively weak, highly flammable, and generally requires dry cleaning. Wool is relatively expensive and also requires dry cleaning. In contrast, acrylic, because of its

Table 29.3 Types and Sizes of Sheets and Pillowcases	
Type and Name	Inches (width × length)
Flat sheets	
Crib	45 × 68
Twin	66 × 104
Double or full	81 × 104
Queen	90 × 110
King	108 × 110
Fitted sheets	
Crib	29 × 54
Twin	39 × 75
Double or full	54 × 75
Queen	60 × 80
King	78 × 80
Pillowcases	
Standard	21 × 35
Queen	21 × 39
King	21 × 44

Table 29.4 Standard Performance Specification for Woven and Knitted Sheeting Products for Institutional and Household Use

Characteristic	Test Method Number	Requirements			
		Woven			Knitted
		Non-flannel		Flannel	Flannel/Non-flannel
		Polyester/Cotton	100% Cotton		
Breaking Force (load)	ASTM D 5034	222 N (50 lbf) min	178 N (40 lbf) min	156 N (35 lbf) min	NA
		222 N (50 lbf) min	178 N (40 lbf) min	156 N (35 lbf) min	
Bursting Force[a] (knits only)	ASTM D 3786	NA	NA	NA	222 N (50 lbf) min
Tear Resistance	ASTM D 1424	7 N (1.5 lbf) min	7 N (1.5 lbf) min	7 N (1.5 lbf) min	NA
Pilling	ASTM D 3512	4.0	NA	NA	4.0
Dimensional Change:	AATCC 135 or AATCC 96				
Durable Press (In Each Direction)		5% max	5% max	3.5% max	4% max
Nondurable Press (Nonpreshrunk)					
Length		8% max	8% max	8% max	
Width		6% max	6% max	6% max	
Preshrunk (In Each Direction)		2% max	3% max	3.5% max	
Laundered Appearance	AATCC 143	Acceptable	Acceptable	Acceptable	Acceptable
Fabric Appearance	AATCC 124	SA 3.0 min[g]	SA 2.2 min[b,g]	NA	SA 3.0 min[g]
Bow and Skew	ASTM D 3882	3% max	3% max	3% max	3% max
Colorfastness to:[c]					
Laundering:	AATCC 61				
Alteration in Shade		Class 4 min[d]	Class 4 min[d]	Class 4 min[d]	Class 4 min[d]
Staining		Class 3 min[e]	Class 3 min[e]	Class 3 min[e]	Class 3 min[e]
Crocking:	AATCC 8 or AATCC 116				
Dry		Class 4 min[f]	Class 4 min[f]	Class 4 min[f]	Class 4 min[f]
Wet		Class 3 min[f]	Class 3 min[f]	Class 3 min[f]	Class 3 min[f]
Light (20 AATCC FU)	AATCC 16				
Perspiration	AATCC 15	Class 4 min[d]	Class 4 min[d]	Class 4 min[d]	Class 4 min[d]
Alteration in Shade		Class 4 min[d]	Class 4 min[d]	Class 4 min[d]	Class 4 min[d]
Staining		Class 3 min[e]	Class 3 min[e]	Class 3 min[e]	Class 3 min[e]
Flammability	ASTM D 1230	Class I	Class I	Class I	Class I

[a]There is more than one standard method that can be used to measure breaking force, bursting force, tear resistance, and lightfastness. These methods cannot be used interchangeably since there may be no overall correlation between them.
[b]Recommended requirement for Easy Care Products which must be ironed.
[c]Class in colorfastness and 5A rating is based on a numerical scale of 5.0 for negligible color change, color transfer, or wrinkling to 1.0 for very severe color change, color transfer, or wrinkling. The numerical rating in Table 29.4 or higher is acceptable.
[d]AATCC Gray Scale for Color Change.
[e]AATCC Gray Scale for Staining.
[f]AATCC Chromatic Transference Scale.
[g]AATCC 3-D Smoothness Appearance Replicas.
Adapted, with permission from D5431-93(2001)E1 Standard Performance Specification for Woven and Knitted Sheeting Products for Institutional and Household Use, copyright ASTM International, 100 Barr Harbor Drive, West Conshohocken, PA 19428, www.astm.org. A copy of the complete standard may be obtained from ASTM International.

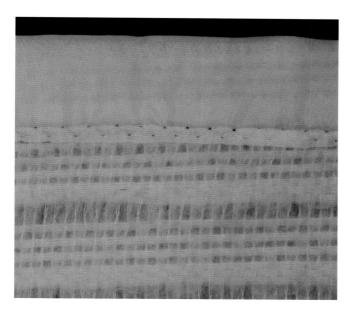

Figure 29.11 Leno-woven thermal blanket.
Courtesy of Amy Willbanks, www.textilefabric.com.

resemblance to wool, without the problems of moths and dry cleaning costs, is a popular choice for blankets.

As detailed in Table 29.1, virtually all fibers used in blankets and blanketing are staple length. These fibers are usually processed into yarns on the woolen or cotton spinning systems.

Weaving Blanketing

Plain weaving and **leno weaving** are used to produce a large amount of blanketing. The leno-woven **thermal blanket** in Figure 29.11 is lightweight and lofty for thermal insulation. The filling yarns were spun on the woolen system and the warp yarns on the cotton system.

Weaving one set of warp yarns and two sets of filling yarns together produces **double-faced blanketing**, or **reversible blanketing**, with different colors on each side. One set of filling yarns is carried to the face and one set to the back. The sets of filling yarns may have different colors or different fiber compositions. If the fiber compositions differ, a cross dyeing operation could be used to produce the two colors in one immersion procedure (see Chapter 8). The additional set of yarns adds strength, which compensates for the weakening effect of the heavy napping used on both sides for warmth.

The blanketing in electric blankets is often produced by interlacing four sets of yarns into a doublecloth fabric.

The interlacing is planned so that pocket-like channels are created, which will prevent the wires from shifting through the structure.

Knitting Blanketing

Knitted blanketing, which is generally constructed on a **raschel knitting** machine, may have a simple or a complex interlooping pattern. The thermal efficiency of this fabric can be engineered by varying the size of the yarns and the knitting gauge used.

Tufting Blanketing

Tufting, used extensively for the production of soft floor coverings and increasingly for upholstery coverings, has been adapted for the production of a small quantity of blanketing. The pile yarns are punched into the base fabric, using a gauge of $5/64$ or $6/32$ inch and six to fourteen stitches per lengthwise inch. By napping the pile surface, the raised fibers have the effect of increasing the diameter of the pile yarns, helping to secure them in the fabric. The back is napped to soften the surface and further stabilize the pile yarns.

Needlepunching Blanketing

The use of a **needlepunching** operation for the commercial production of blanketing began in the mid-1960s. Blanketing fabric is made by cross layering a thick batt with webs of staple-length fibers on each side of a web of yarns. The batt is fed into a machine where pairs of closely spaced, barbed needles punch into the batt, entangling the fibers into a mechanical chain stitch. The extensive needling, approximately 2,000 punches per square inch, reduces the depth of the batt to about ¼ inch. Subsequent napping raises some surface fibers, softening the appearance and improving the thermal efficiency.

Flocking Blanketing

Lightweight, warm blankets can be produced by **flocking** nylon over the surfaces of a thin slab of polyurethane foam. In Figure 29.12a and b, Vellux® blankets manufactured by WestPoint Stevens, nylon flock is embedded on both sides of the foam. Together, the flocked fiber and the cellular foam serve to minimize heat transfer by restricting air flow.

Coloring and Finishing Blanketing

Blanketing may be constructed with colored fibers or yarns or the greige fabric may be piece dyed or printed.

a) Exterior.

Figure 29.12 Velux® blanket.
Courtesy of Amy Willbanks, www.textilefabric.com.

b) Interior.

Whatever fabrication technique is used, virtually all blanketing fabrics are napped.

Constructing Blankets

Most blankets are approximately 84 inches long and they are finished 20 inches wider than the mattress with which they are intended to be used. The side edges may be the fabric selvages or they may be machine overcast, and the ends are enclosed within tightly satin-woven binding. For electric blankets, insulated wires are inserted into the channels before the edges are finished.

Caring for Blankets

Wool blankets must be stored with some type of moth repellent to protect the fibers from attack by moth larvae (see Chapter 9). To avoid **felting shrinkage**, blankets composed of wool fiber should be dry cleaned, unless information on the label directs otherwise. Blankets composed of most other fibers can generally be laundered, unless care instructions voluntarily provided by the producer state otherwise. Electric blankets must always be laundered; dry-cleaning solvents may damage the insulating material covering the heating wires.

Evaluating Blankets

Two ASTM International standards are used to evaluate the performance of blankets. ASTM D 4151 Standard Test Method for Flammability of Blankets details the methodology for testing ignition and flame spread of blankets and ASTM D 5432 Standard Performance Specification for

Blanket Products for Institutional and Household Use is used to evaluate fabrics used in blankets (Table 29.5).

Bedspreads, Quilts, and Comforters

It may be helpful to differentiate among bedspreads, comforters, and quilts. ASTM D 4721 Standard Practice for Evaluation of the Performance of Machine Washable and Drycleanable Bedcoverings and Accessories provides useful distinctions. Bedspreads are defined "as a type of bedcovering that is placed over the blankets and sheets for appearance and warmth," a comforter is described as "a bedcovering assembly, consisting of an insulating filler secured between two layers of fabric, used primarily to reduce heat loss," and a quilt is "a bedcovering assembly used primarily for warmth, consisting of an insulating filler secured between two layers of fabric, but generally lighter in weight and thinner than a comforter."[7]

Commercial Quilting

Both of the commercial quilting techniques of **machine stitching** and **pinsonic melding** were discussed in Chapter 9. Typical stitching patterns are illustrated in Figure 9.13 (p. 149), and a pinsonic quilted fabric is shown in Figure 9.12 (p. 149).

In **patterned quilts**, the several pieces are shaped to create a specific pattern repeat; today, skilled quilters often cut and sew selected fabrics to replicate traditional hand-stitched patterns (Figure 29.13). In **crazy quilts**, the pieces are irregularly shaped and they vary in size and color styling. The patches in **patchwork quilts** are often square or rectangular. Finishing touches differ from quilt to quilt.

Quilting stitches should be uniformly placed to stabilize the layered structure. As shown in Figure 9.13 (p. 149), the stitches may be sewn in parallel rows, in crisscrossing lines, or in undulating waves, or they may follow the outlines of printed motifs or appliqués. Since the stitches create a three-dimensional effect, they may be used to introduce a surface pattern to a solid-colored surface or to augment the visual interest of a printed fabric. With hand-quilted coverings, the fineness and evenness of the quilting stitches are indicative of quality.

Two quilting variations used on interior textile products include trapunto quilting and shadow quilting.

Table 29.5 Standard Performance Specification for Blanket Products for Institutional and Household Use

Characteristic	Test Method Number	Requirements	
		Knits/Flock	Woven/Nonwoven
Breaking force (load) each direction	ASTM D 5034	NA	89 N (20 lbf) min
Bursting force (ball burst)[a]	ASTM D 3787	345 kpa (50 psi) min	NA
Dimensional change: After 5 launderings each direction	AATCC 135 or AATCC 96		
Wool (50% or more)		6.0 max	6.0 max
Cotton		5.0 max	5.0 max
All others		3.5 max	3.5 max
After 3 dry cleanings each direction	ASTM D 2724		
All fabrics		3.5 max	3.5 max
Colorfastness:[b]			
Laundering:	AATCC 61		
Shade Change		Class 4[c] min	Class 4[c] min
Staining		Class 3[d] min	Class 3[d] min
Drycleaning	AATCC 132		
Shade Change		Class 4[c] min	Class 4[c] min
Burnt Gas Fumes (2 cycles)	AATCC 23		
Shade Change		Class 4[c] min	Class 4[c] min
Crocking:	AATCC 116 or AATCC 8		
Dry		Class 4[e] min	Class 4[e] min
Wet		Class 3[e] min	Class 3[e] min
Light (20 AATCC SFU)	AATCC 16	Class 4[c] min	Class 4[c] min
Flammability	ASTM D 4151	Class I	Class I
Thermal Transmittance	ASTM D 1518	Acceptable[f]	Acceptable[f]
Laundered Appearance	---[g]	Acceptable[g]	Acceptable[g]

[a]There is more than one standard method that can be used to measure breaking force, bursting force, and lightfastness. These methods cannot be used interchangeably since there may be no overall correlation between them (see Notes 2–5, and 8).
[b]Class for color change and color transfer is based on a numerical scale of 5 for negligible or no color change or color transfer to 1 for severe color change or color transfer. The numerical rating in Table 1 or higher is acceptable.
[c]AATCC Gray Scale for Color Change.
[d]AATCC Gray Scale for Staining.
[e]AATCC Chromatic Transference Scale.
[f]7.5 Information.
[g]As agreed upon between the purchaser and the supplier.
Adapted, with permission from D5432-93(2000)e1 Standard Performance Specification for Blanket Products for Institutional and Household Use, copyright ASTM International, 100 Barr Harbor Drive, West Conshohocken, PA 19428, www.astm.org. A copy of the complete standard may be obtained from ASTM International.

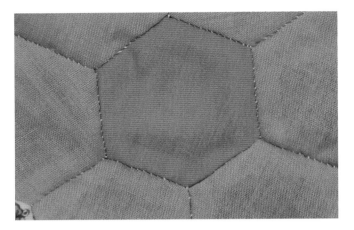

a) Front.

Figure 29.13 Hand-stitched quilt.
Courtesy of Amy Willbanks, www.textilefabric.com.

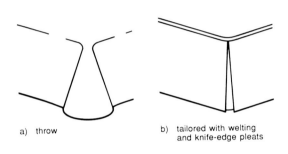

a) throw

b) tailored with welting and knife-edge pleats

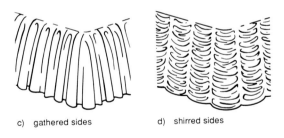

c) gathered sides

d) shirred sides

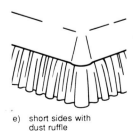

e) short sides with dust ruffle

Figure 29.14 Typical bedspread drops.

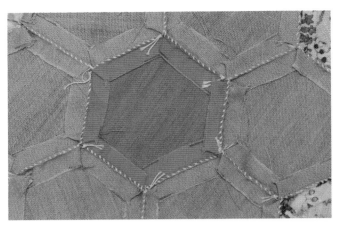

b) Back.

Trapunto quilting is done by placing quilting stitching around a single motif in a pattern repeat. The interior of the quilted shape is then filled by inserting batting material through tiny slits cut in the backing fabric. For long, narrow shapes, a yarn or cord may be drawn between the face and back fabrics. Trapunto quilting is particularly effective when used for decorative pillow coverings with large motifs.

Shadow quilting is done by covering an appliquéd face fabric with a sheer fabric such as organdy or voile. Quilting stitches are then placed around the outlines of the appliqués, joining the layers together. The colored appliqués have a softened or shadowed appearance.

Bedspreads

Most bedspreads are chosen primarily for their styling and decorative fabric. Others, especially quilted ones, are selected for their insulative value.

Styles

Various styles of **drops** seen with bedspreads, ranging from **tailored** to **ruffled** styles, are illustrated in Figure 29.14. The appearance of any of these drops changes dramatically when executed in different fabrics. The qualities of the fabric must always be appropriate for the styling features of the spread. For example, although a heavy fabric would be suitable for use in a throw style, it would not drape properly in a style with **gathered** or **shirred** sides.

Fabrics

Virtually any fabric may be used for a bedspread. Several fabrics, such as **gingham** and printed percale, are flat, essentially two-dimensional, smooth fabrics; others, including **taffeta** and **ribcord**, show a slightly raised rib effect. Clipped dot or spot fabrics, Schiffli embroidered **organdy**, and **eyelet**, have slightly raised designs created by extra yarns. Fabrics such as corduroy, velvet, simulated fur fabrics, and tufted fabrics exhibit the conspicuous depth of a pile layer.

Pile bedspread fabrics are produced by weaving, knitting, or tufting. **Corduroy**, a woven filling-pile fabric, is often used for tailored spreads, and **velvet**, a woven warp-pile fabric, is often used for throw spreads. Pile knitting produces the **simulated fur fabrics** often used for throw style coverings. These three-dimensional coverings are fabricated by incorporating combed fibers into a knitted base fabric.

Tufting is used to produce chenille spreads and candlewick spreads. In **chenille** spreads, the pile tufts are closely spaced and cut, producing the caterpillar-like appearance of chenille yarns; true chenille yarns are not used. After tufting, the level of twist of the pile yarns is reduced, causing them to "bloom" or increase in diameter, and the base fabric is shrunk to effectively lock the pile yarns in position. In **candlewick** spreads, the pile tufts are individually spaced, but, viewed collectively, form a design. The designs resemble those created by a hand-stitching technique in which heavy yarns produced for use as candlewicks are used for the embroidered motifs (Figures 9.7 and 9.8, p. 147).

Quilts and Comforters

As noted above, quilts and comforters are multicomponent bed coverings. Either structure may be used in lieu of a bedspread (Figure 29.15).

Figure 29.15 When using various accents, such as fabric headboard, tab-top panels on canopy, multiple sizes of decorative pillows, and a button-tufted bench, omitting the bed skirt creates an uncluttered, classic design. Courtesy of Ferguson Copeland.

Quilts

Commercially produced **quilts** usually have a printed, solid color or yarn dyed face fabric, a fibrous or polyurethane batting, and a coordinating solid-colored or printed back fabric (Figure 29.16). Patterned machine stitching is normally used to stabilize the layers.

Comforters

Comforters are usually filled with down, feathers, or fiberfill; those filled with down are frequently known as **duvets**. They may also be filled with a loose batting of polyester. The closeup photograph in Figure 29.17 shows the use of a spunbonded backing fabric to prevent **fill leakage**, the migration or penetration of the filling material through the outercovering. Spunbonded fabric can also be used as an interior lining, allowing the use of decorative fabric on both sides of the comforter. To minimize the need for cleaning, manufacturers often recommend that comforters be enclosed in a sheet casing. Sheet cas-

ings have releasable closures that permit them to be easily removed for laundering.

Most comforters are channel quilted to minimize shifting and clumping of the filling. Some products also use a system of crosswise baffles. Sleeping bags are often constructed in this manner, making them, in effect, folded comforters with zipper closures.

Evaluating Bedspread Fabrics, Quilts, and Comforters

Established ASTM International standards may be used to evaluate the performance of bedspread fabrics, quilts, and comforters. These include ASTM D 4037 Standard Performance Specification for Woven, Knitted, or Flocked Bedspread Fabrics (Table 29.6), ASTM D 4721 Standard Practice for Evaluation of the Performance of Machine Washable and Drycleanable Bedcoverings and Accessories, and ASTM D 4769 Standard Specification for Woven and Warp Knitted Comforter Fabrics (Table 29.7).

Figure 29.16 Machine stitched quilt.
Courtesy of Amy Willbanks,
www.textilefabric.com.

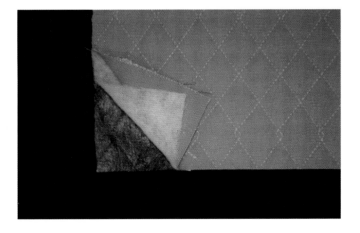

Figure 29.17 Quilted fabric with three quilting layers.
Courtesy of Amy Willbanks,
www.textilefabric.com.

Table 29.6 Standard Performance Specification for Woven, Knitted, or Flocked Bedspread Fabrics

Characteristic	Test Method Number	Requirements	
		Woven	Knit
Breaking strength force (load)	ASTM D 5034	25 lbf (111 N) min	NA
Bursting strength	ASTM D 3786	NA	35 psi (241 kPa) min
Tear strength	ASTM D 2261	1.5 lbf (6.7 N) min	NA
Dimensional change: Laundering and dry cleaning each direction	AATCC 135 and ASTM D 2724		
Tailored type		±3.5% max	±5.0% max
Throw type		±5.0% max	±5.0% max
Fabric appearance (durable press)	AATCC 124	DP 3.5 min	DP 3.5 min
Retention of hand, character, and appearance	AATCC 135 and ASTM D 2724	No significant change**	No significant change**
Durability of back coating	---***	No significant change	No significant change
Colorfastness to:			
Laundering:	AATCC 61		
Shade change		Class 4 min[a]	Class 4 min[a]
Staining		Class 3 min[b]	Class 3 min[b]
Bleaching	AATCC 172 and AATCC 188		
Sodium hypochlorite		Class 4 min[a]	Class 4 min[a]
Nonchlorine		Class 4 min[a]	Class 4 min[a]
Dry cleaning:	AATCC 132		
Shade change		Class 4 min[a]	Class 4 min[a]
Burnt gas fumes (two cycles)	AATCC 23		
Original shade change		Class 4 min[a]	Class 4 min[a]
After one laundering or one dry cleaning shade change		Class 4 min[a]	Class 4 min[a]
Crocking:	AATCC 8 or AATCC 116		
Dry		Class 4 min[c]	Class 4 min[c]
Wet		Class 3 min[c]	Class 3 min[c]
Light (20 AATCC SFU)	AATCC 16	Class 4 min[a]	Class 4 min[a]
Flammability	---	Pass	Pass

[a]Gray Scale for Color Change.
[b]AATCC Gray Scale for Staining.
[c]AATCC Chromatic Transference Scale.
[d]AATCC Durable Press Replicas.
Courtesy of ASTM International.
  *The fabric smoothness (durable-press rating) of such fabrics shall have decreased no more than 0.5 smoothness appearance rating from that of the fabric before it was laundered.
  **Retention of Hand, Character, and Appearance—Fabric tested as directed in laundering and dry cleaning shall not exhibit any significant changes in hand, character, or appearance.
***Durability of Back Coating—A fabric shall exhibit no evidence of cracking or peeling of back coating when subjected to tests in accordance with laundering and dry cleaning.
Adapted, with permission from D4037-02(2008) Standard Performance Specification for Woven, Knitted, or Flocked Bedspread Fabrics, copyright ASTM International, 100 Barr Harbor Drive, West Conshohocken, PA 19428, www.astm.org. A copy of the complete standard may be obtained from ASTM International.

Table 29.7 Standard Specification for Woven and Warp Knitted Comforter Fabrics

Characteristic	Test Method Number	Requirements	
		Woven Fabrics	Warp Knit Fabrics
Breaking Strength (Load)	ASTM D 5034	133 N (30 lbf) min	NA
Bursting Strength (Motor-Driven Diaphragm Tester)	ASTM D 3786 or D 3787	NA	35 psi (155 kPa)
Tear Strength	ASTM D 1424	6.7 N (1.5 lbf) min	NA
Dimensional Change:			
Laundering	AATCC 135	3% max	5% max
Dry Cleaning	ASTM D 2724	3% max	5% max
Fabric Appearance	AATCC 124	D.P. 3.5 min	D.P. 3.5 min
Colorfastness:			
Burnt Gas Fumes (2 cycles)	AATCC 23		
Shade Change After One Laundering or One Dry Cleaning		Class 4[a] min	Class 4[a] min
Laundering:			
Shade Change	AATCC 61	Class 4[a] min	Class 4[a] min
Staining	AATCC 61	Class 3[b] min	Class 3[b] min
Dry Cleaning:			
Shade Change	AATCC 132	Class 4[a] min	Class 4[a] min
Crocking:	AATCC 8 or AATCC 116		
Dry		Class 4[c] min	Class 4[c] min
Wet		Class 3[c] min	Class 3[c] min
Light (20 AATCC SFU)	AATCC 16	Class 4[a] min	Class 4[a] min
Flammability	---*	Pass	Pass
Fill Leakage	---**	Acceptable	Acceptable

[a]AATCC Gray Scale for Color Change.
[b]AATCC Gray Scale for Staining.
[c]AATCC Chromatic Transference Scale.
 *As agreed by purchaser and seller; must meet government mandatory standards where applicable.
**As agreed by purchaser and seller.
Adapted, with permission from D4769-88(2000) Standard Specification for Woven and Warp Knitted Comforter Fabrics, copyright ASTM International, 100 Barr Harbor Drive, West Conshohocken, PA 19428, www.astm.org. A copy of the complete standard may be obtained from ASTM International.

Summary

Several bedding products, including mattresses, mattress pads, quilts, and comforters, are multicomponent structures. They are generally filled with polyester fiberfill, but other filling materials, including loose masses of down or feathers, foamed compounds, and battings composed of wool, cotton, or cotton and polyester, are also used.

Bedding products may be purchased singly or in coordinated ensembles. Some products, such as mattresses and bed pillows, serve functional purposes; other products, such as sheets, pillowcases, and comforters, are selected for their functional and decorative attributes; and still other products, such as decorative pillows and dust ruffles, are completely ornamental.

The performance of beddings may be evaluated using standards such as those published by ASTM International and AATCC. The performance recommended in these standards may be required by an agency having jurisdiction over the selection and use of the products.

Key Terms

all down
backfilled
batting
bedding
blanket, thermal
blanketing, double-faced
blanketing, reversible
candlewick
chenille
comforters
convertible sofa bed
corduroy
down
down cluster
down fiber
drops
drops, gathered
drops, ruffled
drops, shirred
drops, tailored
duplex printing
dust ruffles
duvet
eyelet
feather fiber
feathers
feathers, crushed/chopped/broken
feathers, damaged
feathers, land fowl
feathers, nonwaterfowl
feathers, quill
feathers, waterfowl

felting shrinkage
fiberfill
fill leakage
flannel
flocking
futons
gingham
International Down and Feather
    Laboratory and Institute
    (IDFL)
leno weave
loftiness
mattress, foam-core
mattress, innerspring
mattress covers
mattress pads
muslin
needlepunching
organdy
percale
pillow, bedrest
pillow sham
pillows, bed
pillows, bolster
pillows, boudoir
pillows, breakfast
pillows, European
pillows, king-size
pillows, neckroll
pillows, queen-size
pillows, round
pillows, standard

pillows, Turkish
plumules
pure down
quill
quilting, machine stitching
quilting, pinsonic melding
quilting, shadow
quilting, trapunto
quilts
quilts, crazy
quilts, patchwork
quilts, patterned
raschel knitting
residue
reverse blends
ribcord
sheet casings
sheets, fitted or contour
sheets, flat
simulated fur fabrics
slabs
sofa bed
taffeta
thermal insulation
ticking
tufting
underblankets
USA 2000 Labeling Standards—
    Down and Feather Products
velvet
visco-elastic polyurethane foam

Review Questions

1. Explain the importance of cotton in the bedding products industry.

2. Why is the usage of acrylic popular for blankets?

3. Identify bedding products included and excluded from the provisions of the TFPIA.

4. Why are spun yarns more widely used than filament yarns in bedding products?

5. Distinguish between down and feathers.

6. Do products labeled "down" have to have 100 percent down present?

7. Differentiate among down, all down, and pure down.

8. Explain why filling materials must retain their original loftiness in order to be effective.

9. Compare the positive and negative properties of down, wool, and polyester for use as filling materials.

10. Explain the use of wool underblankets in institutional settings.

11. Why are cigarettes used as the source of ignition in 16 CFR 1632?

12. Explain factors accounting for the changing market shares held by cotton and polyester in the sheetings market.

13. Distinguish between muslin and percale.

14. What is visco-elastic polyurethane foam used for? What are the advantages associated with its use?

15. Is flammability testing of blanketing mandatory or voluntary?

16. How is fill leakage minimized in comforters?

Notes

1. Fiber Economics Bureau, *Fiber Organon*, October 2006, 192.

2. "New Bedding Technology Provides Nighttime Relief for Allergy Suffers," *AATCC Review*, March 2008, 18.

3. "Down and Feather Definitions," International Down and Feather Bureau, *www.idfl.com*.

4. "USA-2000 Labeling Standards—Down and Feather Products (March 2007)," International Down and Feather Bureau, *www.idfl.com*.

5. Fiber, op. cit., p. 195.

6. "You Need to Know: Some Thread Counts Are Bogus," *Consumer Reports*, August 2005, 36.

7. *Annual Book of ASTM Standards*, D 7023-06 Standards Relating to Home Furnishings.

Textile Accessories for Tabletops

CHAPTER **THIRTY**

■ **Because many of today's tabletops** have finishes that are resistant to heat, chipping, and staining, the use of such coverings as tablecloths and placemats is often optional. Nonetheless, these items frequently enrich the dining experience. They may be selected to add warmth and beauty to the table, to carry out a decorative theme, to set a casual or formal mood, or to complement the table service. The use of textile table coverings in such institutional settings as restaurants, for example, adds to the ambiance and to the diners' expectation to pay more for the meal. Even when table coverings are needed to protect fine wood or to camouflage a damaged surface, the assortment of contemporary products is so varied that consumers may choose the items mostly on the basis of their aesthetic features.

At the outset, two terms, napery and linens, should be distinguished. **Napery** is a general term for tablecloths and napkins. Although the term is no longer widely used in commercial activities, it is used in certain standards and labeling rules. In contemporary usage, the term **linens** described sheets, towels, tablecloths, napkins, and related products that formerly were composed entirely or primarily of flax fiber. While the use of flax fiber in these goods has declined significantly, they are still available. Many linen table coverings are not new, but are heirlooms that have been given special care.

Some tabletop accessories are specifically produced for use on dining room tables in homes and in such institutional settings as restaurants and hotels. Several other items are produced for use on tables and other furniture situated throughout interior spaces.

Producing Tabletop Coverings

The assortment of products produced for use on tabletops includes such items as tablecloths, napkins, doilies, placemats, and silencers. With the exception of silencers, all of these items are visible in use; therefore, they are designed to be attractive additions to the table surface, and often to complement the interior setting as well. Silencers, which are placed under tablecloths and concealed from view, serve purely functional purposes.

Components
Most tabletop coverings are composed of textile fibers. Some distinctive nonfibrous structures are also available.

Fibers and Yarns
In reporting fiber consumption in U.S. home textiles production, the Fiber Economics Bureau groups napery products with cotton window shades and insect screening and netting. Between 2001 and 2005, the use of cotton has increased from 19 percent to 23 percent. During the same time period, manufactured fibers remained at the same percentage. Over 90 percent of the manufactured fibers consumed were noncellulosics, including both yarn and staple.[1]

Together with rayon and various noncellulosic fibers, several natural cellulosic fibers, including cotton, flax, ramie, sisal, abaca, and raffia, are used in dining table products, doilies, and dresser scarves. **Raffia**, a fiber obtained from the leaves of various species of palm trees, is used in long, narrow, yarn-like bands to make woven placemats. Abaca comes from the leafstalk of the Abaca plant, which is then stripped and dried. The fibers are flexible, strong, and resistant to damage from salt water, making them very serviceable as woven placemats. **Sisal**, a relatively stiff fiber obtained from the leaves of the agave or yucca plant, is effectively used to produce woven placemats and hot pads. Examples of both abaca and sisal are presented in Figure 30.1.

When stiff fibers, such as **flax** (Figure 30.2), hemp, and **ramie**, are used in large items that are normally folded for storage or use, they may be unable to withstand the repeated flexing, and eventually may split on the crease lines (Figure 3.4, p. 33). To avoid this problem, fabrics composed of these fibers should be stored flat or rolled, and crease positions should be shifted when possible. The need for such storage, in fact, explains the earlier use of special names and spaces for the storage of fine linens (e.g., the linen drawer, the linen closet).

Most yarns used for table products are spun; however, some filament yarns are also used. For economy and ease of care, spinners frequently use staple-length rayon and polyester to produce yarns that resemble those spun of flax. For improved dimensional stability and resiliency, polyester is increasingly used alone or blended with cotton in various sizes of yarns (Figure 30.3).

Nonfibrous Materials
Some contemporary placemats are multicomponent structures, made of a layer of aluminum foil or metallized polymer film faced with a clear fabric, such as Mylar® polyester film produced by DuPont Teijin Films, and backed with a conventional textile fabric; such mats have a mirror-like quality. Several nonfibrous placemats are composed of expanded foam. For increased visual interest, these mats are generally printed with colorful design motifs.

Manufacturing Table Covering Fabrics
Table coverings are produced by weaving, knitting, knotting and twisting, spunbonding, and extrusion. Color may

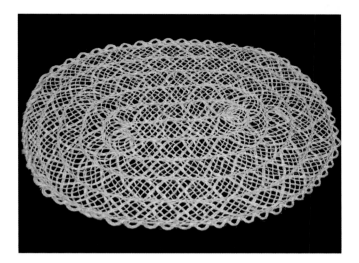

a) Placemat made of abaca.

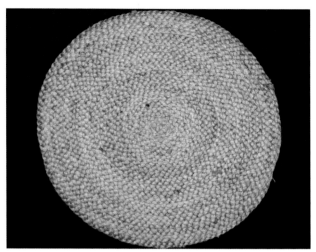

b) Placemat made of sisal.

Figure 30.1 Handmade placemats.
Courtesy of Amy Willbanks, www.textilefabric.com.

be added before or after fabrication, and finishing agents and processes may be used to alter the appearance and improve serviceability.

Fabricating

Woven table coverings may have a casual, contemporary appearance or a formal, traditional appearance; most styles carry no specific fabric name. Elaborate Jacquard interlacing patterns, shown in the tablecloth in Figure 30.4, are used to create the distinctive surfaces of single and double damask. The motifs in **damask** have a five-shaft satin weave, with each warp yarn floating over four filling yarns. Damask is a reversible, Jacquard woven fabric with a satin weave in both the pattern and ground. The ground in these fabrics is generally woven in a twill or sateen interlacing pattern. Damask can be one or two colors. As explained in Chapter 9, **beetling** may be used to flatten the cross sections of the fibers and yarns, increasing the level of light reflection to highlight the motifs (Figure 9.1, p. 143).

Stitch-knitted tablecloths and napkins are produced by chain-stitching across webs of yarns, a technique described in Chapter 7. The technique is fast and economical, but rupturing of the chain stitches can initiate runs.

A wide variety of lace fabrics is produced for use as tablecloths, dresser scarves, and **doilies** (Figure 30.5).

Figure 30.2 Formal Belgian dinner napkins made of 100% flax.
Courtesy of Amy Willbanks, www.textilefabric.com.

Figure 30.3 Cotton and polyester quilted placemat.
Courtesy of Amy Willbanks, www.textilefabric.com.

Figure 30.4 Damask tablecloth.
Courtesy of Amy Willbanks, www.textilefabric.com.

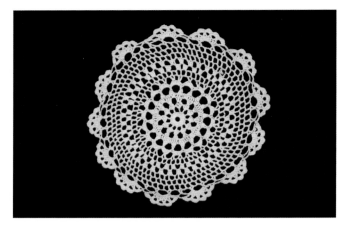

Figure 30.5 Crocheted doily.
Courtesy of Amy Willbanks, www.textilefabric.com.

Machine-made **Nottingham lace**, originally used only for curtains, may be frequently used for table linens. Lace fabrics are placed over a solid-covered fabric for a color accent that emphasizes the intricate motifs in the lace.

Extrusion of such polymer compounds as polyvinylchloride produces film fabrics (Figure 30.6) that are then supported by conventional woven, knitted or nonwoven fabrics and cut for use as tablecloths. Extrusion is also used to produce film structures that are then laminated to produce items like placemats.

Spunbonding is increasingly used for the rapid and economical production of fabrics for table coverings.

Coloring and Finishing

Table covering fabrics may be manufactured from colored

Figure 30.6 Nonwoven backed vinyl tablecloth.
Courtesy of Amy Willbanks, www.textilefabric.com.

components or color may be applied by dyeing or printing the greige goods. Visual interest may also be added with embroidery (Figure 30.7).

Greige fabrics intended for use as **silencers** (Figure 30.8) will be napped to raise the ends of the fibers to the surface, converting the flat goods into thick, flannel-like fabrics. The added thickness will help the silencer to absorb the impact force of dishes and silverware, reducing noise and protecting the table surface.

Fabrics composed of natural and manufactured cellulosic fibers may have small amounts of chemical cross-linking resin added to them to improve wrinkle recovery. The use of these agents is critical for linen fabrics since the untreated fabrics have extremely low resiliency and require a great deal of moisture and pressure in ironing. Fabrics composed of cotton and polyester are often treated with a larger amount of resin for durable press or no-iron performance. Fabrics composed of thermoplastic fibers can be heat set to improve their resiliency and dimensional stability.

Soil release compounds may be used with tablecloths and napkins to help the fibers release food stains (see Chapter 9). Because soil release compounds increase the hydrophilic nature of fibers, they are particularly helpful when used with such hydrophobic fibers as polyester and nylon, and with fabrics having a durable press finish. Durable press resins reduce absorbency and thus lessen the efficiency of the detergent in removing soil. Visa® is a trade name that indicates the use of a soil release treatment developed by Deering Milliken for fabrics composed of 100 percent polyester.

Figure 30.7 Embroidered napkin.
Courtesy of Amy Willbanks, www.textilefabric.com.

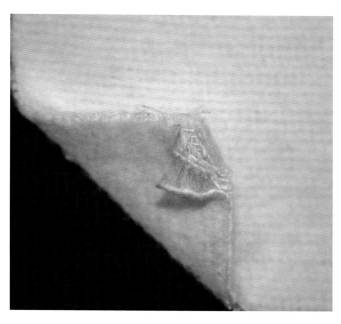

Figure 30.8 Silence cloth.
Courtesy of Amy Willbanks, www.textilefabric.com.

a) Solid color runners.

b) Printed runners.

Figure 30.9 Table runners.
Courtesy of Christian Fischbacher, www.fishbacher.com.

a) Serged edge.

b) Hemmed edge.

Figure 30.10 Edge finishing for napkins.
Courtesy of Amy Willbanks, www.textilefabric.com.

Constructing Tabletop Accessories

Tabletop accessories are constructed in assorted sizes and shapes for different uses. Producers employ various techniques to finish the raw edges.

Types and Sizes

Accessories constructed for use on dining tables include tablecloths, runners, placemats, and napkins. These items are available in square, round, oval, and rectangular shapes in various sizes. **Tablecloths** should be selected to cover the tabletop and drop from 5 to 10 inches on all sides. **Runners** (Figure 30.9a and b) are approximately 12 inches wide, and they, too, should drop from 5 to 10 inches. **Placemats** are generally rectangular, but many are round or oval. Rectangular placemats are typically 12 inches by 18 inches. Small **cocktail napkins** are 5 inches square; larger napkins are 12 to 22 inches square.

Accessories constructed for use on cocktail tables, side tables, end tables, and case pieces include such items as mats, scarves, coasters, and doilies (Figure 30.5). These products, like dining table accessories, are available in a wide variety of sizes and shapes.

Edge Finishes

The raw edges of fabric used for tabletop items may be finished with a small hem, binding, or fringe, or with machine serging, which may be plain or decorative. When plain overcasting stitches are used on fabrics having relatively large yarns, the stitches often cover only one or two yarns. With

continual use and cleaning, the covered yarns and stitching may slide off the edge of the item.

The edges of textile placemats are fringed and reinforced with machine zig-zag stitching, serged with plain or decorative stitching, or finished with a small hem (Figure 30.10a and b). They are also frequently bound with bias-cut fabric.

Evaluating Fabrics for Tabletop Accessories

ASTM D 4111 Standard Performance Specification for Woven Napery and Tablecloth Fabrics: Household and Institutional may be used to evaluate the performance of fabrics intended for use in tablecloths and related items. The specification requirements range from breaking strength (load) to colorfastness to dimensional change (Table 30.1).

Labeling Textile Table Accessories

Textile Fiber Products Identification Act (TFPIA)

The provisions of the TFPIA apply to tablecloths, napkins, doilies, and dresser and other furniture scarves. Specifically exempted are table placemats made principally of plastic. Most textile tabletop accessories therefore must be labeled with the fiber composition and other information required by this act, which was discussed in detail in Chapter 10.

Table 30.1 Performance Specification for Woven Napery and Tablecloth Fabrics: Household and Institutional		
Characteristic	Test Method Number	Requirements
Breaking strength (load) (CRT):	ASTM D 5034 (ASTM D 1682 discontinued)[e]	
Household		133 N (30 lbf), min
Institutional		242 N (55 lbf), min
Yarn distortion	ASTM D 1336	1 mm (0.05 in.), max
Tongue-tear strength:	ASTM D 2261 (ASTM D 2262 discontinued)[e]	
Household		9 N (2 lbf), min
Institutional		13 N (3 lbf), min
Colorfastness:		
Burnt gas fumes—1 cycle:		
Shade change, original fabric	AATCC 23	Class 4[a], min
Shade change, after one laundering		Class 4[a], min
Chlorine Bleach	AATCC 188	Class 4[a], min
Nonchlorine Bleach	AATCC 172	Class 4[a], min
Light (20 AATCC FU)	AATCC 16	Class 4[a], min
Crocking:	AATCC 8 or AATCC 116	
Dry		Class 4[b], min
Wet		Class 3[b], min
Laundering:	AATCC 61	
Shade change		Class 4[a], min
Staining		Class 3[c], min
Dimensional change warp and filling	AATCC 96 or AATCC 135	5%, max
Fabric appearance	AATCC 124	DP 3.5[d], min
Chlorine retention	AATCC 92	
Retention of hand, character, and appearance	---*	Acceptable
Soil release	AATCC 138	Class 4, min

[a]Gray Scale for Color Change
[b]Gray Scale for Staining
[c]AATCC Chromatic Transfer Scale
[d]AATCC Durable Press Replicas
[e]ASTM D 1682 and ASTM D 2262 have been discontinued. These test methods have been replaced by ASTM D 5034 and ASTM D 2261.
*Prior agreement between purchaser and seller
Courtesy of ASTM International. Reprinted with permission.

Summary

Accessories produced for use on tabletops may be composed of textile fibers or nonfibrous materials. Many table covering fabrics are fabricated by weaving, stitch-knitting, knotting and twisting, and, more recently, by spunbonding. Items intended for use on dining tables may have a soil-release finish to help preserve a stain-free appearance.

Items produced for use on occasional tables and case pieces are available in a range of sizes and shapes as varied as that of the dining table accessories.

Virtually all textile tabletop products must be labeled in accordance with the provisions of the Textile Fiber Products Identification Act.

Key Terms

abaca	napery	silencers
beetling	napkins, cocktail	sisal
damask	Nottingham lace	soil release compounds
doilies	placemats	spunbonding
extrusion	raffia	stitch-knitting
flax	ramie	tablecloths
linens	runners	

Review Questions

1. Distinguish between the terms "linen" and "linens."

2. Identify some natural cellulose fibers used in tabletop accessories. Why do some present storage problems?

3. Describe some of the performance properties tested in the evaluation of napery and tablecloths.

4. What problem may be encountered with stitch-knitted fabrics?

5. What is the function of silencers?

6. What types of compounds or finishes may be used with tablecloths and napkins? Why?

Note

1. Fiber Economics Bureau, *Fiber Organon*, October 2006, 192.

UNIT FIVE CASE STUDY

Project Type: Hospital

Statement of the Project:

After nine years of washing and drying, wear and tear, the cubicle curtains in this 376-bed facility needed to be replaced. The existing curtains were a plain, well-washed shade of mauve and did not complement the four different color schemes for patient rooms. They were beginning to show staining and were, in general, not exciting.

Statement of the Problem:

The fabric and mesh of the cubicle curtain needed to be Class A fire rated. State fire codes dictated the distance from the ceiling to the top of the curtain and the size of the openings in the mesh at the top of the curtain to allow for sprinkler coverage on a pulled cubicle curtain. Nylon thread had to be used to prevent breakdown and microbacterial growth. Stainless steel grommets were re-quired to prevent rusting. The top hem was triple reinforced to ensure that the grommets would not rip out with repeated pulling and tugging. The curtains also needed to coordinate with all color schemes, be colorfast, and be reasonably priced.

Selection Criteria:

The recommendation was to choose a patterned fabric, subtle enough to suggest a design, but with enough contrast to make a visual distinction. A strong vertical was not used because some patients suffer from dizziness and it was perceived that the stripes would only add to the condition. Instead a muted and graduated vertical stripe with a faint tree-bark-like design woven into the grey filler threads that create a play on light and shadows was chosen. The graduated colors range from teal, to blue, to rose. This diversity in the colors of this fabric makes for a perfect marriage in all patient rooms.

Product Specifications:
Maharam Textiles

- # 501104 (Mikado Pattern)
- 002 Truffle (Color)
- 100% Trevira®, inherently flame-resistant Polyester
- Width—72″
- 9³/₄″ vertical repeat, 9″ high
- Nylon mesh
- ¹/₂″ opening on the diagonal
- Fabricated by Standard Textiles, Cincinnati, OH

Maintenance and Cost:
The following maintenance guidelines are dictated by the manufacturer. The fabric can be washed in 160 °F temperature and dried up to 110 °F. Bleach or caustic soap should not be used with this fabric. The fabric should not be exposed to excessive heat, to avoid the loss of the fabric's permanent-press feature. The fabric is a midrange product that when properly maintained has an average life cycle of 5 years.

Discussion Questions

1. Identify two of the client's requirements for the design project.

2. Identify aesthetic features of the product that meet the client's requirements.

3. Identify functional features of the product that meet requirements for this application.

4. Discuss the psychological impact of the textile on the user of the space.

5. Research another product that is appropriate for this application. Compare and contrast the cost effectiveness, availability, durability, and maintenance of the new product with the one used in the case study.

Glossary

AATCC Acronym for American Association of Textile Chemists and Colorists, a voluntary scientific association that develops standard test methods.

AATCC Chromatic Color Transference Scale Scale used in evaluations of staining.

AATCC Gray Scale for Color Change Scale used in evaluations of shade changes.

AATCC Gray Scale for Staining Scale used in evaluations of staining.

AATCC Technical Manual Publication that includes AATCC test methods.

Abaca Bast fiber used for cordage; also called Manila hemp.

Abrasion Wearing away by friction or rubbing.

Abrasion resistance Ability of a textile structure to resist damage and fiber loss by friction.

Absorption Penetration of gases or fluids into fibers or within yarn and fabric interstices.

Accordion-pleated shade Window treatment constructed of woven or knitted fabric that has been stiffened and set in a three-dimensional, folded configuration.

Acetate Manufactured cellulose-based fibers made from trees, cotton linters, or bamboo.

Acid print See *burnt-out print*.

Acoustical value The extent to which a structure prevents sound from becoming unwanted noise.

Acrylic A manufactured synthetic fiber which imitates wool.

ACT Acronym for Association for Contract Textiles; a trade association created by members of the contract textile industry to address issues concerning contract upholstery fabrics, including performance guidelines and industry education.

Actual color Color characteristics of hue, value, and intensity are unaffected by such things as the light source, accumulated soil, and textural changes.

Additives agents or compounds added to polymer solutions prior to spinning, e.g., antistatic agents, delusterants, flame retardant agents, softeners, dye pigments, ultraviolet absorbers, optical brighteners.

Advisory practices Labeling practices that are advisory in contrast to being mandatory.

After flame time The time the specimen continues to flame after the burner flame is removed.

Afterglow Smoldering combustion occurring after flames are extinguished.

Airborne sounds Noise radiating directly into the air (e.g., people talking, telephones ringing).

All down Labeling term used when product contains only down; also known as pure down or 100 percent down.

Alpaca Fiber obtained from alpacas, a domesticated animal of the camel family.

Amorphous Molecular arrangement in which the polymer chains are not aligned parallel to each other.

Angora Hair fiber retrieved from Angora rabbits.

Anhydrous glucose Monomer unit in natural cellulose fibers.

Aniline finish Denotes use of aniline dyestuffs with leather; not a finish.

Annual Book of ASTM Standards Seventy-two volumes, divided among 16 sections, that contain approved ASTM standards, provisional standards, and related material.

ANSI Acronym for American National Standards Institute, a private corporation that undertakes the development of standards only when so commissioned by an industry group or a government agency.

Antimicrobial agents Chemical agents used to kill or retard the growth of such microbes as bacteria and fungi; especially useful with mattress covers, mattress pads, and soft floor coverings used in care-type facilities.

Antique Oriental rugs Oriental rugs woven prior to the mid-1800s.

Apparent color Color characteristics of hue, value, and intensity are affected by such things as the light source, accumulated soil, and textural changes so they appear different than they actually are.

Apparent color temperature Visual appearance of a light source expressed in degrees Kelvin (K). The higher the number, the cooler the color or the light.

Apparent volume or bulk Apparent, but not actual, increase in volume or bulk created by texturizing multifilament yarns.

Apparent whiteness or brightness Apparent, but not actual, increase in whiteness or brightness created by the presence of optical brighteners.

Appliqué Shaped piece of fabric placed over a second fabric; raw edges are turned under and secured with blind stitches or embroidery stitches.

Appliqué, reverse Needlework in which artisans layer fabrics and cut decreasing sizes of shaped areas from each fabric, turning the raw edges under and stitching the folded edge to each subsequent layer until the base fabric is reached; used in the production of Molas.

Aramid A manufactured synthetic fiber with high temperature and flame resistance.

Area rugs Soft floor coverings that range in size from 27 inches by 54 inches to 6 feet by 9 feet, and are available in a wide variety of shapes; moveable.

Arm caps Accessories used to protect the arms of upholstered furniture; also called arm covers and armettes.

Armure Jacquard-weave fabrics distinguished by small motifs in which the warp yarns float on the face of the fabrics and the filling yarns float on the back, producing a pebbly surface; two sets of yarns are used.

Artificial silk Name used initially for manufactured fibers invented as substitutes for silk; name discontinued in the mid-1920s when the name rayon was adopted.

Asbestos Natural mineral fiber; although fireproof, use of the fiber has been discontinued because it is a known carcinogen.

ASTM International Acronym for American Society for Testing and Materials; a not-for-profit, voluntary scientific association having 132 committees that develop full-consensus standards for products, materials, or processes.

Astrojets Dye-loaded needles.

Athey shade Variation of the conventional Roman shade in which two shades are used, with one raised and one lowered for full closure.

Atmospheric fading See *fume fading*.

Aubusson rugs French rugs characterized by classic designs, soft pastel colors, and a fine loop pile.

Austrian shade Window covering constructed of textile fabric that is vertically shirred to create lengthwise bands of horizontally draping folds.

Auxochromes Components of dyestuffs that are responsible for the selective absorption and reflection of light waves; determine the hue.

Average density Average density, D, considers pile height (finished thickness) and average pile weight to indicate the true density of floor covering structures; calculated by multiplying the average pile weight in ounces per square yard by 36 and dividing the product by the average pile thickness in inches.

Awnings Rigid structures that may be composed of metal or molded polymer sheeting or of textile fabric stretched and held over a rigid frame; generally mounted as exterior overhead treatments to provide protection from weather elements.

Azlon A manufactured synthetic fiber composed of regenerated naturally occurring proteins.

Backfilled Use of a large amount of sizing on fabrics that generally have lower fabric counts; also known as loading.

Bacteria Extremely simple vegetative plant forms that can react with perspiration to cause odor and can cause infection and slow the healing process; also referred to as a microbe.

Balanced construction   Weave structure in which there is an equal number of warp and filling yarns.

Balloon shades   Window coverings composed of textile fabric that form balloon-like puffs when they are raised.

Bamboo   Family of fast-growing woody grasses found in warm climates and used for the production of rayon.

Base yarn   Foundation yarn in decorative yarns; determines yarn length.

Basket weave   Interlacing pattern in which two or more warp yarns, side by side, interlace with one or more filling yarns.

Bast fiber   Classifies cellulose fibers retrieved from stem portion of plants (e.g., jute, linen, ramie, and hemp).

Batch dyeing   Dyeing relatively small quantities or batches of carpet in a discontinuous-dyeing operations, using a carpet winch, a jet beck, or a horizontal beam-dyeing machine.

Bath mats   Relatively small textile floor covering used to absorb moisture when bathers step on it.

Bath rugs   Relatively small scatter rugs used in the bathroom.

Batik   Hand print produced by artisans who apply melted wax to fabric areas that are to resist dye penetration.

Batons   Rods used manually to open and close curtain and drapery panels; also known as curtain tenders.

Battening   In weaving, beating the filling picks against those already in place, aligning them parallel.

Batting   Three-dimensional fibrous structure that is bonded into a relatively flat nonwoven fabric; three-dimensional fibrous structure used as filling in quilts and comforters.

BCF yarn   See *bulked continuous filament*.

Beam dyeing   Immersing a beam wound with warp yarns or a full width of carpet into a dyebath when the dye liquor is forcibly circulated.

Bearding   Development of long fiber fuzz on loop pile floor coverings; caused by snagging and poor penetration of pile yarn bundle by adhesive.

Beater bar   Loom device used in battening; also known as the lay.

Bedding   Includes sheets, covers, blankets, comforters, pillows, pillowcases, quilts, bedspreads, pads, and all other textile fiber products used or intended to be used on or about a bed.

Beetling   Finish in which heavy wooden planks hammer the surface of linen fabric to flatten the cross section of the yarns to increase the surface reflection.

Below-grade   Below ground level.

Berber yarn   Speck yarn, hand-spun by peoples of northern Africa, composed of naturally colored wool; simulated by spinning fiber-dyed acrylic.

Biaxial weaving   Interlacing in which the warp and filling yarns cross at right angles.

Bicomponent fiber   Fiber composed of two or more generically similar polymer compounds.

Biconstituent fiber   Fiber composed of two or more generically dissimilar polymer compounds.

Binder or tie yarn   Yarn used to secure fancy yarn to base yarn in complex, decorative yarns.

Birdseye piqué   Dobby woven curtain fabric with small, diamond-shaped designs.

Bishop's sleeve treatment   See *pouf window treatment*.

Blanketing, double-faced   Blanketing woven with one set of warp yarns and two sets of filling yarns, with one set of filling yarns carried to the face and one set of filling yarns carried to the back; often has different colors on each side.

Blanketing, thermal   Leno-woven blanket that is lightweight and lofty for thermal insulation.

Bleaching agents   Agents and compounds, such as sunlight, hydrogen peroxide and sodium hypochlorite, used to remove unwanted color.

Bleeding   Loss or migration of color when dye mixes with fluids.

Blended filaments   Yarns formed by combining two generically dissimilar filaments immediately after extrusion.

Block print   Hand print produced by artisans who press a hand-carved, dye-covered block onto fabric surface.

Blotch print   Color style in which fabric background is printed, leaving undyed design motifs.

Bobbin   Device that holds the filling yarns when it is inserted by the shuttle.

Bobbinet   Transparent net with six-sided openings that appear round; produced by raschel stitching; used as a base for Tambour-embroidered appliques.

Bobbin lace   Lace created by artisans manipulating multiple pairs of bobbins to twist and cross yarns.

BOCA   Acronym for Building Officials and Code Administrators.

Boiling off   Washing silk to remove the natural gum called sericin.

Bonded-web fabric   Nonwoven fabric produced by applying adhesive or heat to webs of fibers.

Bottom fabrics   Fabrics used underneath the deck of upholstered furniture to conceal the interior components and give a finished look.

Bouclé yarn   Complex yarn with pronounced, closed loops that vary in size and spacing.

Bow   Indicates an off-grain problem.

Boxing   Wrapping strips of fabric around front and sides of upholstered cushions and throw pillows.

Bracket   Used in Axminster weaving; formed by linking three or four 3-foot spools that carry the pile yarns.

Braiding   Diagonal interlacing of three yarns.

Breaking   Process used in retrieving linen fibers from the flax plant; breaks up or crumbles the rotted woody core.

Breaking force (load)   Indicates the load required to rupture a fiber, yarn, or fabric.

Breaking tenacity   Strength reported as force per unit of linear density, for example, grams per denier (gpd or g/den) or grams per tex (gpt or g/tex).

Broadloom   Carpet produced 54 or more inches wide; does not identify a method of construction and carries no implication of quality.

Browning   Staining of pile yarns as water wicks upward from overwetted jute carpet and rug backing yarns.

Brushing   Aligning pile surfaces using straight wires; introduces pronounced fabric nap or pile sweep.

Brussels   Name used earlier for loop pile carpet woven on a Jacquard loom; now, all carpet woven on a Jacquard loom is called Wilton carpet.

Bulk or apparent volume   See *apparent volume or bulk*.

Bulked continuous filament (BCF)   Filament-length fiber given a multidimensional configuration to increase the apparent volume.

Bullion   Fringe composed of metallic-colored strands; used as decorative trimming.

Bundle penetration   Adhesive penetration of the pile yarns in tufted constructions; helps to prevent individual staple or filament fibers from being pulled out of the yarns and rubbed into fuzz and pills on the carpet surface.

Burling   Repair of imperfections in textile floor coverings.

Burnt-out print   Print produced with acid instead of dyestuff; weak acid is used to etch out or destroy an acid-degradable fiber in selected fabric areas, leaving a transparent ground composed of an acid-resistant fiber; also know as etched-out print or acid print.

Burnt gas fumes   Such atmospheric gases as nitrogen dioxide and sulfur dioxide; may cause fading or color change with colored textiles.

Bursting strength   Force (load) required to rupture or burst a knitted fabric.

Cable yarn Simple yarn formed by plying two or more cords.

CABO Acronym for Council of American Building Officials.

Café curtains Unlined window coverings used alone or in combination with draperies; frequently constructed with scalloped headings and hung by rings looped over a rod.

Calendering Industrial ironing using heated and highly polished cylinders.

Calico Lightweight, plain-woven fabric characterized by small, colorful, printed motifs and solid-colored ground.

California Technical Bulletins California Bulletin #117 (CAL 117) is a small scale upholstery fabric flammability test. California Bulletin #133 (CAL 133) is a full scale upholstered seating flammability test.

Candlewicking An embroidery technique in which the design motifs are created by the extensive use of French knots; collectively, the knots create a recognizable pattern.

Candlewick yarn Four-ply yarns composed of unmercerized cotton.

Cane Long, hollow or pithy, bamboo-like grass retrieved from the rattan, a climbing palm; used in hand-woven chair seats and Roman shades.

Cantonniére Rigid overhead window treatment mounted flush to the wall, framing the window; has a curved cornice and side panels that extend to the floor.

Canvas Base fabric used in needlepoint stitching.

Canvas, coarse Canvas with three to seven meshes per inch; used for rugs.

Canvas, double-mesh Canvas which has closely spaced pairs of warp and filling yarns; also known as penelope canvas.

Canvas, fine Canvas with 18 or more meshes per inch; used for petitpoint work.

Canvas, medium Canvas with 10 to 12 meshes per inch; used for needlepoint items such as chair seat coverings.

Canvas, single-mesh Canvas which is plain woven.

Canvas embroidering See *needlepoint stitching*.

Cape Cod curtains Window treatment in which single-tier café curtains are combined with ruffled, tied-back panels; also known as cottage curtains.

Carbonizing Using weak acid to degrade cellulosic matter (e.g., cockle burrs, twigs, in wool fleece).

Carded yarns Yarns spun of both long and short cotton fibers and having a relatively low degree of fiber alignment.

CARE Acronym for Carpet America Recovery Effort.

Carding Combing fibers to align them in the yarn production process.

Carpet Singular as well as plural form of term used to identify textile floor covering securely attached to the floor; carpets and carpeting are incorrect forms.

Carpet modules Floor coverings, generally 18-inches square, that are laid wall-to-wall; may be installed with no adhesive or with releasable or permanent adhesive.

Carpet winch Vessel used for dyeing full widths of carpet which is folded or plaited and fed into the dye liquor; a type of batch dyeing.

Cascade loop shade Window covering having horizontal tucks in the fabric panels; soft folds form when the shade is raised.

Cascades Nonrigid side window treatments composed of gathered fabric falling in folds of graduated length; normally hung behind ends of swagged valence.

Casement General term for curtain and drapery fabrics that have medium weight and some degree of transparency.

Cashmere Fine, soft fiber retrieved from Cashmere goats.

Casing Opening formed by hemming the upper edge of window covering fabric and through which a rod is inserted.

Cattlehair Natural material used earlier as a filling in upholstered furniture cushions and in carpet cushions.

CC system   Cotton count system; used to indicate the size or count or number of yarns spun on the cotton yarn spinning system; gives the yarn count based on length per unit of weight; is an indirect yarn numbering system.

CDC   Acronym for Centers for Disease Control.

Cellubiose unit   The basis repeating unit in natural cellulose fibers.

Certification marks   Coined names and stylized logos that may be used on the labels of end products that conform with fiber content specifications or performance specifications established by the owner of the mark.

CFR   Acronym for Code of Federal Regulations.

Chain warp yarns   Warp yarns used in machine-woven floor coverings.

Char length   The distance of fabric damage produced by flame in standard flammability test methods.

Cheeses   Yarn packages.

Chemical washing   Use of chlorine or acetic acid and glycerin to simulate the prized sheen and soft luster of older Oriental rugs that were dyed with natural rather than synthetic dyestuffs; also known as culturing and luster washing.

Chenille carpet   Soft floor covering woven with chenille yarns as the pile yarns.

Chenille spread   Bedspread fabric produced with closely spaced pile tufts inserted by tufting.

Chenille yarn   Yarn-like strand cut from leno-woven fabric that has fine warp yarns and coarse filling yarns; fluffy strand is said to resemble a caterpillar.

Chroma   See *intensity*.

Chromophores   Components of dyestuffs that are responsible for the quantity of waves reflected, influencing the value of the hue.

Circular braids   Narrow, often decorative strands created by interlacing yarns or yarn-like strands around a textile cord.

Cleaning code   Letter codes used with upholstery fabric to identify the recommended method of cleaning.

Clipped dot or spot   See *dot or spot weave*.

Cloth beam   Cylinder on the loom that holds the woven fabric.

Coarse canvas   See *canvas, coarse*.

Codes   Mandatory practices concerned with the safety and well-being of the general population; they are laws enacted by federal, state, and local governments.

Cohesiveness   The ability of textile fibers to adhere to one another mechanically.

Coir   Fiber retrieved from husk of coconuts; used in pile layer of track-off mats.

Collagen   Protein compound in leather fibers.

Colorants   Dyestuffs used to color textiles.

Color characteristics   Distinguishing features of colors, including hue, value, and intensity.

Colorfastness   Ability of a colorant or dyestuff to retain its original color characteristics.

Color rendering index (CRI)   Scale of 0 to 100, indicating how accurately colors appear under a light source, with a CRI of 100 being the truest color rendering.

Color sealed   Term used to identify solution-dyed fibers.

COM   See *customer's own material*.

Combed yarns   Yarns spun of long cotton fibers having a relatively high degree of fiber alignment.

Combing   Combing fibers to align them and to separate the shorter staple-length fibers in a yarn production process.

Combustible   Material capable of undergoing combustion.

Combustion   Chemical process in which combustible material combines with oxygen to produce heat and light (flame).

Combustion, flameless   Combustion in which no flames are evident (e.g., glowing, smoldering).

Combustion, flaming Combustion in which flame and heat are being produced.

Comforters Bed covering having a face fabric, lofty filling, and a backing fabric.

Commercial interiors Includes stores, shopping centers, offices, schools, hospitals, hotels and motels, libraries and public buildings, religious buildings, restaurants, penal institutions, and the like.

Commercial quilting See *quilting, machine stitching*.

Common names Names of natural fibers (e.g., wool, silk, flax, cotton).

Compacted selvage Selvage in which the number of warp yarns is relatively high to increase the compactness of construction.

Compactness of construction Refers to the number of meshes per inch in needlepoint stitching.

Completion Application of upholstery fabric so the pattern flows uninterrupted down the back pillows, the seat cushions, the seat boxing, the seat front, and the skirt.

Complex cords Decorative yarns composed of two or more complex ply yarns.

Complex plies Decorative yarns composed of two or more complex single or ply yarns.

Complex single yarns Decorative yarns composed of one complex yarn.

Complex yarns Decorative yarns having a base yarn, a fancy yarn, and/or a binder or tie yarn; may be single, ply, or cord.

Compressibility The ease with which a textile structure can be crushed or reduced in thickness.

Compressional loft Ability of a textile structure to recover from compression and regain its original loft; also known as compressional resiliency.

Compression deflection The extent to which a structure resists compression force.

Compression load deflection (CLD) The force required to deflect or compress a specimen assembly a given percentage of its original thickness; reported as the average number of pounds per square inch.

Compression loss The extent to which a structure fails to recover its original thickness after being compressed under a static load; also known as compression set.

Compressional resiliency See *compressional loft*.

Compression set See *compression loss*.

Compressive shrinkage treatment Mechanical treatment used to improve the dimensional stability of fabrics composed of cotton.

Conditioning, textile Placing test specimens in a controlled atmosphere of 70 + or − 2 °F and 65 + or − 2 % relative humidity for a minimum of 24 hours prior to measuring a given property.

Conduction Mechanism by which heat energy, electrical charges, and sound waves are transmitted through solids, liquids, and gases.

Conductors Materials, including textile fibers, that keep electrons flowing, minimizing their accumulation.

Consumer The person or corporation who ultimately pays for a product or service.

Continental rod Flat curtain rod typically 2½ to 4½ inches wide and projecting from the wall surface.

Continuous dyeing Dyeing operation that includes wetting the carpet, applying the dyestuff, steaming, washing, drying, and rolling up the dyed and dried goods; used for large quantities of greige goods.

Continuous filament See *filament*.

Contract design The design of commercial spaces.

Convection Transmission of heat energy by air movement.

Conventional selvage Selvage formed by the continuous filling yarn being turned at each edge to produce a finished, nonraveling edge.

Converters Textile finishers; convert greige goods into finished fabric.

Convertible sofa bed An upholstered sofa with a mattress concealed under the cushions.

Copolymer   Fiber composed of two different monomer units (e.g., polyester, nylon).

Cord yarn   Simple yarn formed by plying two or more plied yarns.

Core-spun yarn   Yarn formed by spinning staple-length fibers around an elastomeric filament.

Corium   The central portion of hides and skins; composed of a network of interlaced bundles of tiny fibers.

Corkscrew yarn   Complex yarn formed by twisting a fine yarn around a heavy yarn; also known as spiral yarn.

Cornice   Rigid overhead treatment mounted over drapery heading and hardware.

Cortex   The main part of a wool fiber that contains cortical cells.

Cottage curtains   See *Cape Cod curtains*.

Cotton   A seed fiber from the boll of the cotton plant.

Cotton felt   Three-dimensional batting structure used as a filling in upholstered furniture.

Cotton spinning system   Spinning system used to spin cotton fibers into yarns.

Courses   Crosswise rows of loops in a knitted fabric.

Covered-core yarn   Yarn formed by wrapping or braiding filaments around an elastomeric filament.

Covering power   The ability of a textile structure to cover or conceal a surface without undue weight.

CPSC   Acronym for Consumer Product Safety Commission; federal agency concerned with the safety of most consumer products; governs marketing of consumer products, including flammable textiles.

Crackle effect   Striated appearance seen with batik prints; created by cracking the wax to allow the dye liquor to run through the cracks.

CRE   Acronym for constant-rate-of-extension.

Crease resistance   Misnomer: creases are planned, wrinkles are not.

Creel frame   Device used to hold the yarn cheeses as the warp yarns are wound onto the warp or loom beam.

Crewel yarns   Fine, two-ply strands composed of wool; used in hand embroidery.

CRT   Acronym for constant-rate-of-traverse.

Critical radiant flux   (CRF) Numerical value determined by converting the distance of flame spread to watts per square centimeter after completion of the flooring radiant panel test; indicates the minimum heat energy necessary to sustain burning of a floor covering that leads to flame propagation.

Crocheting   Interlooping yarns with one needle, in contrast to interlooping yarns with two needles as in knitting.

Crocking   Transfer of color from one material to another as a result of surface rubbing.

Crockmeter   Machine used to measure the colorfastness to crocking.

Cross-sectional shape   Lateral shape of textile fibers (e.g., round, trilobal).

Cross dyeing   Variation of piece dyeing in which a fabric composed of two or more different and strategically placed fibers is immersed into a dyebath formulated with dyestuffs that will be selectively accepted and rejected; produces a multicolored fabric from one immersion process; also known as differential dyeing.

Crystalline   Parallel arrangement of polymer chains anchored by lateral bonds.

Culturing   See *chemical washing*.

Cuprammonium   Conventional rayon fiber.

Curing   Salting the raw hides to retard bacterial action; initial process of converting hides and skins into leather.

Curtain tenders   See *batons*.

Curtains   General term for textile window covering fabrics hung without linings.

Customer's own material (COM)   Textile or nontextile fabric supplied to end-product manufacturers by consumers.

Cuticle Wax-like film that coats the primary wall of cotton.

Cystine An amino acid found in wool fibers.

Dead and buried yarns Yarns carried in the back portion of a Wilton carpet; contribute weight and resiliency.

Deck Portion of furniture frame that supports the seat cushions.

Degree of polymerization The extent to which monomers link to form polymers; the average number of monomer units in the polymer chains of a fiber.

Delamination Separation of attached layers in a textile structure.

Delamination strength The force required to separate the primary and secondary backings of tufted floor coverings.

Delusterants Titanium dioxide particles added to the polymer solutions of manufactured fibers.

Den number Yarn number determined with the denier system; numerically equal to the weight in grams of 9,000 meters of the strand.

Denier Direct yarn numbering system; gives weight per unit of length measurement of a fiber or yarn.

Density Mass or amount of matter per unit of volume of a fiber or other textile structure; reported as pounds per cubic inch or grams per cubic centimeter.

Density factor Product resulting from the multiplication of yarn size, needle count, and stitches per inch used in a pile floor covering.

Density index See *density factor*.

Dents Openings in the reed through which the warp yarns are threaded; help to keep the warp yarns aligned and ensure grain straightness.

Dents per inch Number of openings per inch in a reed; determines compactness of the warp yarns.

Design elements Color, texture, pattern, light, form, and shape; provide a way to evaluate aesthetic considerations for an abstract problem.

Design principles Balance, harmony, rhythm, emphasis, contrast, scale, and proportion; provide a way to evaluate aesthetic considerations for an abstract problem.

Dhurrie (durrie, durry) rugs Flat, hand-woven rugs having a plain, twill, or tapestry interlacing.

Differential dyeing See *cross dyeing*.

Dimensional stability The ability of a textile structure to maintain its size and shape after use and care.

Dimity Sheer, warp-rib woven curtain fabric.

Directional pile lay See *nap*.

Direct yarn numbering system Systems that give the yarn number as weight per unit of length; as yarn number increases, yarn size increases; examples include the denier and tex systems.

Discharge printing Operation in which fabric is piece dyed before the selective application of an agent that will remove the dye, creating undyed motifs and a solid colored ground.

Discontinuous dyeing Dyeing operation in which the wet carpet must be removed from the dyeing machine and dried elsewhere; also known as batch dyeing.

Discretionary income Income available to spend on the basis of want rather than need.

Disposable income Income available to spend after taxes; also known as real income.

Disposable toweling Toweling produced by bonding webs of fibers; may be reinforced with a scrim.

Distortion of yarn Yarns shifting, slipping, or sliding over others, producing areas having different levels of transparency.

Disulfide cross links Linkages (—S—S—) contained in cystine that are attractive to moth and carpet beetle larvae.

Dobby weave Decorative weave requiring many harnesses; distinguished by small, geometric woven-in motifs.

DOC Acronym for Department of Commerce.

Doctor blade   Squeegee-like metal blade used to clean nonengraved portion of metal-covered printing rollers or to transfer dye liquor from a roller to the surface of greige goods.

Document fabrics   Accurate reproduction of historic fabrics using true colors, replicated patterns, and the same fiber composition and fabric construction.

Doilies   Small, decorative tabletop accessories; used under artifacts, fruits, cheeses, etc., or for decoration; often lace.

Dope dyeing   See *solution dyeing*.

Dot or spot weave   Surface figure weave in which extra yarns interlace with the base yarns to create a small motif; yarns floating between the motifs may be clipped away (unclipped dot or spot weave) or left in place (unclipped dot or spot weave).

Doublecloth construction technique   Fabrication in which pile yarns are alternately interlaced in an upper fabric and a lower fabric; as the weaving progresses, the pile yarns joining the two fabrics are cut, resulting in two lengths of fabric.

Double-mesh (penelope) canvas   See *canvas, double mesh*.

Double rubs   A forward and backward oscillation of the cylinder used in the Wyzenbeek test method; equivalent to one cycle.

Down   The undercoating of waterfowl, consisting of clusters of light, fluffy filaments.

Down, all   Labeling term used only when product contains only down.

Down cluster   Consists of down, nestling down, and plumule.

Down fiber   The detached barbs from down and plumules and the detached barbs from the basal end of waterfowl quill shaft, which are indistinguishable from the barbs of down.

Downstream segments   Firms and personnel in the latter part of the production pipeline (e.g., end-product producers), in contrast to those in the earlier portion of the pipeline (e.g., fiber manufacturers).

DPF   Denier per filament.

Drapability   The ability of a fabric to form graceful configurations, such as folds in curtain and drapery panels.

Draperies   Lined textile fabric panels hung to drape gracefully at windows.

Drapes   A verb meaning "hangs gracefully"; incorrectly used as a synonym for draperies.

Draw curtains   Unlined window treatment panels that are drawn in one direction, stacking on one side of the window, or in two directions, stacking on both sides of the window.

Drawing   Stretching a manufactured filament to improve its interior order, especially to increase the orientation of the polymer chains.

Drawing out   In yarn spinning, combining several slivers into one new sliver.

Drop-match patterns   Patterns that repeat themselves diagonally across the width of the carpet; may be half-drop or quarter-drop.

Drops   The portion of a bedspread that hangs vertically from the bed surface to the floor; may be tailored, ruffled, gathered, or shirred.

Drop wire   Device used on industrial looms to stop the weaving when a warp yarns ruptures.

Drum dyeing   Rotating leather in dye liquor rotating in large vessels.

Drycleaning and Laundry Institute International   A service organization which provides education, research, legislative representation, and industry-specific information to its members on dry cleaning and care procedures related to dry cleaning.

Dry extraction cleaning   Absorbent powder that contains water-based cleaning fluids or detergents and a small amount of solvent is sprinkled on the carpet, releasing and absorbing the soil, which is subsequently removed by vacuuming.

Dry foam cleaning   Water-based shampoo in foam form is sprayed onto the carpet, mechanically worked in, and the soil-foam residue is subsequently removed by vacuuming.

Dry spinning   A volatile solvent is used to dissolve the polymer compound, then evaporated after extrusion to allow the filaments   to solidify.

Duplex printing   Printing on both sides of a fabric.

Duppioni silk   A type of silk that results when two silkworms spin their cocoons together.

Durable press finishing   Chemical treatment used to improve the resiliency of fabrics composed of cellulose fibers; creates strong cross-links.

Dust ruffles   Fabric panels dropping from the top of box springs to the floor.

Duvet   Comforters filled with down.

Dye beck   Pressure cooker-like vessel used in dyeing.

Dye liquor   Combination of dyestuff and relatively large quantities of water; used in immersion dyeing operation.

Dye migration   Movement of dye liquor through fabric; necessary for uniform application of the dye; creates uneven level of dye intensity if in-use cleaning agents or procedures promote such movement.

Dye paste   Combination of dyestuff and relatively small quantities of water; used in printing operations.

Dye pigments   Insoluble dyestuffs that may be added to polymer solutions prior to spinning.

Dyes or dyestuffs   Color-producing compounds that are normally soluble in water.

Dyed-in-the-wool   Old adage meaning deeply ingrained and staunchly dedicated; arose from the observation that wool fibers dyed prior to spinning had richer and deeper colors than those produced by dyeing yarns or fabrics.

Dyeing ranges   Systems used in continuous dyeing operations, includes units for all stages of the dyeing and drying operation.

Edge abrasion   Wear caused by friction where the fabric is folded, as is the case at seamlines.

Effect yarn   Fancy or decorative yarn found in complex decorative yarns.

Effective face yarn weight   Weight of the pile yarns in the wear layer of a textile floor covering, not in the backing.

Egress   The act of leaving an interior in the event of fire; the exit way or means of egress should be free of obstructions.

Egyptian cotton   Cotton fiber which originated in the Nile Valley; up to 1½ inches in length.

Elasticity   The ability of a textile structure to be extended and to recover from the extension; also known as stretchability.

Elastic modulus   Initial resistance to deformation stress exhibited by a fiber or other textile structure.

Elastic recovery   The extent to which a fiber, yarn, or fabric recovers from extension.

Electrical conductivity   The relative ease with which a fiber conducts the flow of electrons.

Electrical resistivity   The relative ease with which a fiber resists the flow of electrons.

Electromagnetic spectrum   Range of waves of electromagnetic energy, from extremely short cosmic and gamma rays to relatively long radio waves.

Electrostatic flocking   Using an electrostatic field to induce flock to embed itself into a fabric coating.

Elevator effect   Euphemism for the sagging and shrinking of curtain and drapery panels composed of conventional rayon fibers when the level of relative humidity fluctuates; also known as hiking and yo-yo effect.

Elongation   The ability of a fiber, yarn, or other textile structure to extend or elongate; normally measured and reported as percent elongation at the rupture point.

Embodied energy   Total energy used in the production and delivery of a product.

Embossing   Mechanical treatment used to introduce convex and concave design forms to two-dimensional fabric.

Embroidering Hand or machine stitching of colored yarns in decorative patterns on a portion of a base fabric.

Emerizing See *sueding*.

End One warp yarn.

End-product producers/designers Members of the interior textile industry who design and manufacture textile end products for use in residential or commercial interiors.

EPA Acronym for Environmental Protection Agency; established to protect human health and safeguard the natural environment (air, water, and land), upon which life depends.

Epidermis The top layer of hides and skins.

Etched-out print See *burnt-out print*.

Even twill Twill fabric in which an equal amount of warp and filling are visible on the face of the fabric.

Expanded polymer solutions Polymer solutions having air incorporated to increase the apparent volume.

Extrusion Mechanical spinning of manufactured filaments; polymer solution is extruded or forced through openings in a spinneret.

FAA Acronym for Federal Aviation Administration; controls the flammability of items used in airplanes.

Fabrication techniques Ways to make fabrics (e.g., weaving, knitting, felting, braiding, needlepunching).

Fabric count Numerical indication of compactness of construction; equal to the number of warp and filling yarns per square inch of greige goods; also known as thread count.

Fabric nap See *nap*.

Fabric openness The ratio of the open areas of a fabric to its total area.

Fabric panel Portion of a window treatment in which a number of fabric widths, and, if necessary, a partial width are seamed together.

Fabric stylists Personnel who identify the aesthetic features preferred by contemporary consumers, interpret and forecast trends, and design fabrics that will meet end-use requirements and expectations.

Fabric weights Weights that are placed in the lower hem areas of fabric panels to improve the draping quality.

Face yarns Yarns in the face or pile portion of a fabric or floor covering.

Fade-Ometer® Equipment used in accelerated testing for lightfastness.

Fading Loss of or weakening of the original color characteristics.

False-twist coiling Texturing technique involving continuous twisting, heat setting, and untwisting; introduces apparent volume and bulk but little or no stretch.

Feather fiber The detached barbs of feathers that are not joined or attached to each other.

Feathers The plumage or outgrowth forming the contour and external covering of fowl, which are whole in structure and have not been processed in any manner other than by washing, dusting, chemical treatment, and sanitizing.

Feathers, crushed, chopped, or broken Feathers that have been processed by a curling, crushing, or chopping machine, which has changed the original form of the feathers without removing the quill; the term also includes the fiber resulting from such processing.

Feathers, damaged Feathers that have been damaged by insects, or otherwise materially injured.

Feathers, land fowl Nonwaterfowl feathers derived from chickens, turkeys, and other land fowl.

Feathers, nonwaterfowl See *feathers, land fowl*.

Feathers, quill Feathers that are over 4 inches in length or that have a quill point exceeding 6/16 inch in length.

Feathers, waterfowl Feathers derived from ducks and geese.

Federal Trade Commission (FTC) U.S. federal governmental agency empowered and directed to prevent unfair methods of competition in commerce.

Felting Interlocking of the scales covering wool fiber that results in matting and shrinking of the yarns and fabric; caused by heat, agitation, and moisture.

Fenestration Design, arrangement, and proportions of the windows and doors in an interior.

Festoon Ornamental trimming draped over a valence or other overhead window treatment.

FFA Acronym for Flammable Fabrics Act.

FHA Acronym for Federal Housing Administration; has jurisdiction over the materials used in the interiors of such places as elderly and care-type housing, low-rent public housing projects, and structures insured by FHA.

Fiber cohesiveness Ability of fibers to adhere to one another; affected by such inherent features as the twist in cotton and the scales covering wool; may be introduced with texturing.

Fiber dyeing Immersing loose masses of fiber into dye liquor; frequently used with wool fiber; also known as stock dyeing.

Fiber toughness The ability of a fiber to resist abrasion; determined by a combination of strength and elongation.

Fiber variant Manufactured fiber that is chemically related to other fibers in its generic class but distinguished by a structural feature, such as diameter or cross-sectional shape, or by the inclusion of a polymer additive.

Fiberfill Loose, lofty masses of staple or tow used as filling for pillows; generally polyester.

Fibrillation Breaking off of minute slivers of glass from high-denier glass filaments as a result of flexing and abrasion.

Fibrils Tightly knit bundles of polymer chains in cotton and linen.

Fibroin Protein found in silk.

Fibrous batts 1. Three-dimensional arrangement of webs of fibers that can be bonded with adhesive or heat into essentially flat structures (e.g., nonwoven interfac-

ing fabric). 2. Three-dimensional arrangement of webs of fibers that are stabilized and used as filling or padding in upholstered furniture, quilts, or as carpet cushions.

Filament An extremely long textile fiber, measured in yards, meters, miles, or kilometers; also known as a continuous filament.

Fill leakage The migration or penetration of the filling material through the outercovering; minimized by using a spunbonded interior lining fabric.

Filling-faced satin weave Interlacing pattern in which the filling yarns float over the warp yarns; also known as sateen weave.

Filling knitting Fabrication in which fabric is produced by continuously interlooping one or more yarns from side to side, creating one course after another; also known as weft knitting.

Filling or weft shots Crosswise yarns in woven carpet; used in pairs in Axminster carpet.

Filling pile fabric Fabric in which the pile layer is created with extra filling yarns (e.g., velveteen and corduroy).

Filling-rib weave Variation of the plain weave in which larger or grouped filling yarns create a ribbed or ridged effect in the crosswise fabric direction.

Filling yarns Crosswise yarns in woven fabric; also known as weft yarns and woof yarns.

Film sheeting Nontextile fabric produced by forming polymer solutions into a thin film.

Fine canvas See *canvas, fine*.

Finials Decorative pieces attached to the ends of curtain and drapery rods.

Fireproof fiber A fiber that is unaffected by heat (e.g., asbestos).

Flame propagation Flame spreading (e.g., from original source of ignition to other items within an interior).

Flame-resistant fiber Fiber exhibiting relatively high decomposition and ignition temperatures.

Flame retardant   Agents added to fibers to increase their relative flame resistance.

Flame spread   Distance flame spreads from site of ignition; measured in several flammability test methods.

Flame yarn   Complex yarn produced by twisting a simple yarn around a single slub yarn that has large and elongated areas of low twist.

Flameless combustion   See *combustion, flameless.*

Flaming combustion   See *combustion, flaming.*

Flammable fiber   Fiber that is relatively easy to ignite and sustains combustion until it is consumed.

Flashover   Situation in which all combustible materials burst into flame.

Flat abrasion   Abrasion of a textile while it is fairly flat, such as on the seat cushions of automobiles and interior furniture items.

Flat-bed screen printing   Printing the textile surface by forcing dye paste through openings in a screen mounted above the surface; screens have been treated to resist flow through of the paste wherever the fabric is not to be printed.

Flat braid   Narrow, often decorative strand formed by interlacing a minimum of three yarns or yarn-like strands.

Flaw   Defect in finished fabric.

Flax   A natural cellulose fiber obtained from the stem of the flax plant.

Flesh tissue   The bottommost portion of hides and skins.

Flex abrasion   Abrasion of a textile while it is bent or curved, such as on the arms and curved portions of seat and back cushions, as well as with that covering prominent welts.

Flexibility   Pliability; improves with fiber fineness; needed for freedom of movement.

Flock   Extremely short fibers.

Flocking   Embedding extremely short fibers, known as flock, into an adhesive or resin compound.

Flock or flake yarn   Complex yarn having enlarged segments created by periodically binding thin bits of roving between plied single yarns.

Flokati (Flocati) rugs   Long-pile wool floor coverings woven in Greece; after the pile is formed, the rugs are immersed in a pool of water beyond a waterfall where the swirling waters cause felting of the pile tufts.

Floss yarns   Loosely twisted, six-ply strands composed of mercerized cotton; used in hand embroidery.

Flossa stick   Stick used in weaving rya rugs; pile is formed over the stick to ensure uniform pile height.

Fluorescent compounds   Agents that absorb invisible ultraviolet light and emit visible blue or violet light; used to neutralize the natural yellow hues of wool or yellowed laundered fabrics; create apparent whiteness and brightness; also known as optical brighteners.

Fluorocarbon compounds   Agents used to lower the critical surface energy of fibers so dirt and lint do not adhere to their surface and fluids bead up rather than pass into the fibers.

Flying shuttle loom   Loom having devices to hammer the canoe-like shuttle in the picking operation to send it "flying" through the shed.

FPLA   Acronym for Fur Products Labeling Act.

Foot traffic units   In floor coverings testing, the number of passes by human walkers, not the number of times each specimen is stepped on.

Frames   The number of colors in a Wilton carpet is denoted by the number of frames (e.g., 3-frame, 4-frame).

Free-lay installation   Installation of carpet modules or squares in which the modules are held in place by gravity, not by adhesive.

Frictional heat energy   With floor coverings, for example, the rubbing of the soles on carpet and rug fibers creates frictional heat energy which causes negatively charged electrons to transfer from the fiber surfaces to the body.

Frostiness   Absence of dye on yarn tips; planned and executed by gum printing operations.

Frosting Loss of color as a result of abrasion-induced fiber loss.

FTC Guides for the Household Furniture Industry See *Guides for the Household Furniture Industry*.

Fugitive dye Textile colorant exhibiting poor color-fastness.

Full-grain leather Leather having unaltered grain markings.

Fulling Conversion process used to encourage yarns in fabrics composed of wool to relax and shrink, resulting in a more compact fabric.

Fullness Yardage added when calculating the measurement of the fabric panels.

Full-scale testing Flammability testing done in facilities constructed to replicate a room or a corridor.

Full warranty See *warranty, full*.

Fume or gas fading Color change typically seen with acetate dyed blue, brown, or green with disperse dyestuffs and exposed to oxides of nitrogen or sulfur; blues turn pink, browns turn reddish, and greens turn brownish yellow; can be avoided by solution dyeing the fibers; also known as gas fading and atmospheric fading.

Fungi Extremely simple vegetative plant forms, such as molds and mildew; they feed on cellulosic fibers and sizing, producing stains and odors and weakening and rotting fibers; also referred to as microbes.

Fused selvage Selvage in which the ends of the filling yarns, which must be composed of thermoplastic fibers, are heated to fuse them together; often used with water-jet looms.

Fusion bonding Fabrication technique in which pile yarns are embedded into a vinyl compound coating a base fabric.

Fusion printing Using heat to secure colored acrylic resins to the surface of glass fiber fabrics.

Futons Flexible mattresses typically filled with cotton batting.

Galloon Narrow, tape-like length of trimming; often contains metallic strands.

Garneting A recycling process in which wool yarns and fabrics are shredded and converting them back to fibers.

Gas fading See *fume fading*.

Gasfastness Stability of colorants when exposed to gases.

Gassing-off Period of time that allows the gases and pollutants from new furnishing and finishes to permeate the air while the space is still vacant; ensures less toxicity for the occupants.

Gauge 1. Fractional distance between needles on tufting machines; reported in whole-number fractions. 2. Number of loops per inch of width in knitted constructions. 3. Thickness of polymer film sheeting.

Gauze See *theatrical gauze*.

Gear crimping Texturing process in which intermeshing gears introduce a planar or two-dimensional crimp to filaments; used to improve fiber cohesiveness.

GEI Acronym for Greenguard Environmental Institute.

Generic class Class or name of manufactured fibers; defined in terms of chemical composition (e.g., nylon, polyester, acetate, acrylic, spandex).

Genetically modified cotton A cotton seed that has be genetically modified to resist natural pests.

Genuine suede Suede produced by processing the flesh side of hides and skins.

Ghiordes knot Hand-tied knot used in the production of rya rugs and some Oriental rugs; also known as Turkish knot.

Gimp yarn Yarn formed by spirally wrapping one yarn around another, or by braiding three or more strands around one central yarn; interior yarn is completely covered and outer yarns are often metallic strands.

Ginning Mechanical process used to separate cotton fibers from the cotton seeds.

Glass A manufactured synthetic fiber used in drapery for its flame resistance.

Glass curtains Sheer curtains hung next to the window glass; may or may not be composed of glass fiber; also known as sheers.

Glass transition temperature   Temperature at which lateral bonds within a fiber are disturbed, allowing the position of the polymer chains to be shifted.

Glazed leather   Leather having a high gloss created by the application and polishing of resins, waxes, or lacquer-based compounds.

Glazing   Finishing treatment in which glue, shellac, or resin is added to fabric to create a hard, high shine. See also *chintz*.

Glowing   See *combustion, flameless*.

Glue-down installation   Installation of carpet or carpet modules in which a permanent or releasable adhesive is used; no pad is used; provides greater stability when rolling traffic is present.

Grain   The relationship of warp yarns to filling yarns.

Grain markings   The pores that are exposed when the hair is removed from hides and skins.

Grain, straight   Characteristic of woven fabric in which all warp yarns are parallel and all warp and filling yarns cross at right angles.

Grams per denier   Indicates force per unit of linear density necessary to rupture a fiber, yarn, or thread; also gpd and g/den.

Grams per tex   Indicates force per unit of linear density necessary to rupture a fiber, yarn, or thread; also gpt and g/tex.

Grassing   Using sunshine to bleach fabrics of linen.

Green cotton   Cotton fabric that has not been bleached or treated with any other chemicals, finishes or dye products.

Green standard   A guide to environmentally safe products.

Greenguard Environmental Institute (GEI)   The GEI is an ANSI authorized standards developer that establishes acceptable indoor air standards for products.

Greige goods   Unfinished fabrics.

Grin   Exposure of the backing in floor covering with low pile construction density.

Growth   Unrecovered elongation.

GSA   Acronym for General Services Administration; oversees the selection of materials for federal facilities.

Guide bars   Devices used in warp knitting to position the yarns around the hooks of the needles; as the number of guide bars is increased, the complexity of the interlooping can be increased.

Guides   Collection of labeling provisions issued by the FTC; serve to inform members of a limited portion of the interior textile industry how to avoid engaging in unfair and deceptive labeling practices; advisory in nature.

Guides for the Feather and Down Products Industry   Labeling guidelines that include definitions of terms and recommended procedures for labeling products filled with feather and down.

Guides for the Household Furniture Industry   Labeling guidelines that include advisory practices regarding disclosure of the composition of furniture.

Gum printing   Application of a gum compound to the tips of pile yarns prior to dyeing to prevent dye absorption and migration; develops a frosted appearance.

Gypsum   A high-density, uncrystallized plaster used to coat the back of open-weave burlap wallcovering.

Hackling   Aligning linen fibers prior to spinning.

Hand   The tactile qualities of a fabric, perceived by touch.

Hand embroidering   See *embroidering*.

Harnesses   Devices on looms that support the heddles and form the shed.

Hawser yarn   Simple yarn formed by twisting two or more ropes together.

Head covers   See *antimacassars*.

Headings   Treatments used at the top of curtain and drapery panels to finish the upper edge and distribute fullness evenly across the finished width.

Heat conductivity   Rate at which a material conducts heat; reported as K-value; reciprocal of heat resistivity; synonymous with heat transmittance.

Heat of combustion values   Amount of heat energy generated by burning materials that could cause burn injuries as well as maintain the temperature required for further decomposition and combustion; reported as BTUs/lb.

Heat resistivity   Rate at which a material resists heat flow, that is, how effectively it insulates and prevents heat exchange; reported as R-value; reciprocal of heat conductivity.

Heat sensitivity   See *thermoplasticity*.

Heat setting   Use of heat to stabilize thermoplastic fibers, improving their dimensional stability and that of yarns and fabrics composed of them; also improves resiliency.

Heat transfer printing   Transfer of dyestuff from printed paper to fabric surface; heat is used to cause the dyestuff to sublime, that is, change from a solid on the paper to a gas to a solid on the fabric.

Heat transmittance   See *heat conductivity*.

Heather   Color styling in which two or more colors of fibers are uniformly distributed along the length of a spun yarn or in which two or more colors of filaments have been thrown.

Heddles   Devices on looms through which the warp yarns are threaded; the threading and shedding patterns determine the interlacing pattern.

Held-back draperies   Window treatment in which the panels are held to the side by such devices as cords, chains, and medallions.

Hemp   A natural cellulose fiber produced by the stem of a hemp plant.

Herringbone   1. Variation of the basic twill weave in which the direction of the visual diagonal is continually reversed. 2. Upholstery fabric produced with a herringbone weave.

Hides   Animal hides retrieved from such large animals as deer, horses, and cattle.

High-low   Name given to some multilevel cut and loop carpet surface textures; the higher tufts may have the appearance of shag textures.

High surface tension   See *surface tension*.

Hiking   See *elevator effect*.

Hollow fibers   Manufactured fibers engineered to have hollow interiors for insulation without undue weight.

Homophones   Polymers composed of one type of monomer (e.g., polyethylene).

Honeycomb cellular shade   Window treatment composed of spunbonded polyester fabric which is permanently pleated and paired to create a single- or double-cell structure with an insulating layer of air.

Horsehair   Natural material used earlier as a filling in upholstered cushions.

Hot water extraction cleaning   Properly diluted shampoo is driven into the pile as a spray by high-pressure jets; it is then immediately extracted by the vacuum component of the machine; also called steam extraction.

Houndstooth check   Broken-check motif said to resemble the tooth of a dog; produced by interlacing different colors of strategically placed yarns in a twill weave.

Household textiles   Textile products used in residential interiors, including beddings, towelings, and such tabletop accessories as napkins, tablecloths, and runners.

Huck toweling (*huckaback*)   Toweling woven on a dobby loom and having small filling floats that improve the drying efficiency of the towel.

Hue   Color (e.g., blue, red, green, yellow).

Hydrophilic fiber   Fiber having strong attraction for water; also known as water-loving fiber.

Hydrophobic fiber   Fiber having low attraction for water; also known as water-hating fiber.

Hygroscopic   Fibers that absorb moisture without feeling wet.

IAQ   Acronym for indoor air quality.

ICBO   Acronym for International Conference of Building Officials; publishes the Uniform Building Code.

ICC Acronym for International Codes Council; seeks to establish a single coordinated set of national codes.

Ignition temperature Temperature at which a combustible material combines with oxygen, igniting to produce heat and such other combustion by-products as light and smoke; also known as kindling temperature.

Ikat Hand print produced by artisans who tie off selected areas of bundled warp yarns and dye them prior to weaving.

Impact or structurally borne sounds Sounds generated by impacts, such as walking, jumping, dropping items on the floor, etc.; concern is for their transmission as noise to interior spaces below.

Impact insulation class (*IIC*) Numerical value used to indicate the effectiveness of a floor, carpet, cushion, or combination in reducing noise transmission; IIC values are roughly equal to the INR values plus 51.

Impact noise rating (*INR*) Numerical value used to indicate the effectiveness of a floor, carpet, cushion, or combination in reducing noise transmission; INR values are roughly equal to IIC values minus 51.

Implied warranty See *warranty, implied*.

Indirect yarn numbering systems Systems in which the yarn number is determined as the length per unit of weight; as yarn number increases, size decreases; examples include the cc system, ll system, wc system, and wr system.

Inflation Demand exceeds supply and prices rise.

Ingeo™ Registered trademark of Cargill for natural flame-resistant PLA.

Inherent color Natural color of fibers; may be retained for their natural beauty or removed to avoid interference with fashion colors.

Initial cost Includes such variables as product price, accessories prices, fees for design professional, delivery charges, and installation charges.

Institutional textiles Products such as beddings, towelings, and tabletop accessories designed and selected for use in such hospitality settings as motels, hotels, and restaurants; in such care-type facilities as hospitals; and in such commercial settings as penal institutions and dormitories.

Institutional toweling Twill-woven toweling produced with brightly colored stripes on each long side and constructed into towels used in restaurants.

Insulation See *R-value*.

Insulative value Numerical indication of the ability to prevent the transfer of heat.

Insulators Materials, including textile fibers, that offer resistance to the flow of electrons, allowing them to "pool" on their surfaces, readily available for transfer.

Intensity Terms used to describe the purity or strength of a color (e.g., strong, weak); also known as chroma.

Interim maintenance Maintenance activities designed to assure a high level of appearance retention for an extended period of time and to delay the need for restorative procedures.

Interior acid rain Formed when vapor-phase moisture reacts with such gases as sulfur oxide and nitrogen oxide and forms weak sulfuric acid and weak nitric acid; may attack chemical bonds within fibers, rupturing the polymer chains and weakening the fibers.

Interlock stitch Interlooping yarns to create the appearance of two interknitted fabrics.

In-the-muslin Furniture offered covered in muslin so it subsequently can be covered with a variety of decorative slipcovers.

In-use performance Level of serviceability of a textile product while being used by the customer or client.

ISO Acronym for International Organization for Standardization; engages in the development of standards to help foster international textile trade.

Jabots Nonrigid side window treatments composed of pleated fabric; lower end may be level or angled; normally hung in front of ends of swagged valance.

Jacquard weave   Decorative weave in which independent control of each warp yarns provides for an infinite variety of sheds, and, thus, extremely complex interlacing patterns.

Jaspé   Descriptive of color style in which space-dyed yarns are woven in narrow, lengthwise bands to produce the effect of irregularly placed stripes; similar to strié.

Jersey stitch   Filling knitting stitch distinguished by herringbone-like wales on the fabric face and crescents or half-moon courses on the fabric back; subject to running.

Jet beck   Vessel used in the discontinuous dyeing of carpet in rope form; dye is introduced by jets.

Jet printing   Using jets precisely to deliver dye liquor to create detailed designs and pattern repeats.

Jet spraying   Using pressurized dye jets to spray dye liquor onto skeins of yarns.

Jute   A natural cellulose fiber used in carpet backing.

Kapok   A cellulosic fiber obtained from the seed pods of the kapok tree; use as a filling material has diminished.

Keratin   Protein found in wool fibers; composed of 18 alpha amino acids.

Khilim (Kelim, Kilim) rugs   Rugs woven in eastern European countries; may have stylized designs depicting flowers, animals, and other natural things; may have slits; reversible.

Kindling temperature   See *ignition temperature*.

Knap yarn   See *nub yarn*.

Knee-kicker   Device used to grip and anchor the edges of carpet over the pins in tackless strips.

Knife-edge treatment   Use of a plain seam to join the fabric pieces of upholstery cushions.

Knit-de-knit crinkling   Texturing technique in which multifilament yarns are first knitted into a fabric that is then heat set and, subsequently, de-knitted or unraveled; introduces a wavy configuration.

Knit-de-knit space dyeing   Combining jet spraying with knit-de-knit crinkling to produce a texturized, space dyed (variegated) yarn.

Knitting   Interlooping yarns to create a fabric.

Knop or knot yarn   Complex yarns in which bits of tightly compacted and contrastingly colored fibers are incorporated into nubs.

Kraftcord   Heavy, cord-like strands used in the back layers of woven floor coverings.

K-value or K-factor   Numerical value that reports the rate at which a material conducts heat.

Lambrequin   Rigid overhead window treatment with a straight cornice and side panels that protrude some distance from the wall and extend some distance down the sides of the window.

Lappet weave   Surface-figure weave in which extra warp yarns are shifted laterally to create a zigzag surface pattern that resembles hand embroidery.

Large-scale test methods   Laboratory procedures which require large test specimens, in contrast to small-scale testing which requires small test specimens.

Lastrol   A generic subclass of elastic olefin.

Latex foam   Natural rubber or synthesized rubber having tiny, air-filled cells; used as an upholstered cushion filling material and as a carpet cushion material.

Launder-Ometer®   Equipment used in accelerated testing for colorfastness to laundry and dry-cleaning agents.

Lay   See *beater bar*.

Leadership in Energy and Environmental Design (LEED)   Green Building rating system for developing high performance, sustainable buildings.

Leaf   Classifies cellulose fibers retrieved from the leaf portion of plants (e.g., abaca, banana, sisal).

LEED   Acronym for Leadership in Energy and Environmental Design.

LEED Accredited Professional Accredited design professionals who have the knowledge and skills to supervise the LEED certification process.

Left-hand twill Twill interlacing in which the visual diagonal ascends from left to right.

Leno-reinforced selvage Selvage in which a leno weave is used in the selvage areas.

Leno weave Decorative weave in which paired warp yarns cross as they encircle and secure the filling yarns.

Level of light transmission Degree to which light can pass through a medium.

Level of openness Relative opacity of fabric; see also *fabric openness*.

Licensing programs Voluntary programs in which companies sell the right to use their company-owned processes.

Life-cycle cost (*LCC*) The total cost of a product during its expected use-life; includes initial purchase costs, installation charges, and long-term maintenance expenses; the total LCC values of several products may be amortized according to their respective life expectancies to show the annual use-cost of each.

Lightfastness Colorfastness to light.

Light reflectance factor (*LRF*) Numerical value indicating the percentage of incident light being reflected by a carpet surface; complement of the LRF indicates the percentage of incident light being absorbed.

Light transmittance value Numerical value indicating the amount of light passing through smoke generated during flaming and nonflaming conditions; values are converted into specific optical density values.

Limited warranty See *warranty, limited*.

Limiting oxygen index (*LOI*) Numerical value identifying the amount of oxygen required to support the combustion of a textile fiber.

Line Extremely long linen fibers, ranging from 12 inches to more than 24 inches.

Linear density Weight or mass per unit of length; denier and tex indicate linear density.

Linens In earlier years, used as a collective term for sheets, towels, table cloths, napkins, and related products composed entirely or primarily of linen fibers; although the use of linen fabric in these goods has declined significantly, the term continues to be used.

Liquor ratio Ratio of pounds of dye liquor to pounds of greige goods.

Llama Hair fiber retrieved from the South American llama, a domesticated animal of the camel family.

LL system Linen lea yarn numbering system; used to determine number of yarns produced on the linen spinning system; the ll number is equal to the number of 300-yard hanks of yarn produced from one pound of fiber.

Lofty Quality of bulk without weight.

Loom beam Cylindrical device used on the loom to hold the supply of warp yarns.

Longitudinal configuration Lengthwise shape and form of textile fibers.

Loop or curl yarn Complex yarns with open, airy loops.

Loose-pillow styles Style of upholstered furniture having pillows that can be shifted or removed.

Lumen Hollow core of cotton fibers that becomes smaller as the fiber grows and matures.

Luminosity See *value*.

Luster The brightness of a fiber, yarn, or fabric; affected by cross-sectional shape, surface texture, presence or absence of delusterants, finishing agents, directional pile lay, etc.

Luster washing See *chemical washing*.

Lyocell Manufactured cellulose-based fibers composed of cellulose derived from trees grown on managed tree farms.

Machine embroidering See *embroidering*.

Machine stitching See *quilting, machine stitching*.

Macramé Relatively heavy fabric constructed by knitting and twisting textile cords.

Magnuson-Moss Warranty Act U.S. Congressional law governing product warranties.

Malipol Mali technique in which pile yarns are incorporated into the chain-stitched layers of base yarns.

Manufactured fiber producers Members of the industry who manufacture usable fiber forms using monomers extracted or synthesized from natural compounds.

Marled Descriptive of the color styling produced by spinning together two differently colored rovings.

Martindale abrasion test method Method used to evaluate the flat abrasion resistance of fabric.

Material Safety Data Sheet Documentation that identifies hazardous chemicals and the health hazards for individuals coming into contact with such items.

Mattress covers Beddings designed to completely encase the mattress or to cover only the exposed surfaces; may have vinyl film sheeting to protect against moisture.

Mattress, foam-core Mattresses filled with a slab of rubber or urethane foam; support determined by the foam density.

Mattress, innerspring Mattress filled with metal springs that are anchored to one another with metal clips or encased in fabric and sewn together.

Mattress pads Beddings designed to provide extra cushioning and to protect the mattress; generally a multi-component quilted structure.

Mechanical flocking Sifting flock through a screen to embed itself in a coated surface.

Medium canvas See *canvas, medium*.

Medulla Soft, central tissue in plant stems.

Melt spinning Heat is used to dissolve the polymer compound; cold causes the filaments to solidify following extrusion.

Members of the trade Interior designers, architects, and other industry members who serve clients and con-

sumers; have access to showrooms that are not open to the ultimate consumer.

Mercerization Treatment of cotton or linen fibers, yarns, or fabrics with NaOH and tension to improve the strength, absorption, or luster.

Meshes per inch Refers to one intersection of yarns used in canvas; number of meshes per inch indicates the compactness of construction.

Metallic yarns Yarns made of colored particles or colored foil encased in clear sheeting that is then slit into thin, yarn-like strands.

Methenamine tablet test Flammability test method in which a methenamine tablet is used as the ignition source, simulating a burning match, an ignited cigarette, or a glowing ember; also known as the pill test.

Microbes See *bacteria* and *fungi*.

Microfiber A fiber with denier of less than 1.

Microscopic voids Minute tunnels or conduits that are lengthwise within fibers; deflect incident light waves, obscuring the appearance of soil.

Migration Movement of dye through fabric; results in varied levels of intensity.

Mildew Growth caused by spore-forming fungi; may result in discoloration, odor, and fiber tendering.

Modacrylic A manufactured synthetic fiber with relatively high flame resistance.

Modal® A registered trade name for a variety of rayon derived exclusively from beech trees.

Modern rugs Oriental rugs produced during the twentieth Century.

Mohair Hair fiber retrieved from Angora goat; often used in loop yarns.

Moiré Finish characterized by a wood-grain or water-marked effect.

Moisture absorbency Ability of textiles to absorb moisture; affects dyeability, static buildup, cleanability.

Moisture regain values Calculations of the ability of fibers to absorb vapor-phase moisture; % moisture regain is determined by subtracting the dry weight of a specimen from its conditioned weight, dividing the result by the dry weight, and multiplying by 100.

Molas Textile accents created with a reverse appliqué technique.

Monofilament yarn Simple yarn composed of a single filament; used in sheer curtain fabrics and as transparent sewing thread.

Monomer Basic building block of textile fibers; several monomers are linked end-to-end to form polymers.

Mordant Compound, usually metallic salt, used to increase the attraction between fibers and dyestuffs.

Moresque Descriptive term used to identify color effect of ply yarn formed by twisting different colors of single yarns.

Mosquito netting Transparent leno-weave fabric used as a curtain-like bed canopy in tropical climates, forming a barrier against mosquitoes.

Moth resistance Ability of wool fibers to resist attack by moth larvae; may be permanently incorporated by introducing a methane group between the sulfur atoms.

Multifilament yarn Simple yarn composed of several filaments.

Multi-tier café curtains Window treatment style in which tiers of café curtains overlap one another.

MVSS 302 Acronym for Motor Vehicle Safety Standard No. 302; designed to reduce deaths and injuries to motor vehicle occupants caused by vehicle fires, especially those originating in the interior of the vehicle from sources such as matches or cigarettes.

Nailhead trimming Using nails to secure heavier upholstery coverings, such as genuine leather to framework.

Nanometer Unit of measure equal to one billionth of a meter.

Nanotechnology A study of the control of matter on an atomic or molecular scale.

Nap Directional orientation of yarns in pile layers; also known as pile sweep, pile lay, and directional pile lay.

Napery General term for tablecloths and napkins.

Naphthalene Agents used to make wool moth resistant.

Napkins, cocktail Small napkins, generally five inches square.

Napping Conversion operation in which fiber ends are teased to the surface, making it fuzzy, soft, and warmer.

Natural colored cotton Cotton grown naturally in colors of browns, greens, tans, green and rust.

Natural fiber suppliers Members of the industry who retrieve fibers from such natural sources as sheep, cotton and flax plants, and cocoons.

Natural rush Strands produced by twisting two or three flat cattail leaves together.

Needle count Number of needles per crosswise inch on tufting machines.

Needlepoint stitching Embroidering on canvas.

Needlepoint weave Misnomer; used for Jacquard-woven tapestry having the appearance of hand-stitched needlepoint.

Needlepunching Fabrication techniques in which barbed needles are used to introduce a mechanical chain-stitch in a fibrous batting.

NEISS Acronym for National Electronic Injury Surveillance System.

New wool See *wool, new.*

NFPA Acronym for National Fire Protection Association; voluntary scientific association concerned with fire safety.

NFPA 101® Life Safety Code Publication of the NFPA; includes recommendations to reduce the extent of injury, loss of life, and destruction of property from fire; includes the design of egress facilities permitting the prompt escape of occupants from burning buildings or into safe areas within the buildings.

NFPA 701 Standard methods of fire tests for flame-resistant textiles and films; includes small-scale and large-scale test methods.

NHTSA Acronym for National Highway Traffic Safety Administration; oversees the flammability of items used in motor vehicles.

NIST Acronym for the National Institute for Standards and Technology.

Noil Relatively short cotton staples; separated and removed when producing combed cotton yarns.

Noise Unwanted sound.

Noise reduction coefficient (*NRC*) Numerical value that indicates the effectiveness of textile floor and wallcoverings at absorbing sound.

Noise transmission Transmission of unwanted sound to other interior areas; especially important in multilevel structures, where impact sounds can be transmitted to the interior spaces below.

Noncellulosic manufactured fibers Fibers manufactured from compounds other than cellulose; includes such fibers as nylon, polyester, acrylic, and spandex.

Noncombustible fiber Fiber that does not burn or contribute significant amounts of smoke; may undergo pyrolysis.

Nonwaterfowl feathers Feathers derived from chickens, turkeys, and other land fowl.

Nonwoven fabric Fabric produced by stabilizing fibrous batts.

Nottingham lace Flat lace or net with warp and filling yarns; machine-made.

Nub yarn Complex yarn with tightly compacted projections created at irregular intervals along its length; also known as spot or knot yarns.

Nylon A manufactured synthetic fiber commonly used in carpeting and upholstery fabric.

Nylon cap Web of nylon fibers needlepunched into face of primary backing; color-coordinated with pile yarn.

Off-grain Yarn alignment that exhibits filling bow or filling skew.

Off-grain fabric A fabric in which the warp and filling yarns do not intersect at a right angle.

Oil-borne stain Stain carried by an oily compound.

Olefin A manufactured synthetic fiber used in wallcovering, rugs and upholstered furniture.

Oleophobic Oil-hating; resistant to oily soil.

Ombré Descriptive of the color styling produced by a gradual change in the level of intensity of a single hue.

One-way draw draperies Window treatment on a traverse rod that allows the movement all of the fabric to one end of the rod.

Opacity Level of fabric openness in which light is not permitted to pass through fabric.

Opening and cleaning Initial operation in yarn spinning process; opening the bale of cotton and cleaning the fibers.

Optical brighteners See *fluorescent compounds*.

Optical properties Fiber characteristics such as color, luster, apparent whiteness and brightness, and soil hiding.

Organic cotton Cotton grown without synthetic chemicals.

Organic wool Wool that is produced in accordance with federal standards for organic livestock production.

Organically grown Fibers cultivated on land that has been chemical free for a minimum of three years, and without the use of chemicals.

Oriental design rugs Machine-made rugs having traditional Oriental patterns; generally woven on an Axminster loom.

Oriental rugs Hand-woven rugs having hand-knotted pile tufts; see **Ghiordes knot** and **Sehna knot**.

Oriented Polymer arrangement in which the polymer chains are aligned in the direction of the long axis of the fiber.

Oscillatory Cylinder Method   Test method used to measure the abrasion resistance of textile fabrics; also known as ASTM D 4157 and the Wyzenbeek test method.

OSHA   Acronym for Occupational Safety and Health Administration; has goal of saving lives and preventing and controlling disease, injury, and disability.

Ottoman   Filling-rib woven upholstery fabric; has large, flat ribs of equal size and spacing or of unequal size and spacing.

Outline quilting   See *quilting, outline*.

Overdraperies   Draperies that are hung in combination with sheers.

Overprinting   Printing dye paste or pigments over an initial color application.

Over-the-counter fabric   Refers to lengths of piece goods or fabric sold by retail distributors; also called OTC fabric.

Over-the-wire construction technique   Fabrication in which the pile yarns are supported by wires during weaving; knives have smooth or sharp ends to leave the pile in loops or cut tufts as they are removed.

Ozone fading   Color loss as a result of exposure to ozone.

Package dyeing   Immersing yarns wound on perforated cylinders, that is, packages, into dye liquor held in a dye beck.

Package-injection technique   Using astrojets to repeatedly "inject" packages of yarn with dye liquor.

Palm grass   A natural fiber often used for wooden frame chair seats.

Pattern quilting   See *quilting, pattern*.

Paragraph 25.853   Federal Aviation Administration standard intended to improve the crashworthiness and emergency evacuation equipment of airliners.

Partial blackout   Reduction of the level of light transmission in which most of the incident rays are blocked.

Pattern drafts   Graphic representations of interlacing patterns; also known as point designs and print designs.

Pattern repeat   In patterned goods, a repetition of the full pattern of motifs and ground.

Peace silk   Cultivated silk that is obtained without destroying the silk worms.

Pearl yarns   Fine cords formed by plying three two-ply yarns composed of mercerized cotton; used in hand embroidering.

Permanent press   See *durable press*.

Permeability principle   With respect to the acoustic value of carpet, cushions, and carpet/cushion assemblies, the more permeable the structures, the more efficiently they will absorb sound, lessening the level of noise within an interior; at the same time, the more permeable the structures, the more likely they will allow noise to be transmitted to interior spaces below.

Permethrin   Compound used to modify the disulfide linkages in wool, making the fibers mothproof.

Persian knot   Knot used in authentic Oriental rugs; can be tied to slant to the left or to the right; also known as the Sehna knot.

Persian yarns   Loosely twisted three-ply strands composed of wool; used in needlepoint stitching.

Pick   One filling or weft yarn.

Picking   The second step in weaving in which the filling yarn or pick is inserted through the shed.

Piece dyeing   Immersing piece goods into dye liquor.

Pigment print   Color styling in which opaque pigments are applied.

Pigments   Insoluble dyestuffs.

Pile construction density   Value indicating number of pile tufts per square inch; with tufted constructions, calculate by multiplying the needle count by the stitches per inch; with woven constructions, calculate by multiplying the pitch divided by 27 by the number of rows or wires per inch.

Pile height   The length of the pile tufts above the backing.

Pile lay   See *nap*.

Pile reversal Pile yarns crushed to lay in opposing directions; area appears as a large stain; also known as watermarking, shading, and pooling.

Pile sweep See *nap*.

Pile thickness Average thickness of the pile material above the backing.

Pile warp yarns Warp yarns used to form pile layer; used with velvet and most woven floor coverings; also known as face yarns.

Pile yarn integrity Ability of pile yarns to retain their original level of twist.

Pile yarn weight The weight of the yarns used in the wear layer and those portions of the pile yarns that extend into the backing layer; expressed in ounces per square yard.

Pile yarns See *face yarns*.

Pilling The formation of pills on the surface of textile fabrics.

Pillow sham Decorative casing used for bed pillows for daytime display.

Pillow, bedrest Pillow rest having back and arms.

Pillows, bed Pillows used for sleeping; generally 20 to 21 inches wide and varying in length.

Pillows, bolster Cylindrical or lozenge-shaped pillows that may be from 40 to 50 inches in length.

Pillows, boudoir Rectangular pillows, 12 inches by 16 inches; also known as breakfast pillows.

Pillows, breakfast See *pillows, boudoir*.

Pillows, European Pillows that are 12-inches square.

Pillows, king-size Bed pillows constructed for use with king-size mattresses; 37 to 38 inches long.

Pillows, neckroll Cylindrical pillows that range from 6 inches by 14 inches to 7 inches by 17 inches.

Pillows, queen-size Bed pillows constructed for use with queen-size mattresses; 30 to 31 inches long.

Pillows, round Decorative pillows that are normally 12 inches in diameter.

Pillows, standard Bed pillows that are constructed for use with twin- or double-size mattresses; 26 to 27 inches long.

Pillows, Turkish Decorative pillows which have gathered corners and are 16-inches square.

Pills Unsightly bunches or balls of fiber formed on fabric surfaces.

Pima cotton Cotton grown in the American southwest; fine and up to $1\frac{5}{8}$ inches in length.

Piña A leaf fiber obtained from the pineapple plant.

Pinned-up panels Window treatment style in which the fabric panels are held by two-piece, stylized magnets or by decorative pins that function like large tie-backs.

Pinsonic melding See quilting, pinsonic melding.

Pitch Number of pile tufts per 27 inches of width in a woven floor covering.

PLA A manufactured dextrose fiber made produced from corn.

Placemat A mat of fabric, paper, vinyl or other materials place at each set of a dining table; typically rectangular, oval or round; may be used instead of a tablecloth.

Plaid Fabric with linear patterns that intersect at right angles to each other.

Plain piqué See *pinwale piqué*.

Plain weave Simple interlacing in which warp and filling yarns alternately cross one another; also known as tabby weave and homespun weave.

Planting Periodically substituting a colored pile yarn for a basic pile yarn in Wilton carpet weaving; reduces quantity of buried yarns and, thus, yarn costs.

Plied slub yarn Complex ply yarns have a decorative slub yarn plied with a simple ply yarn or with a second slub yarn.

Plumules Down waterfowl plumage with underdeveloped soft and flaccid quill with barbs indistinguishable from those of down.

Plush One level, cut pile surface texture; pile height ranges from 0.625 inch to 0.750 inch; also known as velvet and velvet plush.

Ply yarn Yarn formed by twisting two or more single yarns.

Pockets Areas in Jacquard-woven, doublecloth fabrics in which the face yarns and back yarns are not mutually interlaced.

Point designs See *pattern drafts*.

Pollutant gases Atmospheric gases such as oxides of nitrogen and oxides of sulfur that react with vapor-phase moisture to form weak acids; cause shade changes and fiber tendering.

Polyester The most widely used manufactured synthetic fiber.

Polylactic Acid A manufactured fiber made from corn.

Polymer Compound composed of extremely long, chain-like molecules.

Polymer additives Compounds added to polymer solutions to engineer specific properties (e.g., reduced luster, reduced static propensity, colorfastness). See also *additives*.

Polymer ribbons or tape Yarn-like structures produced by slitting film sheeting into long strands of the desired width.

Polypropylene Term commonly used in the interior design industry for olefin fibers and fabrics.

Polyurethane foam Synthesized compound used as a filling for upholstered furniture and as a carpet cushion.

Pooling Collecting of electrons on fiber surfaces, making them readily available for transfer to shoe soles or other surfaces.

Pouf or bishop's sleeve treatment Drapery treatment in which tiers of bouffant or billowed-out areas are created by periodically gathering the fabric panels; also known as bishop's sleeve treatment.

Power stretcher Device used to place uniform stretch over carpet in wall-to-wall installations.

Preventive maintenance Protective cleaning procedures intended to capture soil and grit in track-off, funnel, and concentrated traffic areas.

Primary backing Base fabric into which pile yarns are tufted.

Print design Graphic representation of color positions in textile structures.

Priscilla curtains Window treatment in which ruffled panels overlap at their upper edges and are held-back by ruffled tie-backs.

Producer colored Term used to identify a solution-dyed fiber.

Product showroom Showroom where end-product manufacturers display their merchandise for members of the trade.

Project bid Detailed price listing of all products specified for a particular project.

Project specification A listing of multiple performance criteria that should lead to a single product specification.

Pure down See *all down*.

Pyrolysis Process in which high temperature causes the decomposition of textile fibers and other organic materials.

Quality control work Work undertaken by members of the industry to ensure the quality of their products; often use standard methods of testing and performance specifications.

Quill Device used to hold the filling yarns during weaving; also known as a bobbin.

Quilting To stitch two pieces of fabric and a filling material together; stitches may create a decorative surface pattern.

Quilting, channel See *quilting, machine stitching*.

Quilting, machine stitching Commercial quilting using many needles to join separate components and to impart a surface pattern.

Quilting, outline   See *quilting, machine stitching*.

Quilting, pattern   See *quilting, machine stitching*.

Quilting, pinsonic melding   Commercial quilting using heat and sound waves to meld separate components at specific points; meld points simulate the appearance of sewn quilting stitches.

Quilting, shadow   Hand quilting stitches are used to secure a sheer fabric over an applique to join the layers and give a softened or shadowed appearance.

Quilting, trapunto   Hand technique in which quilting stitches are placed around a single motif in a pattern repeat; subsequently, batting material is inserted into the quilted shape.

Quilts   Multicomponent bed coverings usually having a face fabric, a fibrous or polyurethane batting, and a back fabric; layers are secured with hand or machine quilting stitches.

Quilts, crazy   Quilts in which the fabric pieces are irregularly shaped and vary in size and color styling.

Quilts, patchwork   Quilts in which the fabric pieces or patches are often square or rectangular.

Quilts, patterned   Quilts in which several fabric pieces are shaped and sewn together to create a specific pattern repeat.

Quivit   Fine fiber obtained from the underbelly of the domesticated musk ox.

Radiant energy   Energy, such as heat or light, which is transmitted in waves.

Radiant heat   Heat that is transferred in the form of waves or rays.

Radiation   Mechanism by which heat is transferred in the form of waves or rays.

Raffia   A fiber obtained from the leaves of various species of palm trees; used in long, narrow, yarn-like bands to make woven placemats.

Railroad   See *to railroad*.

Raised fiber surfaces   Fabric surfaces that have been napped or brushed to raise fibers from yarns to give a soft, fuzzy hand; examples are flannelette and flannel.

Ramie   Cellulosic fiber retrieved from stem portion of plants; also called China grass.

Random shear   Multilevel, cut and loop pile in which the uppermost portions of some of the higher yarn tufts are sheared.

Rapier   Device used in picking to carry the filling yarn to the center of the shed where it is picked up by a second rapier and carried to the opposite selvage.

Raschel knitting   Warp knitting operation using up to 30 guide bars; used for knitting fabrics ranging from hairnets to power net to rugs.

Ratiné yarn   Complex yarn with small, uniformly spaced loops of equal size.

Raw silk   Silk from which the natural gum, sericin, has not been removed.

Rayon   A manufactured fiber composed of regenerated cellulose.

Reclined diagonal   Visual diagonal in a twill weave fabric that falls at an angle less than 45 degrees to the fabric grain.

Recycled wool   See *wool, recycled*.

Reed   Comb-like device held by the beater bar; has openings through which the warp yarns are threaded.

Reeling   Silk process in which the natural gum, sericin, is softened and skilled technicians collect the filaments and unwind the cocoons.

Regular diagonal   Visual diagonal in a twill weave fabric that falls at an angle of 45° to the fabric grain.

Regulatory agencies   Municipal, state, or federal agencies that have jurisdiction to oversee and power to regulate product selection and/or marketing.

Relative humidity   The proportion of vapor-phase moisture present in air to the maximum possible at a given temperature; expressed as a percentage.

Relaxation shrinkage Shrinkage of yarns; occurs when yarns recover or relax from strains imposed by manufacturing stresses.

Reprocessed wool See *wool, reprocessed*.

Residential interiors Interiors in private residences (e.g., mobile homes, apartments, condominiums, town homes, free-standing homes).

Residual shrinkage Shrinkage of fibers; fibers become progressively shorter during use and care.

Residue Matter that remains at the end of a burning test.

Resiliency Ability of a textile structure to recover from deformations other than elongation; recovery from folding and bending is commonly referred to as wrinkle recovery and recovery from compression is commonly referred to as crush recovery; see also *compressional loft*.

Resilient batting Three-dimensional fibrous structure that springs back into its original shape after being compressed.

Resin compounds Compounds used to improve the resiliency and dimensional stability of fabrics composed of cellulosic fibers.

Resist printing Immersing a fabric that has been selectively printed with an agent that will resist penetration of the dye liquor.

Restorative maintenance Maintenance involving overall or wall-to-wall cleaning.

Retting Process in which moisture and bacteria or chemicals are used to dissolve the binding agents, known as pectins, in the bark-like covering of flax stalks.

Reused or indirect light Light being reflected from light-colored walls, ceilings, doors, and furnishings.

Reused wool See *wool, reused*.

Reverse blends Fabrics that earlier had been composed of 65 percent polyester and 35 percent cotton are now composed of 65 percent cotton and 35 percent polyester; consumer demand brought about the shift.

Right-hand twill Twill interlacing in which the visual diagonal ascends from right to left.

Rippling Process in which flax stalks are pulled through a coarse metal comb to remove the seeds, which will be processed to retrieve linseed oil.

Roller printing Using engraved copper-covered rollers to transfer dye paste to the surface of fabrics.

Roller shade Fabric or other material mounted on a spring-loaded cylinder mounted on a window frame, allowing the fabric to be pulled down to cover the window or rolled up on the cylinder.

Rollgoods Soft floor coverings available in widths of 9, 12, and 15 feet and long lengths.

Roman shades Window coverings that hang flat at the window until pleats form when panels are raised; may be constructed of textile fabric or woven wood.

Room-fit rugs Loose-laid rugs designed or cut to come within one or two inches of the walls.

Room-size rugs Loose-laid rugs that are designed or cut to come within 12 inches of each wall.

Rope yarn Simple yarn formed by plying two or more cable yarns.

Rotary screen printing Printing textile surfaces by forcing dye paste through openings in cylindrical-shaped screens; selected areas of the screens are treated to resist flow through of the dye paste.

Routine maintenance Practices such as regular vacuuming to remove accumulated dust.

Rows per inch The number of crosswise rows of pile tufts per lengthwise inch in Axminster and chenille floor coverings.

Ruffled, tie-back curtains Window treatments in which ruffled panels do not cross at their upper edges.

Rug Soft floor covering that is loose-laid on floor or over wall-to-wall carpet.

Runner A long, narrow form of a room-fit rug installed in hallways and on stairs.

Rush A wiry stemmed grass which can be woven to made chair seats or backs.

R-value (R-factor) Numerical value indicating how effectively a structure resists heat flow, that is, how effectively it insulates and prevents heat exchange; R-value equals the thickness of the structure divided by its K-value.

Rya rugs Hand-knotted rugs; originated in Scandinavian countries; pile may be from one to three inches.

Rya stick See *flossa stick*.

Salvage maintenance Maintenance procedures used for extremely soiled carpet or for removing built-up residue.

Saran A manufactured synthetic with excellent weathering properties.

Sash curtains Window treatment in which the panels are anchored at their upper and lower edges; typically used on French doors.

Savonnerie rugs French Oriental rugs originally made in a factory used earlier for the production of soap; distinguished by classic designs and soft pastel colors.

Saxony One level, cut pile surface texture; pile height ranges from 0.625 to 0.750 inches; yarn twist is stabilized by heat setting.

SBCCI Acronym for Southern Building Code Council International.

Scales The outer covering of a wool fiber resembling fish scales.

Scatter rugs Small rugs, often 2 feet by 3 feet; often decorative accents.

Schreinering Calendering process in which etched rollers impart minute diagonal "hills and valleys" into the fabric surface; gives soft luster.

Screen printing See *flat-bed screen printing and rotary screen printing*.

Scrim Flat woven fabric with low fabric count; used as backing in tufted floor coverings and as reinforcing layer in needlepunched carpet, hair cushions, and spunbonded fabrics.

Sculptured Multilevel cut and loop pile surface texture; in most cases, the higher loops are all cut and the lower loops are all uncut.

Scutching Linen processing in which the degraded woody core of the flax plant is removed from the linen fiber bundles.

Sea grass Yarn-like structure produced by twisting plied strands of grass into a cord; used in wallcoverings.

Sea Island cotton Variety of cotton grown originally off the coast of Georgia; up to 2½ inches in length.

Seacell® A modified lyocell fiber with a natural anti-inflammatory and skin protection additive.

Secondary backing See *scrim*.

Seed fibers Natural fibers retrieved from the seeds of plants (e.g., cotton, kapok, coir).

Seed yarn Complex yarn with tiny nubs.

Sehna (Senna) knot Hand-tied knot used in the production of some authentic Oriental rugs; also known as Persian knot.

Self-deck treatment Use of the exposed outercovering fabric to cover the deck.

Self-extinguishing fiber Fiber that stops burning when the source of ignition heat is removed.

Selvages Narrow band on each side of a woven fabric; see also *compacted selvage, conventional selvage, leno-reinforced selvage*, and *tucked-in selvage*.

Semi-antique rugs Oriental rugs woven during the latter part of the nineteenth century.

Serging Machine overcasting.

Sericin Natural gum binding silk filaments into a cocoon.

Sericulture The growth of silkworms and the production of cultivated silk.

Set-match patterns Patterns that repeat themselves across the width of carpet or wallpaper; the crosswise repeats may be fully completed or partially completed.

SFU   Acronym for standard fading unit.

Shade   Color feature produced by adding a compound known to absorb all wavelengths, creating black, to a colorant, decreasing its value and luminosity.

Shade changes   Fading of original hue after exposure to such things as sunlight, laundry, and gases; may be evaluated, for example, with the AATCC Gray Scale for Color Change.

Shading   See *pile reversal*.

Shading coefficient (S/C)   Numerical rating that indicates light transmission in relation to temperature flow; calculated by dividing the total amount of heat transmitted by a window and window covering combination by the total amount of heat transmitted by a single pane of clear glass ⅛ inch in thickness.

Shag   One level, cut pile surface texture; pile height may be as high as 1.250 inches; pile density is lower than that of plush and saxony textures.

Shearing   Conversion operation in which raised fiber and pile surfaces are cut to be level.

Shed   V-shaped opening of the warp yarns through which the filling pick is inserted.

Shedding   1. Occurs with new carpet when short lengths of fibers that have accumulated during manufacturing work to the surface; fiber loss is not significant. 2. In weaving operations, using the harnesses to raise some warp yarns and lower others, creating the shed.

Sheers   See *glass curtains*.

Sheet casings   Covers that protect comforters from soil accumulation and abrasion; their releasable closures permit easy removal for laundering.

Sheets, fitted or contour   Sheets constructed with four contour corners to fit the mattress.

Sheets, flat   Sheets constructed with hems at both ends; may be used as top or bottom sheets.

Shift mark   Distorted yarn group.

Shirring   Gathering fabric; seen with Austrian shades and bedspread drops.

Shots   Filling yarns used in machine-woven floor coverings.

Shrinkage   See *relaxation shrinkage*, *residual shrinkage*, and *felting shrinkage*.

Shutters   Decorative panels hung at the sides of windows; may be stationary or unfolded to cover the glass to reduce heat exchange.

Shuttle   Canoe-shaped device used to carry the filling picks through the shed.

Shuttleless looms   Looms which have devices other than shuttles to carry the filling picks through the shed (e.g., grippers, rapiers, jets of water, jets of air).

Silencers   Felt or heavily napped fabric placed under tablecloths; cushion the impact force of dishes, artifacts, etc.

Silicone compounds   Agents used to impart water repellency.

Silk   A natural protein fiber produced by the larva of silk moths; used in apparel and home furnishings.

Silk Latte®   A registered trade name for an azlon fiber; made from milk protein.

Simple cord yarns   Simple yarns formed by twisting or plying together two or more simple ply yarns.

Simple ply yarns   Simple yarns formed by twisting or plying together two or more simple single yarns.

Simple single yarns   Simple yarns formed by spinning staple fibers into a simple yarn or by combining several filaments into a simple yarn with or without twist.

Simple yarns   Yarns having a smooth appearance and a uniform diameter along their length.

Simulated fur fabrics   Pile fabrics formed by incorporating fibers or yarns among base yarns, creating a three-dimensional structure; fiber composition is often acrylic or modacrylic.

Simulated leather   Fabric manufactured by coating a base structure with foam or bonding a base structure with film sheeting; often embossed to impart grain markings.

Simulated suede Fabric manufactured by emerizing a coated fabric to roughen the surface, imparting a suede-like hand and appearance.

Singeing The burning of fiber ends projecting from the surface of a fabric to reduce pilling.

Single-mesh canvas See *canvas, single-mesh.*

Sisal A natural cellulosic, relatively stiff fiber retrieved from the leaves of the agave or yucca plant; used for ropes and placemats.

Skein dyeing Immersing skeins of yarns into a dyebath.

Skew Distorted yarn alignment in woven fabric; filling yarns slant below straight crosswise grain.

Skins Animal skins retrieved from such small animals as lambs, goats, and calves.

Slabs Three-dimensional structure generally composed of synthesized rubber or polyurethane foam; used as filling layer in mattresses and quilts.

Slack tension technique Weaving technique in which the base warp yarns are held under regular (high) tension and the pile warp yarns are held under slackened tension; used to produce terry toweling.

Slashing Adding starch or sizing to the warp yarns prior to weaving to make them smoother and stronger.

Slipcovers Furniture coverings that are cut, seamed, and fitted over the permanently-attached coverings; used for protection and/or decorative purposes.

Slub yarn Complex single yarn with fine and coarse segments along its length, which are produced by varying the level of twist used in spinning.

Smoke density Concentration of smoke passing through light measured numerically as the light transmission value and reported as optical density value.

Smoldering Flameless combustion.

Smoothing Laying pile yarns in one direction after the surface has been brushed.

Sofa bed An upholstered sofa with a hinged back that swings down flat with the seating cushions to form the sleeping surface.

Soil Dirt or other foreign matter that is mechanically held and comparatively easy to remove.

Soil hiding The ability of a fiber or coloration to hide or camouflage dirt; carpet, for example, will look cleaner than it is.

Soil magnification Occurs when soil particles reflect incident light waves through round, nondelustered fiber; carpet, for example, will look dirtier than it is.

Soil reduction Reduction of the quantity of soil accumulated; achieved by chemical finishing agents or by using an extra large denier per filament.

Soil release compounds Fluorocarbon-based compounds increase the surface energy of the fibers, making them more hydrophilic so the water can more readily carry the detergent molecules into the fiber crevices and emulsify and remove the soil material.

Soil repellency Fluorocarbon compounds make textile compounds more oleophobic or oil-hating, as well as more hydrophobic.

Soil shedding Reduction of the quantity of soil accumulated; achieved by using a trilobal fiber that has a microrough surface.

Solution dyeing Adding dye pigments to the spinning solution of manufactured fibers prior to spinning; also known as dope dyeing and producer colored.

Solvent spinning Manufactured fiber spinning technique in which a solvent is used to dissolve the polymer and the solution is extruded into a solvent that is recovered for continued use; used to produce lyocell fibers.

SoySilk® A trade name for Azlon; made from the soybean waste from the tofu manufacturing project.

Space dyeing Dyeing spaces or segments of yarns; produces variegated color styling.

Spandex A manufactured synthetic fiber with excellent elongation and elastic recovery.

Specialty wools   Wool fiber from the goat, camel and rabbit families.

Specific gravity   The density of a fiber relative to that of water at 4°C, which is 1.

Specification listing   A listing of preferred or required features of a product, including such things as appearance, composition, construction features, functional benefits, and performance properties.

Speck yarn   Complex single yarn having small tufts of differently colored fibers incorporated along its length; also known as tweed or flock yarn.

Spike yarn   Complex, loop-type yarns composed of yarns having different levels of twist; the more highly twisted yarn is introduced at a faster rate, causing the extra length to form well-defined kinks or loops; also known as snarl yarns.

Spillover   Refers to the migration of fire from the room of origination to other rooms and/or corridors.

Spinneret   Shower head-like device used for mechanically spinning manufactured fibers.

Spinners   Members of the industry who align and spin staple fibers into spun yarns.

Spinning and twisting   Process in yarn spinning in which fibers that are aligned in yarn-like structures are spun and twisted into a yarn; twisting introduces strength.

Spike yarn   A complex yarn composed of yarns having different levels of twist, also called a snarl yarn.

Spiral yarn   Complex yarn formed by twisting a heavy yarn around a fine yarn; also known as a corkscrew yarn.

Splash yarn   Complex yarn having elongated nubs along its length.

Split leather   Leather fabric produced from an inner layer of hide; lacks natural grain markings.

Spoken warranties   See *warranties, spoken*.

Spontaneous combustion   Combustion process initiated by heat rather than flame.

Spools   Three-foot-long spools that are linked end-to-end to form a bracket; used in Axminster carpet weaving.

Spot yarn   See *nub yarns*.

Sprouting   The protrusion of a tuft above the surface of the wear layer of carpet.

Spunbonding   Fabrication technique in which a web of filaments is stabilized with heat or adhesive binders.

Spunlacing   Fabrication technique in which webs of fibers are mechanically entangled.

SSA   Acronym for Social Security Administration; administers the Medicare and Medicaid programs.

Stackback space   Distance on one or both sides of a window that is allowed for the panels to remain when drawn open.

Stage 1 Fire   Characterizes a fire when only the ignited item is burning.

Stage 2 Fire   Characterizes a fire when all combustible items in a room burst into flames, producing a situation known as flashover.

Stage 3 Fire   Characterizes a fire when the flames spread beyond the burning room into the corridor or passageway.

Stain   Dirt or other foreign matter that is chemically bonded to the fiber surfaces and is comparatively difficult to remove.

Stair tread test   A long-term, service exposure test; carpet specimens are installed without a cushion on heavily used stairs.

Stalwart roller printing   Using large cylinders covered with three-dimensional sponge forms, each cut in the shape of the planned motifs, to print the surface of pile fabric.

Standard performance specification   A performance specification established by, for example, a voluntary scientific association; see also *performance specification*.

Standard test method   A prescribed procedure for measuring a property; established by, for example, a voluntary scientific association.

Staple A relatively short textile fiber; measured in inches or centimeters.

Static propensity Ease with which materials such as textile fibers accumulate electrons and develop electrostatic charges.

Stationary casement panels Window treatments made of open weave fabric which are not designed to be opened and closed.

Steep diagonal Visual diagonal in a twill weave fabric that falls at an angle greater than 45 degrees to the fabric grain.

Steiner tunnel test method See *tunnel test*.

Stiffness Degree of flexibility exhibited by fibers; affects fabric draping quality.

Stitch-bonding Fabrication technique in which knitting stitches are used to stabilize webs of fibers.

Stitch-knitting Fabrication technique in which knitting stitches are used to anchor webs of yarns; also known as knit-sewing.

Stock dyeing See *fiber dyeing*.

Stretch-in installation Technique used to install rollgoods wall-to-wall; see also *power stretcher*.

Strié (*striaé*) Descriptive of color style in which yarns of various shades of the same hue are woven in narrow, lengthwise bands to produce the effect of irregularly placed stripes; similar to jaspé.

Stuffer-box crimping Texturing technique in which yarns are rapidly stuffed into a heated, box-like chamber, backing up on themselves; develops a three-dimensional crimp.

Stuffer yarns 1. Extra warp yarns running in a plane and supporting wales or other woven-in dobby designs. 2. Extra warp yarns running in a plane in the back of woven floor coverings, adding weight, strength, dimensional stability, and thickness.

S twist A left-handed or counterclockwise direction of yarn twist.

Sublimation Occurs when heat causes a dyestuff to change from a solid to a gas to a solid; occurs in heat transfer printing.

Sublistatic printing See *heat transfer printing*.

Sueding Revolving sandpaper-covered disks against a flocked surface; also known as emerizing.

Surface dyeing Staining the surface of leather to impart a fashion color.

Surface noise radiation Movement of surface noise created by such activities as walking, running, and shuffling throughout an interior space.

Surface tension Determined by the affinity that molecules in a compound have for one another, in contrast for a second surface.

Surface texture Visual and textural characteristics of a textile surface (e.g., smooth, rough, short pile, fuzzy, etc).

Susceptibility to heat Characteristic of being affected by heat (e.g., scorches).

Swags Softly draping lengths of fabrics hanging at the sides of windows.

Swivel weave Surface-figure weave in which extra yarns encircle the base yarns to create a motif.

Tabby weave See *plain weave*.

Tablecloths Table coverings produced by weaving, stitch-knitting, knotting and twisting, spunbonding, and extrusion; used for dining and decoration.

Tackless strips Pin-holding strip used in stretch-in tackless installation projects.

Taking up and letting off In the weaving operation, taking up woven fabric and letting off warp yarns.

TAK printing Adding droplets of intense color to the already-colored pile surfaces.

Tambour embroidering Machine stitching that resembles hand chain-stitching.

Tanning Leather processing in which selected mineral substances react with the collagen, rendering the fibers insoluble.

Tapestry weave   Plain weave in which the filling or weft yarns are crammed to completely cover the warp yarns.

Tapestry yarns   Highly twisted, four-ply yarns, which are used without being separated; used in needlepoint stitching.

Tatting   Hand technique in which artisans manipulate one small bobbin to twist fine yarns into open, highly decorative lace.

Tear strength   Force required to continue or propagate a tear in a fabric; can be used to predict the likelihood that a small cut or puncture would become a large tear with continued use of the fabric.

Tenacity   The force per unit of linear density necessary to rupture a fiber, yarn, or thread; reported as grams per denier (gpd or g/den) or grams per tex (gpt or g/tex).

Tencel®   Registered trade name for lyocell by Lenzing Fibers Inc.

Tendering   Weakening of fibers by, for example, sunlight or chemicals.

Tentering   Mechanical treatment used to improve the grain of woven fabrics.

Tensile strength   The force per unit of cross-sectional area necessary to rupture a fabric; reported as pounds per square inch (psi) or grams per square centimeter.

Terry toweling   Toweling having a loop pile on one or both sides of the fabric; also known as Turkish toweling.

Terry velour toweling   Toweling having a loop pile on one side and a cut pile on the other side of the fabric.

Tetrapod walker   Device used in the accelerated testing of carpet for changes in texture and fiber loss; has four, plastic-tipped "feet" that tumble against the carpet surface to simulate foot traffic.

Tex number   Weight per unit of length measurement of a fiber of yarn; numerically equal to the weight in grams of 1,000 meters of the strand.

Textile   Formerly used only in reference to woven fabrics; now applied to fibers, yarns, and fibrous fabrics manufactured in various ways; not applicable to leather and film fabrics.

Textile colorists   Members of the industry who add fashion colors to textiles.

Textile designers   Members of the industry who design textile fabrics.

Textile end products   Goods that are ready for consumer purchase and use; includes such items as apparel, apparel fabric, upholstery fabric, upholstered furniture, curtains and draperies and curtain and drapery fabrics; soft floor coverings, household and institutional textiles, and wallcoverings.

Texturing   Introducing multidimensional configurations to otherwise parallel and smooth filaments.

TFPIA   Acronym for Textile Fiber Products Identification Act.

Theatrical gauze   Plain-woven, stiffened curtain fabric having slightly higher fabric count than cheesecloth; also known as gauze.

Thermal insulation   Heat insulation.

Thermoplasticity   Property that allows a fiber to be softened and stabilized with controlled heat and that results in melting at higher temperatures; also known as heat sensitivity.

Thick-and-thin yarn   Complex single yarn characterized by variations in diameter that are created by varying extrusion pressure.

Thread   Fine, yarn-like strand used for sewing.

Threshold of human sensitivity   The level of static voltage that produces a noticeable shock for most people when it discharges from their bodies; the level is normally 2,500 static volts.

Throwing   In yarn production, plying or twisting monofilaments into multifilaments.

Throwsters   Members of the industry who work in yarn throwing production.

Tidies   Decorative covers placed on the backs and arms of furniture.

Tied-back panels Drapery panels tied back to the sides of the window by such items as cords, chains, and medallions.

Tie-dye print Hand print produced by artisans who tie off selected areas of fabric so that they resist penetration of dye liquor.

Tight-pillow styles Style of upholstered furniture having pillows that cannot be shifted or removed.

Tint Color feature created by adding a compound known to reflect all wavelengths, creating white, to colorants, increasing its value and lumninosity.

Tinting Adding colorants that neutralize the natural color (e.g., violet tints may be used to neutralize the natural yellow hues of wool fiber).

Tip shear One level, cut pile surface texture produced by selectively shearing the uppermost portion of some yarn loops.

Tippiness Unwanted concentration of dye on yarn tips; result of poor dye migration.

Titanium dioxide Minute white particles used to deluster manufactured fibers.

Top-grain leather Leather having minor corrections of the natural grain markings.

To railroad Cutting upholstery fabric so that the lengthwise grain aligns crosswise on the cushions, given that the fabric motifs and repeats do not directional features.

Total blackout Complete blockage of light transmission.

Total weight The total weight of a floor covering including the weight of the pile yarns as well as the weight of the backing yarns, backing fabrics, and backcoatings.

Tow 1. A rope-like bundle of manufactured filaments having crimp but no twist. 2. Linen fibers approximately 12 inches long.

Toxicants Materials or compounds that are toxic or hazardous, especially when inhaled.

Toxic gases Gases that are hazardous when inhaled; generated in the combustion of such things as fibers.

Trade associations Organizations that represent, protect, and promote the interests of their members who provide financial support for the operation and activities of the associations.

Trademarks Distinctive names, words, phrases, and stylized logos that are used to promote product recognition and selection.

Trade practice rules Collection of labeling provisions issued by the FTC in response to requests by members of a limited segment of the industry; advisory in nature; several trade practice rules have been superseded by guides.

Trade regulation rules Collection of mandatory labeling provisions issued by the FTC.

Transfer printing See *heat transfer printing*.

Triaxial weaving Fabrication technique in which two sets of warp yarns and one set of filling yarns are interlaced at 60-degree angles.

Tricot stitch Warp knitting stitch produced with spring needles and one or two guide bars; nonrun and stable; distinguished by herringbone-like wales on the face of the fabric and herringbone-like courses on the back of the fabric.

True bias Fabric position falling at 45 degrees to the lengthwise and crosswise grains of woven fabric; position of highest stretch.

Tucked-in selvage Fabric edge finish in which the ends of the cut filling picks are turned back into the next shed; creates a finished edge that resembles that of a conventional selvage.

Tuft bind Average force required to remove a pile tuft from tufted structures.

Tufted trimming Using buttons to secure the outer-covering and filling tightly in a deeply indented three-dimensional pattern.

Tufting Fabrication technique in which pile yarns are inserted into a preformed base fabric.

Tufts per square inch Indicates pile construction density; calculated by multiplying the needle count by the number of stitches per inch in tufted constructions and by multiplying the number of rows or wires per inch by the pitch divided by 27 in woven constructions.

Tunnel test Flammability test method that measures the surface burning characteristics of building materials; assesses flame spread and smoke generation; also known as the Steiner tunnel test method.

Turkish knot See *Ghiordes knot.*

Turkish toweling See *terry toweling.*

Turns per inch (*tpi*) Numerical indication of the level of yarn twist.

Tussah silk A type of wild silk.

Tweed A fabric containing speck or tweed yarns.

Twill weave Basic weaving pattern in which the warp and filling yarns are interlaced to create a visual diagonal.

Twisting Used to introduce strength to spun yarns; used to combine monofilaments into multifilaments.

Two-way draperies Window treatment style in which the drapery panels are drawn to stack on both sides of the window.

UFAC Acronym for Upholstered Furniture Action Council.

Unclipped dot or spot fabric See *dot or spot weave.*

Underblankets Fleece-like mattress pad having a knitted base and pile of lamb's wool; placed under the bottom bed sheet to provide softness, warmth, and moisture absorption.

Uneven filling-faced twill Twill fabric in which more filling yarn than warp yarn shows on the face of the fabric.

Uneven warp-faced twill Twill fabric in which more warp yarn than filling yarn shows on the face of the fabric.

Union dyeing Variation of piece dyeing in which a fabric composed of two or more different and strategically placed fibers is immersed into a dyebath formulated with dyestuffs

that will be selectively accepted and rejected; produces a single, uniform color from one immersion process.

Upland cotton Variety of cotton ground inland, in contrast to on an island; most fibers are a relatively short $13/16$ inch in length.

Upstream segments Firms and personnel in the earlier part of the production pipeline (e.g., fiber manufacturers and suppliers), in contrast to those in the latter part of the pipeline (e.g., end-product producers).

Up-the-bolt Cutting upholstery fabric so that the lengthwise grain runs vertically on the cushions, given that the motifs and repeats have a directional feature.

U.S. Green Building Council (USGB) Non-profit organization providing green building resources, educational courses, research, statistical information, and the Leadership in Energy and Environmental Design (LEED).

Usable fiber form Relatively long and thin form, in contrast to being relatively short and thick; affects flexibility.

U-values Numerical indications of how much heat actually does pass outward through windows in winter and inward in summer.

V pattern interlacing Pile interlacing in which the pile yarn is anchored by one base filling yarn.

Valance Fabric window treatment at the top of the window which may stand alone or serve to cover drapery hardware; usually pleated or shirred.

Value Color characteristic referring to the quantity of light being reflected from a textile or other surface; also known as luminosity.

Vapor-phase moisture Water vapor held in the air.

Variegated yarns Space-dyed yarns having a variety of colors along their lengths.

Velvet carpet weaving Weaving floor coverings using an over-the-wire-construction technique; pile may be conventional or woven-through-the-back.

Venetian blinds Window coverings made up of horizontal slats or louvers laced together with textile cords.

Vertical blinds Window coverings in which the louvers or vanes are suspended vertically and may be rotated 180°.

Vinuca Fiber obtained from the hair of the vicuna, a rare wild animal of the camel family.

Vinyon A manufactured synthetic fiber also known as polyvinyl chloride or PVC.

Vinylized fabric Fabric given a vinyl coating to protect it from such things as soil and spilled fluids.

Virgin wool See *wool, virgin*.

Visco-elastic polyurethane foam Open cell foam of polyurethane which has a slow recovery time when compressed and is sensitive to heat; commonly known as "memory foam."

Visible spectrum Portion of the electromagnetic spectrum containing wavelengths that can be interpreted by the eye when reflected.

Visual diagonal Surface feature created with twill interlacing patterns.

VOC Acronym for volatile organic compounds.

Vulcanizing Heating latex with sulfur to introduce strong chemical cross links that stabilize the shape and add strength.

Wales Ridge-like features created in filling pile weaving (e.g., pinwale corduroy) or dobby weaving (e.g., pinwale piqué).

Walk-off mat Floor covering used in entrance areas subjected to high traffic levels to capture tracked-in dirt and grit, protecting the carpet from abrasion and apparent changes in color.

Wall-to-wall installation Installation of carpet to cover the entire floor space, baseboard to baseboard.

Warp knitting Fabrication in which adjacent warp yarns are interlooped.

Warp pile fabric Fabric in which the pile layer is created with extra warp yarns (e.g., velvet, terry, terry velour, friezé, grospoint).

Warp print Color style produced by printing the warp yarns prior to weaving; distinguished by striated or blurred appearance; used for draperies.

Warp yarns Lengthwise yarns in a woven fabric; also known as ends.

Warp-rib weave Variation of the plain weave in which larger or grouped warp yarns create a ribbed or ridged effect in the lengthwise fabric direction.

Warranty or guarantee programs Program offering some level of protection from defective or faulty merchandise; most warranties are legally binding. See also *warranty, full*; *warranty, implied*; *warranty, limited*; *warranty, spoken*; and *warranty, written*.

Warranty, full Guarantee program designation that indicates what the warrantor agrees to do for the purchaser, as well as what is expected of the purchaser; gives more than a limited warranty.

Warranty, implied Guarantees that come automatically with every sale unless the product is sold "as is"; rights are provided by state law.

Warranty, limited Guarantee program designation that indicates what the warrantor agrees to do for the purchaser, as well as what is expected of the purchaser; gives less than a full warranty.

Warranty, spoken Verbal promise; virtually impossible to enforce.

Warranty, written Legally binding promise that the warrantor is ensuring quality and performance; subject to the provisions of the Magnuson-Moss Warranty Act.

Washfastness Resistance of colored textiles to fading, bleeding, migration, and/or color change when laundered.

Water-borne stain Stain carried by water.

Waterfowl feathers Feathers derived from ducks and geese.

Watermarking See *pile reversal*.

Water resistance Characteristic of repelling water, delaying absorption.

WC system   Worsted count (wc) yarn numbering system.

Wear layer   The face or pile yarns above the backing in pile floor coverings.

Weather-Ometer®   Apparatus used for the accelerated laboratory testing of textile fabrics to be installed outdoors.

Weft insertion   Fabrication technique in which weft or filling yarns are inserted through loops of a tricot-stitched fabric.

Weft knitting   See *filling knitting*.

Weft yarns   Another name for filling yarns; also known as woof.

Weight density   Product of the average pile weight in ounces per square yard and the average density of soft floor coverings.

Welt   Fabric-covered cord inserted in seam lines of upholstered furniture coverings.

Wet shampoo cleaning   Restorative maintenance procedure in which a diluted detergent solution or foam is driven into the pile with rotating brushes, followed by a thorough vacuuming.

Wet spinning   Manufactured fiber spinning technique in which a basic solvent is used to dissolve the polymer and the solution is extruded into a weak acid bath where filaments coagulate.

Wickability   The ability of a fiber to transport moisture along its surface by capillary action.

Wicking   The ability of a textile fiber to transport moistue along its surface by capillary action.

Wild Silk   Fiber obtained from the cocoons of silk moths found in the wild.

Wilton   Carpet woven on a Jacquard loom; distinguished by having buried pile yarns.

Wires per inch   The number of wires used per lengthwise inch in the construction of Wilton and velvet carpet; also the number of crosswise rows of tufts per lengthwise inch in Wilton and velvet carpet, since one wire is used per row of tufts.

Woof yarns   See *weft yarns*.

Wool   Labeling term that means the fiber from the fleece of the sheep or lamb has never been reclaimed from any woven or felted wool product.

Wool, new   See *wool, virgin*.

Wool, recycled   Labeling term used to identify the resulting fiber when wool or reprocessed wool had been spun, woven, knitted, or felted into a wool product that, without ever having been used or after having been used by a consumer, subsequently had been returned to a fibrous state; replaced in 1980 by the term "recycled wool."

Wool, virgin   Labeling term that means the constituent fibers have undergone manufacturing only once; they have not been reclaimed from any spun, woven, knitted, felted, braided, bonded, or otherwise manufactured or used product; synonymous with "new wool."

Woolen yarn   Yarn spun of both long and short wool fibers and exhibiting a relatively low degree of fiber alignment.

Worsted yarn   Yarn spun of long wool fibers and exhibiting a relatively high degree of fiber alignment.

Woven-through-the-back   Velvet carpet in which the pile yarns are anchored by both the upper and lower filling shots.

W pattern interlacing   Pile interlacing in which the pile yarn is anchored by three base filling yarns.

WPLA of 1939   Acronym for Wool Products Labeling Act of 1939.

WR system   Woolen run (wr); yarn numbering system used to determine yarn number of yarns spun on the woolen spinning system.

Wrinkle recovery   Recovery from folding and bending deformations, minimizing fabric mussiness; see resiliency.

Written warranty   See *warranty, written*.

Wyzenbeek test method   See *Oscillatory Cylinder Method*.

Yak   Fiber obtained from a large Tibetian ox; used for blanketing.

Yarn count   See *yarn number.*

Yarn Distortion   Yarn Slippage.

Yarn dyeing   Dyeing in the yarn stage. See also *package dyeing*, *beam dyeing*, *skein dyeing*, and *space dyeing.*

Yarn number   Numerical designation of the fineness or size of a yarn; based on length per unit of mass (weight) or mass (weight) per unit of length; also known as yarn count.

Yarn raveling   Yarn falling from a raw edge of fabric.

Yarn slippage   Moving or "traveling" of warp or filling yarns.

Yarn splay   Untwisting of yarns, resulting in a loss of tuft definition.

Yo-yo effect   See *elevator effect.*

Zimmer flat-bed screen printing   Flat-bed screen printing in which a vacuum system is used to pull the dye paste into the pile yarns.

Z twist   A   right-handed or clockwise direction of yarn twist.

Bibliography

AATCC Technical Manual. Research Triangle Park: NC. American Association of Textile Chemists and Colorists, published annually.

Annual Book of ASTM Standards. Philadelphia: ASTM International, published annually.

Axelson, Kirk B. and Barbara Talmadge, (2006). *Elements of Soft Treatments*, Denver: Precision Draperies Education.

Binggeli, Corky, *Materials for Interior Environments*, Hoboken, NJ: John Wiley and Sons, Inc., 2008

Carpet Specifier's Handbook, 3rd ed., Dalton, GA: Carpet and Rug Institute, 1992.

Cohen, Allen C. and Ingrid Johnson. (2010). *J.J. Pizzuto's Fabric Science*, 9th ed. New York: Fairchild Books.

Collier, Billie J., Martin Bide and Phyllis Tortora. (2009) *Understanding Textiles, 7th ed*. New Jersey: Pearson Education, Inc.

CRI 104—Standard for Installation Specification of Commercial Carpet, Dalton, GA: Carpet and Rug Institute, 2002.

CRI Technical Bulletin: Acoustical Characteristics of Carpet, Dalton, GA: Carpet and Rug Institute, May 2008.

CRI Technical Bulletin: Recommended Indoor Air Quality Specifications, Dalton, GA: Carpet and Rug Institute, February 2001.

CRI Technical Bulletin: Static Control, Dalton, GA: Carpet and Rug Institute, June 2000.

CRI Technical Bulletin: Antimicrobial Carpet Treatments, Dalton, GA: Carpet and Rug Institute, June 2007.

Elsasser, Virginia Hencken, *Know Your Home Furnishings*, New York: Fairchild Publications Inc., 2004.

Elsasser, Virginia H. (2005). *Textiles: Concepts & Principles*, 2nd ed. New York: Fairchild Books.

Godsey, Lisa, *Interior Design Materials and Specifications*, New York: Fairchild Books, Inc., 2008.

Harmon, Sharon Koomen, and Katherine E. Kennon. (2009). *The Codes Guidebook for Interiors*, 3rd ed. Hoboken, NJ: John Wiley and Sons.

Ireland, Jeannie. (2008) *History of Interior Design*. New York: Fairchild Books.

Jackman, Dianne, M. Dixon, and J. Condra. (2003). *The Guide to Textiles for Interiors*, 3rd ed. Winnipeg: Portage and Main Press.

Jones, Louise, ed., *Environmentally Responsible Design*, Hoboken, New Jersey: John Wiley sons, Inc., 2008.

Jones, Lynn and Phyllis S. Allen. (2009) *Beginnings of Interior Environments*, 10th ed. Upper Saddle River, NJ: Pearson Education.

Kadolph, Sara J. (2007). *Textiles*, 10th ed., Upper Saddle River, NJ: Pearson Education.

Kopec, DAK. (2008) *Health, Sustainability, and the Built Environment*. New York: Fairchild Books.

Koe, Frank T. (2008). *Fabrics for the Designed Interior*. New York: Fairchild Books.

Liles, J. N. (2001). *The Art and Craft of Natural Dyeing: Traditional Recipes for Modern Use*, Knoxville, TN: University of Tennessee Press.

McGowan, Maryrose. (2006). *Specifying Interiors: A Guide to Construction and FF & E for Commercial Interior Products*, 2nd ed. Hoboken, NJ: John Wiley & Sons.

Meller, Susan and Joost Elffers. (2002). *Textile Designs, 2nd ed*. New York: Harry N. Abrams, Inc.

Neilson, Karla J. (2007). *Interior Textiles: Fabrics, Applications & Historic Style*. Hoboken, New Jersey: John Wiley & Sons, Inc.

Neilson, Karla J. and David A. Taylor. (2006). *Interiors: An Introduction*, 4th ed. New York: McGraw-Hill.

NFPA 701: Standard Method of Fire Tests for Flame Propagation of Textiles and Films, Quincy, MA.: National Fire Protection Association, 2004

NFPA 101: Life Safety Code, Quincy, MA: National Fire Protection Association, 2006.

Peglar, Martin. (2006) *The Fairchild Dictionary of Interior Design*, 2nd ed. New York: Fairchild Books.

Pile, John. (2005). *A History of Interior Design*, 2nd ed. Hoboken, NJ. John Wiley & Sons.

Randall, John T. (2006). *The Encyclopedia of Widow Fashions*, 6th ed. San Clemente, CA: Randall International.

Reznikoff, S. C., *Specifications for Commercial Interiors, Professional Liabilities, Regulations, and Performance Criteria*, New York: Whitney Library of Design/Watson-Guptill Publications, 1989.

Rodie, Janet B. (2008). Going Green: Beyond Marketing Hype. *Textile World*, November/December, 28–32.

Rosenfield, Jeffery and Wid Chapman. (2008) *Home Design in an Aging World*. New York: Fairchild Books.

Rupp, Jurg. (2008). Manmade Fibers: New Attitude. *Textile World, November, December*, 33–37.

The Carpet Primer, Dalton, GA: Carpet and Rug Institute, 2003.

The Carpet Industry's Sustainability Report, Dalton, GA: Carpet and Rug Institute, 2003.

TECHNICAL BULLETIN 133: Flammability Test Procedure for Seating Furniture for Use in Public Occupancies, North Highlands CA: State of California Department of Consumer Affairs, Bureau of Home Furnishings and Thermal Insulation, January 1991.

TECHNICAL BULLETIN 116: Requirements, Test Procedure and Apparatus for Testing the Flame Retardance of Upholstered Furniture, North Highlands CA: State of California Department of Consumer Affairs, Bureau of Home Furnishings and Thermal Insulation, January 1980.

Thiry, Maria C. (2009). Unsung Heroes: Antimicrobials Save the Day. *AATCC Review*, Vol 9, No. 5, 20–27.

Thiry, Maria C. (2009). Everything Old is New Again: Recycling, Recycled, and Recyclable Fibers. *AATCC Review*, Vol 9, No. 3, 20–26.

Thiry, Maria C. (2008). Tag, You're It." *AATCC Review*, Vol 9, No. 5, 22–28.

Thiry, Maria C. (2006). Smarter Than You Think. AATCC *Review*, Vol. 6, No. 12, 18–23.

U. S. Customs and Border Protection. (2006). *What Every Member of the Trade Community Should Know About: Fiber Trade Names and Generic Terms: An Informed Compliance Publication*. 1–27.

Von Tobel, Jackie, *The Design Directory of Window Treatments*, Salt Lake City: Gibbs Smith, 2007.

White, Christine (2007). *Uniquely Felt*, North Adams, MA: Storey Publishing.

Winchip, Susan, *Designing a Quality Lighting Environment*, New York: Fairchild Publications, 2005.

Yates, Mary P. (2002). *Fabrics: A Guide for Interior Designers and Architects*. New York: W.W.Norton, 2002.

Periodicals

AATC Review
Textile Chemists and Colorists
P.O. Box 12215
Research Triangle Park, NC

Consumer Reports
Consumers Union of U.S., Inc.
101 Truman Avenue
Yonkers, NY 10703-1057

Draperies and Window Coverings Magazine
840 U.S. Highway 1, Suite 330
North Palm Beach, FL 33048

Fiber Organon
Fiber Economics Bureau, Inc.
1530 Wilson Blvd., Suite 690
Arlington, VA 22209

Furniture World
P.O. Box 16044
St. Louis, MD 63105

High Performance Textiles
Elsevier International Bulletins
Journal Information Center
52 Vanderbilt Avenue
New York, NY 10017

Home Furnishings Daily
Fairchild Publications, Inc.
750 Third Avenue, 6th Floor
New York, NY 10017

Interiors
Affiliated Publications
854 West Waverland, Suite 2
Chicago, IL 60613

Interiors and Sources
P.O. Box 1888
Cedar Rapids, IA 52406-1888

Modern Textile Business (formerly *Modern Textiles*)
Vista Publications Inc.
9600 West Sample Road
Coral Springs, IL 33065

Textile Chemist and Colorist
P.O. Box 12215
Research Triangle Park, NC 27709

Textile Organon
Textile Economics Bureau, Inc.
101 Eisenhower Parkway
Roseland, NJ 07068

Textile World
Billian Publishing Company
2100 Powers Ferry Road
Atlanta, GA 30339

Window Fashions
4215 White Bear Parkway, Suite 100
St. Paul, MN 55110

Scientific Organizations

American Association of Textile Chemists and Colorists
(AATCC)
P.O. Box 12215
Research Triangle Park, NC 27709

American College of Allergy, Asthma & Immunology
www.acaai.org

American National Standards Institute, Inc. (ANSI)
1403 Broadway
New York, NY 10018

ASTM International
1916 Race Street
Philadelphia, PA 19103

Efficient Windows Collaborative
www.efficientwindows.org

International Down and Feather Laboratory and Institute
1455 South 1100 East
Salt Lake City, UT 84105

International Organization for Standardization (ISO)
1, ch. de la Voie-Creuse, Case postale 56
CH-1211 Geneva 20, Switzerland

Mayo Foundation for Medical Education and Research
www.mayoclinic.org

National Fire Protection Association, Inc. (NFPA)
1 Batterymarch Park
Quincy, MA 02169

Government Agencies

Centers for Disease Control and Prevention
U.S. Department of Health and Human Services
1600 Clifton Road
Atlanta, GA 30333

Federal Aviation and Administration (FAA)
U.S. Department of Transportation
800 Independence Avenue, SW
Washington, DC 20591

Federal Emergency Management Agency (FEMA)
500 C. Street, SW
Washington, DC 20472

Federal Housing Administration (FHA)
U.S. Department of Housing and Urban Development
451 7th Street, SW
Washington, DC 20410

Federal Trade Commission (FTC)
600 Pennsylvania Avenue, NW
Washington, DC 20580

General Services Administration
1800 F Street, NW
Washington, DC 20405

National Highway Traffic Safety Administration
U.S. Department of Transportation
1200 New Jersey Avenue, SE
West Building
Washington, DC 20590

National Institute of Standards and Technology
100 Bureau Drive, Stop 1070
Gaithersburg, MD 20899-1070

National Technical Information Service
U.S. Department of Commerce
5285 Port Royal Road
Springfield, VA 22161

Office of Civil Rights
U.S. Department of Health and Human Services
200 Independence Avenue, SW
Washington, DC 20201

Office of Energy Efficiency and Renewable Energy
(EERE)
Mail Stop EE-1
Department of Energy
Washington, DC 20585

United States Access Board
1331 F Street, NW, Suite 1000
Washington, DC 20004-1111

U.S. Consumer Product Safety Commission (CPSC)
4330 East West Highway, Suite 523
Bethesda, MD 20814

U.S. Department of Commerce
5285 Port Royal Road
Springfield, VA 22161

U.S. Department of Energy
1000 Independence Avenue, SW
Washington, DC 20585

U.S. Department of Labor
Occupational Safety and Health Administration
200 Constitution Avenue
Washington, DC 20210

U.S. Environmental Protection Agency
Ariel Rios Building
1200 Pennsylvania Avenue, NW
Washington, DC 20460

U.S. Government Printing Office
732 North Capitol Street, NW
Washington, DC 20401

Trade Associations

The Academy of Textiles and Flooring
12430 E. Whittier Boulevard
Whittier, CA 90602

American Fiber Manufacturers Association, Inc.
1530 Wilson Boulevard, Suite 690
Arlington, VA 22209

American Furniture Manufacturers Association
P.O. Box HP-7
High Point, NC 27261

American Home Furnishings Alliance
317 W. High Avenue, 10th Floor
High Point, NC 27260

American Manufacturing Trade Action Coalition
910 16th Street, N.W., Suite 760
Washington, DC 20006

Association for Contract Textiles
Headquarters
P.O. Box 101981
Fort Worth, TX 76185

Association for Linen Management
2161 Lexington Road
Suite 2
Richmond, KY 40475

Australian Wool Innovation Limited
1156 Avenue of the Americas
Suite 701
New York, NY 10086

BIFMA International
2680 Horizon Drive, S.E.
Suite A-1
Grand Rapids, MI 49546-7500

Bureau of Home Furnishings and Thermal Insulation
3485 Orange Grove Avenue
North Highlands, CA 95660

California Furniture Manufacturers Association
1240 N. Jefferson Street, Suite G
Anaheim, CA 92807

Canadian Carpet Institute
1064 Cadboro Road
Ottawa, ON K1J 8E1

Carpet and Fabricare Institute
P.O. Box 758
Escondido, CA 92033

Carpet and Rug Institute
P.O. Box 2048
Dalton, GA 20720

Carpet Cleaners Institute of the Northwest
2421 S. Union Ave. Suite L-1
Tacoma, WA 98405

Carpet Cushion Council
23 Courtney Circle
Bryn Mawr, PA 19010

Carpetcycle, LLC
447 Schiller Street
Elizabeth, NJ 07206

CELC—MASTERS OF LINEN
15, rue du Louvre
75001 Paris
France

Cotton Incorporated
World Headquarters
6399 Weston Parkway
Cary, NC 27513

Cycle-Tex, Inc.
2104B Fiber Park Drive
Dalton, GA 30720

Drycleaning & Laundry Institute International
14700 Sweitzer Lane
Laurel, MD 20707

GREENGUARD Environmental Institute
2211 Newmarket Parkway, Suite 110
Marietta, GA 30067

Industrial Fabrics Association International
1801 County Road B W.
Roseville, MN 55113

Institute of Inspection Cleaning and Restoration
Certification
IICRC Administrative Office
2715 E. Mill Plain Boulevard
Vancouver, WA 98661

International Furnishings and Design Association
International Headquarters
150 S. Warner Road, Suite 156
King of Prussia, PA 19406

International Home Furnishings Representatives
209 S. Main Street
IHFC M001LL
P.O. Box 670
High Point, NC 27261

Jute Carpet Backing Council
P.O. Drawer 8
322 Davis Avenue
Dayton, OH 45401-0008

Jute Carpet Backing Council Inc.
632 Plymouth, N.E.
Grand Rapids, MI 49505-6032

Jute Manufactures Development Council
Government of India Organisation
3A Park Plaza, 71 Park Street
Kolkata 700 016

Kruse Carpet Recycling
4800 W. 96th Street
Indianapolis, IN 46268

National Association of Decorative Fabrics Distributors
One Windsor Cove, Suite 305
Columbia, South Carolina 29223

National Cotton Batting Institute
4322 Bloombury Street
Southaven, MS 38672

National Cotton Council of America
7193 Goodlett Farms Parkway
Cordova, TN 38016

National Fenestration Rating Council
6305 Ivy Lane, Suite 140
Greenbelt, MO 20770

National Home Furnishings Association
3910 Tinsley Drive, Suite 101
High Point, NC 27265-3610

North American Association of Floor Covering
Distributors
401 N. Michigan Avenue, Suite 2400
Chicago, IL 60611-4267

ReSource Commercial Flooring Network, LLC
23461 E. Otero Drive
Aurora, CO 80016

SF Carpet Recycling
1588 Carroll Avenue
San Francisco, CA 94124

The Society of the Plastics Industry, Inc.
1667 K Street, N.W., Suite 1000
Washington, DC 20006

Synthetic Turf Council
400 Galleria Parkway, Suite 1500
Atlanta, Georgia 30339

Synthetic Yarn and Fiber Association
P.O. Box 66
Gastonia, NC 28053-0066

Upholstered Furniture Action Council
Box 2436
High Point, NC 27261

U.S. Green Building Council (UFAC)
2101 L Street, NW, Suite 500
Washington, DC 20037

Window Coverings Association of America (WCAA)
2646 Highway 109, Suite 205
Grover, MO 63040

Appendix A

Federal Trade Commission Generic Fiber Names

Acetate
Acrylic
Anidex*
Aramid
Azlon*
Fluoropolymer
Glass
Lastrile*
Lyocell
Melamine
Metallic
Modacrylic
Novoloid
Nylon
Nytril*
Olefin
PBI
PLA
Polyester
Rayon
Rubber
Saran
Spandex
Sulfar
Triacetate*
Vinal*
Vinyon*

*No longer produced in the United States

Appendix B

The International System of Units-SI/Metric

The information in this appendix is courtesy of PPG Industries, Inc., 1984.

SI Base Units

Quantity Measured	Unit of Measure	Symbol
Length	meter	m
Mass[a]	kilogram	kg
Time	second	s
Electric current	ampere	A
Thermodynamic temperature[b]	kelvin	K
Amount of substance	mole	mol
Luminous intensity	candela	cd

[a]The kilogram is the unit of mass but not of force. The Newton (N) is the unit of force. (For more detailed explanation of mass and force, refer to ASTM E 380.)
[b]While the kelvin is the correct SI unit of thermodynamic temperature, in practice, degree Celcius (°C) is most commonly used (1K = 1°C).

Prefixes Used With The SI Metric System

Prefix	Symbol	Multiplying Factor	
tera	T	1000 000 000 000	$= 10^{12}$
giga	G	1 000 000 000	$= 10^{9}$
mega	M	1 000 000	$= 10^{6}$
kilo	k	1 000	$= 10^{3}$
hecto	h	100	$= 10^{2}$
deka	da	10	$= 10^{1}$
deci	d	0.1	$= 10^{-1}$
centi	c	0.01	$= 10^{-2}$
milli	m	0.001	$= 10^{-3}$
micro	μ	0.000 001	$= 10^{-6}$

For additional prefixes, refer to ASTM E 380.

Customary Inch-Pound Measures and Equivalent SI Units

Inch-Pound Measure and Symbol

inches	in
inches	in
feet	ft
yards	yd
miles	mi
square yards	yd^2
ounces (avdp.)	oz
pounds (advp.)	lb

Equivalent Metric Measure and Symbol

centimeters	cm
millimeters	mm
meters	m
kilometers	km
square meters	m^2
grams	g
kilograms	kg

Customary Units of Measure In SI Units

Length

1 meter (m) = 100 cm	=	1000 mm
1 millimeter (mm)	=	0.001 m
1 centimeter (cm)	=	0.01 m
1 decimeter (dm)	=	0.1 m
1 dekameter (dam)	=	10 m
1 hectometer (hm)	=	100 m
1 kilometer (km)	=	1000 m

Weight

1 gram (g) = 100 cg	=	1000 mg
1 milligram (mg)	=	0.001 g
1 centigram (cg)	=	.01 g
1 decigram (dg)	=	0.1 g
1 dekagram (dag)	=	10 g
1 hectogram (hg)	=	100 g
1 kilogram (kg)	=	1000 g

Capacity

1 liter (L) = 100 cL	=	1000 mL
1 milliliter (mL)	=	0.001 L
1 centiliter (cL)	=	0.01 L
1 deciliter (dL)	=	0.1 L
1 dekaliter (daL)	=	10 L
1 hectoliter (hL)	=	100 L
1 kiloliter (kL)	=	1000 L

Selected Inch-Pounds/SI Metric Conversion Factors and References

Quantity	Inch-Pound Units	SI units	To Convert Inch-Pound units to SI	SI Units to Inch-pound
			Multiply By:	**Multiply By:**
	inch	mm	25.400	0.03937
	inch	cm	2.5400	0.3937
Length	foot	m	0.3048	3.2808
	yard	m	0.9144	1.0936
	mile	km	1.6093	0.6214
	ounce (avdp.)	g	28.3495	0.0353
	pound (avdp.)	kg	0.4536	2.2046
Mass	ton (2,000 lbs.)	t	0.9072	1.1023
	ton (2,240 lbs.)	t	1.0161	0.9842
Force	pound	N	4.4482	0.2248
	ounce (fluid	mL	29.5735	0.0338
	Quart (liquid)	L	0.9464	1.0567
	gallon	L	3.7854	0.2642
Volume	quart (dry)	L	1.1012	0.9081
	bushel	L	35.2391	0.0284
	inch^3	cm^3	16.3871	0.0610
	feet^3	dm^3	28.3168	0.0353
	yard^3	m^3	0.7646	1.3079
	inch^2	cm^2	6.4516	0.1550
	feet^2	m^2	0.0929	10.7639
Area	yard^2	m^2	0.8361	1.1960
	acre	hectare	0.4047	2.4710
Temperature	°F	°C	5/9(°F−32°)	9/5°C + 32°
	lb/in^3	g/cm^3	27.6799	0.0361
Density	lb/ft^3	kg/m^3	16.0185	0.0624
	ft/sec	m/s	0.3048	3.2808
Velocity	yd/min	m/min	0.9144	1.0936
	mi/hr	km/h	1.6093	0.6214
	ft lb	J	1.3558	0.7376
Energy	BTU	kJ	1.0551	0.9478
	kWh	MJ	3.6000	0.2778
Pressure	lb/in^2	kPa	6.8947	0.1450
	oz/yd	g/m	31.0034	0.0323
	oz/yd^2	g/m^2	33.9057	0.0295
Textile	turns/in(tpi)	turns/m(tpm)	39.3700	0.0254
	yds/lb	m/kg	2.0159	0.4961

*Definitions and symbols for the complete international system are given in ASTM E 380.

Index

Page numbers in italics indicate figures.